CRITICAL SURVEY
OF GRAPHIC NOVELS

INDEPENDENTS AND
UNDERGROUND CLASSICS

CRITICAL SURVEY OF GRAPHIC NOVELS

INDEPENDENTS AND UNDERGROUND CLASSICS

Volume 2
Ice Haven – Shenzhen: A Travelogue from China

Editors

Bart H. Beaty
University of Calgary

Stephen Weiner
Maynard, Massachusetts

SALEM PRESS
Ipswich, Massachusetts Hackensack, New Jersey

Cover images: Top Left: *My Mommy Is in America and She Met Buffalo Bill* (Ponet Mon S.L.) Top Right: *Blueberry* (Editions Darguard) Bottom Right: *Strangers in Paradise* (Abstract Studios) Bottom Left: *Flaming Carrot* (Dark Horse)

Critical survey of graphic novels : independents and underground classics / editors, Bart H. Beaty, Stephen Weiner.
    p. cm.
 Includes bibliographical references and index.
 ISBN 978-1-58765-950-8 (set) -- ISBN 978-1-58765-951-5 (vol. 1) -- ISBN 978-1-58765-952-2 (vol. 2) -- ISBN 978-1-58765-953-9 (vol. 3)
 1. Graphic novels. 2. Comic books, strips, etc. I. Beaty, Bart. II. Weiner, Stephen, 1955-
PN6725.C754 2012
741.5'0973--dc23
                                                                        2011051380

First Printing

Printed in the United States of America

CONTENTS

Master List of Contents..............................vii

Ice Haven 369

Incognegro: A Graphic Mystery 374

I Never Liked You: A Comic-Strip Narrative 378

In the Shadow of No Towers 382

It Rhymes with Lust 386

It's a Bird 390

It's a Good Life, If You Don't Weaken 393

It Was the War of the Trenches 397

Jar of Fools: A Picture Story 402

Jew in Communist Prague, A 406

Jew of New York, The 410

Jimmy Corrigan: The Smartest Kid on Earth 414

Journey: The Adventures of Wolverine MacAlistaire 419

Journey into Mohawk Country..................424

Julius Knipl, Real Estate Photographer: Stories......429

Kabuki 433

Kafka 438

Kampung Boy 443

Kane 448

King: A Comics Biography 452

Kings in Disguise 456

Laika 460

La Perdida..465

Last Day in Vietnam: A Memory..............470

Leave It to Chance 474

Life and Times of Scrooge McDuck, The 479

Life Sucks 483

Like a Velvet Glove Cast in Iron 486

Long Time Relationship 489

Lost Cause: John Wesley Hardin, the Taylor-Sutton Feud, and Reconstruction Texas......493

Lost Girl...497

Lost Girls 501

Louis..506

Louis Riel: A Comic-Strip Biography 512

Love and Rockets 517

Lucky 525

Mail Order Bride 530

Market Day 534

Maus: A Survivor's Tale 538

Metropol: The Complete Series + Metropol A.D. 543

Minor Miracles 548

Monologues for the Coming Plague 552

Mouse Guard..556

My Mommy Is in America and She Met Buffalo Bill..............................562

Nat Turner..566

Night Fisher 571

9/11 Report, The: A Graphic Adaptation 575

Notes for a War Story.............................579

Omaha the Cat Dancer............................583

One! Hundred! Demons!..........................588

Our Cancer Year 592

Owly 596

Palestine 601

Palomar: The Heartbreak Soup Stories 606

Passionate Journey 611

Paul 615

Pedro and Me: Friendship, Loss, and What I Learned 620

Percy Gloom 623

Perfect Example 627

Persepolis...631

Photographer, The: Into War-Torn Afghanistan with Doctors Without Borders 636

Plain Janes, The.....................................641

Playboy, The...644

Poor Bastard, The 647

Predator 652

Pride of Baghdad: Inspired by a True Story..........656

Pyongyang: A Journey in North Korea..................660

Queen and Country 664

Rabbi's Cat, The 671

Rex Mundi 677

Richard Stark's Parker............................683

Road to Perdition 687

Robot Dreams 691

Rose: Prequel to Bone.............................695

Safe Area Goražde 699

Scary Godmother: The Boo Flu 704

Scott Pilgrim 707

Shenzhen: A Travelogue from China......................713

MASTER LIST OF CONTENTS

Volume 1

Contents v
Publisher's Note xi
Introduction xv
Contributors xvii
A.D.: New Orleans After the Deluge 1
Adventures of Luther Arkwright, The 6
Adventures of Tintin, The 10
Age of Bronze: The Story of the Trojan War 16
Age of Reptiles 21
Airtight Garage of Jerry Cornelius 26
Alan's War: The Memories of G.I. Alan Cope 29
Alec: The Years Have Pants 33
Alice in Sunderland: An Entertainment 38
Aliens 42
American Born Chinese 47
American Splendor: From off the Streets
     of Cleveland 51
Arrival, The 56
Asterios Polyp 60
Asterix 65
Aya of Yopougon 70
Bacchus 75
Ballad of Doctor Richardson, The 81
Berlin: City of Stones 85
Binky Brown Sampler 89
Black Hole 94
Blackmark 99
Blankets: An Illustrated Novel 103
Blueberry 107
Bone 115
Book of Genesis, The 120
Boulevard of Broken Dreams, The 125
Box Office Poison 130
Burma Chronicles 134
Cages 139
Cancer Vixen: A True Story 144
Cartoon History of the Universe, The 149
Castle Waiting 153
Chicken with Plums 158
City of Glass 163
Clumsy 167
Color Trilogy, The 171

Complete Essex County, The 175
Complete Fritz the Cat, The 179
Contract with God, And Other Tenement
     Stories, A 184
Curious Case of Benjamin Button, The 189
David Boring 193
Dead Memory 197
Dear Julia 201
Deogratias: A Tale of Rwanda 205
Diary of a Mosquito Abatement Man 209
Dropsie Avenue: The Neighborhood 212
Dykes to Watch Out For 216
Ed the Happy Clown: The Definitive
     Ed Book 221
Elk's Run 225
Embroideries 230
Epileptic 235
Ethel and Ernest: A True Story 240
Exit Wounds 244
Far Arden 248
Fax from Sarajevo: A Story of Survival 252
The Fixer: A Story from Sarajevo 256
Flaming Carrot Comics 261
Flood! A Novel in Pictures 267
Footnotes in Gaza: A Graphic Novel 271
Frank Book, The 275
From Hell: Being a Melodrama in
     Sixteen Parts 279
Fun Home: A Family Tragicomic 285
Gemma Bovery 290
Get a Life 295
Ghost World 299
Give It Up! And Other Short Stories 305
Glacial Period 309
Golem's Mighty Swing, The 313
Good-Bye, Chunky Rice 318
Hard Boiled 322
Harum Scarum 326
Harvey Kurtzman's Jungle Book 331
Hate 336
Haunted 342
He Done Her Wrong 347

Hey, Wait 352
Hicksville 356

History of Violence, A 361
Houdini: The Handcuff King 365

Volume 2

Contents v

Ice Haven 369
Incognegro: A Graphic Mystery 374
I Never Liked You: A Comic-Strip Narrative 378
In the Shadow of No Towers 382
It Rhymes with Lust 386
It's a Bird 390
It's a Good Life, If You Don't Weaken 393
It Was the War of the Trenches 397
Jar of Fools: A Picture Story 402
Jew in Communist Prague, A 406
Jew of New York, The 410
Jimmy Corrigan: The Smartest Kid on Earth 414
Journey: The Adventures of Wolverine
    MacAlistaire 419
Journey into Mohawk Country 424
Julius Knipl, Real Estate Photographer: Stories 429
Kabuki 433
Kafka 438
Kampung Boy 443
Kane 448
King: A Comics Biography 452
Kings in Disguise 456
Laika 460
La Perdida 465
Last Day in Vietnam: A Memory 470
Leave It to Chance 474
Life and Times of Scrooge McDuck, The 479
Life Sucks 483
Like a Velvet Glove Cast in Iron 486
Long Time Relationship 489
Lost Cause: John Wesley Hardin, the Taylor-Sutton
    Feud, and Reconstruction Texas 493
Lost Girl 497
Lost Girls 501
Louis 506
Louis Riel: A Comic-Strip Biography 512
Love and Rockets 517
Lucky 525
Mail Order Bride 530
Market Day 534
Maus: A Survivor's Tale 538
Metropol: The Complete Series +
    Metropol A.D. 543

Minor Miracles 548
Monologues for the Coming Plague 552
Mouse Guard 556
My Mommy Is in America and She Met
    Buffalo Bill 562
Nat Turner 566
Night Fisher 571
9/11 Report, The: A Graphic Adaptation 575
Notes for a War Story 579
Omaha the Cat Dancer 583
One! Hundred! Demons! 588
Our Cancer Year 592
Owly 596
Palestine 601
Palomar: The Heartbreak Soup Stories 606
Passionate Journey 611
Paul 615
Pedro and Me: Friendship, Loss, and What
    I Learned 620
Percy Gloom 623
Perfect Example 627
Persepolis 631
Photographer, The: Into War-Torn Afghanistan
    with Doctors Without Borders 636
Plain Janes, The 641
Playboy, The 644
Poor Bastard, The 647
Predator 652
Pride of Baghdad: Inspired by a True Story 656
Pyongyang: A Journey in North Korea 660
Queen and Country 664
Rabbi's Cat, The 671
Rex Mundi 677
Richard Stark's Parker 683
Road to Perdition 687
Robot Dreams 691
Rose: Prequel to Bone 695
Safe Area Goražde 699
Scary Godmother: The Boo Flu 704
Scott Pilgrim 707
Shenzhen: A Travelogue from China 713

Volume 3

Master List of Contents...vii
Shortcomings...717
Shutterbug Follies...722
Signal to Noise..726
Sin City...730
Skim...735
Skitzy: The Story of Floyd W. Skitzafroid...............739
Sloth..743
Small Killing, A..746
Snowman, The..750
Stitches: A Memoir..753
Strangers in Paradise...757
Stray Bullets...763
Stray Toasters..768
Streak of Chalk...772
Stuck Rubber Baby...776
Suckle: The Status of Basil...780
Summer of Love, The...785
System, The...790
Tale of One Bad Rat, The..794
Tales of the Beanworld:...798
Tamara Drewe..802
Tank Girl...806
Tantrum...810
30 Days of Night..814
Three Fingers...818
300...822
Three Shadows...826
Tragical Comedy or Comical Tragedy
    of Mr. Punch, The...831

Transit...835
Treasury of Victorian Murder, A.......................................839
Tricked...844
Twentieth Century Eightball...849
Violent Cases...854
Walking Dead, The...858
Wall, The: Growing Up Behind the
    Iron Curtain..863
Waltz with Bashir: A Lebanon War Story................................867
We Are on Our Own...871
What It Is..875
When the Wind Blows...879
Whiteout..883
Why I Hate Saturn...888
Wilson..891
Xenozoic Tales..896
Yossel: April 19, 1943..900
You Are Here..903
You'll Never Know: Book One: A Good
    and Decent Man..906
Zombies Vs. Robots..911
Zot!..914
Bibliography..919
Guide to Online Resources...943
Timeline..945
Major Awards..949
Works by Artist...1014
Works by Author...1026
Works by Publisher..1033
Index...1039

CRITICAL SURVEY
OF GRAPHIC NOVELS

INDEPENDENTS AND
UNDERGROUND CLASSICS

I

ICE HAVEN

Author: Clowes, Daniel
Artist: Daniel Clowes (illustrator)
Publisher: Pantheon Books
First serial publication: 2001
First book publication: 2005

Publication History

Ice Haven first appeared in issue 22 (2001) of *Eightball*, an alternative comic book published by Fantagraphics Books that was written and drawn by Daniel Clowes. Issue 22 was the first issue of *Eightball* to feature one story in its entirety and was divided into chapters designed to look like old newspaper comic strips, using a variety of connected characters and graphic styles. The 2005 Pantheon Books publication included all the original material from *Eightball*, issue 22, along with eight new strips. Some of the original strips were edited and redrawn, and a new cover, title sequence, and final chapter were added. The closing sequence illuminates the central mystery of the story, the disappearance and reappearance of a young boy.

Plot

Ice Haven begins with a walking tour led by Random Wilder, a pompous poet dressed in a seersucker jacket and straw hat. Wilder reveals his rivalry with Ida Wentz, a cheerful grandmother whose more popular poetry he scorns. Wilder is horrified to learn that Wentz has received a poetry prize.

In a sequence titled "Our Children and Their Friends," adults appear only as offstage voices. David Goldberg, a strange and silent child, is encouraged (presumably by his mother) to play with Charles, a serious-looking boy who is bouncing a baseball. David runs away, and Charles is next approached by Carmichael, a belligerent boy who claims to have had

Ice Haven. (Courtesy of Pantheon Books)

sex with Paula, a girl in their class. Carmichael gives Charles a paperback book, *The True Story of Leopold and Loeb*, a true-crime story that is dramatized in the next strip, complete with a 1950's-style cover. The book describes the famous 1924 murder of a boy by two young men who killed to prove their superior intellect. Following the Leopold and Loeb sequence, Clowes cuts to Random Wilder watching a television news report about the real-life 1996 murder of child model JonBenét Ramsey (one of the few modern references in *Ice Haven*). Wilder is most interested in the close study given to the ransom note and wonders aloud whether child murder is the only way for a writer to get an attentive reading of his work. Wilder writes an anonymous note to his neighbors, complaining about their teenage sons' band.

Love-obsessed teenage girl Violet van der Platz is introduced in the next strip, "Seventeen." Violet is Charles's new stepsister, as her mother has married Charles's father. Unhappy in her new high school, Violet spends her time daydreaming about her boyfriend, Penrod, and writing letters begging him to run away with her.

Meanwhile, Charles learns that David Goldberg is missing. He suspects that Carmichael killed David and imagines he will be killed by Carmichael or accused of collaborating with him. Two short sequences follow: a black-and-white cartoon about the further adventures of Leopold and Loeb and a scene in which Paula tells Charles that David Goldberg is better off dead, since kidnapped children who do return are psychologically damaged. The next chapter, "Vida and Her Grandmother," focuses on Ida Wentz's visiting granddaughter, a recent college graduate who self-publishes a small "'zine" about her life. Unemployed and bored, Vida becomes obsessed with Random Wilder and spends a day following him.

In the next section, "Mr. and Mrs. Ames, Detectives for Hire" come to investigate David Goldberg's kidnapping, but internal tensions dominate this sequence; Mrs. Ames feels neglected, and Mr. Ames threatens a hotel guest with a gun for playing the radio too loud. In the moody, monotone strip that follows, Charles

confesses his desire for his stepsister, Violet, who secretly marries Penrod in the next chapter, "Violet in Love." Following the ceremony, she returns to her stepfather's house without telling anyone she is married. Mr. Ames investigates Harry Naybors, a comic book critic who is defensive about his occupation.

In "The Hole," Carmichael and Charles visit a landmark rock formation. Carmichael confesses to Charles that he killed David Goldberg and threw his body in a hole; he then threatens to kill Charles if he tells anyone else.

In "Seersucker," Vida works up the courage to give her writing to Random Wilder, who accepts her magazine politely, then tosses it aside contemptuously when he goes inside. Meanwhile, Mr. Ames continues to investigate Ice Haven's citizens and to ignore the significance of finding what looks like his wife's panties on a town police officer's bed. In a moody sequence drawn in shades of pale red, Charles agonizes over his guilt and thwarted longing for Violet. In "Convenience

Ice Haven. (Courtesy of Pantheon Books)

Store," Kim Lee, a young Korean shopkeeper, displays his contempt for his customers, either pretending not to speak English or commenting on embarrassing purchases such as condoms.

Random Wilder finally reads Vida's writing and finds it so much better than his own that he is thrown into despair. He throws her magazine in the trash, where Vida later finds it. Charles sees a therapist who tells him to imagine the ideal solution to his problems; Charles fantasizes Carmichael's death and the divorce of his father and stepmother, leaving him free to marry Violet.

Mr. and Mrs. Ames appear on a television talk show to discuss the ransom note given to David Goldberg's parents, and their analysis drives Wilder into a frenzy of self-hatred. He tries to flush his poems down the toilet, and, failing that, attempts suicide by carbon-monoxide poisoning.

In the next chapter, "David Goldberg Is Alive," all of Ice Haven celebrates when the boy is found alive in the park. Carmichael tells Charles that he has had a religious awakening and now loves everybody; Violet realizes that her relationship with Penrod is over, and, soon after, her mother and Charles's father divorce. Violet looks forward to moving to Hawaii, and she rides away, leaving a heartbroken Charles behind. Vida, too, leaves Ice Haven, happily willing to sell out when an unexpected Hollywood offer comes along.

Clowes includes two additional chapters: "Harry Naybors Explains It All," which appeared in the original issue of *Eightball*, and an untitled sequence with David Goldberg, which was added for the book publication. In the first, the fictional comic book critic discusses the story in which he has just appeared. In the second, a sequence powerful in its stillness and understatement, David Goldberg speaks his first words, a poem.

Characters

- *Random Wilder* is a pompous poet who serves as a narrator for only his own chapters. A middle-aged, pudgy eccentric, he lives alone. Though he seems to be a harmless, comical character, his need for recognition sets the story's main event, the kidnapping, in motion.

- *Vida*, is the visiting granddaughter of Ida Wentz. She chronicles her life in an ongoing magazine and sends review copies to major magazines, hoping to be discovered.

- *Charles* is a young boy and has a secret love for his teenage stepsister, Violet, and worries about his complicity in the imagined murder of David Goldberg. Around adults and his peers, he is quiet and spends most of his time bouncing a baseball.

- *Violet van der Platz*, Charles's stepsister, is a teenager who spends most of her time writing to her old boyfriend, Penrod, and daydreaming of him coming to her school to take her away with him.

- *Mr. Ames* is a private eye who is cynical and quick to anger.

- *Carmichael*, a friend of Charles, is a troubled boy.

- *David Goldberg* is a silent, socially withdrawn boy who is a small, pudgy child with long hair, a fuzzy sweater, and a perpetually miserable expression.

- *Harry Naybors*, is a comics expert and a nerdy type with thick glasses and a wall-to-wall collection of comics. In a final metafictional twist, he appears at the end of *Ice Haven* to analyze the story and its author.

Artistic Style

Clowes deliberately varies the look of each chapter, using subtle variations in inking, shading, lettering, and detail to give each character's story a distinctive look. The chapter "Harry Naybors, Comic Book Critic," for example, uses a three-dimensional "superhero" title font and dresses the characters in bright primary colors of yellow, blue, and green to give a 1950's or 1960's feel. The sequences with Mr. Ames use darker colors, with panels depicting blue-shaded night and rain scenes reminiscent of a 1940's noir film.

Some sequences pop with a bright, four-color comic-book palette; others have a blue-shaded or red-shaded monotone style, similar to Clowes's *Ghost World* (1997); still others use pale, faded colors that give them the feeling of Sunday comic pages from old newspapers.

Chapters featuring Charles have a stripped-down and cartoony look, reflecting a child's view of the world. In one panel, a giant exclamation point appears over Charles's head to indicate surprise; in another, flying sweat droplets illustrate worry. Violet's segments are relatively realistic, with a warm range of colors, but her daydreams of Penrod are rendered in wistful shades of blue. Despite the medley of styles, *Ice Haven* is colorful and light in tone. The lines are clean and classic. Taken as a whole, the comic has a retro look that is also essentially timeless. Little in *Ice Haven* would be out of place in 1965, for example, yet there are no overtly nostalgic details.

Themes

Ice Haven explores themes of community and isolation, innocence and experience, and the meaning that art can give to life. Significantly, many of the major characters in *Ice Haven* are writers: Random Wilder and Ida Wentz are poets, Vida writes both prose and poetry, Harry Naybors writes critical essays on comic books, and Violet pours her teenage heart into love letters to her boyfriend.

Innocence and its loss is another major motif in *Ice Haven*. A quick glance at the lettering and style of "Our Children and Their Friends," one of the Charles chapters, might lead readers to expect a cheery comic strip. Instead, Charles is wrestling with adult questions of sex and death. When he imagines Carmichael having sex with Paula, he pictures them standing next to each other, motionless and fully clothed. Later, Charles daydreams about Carmichael's death. When he dreams of meeting Violet in the future, he pictures them in a *Jetsons*-style future, with moon rockets and flying-saucer-shaped buildings.

The difficulty of truly connecting with other people is perhaps the overriding theme of *Ice Haven*. Each character inhabits a vivid but solitary world, where self-knowledge is a struggle and knowledge of others almost impossible. Many of these people are literally neighbors, yet their interactions with each other are awkward and distant. Vida is crushed when she finds her work in Wilder's trash, never knowing that her

words have so moved Wilder that he loses all faith in his own work and attempts suicide. Mr. Ames claims to love his wife, yet he remains oblivious to her growing boredom and unhappiness. Violet romanticizes Penrod in her letters and daydreams, but after one night together, they drift apart, and by the end of the story she can no longer remember what he looks like. At the same time, Violet is completely unaware that Charles has feelings for her.

David Goldberg is the ultimate symbol of Ice Haven's isolation. He refuses interaction with other children and does not even respond to his parents. Ironically, this solitary child's kidnapping and return bring the town together. In a scene presaged by the cartoony "Leopold and Loeb" sequence, David Goldberg's return makes Ice Haven's residents smile and embrace each other. In a panel reminiscent of classic children's holiday cartoons like *A Charlie Brown Christmas* (1965), all the people of Ice Haven are shown holding hands and singing, faces lifted to the stars.

Impact

Although *Ice Haven* is not as sexually explicit as many of Clowes's other works, it gained notoriety when a high school teacher in Connecticut was targeted for a police investigation after giving the book to a thirteen-year-old student. The teacher ended up leaving his job, and the censorship story made national headlines when the student's father described *Ice Haven* as pornography. Clowes declined to comment on the specifics of the case or the merits of his work but simply said that the disregard for the teacher's career was an obscenity greater than anything he had ever drawn in a comic.

When *Ice Haven* was revised, expanded, and published as a graphic novel in 2005, critical reception was favorable. A few reviewers found the book overly fragmented and self-referential, but most praised Clowes for his range of styles, his ability to pay homage to vintage comics without parody, and his use of the town as a kind of character in the story.

Kathryn Kulpa

Further Reading

Burns, Charles. *Black Hole* (2005).
Tomine, Adrian. *Sleepwalk: And Other Stories* (1998).

Ware, Chris. *Jimmy Corrigan: The Smartest Kid on Earth* (2000).

Bibliography

Clowes, Daniel. "Conversation Four: Daniel Clowes." Interview by Mike Sacks. *McSweeney's*, 2009. http://www.mcsweeneys.net/links/sacks/clowes.html.

Clowes, Daniel, Ken Parille, and Isaac Cates. *Daniel Clowes: Conversations*. Jackson: University Press of Mississippi, 2010.

Hignite, Todd. "Daniel Clowes." *In the Studio: Visits with Contemporary Cartoonists*. New Haven, Conn.: Yale University Press, 2006.

Lukich, Mike. "Ice Haven," *PopMatters*, February 6, 2006. http://www.popmatters.com/comics/ice-haven.shtml.

Parille, Ken. "A Cartoon World." *Boston Review*, January/February, 2006.

Schwartz, Ben, ed. *The Best American Comics Criticism*. Seattle: Fantagraphics, 2010.

See also: *David Boring; Ghost World; Black Hole; Jimmy Corrigan, the Smartest Kid in the World*

INCOGNEGRO: A GRAPHIC MYSTERY

Author: Johnson, Mat
Artist: Warren Pleece (illustrator); Clem Robins (letterer); Steven John Phillips (cover artist)
Publisher: DC Comics
First book publication: 2008

Publication History

Published by DC Comics' Vertigo imprint in 2008, *Incognegro* is the product of both history and personal experience. Author Mat Johnson, an African American who is often mistaken for a Caucasian, traces the evolution of the novel in the author's note preceding the text. Inspired not only by his own experience but also by journalist and activist Walter White and by the birth of Johnson's twins (one of whom is "brown-skinned with black Afro hair, the other with the palest of pink skins"), the novel, while subtitled *A Graphic Mystery*, is also a significant commentary on race in the United States. Johnson bases his protagonist, Zane Pinchback, on White's legacy, yet places him in the context of Johnson's own children: Zane is the lighter-skinned twin who can pass as white.

The graphic novel has been well received. Its cover features praise by academic Cornel West and writers Walter Mosley and George P. Pelecanos, cementing Johnson's prominence as a twenty-first-century voice of the African American experience and a respected author of fiction. Artist Warren Pleece (*Hellblazer*, issues 115-128; *Life Sucks*), a frequent contributor to the Vertigo imprint, accompanies Johnson's text with stark images that are reminiscent of the black-and-white art of *Maus: A Survivor's Tale* (1986), yet clearly influenced by more traditional comics art.

Plot

Incognegro follows Harlem journalist Zane Pinchback as he travels to Tupelo, Mississippi, to help exonerate his brother, who has been accused of murder. Zane infiltrates lynchings and then reports on them as "Incognegro," a nom de plume that protects his identity.

Part I begins as Zane describes his experiences to two friends, introducing readers to the horrors of

Incognegro is partly inspired by American civil rights leader Walter White (1893-1955), former head of the National Association for the Advancement of Colored People. (Getty Images)

lynchings as well as to his role in reporting them. He explains his transformation into Incognegro and introduces the concept of "passing." While recognizing the importance of the work he does, Zane craves recognition and tells his editor that he will no longer report as Incognegro. He travels to the South one last time to exonerate his brother, Alonzo "Pinchy" Pinchback, who has been jailed for the murder of his white girlfriend, Michaela Mathers. Zane's friend Carl, also able to pass as white, accompanies him, complicating Zane's practiced presence in the South by calling attention to the two of them and putting them both in danger of being discovered. While Pinchy maintains his innocence, Zane begins investigating Michaela's murder and soon encounters Michaela, alive. As Part I ends, Zane and Carl watch as men begin to gather around the jail, intent on lynching Pinchy. Zane starts to investigate the disappearance of a sheriff's deputy, Deputy White, whom he believes is somehow connected to the murder of the unidentified woman.

In Part II, Zane finds himself held captive by Deputy White's family, the secluded Jefferson-Whites. As he pleads with the family's leader, Seamus, to let him go, he discovers that the missing deputy is in fact Seamus's daughter Francis, who has been masquerading as a man. Escaping the Jefferson-Whites and returning to town, Zane resolves the identity of the murdered woman: Francis Jefferson-White. The sheriff continues to press Pinchy for information, believing he is innocent but eager to know what happened to Francis. While Zane has been investigating, Carl has been misidentified as Incognegro by a local Ku Klux Klan (KKK) leader and is led to his own lynching.

Carl is hung in Part III. Zane returns to the jail to explain his discoveries to the sheriff and is joined by Michaela, who admits to killing Francis when she caught her investigating Michaela and Pinchy's still. The sheriff shoots Michaela, avenging Francis's death, and admits that he knew Francis's secret. Zane and Pinchy return to Harlem, where Zane receives a promotion from his surly but supportive editor and publishes an article that identifies the KKK leader who lynched Carl as Incognegro.

Characters

- *Zane Pinchback*, a.k.a. *Incognegro*, the protagonist, is an African American who can pass as white, a transformation indicated primarily by a change in his hairstyle early in the novel. Fulfilled but emotionally exhausted from reporting on lynchings for a Harlem-based newspaper, he travels to the South to free his brother from jail.
- *Carl*, Zane's friend and unexpected companion on the journey to Mississippi, wants to go with Zane so that he can take over as Incognegro. While in Tupelo, he poses as a foreign dignitary,

helping Zane gather information, but he eventually proves to be a liability when he cannot keep up the act. He is lynched toward the end of the novel.
- *Alonzo Pinchback*, a.k.a. *Pinchy*, Zane's darker-skinned twin brother, is a serial troublemaker who is in jail for murdering his white girlfriend, Michaela Mathers. He maintains his innocence in the face of a lynch mob and is supported by the town's sheriff.
- *Francis Jefferson-White*, a.k.a. *Deputy White*, a woman passing as a man and serving as a sheriff's deputy, is missing. She was murdered by Michaela when she discovered Pinchy and Michaela's still. It is her body that Pinchy finds and mistakes for Michaela's.
- *Michaela Mathers*, Pinchy's girlfriend, killed Francis. Wanted by the police for making moonshine, she disguised Francis's body as her own in order to flee Tupelo.
- *The sheriff*, who believes that Pinchy is innocent, is Francis Jefferson-White's lover and the only one who knows that she is really a woman. He shoots Michaela after learning that she killed Francis.

Artistic Style

In an interview about his work on *Incognegro*, Pleece expressed his satisfaction with Vertigo's decision to leave his drawings in stark black and white instead of adding halftones, assuming that the choice was made intentionally. The intentionality of that choice is clear for two reasons: one, the noir style of the artwork reflects the aesthetic of the setting; and two, the contrast and tension between the black and white of the imagery reflects one of the most prominent themes of the novel, the contrasts between the black and white experiences of the South.

Just as the images are constructs, Johnson claims, through the voice of protagonist and narrator Zane, that race is a fallacy and a construct: "That's one thing that most of us know that white folks don't. That race doesn't really exist . . . race is a strategy. The rest is just people acting. Playing roles." The imagery, then, reflects the central point of the novel. The book is subtitled *A Graphic Mystery*, and the style recalls the dark shadows of noir style: Night scenes are not just dark, they are black; shadows do not merely muffle faces and figures, they bury them in darkness. While the mystery of the novel is heightened by this imagery, the contrasts of the images serve another, more significant purpose, as a literal manifestation of the contrasts between white and black Americans.

Central to understanding both black and white experiences of the South is the protagonist's ability to pass as white, illustrated in a one-page, eight-panel progression in which Zane becomes Incognegro, the white man who infiltrates lynchings. The allusion to superhero transformations, from everyday citizen to superhuman, is clear. The page begins with Zane's affirmation, "I am Incognegro," and follows with his clarification that he wears neither a mask nor a cape. Still, he is a superhero; a transparent American flag waves over him as he explains his power, invisibility, made possible only by white America's blindness to its past.

Pleece's style reinforces that blindness so that readers see what white America sees. Zane is, literally, white, as are the other African American characters in the novel. The absence of halftones means that skin tones are absent, and readers can only assume or perceive a character's race from the way others treat him or speak to him, from the way he treats or speaks to others, and from other verbal clues. As Zane tells us, "race is a strategy," and it is no less a strategy in this novel than it is in American society. While this style makes differentiating characters difficult, Pleece uses visual clues to make each character distinct: Carl has a moustache, Pinchy wears suspenders, and some white characters, such as Michaela, have white hair. Such distinctions indicate that, even had Pleece expected the publisher to wash the pages in halftones, his own intention was to draw in stark black and white to complement the content of the novel.

Themes

Incognegro is clearly a story about race, but it is more specifically a story about passing. Characters, both major and minor, pose as something other than they are, and what they really are is not always clear. Even the mystery

of the novel, the unsolved murder, is complicated by passing and by disguise: Michaela disguises Francis's body as her own so that she may safely escape Tupelo; when Zane first encounters Michaela, she appears to be a man, dressed in a trench coat and pants, with a hat placed low over her brow; a cash-poor resident of Tupelo pretends that he is a wealthy man to persuade Carl, himself passing as an English duke, to buy his land.

The most prominent and intentional example of passing is Zane, who transforms himself so that he can more easily pass as a white man. His motive is clear from the opening pages of the story. As he narrates his transformation for Carl and Carl's fiancé, the story he tells them is illustrated for readers: He easily blends in among the participants and spectators at a lynching and is betrayed only by his actions, not his appearance. His motivation is to write articles about lynchings for primarily northern newspapers, pointing out that lynching is no longer newsworthy in the South. Carl's fiancé marvels at Zane's heroism, reinforcing the idea that Zane is a superhero, donning a disguise and putting himself at risk for the greater good. This risk is great, as Carl is lynched when a local Klan leader thinks that he is Incognegro.

The risks of passing are also evidenced by Francis. While she is not murdered because she is passing as a man, her murder hints at the dangers inherent in fooling others: Zane and a local man are imprisoned by Francis's family because the two men misidentify her gender; the sheriff is robbed of Francis, his lover, because of her secret identity. Carl's situation is much the same, for it is not just because he is African American that he is lynched but because he is an African American who made prominent Caucasians of Tupelo feel foolish: Women wanted to marry him, he was invited to dinner, and he fraternized with a Klan leader. While their hatred of African Americans is undeniable, these men and women become violent when they feel that they have been wronged or tricked by someone whom they deem to be less intelligent or less capable than themselves, for lynching is used to assert the power of white over black.

A less prominent, but no less important, theme of the novel is that of the role of the media in public knowledge and public reaction. The resolution of the story calls into question media ethics and the media's responsibility for reporting the truth, as the Klan leader who sees through Zane's cover at the opening of the novel and later mistakes Carl for Incognegro is himself outed as Incognegro. Zane's outing of the Klan leader is clearly a breach of ethics, but in the context of the novel, it seems justified. This man is responsible for the deaths of many, including Carl; that he will die in the same horrific manner is somehow satisfying, and he would never have been punished for his crimes otherwise. Zane uses the power of the media, including the public's willingness to believe what it reads, to mete out punishment. The subtitle of the novel belies the complexity and importance of the story, as its central mystery becomes secondary to the horrors of lynching and the complicated questions of race, gender, passing, and, ultimately, justice.

Impact

Since its publication in 2008, *Incognegro* has been embraced by academics and readers of serious graphic novels alike. Author Johnson works from both an academic and a personal perspective, combining his study of the Harlem Renaissance with his own experiences as a light-skinned African American to create a novel that speaks to readers on many levels: as a mystery, as historical fiction, and as social and political commentary. While not as widely read or recognized as some of its

counterparts, Johnson's text has been used in history and literature classrooms to teach students about African American history, southern history and culture, and racism, while simultaneously introducing more modern themes such as gender crossing and media ethics. The novel has also contributed to the growing reputation of works of graphic fiction, joining such well-respected works of graphic nonfiction as *Maus* and *Persepolis* (2003) in legitimizing the graphic literature genre in academic institutions and libraries. Because Johnson is an academic and writer himself, his own reputation contributes significantly to the reception of the text.

Theresa Fine-Pawsey

Further Reading

Laird, Roland, Taneshia Nash Laird, and Elihu Bey. *Still I Rise: A Graphic History of African Americans* (1997).

Johnson, Mat, and Simon Gane. *Dark Rain: A New Orleans Story* (2010).

Satrapi, Marjane. *Persepolis* (2003).

Spiegelman, Art. *Maus: A Survivor's Tale* (1986).

Bibliography

Chaney, Michael A. "Drawing on History in Recent African American Graphic Novels." *MELUS: The Journal of the Society for the Study of the Multi-Ethnic Literature of the United States* 32, no. 3 (2007): 175-200.

Coogan, Peter. "The Definition of the Superhero." In *A Comics Studies Reader*, edited by Jeet Heer and Kent Worcester. Jackson: University Press of Mississippi, 2009.

Johnson, Charles. "Foreword: A Capsule History of Blacks in Comics." In *Still I Rise: A Graphic History of African Americans*, by Roland Laird, Taneshia Nash Laird, and Elihu Bey. New York: Sterling, 2009.

Lutes, Jean M. "Lynching Coverage and the American Reporter-Novelist." *American Literary History* 19, no. 2 (Summer, 2007): 456-481.

See also: *Persepolis; Maus: A Survivor's Tale; A.D.: New Orleans After the Deluge*

I Never Liked You: A Comic-Strip Narrative

Author: Brown, Chester
Artist: Chester Brown (illustrator)
Publisher: Drawn and Quarterly
First serial publication: 1991-1993
First book publication: 1994

Publication History

I Never Liked You was originally serialized in issues 26-30 (October, 1991, to April, 1993) of Chester Brown's comic book *Yummy Fur* under the title *F----*. *Yummy Fur* began as a self-published minicomic in 1983 and was picked up by Toronto-based Vortex Comics in 1986. The series later transitioned to Montreal-based Drawn and Quarterly beginning with issue 25. While early issues included an eclectic mix of shorter, humorous pieces along with regular installments of the surreal *Ed the Happy Clown* (1989) and the biblical adaptation *The Gospel of Mark* (1987), *Yummy Fur* eventually became an outlet for Brown's autobiographical work, a volume of which was published as *The Playboy* by Drawn and Quarterly in 1992.

I Never Liked You was first collected under that title in hardcover and paperback editions published by Drawn and Quarterly in 1994. The first edition maintained the series' original black backgrounds, but the book was reformatted with white backgrounds for a second Drawn and Quarterly paperback edition in 2002. Known as "The New Definitive Edition," the second edition also incorporates an important cover image into the narrative proper and includes two pages of endnotes, providing context for both the story and its production. A third and similar paperback edition was published by Drawn and Quarterly in 2007.

Plot

Set in the Montreal suburb of Châteauguay in the mid-1970's, *I Never Liked You* is an autobiographical story from Brown's teenage years, focusing especially on his relationships with his mother and a number of neighborhood girls. A prologue set in 1969, when Brown was nine years old, sets the impressionistic and understated narrative in motion by introducing both

I Never Liked You: A Comic-Strip Narrative. (Courtesy of Drawn and Quarterly)

Connie, the older of two girls living across the street, and Brown's mother, who chastises him for swearing. The story then skips a few years ahead and introduces Carrie, Connie's younger sister, who has an obvious crush on Brown but does not act on it. Because of the sparse narrative and dispassionate authorial voice of the novel, Brown's own feelings are at first difficult to determine. He spends time with Connie and Carrie as well as another girl, Sky. Brown eventually develops a crush on Sky, and a few scenes demonstrate his initial inability to communicate his feelings to her. When he finally does, she reacts positively, but Brown subsequently withdraws, seemingly unable to develop their relationship. Making up excuses for not spending time with her, he finally rejects her outright in favor of listening to the new Kiss record.

Meanwhile, Carrie's crush continues. However, when she hears about Brown's declaration to Sky, she attacks him in a fit of anger and screams the words that give the book its title. Connie remains an enigmatic figure, and her relationship with Brown is never defined. He admits to not liking her much, except when the two form a team and play hide-and-seek in the fields with the other neighborhood children. At school, Brown is constantly teased for his refusal to use swear words, and the other children's numerous attempts to trick him into swearing become a running gag.

A second important plot strand concerns Brown's relationship with his mother, who is suffering from schizophrenia. Her relatively few appearances in the story are clearly of intense emotional importance to Brown and include such instances as her attempt to talk to her two teenage sons about the female body and Brown's refusal to run a small errand for her because he would rather watch television. She commits herself to a hospital near the end of the story. When the family visits, Brown fails at his attempt to tell her he loves her, despite having practiced on the way to the hospital. She dies shortly after, and Brown tries to cry but can only force a single tear to come.

Characters

- *Chester Brown*, the autobiographical protagonist, is a skinny, long-haired teenage boy living in the Montreal suburb of Châteauguay, Quebec, during the 1970's. He is quiet and emotionally reserved and relates awkwardly to the other characters. His relationship with his mother is particularly strained, and he is unable to show her any affection. His refusal to use swear words stems from his religious upbringing.
- *Chester Brown's mother* is devoutly religious and suffers from schizophrenia. She looks older than she is and is insecure in her relationship with Brown. She often talks to her two sons about matters that embarrass them, but it is clear that she craves their affection. At the end of the story, she checks herself into a hospital for treatment, but she dies there shortly afterward.

- *Connie* is the older of two girls living across the street. She is one year younger than Brown and has a somewhat bossy demeanor. Her relationship with Brown remains unclear, but they often spend time together despite having little to talk about.
- *Carrie* is Connie's younger sister. She is two years younger than Brown and has an unspoken yet obvious crush on him that is not reciprocated. Her many attempts to win his affection are unsuccessful, and she finally attacks him in a fit of rage after she hears that he has confessed his love to Sky. She has a boyfriend at the end of the story.
- *Sky* is a girl who lives next door. She is two years younger than Brown and in the same grade as his brother, Gordon. She stands out from the other girls because of her large breasts and dark hair, and Brown masturbates while thinking about her. She often sits next to Brown in the library. She returns his declaration of love but grows impatient when he is unable to act on it.

Artistic Style

I Never Liked You is drawn in a minimalist style, exhibiting an extraordinary sense of restraint. The pared-down visuals are a natural development from Brown's earlier autobiographical work in *The Playboy*, which itself is a departure from his earlier, more cartoonlike and detailed work in *Ed the Happy Clown*. Despite being fully formed and highly proficient on a technical level, the evocative black-and-white drawings often resemble sketches drawn from an incomplete recollection, an approach that underscores the narrative's highly personal involvement with childhood memory.

Brown's quavering and fragile lines cause characters to seem small, insecure, and insignificant, none more so than Brown himself. While the backgrounds are highly naturalistic, characters are most often drawn as exceedingly thin and depicted with large heads and blank stares, adding to the overall evacuation of emotional investment. An exception is the voluptuous Sky, whose curvy appearance adds gravity to her presence and underlines her prominence in Brown's memories. The skilled use of contrast and large areas of negative space gives the book an ephemeral feel that fits perfectly with the impressionistic and sparse narrative.

Brown is known for his inventive use of irregularly spaced panels and for his untraditional way of arranging them on the page. While most single images are of a similar size, the number on each page varies greatly, from one to as many as seven or eight. Brown drew each panel on a separate piece of paper and assembled the pages afterward, a technique that allows for great flexibility with pacing and gives each image

I Never Liked You: A Comic-Strip Narrative. (Courtesy of Drawn and Quarterly)

the potential for heightened significance depending on where it is placed.

Themes

The main theme of *I Never Liked You* is Brown's inability to form personal relationships in his teenage years. An uncommunicative and emotionally reticent boy, Brown finds it impossible to relate to both his peers and his mother, and the book is tinged with a sense of Brown's regret at having failed at both. The scene in which Brown visits his mother in the hospital is especially powerful, as he practices telling her he loves her, imagining the healing effect of his words, only to fail at the last minute.

Speech itself appears as a secondary theme and is evident in both the imagined significance of declarations of love and affection and Brown's refusal to swear. It is suggested that his religious upbringing might have influenced his inability to communicate strong feelings to the people in his life. The book's preoccupation with the confused verbal silences of adolescence is mirrored in the many blank visual spaces, which often isolate characters physically from the rest of the narrative and depict them as dwarfed by their surroundings.

The difficulty of communicating through the means of language is underscored by a sequence in which Brown draws an image of a skeleton reaching for a bird as a present for Sky. In this image, the bird represents Sky and the skeleton Brown. He is perfectly articulate when describing its meaning to himself, but when questioned by Sky, he denies that it carries any special significance and later claims never to use symbolism. Only through art can Brown express himself, and, thus, *I Never Liked You* documents an important step in his realization of artistic purpose and also serves as a belated attempt to communicate with those he feels he has let down, including his adolescent self.

Impact

I Never Liked You, along with its predecessor *The Playboy*, was part of a late 1980's and early 1990's surge in autobiographical comics. Inspired by the 1960's and 1970's underground artists Robert Crumb, Harvey Pekar, and Justin Green and frequently emerging from 1980's "zine" culture, artists such as

Joe Matt, Seth, Julie Doucet, Lynda Barry, and Mary Fleener began depicting events from their pasts and daily lives in quotidian and often uncomfortable detail. Dedicated to factual and emotional truth, artists such as Brown and Matt became known for their unflattering self-portraits as pornography and masturbation addicts, and the simple aesthetic of the black-and-white images was often seen as underscoring the authenticity of the work and lending credibility to the project of exposing the artists' most private sides. This convenient but facile and superficial analysis belies the fact that many of these stories are in fact artfully crafted narratives drawn in a highly sophisticated visual style, as is the case with *I Never Liked You*.

Brown's shift to autobiography was brought about by his interest in the work of Matt and Doucet, while his pared-down style was influenced by the simple and slightly old-fashioned style of Seth. In the years since the publication of *I Never Liked You*, autobiography has become one of the most lasting and artistically fertile genres in the world of comics. Artists such as Jeffrey Brown and Ariel Schrag continue the project of documenting painful personal history in a sparse visual style, while Anders Nilsen's masterful use of negative space is indebted to the absences and large empty spaces of *I Never Liked You*.

Frederik Byrn Køhlert

Further Reading

Brown, Jeffrey. *Funny Misshapen Body* (2009).
Matt, Joe. *Fair Weather* (2002).
Schrag, Ariel. *Potential* (2000).

Bibliography

Daly, Mark, and Rich Kreiner. "Seth, Brown, Matt." *The Comics Journal* 162 (1993): 51-56.
Grammel, Scott. "Chester Brown: From the Sacred to the Scatological." *The Comics Journal* 135 (1990): 66-90.
Hatfield, Charles. "The Autobiographical Stories in *Yummy Fur*." *The Comics Journal* 210 (1999): 67.
Juno, Andrea. "Chester Brown." In *Dangerous Drawings: Interviews with Comix and Graphix Artists*. New York: Juno Books, 1997.
Levin, Bob. "Good Ol' Chester Brown: A Psycho-Literary Exploration of *Yummy Fur*." *The Comics Journal* 162 (1993): 45-49.
Wolk, Douglas. "Chester Brown: The Outsider." In *Reading Comics: How Graphic Novels Work and What They Mean*. New York: Da Capo Press, 2007.

See also: *Ed the Happy Clown; The Playboy; The Complete Fritz the Cat; American Splendor*

IN THE SHADOW OF NO TOWERS

Author: Spiegelman, Art
Artist: Art Spiegelman (illustrator)
Publisher: Pantheon Books
First serial publication: 2002-2004
First book publication: 2004

Publication History

Art Spiegelman's graphic novel *In the Shadow of No Towers* began as a series of comic strips, published by the German weekly broadsheet newspaper *Die Zeit*, that ran from 2002 to 2004. The strip was later picked up by such publications as *Courrier International*, *The London Review of Books*, and *Internazionale*. Because of the work's sensitive subject matter, major publications such as *The New York Times*, *The New Yorker*, and *The New York Review of Books*, to which Spiegelman was a regular contributor, shied away from publishing the strips. Spiegelman eventually found willing American publishing outlets for his nonfiction political comics in the Jewish weekly broadsheet newspaper *The Forward*, *The LA Weekly*, *The Chicago Weekly*, and the semiannual political "comix" magazine *World War Three Illustrated*.

In 2004, Pantheon Books, a division of Random House, published a collection of the ten strips, combined with a supplement of early twentieth-century Sunday comics such as *The Katzenjammer Kids* and *Happy Hooligan*, which had given Spiegelman comfort in the days following the terrorist attacks of September 11, 2001 (9/11), and which he integrated into his strips. The early comics employed within the twenty-first-century pages of Spiegelman's work serve to reconnect the modern reader with America's cultural and artistic past through the medium of comics.

All of the artistic works contained in the book are the products of Spiegelman, with the exception of the early twentieth-century plates that compose "The Comic Supplement" and the latter half of the book. These images are from *The Kin-der-Kids Abroad* (1906), illustrated by Lyonel Feininger; *The War Scare in Hogan's Alley* (1896), illustrated by Richard Felton Outcault; *The Upside-Downs of Little Lady Lovekins and Old Man Muffaroo* (1904), illustrated by Gustave Verbeck; *The Glorious Fourth of July!* (1902), illustrated by Gene Carr, Rudolph Dirks, Frederick Burr Opper, and Carl Edward Schultze; *Happy Hooligan* (1911), illustrated by Opper; *Little Nemo in Slumberland* (1907), illustrated by Winsor McCay; and *Bringing Up Father*, illustrated by Geo McManus.

Plot

A postmodern version of one man's struggle with post-traumatic stress disorder, *In the Shadow of No Towers* is Spiegelman's sardonic analysis of the culpability for and the nation's reactions to the September 11, 2001, terrorist attacks on the United States, illustrated through the panicked portrayal of his own personal experience. Once a self-declared "rootless cosmopolitan," Spiegelman narrates the events of 9/11 in a way that causes his own perception of himself and his home city to change. In struggling to maintain his own sanity while grappling with the grim realities and causalities of the attacks, Spiegelman renounces his transient status in favor of that of a "rooted cosmopolitan." The traumatic alteration of the New York City skyline and the vast confusion and disarray of the lower Manhattan landscape, the author's home, sets Spiegelman's artistic wheels spinning as he seeks a way to cope with the devastation that engulfed his city in particular and the country as a whole.

Both Spiegelman's narrative and the strip panels are fragmented, as paranoia takes hold of him and conspiracy theories abound. Following the 2000 election, which the author refers to as a "coup d'état," he is distrustful of the U.S. government, principally the Republican Party and the George W. Bush presidential administration. Spiegelman is highly suspicious of President Bush and his motivations for declaring war on Iraq, claiming that the tragic events of 9/11 were used as a catalyst to declare war not for justice, but for Middle Eastern oil. In numerous panels throughout *In the Shadow of No Towers*, the author depicts Bush as a villain and a threat to the very country he was elected to lead and protect.

After the Twin Towers collapsed upon themselves, and apparently before the dust even had a chance to settle, the sales of American flags and other such patriotic paraphernalia skyrocketed. To Spiegelman, this does not signal patriotism so much as the mass disillusion of Americans, who pushed the vision of the falling towers to the back of their minds as they moved forward in the myriad lines of stores and street vendors peddling "I Love NY" kitsch.

Spiegelman's varied, almost schizophrenic panels are the means by which the author seeks to know himself as an American and as a New Yorker. Searching for solace and a sense of grounding, he turns to the founding fathers of his profession, resulting in his constant references to the late-nineteenth- and early twentieth-century comic-strip characters that abound throughout his ten strips and make up "The Comic Supplement" and the latter half of the novel.

Characters

- *Art Spiegelman*, the protagonist, is the author and illustrator of the work. He is a chain-smoker and conspiracy theorist whose paranoia is often justified and heightened by his obsession with the news. In a reference to his Pulitzer Prize-winning graphic novel *Maus: A Survivor's Tale* (1986), which chronicles his father's survival of the Holocaust, Spiegelman depicts himself as a mouse when he notes parallels between the Holocaust and the 9/11 attacks and as he struggles with the task of translating his emotions into the comic form.
- *Françoise Mouly* is Spiegelman's wife and the mother of his children, Nadja and Dashiell. The art editor of *The New Yorker*, Mouly commissioned the black-on-black afterimage of the Twin Towers that would later become the front cover of *In the Shadow of No Towers*.
- *Nadja Spiegelman* is Spiegelman's teenage daughter and the focus of several panels. She had just started high school at the foot of the Twin Towers three days prior to the attacks, and Spiegelman recounts his and his wife's hysterical search for their daughter.
- *George W. Bush*, the antagonist, is the president of the United States from 2001 to 2009.

As Spiegelman is angry about the suspicious circumstances surrounding Bush's election to the presidency and distrustful of his position as both a politician and a businessman, Bush is the source of much of Spiegelman's anxiety and the target for his blame and cynicism.
- *The Katzenjammer Kids* are two comic pranksters named Hans and Fritz who were created by Dirks in 1897. They serve as personifications of the Twin Towers throughout the graphic novel.
- *Happy Hooligan* is a loveable but unlucky cartoon character created by Opper in 1899. Having looked to old comics for solace following the 9/11 attacks, Spiegelman posits himself as the bumbling Hooligan in the collection's final strip.

Artistic Style

With the exception of the haunting black-on-black book cover featuring the afterimage of the towers, almost every part of every panel is filled with color. The book's central image is one created from Spiegelman's memory: "the image of the looming north tower's glowing bones just before it vaporized." In several instances, the glowing orange of the tower's skeletal remains is contrasted with surrounding panels painted red, white, and blue, intentionally evoking simultaneous feelings of patriotism and destruction.

The individual panels within each strip often appear erratically positioned, so as to physically mirror Spiegelman's mentally and emotionally frantic state. Panels overlap other panels throughout the pages, lending a chaotic scheme to the overall design without hindering readability. Often, the reader may jump from one set of panels to another because the eyes become distracted, but again, this is symbolic of the author's disjointed experience.

The character designs and the lettering are not complex; rather, they are simplified because the message of the work is what most concerns the author. Although the characters are more cartoonlike than realistic, every page contains a mixture of characters and mediums, from different types of self-portraits of the author and the inclusion of multiple late-nineteenth- and early twentieth-century comic characters to the addition of photographs, Topps cards, and billboards. Unlike the traditional 6.75 x 10-inch comic book, the 17 x 22-inch broadsheet newspaper allows for greater experimentation regarding layout and the amount of media that can be placed on a single page.

Themes

In the Shadow of No Towers focuses on a dreaded anticipation, or as Spiegelman puts it, "waiting for the other shoe to drop." The fear and paranoia that the author expresses is not fabricated but is a very real part of his trauma following 9/11. This anxiety is the result of familial crisis and the traumatic memory that is inextricably linked to it. Just as Spiegelman struggles to narrate his father's Holocaust experiences in *Maus*, he wrestles with his own fears of loss and historic devastation in *In the Shadow of No Towers*. In an attempt to foresee the next catastrophe and protect his family, Spiegelman becomes increasingly suspicious of the rhetoric of mainstream media and politicians.

Spiegelman's distrust of the U.S. government and President Bush weighs heavily on his mind. His conspiracy theorizing results in the creation of several disturbing images that posit the president as a traitor, warmonger, and murderer. Spiegelman also notes the presence of a giant billboard for the Arnold Schwarzenegger film *Collateral Damage* in the foreground of his view of the burning Twin Towers, hinting that those who die and suffer as a result of the attacks are merely anticipated losses in an oil war waged under the guise of justice and retribution. As history has shown, in times of war, people seek comfort in simpler eras and past pleasures; Spiegelman initially delves into antique comics for this very reason. In integrating these apparently delightful reminders of the comic's past into Modern Age "comix," the author pays tribute to the tragedy of 9/11 while reinforcing the importance of the genre and its ability to serve as a unique means of social and political critique.

Impact

In a narrative fashion similar to that of his groundbreaking work *Maus*, Spiegelman again constructs a family's firsthand account of epic acts of terrorism and the effects of living in and coping with the aftermath. Spiegelman must continually relive the trauma of 9/11 in order to capture the realism of that day and translate it onto the comic book page. The more the author dwells on the terrorist attacks, the more he begins to view the U.S. government as a part of the terrorist cell responsible for the deaths of thousands of people. For Spiegelman, 9/11 was not only a day that altered American history and consciousness but also one on which "the world ended."

There is no shortage of material to analyze on each page. Therefore, the book requires several readings, without which the reader is certain to miss a large portion of the nuanced information Spiegelman meticulously places in every panel sequence. Spiegelman's requirement of a certain amount of effort from his readers is in line with his own close examination of the happenings during and after the 9/11 attacks. As he focuses on the minutiae of every speech, newscast, advertisement, and public-service announcement, so too does he wish his reader to take in and seriously consider the meanings behind and the overall effect of the media presented on each page.

To some readers, the oversized pages, overly dramatic conspiracy theory-driven images, and overtly sweating characters may seem over-the-top and, thus, lacking in depth. However, many critics view the book as a painfully honest and unmitigated biographical production that not only serves as a kind of follow-up to *Maus* but also continues Spiegelman's personal journey in which he is forced to deal with familial grief and traumatic memory. With *In the Shadow of No Towers*, Spiegelman revolutionizes the way readers see comics and comix, seamlessly incorporating vintage and contemporary illustrations and the themes within them into his biographical account of living through tragedy. The media through which Spiegelman expresses himself constantly offer new aspects to analyze, from their artistic and aesthetic value to their cultural and sociopolitical significance. *In the Shadow of No Towers* is a unique and artistic rendering of one man's battle with terror, authority, grief, and memory.

Lydia E. Ferguson

Further Reading

McCloud, Scott. *Understanding Comics: The Invisible Art* (1994).
Satrapi, Marjane. *The Complete Persepolis* (2006).
Yang, Gene Luen. *American Born Chinese* (2006).

Bibliography

Chute, Hillary. "'The Shadow of a Past Time': History and Graphic Representation in *Maus*." *Twentieth Century Literature* 52, no. 2 (Summer, 2006): 199-230.

Hirsch, Marianne. "Editor's Column: Collateral Damage." *PLA* 119, no. 5 (October, 2004): 1209-1215.

Orbán, Katalin. "Trauma and Visuality: Art Spiegelman's *Maus* and *In the Shadow of No Towers*." *Representations* 97 (Winter, 2007): 57-89.

See also: *Maus: A Survivor's Tale; The 9/11 Report;*

IT RHYMES WITH LUST

Author: Waller, Drake (pseudonym of Arnold Drake and Leslie Waller)
Artist: Matt Baker (illustrator); Ray Osrin (inker and letterer)
Publisher: Dark Horse Comics
First book publication: 1950

Publication History

Originally published in 1950 as the first of a proposed series of what St. John Publications called "picture novels," *It Rhymes with Lust*, written by Arnold Drake and Leslie Waller (as Drake Waller), was part of a short-lived experiment in creating a mature comic book series for adults, using a small paperback format. As such, it is seen by some as the first graphic novel, particularly as it combined text and images in a way that precursors of the form had not. The book remained out of print for many years, making it a valuable rarity that commanded a high price in *The Overstreet Comic Book Price Guide*. As interest in the graphic novel and its development grew, the book was reprinted by Dark Horse Comics in 2007, in a close facsimile edition with short biographies of Drake, Waller, and illustrator Matt Baker and an afterword by Drake.

Plot

The story opens with reporter Hal Weber returning to his hometown, Copper City, at the behest of an old flame, Rust Masson. He arrives to find Rust attending the funeral of her husband, Buck Masson, a rich businessman and boss of the local political machine. Rust offers Hal the job of editing a local newspaper, *The Express*, which she secretly owns and plans to use to discredit Marcus Jeffers, who hopes to inherit Buck Masson's empire. Almost immediately, Marcus Jeffers tries to persuade Hal to double-cross Rust.

Hal then goes on a date with Rust's attractive stepdaughter, Audrey Masson, to the expensive Club Gaucho; there is a strong attraction between them. She warns Hal about Rust, but Hal continues to do Rust's bidding; despite some reservations, he searches for dirt on Jeffers. He meets Audrey again, and she continues

It Rhymes with Lust. (Courtesy of Dark Horse Comics)

to make him feel guilty, especially when they talk about Hal's father, an honest newspaper man.

Hal receives a tip that Jeffers runs an illegal gambling den, and when he passes this information to Rust, she assures him that she will arrange for the place to be raided. Instead, she arranges for her hired thug, Monk Shirl, to bomb the gambling den. Aware of who has destroyed his club, Jeffers confronts Rust, but she reveals that she has incriminating evidence that she can use to blackmail him.

Meanwhile, Hal refuses to believe that Rust had anything to do with the bombing. (An innocent paperboy is killed in the blast.) Jake, his assistant at *The Express*, persuades him to suspect Rust. Hal is taken to Masson's mines by Pop, the local taxi driver; when they are nearly killed in a cave-in, he has evidence against Rust that he can print in his newspaper. However, when he confronts her, the combination of her denial and her sexual allure persuades him he is wrong.

Audrey witnesses this, and, after Hal leaves, she confronts Rust, who slaps her in the face. Later, seeing

Audrey's injuries, Hal takes her back to confront Rust. They arrive just in time to see Monk Shirl and another thug, Tiny, killing Marcus Jeffers. In perhaps the most implausible twist in the plot, Hal not only fails to stop the killing, thereby driving Audrey away, but he also agrees to help Tiny dump the body.

It Rhymes with Lust. (Courtesy of Dark Horse Comics)

Alone in his apartment, Hal confronts his own weakness, not only for Rust but also for alcohol. With a bottle of liquor in one hand and Audrey's glove in the other, he makes a choice and smashes the bottle against the wall. He returns to the newspaper office and begins to write a full exposé. Hal arranges for the newspapers to be delivered. Meanwhile, a badly injured Marcus Jeffers has survived and hitches a ride on a truck.

While Jeffers plans his revenge, Rust is woken by Monk Shirl who is holding a copy of the *Express* newspaper. She discovers that her former allies are beginning to desert her. She then has to employ Monk and his thugs to help her confront the miners who are refusing to work. In a confrontation at the mine, Rust and Monk mount one of the automated mine buckets to address the miners. At this point, Jeffers arrives, and, as he hears Rust blaming him for all the previous events, he switches the power, putting the bucket in motion. Monk shoots Jeffers, but the bucket tips Rust and Monk, and all three die. The novel finishes with a conventional happy ending: Audrey forgives Hal and they appear to settle down to domestic bliss.

Characters

- *Rust Masson* is prepared to use violence to achieve her aims, whether directly or indirectly. Judging by the color cover, Rust's name derives from her hair, which is red and is cut in a short, assertive style. As drawn by Baker, she has all the attributes of an attractive but deadly femme fatale.
- *Hal Weber* is an archetypal American alpha-male hero, but his weakness is clearly women, particularly the manipulative Rust. He is tortured by his guilt for much of the novel and is unable to escape the wiles of Rust.
- *Audrey Masson* is the daughter of Buck Masson's first marriage and is at loggerheads with her stepmother, whom she knows married her father only for his money and power. She has long flowing hair and is the more traditionally feminine counterpart to the assertive Rust.
- *Monk Shirl* is Rust's main thug who is prepared to follow her orders to the letter. He would like to

be more than just her hired gun, but Rust resists his advances.
- *Marcus Jeffers* is an obese, corrupt businessman who is less under the influence of Rust than others but is driven by the desire for power.

Artistic Style

Baker, an African American illustrator, a rarity in mainstream comics during the 1950's, is best known for drawing comics with beautiful heroines, a genre known as "Good Girl Art." His most famous characters were the leads in *Sheena, Queen of the Jungle* and *Phantom Lady*; the pneumatic figure of the latter was cited by Frederic Wertham in his 1954 book *The Seduction of the Innocent* as having a detrimental effect on the nation's youth. The two main female characters in the book, Rust and Audrey, are drawn in Baker's usual style, both rendered as beautiful and sensual, with the shapely figures that were fashionable in the 1950's.

It Rhymes with Lust is drawn in the bold style typical of many mainstream comics of the period, with strong brush-inked lines and solid blacks. Baker is more comfortable with figures, and his landscapes and street scenes are perhaps less convincing, hampered by the small scale of the book and the fact that most pages have three or four panels.

Full-page panels are used for dramatic effect, such as the bombing scene and the deaths of Rust and Monk. Baker is more confident with interiors, and the artwork uses detailed tone effects that allow various shades of gray to be introduced where necessary. This technique is used to great effect on some interior scenes, creating depth and atmosphere. For example, Hal is shown sitting in an office that is almost entirely rendered in tone with no line artwork, giving the room a gray, bleak feeling. Elsewhere, this effect is used to create a sense of depth, with either figures or backgrounds atmospherically rendered entirely in tone.

Themes

As suggested by the title, the book's central theme is lust, both in a sexual context and also in terms of lust for power. The themes of the book are typical of those in "hard-boiled" detective fiction and film noir popular in the United States in the 1930's and 1940's. The story

Arnold Drake

A prolific writer for Marvel and DC Comics in the 1960's, Arnold Drake created several seminal characters, including Deadman, the Doom Patrol, and the Guardians of the Galaxy, which are still regularly published today. In the 1950's, he helped pioneer the graphic novel form with the adult crime story *It Rhymes with Lust*. Known for his tight plotting, characterization, and subversive humor, Drake received several fan awards both during his lifetime and following his death in 2007.

deals with a central, sexual relationship between two people set in an evil, crime-ridden world.

The plot is driven by Rust Masson, the femme fatale. She is a typical femme fatale, in that she is prepared to achieve her aims by any means necessary, including murder; in particular, she will use her sexual charms to control the men she meets. This archetype has attracted criticism from feminist writers, who see the femme fatale as a strong, sexualized woman who is punished for these characteristics by a patriarchal society. This punishment is usually extreme and, as in the case of Rust Masson, often ends in the death of the character.

Meanwhile, the central male character, Hal Webber, is initially in the thrall of Rust, and the events that unfold are largely out of his control. This is typical of film noir, in that the evil events that happen are not caused by the hero or victim but happen for no good reason.

The sexual nature of the relationship between Rust and Hal is clear, but even though the book is aimed at adults, the extent of their affair is not shown overtly. They are shown in a torrid, virtually horizontal kiss, for example, taking up the whole of the page, but on the next page, they are shown talking, with Hal in his shirtsleeves and a glass in his hand. The shift in time and space is subtle but can be read as the equivalent of the "fade" used in films of the time and that implied sexual activity that the censor would not allow to be shown. Hal in particular deals with the tension between integrity and lustful and financial temptation.

Impact

The book and the following picture novel, *The Case of the Winking Buddha* (1950), were not commercially successful. Low sales meant that the experimental series was stopped after those two titles. The time may have not been right for the acceptance of a graphic novel, even in a paperback book format. A similar attempt was made in 1950 by Gold Key Comics, but its title, *Mansion of Evil*, by Joseph Millard, was also a failure even though it used interior color. Had any of these books been successful, they might have changed the history of the form, spawning a range of imitators. The picture books' impact was therefore limited, other than perhaps discouraging other publishers from undertaking similar experiments. Nevertheless, the picture books can be seen as an attempt, allied with the experiments of EC Comics and others, to produce more sophisticated and adult comics in the decade after World War II.

David Huxley

Further Reading

Kane, Gil. *His Name Is . . . Savage!* (1968).

Millard, Joseph. *Mansion of Evil* (1950).

Stokes, Manning Lee, and Charles Raab. *The Case of the Winking Buddha* (1950).

Bibliography

Gilbert, Michael T., and Ken Quattro. "It Rhymes with Lust." *The Comics Journal* 277 (July, 2006): 78.

Jourdain, Bill. "Comics' First Great African American Artist." *Golden Age of Comic Books*, June 17, 2009. http://goldenagecomics.org/wordpress/2009/06/17/comics-then-5-comics-first-great-african-american-artist.

Stout, Tim. "*It Rhymes with Lust* Story Structure." *Tim Stout*. http://timstout.wordpress.com/story-structure/it-rhymes-with-lust-story-structure.

See also: *He Done Her Wrong*

IT'S A BIRD . . .

Author: Seagle, Steven T.
Artist: Teddy H. Kristiansen (illustrator); Todd Klein (letterer)
Publisher: DC Comics
First book publication: 2004

Publication History

It's a Bird . . ., written by American Steven T. Seagle and illustrated through paintings by Danish artist Teddy Kristiansen, was originally released as a hardcover graphic novel from DC Comics' Vertigo line in 2004. It was released as a paperback in 2005. Seagle and Kristiansen had previously collaborated on *House of Secrets* (1996-1998) for Vertigo.

Plot

In some ways, *It's a Bird . . .* is a graphic novel about Superman, but the story of Superman is never told. Steve, the main character, is a comic book writer, and Seagle admits that the story is highly autobiographical.

The story starts with a flashback in which Steve is remembering his first encounter with a *Superman* comic book. He and his brother are children and are at the hospital where his father's mother is dying of the genetic disorder Huntington's disease. In an attempt to keep the two boys entertained and out of trouble, Steve's father gives them a *Superman* comic book to share. The story then jumps to present day and the adult Steve receives two phone calls that serve to merge the two interconnected plotlines together.

The first call is from Jeremy, Steve's editor, who offers Steve the job of writing for *Superman*. Steve tells Jeremy he's not interested, but Jeremy will not be deterred. The second phone call is from Steve's mother who is worried and wants to see Steve, who promises to come see her as soon as he's able. Steve then sees his girlfriend, Lisa, and starts to think about Superman and what the character means to people. Steve also visits his doctor and discusses his concern about developing Huntington's disease.

Steve visits his mother; she tells him his father is missing and that she wants Steve to go looking for

Steven T. Seagle

Writer Steven T. Seagle became one of the hallmark creators associated with DC Comics' Vertigo imprint when he took over from Matt Wagner as the writer of *Sandman Mystery Theatre*. In 1996, he launched *House of Secrets*, a horror title with artist Teddy Kristiansen, and in 2006 he created *American Virgin* with Becky Cloonan, both of which were produced by Vertigo. His graphic novel *It's a Bird . . .*, with Kristiansen, presented a highly unusual take on Superman through the lens of autobiographical writing. Despite his many successes in mainstream comics, Seagle's writing has always been somewhat on the periphery of the genres that he is asked to write in, and his work is often characterized by a more introspective take on genre conventions than is normally associated with superheroes and horror. Seagle is a member of the Man of Action group with Duncan Rouleau, Joe Casey, and Joe Kelly, and collectively created the *Ben 10* television franchise for the Cartoon Network.

him. He promises he will, but first he has to meet with Jeremy. In his meeting with Jeremy, he again refuses the *Superman* assignment on the grounds that Superman is not a realistic character. Jeremy still will not accept his refusal and gives him copies of *Superman* to read.

Steve asks his friend Raphael for a ride to Long Island to search for his father. The last time his father vanished, he had gone to see his sister Sarah. Steve decides to go to his Aunt Sarah's house, but he finds it abandoned. Raphael returns Steve to the city, and he meets with the current writer of *Superman*. Steve gets into a fight with the editor and punches him.

Steve meets with Jeremy the following day, and they go to the gym. Jeremy gives Steve another few days to come up with his plans for *Superman*. Leaving the gym, Steve runs into Marco, a friend from film school who has just written a play about Huntington's disease, which also runs in his family. When Steve goes home that night, he has a fight with Lisa, who walks out on him.

Steve spends the next few days in bed in a deep depression until his brother, Dave, comes over. Steve tells Dave about their father, and they go looking for him. They trace him to a bar, and even though their dad isn't there when Steve and Dave arrive, they're directed to a nearby nursing home. Steve and Dave discover that Aunt Sarah is a patient at the nursing home, and their father has been spending most of his time there with his sister.

Steve goes to his aunt's room and finds that she is in the final stages of Huntington's disease. His father comes back to the room and is angry that his sons have found him. Steve and his father get into a fight; finally, Steve confronts his father about what he said when his own mother died: If he had known about the disease and that it ran in his family, he never would have had his boys. The family confrontation ends with Steve and his father reconciling and with Steve coming to terms with the disease that is haunting his life. He returns home to Lisa, and they soon move into a new apartment. Finally, Steve takes the job of writing *Superman*.

Characters

- *Steve*, the protagonist, is a comic book writer who is asked to write *Superman*. He finds, however, that he cannot relate to the character since his family is dealing with the devastating effects of Huntington's disease.
- *Lisa* is Steve's understanding girlfriend who wants their relationship to move forward and who is unaware that Huntington's disease runs in Steve's family.
- *Jeremy* is Steve's editor who offers him the job of writing *Superman* comics and cannot understand why Steve is refusing the offer.
- *Dave* is Steve's brother and an electrician.
- *Steve's mom* is worried when her husband goes missing and refuses to talk about Huntington's disease or its effect on her family.
- *Steve's dad* carries guilt about the fact that Huntington's disease runs on his side of the family, and he leaves home to take care of his sister, who is dying from the disease.

- *Raphael* is a cab driver that Steve relies on for transportation. He is an avid comic book fan who likes to ask who would win matchups between characters.
- *Aunt Sarah* is Steve's aunt (his father's sister) and is in the final stages of Huntington's disease.

Artistic Style

The artwork for *It's a Bird . . .* is painted by Kristiansen, who employs many different styles, depending on whether the scene depicted is the main story arc, a flashback, or one of the many commentaries on Superman. The art for the main plotline is an example of what comics creator and scholar Scott McCloud refers to as "iconic." While characters are identifiable—for example, Steve has glasses and dark hair and always wears black—they are not completely realistic visually. This technique is useful for a comic book that deals with heavy themes; for example, it masks the toll that Huntington's disease has taken on Aunt Sarah. Kristiansen gives Sarah just enough detail to make her appear individual and human. The artwork then leaves readers with a haunting image of the disease that is taking over her body.

The flashbacks are rendered in lighter colors than the scenes that take place in the present, reflecting the childhood perspective of a five-year-old Steve. The interludes, or short stories, that discuss the different aspects of Superman are illustrated in a variety of scenes and colors. Many are dark and foreboding. Many of the people are rendered in the aforementioned iconic fashion, such the boy who wears a Superman costume to school.

The section about invulnerability and Achilles is modeled after Greek vase drawings. One of the brightest spots of color used throughout the book is the conventional red "S" from Superman's costume. The last scene, which is Steve's memory of the first *Superman* story he read, is told in vibrant color to reflect the newfound hope in Steve's life. Similarly, the final pages are in lighter and brighter colors as he moves on in his life with Lisa. Word balloons are slightly shaded instead of white when Steve talks directly to the reader.

Themes

There are two major themes in *It's a Bird . . .*, which correspond to the two plotlines. The first theme is the effect a major disease has on a family and an individual and the ways in which people deal with it. Huntington's disease overshadows everything that Steve does. He says he used to write for mutant titles until he realized that not all genetic mutations brought superpowers; sometimes the genes hid monstrous diseases. His family will not talk about the disease because they feel shame about the illness and, in his parents' case, dread that they have passed a death sentence on to their sons.

When Steve meets Marco, the two discuss the fact that no one wants to talk about the disease, which is why Marco has written a play about it. The horrors of the disease are brought home when Steve visits Aunt Sarah in the nursing home and sees her contorted body. She is mostly rendered in an outline, filled with white space; red rings her eyes and lips. She is cadaverous and haunting. Steve's compassion for her is a poignant moment in the graphic novel.

The second major theme is how Superman relates to the average person, particularly to the average American. The story has segments reflecting on the history of Superman as well as the history of the concept of the super man—from Achilles to Friedrich Nietzsche's *Übermensch*. Seagle looks at Superman's costume and the significance of its colors. He compares being an alien from Krypton to being Jewish, black, or gay. He examines Kryptonite and how silly the idea seems.

Throughout the story, Steve's reluctance to write *Superman* comics stems from his inability to understand why the character is a cultural icon; because of the Huntington's disease that runs in his family, he cannot relate to a perfect or indestructible character. He finally realizes that Superman is important to so many because the character continuously faces down obstacles.

Impact

It's a Bird . . . follows in the vein of Art Spiegelman's *Maus* (1986) and Harvey Pekar's *American Splendor* (1987) in its use of autobiographical elements. However, its originality stems from its narrative aspects. This blending of genres could have occurred only with the permission of a major comic book publisher, in this case, DC Comics. In fact, Seagle has joked that DC now owns the rights to part of his life story. The limitation set by copyright restrictions makes it difficult to replicate the book's success.

The real importance of *It's A Bird . . .* was its reception by a mainstream audience outside of the usual comic book and graphic novel audience. The book was reviewed by *The New Yorker, Newsday, People* magazine, and other mainstream media. Seagle was interviewed on National Public Radio's *Fresh Air with Terry Gross*. His goal was to write a Superman book his mother could read, meaning one that anyone could read, even if they had never read a Superman comic in their life.

P. Andrew Miller

Further Reading

Mack, David. *Kabuki: The Alchemy* (2008).
Pekar, Harvey. *American Splendor: The Life and Times of Harvey Pekar* (2003).
Spiegelman, Art. *Maus: A Survivor's Tale* (1986).

Bibliography

Claudio, Esther. "*It's a Bird*—Steven T. Seagle and Teddy Kristiansen." *The Comics Grid*, March 7, 2011. http://www.comicsgrid.com/2011/03/steven-t-seagles-its-a-bird.

Kyler, Carolyn. "Mapping a Life: Reading and Looking at Contemporary Graphic Memoir." *The CEA Critic* 72, no. 3 (Spring/Summer, 2010): 2-20.

Seagle, Steven T. "Sex and Death: The Steven T. Seagle Interview." Interview by Shaun Manning. *Comics Bulletin*. http://www.comicsbulletin.com/features/113807922497512.htm.

See also: *American Splendor; Maus: A Survivor's Tale; Persepolis; Kabuki*

It's a Good Life, If You Don't Weaken:
A Picture Novella

Author: Seth (pseudonym of Gregory Gallant)
Artist: Seth (illustrator)
Publisher: Drawn and Quarterly
First serial publication: 1993-1996
First book publication: 1996

Publication History

It's a Good Life, If You Don't Weaken was originally published in the comic book series *Palooka-Ville* (1991-2003), issues 4-9, between 1993 and 1996. Drawn and Quarterly in Montreal, Canada, published it as a single book in 1996 and has produced several subsequent editions.

Plot

In *It's a Good Life, If You Don't Weaken*, the fictionalized protagonist and narrator, Seth, is a frustrated cartoonist who appreciates the beauty of certain objects and art styles not often valued by others, including old architecture and the comics styles of the past. The narrative opens with Seth's visit with his mother and brother, during which he experiences a sense of displacement, accompanied by the knowledge that he has grown up and must move beyond his own youth and past. When he discovers the cartoon work of Jack "Kalo" Kalloway in an independent bookstore, he embarks on a search to uncover more of Kalo's comics, life, and career. During his search, he meets an attractive, intelligent woman named Ruthie, and they begin dating. Ruthie takes an interest in Seth's quest and is able to provide him with more clues that eventually lead him to a meeting with Kalo's surviving family members.

As Seth discovers more about Kalo, the antihero in Seth explores and discovers his own philosophical ideas about humanity, his nostalgia, and the world. He discusses his aesthetic values and his feelings of failure and loneliness with his friend Chet. Seth realizes that his artistic obsessions and general angst about the world often play roles in ending his relationships with women, while his

It's a Good Life, If You Don't Weaken: A Picture Novella. (Courtesy of Jonathan Cape)

devotion to his art only grows stronger. His disconnection from women is made obvious when he fails to maintain his relationship with Ruthie for no apparent reason.

Both Ruthie and Chet provide critiques of Seth's behavior as he works through his own alienation and feelings of inadequacy. Clearly, Seth feels deeper connections with the deceased Kalo, elements of the vanished past, and his art than with most of the people in his life. In the end, there is a parallel struck between Kalo the cartoonist and Seth the protagonist, and their similarities and differences further reveal the life of a cartoonist.

Characters

- *Seth*, the protagonist and narrator, is a fictionalized version of the author, a Canadian cartoonist living in Toronto who dresses in 1940's-style attire. He loves many elements of the vanishing and vanished past, including old architecture, jazz music, retro fashions, bookstores, comic books, and the cartoon and illustration styles of the 1930's and 1940's, specifically as featured in *The New Yorker*. His interests are treated as obsessions, as they lead him on a search for more information on the mostly unknown cartoonist Jack Kalloway.

- *Chet* is Seth's best friend, also a cartoonist, who has long hair and a funky style. While he

It's a Good Life, If You Don't Weaken: A Picture Novella. (Courtesy of Jonathan Cape)

and Seth have contrasting tastes and beliefs, their friendship is clearly based on their similar appreciation of cartooning. He works as a sounding board for Seth's preoccupations, his worry about his "vague depression," and his concerns about dating and women.

- *Seth's mother* is a minor character. She is a generous person who volunteers in the community, loves her two sons without seeing their flaws, and is happy to cook for them. She does not understand why neither of them have married.

- *Stephen*, Seth's brother, is an overweight, fun-loving adult who seems more boy than man. He is slovenly, lives in his mother's home, tells silly jokes that annoy Seth, dresses carelessly, and seems oblivious to the world around him.

- *Ruthie* is a dark-haired, attractive woman who is briefly involved with Seth. She is a student who enjoys reading and is majoring in French. Ultimately, she becomes yet another of Seth's failed possible relationships.

- *Jack Kalloway*, a.k.a. *Kalo*, is a dead Canadian cartoonist who once had a few cartoons in *The New Yorker*. Seth discovers his work while looking at comics in a bookstore and becomes interested in his style and career.

- *Susie* is Kalo's daughter, an attractive woman with black hair. A realtor and a businesswoman, she does not know the side of her father that was a cartoonist.

- *Ken* is an old friend of Kalo who says that his real talent was for business, not cartooning.

- *Mrs. Kalloway* is Kalo's mother. She describes her son, "Jackie," as being interested in drawing and reading and loving comics, just like Seth.

- *Boris* is one of Seth's cats and the "best thing that ever happened" to him.

Artistic Style

The style is evocative of the *New Yorker* cartoons of the 1930's and 1940's, with entirely hand-drawn images and hand-lettered text. The story is told in traditional comic frames and panels, drawn in black line with muted gray-blue on dark beige paper, with much attention to shadows, architecture, and landscape. This creates a mood that captures the ennui of the protagonist and accentuates his nostalgia for a lost time, serving as a tribute to a fading, past world. Mostly blue shading adds to the depth of the drawings and to their evocation of earlier cartoon styles and old catalog illustrations.

Background landscapes, architecture, and Canadian sites of interest add another dimension to the story, unfolding time via the use of Japanese-style seasonal panoramas that create a sense of the world that the protagonist experiences. This includes details of streetscapes, storefronts, objects, clothing, and landscaping. The backgrounds are often evocative of the narrator's emotional experiences and capture the sense of memory and a fading world that is thematically predominant.

Themes

It's a Good Life, If You Don't Weaken is concerned with the history of comics and cartoons, *The New Yorker* cartoonists, the daily life of the artist, the general ennui of being an adult and forming relationships, and a

---

Seth

One of the best-known cartoonists to have emerged from Canada in the 1990's, Seth (Gregory Gallant) began his career as the artist on *Mister X* before developing his own comic book series, *Palookaville*, at Drawn and Quarterly. It was in that title that he serialized *It's a Good Life, If You Don't Weaken*, a fictionalization of his own life that revolves around his search for a *New Yorker* cartoonist. Seth has published two books based on comics that he produced in his sketchbooks, both of which deal with the culture of cartooning and comic book collecting: *Wimbledon Green* and *The Great Northern Brotherhood of Canadian Cartoonists*. His work *George Sprott* was serialized in the *New York Times Magazine* between 2006 and 2007 before being collected, with additional material, as a graphic novel. Seth's style is self-consciously retro in its orientation. His stories, including the ongoing serial *Clyde Fans*, express a deep admiration for American culture of the early twentieth century, and his drawing style is strongly influenced by magazine illustrators from that era.

sadness for the "vanished past." The title, a common saying that Seth often heard repeated by his mother, links the book thematically to the past and to personal existentialism.

Late in the book, the protagonist defines the "good life" as "going from one children's parade to another." Attention is paid to objects and to collecting, to the philosophical questions of everyday life, and to the strangeness of a changing, evolving world.

Additionally, the theme of obsessive collecting versus establishing deeper adult relationships adds to the story, working as a type of bildungsroman of the heterosexual male artist contemplating his failed sexual relationships and trying to grow as an artist. The novella also has a postmodern metafictional element: The narrative comments on the medium in which it is told, exploring comics and comics styling; and the fictionalized Seth, the protagonist of the narrative, is also the author and illustrator of the book itself.

Impact

This work, published in the Modern Age of comics, had a significant effect on what would shortly become a boom in memoir-style graphic novels. Focused thematically on comics and the history of cartooning, it argues for the importance of the genre and its worthiness as a subject for serious study and exploration. Its unique elements include drawings of old cartoons and a glossary of notable cartoonists. The artistic style reinforces the value of "old world" comics that featured hand drawing and lettering.

It's a Good Life, If You Don't Weaken presents a kind of literary and artistic critical analysis of comics via its characters, who critique many kinds of cartooning, both thematically and aesthetically. Targets of this critique include the treatment of women in comics, typical plots and jokes, and superhero protagonists. Because this graphic novel does not have a high-action plot but instead features the emotional, philosophical, and aesthetic concerns of an antihero protagonist, it offered groundbreaking possibilities for the genre.

Additionally, unlike many memoir-based graphic novels that followed, the trials and actions of the protagonist are not dramatic, nor do they serve to make him "special," as either hero or victim. The story resists any impulse to turn melodramatic or sentimental. While there is nostalgia for certain elements of beauty in the past, that very notion is critiqued as well. The book also contributed to the reputation of the Canadian publishing house Drawn and Quarterly, begun by Chris Oliveros, which has set a standard for excellence in comics art.

Catherine Kasper

Further Reading

Gallant, John, and Seth. *Bannock, Beans, and Black Tea: The Life of a Young Boy Growing Up in the Great Depression* (2004).

Seth. *Clyde Fans: Book One* (2004).

_____. *Vernacular Drawings: Sketchbooks* (2001).

_____. *Wimbledon Green* (2005).

Bibliography

Grenville, Bruce, et al., eds. *Krazy! The Delirious World of Anime and Comics and Video Games and Art.* Berkeley: University of California Press, 2008.

Hannon, Gerald. "Retro Man." *Toronto Life*, November 29, 2010, p. 1-5. http://www.torontolife.com/features/retro-man.

Hignite, Todd. *In the Studio: Visits with Contemporary Cartoonists.* New Haven, Conn.: Yale University Press, 2006.

Mullins, Katie. "Questioning Comics: Women and Autocritique in Seth's *It's a Good Life, If You Don't Weaken.*" *Canadian Literature* 203 (Winter, 2009): 11-29.

Schneider, Greice. "Comics and Everyday Life: From *Ennui* to Contemplation." *European Comic Art* 3, no. 1 (2010): 37-63.

See also: *Ed the Happy Clown; I Never Liked You; Louis Riel*

IT WAS THE WAR OF THE TRENCHES

Author: Tardi, Jacques

Artist: Jacques Tardi (illustrator); Ian Burns (letterer); Brittany Kusa (letterer); Gavin Lees (letterer)

Publisher: Casterman (French); Fantagraphics Books (English)

First book publication: *C'était la guerre des tranchées: 1914-1918*, 1993 (English translation, 2010)

Publication History

Born in 1946 in Valence, France, Jacques Tardi began his career by drawing for the French comics magazine *Pilote*, which is most famous for *Asterix* (1959-2010) and *Lucky Luke* (1946-   ). Tardi went on to draw for the more radical, adult-oriented *Métal Hurlant*, co-founded by Moebius (also known as Jean Giraud) in 1975. An award-winning comics creator, he has attracted the attention of European comics theorists such as Thierry Groensteen, author of *Tardi* (1980). Tardi is known for writing and drawing several series, including *Les Aventures extraordinaires d'Adèle Blanc-sec* (1976-2007; *The Extraordinary Adventures of Adèle Blanc-Sec*), and for adapting stories by the surrealist crime-fiction writer Léo Malet into the *Nestor Burma* (1982-2000) volumes.

First published in 1993 by Casterman as *C'était la guerre des tranchées: 1914-1918*, the graphic novel published in English as *It Was the War of the Trenches* combines two narratives; the opening nineteen-page story was created during the 1970's and published in 1984 by Imagerie Pellerin as *Le Trou d'obus* (*The Bombshell Crater*). Like all of Tardi's works based on World War I, *It Was the War of the Trenches* is inspired by the experiences of his grandfather. The historian and World War I specialist Jean-Pierre Verney collaborated with Tardi on the final version of the novel.

Plot

A foreword by Tardi precedes the first section of *It Was the War of the Trenches*, clarifying that the book is a protest against war rather than a historical or even chronological account of World War I. Consequently, there is no protagonist; the narration follows the final

It Was the War of the Trenches. (Courtesy of Fantagraphics Books)

moments of several soldiers, their commonality being their unwilling participation in the war. Most of the soldiers are essentially types, resembling one another both in their physicality, being men of a similar age, and temperamentally, with their antiwar stances and fear of death. Other individual traits are rarely highlighted. Consequently, their distinguishing features are their actions and experiences.

The first section concentrates on Binet, beginning with a panel showing his corpse and proceeding to alternate between his immediate past on the battlefield and his previous, ordinary civilian life in an apartment house in Paris with advertisements painted over its front. While camping near a village, Binet watches a dogfight with a local boy. The same night, he is haunted by grotesque nightmares as he worries about Faucheux, sent to an outpost that had stopped communicating. Binet decides to search for him alone; he not only finds him dead, but also loses his own life in the firing. In a twist on the last page of the first section, the narrator is revealed to be a soldier who appears after his comrade mistakenly kills the village boy.

It Was the War of the Trenches. (Courtesy of Fantagraphics Books)

The second section, separated from the first by a two-page commentary by Tardi, has its narration divided among several soldiers. The story begins in 1916 and alternates between a French and a German soldier relating the death of a soldier; it then shifts to 1914, as Lafont, sitting in the trenches, recounts the day of immobilization and the destructive collective hatred aroused by the lack of patriotic display. Lafont's death in a blast is followed by the even briefer story of Gaspard, who, unlike the others, dies from eating rats in 1917. A 1916 military charge is shown, during which the narrative voice is replaced by patriotic quotes from Abbot Sertillanges and General Rebelliot. The charge continues for three pages, coming to a standstill when most of the members of the Third Company are killed by a bomb, fired not by the Germans but by the French; later, the remaining members of the Third Company, rendered almost identically, are court-martialed and shot.

In another scene showing the death of a soldier, the narrative captions by Soufflot tell of his own survival and the death of his friend Grumeau. Huet's guilt-ridden story is next, after which a longer set of events are focalized through the injured Mazure in 1914. Seeking refuge in an abandoned church, Mazure is taken prisoner by Werner, a German soldier. Both realize the interchangeability of their situation, and while Werner is immediately shot by the French soldiers who discover them, Mazure is killed after facing the military court.

A scene opening in 1916 begins with the narrator, Ducon, landing in the entrails of a dead German soldier following an explosion. The grotesque imagery extends to further detailed scenes of death and destruction on the battlefield and in the villages, where Ducon sees another soldier die in an explosion. After a two-year leap, the story of Bouvreuil is told. A blacksmith who spent his spare time in the army forging knickknacks out of metal debris, Bouvreuil also corresponds with his wife, Edith, giving readers their only glimpse of a soldier's relationship beyond the war front. Injured and trapped by barbed wires, Bouvreuil is finally shot by his friend Prunier out of mercy. An explosion of poisonous gas kills and injures more soldiers, returning the narrator to the hospital bed from which he began telling the story.

In the remaining twelve pages, a tirade against the war lists the casualties, weapons used, and nations involved, thus revealing the primary purpose of the graphic novel. The book is accompanied by a filmography and bibliography, listing the key literary and cinematic works on World War I.

Characters

- *Binet* is a private in the French army.
- *Faucheux* is Binet's companion.
- *Village boy* is a child who watches a dogfight with Binet and later loses his life while wearing Faucheux's uniform.
- *Unnamed soldier-narrator* is a member of Binet's company and tells Binet's story.
- *Lafont* is a soldier who recounts the immobilization frenzy.
- *Gaspard* is an unpopular soldier with an insatiable appetite.
- *Huet* is a soldier haunted by the possibility of having killed a Belgian woman and her child, used as human shields by the Germans but nonetheless shot at by the French army.
- *Helmut* is a notorious German sniper who is never shown from the front and who kills Huet.
- *Ackermann* is a soldier killed by Helmut while trying to remove Huet's body from the barbed wire beyond the trenches.
- *Mazure* is a French soldier who meets a German soldier, Werner, while seeking refuge in an abandoned church. Both are eventually killed by the French.
- *Ducon* is a soldier who describes his own and his comrades' traumatic experiences in the longest section of the book.
- *Bouvreuil* is a creative blacksmith whose regular letters to his wife, Edith, are narrated in detail.
- *Prunier* is a friend of Bouvreuil who shoots him out of mercy and is last shown shouting for help amid the wreckage of an explosion.

Artistic Style

Tardi's works are almost always situated in the belle époque and the first half of the twentieth century. While many of his works are vividly colored, *It Was the War of the Trenches* is in black and white. This befits the somber theme of the book, even though Tardi's other works on the war are colored. Complementing the nightmarish content of the scenes, color is replaced by strong chiaroscuro effects. The increasingly macabre imagery also differs starkly from the often humorous noir atmosphere of his works not set in the belle époque.

Moebius's influence on Tardi is particularly evident in the dynamic page layouts and the frequently curvilinear panel shapes that alternate with the regular row-long panels. However, Tardi's panels distinguish themselves from Moebius's radical forms by emphasizing the action over the ornamentation.

The layout is more consistent in the second section of the graphic novel, with each page typically divided into three rows. Aside from creating a rhythmic reading pace, the division into three parts alludes to both the French flag and the Christian holy trinity. The panel variations, including the varying dramatic foci, recall the cinematic tool of shifting viewpoints.

Similarly, the deliberate distance between the events and the narration is made obvious in the first section, in which the narrator likens the war to a theater experience. The soldiers are rarely seen from a perspective closer than medium range. There is a lack of smooth transitions between the panels, making each panel resemble a photograph or a film still, in keeping with the book's themes of recording and remembering.

Themes

The documentary mode of the visuals and narration emphasizes the story's incorporation of a major event ensconced in collective memory. This is also supported by the accurate visual details and quotations of prominent political and literary figures of World War I.

The book's central theme is the horror of war and the inexcusability of the extensive human suffering and costs involved. The protest against warfare is realized by the detailed depictions of death and destruction. The word-image narration is also marked by other concepts that come to the forefront during war, such as dehumanization, lack of individuality, and the human tendency toward brutality seen in the modern era.

The emptiness of patriotism is also evident from the beginning, via Binet's remarks, and is later emphasized

---

Jacques Tardi

One of the legendary figures in the history of French comics production, Jacques Tardi began publishing in *Pilote* in 1969 at the age of twenty-three. One of the most influential visual stylists in the second half of the twentieth century, Tardi is a notable chronicler of the history of Paris. His best-known series, the adventures of Adèle Blanc-Sec, features supernatural elements set in Paris between the world wars. His adaptations of Léo Malet's Nestor Burma crime novels depict a hardboiled Paris after the end of the Second World War. He has produced well-received historical comics depicting the horrors of the First World War (*It Was the War of the Trenches*) as well as a four-part history of the rise and fall of the Paris Commune (*Le cri du peuple*). Strongly influenced by Hergé's clear-line style, Tardi is known for a round line and characters that seem lumpy or rumpled. His page designs are some of the most ornate in comics.

---

through the juxtaposition of excerpts from patriotic speeches with images of dying soldiers. The soldiers' stories beyond the front lines are rarely elaborated upon, and the frequent transitions between narrators and years emphasize the soldiers' commonalities as unwilling participants destined to lose their lives in a senseless war. The fact that some of the soldiers are killed by their own countrymen exacerbates the absurdity of the situation. Likewise, the guilt and pangs of conscience that soldiers such as Huet and Ducon are unable to overcome link collective suffering with collective responsibility, which is also underscored in most of the narrators' direct statements to the reader.

Impact

Tardi is one of the exemplary artists whose work simultaneously displays the influence of and subverts the tenets of Belgian artist Hergé's clear-line style of art. In addition, *It Was the War of the Trenches* exemplifies the move away from brief, lighthearted comics toward longer narratives that explore serious themes. At more than 120 pages, the graphic novel is almost triple the length of the typical French comic book.

It is significant that almost a decade separates the creation of the two sections of the book and that this time period corresponds roughly to the zenith of the alternative comics movement and the popularization of the term "graphic novel." Consequently, *It Was the War of the Trenches* exemplifies the use of comics as a medium of protest, breaking away from the conventional formats of comic books characterized as graphic novels.

This change within the work of Tardi is highlighted by not only a more symbolically dense artistic style but also the inclusion of quotes from literary works such as Louis-Ferdinand Céline's *Voyage au bout de la nuit* (1932; *Journey to the End of the Night*, 1934) and Gabriel Chevallier's *La Peur* (1930; *Fear*, 2009) and from contemporaneous patriotic speeches. Similarly, the second section of the graphic novel also employs visual symbols, predominantly that of Christ on the cross. Functioning as an ironic complement to the Abbot's words, additional Christian allusions include the blood-stained shirt, reminiscent of the Veil of Veronica, held up on the book's penultimate page. Notably, despite the destruction shown in the beginning of the book, the first onomatopoeic instance is Binet's scream during his nightmare. The avoidance of this comics convention is yet another indicator of the gravity of the subject matter. In retrospect, the book, with its weighty content and multilayered visual and verbal techniques, can be seen as a predecessor of later graphic novels with rebellious and journalistic strains, such as Joe Sacco's *Palestine* (1996) and Emmanuel Guibert's *The Photographer* (2009).

Maaheen Ahmed

Further Reading

Folman, Ari, and David Polonsky. *Waltz with Bashir: A Lebanon War Story* (2009).

Guibert, Emmanuel. *Alan's War: The Memoires of G.I. Alan Cope* (2008).

Manchette, Jean-Patrick, and Jacques Tardi. *Like a Sniper Lining Up His Shot* (2011).

Bibliography

Beaty, Bart. *Unpopular Culture: Transforming the European Comic Book in the 1990's*. Toronto: University of Toronto Press, 2007.

Groensteen, Thierry. *The System of Comics*. Translated by Bart Beaty and Nick Nguyen. Jackson: University Press of Mississippi, 2007.

McCloud, Scott. *Understanding Comics: The Invisible Art*. New York: HarperCollins, 1994.

Screech, Matthew. *Masters of the Ninth Art: Bandes Dessinées and Franco-Belgian Identity*. Liverpool, England: Liverpool University Press, 2005.

See also: *Waltz with Bashir; Alan's War; Palestine; Photographer; Safe Area Goražde*

J

JAR OF FOOLS: A PICTURE STORY

Author: Lutes, Jason
Artist: Jason Lutes (illustrator); Kristian Grønevet (cover artist); Michel Vrana (cover artist)
Publisher: Drawn and Quarterly
First serial publication: 1993-1996
First book publication: 1996

Publication History

Jar of Fools, Jason Lutes's first book, was originally serialized in the Seattle, Washington, *The Stranger* and the Providence, Rhode Island, *Nicepaper* weekly newspapers between 1993 and 1996. It was self-published in an incomplete edition in 1994 through Penny Dreadful Press, which was created by Lutes and schoolmates at the Rhode Island School of Design. Penny Dreadful Press lasted for only about seven issues, which were sold at the school, to small comic shops, and in a mail network. *Jar of Fools* was then collected, in its entirety, by Black Eye Productions, also known as Black Eye Books, a short-lived Canadian comic book publishing company, in 1996. In 2001, *Jar of Fools* was published by Drawn and Quarterly.

Lutes is entirely responsible for writing, illustrating, penciling, inking, lettering, and creating backgrounds for *Jar of Fools*. The cover of the Drawn and Quarterly edition is a photo from istockphoto.com by Kristian Grønevet. However, the cover of the first complete printing of *Jar of Fools* by Black Eye Books is based on the collaboration between Lutes and Michel Vrana. The only changes between printed editions are the covers; the amount of strips collected; and, according to Lutes, two pages of changes in the drawings.

Plot

Jar of Fools was spurred by Lutes's interest in the magician Harry Houdini and was written in an exploratory fashion: Lutes did not outline a plot, making intuitive

Jar of Fools: A Picture Story. (Courtesy of Drawn and Quarterly)

choices along the way. In general, Lutes's goal is to capture the untapped market—the audience that does not read comics—by creating a clear and focused product. *Jar of Fools* tells the story of a group of disillusioned people who come together to affect changes in one another's lives.

Jar of Fools opens with Ernie Weiss dreaming about his estranged girlfriend, Esther, only to awaken on a park bench as an unshaven, depressed, and slightly alcoholic washed-out magician. Escaping the rain in the park, he returns to his rundown apartment and falls asleep to the television, which morphs into a dream of his brother's death during an underwater escape stunt (which may or may not have been suicide). He is woken up by his neighbor, who says he has a phone call from his mentor, Al Flosso, who has escaped a retirement home once again. Ernie returns with Al to the apartment and discovers a letter and cassette sent by Esther.

The next section deals with Esther, who is first seen in bed with a man for whom she feels little. On her way to work, she seems to hinder a suicide. There is a young woman staring into the river from the bridge Esther crosses. The women share a brief conversation about the last person to die at the bridge, which was Ernie's brother. Esther then goes to work at the coffee shop. Time goes slowly; when she returns home, she tells her boyfriend she would like to disappear. She goes to bed

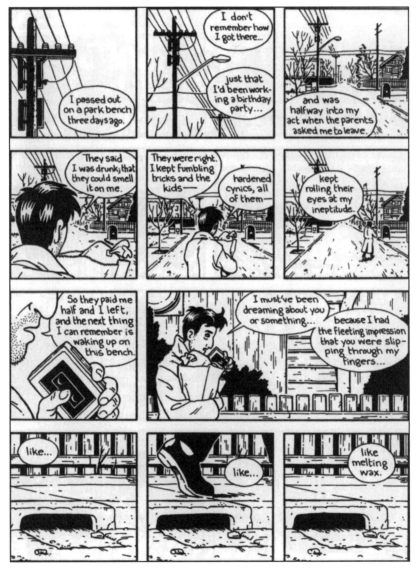

Jar of Fools: A Picture Story. (Courtesy of Drawn and Quarterly)

and dreams of Ernie. The following day at work, a con artist tricks her, and when she cannot catch him or get his license-plate number, in a fit of anger she punches a man who makes a sexual comment about her.

The story returns to Ernie, who is creating a cassette to send back to Esther. Still living with Ernie, Al persuades him to dress up and practice his magic tricks. Ernie leaves the apartment to wander the town and discovers two men from the retirement home have come to pick up Al. Ernie tries to warn Al; in the nick of time, the con man, Mr. Lender, whom Ernie first encountered during his stroll home in the opening scene, pulls up with a car (his daughter, Claire, is with him) and rescues the pair.

At the end of part 1, Esther has a broken hand and is frustrated with her life. Ernie and Al are with Mr. Lender and Claire. They are homeless and living out of their car while hiding under a freeway overpass. Mr. Lender wants Ernie to teach Claire magic tricks so she can learn to con people better. Mr. Lender also shows Ernie the same straightjacket and ball and chain that belonged to Ernie's brother. The scene closes with the four people falling asleep in the car under the overpass as it rains.

In part 2, Ernie teaches Claire magic tricks in exchange for Mr. Lender's help with Al. Ernie also visits the junk shop where Mr. Lender found the straitjacket. He gets little information about the man who brought it in. Meanwhile, Mr. Lender watches over Al, who is suffering from senility—he thinks he is young again and that his magician friends are still alive.

In the meantime, Claire has left her job, apartment, and boyfriend to search for Ernie, whom she finds. Ernie has a mental breakdown and is on the bridge about to try the same trick his brother attempted. Esther stops him. Claire and her father go on one final con; it goes wrong, and Mr. Lender gives himself up to the police to save Claire. Claire is left with Esther; they take the car and try to find Claire's mother. Al and Ernie go into the city together to start a new life.

Characters

- *Ernie Weiss*, a.k.a. *the Amazing Ernesto*, the protagonist, is an unshaven down-and-out magician tormented by his older brother's death. He misses his girlfriend, Esther. He takes in his former mentor, Al Flosso, and tries to take care of the elderly man.

- *Esther O'Dea* is Ernie's former girlfriend. She is dissatisfied with her life. She stops Ernie's suicide attempt. She later takes Claire back to her mother.

- *Al Flosso* is Ernie's former magic mentor. He escapes from a retirement home and is the major catalyst for everything that happens in the story. He might be suffering from dementia or Alzheimer's disease. He coaxes Ernie to start over instead of remaining stuck in his old life.

- *Nathan Lender* is a con man living out of his car. His daughter is Claire. He saves Al and Ernie, and, in exchange, Ernie and Al teach Claire magic tricks. He cons Esther but later apologizes and asks her to take Claire back to her mother. He saves everyone by distracting the police and allowing the police to arrest him.

- *Claire Lender* is Mr. Lender's child. She misses her mother and is unhappy in the unstable life her father provides. She is often part of her father's cons, either keeping the car running or creating a diversion. She learns magic tricks in order to help her father with bigger cons.

Artistic Style

As published by the Penny Dreadful Press, *Jar of Fools* was originally serialized in black and white. Lutes uses clear-line technique. He is heavily influenced by European comics artists such as Hergé, the creator of *The Adventures of Tintin* (1929-1976), as well as Art Spiegelman's comics anthology *RAW*. Lutes's approach to comics production, in terms of going against the mainstream both in content matter and art style, exemplifies Spiegelman's influence. Neatly proportioned panels offer a variety of viewpoints from characters instead of simple third-person views. Lutes believes clarity is the most important thing in the work, which affects the visuals of speech: There is never more than a sentence or two in a word balloon, and conversations are staged at the eye level with careful attention paid to body language and the facial expressions of those in the panel. He also provides inflection on the conversation with the angle or frame of the drawn panel.

Themes

Jar of Fools is primarily concerned with love: between a man and a woman, between brothers, between a father and a child, and between mentor and protégé. There are criminal elements to the story (magic is used to con people), but the story is also one of acceptance of the past such as when Ernie the failed magician comes to realize he may never know whether or not his brother's death was suicide.

Jar of Fools is concerned with peoples' lives and the grittiness of them. Also present is a coming-of-age theme, though in general, the characters are either older or younger than characters that readers would associate with a bildungsroman. Characters quit drinking, go to jail for the right reasons, return to an abandoned family, and move on to new lives—all signs of maturation.

Magic is also a prominent theme in *Jar of Fools*. This is personified by the main character, Ernie Weiss, whose name references Houdini's given name, Ehrich Weiss. Magic is also used to con people. Furthermore, Al's antics and mental instability are centered on magic.

Impact

Jar of Fools is Lutes's first mainstream success and is a novel published in the Modern Age of comics. When *Jar of Fools* was first produced, it was atypical of the age, particularly because it is a tragicomedy; this is a comics subgenre that has become more common, as realist comics artists have come to the forefront.

Lutes's writing style has been compared to Ernest Hemingway's. The characters' psychological makeups and their backstories are interchangeable— much like Hemingway's characters—and provide readers with a greater sense of story and mood.

Lutes has worked as an artist on other graphic novels such as *The Fall* (2001), written by Ed Brubaker. His art style has given a clean visual story line to Brubaker's work. Lutes's work has evolved since *Jar of Fools*, a fact that can be seen in later works such as the critically acclaimed *Berlin: City of Stones* (2000). His work has been published in multiple languages and editions. *Jar of Fools* has garnered positive criticism, and after the success of *Berlin*, many critics and scholars are returning to *Jar of Fools*.

Jason Lutes

Formerly the art director of the Seattle-based weekly *The Stranger*, Jason Lutes began serializing *Jar of Fools* in the pages of that paper in 1993. The story of frustrated magician Ernie Weiss and his mentor, Al Flosso, was widely acclaimed and has been published in collected editions by a number of publishers. After a hiatus, Lutes embarked on the epic graphic novel *Berlin*, a detailed portrait of the decline of the Weimar Republic. Begun in 1996 as a proposed series of twenty-four comic books, two collected volumes—*Berlin: City of Stones* and *Berlin: City of Smoke*—have been published to date. With writer Ed Brubaker, Lutes produced the graphic novel *The Fall*, and he wrote a graphic novel about Harry Houdini's escape from the Charles River (illustrated by Nick Bertozzi), *Houdini: The Handcuff King*. Lutes's drawings are highly influenced by the clear-line style of Hergé, and his backgrounds are highly detailed and extensively researched.

Michelle Martinez

Further Reading

Folman, Ari, and David Polonsky. *Waltz with Bashir* (2009).

Lutes, Jason. *Houdini: The Handcuff King* (2007).

Tomine, Adrian. *Shortcomings* (2007).

Bibliography

Hatfield, Charles. *Alternative Comics: An Emerging Literature*. Jackson: University Press of Mississippi, 2005.

Heer, Jeet, and Kent Worcester. *A Comics Studies Reader*. Jackson: University Press of Mississippi, 2009.

Lutes, Jason. "Walrus Comix Presents: An Exclusive Interview with Artist Extraordinaire, Missoula, Montana's Comix Laureate Jason Lutes." *Walrus Comix*. http://www.walruscomix.com/interview-lutes.html.

See also: *Houdini; Waltz with Bashir; Berlin*

JEW IN COMMUNIST PRAGUE, A:
1. LOSS OF INNOCENCE

Author: Giardino, Vittorio
Artist: Vittorio Giardino (illustrator)
Publisher: Rizzoli Lizard (Italian); NBM (English)
First book publication: *Jonas Fink: L'infanzia*, 1994 (English translation, 1997)

Publication History

A Jew in Communist Prague: 1. Loss of Innocence was written in Italian by Vittorio Giardino and published in 1994 under the title *Jonas Fink: L'infanzia* (*Jonas Fink: Childhood*). The Italian version was published by Rizzoli Lizard, which specializes in graphic novels by Italian writers. Based in Milan, the company was founded by Hugo Pratt in 1993. Rizzoli Lizard has also published graphic novels by Pratt, Hergé, Milo Manara, and Marjane Satrapi.

Jonas Fink: L'infanzia was translated by Jacinthe Leclerc and published under the strikingly different title *A Jew in Communist Prague: 1. Loss of Innocence* in 1997 by ComicsLit, an imprint of NBM. The next two novels in the series, *A Jew in Communist Prague: 2. Adolescence* and *A Jew in Communist Prague: 3. Rebellion* were subsequently published by ComicsLit. NBM is known as an "alternative" comics publisher for the simple reason that it does not publish superhero comics. ComicsLit specializes in graphic narratives that are psychological explorations of ordinary people's lives. Other ComicsLit titles include adaptations of *À la recherche du temps perdu* (1913-1927; *Remembrance of Things Past*, 1922-1931) by Marcel Proust and *The Jungle* (1906) by Upton Sinclair. ComicsLit also published translations of Giardino's Max Friedman series of spy graphic novels.

Plot

A Jew in Communist Prague is a historical novel set in 1950 in the city of Prague in communist Czechoslovakia. The police arrest Dr. Finkel, a Jewish, middle-class professor. No cause for the arrest is given, nor is any information about his welfare relayed to his wife and thirteen-year-old son, Jonas.

A Jew in Communist Prague: 1. Loss of Innocence. (Courtesy of Nantier Beall Minoustchine Publishing)

The innocent Jonas suffers as a result of his father's arrest. Many of his peers ostracize him, and some attack him. Jonas is discriminated against by both children and adults. He is refused entry into college, despite his intelligence and high marks. When his teacher appeals to the director of his school board to let Jonas enroll, the director bluntly states that not everyone can be provided with an education and that "inevitably, there must be some outcasts." Although the government officials claim that they distrust the Finkels because of their affluent background, it becomes increasingly obvious that they are motivated by anti-Semitism.

While Jonas struggles for acceptance from his peers, his mother, Edith, seeks justice for, or at least some news of, her husband. Her persistence yields few results. She writes letters to the authorities, including the justice department, various party committees, and the presidium. She receives no response and no explanation, only threats and castigation from Comrade Commissioner Murad, the government official assigned to her case.

The Finkels also struggle financially, and their bank account is frozen. While Edith worked as a French tutor before her husband was incarcerated, Comrade Murad forbids her from teaching without a license and insists that she find work at a factory instead. Jonas becomes an errand boy for a seamstress, but he is soon fired. A middle-aged client of the seamstress seduces Jonas. When her husband catches the two locked in an embrace, she claims that the boy assaulted her, and Jonas loses his job as a result.

Finally, the family receives news from an elusive stranger who was imprisoned with Dr. Finkel. The stranger tells Edith that her husband will be released in ten years. Although this is hardly the verdict for which they were hoping, Edith and Jonas have already suffered so deeply that even this scrap of information is a great consolation.

Characters

- *Jonas Finkel*, the protagonist, is a thirteen-year-old boy with green eyes and black hair. Before his father is taken prisoner, he is a happy, well-adjusted boy, but as his life becomes increasingly bleak, he grows sullen and occasionally violent. He is fond of toy airplanes and spends hours building and launching them. Midway through the novel, he has a sexual awakening with Mrs. Laparik.
- *Dr. Finkel* is Jonas's father and a wise, kind professor with blond hair and glasses. He is arrested for mysterious reasons and eventually imprisoned. It is rumored that he faces charges of counterrevolutionary activities and espionage, although he has never been involved in such activities.
- *Edith Finkel* is the wife of Dr. Finkel and a dark-haired beauty with clear blue eyes. Bold and tenacious, she is determined to do all she can to help her husband, or at least find out what the justice system

has accused him of. She lost all her relatives during the Holocaust.
- *Hanka* is a close friend of Edith Finkel. While nearly all of Edith's friends abandon her out of fear of being found "guilty by association," Hanka helps Edith and her son make ends meet. Hanka finds Jonas a job working for her seamstress.
- *Comrade Commissioner Murad*, an antagonist, is a haughty, cruel, and anti-Semitic government official who impedes Edith Finkel's efforts to determine what happened to her husband. He is an archetype of Communist hypocrisy.
- *Mrs. Laparik* is a chubby, middle-aged married woman who seduces Jonas. Although she is clearly attracted to Jonas and is flattered by his attention, she treats him callously and lies to her husband about who initiated the relationship.
- *The nameless former prisoner* is an emaciated middle-aged man who shared a prison cell with Dr. Finkel. He tells Jonas and his mother that Dr. Finkel will be released from prison in ten years.

Artistic Style

A Jew in Communist Prague is a work of realistic fiction, and its artwork is similarly realistic. The illustrations are reminiscent of cinematography, as the story moves smoothly from frame to frame. Giardino introduces pauses in the action by repeating images that show subtle changes in characters' movements and faces. This technique is particularly effective in a scene depicting Dr. Finkel pacing silently back and forth in a prison cell. Giardino takes his time with the unfolding narrative, allowing the reader to delve into the images and reflect on the rich, subtle metaphors contained within.

The first few pages of the novel contain vividly colored illustrations of a family picnic in a green meadow, contrasting with the setting of the rest of the narrative. After Dr. Finkel is arrested, colors become muted, even stark, and reflect the weary, melancholic mood of the characters and the era. Although the narrative cycles through the seasons, most of the scenes take place in winter. The lush green that begins the novel is never revisited. When Giardino depicts grass in outdoor scenes, there is barely any of it, and it is full of detritus.

Giardino conveys the characters' thoughts and feelings through subtle changes in their facial expressions. He is particularly attentive when drawing his characters' eyes, close-ups of which frequently punctuate critical points in the plot. Characters rarely smile and frequently appear worried or otherwise troubled.

The frames are arranged in a conventional, sequential manner, with occasional deviations in frame shape and size for dramatic effect. The lettering is tight and orderly and always confined to a speech bubble. One exception is the novel's preface, which is depicted as a letter penned by a fictionalized version of the author.

Themes

The story exposes the injustice and hypocrisy of the Communist junta in Czechoslovakia in 1950.

Giardino continually juxtaposes the Communist rhetoric about freeing the people with the reality: These Communist leaders are no less oppressive than their predecessors.

The central theme of the novel is captivity and the resulting demoralization. Before his arrest, Dr. Finkel shows his son a cicada. The cicada flies away, and Dr. Finkel explains that cicadas do not trust humans because children often capture them and confine them in jars. He tells Jonas that cicadas cease to sing when they are in captivity. The same is true of Dr. Finkel; in a scene depicting his imprisonment, he is entirely silent. After Dr. Finkel has been imprisoned for a while, Jonas kills a cicada by squashing it with his shoe. Thus, a victim of violence becomes a perpetrator of violence. However, by killing the cicada, Jonas also prevents it from being caught and imprisoned like his father.

A Jew in Communist Prague: 1. Loss of Innocence. (Courtesy of Nantier Beall Minoustchine Publishing)

Another key symbol is Jonas's toy plane. Jonas continually tries to launch the plane into the air, but he encounters various obstacles. At one point, a playground bully tries to take Jonas's airplane. As Jonas struggles to get it back, he inadvertently rips it. After this, the bully and his friends beat up Jonas and his friend Jiri. Jiri distances himself from Jonas, possibly to protect himself from further injury. Jonas finally gets the plane to fly, but by that point, Jiri has abandoned him. As a result, Jonas loses interest in the plane and gives it to the boys who bullied him. Thus, the story implies that although Jonas has learned to fly, this achievement is of no value to him without a friend to share in his success.

Anti-Semitism is a key aspect of the story. Government officials claim that they have just cause for targeting Dr. Finkel, but their contempt for Finkel's cultural background evidently plays a significant role in their actions. By depicting this prejudice, Giardino critiques the motives of Communist leaders at the time.

Impact

In genre and structure, *A Jew in Communist Prague: 1. Loss of Innocence* can be described as a bildungsroman, a novel about a character's formative years. Typically, the protagonist of a bildungsroman wrestles with ethical and identity crises throughout his or her growth from childhood to adulthood. Frequently, bildungsroman protagonists must reject the social mores of the people who surround them in order to live authentically and achieve self-realization. Although the bildungsroman structure is common in literary fiction, it is relatively rare in graphic novels; *A Jew in Communist Prague: 1. Loss of Innocence* was one of the first. A number of bildungsroman graphic novels were published in the early 2000's, including *Paul Has a Summer Job* (2003) by Michel Rabagliati and *Persepolis* (2000) by Marjane Satrapi.

A Jew in Communist Prague: 1. Loss of Innocence received enthusiastic praise from *The Washington Post*, *Booklist*, and *Kirkus Reviews*. *Publishers Weekly* rated it one of the best comics of 1997. The other graphic novels in the trilogy also enjoyed critical acclaim.

Bettina Grassmann

Further Reading

Kuper, Peter. *Give It Up! and Other Stories by Franz Kafka* (1995).

Lutes, Jason. *Berlin: City of Stones* (1996-2000).

Satrapi, Marjane. *Persepolis* (2000).

Bibliography

Curtis, Michael. "Antisemitism." In *The Oxford Companion to the Politics of the World*, edited by Joel Krieger. New York: Oxford University Press, 1993.

Morgenstern, Karl. "On the Nature of the Bildungsroman." Translated by Tobias Boes. *PMLA: Publications of the Modern Language Association of America* 124, no. 2 (March, 2009): 647-659.

Schwarz, Gretchen, and Christina Crenshaw. "Old Media, New Media: The Graphic Novel as Bildungsroman." *Journal of Media Literacy Education* 3, no. 1 (2011).

Wolchik, Susan L. "Czechoslovakia." In *The Oxford Companion to the Politics of the World*, edited by Joel Krieger. New York: Oxford University Press, 1993.

See also: *Berlin: City of Stones; Give It Up! and Other Stories by Franz Kafka; Persepolis; Maus*

Vittorio Giardino

One of the most acclaimed Italian comics artists of the 1980's and 1990's, Vittorio Giardino did not begin working in the industry until he left his job as an electrical engineer at the age of thirty. Renowned for his incredibly detailed clear-line drawings and complex espionage plots, Giardino produces work at a slow pace. In 1982 he introduced the character Max Fridman in *Hungarian Rhapsody* and began telling the story of the former spy's involvement in the political struggles that defined Europe before the outbreak of the Second World War. He is also well known as the creator of Jonas Fink, the titular lead in *A Jew in Communist Prague*. This award-winning series examined life under Stalinist oppression in the 1950's. Giardino has also worked extensively in the field of erotic comics, where his character Little Ego—a female version of Winsor McCay's Little Nemo—is the star of sex-themed, single-page stories.

JEW OF NEW YORK, THE:
A HISTORICAL ROMANCE

Author: Katchor, Ben

Artist: Ben Katchor (illustrator); Misha Beletsky (cover artist); Chip Kidd (cover artist)

Publisher: Pantheon Books

First serial publication: 1992, 1993

First book publication: 1998

Publication History

Ben Katchor's *The Jew of New York* first appeared in segments in *The Forward* in 1992 and 1993. The first edition of the complete work was published in 1998 by Pantheon Books. A paperback edition was released the following year. The graphic novel has been translated into French, Spanish, and Dutch.

Plot

The Jew of New York begins after the 1825 failure of Major Mordecai Noah to establish a Jewish homeland named Ararat on Grand Island, New York, an island near Buffalo and Niagara Falls. After much fanfare, Noah gave up suddenly and never set foot on Grand Island. Katchor uses this historical fact as the starting point of his graphic novel, the remainder of which is fictional.

Disgraced butcher Nathan Kishon has followed Noah to Buffalo. After Noah relinquishes his ambitious plan, Kishon ventures into the wilderness, where he meets successful fur trader Moishe Ketzelbourd, who has trapped thousands of beavers. Ketzelbourd collects beaver pelts and theatrical prints of his idol, the aged, one-legged actress Miss Patella. Kishon begins to work for Ketzelbourd, who pays him with beaver pelts rather than money.

Kishon, who narrates much of the first half of the book to Mr. Abel Marah, moves to New York City and checks into the Gibraltar Hotel, but he does not reside there. He has become so accustomed to the wilderness that he no longer feels comfortable wearing clothes or sleeping in a bed, so he replaces his clothes with a blanket and sleeps on the grass outside the hotel. Kishon tells Marah that he and Ketzelbourd visited Septum Dandy's oxygen-worshipping commune, where the

The Jew of New York: A Historical Romance. (Courtesy of Pantheon Books)

inhabitants adore scientist Joseph Priestley, but were exiled after Kishon slaughtered a wild turkey.

Ketzelbourd follows the scent of pickled herring to a rehearsal of the play *The Jew of New York*, written by the famous anti-Semite Professor Solidus, and sees the woman he adores, actress Miss Patella. She is performing in Solidus's satire, which attacks Jews and refers to Major Noah as Major Ham. While trying to meet Miss Patella, Ketzelbourd is shot and killed.

Due to the changes that the wilderness effected on him, Ketzelbourd, who has seemingly adopted beaver traits, is believed to be a wild animal unlike any seen before. Thus, he is stuffed, glued to a "reconstructed" animal tail, and placed as an exhibit in Hiram's Museum, becoming the only circumcised wild animal in the museum.

Marah attends Dr. V. Petersham's Conserve Our Nation's Manhood rally on August 10, 1830, where Petersham gives a public lecture against masturbation for his antimasturbation society, claiming that the act is bad for the economy and that masturbation should be considered an act of treason punishable by death. Meanwhile, Francis Oriole attempts to find financial backers so he can carbonate Lake Erie and pipe soda water to every home in New York. Marah agrees to invest but never follows through. Instead, he fakes his own death and moves to London, where he renames himself Ludwig Hullar.

Characters

- *Nathan Kishon* is a disgraced butcher who was found to have mixed kosher beef tongues with nonkosher ones. After his wife is hit by a falling

The Jew of New York: A Historical Romance. (Courtesy of Pantheon Books)

tree and dies, he follows Noah to Buffalo and then works for Ketzelbourd. He is a born follower and has a propensity to slaughter animals. He wears no clothes, sleeps outside, and has amassed a fortune in beaver pelts.

- *Mr. Abel Marah* is an unscrupulous businessman who leaves his family and breaks off his business partnerships with Ketzelbourd and Oriole by faking his death. He loves get-rich-quick schemes but fails to follow through on them. He pretends to go to upstate New York to retrieve Kishon's beaver pelts, but he instead checks into the American Hotel on Broadway and rests there before faking his death and moving to London.

- *Miss Patella* is an actress with one leg. She appears in the play *The Jew of New York* as part of her farewell tour. She is the object of Ketzelbourd's and Marah's desire, but the text never indicates why men find her attractive.

- *Moishe Ketzelbourd* is a fur trader who lives in the wilderness of upstate New York, where he kills beavers. He regrets the depletion of the beaver population, essentially caused by him, and starts to act a bit like a beaver, mirroring the animals' behavior. He is killed in the theater while trying to approach Miss Patella and is stuffed and displayed in Hiram's Museum.

- *Professor Solidus* is the anti-Semitic author of *The Jew of New York*, which satirizes Noah. He wears a veil and has numerous phobias. He laments Jewish assimilation because he fears that if Jews intermarry, the children will lose their particularly Jewish physical and cultural features, thus depriving him of valuable material for his anti-Semitic writings.

- *Hershel Goulbat* is the man responsible for teaching Hebrew to an American Indian, Elim-Min-Nopee, and arranging for him to speak Hebrew before spectators at Hiram's Museum. People are amazed that Elim-Min-Nopee can speak Hebrew, fueling speculation that American Indians are descendants of the lost tribes of Israel.

- *Isaac Azarael* is a middleman in the button business who awaits a shipment of buttons from a ship called the *Palambrom*, not knowing that it

has sunk. He beats Hershel Goulbat with a stick to save Kishon from a beating.

- *Francis Oriole* is the president of the Lake Eric Soda Water Company. He intends to carbonate Lake Erie and make a fortune piping soda water into people's homes. He tells potential investors and customers that carbonated soda water aids in proper digestion.

- *Major Mordecai Noah* is a man of the theater who decided to found Ararat, a new Jewish homeland on Grand Island, but abruptly gave up. He attends a rehearsal of Solidus's play, *The Jew of New York*.

- *Vervel Kunzo*, a.k.a. *the Man in an India Rubber Suit*, is a German academic who travels to New York to write a cultural report on what makes Jews in New York so unique. He interviews Kishon as part of his research. He exercises by swimming in his India rubber suit.

- *Yosl Feinbroyt* is a latter-day kabbalist who believes that all languages are corruptions of the original Hebrew. He collects spontaneous utterances and sounds of people eating and drinking and attempts to add these words to the dictionary. He believes that his transcription of these sounds will bring him close to God's original language.

- *Enoch Letushim* is a Palestinian seller of soil. He has recently arrived in New York and wishes to sell his soil to people who want to be buried with soil from the Holy Land.

Artistic Style

Katchor combines comic panels with advertising flyers used by his characters to sell their products or advertise upcoming events. As with Katchor's comic strip *Julius Knipl: Real Estate Photographer* (1988-), *The Jew of New York* effectively employs light and shadow. The characters in the graphic novel are designed to appear stereotypically Jewish, in keeping with the novel's subject matter and themes. Marah, for instance, is drawn with a stereotypically large, sharp, and pointy nose. Distinguishing between the characters is sometimes difficult, as they look similar to one another, but their distinctive hats aid in recognition.

Themes

A major theme in *The Jew of New York* is the influence of capitalism in a growing New York City. Characters attempt to market beaver pelts, soda water, soil from the Holy Land, lozenges made from secretions from the anal glands of male beavers, a Hebrew-speaking Indian theatrical show, buttons, and Jewish cultural items such as phylacteries and tzitzit. Hiram's Museum, desperate for an exhibit, displays Ketzelbourd's body, claiming it is a wild animal. The book is also about New York itself, providing a semihistorical interpretation of what the city may have been like in 1830.

Katchor indicates that human beings are inextricably tied to their obsessions and idols, whether those are money, religious artifacts, cultural ideals, or even one-legged actresses. When the desires of humans become compulsive, as do Ketzelbourd's desires to amass thousands of beaver pelts and to meet Miss Patella, they end in tragedy or heartbreak.

Katchor's book also deals with self-interest. Human beings are egocentric and always look out for themselves. When Kishon wears nothing but a blanket and sleeps outdoors, the Shearith Batsal Mutual Aid Society wishes to help him not because its members care about his welfare, but because the idea of a Jew living like an animal reflects poorly on the organization. Therefore, the society attempts to marry him to a widow in order to make itself look good and demonstrate to New York that Kishon does not represent all Jews. The society never considers whether a widow would want to marry a man who wears nothing but a blanket, sleeps outdoors, and has a desire to kill animals.

Impact

Katchor has influenced other comic book writers who share his interest in Jewish studies, satire and iconoclasm, historical graphic fiction, and the history of New York and other cities with rich historical pasts. His speeches on comic book writing at venues such as the Albany Institute of History and Art have sparked interest in the comics medium, and he has influenced budding comics writers and artists through his work as an associate professor at The New School for Design in New York. Katchor has influenced Steve Sheinkin, David Gantz, Michael Chabon, James Sturm, Neil Kleid, and Jake Allen, among other notable figures.

Eric Sterling

Further Reading

Eisner, Will. *The Contract with God Trilogy: Life on Dropsie Avenue* (2006).

Gantz, David. *Jews in America: A Cartoon History* (2001).

Sturm, James. *The Golem's Mighty Swing* (2001).

Bibliography

Hoberman, J. "Gaslight: Ben Katchor's New Graphic Novel Is Set in a Shadowy New York of the 1830's." *The New York Times*, January 10, 1999. http://www.nytimes.com/books/99/01/10/reviews/990110.10hobermt.html.

Jones, Malcolm. "New York's Comic-Book Hero." *Newsweek,* February 27, 2011. http://www.newsweek.com/2011/02/27/new-york-s-comic-book-hero.html.

Katchor, Ben. "Ben Katchor." Interview by Alexander Theroux. *BOMB* 88 (Summer, 2004). http://bombsite.com/issues/88/articles/2668.

See also: *Maus: A Survivor's Tale; The Golem's Mighty Swing; A Contract with God, and Other Tenement Stories; Dropsie Avenue*

JIMMY CORRIGAN: THE SMARTEST KID ON EARTH

Author: Ware, Chris
Artist: Chris Ware (illustrator)
Publisher: Pantheon Books
First serial publication: 1993-2000
First book publication: 2000

Publication History

Chris Ware's first full-page comic featuring the Jimmy Corrigan character appeared in the Chicago arts weekly *New City* in 1992. Between 1993 and 2000, Ware chose selections of these comics and published them with Fantagraphics as the *Acme Novelty Library*, issues 1-14. The Jimmy Corrigan episodes from *Acme Novelty Library* and *New City* were revised, omitted, or included as they originally appeared to create the 380-page graphic novel *Jimmy Corrigan: The Smartest Kid on Earth*, published by Pantheon in 2000. In 2003, Pantheon released a paperback version that includes two additional pages about Amy Corrigan, after the "Corrigenda" on the endpapers. In 2005, Ware began publishing his comics out of Chicago under his own Acme Novelty Library imprint.

Plot

Two main story lines interrupt and inform each other: One takes place in the present and concerns the trials and tribulations of Jimmy Corrigan in 1980's Chicago; the other is set at the turn of the twentieth century and follows Jimmy's grandfather, James Reed Corrigan, and great-grandfather, William Corrigan, against the backdrop of preparations for the World's Columbian Exposition (also known as the Chicago World's Fair) of 1893.

In the dominant, framing story line, the protagonist, Jimmy Corrigan, is a thirty-six-year-old bachelor who lives alone and is wasting his life in an office cubicle at an unfulfilling job. Jimmy's main preoccupations are dodging phone calls from his overbearing mother; staring out the window; attempting to ingratiate himself to Peggy, the unreceptive mail clerk; and daydreaming. His life takes a dramatic turn when his estranged father, James William Corrigan, who left his mother when

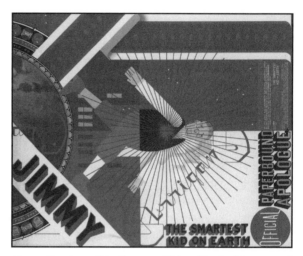

Jimmy Corrigan: The Smartest Kid on Earth. (Courtesy of Pantheon Books)

Jimmy was still a toddler, unexpectedly sends him a letter inviting him to visit. Without telling his mother where he is going, he accepts this unusual invitation and flies to Waukosha, Michigan, to see the father he never knew. During his visit, Jimmy discovers that he has an adopted African American sister, Amy Corrigan, whom he meets for the first time. The possibility of a familial reconciliation and a happy ending is dashed when James Corrigan is fatally injured in a car crash, and Jimmy returns home to Chicago.

A second story line concerns the father-son relationship between William Corrigan, a second generation Irish immigrant and a veteran of the Civil War, and his son, James Reed Corrigan. William, who must raise James alone because his wife died in childbirth, proves to be a stern and unsympathetic father. The only other member of the household is May, the African American maid, who is revealed to be Amy Corrigan's ancestor. While William is at work as a glazier, James is left to defend himself against the taunts of school bullies. James's fleeting moments of happiness are continually overshadowed by his father's disapproval and neglect. Ultimately their troubled relationship comes to a dramatic end when William abandons James at the World's Columbian Exposition on his ninth birthday.

Characters

- *Jimmy Corrigan*, the protagonist, whose simple, potato-shaped head and naïve expression recalls both an infant and an old man, is a timid, unassuming thirty-six-year-old man with a nondescript office job. Painfully shy and awkward, he yearns for romance, but his efforts to attract any female attention are dismally unsuccessful. He lives alone in a modest Chicago apartment and has no social life.

- *James William Corrigan*, who refers to himself as "Jim," lives in Waukosha, Michigan, and works as a bartender in the Landing Field, an airport bar. Although father and son resemble each other physically, their personalities are completely different. Jim is full of masculine bluster and confidence. Nonetheless, in his own clichéd and awkward manner, he tries to make amends with Jimmy and feels some remorse for abandoning him. A more sympathetic side of his character emerges when it is revealed that he remarried and adopted an African American girl, Amy Corrigan.

- *James Reed Corrigan*, born in 1884, is Jim's father and Jimmy's grandfather. His mother died in childbirth, a tragedy for which his father, William Corrigan, has not forgiven the boy. In one of the main story lines, the young James is at the mercy of his stern and unloving father, who punishes him for the smallest infraction. He is depicted both as a child growing up in Chicago during the World's Columbian Exposition of 1893 and during the 1980's, when he is an old man, thus providing the link between the two intersecting story lines.

- *William Corrigan*, whose father was an Irish immigrant, fought for the Union army in the Civil War. Despite the fact that he enjoys boasting about his war exploits to his son, the truth is that he shot off one of his fingers in order to be discharged from the army. He becomes a glazier and works on various construction jobs in Chicago, the most important of which is the World's Columbian Exposition of 1893.

- *J. Corrigan*, originally Irish, is a physician who immigrates to the United States in the nineteenth century. Although he initially can find only construction jobs, he eventually is able to practice as a doctor. His son, William Corrigan, is Jimmy Corrigan's great grandfather.

- *Amy Corrigan*, an African American teenager, is Jim's adopted daughter and Jimmy Corrigan's stepsister. Jimmy and Amy are distant blood relations because William Corrigan fathered a child with his African American maid, May. One of the central ironies in the book is that only the reader has knowledge of this connection.

Artistic Style

Like the two interwoven time frames that comprise *Jimmy Corrigan*, Ware's meticulous craftsmanship and intricate aesthetic paradoxically manage to be simultaneously contemporary and old-fashioned, recalling both Sears Roebuck's catalogs from the early twentieth century and the nonlinear acrobatics of hypertext. The graphic design of fake advertisements and the ornate lettering found in *Jimmy Corrigan* are often painstakingly hand copied from original newspapers and advertisements. Along with Art Spiegelman, Ware is part of a group of artists who are inspired by early twentieth-century newspaper cartoonists Winsor McCay, Frank King, and George Herriman.

Narrative time in *Jimmy Corrigan* is measured in discreet moments of everyday life that ordinarily escape notice, and it frequently shifts between dream and reality with little warning. A telephone ringing, subtle gradations of color in the changing dawn sky, or the awkward wait in a doctor's examining room can occupy several panels and establish the mood or feeling surrounding a particular character. Ware typically uses vivid primary colors as the background when Jimmy is experiencing a particularly strong emotion—most often fear, embarrassment, or panic. Page layouts are intricate structures based on grids of varying dimensions.

To describe the principles behind his panel compositions, Ware invokes analogies from music and architecture. He explains that just as sheet music comes alive when the notes are played aloud, a comic strip comes alive when it is read. Similarly, Ware suggests that a comic strip can be viewed as one would a façade of a building—turning it around in the mind to see all sides at one time. In *Jimmy Corrigan*, one can find examples of visual analogies between panels and windows, buildings, and photographs.

The original hardback edition of *Jimmy Corrigan* includes a dust jacket with an elaborate map that traces the lineages of four generations of the Corrigan family as they intersect in time and space across Ireland, Africa, and the United States. Within the pages of *Jimmy Corrigan*, one can find cut-out designs for a zoetrope (a cylinder with slits and images in the interior that creates a simple circular animation), a diorama of William

Corrigan's house, and complex diagrams that chart the relationships between generations. These pages may initially seem to be baffling interruptions or digressions, but the careful reader will be able to discern striking connections to themes and revelations concealed in the plot. The cut-out toys function as games and souvenirs from childhood but are also a reflection of the melancholy plight of Jimmy as he limps through life like the robot on crutches depicted in the zoetrope. Maps and diagrams reveal the maid May's heritage as the descendant of slaves; Amy Corrigan's biological relationship to William Corrigan and his maid, May; William Corrigan's discharge from the Union army;

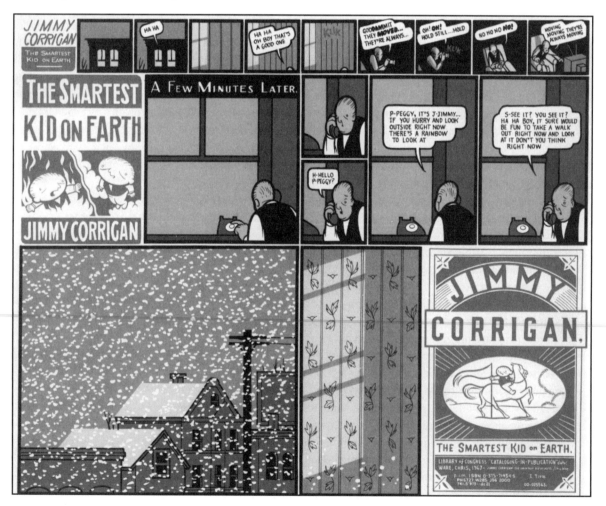

Jimmy Corrigan: The Smartest Kid on Earth. (Courtesy of Pantheon Books)

and J. Corrigan's original immigration from Ireland to the United States.

Themes

Above all, *Jimmy Corrigan* is about missed connections among family members. James William Corrigan attempts to reunite with his son, Jimmy, but the differences between them are too great to develop any meaningful relationship. There is a clear parallel to the second story line set in the nineteenth century that represents the strained relationship between William and James from the perspective of James, the neglected and abused child. This lack of familial bonding is magnified in the context of the World's Columbian Exposition, which is supposed to signify mankind's greatest social, cultural, and technological achievements.

Conspicuously absent from the story are sympathetic, positive female characters, with the possible exception of Amy Corrigan. Jimmy's mother nags her son incessantly and makes him feel guilty. Amy makes an effort get to know Jimmy and befriend him, although this nascent friendship is dashed when she turns him away after their father's death. The final missed connection, which is available to the reader but not to the characters, is the revelation that Amy and Jimmy are distant blood relations.

Another crucial theme concerns the impossibility of a credible superhero. *Jimmy Corrigan* begins with a prologue in which the young Jimmy, full of naïve enthusiasm, goes to a car show to get the autograph of a television actor who played Superman. The actor, who seduces Jimmy's divorced mother for a one-night stand, is not a model hero. Throughout the graphic novel, there are repeated episodes of disillusionment involving images of superheroes that poignantly echo Jimmy's own search for a father figure. When Jimmy wears a Superman shirt, it only serves to emphasize how absurdly pathetic he is.

Under the heading "Corrigenda" in the endpapers, a third, autobiographical theme emerges. Owing to a bizarre coincidence, Ware was contacted by his estranged father—just like his character Jimmy was—while he was working on the graphic novel. Father and son met briefly once, but their conversation was

> ## Chris Ware
>
> Award-winning writer and illustrator Chris Ware has created some of the most depressing adult comic books ever written—which doesn't mean they're not entertaining. A master of intricately designed pages, Ware often experiments with a wide variety of formats and flowchart-like panels in his work. His characters often suffer from indecision, oppressive figures, or violence being visited upon them—but the resulting stories are often beautiful to watch unfold.

as strained and awkward as the relationship depicted in the novel; a year later, Ware learned that his father had died. He concludes with the observation that the four or five hours it takes to read Jimmy Corrigan "is almost exactly the total amount of time I ever spent with my father."

Impact

Jimmy Corrigan has helped to elevate the status of the graphic novel to the attention of the general reading public. Thanks to the American Book Award (2001) and Guardian Book Awards (2001), readers who might never have read a graphic novel before bought *Jimmy Corrigan*, which helped make it a best seller. Based on its formal complexity and its focus on the humiliations of everyday life, Ware's work has been compared to Gustave Flaubert's *Madame Bovary* (1886) and James Joyce's *Ulysses* (1922).

Since the publication of *Jimmy Corrigan*, Ware's aesthetic has been recognized and celebrated in the fields of graphic design and fine art. His artwork has appeared on the cover of *The New Yorker*, the *Virginia Quarterly Review*, *McSweeney's Quarterly Concern*, and the Penguin deluxe edition of Voltaire's *Candide*. Museums and galleries have begun to display his artwork, most notably when it was part of the Whitney Biennial of American Art (2002) and also in solo exhibitions at the Museum of Contemporary Art in Chicago (2006) and the University of Nebraska's Sheldon Memorial Art Gallery (2007).

Ware's interest in architecture and particular fondness for Louis Sullivan's buildings is evident in his collaboration with National Public Radio host Ira Glass and cultural historian Tim Samuelson on *Lost Buildings* (2004), a book and DVD that document the destruction of historic buildings in Chicago. Between 2005 and 2006, his series "Building Stories," a narrative that recounts the intertwined lives of the residents of one Chicago row house, was published in *The New York Times Magazine*.

Martha B. Kuhlman

Further Reading

Clowes, Daniel. *Ghost World* (1997).

_____. *Twentieth Century Eightball* (2002).

Katchor, Ben. *Julius Knipl, Real Estate Photographer* (1996).

Seth. *It's a Good Life, If You Don't Weaken* (1993-2003).

Ware, Chris, ed. *Best American Comics* (2007).

_____. *McSweeney's Quarterly Concern Issue 13* (2004).

Bibliography

Ball, David M., and Martha Kuhlman, eds. *The Comics of Chris Ware: Drawing Is a Way of Thinking*. Jackson: University Press of Mississippi, 2010.

Bredehoft, Thomas. "Comics Architecture, Multidimensionality, and Time: Chris Ware's *Jimmy Corrigan: The Smartest Kid on Earth*." *Modern Fiction Studies* 52, no. 4 (Winter, 2006): 869-890.

Carlin, John, Paul Karasik, and Brian Walker, eds. *Masters of American Comics*. New Haven, Conn.: Yale University Press, 2005.

Raeburn, Daniel K. *Chris Ware*. New Haven, Conn.: Yale University Press, 2004.

See also: *Ghost World; It's a Good Life, If You Don't Weaken; Maus: A Survivor's Tale; I Never Liked You*

JOURNEY: THE ADVENTURES OF WOLVERINE MACALISTAIRE

Author: Messner-Loebs, William

Artist: William Messner-Loebs (illustrator); James Bleeker (letterer); James A. Osten (letterer)

Publisher: IDW Publishing

First serial publication: 1983-1984, 1985-1986

First book publication: 2008 (Volume 1); 2009 (Volume 2)

Publication History

The first fourteen issues of *Journey*, created by William Messner-Loebs, were published by Aardvark-Vanaheim in 1983, during the rise of independent comics in the direct-sales market. Teaser pages of *Journey* appeared as a backup feature in issues 48 and 49 of *Cerebus* (1977-2004) under the title "Unique Stories." In 1984, a four-page *Journey* story appeared in *AV in 3D*, an anthology featuring characters from the Aardvark-Vanaheim line, with 3D rendering provided by Ray Zone.

Fantagraphics Books published issues 15-27 of *Journey*, as well as several related projects. Two issues of a proposed six-issue miniseries entitled *Journey: War Drums* came out in 1987. The rest of the series never appeared. An original short story featuring Wolverine MacAlistaire, the protagonist of *Journey*, appeared in issue 5 of the anthology series *Anything Goes!* (1986-1987). That same year, a magazine-size trade-paperback reprinting of the first three issues of *Journey* appeared under the title *Journey: Tall Tales*. A second volume, *Journey: Bad Weather*, was published in 1990.

IDW Publishing released the entire original series in two trade-paperback volumes in 2008 and 2009. Volume 1 contains issues 1-16, and Volume 2 completes the set with issues 17-27.

Plot

Journey is the story of frontiersman Joshua "Wolverine" MacAlistaire. Set in the early nineteenth century in what was then the far western frontier of Michigan, *Journey* is a combination of historical fiction and American tall tale. *Journey* was originally designed as an ongoing series; thus, the stories in the two IDW

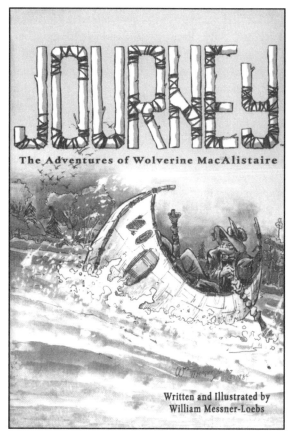

Journey: The Adventures of Wolverine MacAlistaire. (Courtesy of Fantagraphics Books)

volumes are episodic. Many small stories take place within the context of MacAlistaire's journey across Michigan to deliver a mysterious package. Early in the series MacAlistaire meets a group of Mennonites who are traveling to Canada. He directs them instead to the nearer Fort Miami. At this point, the plot diverges to follow two separate story lines.

The first story line involves MacAlistaire and his tale of survival in the wilderness. In these vignettes, his role as a larger-than-life American mythological character in the tradition of Paul Bunyan is made clear. He meets Jemmy Acorn, an obvious parody of Johnny Appleseed. He lives briefly with a woman who believes he is her dead husband. He spends part of the winter with old friends Crawfish Martin and his Indian wife, Sparrowdark. He is chased by a bear, negotiates a treaty between Native Americans and a tribe of Sasquatch, and hears a story told by a dead man's skull. He survives an earthquake, lives through a blizzard in a handmade ice cave, and is flung miles through the air by a tornado.

The secondary story begins slowly, but it gradually takes over the main narrative of the book, almost to the exclusion of MacAlistaire, who plays no part in this tale at all. Elmer Craft and the Mennonite Ilse Keiffer arrive at Fort Miami where a large cast of characters is introduced.

The main plot of this story arc involves the relationship between the inhabitants of the fort and the Native Americans. While no actual historical figures appear, this plotline is set against the backdrop of the Shawnee Indian Tecumseh's and his brother the Prophet's doomed attempt to unite the tribes against European American expansion into their territory.

Mary, the fort's American Indian cook (considered a "tame Indian" by its inhabitants), is actually Wolf Marie, a supporter of Tecumseh's cause. She plots with the tribes to destroy Fort Miami. The tensions and politics of this situation, tied to the basic need for survival on the frontier, form the core story of this section of *Journey*.

Three specific historical events are woven into the tale. The first, an eclipse of the sun predicted by the Prophet, signals the beginning of actual conflict between the settlers and the American Indians. The second, a series of severe earthquakes that shook Michigan and Ohio in 1811, destroy Fort Miami and mark the end of the first volume.

Volume 2 begins with the chapter appropriately titled "Diaspora." The characters at Fort Miami disperse after the earthquake, most of them disappearing from the series. One group heads for Prophetstown on the banks of the Tippecanoe River to join Tecumseh, only to discover that the settlement has been wiped out by American forces led by future president William Henry Harrison.

Elmer Craft, lost in the woods after the earthquake, meets MacAlistaire once again. The two travel together to the small town of New Hope. Most of the remaining story is a convoluted murder mystery set in that town.

The content of MacAlistaire's package is finally revealed to be a Bible containing clues to the identity of the killer. The series ends on an inconclusive note, indicating that there were many more MacAlistaire stories to be told.

Volumes

- *Journey: The Adventures of Wolverine MacAlistaire,* Volume 1 (2008). Collects *Journey* issues 1-16. Follows MacAlistaire on his adventures and introduces readers to the group of Mennonites that cohabit with the American Indians of the area.
- *Journey: The Adventures of Wolverine MacAlistaire,* Volume 2 (2009). Collects *Journey* issues 17-27. Characters flee Fort Miami after a devastating earthquake, and Craft and MacAlistaire journey together.

Characters

- *Joshua MacAlistaire*, a.k.a *Wolverine*, the protagonist, is a tall, rugged frontiersman with shaggy braided hair and an enormous handlebar mustache. He hates civilization, preferring the wilderness. He is educated and well-read and has a dry wit and laconic manner. He typically finds himself involved in other people's plots, much to his displeasure. Only by agreeing to deliver a mysterious package does he further the plot.
- *Jemmy Acorn*, a wandering madman, wears rags and a tin pot for a hat. He speaks in anachronisms and serves primarily as comic relief.
- *Elmer Craft*, an educated Boston poet, is a foil for MacAlistaire. Initially a parody of H. P. Lovecraft, his unrealistic and romantic notions about the frontier clash with the reality of his experience.
- *Hans Keiffer*, a Mennonite, is a weak, ineffectual man. He spends months lost in the woods, surviving with the help of Fitzhugh, a cannibalistic wild man. The experience changes him for the better.
- *Ilse Keiffer* takes shelter at Fort Miami. The reality of survival there compromises her rigid beliefs, allowing her to live more fully in the

Journey: The Adventures of Wolverine MacAlistaire. (Courtesy of Fantagraphics Books)

world. Believing her husband Hans to be dead, she begins an affair with Henri Lenoir, commandant of the fort.

- *Crawfish Martin*, a friend of MacAlistaire, wants to leave the wilderness and open a store. MacAlistaire spends the winter in his home.
- *Sparrowdark*, Martin's Algonquin wife, represents the conflict between ideas of civilization and savagery, Europeans and American Indians, and individualism and social and familial responsibility.

- *Wolf Marie,* a.k.a. *Mary*, is a Shawnee Indian who serves as cook at Fort Miami. Considered harmless, she is actually a follower of Tecumseh and wants nothing more than the death of all white people. Her machinations lead to much of the unrest and violence that plagues the fort.
- *B. K.*, a young soldier at Fort Miami, is drawn in a simplified, iconic style to convey his wide-eyed innocence. He maintains an inner dialogue, telling the story of his great wilderness adventure. He is a counterpoint to Craft in maintaining a romantic delusion of frontier life. Unlike Craft's story, which is a contemptuous chronicle of what he witnesses, B. K.'s story is an effort to

protect himself from the deprivations, violence, and horror he experiences.

- *Ellinore Trent* was once a Boston socialite. The recipient of Craft's affection, he keeps Ellinore on a pedestal as his muse and romantic ideal. Her frontier experiences and the murder of her husband have made her cold, heartless, and bent on revenge.

Artistic Style

The entire *Journey* saga was drawn by series creator Messner-Loebs and published as a black-and-white comic. His sense of design and storytelling owes much to *The Spirit* (1940-1952) creator Will Eisner. Like Eisner's work, there is a lithe dynamism to his characters, suggesting motion that leads the eye across the page. Beyond the surface similarities, however, Messner-Loebs has made the style his own.

The character designs, while cartoony, run the gamut from detailed features to the grotesquely exaggerated to the simplified, almost to the point of iconic abstraction. His portrayal of people on the frontier is not idealized. The look of his characters can be off-putting; they are ugly and utterly human. No matter how far Messner-Loebs strays from the realistic, however, the characters stay consistent and express a wide array of emotions.

The primary appeal of Messner-Loebs's art is his masterful use of the brush for inking. His lines are loose and expressionistic, with few hard edges. Though his figures are caricature, he spares no detail in their rendering. Through a variety of brush techniques, such as feathering, cross-hatching, and dry-brush, Messner-Loebs delineates a complete world. The textures of tree bark, animal fur, and leather clothing, as well as the elements of rain, snow, and fog are differentiated under his skillful hand. There are times when the black bleeds across the page, creating a sense of claustrophobia and foreboding. His use of white space is carefully calculated and is used to accentuate the mood. The extreme contrast conveys the themes of inner darkness and outer conflict that run throughout the story.

As the series progressed, the art became much looser and less detailed. Whether this was a conscious choice or came about because of the pressures of producing on a monthly deadline is unclear. Artist Don Simpson lent an inking assist on a single issue. His lines, while expressive, are more controlled than Messner-Loebs's.

Themes

Journey is the story of the frontier. The exploration of the actual, historical frontier of early nineteenth-century America is the most obvious example of this. However, the idea of the frontier as the place where old ideas clash with new, as the meeting place of conflicting ideologies and worldviews, plays out in ways both overt and subtle throughout the series.

MacAlistaire, and many other characters, have gone into the wilderness to escape encroaching civilization. Nonetheless, wherever humanity goes, it brings civilization with it, which leads to the question of what is actually "civilized" needing to be addressed. The physical needs of survival in the natural world play against the purely man-made political and social intrigues that plague both Fort Miami and the village of New Hope.

The contrast between nature and civilization is also seen in the cultural clash between the white frontier people and the American Indians. The settlers see the Indians as uncivilized, either vilifying them as barbarians or idealizing them as "noble savages." However, the narrative makes clear that neither is true. The Indians are portrayed, like the white settlers, as fully human, replete the political and social issues that are the hallmarks of civilization.

Early in the story, MacAlistaire says "the only darkness in the wilderness is what man brings with him." In dreams, he is chased by the Dark Man, the only thing MacAlistaire fears. It is revealed that the Dark Man represents his father, an abusive man who once tried to drown MacAlistaire in a barrel of water.

Impact

Journey appeared during the first bloom of independent comics publishing, which was made possible by the birth of the direct market in the early 1980's. At the time, it was difficult to find a comic book that did not involve a superhero or fantasy-inspired themes. The only real alternative was the teen humor world of Archie Comics.

Freed from the constraints of the Comics Code

William Messner-Loebs

Best known in the world of superhero comics as a longtime writer of a variety of DC Comics titles, William Messner-Loebs first established his reputation as a cartoonist by producing *Journey: The Adventures of Wolverine McAlistaire* from 1983 to 1986, one of the most influential independent adventure comics of the period. The comic featured the adventures of Michigan frontiersmen in the nineteenth century and its twenty-seven issues have been collected on multiple occasions. After writing for *Jonny Quest*, Messner-Loebs moved to DC Comics as the writer of *The Flash* and *Dr. Fate*. In the 1990's he wrote a very well-received run on *Wonder Woman* (with artist Mike Deodato) and subsequently worked as the writer of *Hawkman* and *Impulse*. Messner-Loebs's style was cartoonishly realistic, with rounded lines and exaggerated expressions recalling the classic illustrators of *MAD* magazine.

Authority, independent publishers were able to create a wider variety of content and had greater leeway in the expression of personal vision. Nonetheless, numerous creators had been inspired by the mainstream, and many of the new titles were still variations on the tropes of science fiction, fantasy, and the superhero. *Journey* was one of the earliest exceptions to this trend.

Messner-Loebs created a world and populated it with characters based on his personal interest in American history and folklore. The elements of the fantastic that do appear are traceable to tall tales and the oral storytelling tradition of exaggeration more than to any comics-inspired clichés. While not singular in its approach—Larry Marder's *Tales of the Beanworld* (1985-1993) and Arn Saba's *Neil the Horse* (1983-1988) are other examples from this time period of the type of comic that Messner-Loebs was

creating—*Journey* proved that comic books can accommodate any style or vision.

Messner-Loebs, like MacAlistaire, was on the frontier of a new world. Unlike his protagonist however, Messner-Loebs left the unexplored wilds for comparative civilization. While critically acclaimed at the time, *Journey* never found a wide audience. Messner-Loebs joined the mainstream comics world and became a well-respected writer. In addition to a number of miniseries and titles for various companies, he helmed the 1980's DC Comics relaunch of *The Flash* and wrote an influential run of *Wonder Woman*.

Wayne Wise

Further Reading

Bertozzi, Nick. *Lewis and Clark* (2011).

Messner-Loebs, William, and Sam Kieth. *Epicurus the Sage* (2003).

Truman, Timothy. *Wilderness: The True Story of Simon Girty, Renegade* (1992).

Bibliography

Messner-Loebs, William. "Bill Messner-Loebs: A Career Retrospective (Part I)." Interview by Darren Schroeder. *Comics Bulletin.* http://www.comicsbulletin.com/storytelling/95852385995680.htm.

Sanders, Joe Sutliff. "A Western Legend." *Teacher Librarian* 37, no. 1 (2009): 29.

Wheeler, Andrew. Review: "*Journey,* Volume 1 by William Messner-Loebs." Review of *Journey: The Adventures of Wolverine MacAlistaire,* Volume 1 by William Messner-Loebs. *Comicmix. com,* September 22, 2008. http://www.comicmix.com/news/2008/09/22/review-journey-vol-1-by-william-messner-loebs.

See also: *Tales of the Beanworld; Louis Riel; Journey into Mohawk Country*

JOURNEY INTO MOHAWK COUNTRY

Author: Bogaert, Harmen Meyndertsz van den
Artist: George O'Connor (illustrator); Hilary Sycamore (colorist)
Publisher: First Second Books
First book publication: 2006

Publication History

George O'Connor's *Journey into Mohawk Country* was published in September of 2006 by First Second, an imprint of Roaring Brook Press, which is a division of Holtzbrinck Publishers. First Second was established in 2004 under editorial director Mark Siegel to develop graphic novels. The entire text of O'Connor's book was a twenty-two-page journal written by Dutch trader Harmen Meyndertsz van den Bogaert in 1634. Bogaert's journal was translated into English by Charles T. Gehring and William A. Starna in 1988 and published by Syracuse University Press as *A Journey into Mohawk and Oneida Country, 1634-1635*. Every word that appears in O'Connor's book is taken directly from the Gehring and Starna translation of the original; O'Connor has not changed (either adding or excising) anything in the original text. However, he has done more than simply "illustrate" it; as O'Connor explains in his publisher's blog about the development of the project, his panels "fill in the gaps of his story, as they were suggested by what [Bogaert] wrote."

Plot

The journal on which O'Connor's book is based was written over a two-month period in the winter of 1634-1635 by Bogaert, a barber-surgeon who was stationed at Fort Orange in New York. He traveled through Mohawk and Oneida Indian territory in an attempt to secure trade relations with the natives, who the Dutch believed had begun trading with the French. Although brief, the original journal is full of impressive detail about Native American culture that Bogaert observed in his travels.

Bogaert opens his narrative by explaining the reasons for his travels and introducing his companions, Jeromus La Croex and Willem Tomassen. Dressed in

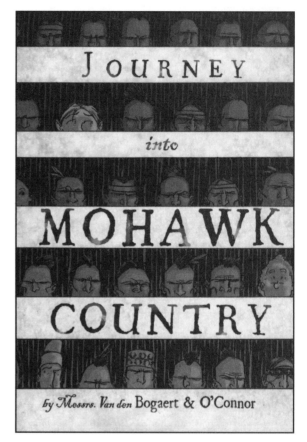

Journey into Mohawk Country. (Courtesy of First Second Books)

knee breeches, collared shirts, and fancy shoes and hats, the three men begin a difficult and extremely cold journey, immediately facing privation and physical challenges. Their physical appearances become more and more ragged as their adventure proceeds. The plotline of the book involves them moving from one Native American settlement to the next, engaging in conversations about trade and learning more about the various indigenous groups and their habits. After gathering all the information they can, the men return home to Fort Orange, where Bogaert ends his diary.

O'Connor's interpretations often add humor and irony to what is sometimes dull text. For example, early in the journal, Bogaert explains the purpose of his journey in plain terms; O'Connor uses a whole page to illustrate what is going on behind the dry journal text. Between the text box that reads "I went with Jeromus La Croex and Willem Tomassen" and the text box "May the Lord Bless our Journey," the reader sees Jeromus and Willem in a sort of slapstick, bumbling attempt to cross a river that devolves into them fighting. The text of the original journal is reproduced faithfully, but O'Connor's images change the tone of the journal, adding visual humor and irony to the writing.

Throughout their travels, the men rely upon the Native Americans they meet to serve as guides and to help them find shelter and food. Bogaert also provides detailed descriptions of the Native Americans' settlements, including the buildings where they lived, stored food, slept, and entertained. O'Connor's illustrations use both the information from Bogaert's text and the footnotes from the scholarly edition of the book, providing excellent and well-researched background scenery that fleshes out the sketch provided by Bogaert.

Characters

- *Harmen Meyndertsz van den Bogaert*, the protagonist, is a Dutch trader leading an exploration of Mohawk settlements, seeking to improve trade in beaver pelts. He is portrayed as young and attractive with blond hair; he is considerably shorter than his traveling companions and most of the indigenous people he meets. In the text, he relates his experience in a matter-of-fact tone. In the images, he is a much more lively figure, portrayed as frequently surprised by the things and people he encounters. He is the keeper of the journal; thus, he is the filter through which the reader learns everything in the story.

- *Jeromus La Croex* is one of Bogaert's two companions on his travels. His name is sometimes spelled "Jeronimus." O'Connor portrays him as portly and round. He repeatedly—and apparently needlessly—becomes alarmed about the behaviors of the Native Americans, worrying at one point "that an Indian was planning to kill him with a knife" and later fearful "that the Indians were arming themselves" to attack them, when in reality they were preparing for war games. He

provides some comic relief in O'Connor's illustrations of the journal.

- *Willem Tomassen* is the other of Bogaert's two companions. O'Connor portrays him as tall and slender. Although the text itself does not mention this, O'Connor's images show him commencing a romantic relationship with one of the native women, whom he ultimately brings back to Fort Orange with him at the end of their travels.

- *Marten Gerritsen* is the commissary of Fort Orange who sends the men on their mission. Although he does not actually appear as a character in the story, he sends the Dutch travelers several letters over the course of their travels, and they report to him on their progress.

Artistic Style

Although the book is based on real events, the illustrations are not particularly realistic, veering occasionally into an almost superhero style; at times, the images of the Native Americans are quite stylized and even stereotyped. *Kirkus Reviews* wrote that "Several facial expressions are presented with exaggerated juvenile quirkiness, marking the work's interest level as definitely middle school." Although at times comic, the illustrations are detailed in their portrayal of various clothing styles and the tools and homes of the Native Americans.

The color choices throughout the book serve to further emphasize the differences between the Native Americans and the Dutch explorers. Warm brown and orange earth tones are used to portray the natives, while the Dutchmen wear black, white, red, and purple. Color also serves to underscore tone and emotions. During the intense rituals of the medicine men, the color contrasts are stark with black, red, purple, and yellow creating frightening scenes in darkened, fire-lit tents. During one of the passages describing the Native Americans singing, the illustrations depict Bogaert dreaming; the color palette changes to pastels and the illustrations become even more simple and childlike, as Bogaert imagines all his dreams for success coming true.

Color is also used effectively to signal the temperature; inside the natives' huts, warm browns and oranges signal warmth, in contrast with the blues of the frigid outdoors. Toward the end of the book, Bogaert strikes out on his own on a particularly cold and stormy night. Unable to start a fire, he explains, "I had to walk around all night to keep warm." Following this statement are six, near-wordless full pages portraying Bogaert cold

and terrified, being either haunted by or hallucinating a native man who appears to give him directions.

Themes

The original journal is simply a recounting of daily life as an explorer and trade ambassador to the Mohawk

Journey into Mohawk Country. (Courtesy of First Second Books)

Indians. One major theme for the book can be seen as a questioning of what "really" happened compared to what Bogaert chooses to tell (or what O'Connor chooses to illustrate). While the original journal can be read as "just-the-facts" reporting, O'Connor's version is adept at bringing out some of the curious resonances between the two supposedly alien cultures, showing them to be foreign not only to each other but also to modern readership.

Notions of religion, superstition, and medical treatment are notably intertwined within both the Dutch and the native culture. Bogaert describes some of the native religious rituals and worship of animal idols, but also mentions his own, such as shooting off his gun "in honor of our Lord and Redeemer, Jesu Christo." Clearly both the natives and the Dutch hold to traditions and rituals that, to outsiders, may seem silly. Early in the book, Willem Tomassen's leg "had swollen from walking," and so Bogaert "made some cuts with a knife . . . and then smeared it with bear's grease." Bogaert's supposed healing is juxtaposed with another incident when he observes a healing ritual in which one of the doctors—called "sunachkoes"—put a stick down his throat "and vomited on the patient's head and all over his body." Modern readers see both of these practices as disgusting and of questionable medical value.

Another central issue throughout the book is the ongoing misunderstandings between the two cultures. The Native Americans repeatedly provide the three Dutchmen with hospitality, yet despite the fact that they never encounter any violence at the hands of the natives, the Dutchmen repeatedly indicate their fears of them, both in the original text and in O'Connor's illustrations. Bogaert notes during one gathering "if they had wanted to do anything to us we could have done nothing" and at another "had they any malicious intentions, they could have easily grabbed us with their hands and killed us without much trouble." There is an undercurrent of a threat in the original journal, although it never amounts to anything. O'Connor picks up on this tension and amplifies it, showing the real and, more so, imagined fears of the three men. Bogaert describes entering a Native American settlement that is decorated with "three locks fluttered that they had cut

from the heads of slain Indians." In the image paired with this text, the reader sees three dangling scalps that match the hair colors and styles of the three Dutchmen, which they eye with concern.

The most substantial (and possibly controversial) addition that O'Connor provides is a love story playing out in the background between Tomassen and a Native American woman. In several early scenes, it becomes clear that Tomassen is flirting with her, despite the fact that there is no mention of this in the original text. Later, Bogaert's journal indicates "I found many acquaintances," and in the illustration, he looks on approvingly while his friend and his romantic companion are reunited. Later, while Bogaert explains his trade negotiations with the natives, the action in the images turns to the blooming relationship between Tomassen and his native girlfriend, who walk holding hands and who play games while Bogaert and La Croex negotiate the deal.

Impact

Journey into Mohawk Country is a unique collaboration between an author and illustrator, since the author was dead for three hundred years before the illustrator began his work. It is a singular example of a primary document being made into a graphic novel. Reception of *Journey into Mohawk Country* has been generally positive, with many librarians and teachers praising it as a way to get younger students to read history.

This was O'Connor's first graphic novel. Prior to this book, he was known for children's books, including *Ker-Splash* (2005) and *Sally and the Something* (2006). Since the publication of *Journey into Mohawk Country*, O'Connor has begun a graphic novel series with First Second Books called *The Olympians*, which focuses on retelling Greek mythology.

Bridget M. Marshall

Further Reading

Bechdel, Alison. *Fun Home: A Family Tragicomic* (2006).

Lat. *Kampung Boy* (2006).

Neufeld, Josh. *A.D.: New Orleans After the Deluge* (2010).

O'Connor, George. *Zeus: King of the Gods* (2010)
_____. *Olympians* (2010).

Bibliography

Abler, Thomas S. Review of *A Journey into Mohawk and Oneida Country, 1634-1635. Ethnohistory* 38, no. 3 (Summer, 1991) 340-343.

Bogaert, Harmen Meyndertsz van den. *A Journey into Mohawk and Oneida Country, 1634-1635: The Journal of Harmen Meyndertsz van den Bogaert.* Translated and edited by Charles T. Gehring and William A. Starna. Syracuse, N.Y.: Syracuse University Press, 1988.

Jackson, Tom, and Emily S. Rueb. "From Dutch to Drawings." *The New York Times*, December 28, 2009. http://www.nytimes.com/interactive/2009/12/28/nyregion/200912-MOHAWK-ILLOS.html

"O'Connor, George: *Journey into Mohawk Country*." *Kirkus Reviews* 74, no. 17 (September 1, 2006): 910.

Schwartz, E. A. "*A Journey into Mohawk and Oneida Country, 1634-1635: The Journal of Harmen Meyndertsz van den Bogaert.*" *The American Indian Quarterly* 18, no. 1 (Winter, 1994): 119. http://find.galegroup.com.libproxy.uml.edu/itx/start.do?prodId=AONE.

Sheyahshe, Michael A. *Native Americans in Comic Books: A Critical Study.* Jefferson, N.C.: McFarland, 2008.

See also: *Fun Home: A Family Tragicomic; Kampung Boy; A.D.: New Orleans After the Deluge*

JULIUS KNIPL, REAL ESTATE PHOTOGRAPHER: STORIES

Author: Katchor, Ben
Artist: Ben Katchor (illustrator)
Publisher: Little, Brown
First book publication: 1996

Publication History

Ben Katchor created *Julius Knipl, Real Estate Photographer* at the urging of Art Spiegelman, who had previously worked with Katchor at *RAW*, the comics anthology that Spiegelman edited with his wife, Françoise Mouly, from 1980 to 1991. Spiegelman had been contacted by the publisher Russ Smith, who was looking for alternative comic strips for his fledgling weekly, *New York Press;* Spiegelman recommended Katchor for the job.

The first *Julius Knipl, Real Estate Photographer* comic strip appeared in 1988. Katchor has been writing it weekly ever since, and it is published in numerous alternative weekly newspapers, most notably *The Forward*. Although the comic strip has never achieved mainstream success, it does have a devoted following, particularly in New York City. For example, there was a minor uproar when the new editor of *The Village Voice* decided to drop the strip from the paper in 1995. From 1995 to 1996, the National Public Radio news show *Weekend Edition* produced audio versions of *Julius Knipl, Real Estate Photographer*, narrated by Katchor with comedian Jerry Stiller as Julius Knipl.

Julius Knipl, Real Estate Photographer is the second anthology of Katchor's comic strip, following the 1991 publication of *Cheap Novelties: The Pleasures of Urban Decay* by Penguin (as a *RAW* one-shot.) It has since been followed by a third anthology, *Julius Knipl, Real Estate Photographer: The Beauty Supply District*, published in 2000 by Pantheon Books.

Plot

There is no central plot to *Julius Knipl, Real Estate Photographer*. Since the book is simply a collection of Katchor's weekly strips, the individual stories are often concluded within a single page of the book. On occasion, a story arc will continue across two or even three

(AP Photo)

Ben Katchor

An early contributor to *RAW*, Ben Katchor published two issues of the anthology *Picture Story* before embarking on the work for which he is best known: the comic strip *Julius Knipl, Real Estate Photographer*. Published in *The Forward* and several other weekly newspapers, the strip exudes a love for the failing urban landscape of New York City, expressed as a poetic collection of whimsical observations and gray-washed drawings. Three collections of the strip have been published to date. In 1999, Katchor published his first graphic novel, *The Jew of New York*, which tells a story based on Mordecai Manuel Noah's attempt to establish a Jewish homeland in Grand Island, New York, in the 1820's. *The Cardboard Valise*, a 2011 graphic novel, follows the adventures of two neighbors, the compulsive vacationer Emile Delilah and Elijah Salamis, who dresses only in underwear, no matter the weather. Katchor, who is the only cartoonist to have been awarded the prestigious MacArthur Fellowship, has also received a Guggenheim Fellowship. Katchor is among the most acclaimed contemporary cartoonists.

weekly strips, but this is the exception rather than the rule. The only two consistent elements throughout *Julius Knipl, Real Estate Photographer* are the unnamed city in which all the strips are set and the character Julius Knipl, who appears somewhere in every strip (even if just in the background of a panel). Most of the strips depict a forgotten corner of an unnamed urban center, based on New York City. During his travels, Knipl comes upon the Holey Pocket League, a group of men who ruminate on the cosmic significance of their pockets; a physiognomist in search of an authentic facial expression; the Public Directory of the Alimentary Canal, which lists the gastrointestinal condition of all the city's residents for a given week; and the Stasis Day Parade, where the city celebrates the most quotidian elements of urban living.

At the end of the book, Katchor does create one sustained narrative, "The Evening Combinator," which extends for seventeen pages. In this story, Julius Knipl comes to believe that his apartment is no longer conducive to sleep and begins sleeping in his office instead. On the way to his office one night, Knipl finds a discarded copy of *The Evening Combinator*, a newspaper that reports on dreams of the city's residents, on a subway seat and begins to read it. Once he arrives at his office, Knipl discovers Victor Rubicon, who has similarly decided to sleep in his office that evening. Rubicon explains something has seemed amiss ever since he purchased a new mattress and his dreams started being printed in *The Evening Combinator*.

Meanwhile, across town, Ormond Bell is speaking to his followers in the Stay-Awake-Atorium of the perils of sleep and his mission to provide every man, woman, and child in the city with a daily moment of wakefulness. He eventually reveals that he has organized a series of coordinated explosions intended to wake up the entire city. At the same time, Selladore, a highly eccentric architect, is searching for Rubicon, whose published dreams often involve a man named "Selladore" who engages in salacious and vulgar acts; the publication of these dreams has resulted in funders backing out of Selladore's new design, "Carfare City," believing he is the same man as in Rubicon's dreams. Selladore eventually finds Rubicon and Knipl in Rubicon's office, and Rubicon apologizes for the mix-up. As

the three men decide to walk to an all-night cafeteria, they hear the sounds of one of Bell's explosions in the distance—two of Bell's followers have set a bomb in the foundation of Carfare City.

Characters

- *Julius Knipl*, the protagonist, is a real estate photographer. He is noted for being a mostly passive observer of the curiosities of the city and makes an appearance in every strip.
- *Victor Rubicon* is a brassiere-strap adjuster whose office is in the same building as Julius Knipl's. The two meet when they both decide to sleep in their offices.
- *Ormond Bell* is the proprietor of the Stay-Awake-Atorium. He goes days without sleeping and spreads a gospel of wakefulness and awareness across the city.
- *Dr. Pharos* is the editor-in-chief of *The Evening Combinator*, a newspaper that prints stories about people's dreams.
- *Selladore* is an architect who concocts elaborate and surreal ideas for buildings, few of which are actually built. Coincidentally, he has the same name as a figure who appears in Victor Rubicon's dreams.
- *Morris Borzhak* is a friend of Julius Knipl with an addiction to putting various goods on layaway.
- *Arthur Mammal* is a retailer of surgical supplies who cannot help but see and diagnose the ailments of each person he passes during the day.
- *Fetor Maracas* composes music to be played using the steam that escapes from a building's radiator.
- *Harold Alms* is a lecturer who only decides upon the subjects of his lectures by listening to the conversations of the crowd in the hour before his lecture. He goes to great pains to ensure that he does not think about the subject of his lecture any earlier than this.
- *Gustave Vint* is an inventor who has created a briefcase that doubles as a wastepaper basket.
- *Doctor Tarmooti* is a man that Julius Knipl meets at the toothpick resort. The two become

lost in the woods and despair after running out of toothpicks.

Artistic Style

The most distinctive element of *Julius Knipl, Real Estate Photographer* is the gray watercolor wash that Katchor uses to illustrate all of his strips. Instantly evocative of the cityscape in which *Julius Knipl, Real Estate Photographer* is set, the images that Katchor creates are often reminiscent of Edward Hopper paintings in their composition and tone. The eight or nine sketched panels that compose each strip frequently depict loosely drawn men in baggy suits shambling their way across shadowy sidewalks and run-down stores and warehouses.

While Katchor's figures may seem quickly sketched, the city they inhabit is depicted in deep perspective. While many newspaper strips use their backgrounds almost like dioramas, in *Julius Knipl, Real Estate Photographer*, Katchor will often use a variety of different viewpoints within one strip. The first panel could begin by surveying the action from the rooftops of the city from a bird's-eye point of view, and then move into a street-level view of a shop in the next panel, before the perspective settles over the shoulders of men engaged in conversation.

Katchor's illustrations often act in concert with the text of the strip. Many of the strips are narrated in horizontal boxes that burst with crooked, handwritten lettering. Along with the narration, Katchor uses dialogue lettered in a diagonal and captured in clunky balloons. One of the most interesting things about *Julius Knipl, Real Estate Photographer* is how the artwork, narration, and dialogue function alongside one another. Instead of using the artwork to illustrate what the words are describing or having the dialogue reinforce the story of the narration, Katchor allows each element to function independently of the other two. Occasionally, the three elements will complement one other, bringing the reader to a single point. More often, however, Katchor explores the tension between word and picture as well as narration and speech by having the elements contradict or comment ironically on one another.

Themes

The central theme of many of the *Julius Knipl, Real Estate Photographer* strips seems to be nostalgia for a bygone (and distinctly Yiddish) version of New York City that, if it ever existed in the first place, has been forgotten. In the place of large corporations, skyscrapers, and franchise restaurants that fill the modern city, Katchor creates a simpler, more idiosyncratic city full of eccentrics, oddities, and surreal businesses selling perversely specific goods that is reminiscent of a time when New York was a city made up of European immigrants. Although the residents of Katchor's city are not without their own dissatisfactions and difficulties, there is a palpable air of longing on Katchor's part, a willful desire to inject an Old World European charm into the modern, relatively sterile urban spreads.

Perhaps most interesting, in *Julius Knipl, Real Estate Photographer*, Katchor is not necessarily nostalgic for a New York City that once existed, but, rather, a version of New York City that never existed. In a sense, Katchor has rewritten history and created a version of New York cut from the same fabric as the Yiddish New York for which he has affection; however, this Yiddish New York is rearranged and reassembled in such a way that the city of *Julius Knipl, Real Estate Photographer* could never actually exist. What makes Katchor's city impossible is how staunchly quotidian it is. Drawing from the most forgotten corners of modern life (all-night cafeterias, salesmen of forgettable products, hard-luck office buildings) Katchor creates a dreamlike New York of a parallel universe.

Impact

As Michael Chabon points out in his introduction to *Julius Knipl, Real Estate Photographer*, Katchor is the creator of arguably the last great American newspaper comic strip. Eschewing many of the staples of modern newspaper comic strips—such as the setup and punch line, an emphasis on the text, art that serves to simply reinforce the dialogue, the diorama-like backgrounds—*Julius Knipl, Real Estate Photographer* traces its heritage to a more traditional type of comic-strip artwork and storytelling that began with Richard Felton Outcault's *Yellow Kid* at the turn of the twentieth century. That this return to an older, forgotten form of graphic storytelling meshes perfectly with Katchor's nostalgic subject matter only adds to the substance of Katchor's mission.

As the last practitioner of a perhaps lost art, Katchor has attracted many fans, though few imitators. Reacting to the strong Yiddish influences in his work ("knipl" itself is a Yiddish word that roughly translates to "nest egg"), he has become a particularly important artist to those concerned with preserving Jewish heritage. In particular, *The Forward*, a weekly magazine that was once a daily Yiddish newspaper, has championed Katchor by not only publishing *Julius Knipl, Real Estate Photographer* but also by commissioning Katchor to write a second serialized comic, *The Jew of New York*, in 1992 and 1993. In 2000, Katchor became the first cartoonist to be awarded a MacArthur Genius grant.

Stephen Aubrey

Further Reading

Auster, Paul, Paul Karasik, and David Mazzucchelli. *City of Glass* (1994).

Eisner, Will. *Invisible People* (2000).

Katchor, Ben. *Julius Knipl, Real Estate Photographer: The Beauty Supply District* (2000).

Bibliography

Buhle, Paul. "Walker in the Imagined City." *The Nation* 271, no. 11 (October 16, 2000): 29-32.

Chabon, Michael. Introduction to *Julius Knipl, Real Estate Photographer*. New York: Little, Brown, 1996.

Op de Beeck, Nathalie. "Found Objects: (Jem Cohen, Ben Katchor, Walter Benjamin)." *Modern Fiction Studies* 52, no. 4 (Winter, 2006): 807-831.

Weschler, Lawrence. "A Wanderer in the Perfect City." *The New Yorker* 69, no. 25 (August 9, 1993): 58-66.

See also: *The Jew of New York; City of Glass; A Contract with God, and Other Tenement Stories; Dropsie Avenue*

K

KABUKI

Author: Mack, David
Artist: David Mack (illustrator); Rick Mays (illustrator); Joe Martin (letterer)
Publisher: Caliber Press; Image Comics; Marvel ICON Comics
First serial publication: 1995-2007
First book publication: 1995-2009

Publication History

David Mack wrote the first volume of *Kabuki* at the age of twenty-one, while still in college. He submitted the work as his senior writing thesis. He attended a university, not a specialized art school, because the art schools to which he applied could not offer free full tuition. According to Mack, this was a blessing, because his well-rounded university education gave him a solid and broad foundation as a writer and illustrator.

The first volume of Kabuki was inspired by many of Mack's favorite subjects at university, including the Japanese language, theater, and world religions. Although *Kabuki*'s main character lives a radically different life than its author, Mack explores some deeply personal issues in the series, notably, the death of his mother, Ida Mack, to whom he dedicates many of the novels. The series changed publishers several times. The first four volumes of the series were published together by Caliber Press, under the name *Fear the Reaper*. Image Press published subsequent volumes, except the last volume in the series, which was published by Marvel Comics, under the Icon label.

Plot

Although heavily influenced by Japanese culture and manga, *Kabuki* is written and drawn by a Western writer and is arguably meant for a Western audience. The Japanese influence is obvious from the title of the series; the character of Kabuki is named after the term

Kabuki: The Alchemy. (Courtesy of Image Comics)

that refers to Japanese popular theater, while Kabuki's agency, the Noh, is named after the term that refers to Japanese classical theater.

In Volume 1: *Circle of Blood*, the curtain opens to a grim vision of modern-day Kyoto, where criminal gangs, or *yakuza*, struggle for power. The government keeps the crime lords in check through a group of seven female assassins called the Noh. The assassins wear masks and red visors that provide information on their surroundings and vital statistics about their targets. Their tight, bulletproof outfits are reminiscent of superhero costumes. They each play specific roles in fighting crime.

Kabuki, the most prominent Noh operative, regularly makes appearances on *Noh TV* as "Little Sister," reporting on sundry news stories as well as delivering threats to various criminals. Her viewers, and even some of her targets, believe that she is merely a trick, perhaps computer-generated, designed by the government to intimidate and control the Japanese populace. However, Kabuki and her cohorts are very real and manage to wipe out many of the crime syndicates in Japan.

Mack devotes almost more attention to the backstory than to the events that happen in the "real time" of the narrative. Kabuki, whose real name is Ukiko, comes from a troubled family, a "circle of blood" that contains both the protagonist and the villain of the novels.

Ukiko's mother, Tsukiko, is of Ainu origin. The Ainu are the indigenous peoples of Japan who were conquered during feudal times and have been the victims of discrimination ever since. During World War II (1939-1945), Tsukiko is taken from her family and enlisted as a "comfort woman" for the Japanese army. Comfort women were normally sent to "comfort stations," where they were often raped by soldiers. However, Tsukiko is spared this indignity, thanks to a wise yet eccentric general. He instructs Tsukiko and the other comfort women in his regiment to perform elaborate Kabuki dramas, and forbids his soldiers from doing anything to the women other than watching them. The soldiers fear him too much to disobey, with the exception of his son, Ryuichi Kai, who molests Tsukiko. As the general's son becomes increasingly contemptuous of the women, the general becomes increasingly entranced by them, especially Tsukiko, his favorite.

After the war, the general rises to power in the government, at the same time that Ryuichi Kai rises to power in the underworld. The general adopts Tsukiko as his ward and eventually becomes engaged to her. Ryuichi Kai is incensed that his father would risk his social position by marrying an Ainu woman. On the eve of Tsukiko's marriage, an unidentified assailant gouges out her eyes and carves the word "Kabuki" on her back. Tsukiko goes into a coma before she is able to tell the general who attacked her. She is left pregnant and dies while giving birth to Ukiko. Since the general never touched Tsukiko, he has little doubt about who the father is. Thus, Ukiko/Kabuki is the daughter of her own archenemy.

Ryuichi Kai does not learn of Ukiko's existence until she is nine years old. When he does, he finds her and cuts the characters for "Kabuki" on her face. Ukiko is brought to the hospital and dies. While she flatlines, she is transported to a zone between living and dying, where she meets with her mother, who tells her to return to life and be like an avenging ghost, in imitation of one of Tsukiko's roles in the Kabuki plays. Ukiko is brought back to life, ignited with determination to carry out her mother's wishes. The general educates Ukiko in the best schools, grooming her for an elite position in an agency he has created–the Noh. Versions of this backstory are repeated many times throughout the series, as Kabuki grasps for an identity that does not involve blood, literally and figuratively.

In the present time of the story, Kabuki's nemesis, Ryuichi Kai, manages to infiltrate the Noh and becomes one of their prominent leaders, disguised with an *oni* mask, a traditional mask worn by the demon characters of Kabuki theater. Using the code name "the Devil," Kai sends the Noh agents to kill prominent members of rival gangs, thus destroying his competition. Eventually, he forms an unholy alliance with the government and even wins over his father.

When Ukiko discovers the deception, she massacres Kai and his entire syndicate against the orders of the Noh. When the Noh directors hold a disciplinary hearing with her, she kills all of them, except the general, who shoots himself. Ukiko is injured by the security guards and flees to her mother's grave.

In *Masks of Noh*, Mack shines the spotlight on the other Noh operatives, who are on a mission to assassinate Ukiko, before she can defame them all. However, before the Noh reach her, Ukiko is spirited away by Control Corps, an agency designed to rehabilitate and reprogram "defective" agents.

When the story returns to Ukiko, she is being interrogated by a psychiatrist at Control Corps, who seems at least as interested in extracting information from her as she is in "helping" her. Ukiko is an inmate of what resembles a prison psych ward, where agents gone wrong wander about the halls, drugged and rambling. Ukiko refuses to speak without her mask; deprived of her protective persona, she feels too vulnerable. She is put in solitary confinement for several weeks, during which time a mysterious inmate named "Akemi" communicates with her by means of notes folded into origami pieces and makes plans for them both to escape.

Eventually, the Noh break into Control Corps. One of the agents poses as Ukiko's doctor in order to kill her, but Ukiko is not fooled. Ukiko murders her would-be assassin and escapes Control Corps with the help of Akemi, with whom she begins to have a physical relationship. Akemi temporarily joins the Noh, impersonating the dead Noh agent, and claims that she has killed Ukiko.

With the Noh no longer after her, Ukiko moves to California and reinvents herself as a children's entertainer and children's book writer. Occasionally she wears a mask, but it is of a much different variety than her previous one: She now plays an animal in a children's play.

Volumes

- *Kabuki: Circle of Blood* (1995). Includes *Fear the Reaper*, issues 1-4, and *Circle of Blood*, issues 1-6. Featuring the rise of the Kai syndicate and its demise at the hand of Ukiko/Kabuki.
- *Kabuki: Dreams* (2002). Collects Volume 2, issues 1-4. Kabuki has a near-death experience and meets with her dead mother.
- *Kabuki: Masks of Noh* (1998). Collects Volume 3, issues 1-4. Account of the Noh operatives' mission to find Kabuki and kill her.
- *Kabuki: Skin Deep* (1998). Collects Volume 4, issues 1-3. Ukiko wakes up in Control Corps to find her mask and Kabuki identity ripped away from her.
- *Kabuki: Metamorphosis* (2000). Collects Volume 5, issues 1-9. Features the infiltration of Control Corps by the Noh and depicts Kabuki's escape with the help of Akemi.
- *Kabuki: Scarab* (2002). Collects Volume 6, issues 1-8. Provides background to the character

of Keiko (Scarab), recounting key events of her childhood and adolescence.
- *Kabuki: The Alchemy* (2009). Collects Volume 7, issues 1-9, during which Kabuki lives in hiding from the Noh and reinvents herself as a writer of children's books.

Characters

- *Ukiko Kai*, a.k.a. *Kabuki*, the protagonist, is a muscular and alluring assassin who plays the role of Kabuki in the elite Noh agency. She wears a mask that is featureless except for a small tear below the right eye. Her costume is decorated with a red sun, the emblem of the imperial flag. Her weapons of choice are sickles, farm tools of the Ainu. The mask and costume give her a stunning, picture-perfect presence, but under her mask, her face is plain and severely scarred. She is intelligent, calculating, and a fierce fighter. She is prone to moodiness and melancholy, and she frequently broods about her past.
- *Ryuichi Kai*, the antagonist and Ukiko's father, is a crime lord and the leader of the Kai syndicate. He is stubborn, and when he does not get his way, he is unmerciful. He is clever and cunning, especially in his infiltration of the Noh. As cultured as he is vicious, he loves to play piano and read philosophy books.
- *The General* is Ukiko's grandfather and Ryuichi Kai's father. Unlike his son, he is deeply respectful of the women in his life. When he was younger, he was wise and refined and a brilliant strategist. As he gets older, he begins to lose his wits and is often seen playing chess with a mannequin he believes to be his dead bride.
- *Tsukiko*, Ukiko's mother, is an Ainu who comes from Hokkaido in northern Japan. As a child, she worked on a farm. When she was ten years old, the Japanese army took her from her family and enlisted her as a "comfort woman." The general, however, has different plans for her and makes her a Kabuki actor.
- *Keiko*, a.k.a. *Scarab*, is a Noh assassin who wears a mask that has a red circle on the forehead, similar to the red sun on the costume that Kabuki

wears and alluding to the "circle of blood" theme that runs throughout the series. Her role in the Noh is to clean up messes left by other Noh operatives, thus filling a niche similar to that of the scarab beetle. As a teenager, she lived on the streets, where she engaged in petty crime, including theft and vandalism. Unlike Ukiko, she is vibrant and gregarious.

- *Siamese*, two Noh assassins, are twins who were once literally joined at the hip. After they were separated, they were both given robotic arms, with long swords as "fingernails." The two are different in character: one is quiet and the other talkative. The characters reference the Asian cyberpunk genre, from which Mack certainly took inspiration.
- *Akemi* is a mysterious and beautiful inmate at Control Corps. Akemi's character has an allegorical significance, which is why Mack named her "Akemi," in imitation of how the Japanese

---

David Mack

Best known for his creator-owned series *Kabuki*, cartoonist David Mack has one of the most distinct visual styles in comics. Working extensively in collage and multilayered artwork, Mack has created images that are fundamentally unlike the work of most of his peers. *Kabuki* was originally launched by Caliber Press in 1994 and has subsequently moved to Image Comics and Marvel Comics. Ostensibly a science-fiction adventure series about a Japanese assassin, *Kabuki* features dreamlike elements in which very little seems to happen. Mack is fond of recycling images and his characters repeatedly revisit past memories. In addition to his work on *Kabuki*, Mack has worked extensively on Marvel's *Daredevil*, serving as the artist (with writer Brian Bendis), as the writer (with artists Joe Quesada and David Ross), and as writer-artist for a short period of time. He is also a highly sought-after cover artist working in the American superhero tradition.

---

pronounce the word "alchemy." She is a veterinarian with a penchant for making origami animals. At the end of the series, she changes her gender and becomes a mailman. Her identity is intentionally ambiguous. Mack makes it unclear whether she is a real person or an aspect of Kabuki's personality that helps her transform and overcome the ghosts of her past.

Artistic Style

Kabuki contains some of the most exquisite and innovative artwork in the graphic novel genre. Mack showed promise in the first volume of the series (*Circle of Blood*), with its skilled and realistic black-and-white drawings. However, in the later volumes, Mack developed and perfected a unique style. Although manga certainly influenced the plot and characters, Mack's style is distinctly, if not stubbornly, non-manga. The pictures are vividly colored and richly textured, with detailed backgrounds that reflect the characters' thoughts, feelings, and personal histories. Just as Mack frequently repeats scenes and events, he also repeats images, weaving them into new contexts as the story unfolds. He experiments extensively with panels, superimposing them, arranging them asymmetrically on the page, or dispensing with them altogether. Mack uses a variety of media, including collage, photographs, and even bamboo cuttings from Japanese fans. He also employs playful storytelling devices that link the illustrations thematically. For example, the last issue of *Metamorphosis* is structured like an alphabet book.

The women of the Noh are all voluptuous and extravagantly provocative in their poses and gestures. Nudity is abundant, to the point that some of the issues border on pornography. However, although the art is certainly drawn for men, the female characters maintain their positions as subjects, with Mack evoking their complex inner lives through moody landscapes and whimsical metaphorical symbols scribbled all over the page. Literally and figuratively, Mack is not an artist who stays inside the lines.

Not all issues are drawn by Mack. Each chapter of *Masks of the Noh* is drawn by a different artist, as a way of showing a distinction among the different characters. Rick Mays illustrates the chapter that focuses on Scarab and Volume 6: *Scarab*, as a way of maintaining character continuity. Mays's manga-informed style is engaging and lively, but it pales in comparison to Mack's highly original illustrations.

Themes

Identity construction and deconstruction represent the primary theme of the series. In the beginning, Ukiko/Kabuki plays a role given to her by others. From beyond the grave, Tsukiko bids Ukiko to act as an avenging ghost. The general facilitates this objective through giving Ukiko the position of Kabuki in the Noh agency.

Ukiko's identity is constructed not only by the people who care about her, but also by one who despises her, namely, Ryuichi Kai, who gives her the name Kabuki by inscribing it on her face. Not only does he manage to infiltrate the Noh, he also meddles with the identity of his daughter.

Ukiko embraces her Kabuki role as if it were a security blanket. The mask and bulletproof costume command attention and authority and give her a sense of safety. With the mask on, Kabuki feels more like herself than without it; she has so embodied her constructed identity that it has become more "real" than the one with which she was born. Most important, the mask hides her scars, the horrors of her past that are literally written on her face.

When Ukiko is kidnapped by Control Corps, she loses her mask, and with it, her sense of self. Slowly, Ukiko creates a new identity for herself with the help of her friend Akemi. This can happen, however, only through accepting what she sees as her imperfections, such as the scars on her face, which are a constant reminder of the brutality of her kin.

The Alchemy, the last volume of the series, takes a different thematic direction, exploring the creative process and the roots of genius. Ukiko is no longer tormented about her identity or lack thereof: She is thoroughly engrossed in her work. She even transforms into it; in one drawing, Mack draws her metamorphosing into one of the creatures that she draws in her picture books. No longer is Ukiko the recipient or victim of an identity imposed on her by outside forces; she has become the author of her own story.

Impact

Kabuki was one of the most critically acclaimed graphic novel series of the 1990's and helped put Mack on *Wizard* magazine's top-ten writers list. Mack has been accused of exoticism and voyeurism, and some criticize him for reducing sophisticated Japanese literature into stereotypes and stock plots. However, he did help introduce Japanese theater to a wide audience in the West.

Certainly the most influential aspect of the series is the artwork. Mack pushed the boundaries of the graphic novel medium, just as he pushed the boundaries of the printed page. Many critics hail Mack's work as fine art, worthy of being hung on gallery walls. Thus, Mack raised the bar for many illustrators to come. The series' strong female characters and their psychological depth make *Kabuki* at least as popular among women as among men, which is itself an achievement for a genre whose readership is often predominantly male.

Bettina Grassmann

Further Reading

Moore, Alan, J. H. Williams, and Mick Gray. *Promethea* (2000-2005).

Koike, Kazuo, and Kazuo Kamimura. *Lady Snowblood* (2005-   ).

Shirow, Masamune. *Ghost in the Shell* (1996).

Bibliography

Bowers, Faubion. *Japanese Theatre*. New York: Hermitage House, 1952.

Casey, Jim, and Stefan Hall. "The Exotic Other Scripted: Identity and Metamorphosis in David Mack's *Kabuki*." *ImageText: Interdisciplinary Comics Studies* 3, no. 1 (2006).

Soh, Chunghee Sarah. "Prostitutes Versus Sex Slaves: The Politics of Representing the 'Comfort Women'." In *Legacies of the Comfort Women of World War II*, edited by Margaret Stetz and Bonnie Oh. Armonk, N.Y.: M.E. Sharpe, 2001.

KAFKA

Author: Mairowitz, David Zane
Artist: Robert Crumb (illustrator)
Publisher: Icon Books; Fantagraphics Books
First book publication: 1993 (*Introducing Kafka*);
2007

Publication History

Kafka was originally published in 1993 by Icon Books
in the United Kingdom as a stand-alone trade paperback
in its "Introducing" series and was issued by its American imprint, Totem Books, in the same year. British
and American editions are known as *Introducing Kafka*
or *Kafka for Beginners*. Subsequent English and non-
English reprint editions may have alternate titles, including *R. Crumb's Kafka*. The 2007 English edition
from Fantagraphics Books has an index and is simply
titled *Kafka*.

Cover design varies among editions but usually includes Robert Crumb's distinctive drawings or details
from illustrations by him. Different editions or versions
exhibit variations in font styles, physical qualities, and
other internal typographic features. Crumb's expressive hand lettering in *Kafka* is lost in translated versions and editions.

Plot

Kafka is a biographical sketch of the Czech writer
Franz Kafka (1883-1924) told in short chapters or sections based on his fiction and augmented with material
from his parables, diaries, and letters. The weird atmo-
spherics associated with Kafka the historical figure and
Kafka the cultural icon are suddenly and graphically
announced early in the book. The title page features a
cartoon portrait of a dapper Kafka in a stylish bowler
followed by an image of the same figure having the
side of his head sliced off with a meat cleaver.

The first section describes the cultural milieu of
Kafka's childhood in a late-nineteenth-century Prague
ghetto, which provides the backdrop for Kafka's
emerging sense of alienation from family, community,
the body, and everyday life. Drawings of Old Town

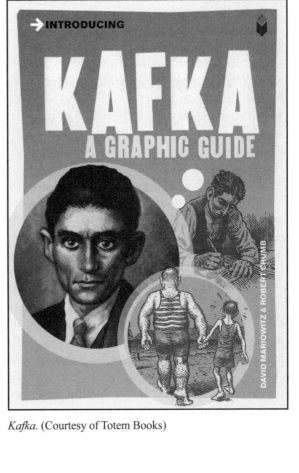

Kafka. (Courtesy of Totem Books)

Prague architecture and aspects of Jewish mysticism
are significant.

The second section, "The Judgment," features a
young man named Georg who lives with his aging father. The relationship between the protagonist and the
abusive father mirrors Kafka's relationship with his father. After telling his father about a letter he has written
to an old friend in Russia announcing his engagement,
the old man begins abusing Georg in sudden, paranoid
outbursts. A sense of revulsion, loathing, guilt, and in-
timidation overwhelms Georg as he confronts the obscene presence of his father's physicality and brutal
personality. Shame over his own body and subsequent
humiliation by his father lead Georg to fantasize about
death or disappearance. He will effectively exploit his

fear of abusive authority for literary purposes, though his ambivalence toward his father will never abate.

Section 3 is based on one of Kafka's most famous novellas *Die Verwandlung* (1915; *The Metamorphosis*, 1936). The main character, Gregor Samsa, awakens one morning transmogrified into a bug. While trying to cope with this unusual situation he is immediately confronted by his parents and some clerks from his firm, whose concern over the fact that he is late for work quickly turns to revulsion when they finally barge into his bedroom and see him as a horrifying insect. Aware of the fear and disgust he provokes in his family, Gregor attempts to elude their gaze even as he experiences wonder over the curious biological features of his new insect body. Alternately, he grieves over his sudden inability to work and provide for his family.

Gregor subsists on scraps and slops of food placed on the floor of his bedroom by his sister, Grete. After bouts of compassion, loathing, and resentment, Grete persuades her parents to let Gregor die from a festering wound caused by a rotten piece of apple lodged in his back. Samsa sympathizes with his family's wish that he disappear. He finally dies, and his corpse is found and disposed of by a charwoman. On vacation soon after his death, Gregor's parents and sister become rejuvenated, happy over the fact that Grete is blossoming into vigorous young womanhood.

The fourth section, called "The Burrow," reflects Kafka's adult life living at home even though he was employed and could have lived on his own. He found it difficult to work on his writing in this environment. The burrow's terror of discovery becomes a metaphor for Kafka's hypochondria, which is connected in these panels to his sense of Jewish self-abasement. To overcome physical insecurities and self-loathing, Kafka engages in various physical fitness schemes and begins the first in a series of tortured epistolary relationships.

Kafka performs important and useful work at the Workman's Accident Insurance Institute in Prague, but this, along with intense focus on his writing, are not enough to allay his irrational fears. In the end, the fantastic molelike creature in "The Burrow" cannot elude its self-imposed torment.

Section five, "In the Penal Colony" ("In der Strafkolonie," 1919; "In the Penal Colony," 1941),

features a Traveler and the chief administrator of a remote penal settlement who demonstrates the workings of justice by describing a frightful execution machine. The reader quickly learns that the administrator of this settlement is both judge and executioner. An abject prisoner whose guilt is never in doubt is gagged and bound to the execution machine, which consists of a vibrating bed positioned under a stationary harrow. The harrow slowly inscribes both the offense and the sentence into the prisoner's flesh before it slices through his body, killing him. The administrator delights in the machine's efficient design features, including the fact that it dumps corpses into an adjacent pit for easy disposal.

The interlude takes a strange twist when the Traveler indicates disapproval of the operation. The administrator then whips a piece of paper out of his wallet, on which is vaguely scribbled the imperative "Be Just," which he shoves in the Traveler's face. The chief administrator next orders the prisoner to be freed, places the scrap of paper on the machine bed, has himself bound and gagged as if he were a condemned prisoner, and promptly orders his own execution. The machine quickly malfunctions and bloody fragments of the administrator's shredded corpse hang from the harrow with a spike rammed through his forehead.

The final sections of *Kafka* examine "The Hunger Artist" (*Ein Hungerkünstler: Vier Geschichten*, 1922; *A Hunger Artist*, 1945). Kafka's death and posthumous reception suggest that Kafka's fiction and other writings are—despite the academic industry and pop-culture iconography that has grown up around him—the best guide to his work.

Characters

- *Franz Kafka* (1883-1924), the biographical subject, is an unmarried author who lives most of his life with his parents in Prague. He works as a claims assessor for the Worker's Accident Insurance Institute for Bohemia.
- *Hermann Kafka* (1852-1931) is Franz's overbearing father, an assimilated Jew, and a Prague shop owner. Father and son never get along well. In response to Hermann's lifelong rejection of

him, Kafka writes his famous *Brief an den Vater* (1952; *Letter to His Father*, 1954).

- *Georg* is the protagonist in Kafka's story "The Judgment," a thinly veiled account of Kafka's troubled relationship with his father.

- *Gregor Samsa* is the protagonist in Kafka's story *The Metamorphosis*. One day, he finds himself mysteriously turned into an insect and is unable to return to work as a traveling salesman. After Gregor has a series of harrowing misadventures at home, his family decides to let him die from a wound.

- *Grete* is Gregor's sister in the *Metamorphosis*. At first, she is shocked by her brother's transformation, but she overcomes her revulsion and brings him scraps of food. Eventually, she persuades her parents to let him die when his continued existence as an insect threatens the family's financial situation.

- *A mole*, in the "The Burrow," is one of various animals used by Kafka to examine the world of terror and alienation and related fantasies of escape.

- *Josef K* is the protagonist in *Der Prozess* (1925; *The Trial*, 1937), the story of a man who wakes up one day to find himself accused of a vague crime, about which he can learn nothing from judicial authorities. After a fruitless struggle to learn the truth about his situation in regard to the law, he is executed.

- *Milena Jesenská* (1896-1944) is one of Kafka's girlfriends. Letters he wrote to her were published after his death.

- *K*, the protagonist in *Das Schloss* (1926; *The Castle*, 1930), is a land surveyor who is mysteriously summoned by inaccessible authorities to a remote castle staffed by bureaucrats who work in a maze. Klamm is one of the officials associated with the castle.

- *Frieda* is Klamm's mistress and a bartender at a village inn near the castle with whom K has a sexual encounter and an even briefer engagement to be married.

- *Olga* and *Amalia* are sisters in *The Castle* who provide K with companionship.

- *Ottla* (1892-1943) was Kafka's younger sister and the person to whom he was closest in his family.

- *Dora Diamant* (1898-1952) is a young woman who lived with Kafka in Berlin at the end of his life.

- *Karl Rossmann* is the emigrant protagonist in Kafka's unfinished novel *Amerika* (1927; *America*, 1938, better known as *Amerika*, 1946), an odd fantasia in which he ends up working for a carnival-like operation improbably called "The Nature Theatre of Oklahoma."

Artistic Style

Crumb and David Zane Mairowitz's collaboration highlights prominent themes from Kafka's life and writings. Crumb's trademark crosshatch drawings and expressive hand lettering convey the claustrophobia and absurdity of Kafka's fictional universe. The photographic record of Kafka's milieu provides the basis for a realistic depiction of period clothing and associated social roles just prior to the dissolution of the Habsburg Empire. Dense cross-hatching suggests a noirish sense of Prague's old buildings and ghetto area. Interiors are oppressive, while both city life and remote locales appear menacing. Nuances of setting and psychology emerge through Crumb's black-and-white cartooning, especially through his precise rendering of the grotesque. Facial expressions are often crazed or oddly impassive. The mise-en-scène evokes irrationality and paranoia, with Mairowitz's factual narrative offering a sharp contrast to Crumb's illustrated narrative.

Crumb's moody drawings are especially effective at highlighting Kafka's conflicted sexual experiences. Recurring erotic escapades goad ambivalent male protagonists into farcical situations. In *The Trial*, Crumb draws a sequence of panels in which a bemused K and a hesitant Kafka attempt to negotiate carnal situations. The same sequence occurs in the chapter on *Amerika*, where Karl Rossmann is first seduced by his uncle's daughter and later bullied by the slatternly Brunelda.

Emotional stress and trauma are represented by the traditional cartooning device of sweat marks and exclamation lines drawn near characters' heads. Crumb's illustrations of crowds and ensembles in *Kafka* suggest the dangers lurking in mob psychology. In this setting, group portraiture becomes a record of panic, cruelty, indifference, and curiosity. In contrast, some of the individual portraits in *Kafka* convey warmth and humanity.

Themes

The themes in *Kafka* are as varied as Kafka's complex personal life and the writing he produced in a relatively short lifetime. The allegorical and the personal are subtly interwoven, though dread is pervasive throughout Kafka's fiction. His use of symbolic animals to explore alienation and consciousness is given vivid expression in Crumb's drawings. Some critics see *The Metamorphosis* and "The Burrow" as allegories of dehumanization and social marginalization. The novels *The Castle* and *The Trial* and the short story "In the Penal Colony" explore an important thematic cluster concerning the "law" and its obscure workings in bureaucratic regimes rooted in guilt, power, and authority. The characters in *Kafka* seem animated by occult forces, but episodes of overt brutality and violence erupt throughout these narratives. Men are usually feckless or authoritarian, while

women are depicted as objects of longing or revulsion and occasionally as benign.

Maneuvering Kafka's problematic fictional world in an attempt to find resolution or clarity seems to evoke the very conditions that undercut such a possibility. Though compelled to do so, Kafka's protagonists are frequently confronted with opaque obstacles or have difficulty decoding meaning. Social roles and processes become subtly distorted or overdetermined. The organization of space and architecture undermines normal expectations. Consequently, transformation plays a central role in Kafka's fiction, as if change into allegorical creatures or sudden flight will offer relief from traumatic or dangerous situations. Karl Rossmann, the émigré hero in the unfinished novel *Amerika*, for example, hopes to find a fresh start in the "new world" after a kerfuffle forces him to leave Bohemia. Since Rossmann's fantasy about life in the United States simply inverts the particular conditions of his old life in Europe, his raw frontier experiences mostly result in alienation. The twist comes with his eventual employment in a kind of vaudeville company called "The Nature Theatre of Oklahoma," an ironic utopia that Crumb depicts as a scene from a 1930's Busby Berkeley musical.

David Zane Mairowitz

David Zane Mairowitz is a writer best known for his work outside of the comics field, including his plays *The Law Circus* and *Flash Gordon and the Angels*. Strongly interested in literature and philosophy, he produced two *Introducing...* books, one on Albert Camus (with artist Alain Korkos) and the other on Franz Kafka (with cartoonist Robert Crumb). Mairowitz's contributions to the *Introducing* series are particularly notable for their thorough engagement with their subjects and their ability to distill complex biographical and philosophical information in a format that is easily digested. Mairowitz was one of the founders of the *International Times*, the London-based underground newspaper in the 1960's. In addition to his creative works, Mairowitz has authored a number of essays on leftwing politics.

Impact

As an individual graphic guide that has been reprinted and translated many times since its original publication in 1993, *Kafka* has provided readers with a concise overview of major themes in Kafka's life and work. Crumb's prominence in the underground comics community and his likely sympathy toward many of Kafka's fixations enhance *Kafka*'s value as a reference guide, particularly since his illustrations easily resonate across cultures.

Bob Matuozzi

Further Reading

Crumb, Robert. *The Complete Crumb Comics* (2011).
_____. *R. Crumb Sketchbook* (1992-).

Bibliography

Crumb, Robert. "R. Crumb, the Art of Comics, No. 1." Interview by Ted Widmer. *The Paris Review*, no. 193 (Summer, 2010): 19-57. http://www.theparisreview.org/interviews/6017/the-art-of-comics-no-1-r-crumb.

Crumb, Robert, and D. K. Holm, ed. *R. Crumb Conversations*. Jackson: University Press of Mississippi, 2004.

Crumb, Robert, and Peter Poplaski. *The R. Crumb Handbook*. London: MQ Publications, 2005.

Holm, D. K.. *Robert Crumb*. North Pomfret, Vt.: Pocket Essentials, 2005.

Schmitz-Emans, Monika. "Kafka in European and U.S. Comics Inter-medial and Inter-cultural Transfer Processes." *Revue de littérature comparée*, no. 312 (2004): 485-505.

See also: *The Book of Genesis; The Complete Fritz the Cat; Give It Up! and Other Stories*

KAMPUNG BOY

Author: Lat
Artist: Lat (illustrator)
Publisher: Berita
First book publication: 1979

Publication History

Kampung Boy was first published in 1979 by the Malaysian company Berita Publishing, under the title *The Kampung Boy*. Lat, whose real name is Mohammad Nor Khalid, was already a well-known editorial cartoonist, and his cartoons had been compiled and published in book form. *The Kampung Boy* was the first book he designed as an extended narrative and that featured new material. The idea for the graphic novel came to Lat in 1977, when he was visiting the United States and was suddenly struck by nostalgia for the village, or *kampung*, where he was born and raised. He worked on the project intermittently for two years. Upon its release, *The Kampung Boy* became an instant best seller. It has been reprinted multiple times and remains immensely popular in Malaysia. *Town Boy*, the sequel to *Kampung Boy*, was published in 1981. Another follow-up, *Kampung Boy: Yesterday and Today*, was released in 1993.

Lat wrote *The Kampung Boy* in English and hand-picked his friend Zainon Ahmad to do the Malay translation. The Malay edition, entitled *Baduk Kampung*, was also released by Berita Publishing. The graphic novel has also been translated into Japanese, French, Portuguese, and German. In 2006, First Second Books released an American edition entitled *Kampung Boy*. First Second is the graphic novel imprint of Roaring Brook Press, a division of Holtzbrink Publishers that specializes in books for children and young adults. The American editors made few changes to the original version, with most alterations involving changing British English to American English.

Kampung Boy. (Courtesy of First Second Books)

Plot

Consisting of a series of anecdotes, *Kampung Boy* describes the rituals and day-to-day experiences that characterize boyhood in a small Malaysian village. The graphic novel relates the story of Mat, a young Muslim boy, who is born and raised in the kampung. As a toddler, Mat is confined to the family's housing compound. One day, he sneaks off the property to investigate the tin dredge, which he has never seen but always hears roaring in the distance. The enormous dredge appears monstrous to him. His mother is infuriated by his disobedience, and she punishes him.

At the age of six, Mat begins attending Tajwid classes to learn how to enunciate Arabic words properly and thus read the Quran. Mat meets the three Meor brothers, and he is impressed by the brothers' sense of adventure and their experience with swimming and fishing. As the years pass, Mat begins to take on more responsibilities at home as well as at the mosque, and he also starts spending more time with the Meor brothers, who are often up to mischief. Mat's parents worry that the brothers are distracting Mat from his studies.

Just before he turns ten, Mat and two of his cousins undergo the ritual of circumcision, which takes place in his grandmother's house. The villagers arrive to celebrate the ceremony. The nervous Mat finds the circumcision itself to be quick and virtually painless.

Mat learns that the Meor brothers have started dulang-washing, or panning for tin. Dulang-washing was considered illegal because it disrupted the operations of the tin company, but it is a good way to make money, and Mat enthusiastically joins the brothers in panning for tin. One day, Mat and the Meor brothers are almost caught by the constable. Mat scurries home and excitedly shows the tin he has collected to his father. His father is furious to learn that Mat has been "stealing tin" and he gives his son a beating. Later, he brings Mat to his rubber plantation. He tells his son that the land was his to inherit, but only if he concentrates on his studies and gets admitted to a boarding school in Ipoh. Mat decides to start spending more time studying and less time with the Meor brothers.

Mat's hard work pays off; he is accepted to the boarding school. He runs home to share the good news, but he sees his father riding off with the land broker. His mother tells him that they were thinking of selling their land to the tin company, because it was rumored that the area was rich with tin.

A few weeks later, it is time for Mat to travel to Ipoh. His family and the Meor brothers take him to the town center for a send-off. Mat suddenly realizes that he will miss his tiny kampung. He wants the kampung to remain unchanged and hopes that the tin company will not find tin on their land. He and his father board the bus. As the bus drives off, Mat looks out the rear window and waves good-bye to his family and friends.

Characters

- *Mat*, the protagonist, is a short, slightly pudgy boy with wiry limbs. His bushy black hair often covers his eyes. Although he sometimes gets into mischief, he is mostly an obedient boy who fulfills his responsibilities and eventually learns to prioritize school over play. He keeps mostly to himself at school and tends to follow the lead of the Meor brothers.

- *Mat's mother* is a somewhat stern woman who hardly smiles and scolds Mat and his father for their misdeeds. Although she is strict, she is also sympathetic toward Mat. She takes care of Mat and his two younger siblings and takes charge of household chores.

- *Mat's father* is a large, round man who likes to play with his children and make them laugh. Although he is fun-loving and less strict than Mat's mother, he is mindful about fulfilling the tasks that Muslim fathers are traditionally expected to perform. He is also deeply concerned about Mat's future and wants to ensure that his son focuses on his studies.

- *Mat's grandmother* is the kampung's official midwife. She delivers Mat and takes an active part in other rituals that mark his childhood, such as his head-shaving and circumcision.

- *The Meor brothers* are Mat's three mischief-making playmates. Although they come in three different sizes, they look alike with their wide, toothy grins and their hair parted in the middle. More confident and experienced than Mat, they act as his mentors and teach him how to swim, fish, and pan for tin.

Artistic Style

Kampung Boy is written in the first person, from the perspective of an adult Mat looking back at his childhood. The text's font is made to resemble penmanship. The point of view and the font create a sense of a familiarity and intimacy, as if Mat were addressing a close acquaintance and allowing her to view his diary or sketchbook.

Much of the graphic novel's humor arises from the incongruity between the words and the pictures. The text has a matter-of-fact tone, while the accompanying black-and-white pictures reveal the characters' comic actions. The pictures also provide parallel narratives that are only hinted at, or not mentioned at all, in the text. Some scenes, for example, show a young girl with curly hair looking in Mat's direction. She is never alluded to in the text, but the pictures suggest she is a potential romantic interest for Mat. Several wordless sequences also highlight the antic movements of the characters.

The characters are drawn as caricatures, with exaggerated facial features and body shapes. Costumes, objects, buildings, and the rural landscape, however, are drawn in a more realistic and detailed style. Such details not only localize the story but also speak to Lat's affection for and his interest in faithfully rendering the kampung setting. The setting's importance is also emphasized by how the characters, including Mat, are often shown to be dwarfed by their surroundings. Mat's smallness in relation to his environment highlights how he is part of the kampung, rather than independent from it.

Kampung Boy's horizontal 6 x 8-inch format deviates from the format of most other graphic novels. Lat uses few word balloons and does not enclose the narration in caption boxes. Few pages are divided into panels, with most pages and even double-page spreads serving as panels themselves. The page-as-panel format allows Lat to create detailed and sometimes panoramic backgrounds, enhancing the notion that the kampung, though small, feels like the whole world to its inhabitants.

Themes

Kampung Boy is a coming-of-age story that shows Mat learning how to prioritize between childhood play and the fulfillment of his obligations to his family and himself. Although Mat dutifully accomplishes many of the tasks he is assigned at home, school, and the mosque, he comes to understand that his actions in the present can have consequences for his future. The final sequence of *Kampung Boy* also suggests that Mat's

This is the split—level back portion of our house, where I spent most of my time. On the lower level is the kitchen. Mum did her cooking on that table.

It was also in the kitchen that Mum bathed me, since I was too young to go to the river.

11

Kampung Boy. (Courtesy of First Second Books)

education can only continue when he abandons the comfort of his family and his familiar surroundings. To mature and learn, Mat needs to discover and interact with the greater world outside his kampung.

Kampung Boy, however, also romanticizes village life. With its strong tone of nostalgia, the graphic novel depicts life in the kampung as pleasant because it is simple, laid back, and close to nature. The kampung is depicted as the ideal place for a child to grow up. The village is also characterized as a strongly knit community that actively participates in raising its children.

The graphic novel alludes to the tension between village life and modernization. On the one hand, the kampung seems to be left behind by modernization, as even the mail train never stops at the village. On the other hand, the graphic novel also shows that a far-flung kampung cannot escape the changes brought about by modern development. The omnipresent tin dredge shows how business and technology are slowly invading the village and transforming the land and the villagers' way of life. In one scene, Mat and his father step off the road to make way for a passing car, suggesting that simple kampung life must inevitably give way to modernization.

Impact

A highly acclaimed cartoonist and revered public figure in Malaysia, Lat is considered the father of modern Malaysian cartoons. He first gained popularity during the 1970's for his editorial cartoons for the *New Straits Times*. He has published more than twenty books, although *Kampung Boy* is probably his best-known and beloved work. He enjoys a wide readership in Malaysia as well as in Singapore and Indonesia, and his work has also been merchandised extensively. Despite his immense popularity in parts of Southeast Asia, Lat's work is not well-known in the United States. The editorial director of First Second Books, Marc Siegel, who first encountered *Kampung Boy* while growing up in France, published an American edition of *Kampung Boy* to introduce Lat to readers in the United States.

Lat's work was partly inspired by his childhood reading of British children's comics such as *The Beano* (1938-   ) and *The Dandy* (1937-   ). He identifies Malaysian comics pioneers Raja Hamzah and Rejab

---

Lat

Malaysia's best-known cartoonist, Lat (Datuk Mohammad Nor Khalid) has published more than twenty volumes of comics since the 1970's. He is most celebrated for *The Kampung Boy* (1979), a story of a young boy growing up in Perak in the 1950's. The book was an immediate success upon its release in Malaysia and helped turn Lat into an international cartooning superstar. The book has generated two sequels: *Town Boy* (1981) continues the story and depicts life in the city; *Kampung Boy: Yesterday and Today* (1993) revisits the settings of the original in order to contrast changes to Malaysian society from the 1950's to the 1980's. Among Lat's many other books are numerous collections of his editorial cartoons. His visual style is quite wide-ranging. Self-taught, he was strongly influence by British humor magazines like *Beano* and *Dandy*, but his later work shows the influence of illustrators like Ralph Steadman and Gerald Scarfe.

---

bin Had as his mentors and British cartoonists Frank Dickens and Ralph Steadman as his influences. Despite his British influences, Lat sought to distinguish his work from the foreign comics and cartoons that filled Malaysian newspapers in the early 1970's. His single-panel comics series for the *New Straits Times*, titled *Scenes of Malaysian Life*, was among the first comics to focus on Malaysian subjects and concerns. He also gave an "Asian look" to his Malay characters, replacing the "big and long noses" typically used in foreign comics with three linked u's. His work and its local flavor may have helped inspire the humor-magazine boom in Malaysia in the mid-1970's, and his style has been widely imitated.

Lat has been honored with retrospectives at Malaysia's National Museum and National Art Gallery. In 1994, the Sultan of Perak conferred the title of Datuk (knighthood) to Lat, in recognition of his artistic contributions. Lat also received the Fukuoka Asian Culture Prize for Arts and Culture in 2002. His critical and commercial success has become the benchmark for many aspiring Malaysian cartoonists.

Television Series

Kampung Boy: The Animated Series. Directed by Frank Saperstein. Matinee Entertainment, 1997-1999. While the graphic novel appeals to a more general readership, the animated series is designed for a juvenile audience. Unlike the black-and-white graphic novel, the series is in full color, and characters are drawn in a softer, rounder style. The original 1950's setting is also updated to present day. Minor characters, such as Mat's sister, have more prominent roles and have different traits. Mat's father, for example, provides comic relief as a wacky inventor. In 1999, one of the series' episodes, "Oh, Tok!," won an award at the Annecy International Animated Film Festival.

Lara Saguisag

Further Reading

Abouet, Marguerite. *Aya of Yopougon* (2005-   ).
Barry, Lynda. *One Hundred Demons* (2005).
Delisle, Guy. *Burma Chronicles* (2008).

Bibliography

Campbell, Eddie. "Campbell Interviews Lat: Part 1." *First Second*, January 11, 2007. http://firstsecondbooks.typepad.com/mainblog/2007/01/campbell_interv.html.

Chuen, Ooi Kok. "Lat: Then, Now, and Forever." *New Straits Times*, December 27, 2003, p. 5.

Krich, John. "Cartoonists—Malaysia: Lats of Laughs." *Far Eastern Economic Review*, April 15, 2004, p. 40.

Lent, John A. "Cartooning in Malaysia and Singapore: The Same, but Different." *International Journal of Comic Art* 5, no. 1 (Spring, 2003): 256-289.

_____. "The Varied Drawing Lots of Lat, Malaysian Cartoonist." *The Comics Journal* 211 (April, 1999): 35-39.

See also: *Aya of Yopougon; One! Hundred! Demons!; Burma Chronicles*

KANE

Author: Grist, Paul
Artist: Paul Grist (illustrator)
Publisher: Dancing Elephant Press; Image Comics
First serial publication: 1993-2001
First book publication: 2004-2006

Publication History

The *Kane* series was first published in the United Kingdom by Dancing Elephant Press. The company, founded by *Kane* creator Paul Grist, printed all thirty-one issues of the series from 1993 to 2001. These issues were later collected in six volumes, published by Image Comics between 2004 and 2006, apart from issue 30, which has yet to be reprinted.

Plot

Kane is seen as a mainly character-driven series, but has several story lines that contribute to the plot. Grist relies heavily on the flashback convention, which leads to several subplots, furthers the story line, and lends detail to the plot with a noir-meets-pulp-fiction pace.

When the series begins, Detective Kane is returning to work after serving a six-month suspension for killing his partner, a crooked cop entangled with crime-syndicate leader Oscar Darke. As Kane's new partner, Kate Felix, is put into action, her backstory is introduced, leading into several memory sequences for both main characters.

A series of bombings victimizes local delivery and taxi-cab outfits. When the suspected terrorist is taken in for interrogation and proves recalcitrant, Kane pulls his gun on the man to get him to talk. Kane and Kate seek the real bomber, Fogle, who has a terminal illness and therefore has nothing to lose; he intends to take Kane with him with one last blast. After he is overpowered, arrested, and escorted out of Silver Stone House, Fogle is ambushed by a sniper who shoots and kills him. Kate then goes undercover as Oscar Darke's waitress at the Garden Restaurant, while several others surveil from a van outside. As the cops prepare to trap Darke, a quirky thug calling himself the Plunderer sweeps the dining area for anything he can rob, compromising the sting.

Later, Mr. Floppsie Whoppsie, a man dressed as a

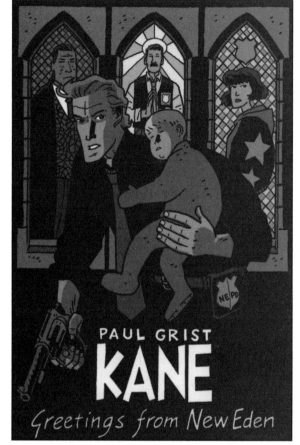

Kane: Greetings from New Eden. (Courtesy of Image Comics)

giant pink bunny, is seen on the lam, running with arms akimbo from the cops in an all-action, no-words hot pursuit. He is eventually caught and arrested. Back at the precinct, plans are in play to deal with Darke's extortion racket, which is housed in the defunct Core Club, a former strip club. Wratz, of Internal Affairs, questions Detective Kane, Officer Perez, and others. Mr. Floppsie Whoppsie agrees to a deal to help set up Darke, but as he delivers the cash, one of Darke's goons interrupts the process, smashing through a two-way mirror, grabbing the rabbit man, and running. Kate and company are on the scene, and after a *Batman*-style fistfight and shoot-out, the setup is revealed and Darke's right-hand men are taken into custody.

When Kane's probationary period ends, he is charged with protecting Oscar Darke, whose life has been threatened. As Darke's history is revealed, Kane and Kate must find whoever attempted to kill him. Next, the histories of others at the Thirty-Ninth Precinct are also revealed, and Kane and Kate must contend with the cocky and dangerous Rico Costas, who is hunted, tracked, and finally shot and killed at the precinct. The lisping Fwankie poses the next threat; then the Blind Man, a sightless person-turned-hit man who uses his acute hearing to stalk his potential prey, nabs Kane. Unable to locate Kane, Kate is compelled to consult with Oscar Darke, who will surely be able to help.

Volumes

- *Kane: Greetings from New Eden* (2004). Collects issues 1-4. Introduces Kane, his backstory, the precinct, select colleagues and superiors, and Grist's particularly mordant brand of humor.

Kane: Greetings from New Eden. (Courtesy of Image Comics)

- *Kane: Rabbit Hunt* (2004). Collects issues 5-8. Features Mr. Floppsie Whoppsie, the egocentric street performer dressed as a giant pink bunny; the archetypal "goodfella" types James "Jimmy-Fix-It" Obe, loan shark Louis Gordo, and their double-fisted fighting goons; and the television superheroes Mega Man and his sidekick, as well as Mark Morris, who is under the delusion that he is Mega Man.
- *Kane: Histories* (2004). Collects issues 9-12. Explores Oscar Darke's character, past, and portended future, the latter of which runs parallel to the fate plotted for Detective Kane; meanwhile, Kane and his new partner, Kate Felix, are called on to protect his archnemesis.
- *Kane: Thirty-Ninth* (2005). Collects issues 13-18. Features Kate Felix's backstory, plus a look at the underpinnings of the Thirty-Ninth Precinct by way of several conventions, including a point-of-view story told from the backseat of the patrol car of officers Miguel Perez and Steve Donahue.
- *Kane: The Untouchable Rico Costas and Other Short Stories* (2005). Collects issues 19-23. Features an assassin called the Blind Man, a monkey giving chase, and an arsonist on the loose.
- *Kane: Partners* (2006). Collects issues 24-29 and 31. Uses continued flashbacks to spotlight Kate's and Kane's stories from before they became cops.

Characters

- *Kane*, the eponymous protagonist, is depicted as a man of great size and presence. A good cop and detective who gives himself to the job whole-heartedly, he must confront the disdain of his colleagues, who misinterpret his shooting and killing of his previous partner, Dennis Harvey.
- *Oscar Darke*, foil to Kane, is the head of a crime syndicate. A stone-faced powerhouse portrayed as a broad-shouldered body double of Kane, he is a dangerous player with deep pockets and a thick Southern, possibly Cajun, accent.
- *Kate Felix*, Kane's new partner, is a tendentious twentysomething detective with a perky face and bobbed hair. She has policing in her blood,

having spent numerous childhood hours at the precinct where her father and uncle were cops.
- *Captain John Dexter*, the head of the Thirty-Ninth Precinct, is an archetypal officer and boss, one who is both sentimental and contradictory in a human yet humorous way.
- *Detective Jimmy Lovett* is a colleague of Kane and Kate and a successful crime fighter. However, he is an implicitly passive-aggressive figure with a disdain for all things Kane-related.

Artistic Style

With little character development and a simple cartoon style that includes generous amounts of black atmosphere and an economy of dialogue, *Kane* delivers, not a thin comic style, but one with much to be revealed. Grist combines discernible imagery and simple lines to give the comic a seedy, gritty reality. The text is in bubbles and is crisp uppercase; logos and emblems on storefronts and products are made just a point or two different to distinguish branding. The panels are montaged, overlapping from left to right, with only a bit of white space to spotlight dialogue, expressions, and actions against generously blacked-out backgrounds; a bush, for example, is inked entirely in black, save for a minimal amount of white lines required to distinguish its flowers. Grist reserves white space for the single spotlight against the wall of darkness that is a police officer's uniform; the rescued infant in contrast to the brawny rescuer; the subtle facial expression visible behind the wide shadow cast across a face; or the hair of a nightclub singer, softened to the point of allure against a contrasting neckline and earlobe.

One distinguishing feature of Grist's work in the *Kane* series is his violation of borders: He denies them, negates them by presenting images without them, and defies them by including elements that overlap or stick out from and beyond their limits. Single panels are devoted to single comments, moments, or events, and a character's size is changed to illustrate the degree of intensity or action or the extent of his or her power and clout. For example, Kane might be depicted in a single, full-page panel, his silence as potent as his proportionately huge outstretched hand; or Kane's burdens as the protagonist will show up in his broad back and

Paul Grist

Paul Grist broke into the British comics scene in the 1980's and his first high-profile success was *St. Swithin's Day* (written by Grant Morrison), the story of an alienated teenager in Margaret Thatcher's England. His work on *Grendel: Devil in Our Midst* (written by Steven Seagle) brought him to mainstream attention in the United States. He subsequently created his own company, Dancing Elephant Press, through which he published *Kane* and *Jack Staff* before moving them to Image Comics. *Kane*, begun in 1993, is a noirish police procedural that follows the adventures of a police detective who is hated by his peers. *Jack Staff* is a superhero comic featuring the exploits of Britain's Greatest Hero, told in a largely nonlinear fashion. Grist's figure drawing is cartoonishly naturalistic but he is noted for his unusual sense of page design, which often includes vast expanses of black. His stories make use of flashbacks and nonlinear storytelling, and eschew many of the tropes of the genres that they explore.

shoulders, an expanse that fills the page and commands the reader's attention.

Thought bubbles, emanata, and other traditional elements are used sparingly, generally to maintain a sense of mystery and danger. At the same time, there is a considerable amount of overheard, sideline, and other talk, framed outside in thin squares, to demonstrate the volume of activity taking place around the characters.

Themes

Several general themes run throughout *Kane*. The text comments on humanity's struggles in a gritty, urban environment, particularly in the police and detective milieu. One theme that pertains to the detective genre is that of the hunter and the hunted. Dualities, such as light versus dark and good versus evil, prevail in New Eden, a tongue-in-cheek antithesis to the biblical Eden. Good cops fight bad guys, but, in another dichotomy, Kane is juxtaposed with his colleagues, who question his motivations for killing his previous partner, Harvey. Kane is emblematic of a good, honest crime fighter who also has a dark side. There are some similarities between Kane and his foil, Oscar Darke,

which challenge the binary constructs of good and evil and question the integrity of the police profession in its entirety.

Perhaps more remarkable is Grist's intertextual inclusion of a passel of literary allusions, postmodern references, and other reflections that highlight humanity, human nature, and the modern human condition. He pays respectful homage to Western popular culture with lines of dialogue that recall Lewis Carroll and Dylan Thomas, while the television crime fighters Mega Man and his sidekick simulate Bob Kane's iconic superhero, Batman.

As is his signature, Grist makes most of his references in context, with the biting, stunning, sometimes seething humor that informs and defines the series. Whether it is with the cheeky "Sesame Safe" television commercial posited as a postmodern reflection of the social intrusiveness of advertisement or with the small-time crook who, while robbing restaurant patrons, comes to Oscar Darke's table and gushingly asks for his autograph, Grist's humor is as potent in entertainment value as it is as social commentary.

Impact

Grist's *Kane* series combines subtle intertextuality with humor. Reportedly influenced by Frank Miller's *Sin City* (1991-2000) and Dave Sim's *Cerebus* (1977-2004), *Kane* has come to demonstrate that self-published comics can thrive. A respectable fan base attests to the entertainment value of *Kane*, as well as of several of Grist's other works, such as the *Jack Staff* collection (2000-   ). Despite this, Grist remains relatively obscure and is considered by graphic novel aficionados to be one of the best-kept secrets of the comics world.

Roxanne McDonald

Further Reading

Brubaker, Ed, and Sean Phillips. *Criminal* (2006-   ).
Lapham, David. *Stray Bullets* (1995-2005).
Miller, Frank. *Sin City* (1991-2000).

Bibliography

Salaman, Jeff. "The Kane Mutiny: Paul Grist Rewrites the Detective Story with *Kane*." *Spin*, July, 1997, 46.
Spurgeon, Tom. "Kane #20." *The Comics Journal* 206 (April, 1988): 36-37.

See also: *Sin City*; *Stray Bullets*; *Hard Boiled*

KING: A COMICS BIOGRAPHY

Author: Anderson, Ho Che
Artist: Ho Che Anderson (illustrator)
Publisher: Fantagraphics Books
First serial publication: 1993 (Volume 1), 2002 (Volume 2), 2003 (Volume 3)
First book publication: 2005

Publication History

King: A Comics Biography, a special-edition comic book originally published in three volumes, took Ho Che Anderson a decade to complete. It was published by Fantagraphics Books, which had previously published Anderson's adult comic *I Want to Be Your Dog* (1990-1991).

Anderson was born in London and raised in Canada. He began creating comics at a young age, approaching publishers such as Vortex when he was in his teens. In the early 1990's, after Fantagraphics Books contacted him about writing a historical graphic novel about Martin Luther King, Jr., Anderson began reading extensively about King and the era in which he led the United States toward a greater awareness of the need for civil rights for all. Initially, the book was planned to be a short volume about King's life and work. After working on the script, Anderson realized his vision for the project exceeded a single volume.

Over a thirteen-year period, three volumes were completed. The first volume, released in 1993, focuses on King's life from childhood through his success as a prominent leader of the Montgomery bus boycott (1955-1956). The second volume, published ten years later, highlights King's complicated negotiations with John F. Kennedy and his involvement with civil rights groups such as the Freedom Riders. The volume ends with his celebrated "I Have a Dream" speech. The final volume begins with Lyndon B. Johnson signing the Civil Rights Act in 1964 and ends with King's murder in Tennessee in 1968. In 2005, a special edition of the book was released, combining the three volumes and including an introduction by Stanley Crouch.

King: A Comics Biography. (Courtesy of Fantagraphics Books)

Plot

King: A Comics Biography has been called an interpretive biography. Anderson dramatizes secondary research and fictionalized details about aspects of King's life, beginning with his childhood in Atlanta, Georgia, during the 1930's. The book opens with a fictionalized black-and-white scene set in 1935 that shows King helping his father don his robe before a sermon, foreshadowing a later scene introducing King's own ministry. Next, a group of fictionalized witnesses, reminiscent of the chorus in a Greek or Shakespearean play, appears. The witnesses are individuals who provide a counternarrative to the national narrative that exists around King. Witnesses throughout the book provide commentary that ranges from admiring praise to envy. Some offer details about the historical context and the tone of the country.

When King appears next, it is more than fifteen years later; he is studying at Boston University and trying to get to know Coretta Scott and a few other women. King and Coretta enjoy a short courtship and move to Alabama after their wedding. There, King becomes pastor of the Dexter Avenue Baptist Church and befriends Ralph Abernathy. When offered the role of president of the Montgomery Improvement Association, King reluctantly takes it, joining E. D. Nixon and others in the Montgomery bus boycott resulting from Rosa Parks's arrest for refusing to give her seat on a bus to a white passenger.

With the success of the boycott behind him, King founds the Southern Christian Leadership Conference (SCLC) in 1957, and in 1960, he begins negotiating with Kennedy, hoping to obtain his support for civil rights efforts in exchange for the black vote during the upcoming presidential race.

Glimpses of King's home life show him to be a loving father and supportive husband, despite his attraction to women other than his wife. King and Coretta bicker about her discontent with moving back to Alabama, her birthplace, but she remains devoted to him. Though King's home life is important, he never strays too far from causes such as the Freedom Riders activist movement and the march in Birmingham.

King's days are spent trying to solve one dispute after another. He urges members of the Student Nonviolent Coordinating Committee (SNCC) to wait patiently for

desegregation to occur, attempts to deflect J. Edgar Hoover's Federal Bureau of Investigation (FBI) surveillance, and works to convince President Kennedy to sign the Civil Rights Act and support the March on Washington for Jobs and Freedom, organized by Bayard Rustin and A. Philip Randolph. A few months later, Kennedy's assassination threatens to choke the momentum of the Civil Rights movement, but

King: A Comics Biography. (Courtesy of Fantagraphics Books)

President Lyndon B. Johnson passes the Civil Rights Act in July of 1964.

In 1966, vigilant in his effort to help all people obtain equal rights, King moves his civil rights work out of the South and into Chicago, where he joins with the locals in a fight for housing equality. There, he meets additional adversity from young activist groups such as the SNCC, which question whether nonviolence is viable or the best course of action. Two years later, King is murdered while standing on a balcony at the Lorraine Motel in Memphis, Tennessee, the day after giving a seemingly prophetic speech titled "I've Been to the Mountaintop."

Characters

- *Martin Luther King, Jr.*, the protagonist, is a preacher from the South and one of the major leaders of the Civil Rights movement.
- *Ralph Abernathy* is a leader in the Civil Rights movement and one of King's closest confidants. A native of Alabama, he is a pastor of a church near King's Dexter Avenue Baptist Church. He supports King and is a founding member of the SCLC.
- *Coretta Scott King* is King's wife. She does not want to live in the South but supports her husband in his efforts to transform it. After King's death, she continues many of his activist efforts and works to preserve his legacy.
- *Rosa Parks* is a woman who is arrested for refusing to relinquish her seat on a Montgomery, Alabama, bus to a white passenger on December 1, 1955. She becomes the catalyst for the formation of the Montgomery Improvement Association and the Montgomery bus boycott.
- *E. D. Nixon* is one of the founding members of the Montgomery Improvement Association. A leader of the National Association for the Advancement of Colored People, he, along with others, organizes a one-day bus boycott four days after Parks's arrest.
- *Bayard Rustin* is one of the organizers of the 1963 March on Washington.
- *A. Philip Randolph* is an activist known for his work on behalf of unions, particularly the

International Brotherhood of Sleeping Car Porters, and an organizer of the 1963 March on Washington.
- *John F. Kennedy* is a senator who supports some of King's civil rights efforts. After becoming president in 1961, he is solicited by King on numerous occasions. His lack of full support is a constant irritation to King.
- *Lyndon B. Johnson* is the president sworn in after Kennedy's assassination in 1963. After much negotiation with King and other leaders, Johnson signs the Civil Rights Act of 1964.
- *J. Edgar Hoover* is the director of the FBI. He requests permission from the attorney general, Robert F. Kennedy, to place King under surveillance. He suspects that King is a communist and identifies King as one of the most powerful African American leaders in the United States.

Artistic Style

Anderson's artistic style and use of color changed over the years. *King* begins in black and white, with an occasional splash of color. For example, when King is stabbed by a woman during a book signing in 1960, King's body is drawn in black and white while a pool of red blood seeps from his chest. Next, two double-page spreads depict King reaching for the sun as he attempts to survive his injury and include the colors yellow, brown, and orange. Color is used again during King's rousing "I Have a Dream" speech; a black-and-white King stands beside a red, white, and blue flag. In contrast, the final section of the book is in full color, complete with blue speech bubbles that indicate when King speaks.

King has a unique style that incorporates photographs, collages, paintings, and cartoons. Anderson has noted that he was interested in a photo-realist style when he began the book but later lost interest in it, resulting in a style that changes from panel to panel. For instance, manipulated photos share a page with cartoons. These familiar photos from historical archives are reminiscent of images in a documentary.

The story line often shifts without warning, making it difficult to determine the event that is taking place and, in some cases, the character who is speaking.

Similarly, the artwork is at times indistinct, making it difficult to distinguish between characters. It is especially difficult to differentiate between King and Abernathy or others in his camp. The female characters, often nameless, are difficult to tell apart as well.

Themes

Throughout the book, panels present the views of witnesses or attesters who provide a commentary, sometimes oppositional, to the events in the main narrative that is King's life and career. The witnesses watch as King develops from a young man into a national hero. In the beginning of the novel, he is reluctant to take on the responsibility of leading the movement in Montgomery; he is content with his role as pastor and family man. However, he quickly ascends and successfully leads the movement that thrusts him into the national consciousness and offers him additional power.

King enjoys immense political power and influence, but he wields spiritual power as well. As a trusted minister, his power leads him to galvanize the South and convince many throughout the nation to support a presidential candidate, protest housing inequity, and question a war. In a climate of violence, he demands nonviolence, leading thousands to put themselves in dangerously precarious positions. However, such power can be intoxicating. On King's journey to self-actualization, his humanity becomes apparent. His ego and questionable morality reveal he is a mere man, not a saint as he is often depicted.

Impact

King: A Comics Biography is an important nonfiction graphic novel that illustrates the versatility of the medium. Critics have lauded it for its appealing cinematic quality and use of multimedia. Anderson offers a multifaceted portrayal of King, depicting aspects of him that few knew existed. *King* continues to be appreciated for its text and art that allow readers to travel with King as he transitions from an unknown preacher in the South to a civil rights hero and Nobel laureate.

KaaVonia Hinton

Further Reading

Laird, Roland Owen, and Taneshia Nash Laird, and Elihu Bey. *Still I Rise: A Cartoon History of African Americans* (1997).

Yang, Gene Luen. *American Born Chinese* (2006).

Yang, Gene Luen, and Thien Pham. *Level Up* (2011).

Bibliography

Anderson, Ho Che. "Interview with Ho Che Anderson." Interview by Dale Jacobs. *International Journal of Comic Art* 8, no. 2 (Fall, 2006): 363-86.

Chaney, Michael A. "Drawing on History in Recent African American Graphic Novels." *MELUS* 32, no. 3 (Fall, 2007): 175-200.

Whyte, Murray. "King's Life in Pictures of Every Kind." *The New York Times*, August 10, 2003. http://www.nytimes.com/2003/08/10/arts/art-architecture-king-s-life-in-pictures-of-every-kind.html.

See also: *American Born Chinese; Nat Turner*

KINGS IN DISGUISE

Author: Vance, James
Artist: Dan Burr (illustrator)
Publishers: Kitchen Sink Press; W. W. Norton
First serial publication: 1988
First book publication: 1990

Publication History

Kings in Disguise was originally released as a six-issue series in 1988 through Kitchen Sink Press. Author James Vance noted that the script for the graphic novel was originally from his play about people during the Depression and was further based on a play sponsored by the Franklin D. Roosevelt-era Works Progress Administration (WPA) of the 1930's.

As Vance worked on the adaptation of his play into a graphic novel, Dan Burr was chosen for his illustration work. Vance wanted someone who could capture the plight of the homeless during the Depression. The six-issue comic book series was later released as a graphic novel in 1990, and it garnered critical acclaim for both the creators and Kitchen Sink Press.

Kings in Disguise was part of a movement to bring to light realistic comics that did not fit the heroic mold but instead looked at actual situations. It was also part of an early wave of graphic novels, including Art Spiegelman's *Maus* (1986), that looked at historical events. *Kings in Disguise* also enjoyed commercial success in Europe, where it was reprinted in several editions and translations. The book was later acquired and republished by W. W. Norton in April, 2006.

Plot

Kings in Disguise focuses on the life of Frederick "Freddie" Bloch, a twelve-year-old boy from California, during the middle of the Depression, specifically 1932. Freddie's great pleasure is watching films, using them as an escape; this fantasy life helps him ignore, or at least diminish, the problems that the Depression is causing in his town. Freddie also escapes from his drunken, yet doting, father and older brother Albert. After witnessing an unemployed man attack a richer

Unemployed and homeless people queue on the "breadline" in New York City in 1932 during the Great Depression. *Kings in Disguise* focuses on the life of a twelve-year-old boy from California, during the middle of the Depression, specifically in 1932. (Getty Images)

man for not providing employment, Freddie becomes far more aware of the troubles that many are facing.

As the Depression affected the entire United States, California was seen as a place where one could find work. However, this was not the case, as increased competition placed more pressure on the jobs that were available. A spiritual person, Freddie's father tried to keep Freddie grounded in his Jewish faith, especially as he neared his Bar Mitzvah, at age thirteen. The death of Freddie's mom prior to the beginning of the story adds more strain to the family and drives his father to drink.

Following a fight between Freddie's father and brother, Freddie wakes to find his father has abandoned them. Albert tries to give Freddie some sense of normalcy, but the situation slowly gets worse. Albert sacrifices much, and ultimately he turns to robbery to gain money to pay bills. The attempt ends when the person whom he is robbing attacks him, hitting him in the head with a bottle; he tells Freddie to run and hide so the authorities do not catch him and send him to an orphanage. Freddie packs and then sets off on his adventure, with the ultimate goal of finding his father, who went to Detroit to find work at the Ford Motor Company plant, according to a postcard the boys received.

As Freddie attempts to join a group of hoboes riding freight trains, he is accosted and assaulted by a man named Joker. As he tries to fight off the physical attack, Freddie is rescued by a man who identifies himself as Sammy the King of Spain, who claims to be traveling in disguise as a hobo. From this point on, the two travel together; Sammy teaches Freddie the ways of the road and helps him look for his father.

Finally, Freddie and Sammy arrive in Detroit. Their trip is ultimately fruitless, as the two do not find Freddie's father or uncle. They become enmeshed in an attempt to unionize at the Ford Motor Company's River Rouge Plant. The Ford union busters use violence to break up the protest. Sammy is hit in the ribs as he and Freddie attempt to escape by train. The two go back to the mission where they had stayed, and Sammy attempts to recuperate. Finally, as the pair gets ready to move, someone gives Freddie "porcupine balls" (opium poppies) to ease Sammy's pain.

In the last part of the book, Freddie tries both to nurse Sammy back to health and to get them back to California. Two fellow hoboes help Freddie by buying a train ticket for him and a box to ship Sammy, who is doped but not dead. As Freddie enjoys the trip and the brief semblance of normalcy, he witnesses a train robbery thwarted by an elderly man with a gun. The man identifies himself as Jesse James. Jesse gets off the train with Freddie and the now-conscious Sammy, and the three travel together. Sammy and Jesse are acquaintances and have traveled together before. The "robbery" is in fact a stunt to gain publicity for Jesse, who then gives lectures, sells books, and holds shooting demonstrations for money.

Characters

- *Frederick Bloch*, a.k.a. *Freddie*, is a twelve-year-old Jewish boy from California. His is a coming-of-age story. Freddie's driving force is to find his father and to either make amends or reprimand him for leaving Freddie and his brother.
- *Sammy*, a.k.a. *the King of Spain*, is a hobo who befriends Freddie at a critical juncture. He is a man running from his past. He has been on the road some time and knows the tricks of the trade. Despite issues with family, friends, and drugs while on the road, he is a stalwart friend to Freddie.
- *Joker* is one of the less-than-honorable hoboes who rides the rails during the Depression. His malevolence early in the story is Freddie's first exposure to the harsh realities of life on the road. His view of life and people has become altered by events, and his actions bring a bad name to those seeking a better life by riding the rails.
- *Jesse James* is an older man who claims to be the infamous outlaw of the same name. Whether he is or not is in dispute, but because the public believes him, he is able to put on shows and make money while traveling. He is an acquaintance of Sammy, which grants Sammy and Freddie access to some money.

Artistic Style

Kings in Disguise is rendered in a realistic style. Since the book discusses the harshness of the Depression, the characters are not drawn in a humorous or distended format. The black-ink illustrations reflect both the style of the films of the 1930's and the iconic images of the Depression published in *Life* magazine during the era, such as the photographs taken by Dorothea Lange. Burr took considerable time and effort to give subtle yet realistic touches to the illustrations, especially with regard to the impromptu housing that the downtrodden assembled out of whatever materials were available.

Burr takes considerable time to give emotion to the characters, which he conveys mostly through their eyes. The reader often sees the desperation brought on by the Depression through those trying to live and survive in those hard times. While the characters may seem somewhat exaggerated, the eyes often tell the true nature of the events. For example, when a crazy traveler attacks Freddie, the look in the man's eyes is one of lust and insanity.

The crowd scenes, full of detail, make readers feel as if they are in the moment. Burr's use of space often makes the depicted circumstances seem cold and foreboding; his artwork successfully conveys the mood.

Themes

The key theme of the book is transition. At the beginning, readers look at the Depression through the eyes of an average twelve-year-old, as Freddie is forced to adapt to several adult situations, including the dangers inherent in the type of travel he has undertaken. Over the course of the story, Freddie transitions from a child to a man. Sammy transitions from a wandering vagabond without responsibility to one who must take care of Freddie. He even transitions from opium addiction to sobriety. The way the other characters are presented emphasizes how they have changed from "regular" folks into something more primal because of the lack of basic necessities during the Depression. Change was

a critical concept in the work world of the 1930's, and real events, such as unionization in the automotive industry in Detroit and racial tensions resulting from the Great Migration of African Americans, become part of the story as well.

The idealization of the past is another theme of *Kings in Disguise*. The idealization of home and what life should be versus the cold reality of what life became during the Depression are key components undergirding the text.

Impact

Kings in Disguise was published during a period in which the superhero genre was still dominant in American comic book culture. It was a mix of historical fact and fictional contrivance and has been seen as an influence on Jason Lutes's *Berlin: City of Stones* (2000), a novel set in the Weimar Republic, and James Sturm's *The Golem's Mighty Swing* (2001), about a fictitious 1920's Jewish American baseball team. *Kings in Disguise* was the type of story that the average reader who was unfamiliar with the comic book genre might gravitate toward.

The book's creators paid close attention to historical detail, rendering things such as WPA projects according to archival documents. The story's realistic tone gained it readership and interest that it might not have had otherwise. Renowned comics creator Alan Moore considered the work important enough to write the introduction to W. W. Norton's reprinted edition. Vance noted that the interest was strong enough that, as of 2011, a sequel was being written. The title of the book was also the inspiration for a popular musical group of some renown.

Cord Scott

James Vance

Best known for his writing on the Eisner and Harvey Award-winning graphic novel *Kings in Disguise*, James Vance brought a broad historical scope to American comics in the early 1990's. *Kings in Disguise* (with art by Dan Burr) tells the story of Freddie Bloch, a young man in Depression-era California who heads out on the road in an effort to locate his alcoholic father. Vance's story weaves real historical events, including the Detroit labor riots, into a story that is highly charged with emotion. Following the completion of this work, Vance worked as a freelance writer for the short-lived Tekno Comics on *Mr. Hero the Newmatic Man*, and scripted comics series based on the *Aliens* and *Predator* movie franchises. Vance's writing is well regarded for its humanity and for its ability to present fully fleshed-out characters in true-to-life situations.

Further Reading

Buhle, Paul, and Nicole Schulman, eds. *Wobblies! The Graphic History of the International Workers of the World* (2005).

Collins, Max Allan, and Richard Piers Rayner. *Road to Perdition* (1998).

Sturm, James. *The Golem's Mighty Swing* (2001).

Bibliography

Arnold, Andrew D. "Return of the Kings." *Time*, April 19, 2006. http://www.time.com/time/arts/article/0,8599,1184802,00.html.

Oklahoma History Center. "James Vance: Writer/Editor, Tulsa." *The Uncanny Adventures of Okie Cartoonists*. http://www.okiecartoonists.org/jvance.html.

Vance, James. "A Short Interview with James Vance." Interview by Tom Spurgeon. *The Comics Reporter*, August 13, 2006. http://www.comicsreporter.com/index.php/resources/interviews/5875.

See also: *Berlin*; *The Golem's Mighty Swing*; *Road to Perdition*; *Maus*

L

LAIKA

Author: Abadzis, Nick
Artist: Nick Abadzis (illustrator); Hilary Sycamore (colorist)
Publisher: First Second Books
First book publication: 2007

Publication History

Though he first hit upon the idea in 2002, British comics creator Nick Abadzis did not complete his first outline of *Laika* until 2005, after doing as much historical research as he could. He then spent some time traveling in and around Moscow to get a visual feel of the locations, before drawing and coloring several test pages to promote the idea to various publishers. These first pages featured a somewhat more anthropomorphized Laika (which Abadzis quickly realized was a mistake after seeing it on paper) than is seen in the published version. First Second, an imprint of Roaring Book Press, expressed interest in the concept and requested additional pages with Abadzis's more canine approach to the titular character. Abadzis obliged, and these slightly more refined pages sold First Second on the idea.

Abadzis continued researching as he wrote, making the novel as accurate as possible; he went as far as creating scale models of several of the period vehicles to ensure he did not miss any details. He completed his first full draft about eight months before he and First Second agreed the work should be finished, in order for publication to coincide with the fiftieth anniversary of Laika's famous flight. The book was released just before the actual anniversary, and Abadzis promoted the book with a slide-show lecture at several locations, including the Smithsonian National Air and Space Museum in Washington, D.C.

Laika. (Courtesy of First Second Books)

Plot

A housekeeper is told to get rid of a litter of puppies from her employer's dog. She is able to pass on all but one of them to local children. The last of them she gives to a friend, suggesting the responsibility might help discipline her son. The boy is outraged but reluctantly takes care of the dog, so as not to incur his father's wrath. In a fit of protest and desperation, the boy takes the dog to the canal and throws her in. The dog survives and scrounges the alleyways as a stray, eventually finding some companionship with another unclaimed dog. The two are sometimes fed by a local butcher, but they are repeatedly forced to flee the dogcatchers.

The dogcatchers' chase goes on for two years, until the butcher's wife finally helps one of them. The catcher secures the smaller dog, but he takes out his frustration by killing the other. He is reprimanded by his superior for his actions, and, since the shelters are already overflowing, the small dog is taken to an air force center that requires dogs for testing purposes.

Oleg Gazenko takes the dog and, walking it down to the kennel, unintentionally interrupts his boss, Vladimir Yazdovsky, who is in the middle of hiring Yelena Dubrovsky as the new dog-training assistant. She takes an immediate liking to the small dog, naming her Kudryavka. As Yelena tends to Kudryavka, Yazdovsky apologizes to Gazenko for hiring her without consultation but talks up her qualifications.

As Yelena begins caring for Kudryavka and several other dogs, Oleg informs her that the dogs are being put through rigorous testing with the ultimate aim of sending one of them into space. For the next year, Yelena sees Kudryavka undergo often painful procedures, only to happily bound back into her arms. After the success of the *Sputnik* satellite, the space program is accelerated, and Kudryavka is selected as one of three final candidates for a space flight, though Sergei Korolev, the chief designer of the space program, renames her Laika.

Oleg and Yelena then learn Laika's trip is deliberately sacrificial, and she will not be returning alive. The two are both heartbroken, but they continue working on the project out of a sense of duty. The rocket launch, with Laika as its sole passenger, goes as planned, which Yelena watches sorrowfully. Within hours, Laika dies from the intense heat.

The news broadcasts all rave about Russia's latest achievement, but the story of Laika's death is distorted with claims that she was euthanized, which causes a fair amount of outrage from several sectors. As the project leaders toast the memory of Kudryavka, Yelena quits her job and walks home, while the dog's space-faring coffin slowly descends into the Earth's atmosphere.

Characters

- *Laika*, a.k.a. *Kudryavka*, is the small, loving dog on which the story is centered. While she is not anthropomorphized, she endears herself to many of the other characters with her unwavering trust and resilience to both emotional and physical duress. She greatly enjoys the company of her caregivers and remains steadfastly loyal to them.

- *Sergei Korolev* is the chief designer in charge of Russia's space program. Having survived wrongful imprisonment in a Siberian gulag, he possesses an almost single-minded determination to overcome the slander he has endured by proving his worth professionally. He constantly pushes his staff to achieve notoriety for the Russian space program, but his dedication often causes others to find him cold and unemotional.

- *Yelena Dubrovsky* is the special assistant for the dog-training sessions and acts as the primary caretaker for the animals. She begins work on the same day Laika arrives and shares a unique bond with the dog. She is an extremely competent worker, but the emotional attachment she forms with the dogs continually weighs on her conscience as she learns more about the space program. Guilt about the fate of the animals she trains causes her to resign after Laika's flight. Of the main characters, she was the only one not based on a real individual; however, after finalizing her look, Abadzis serendipitously discovered there was indeed a real dog trainer in the program who bears a close physical resemblance to his character.

- *Oleg Gazenko* is Yelena's boss at the Institute for Biomedical Problems and acts as the liaison between the dog handlers and the space program. He tries to keep himself emotionally removed from the project, but his attempts at self-control result in more pronounced outbursts as the project continues, forcing him to remain absent from the climactic launch.

- *Vladimir Yazdovsky* is the air force officer in charge of the animal training and testing and is Oleg's superior. Beneath the chief designer in rank, he is the most knowledgeable in the strategic decisions that are being made about the space program. While his work precludes him from working with and thereby growing attached to any of the dogs, he still shows an appreciation for Laika and, ultimately, her memory.

Artistic Style

Abadzis's illustration style seems fairly loose, but this perception belies a deliberate precision. With *Laika*, he wrote the entire book several times, focusing and tightening his story with each pass. The earliest drafts, in fact, were little more than dialogue with an occasional amorphous shape nearby. He followed this with thumbnail layouts, before drawing out full pencils. Though

the pencils remained loose by many artists' standards, Abadzis's inking of his own work allowed him to work at a greater speed by continuing to refine aspects of the story at the inking stage.

Abadzis's figures are fairly simply drawn, but each retains more than enough unique features such that the reader never has any difficulty identifying and distinguishing the characters. The characters resemble the real persons they are intended to represent, but they are not caricatures, as a loose, cartoonlike style such as Abadzis's might suggest. Indeed, Abadzis's figures are considerably more detailed than his earlier work on *Hugo Tate* (1993), where he honed his style, showing a more obvious stylistic progression.

Abadzis created a font specifically for the book, based on his own hand lettering. The text was laid over scans of the pencil art and then printed out; the printouts were then used on a light box as guides while he inked the project. Abadzis shaded minimally at this stage, preferring to focus on his line work and let colorist Hilary Sycamore delineate figures and shapes. Though Sycamore generally used local color based on what Abadzis called "endless exhaustive notes from me" and focused on a slightly muted palette, she helped establish the mood of each scene.

Themes

Abadzis's aim is not only to detail the history of Laika and her space flight but also to make the story emotional and engaging, honoring the dog's sacrifice. Abadzis takes extra care to give all of the characters a great deal of depth, an aspect that is often absent from simple histories. The space race is frequently remembered for the events themselves or the public heroes who took part in the events, but Abadzis ensures that all of the

Laika. (Courtesy of First Second Books)

characters in his graphic text are represented as real people with desires and drives that propel their work and, by extension, the story.

Interpersonal bonds play a key role in the story. Most of the characters presented are based on real individuals who actually worked with Laika. Abadzis's research included learning about both the personalities and professional responsibilities of the people involved. The characters relate to each other on both professional and personal levels. Their interactions are not only those of superior and subordinate but also of friends of varying levels of intimacy.

Even though Laika is portrayed as a regular dog, she is given a distinct personality. The harsh treatment she received as a puppy led to her constant yearning for affection; her desires encourage her to be docile and obedient, which help her to be chosen as the first animal sent into space. Her endearing qualities coupled with the humanity depicted in the other characters produce some particularly emotional scenes, thus making the entire story more memorable.

Nick Abadzis

Nick Abadzis became an editor at Marvel UK at the age of twenty-two, but left that position to become a freelancer after his serial *Hugo Tate* became a success in the British-based comics and style magazine *Deadline*. Hugo Tate, whose adventures were partially collected in the 1993 book *Hugo Tate: O, America*, was a stick-figure character in a naturalistically drawn world. During the 1990's Abadzis produced work for Marvel Comics and DC's Vertigo imprint, including *Millennium Fever* (with Duncan Fegredo). He is best known for the 2007 graphic novel, *Laika*, about the first living creature sent into Earth's orbit. *Laika* is a deeply sensitive and touching account of the dog's impact on his handlers in the years preceding his launch into space. Abadzis has also worked as a creator of children's books, with his *Pleebus Planet* series published in the 1990's.

Impact

Laika was released only a few months after James Vining's *First in Space*, detailing a similarly historic story about Ham, the first chimpanzee launched into space in 1961. Both books capitalized on the fiftieth anniversary of the start of the space race and, together, they paint a fascinating picture of how the approaches of the two superpowers differed. Though they both focus on the actual work being done in the respective programs, there are brief allusions to the competitive aspect at a national level, with occasional references to contemporary news reports.

Of the two graphic texts, *Laika* is perhaps more noteworthy because, in the United States, focus is frequently on American efforts, often downplaying the significance and importance of Russian achievements. Much of what is commonly known about the Russian program is based on inaccurate information or propaganda (both American and Russian), so Abadzis's exhaustive research provides both an unusual point of view and a decidedly more authentic story. It provides a non-Western perspective of the space race, which had largely been examined through the prism of the Cold War.

Reviews of *Laika* were almost unanimously positive, the educational aspect to the story was particularly well received, and many of the book's honors highlighted the fact that the story targeted a young demographic. In 2008, *Laika* earned an Eisner Award for Best Publication for Teens, and the Young Adult Library Services Association named it one of its Top Ten Graphic Novels for Teens.

Sean Kleefeld

Further Reading

Abadzis, Nick. *The Trial of the Sober Dog* (2008).

Ottaviani, Jim, Zander Cannon, and Kevin Cannon. *T-Minus: The Race to the Moon* (2009).

Vining, James, Douglas Sherwood, and Guy Major. *First in Space* (2007).

Bibliography

Dubbs, Chris. *Space Dogs: Pioneers of Space Travel.* New York: Writer's Showcase, 2003.

Harford, James J. *Korolev: How One Man Masterminded the Soviet Drive to Beat America to the Moon.* New York: Wiley, 1999.

Siddiqi, Asif A. *Sputnik and the Soviet Space Challenge.* Gainesville: University Press of Florida, 2003.

See also: *The Wall*; *Persepolis*; *The Photographer*

LA PERDIDA

Author: Abel, Jessica
Artist: Jessica Abel (illustrator)
Publisher: Pantheon Books
First serial publication: 2001-2005
First book publication: 2006

Publication History

La Perdida was originally published in five volumes, titled *La Perdida* Part One through *La Perdida* Part Five, by Fantagraphics Books from 2001 to 2005. In 2006, after numerous small revisions, *La Perdida* was published in hardcover book form in the United States by Pantheon Books, a division of Random House, using the original cover art from Part One of the serial. Later that year, Pantheon published the paperback version. Only the cover art of the first volume has been reprinted, thus helping maintain a market for the original serials, which are sold out from the publisher as of 2011. Several foreign editions of *La Perdida* were published: In 2006, the novel was published in Canada by Random House of Canada, in Spain by Astiberri Ediciones, and in France by Éditions Delcourt. An Italian version was published by Black Velvet Editrice in 2007. *La Perdida* was also anthologized in the first volume of the *Best American Comics* series published in 2006. Author/illustrator Jessica Abel and her husband, cartoonist Matt Madden, edited the 2009 and 2010 volumes of *Best American Comics*. Before *La Perdida*, Abel was best known for her comic book series *Artbabe* (1992-1999). Abel and Madden have combined their talents to co-author a comics how-to text, *Drawing Words and Writing Pictures* (2008).

Plot

La Perdida is the story of Carla, a Mexican American woman who, estranged from her Mexican father, travels to Mexico City in order to connect with and explore her Mexican identity. Upon arrival, she stays with Harry, her privileged former boyfriend (in the mold of William S. Burroughs or Jack Kerouac) who aspires to be a journalist but does more drinking than writing. Carla's involvement with a sketchy crowd of

La Perdida. (Courtesy of Pantheon Books)

people and her questionable decision making and naïve outlook lead to Harry's kidnapping and ultimately to her deportation back to the United States.

The prefatory chapter is set in present-day Chicago, where Carla enters a Mexican restaurant and orders a meal that triggers the memory of her time in Mexico, now two years in the past. Brief flashbacks focus on a moment when she was unable to order a single taco in Mexico without being ridiculed.

The first chapter flashes back to Carla's arrival in Mexico City and her reunion with Harry, with whom she stays. Although he has no problem sleeping with her, two weeks into Carla's stay, Harry pressures her to decide on a departure date. Carla's lack of interest in returning home becomes an increasing point of tension between the two.

Carla meets Harry's friends, who are all expatriate journalists. One of them invites her to a photojournalism exhibition, where she meets Memo, a radical Mexican intellectual who introduces her to Ricardo and Oscar, whom she later discovers are drug dealers. Ricardo is the nephew of El Gordo, a major drug don. Oscar becomes enamored with Carla, competing with Memo for her attention. Although she can barely communicate with him, she finds Oscar compelling.

Harry and Memo immediately cultivate a mutual hatred of one another, engaging in heated political arguments. Harry throws out Carla shortly after she tells him that she plans to stay in Mexico indefinitely. Carla finds an apartment and a roommate, Liana, who moves out three months later. Oscar then moves in. Now obsessed with becoming a disc jockey, he spends his money on records instead of rent and is constantly pestering Carla for her cash.

Shortly thereafter, Rod, Carla's brother, visits Mexico City, signaling a major shift in the narrative, as his facility with the language and upbeat presence encourage Carla to explore new places and meet his friends. Before he returns to the United States, Rod warns Carla to be careful of both Memo and Oscar.

After a Day of the Dead party gone awry, Ricardo pumps Carla for information about Harry. When she reads about Harry's kidnapping in the newspaper, she fails to make the connection. It is not until New Year's Eve, when she is confronted with the battered Harry, that she realizes what has happened. Carla and Harry are eventually rescued, and a month later, she is deported. *La Perdida* ends with a shift back to the present as Carla contemplates her final moments in Mexico and laments a kind of loss of innocence and naïve hope.

Characters

- *Carla Olivares*, the protagonist, is a twenty-something, slim, light-skinned Mexican American woman who travels to Mexico in search of an authentic experience of her cultural heritage. A naïve and often myopic college dropout with good intentions, she has a blind spot for people's

La Perdida. (Courtesy of Pantheon Books)

negative qualities, which inevitably furnishes them with the opportunity to mistreat her. She is so caught up in her quest to fit in and connect with her Mexican identity that she unwittingly facilitates the kidnapping of her former boyfriend.

- *Harry* is Carla's former boyfriend, an Anglo-American journalist who lives in Mexico City. An upper-middle-class expatriate obsessed with emulating his heroes, Burroughs and Kerouac, he only interacts with other expatriates. He is kidnapped by Carla's "friends."

- *Memo* is a tall, lanky, thirty-five-year-old Mexican man. He is a standoffish pseudo-intellectual who immediately challenges Carla's perspective on everything from art to her own identity. An opinionated womanizer who is initially fascinated by Carla, he mocks her relentlessly. He often engages Harry (and others) in heated political arguments.

- *Oscar* is Memo's twenty-year-old, pretty-boy, drug-dealing friend. Handsome and charming, but uneducated and dull, he becomes Carla's live-in boyfriend. Obsessed with becoming a disc jockey, though he has no talent or money for it, he is always broke and constantly pestering Carla for cash.

- *Ricardo* is a minor drug dealer with a mean streak. He strikes Carla at one point in order to silence her and express his power. His uncle is the major drug don El Gordo. He is responsible for gathering information on Harry in order to kidnap him.

- *El Gordo* is Ricardo's uncle and a drug don. Unsavory and always carrying drugs, he offers Carla cocaine at parties and seems interested in her. He is often shadowed by Ray, an expatriate who dislikes Carla.

- *Rod Olivares* is Carla's younger brother. Having lived with their father for several years, he is more familiar with Mexican culture and language than she is. A young skateboarder whose business is going well, he has made many Mexican friends over the Internet. His visit is a major

turning point in the novel and is what leads to Carla's rescue in the penultimate chapter.

Artistic Style

La Perdida is drawn and lettered in black-and-white ink and brush, creating loose, flowing bold lines that focus on character and social interactions rather than extensive background details. Abel used reference photos from her two-year stay in Mexico (1998-2000) as anchor points for drawing backgrounds, simplifying the details in order to maintain the reader's focus on the characters. This style represents a shift from the tighter, more realistic style of Abel's *Artbabe* work. She uses sentence-case idiosyncratic lettering, telling the story entirely in first person, which gives the book a diary feel. Whispered dialogue, most prominently featured near the end of the novel, is set in smaller type, with dashed lines constructing the speech balloons. There are no thought balloons, but emphasized words are written in cursive—there are many of these in the chapter when Rod visits—punctuating Carla's more animated speech.

Early flashbacks are bordered with rough edges, making them distinctive. While the pages often feel slightly crowded, this does not detract from the novel. Instead, these pages mirror Carla's overwhelming experience of taking in her new surroundings. While the characters are drawn simply yet distinctively, there are panels in which Carla's face appears much more detailed and realistic. These are generally during moments of reflection or angst.

The author creates distinctive facial and wardrobe characteristics that convey ethnic identity, but there are no distinctions of skin tone among the characters. While this equalizes the characters visually, it also dismisses important racial characteristics that play into the story textually but not visually.

There is a significant linguistic shift in *La Perdida* from bilingual to principally monolingual material. The novel begins with a signpost in Spanish, and the dialogue in the first quarter of the book is in both Spanish and English. The Spanish dialogue is translated at the bottom of each panel. In the chapter in which Carla moves out on her own, Abel presents Spanish dialogue in English, with actual spoken English dialogue indicated with arrow brackets. While the reasons for this decision are not clear—perhaps the translation process was too labor intensive—the flavor of the narrative changes here.

Themes

La Perdida executes the story of the American in search of an authentic cultural experience. The search is complicated by the desire to connect with an ethnic heritage that is at once foreign and fascinating.

The book enacts both class interaction and class critique throughout the novel. Numerous characters engage in political debates, most notably Harry and Memo, as well as Memo and Carla. These debates center on fundamental questions of capitalism and Marxism. None of these characters can resist assuming the moral high ground and thus each person treats the others condescendingly at every opportunity.

Centrally, the book addresses Carla's slipshod attempt to connect with her ethnic identity. Questions of identity and authenticity permeate *La Perdida*, but none of the characters fits the unquestionable role of the authentic subject. Even Memo, the self-proclaimed radical, reveals the flaws in his thinking when he expresses his "authenticity" by constantly putting Carla down. His participation in Harry's kidnapping also complicates his own claim to both authenticity and ethnic pride.

The book's facile treatment of Mexican drug culture works as an illustration of Carla's lack of awareness, but still poses a problematic snapshot. Most of the characters in *La Perdida* are involved in drugs on some level, and of those characters, the majority are Mexican.

The book also addresses questions of belonging and nationalism. Harry's friends are exclusively expatriates, and Carla is the only Mexican American. Contrary to Carla's notion of immersion, Harry insists that only by distancing himself from Mexicans can he write an authentic piece about them. This contradiction is utterly lost on Harry. A self-proclaimed "crunchy ethnic wannabe," Carla is constantly referred to as a tourist by Memo, further contributing to her sense of alienation as she struggles to belong.

Jessica Abel

Emerging from the minicomics scene in the early 1990's, Jessica Abel became a star in the American alternative comics scene with her anthology title *Artbabe*. After moving to Mexico City in 1998, Abel began serializing the work for which she is best known, *La Perdida*, in 2000. The story of an American expatriate living in Mexico, the work was collected as a book by Pantheon in 2006. In 2008 she released *Life Sucks*, the story of a vampire store clerk, written in collaboration with Gabe Soria and drawn by Warren Pleece. Abel has also produced a number of nonfiction comics, including *Radio: An Illustrated Guide*, which was created in conjunction with the NPR show *This American Life*. As instructors at the School of Visual Arts, Abel and her husband, Matt Madden, have published the textbook *Drawing Words and Writing Pictures*. Abel's comics are strongly realist and are drawn in a naturalistic style, and her stories tend to focus on young people seeking to find their path in life.

Impact

La Perdida, which translates as the "the lost one," is notable for having a Mexican American female protagonist, putting it in limited company. Outside the work of the Hernandez brothers (who are best known for *Love and Rockets*, 1982-1996), Latina characters are few and far between even in twenty-first-century comics. As flawed as Carla is as a character, her very appearance is encouraging. As Carla travels outside the United States, she pushes against the boundaries of traditional gender roles, portraying the quintessential transnational subject.

La Perdida is also notable for its use of both English and Spanish dialogue throughout the first quarter of the novel, as well as its extensive glossary of Spanish words. Rather than requiring the reader to flip back and forth to the glossary, Abel provides immediate extensive translations of these panels, increasing the book's accessibility for English-language readers. One critique of the book is that it would have developed a greater degree of authenticity, particularly to Spanish-language readers, had the author maintained this technique throughout the book.

Critical reception of the book has been generally positive, though it is frequently critiqued for its perceived portrayal of Mexico as a beautiful but flawed land of drug dealers and kidnappers. Additionally, critics and scholars point out that while the novel seems poised as a bildungsroman, Carla does not achieve the necessary maturity to complete the journey. This critique, however, is tempered by the author's contention that both Carla and her journey are intentionally complex and flawed.

Additionally, *La Perdida* is often taken for an autobiographical account of its creator's two years of living in Mexico. Abel herself points out that this is not possible (she is a Caucasian artist), but it does put to rest questions of whether such an author can create a convincing portrayal of an ethnic-identified experience. Many readers of *La Perdida* were initially certain that Abel was indeed a Mexican American artist.

Theresa N. Rojas

Further Reading

Bechdel, Alison. *Fun Home: A Family Tragicomic* (2006).

Clowes, Daniel. *Ghost World* (1998).

Marchetto, Marisa Acocella. *Cancer Vixen* (2006).

Satrapi, Marjane. *The Complete Persepolis* (2007).

Bibliography

Abel, Jessica. "The Jessica Abel Interview." Interviewed by Greg Stump. *The Comics Journal* 270 (August, 2005): 68-106.

Hamilton, Patrick. "Lost in Translation: Jessica Abel's *La Perdida*, the Bildungsroman, and 'That "Mexican" Feel.'" In *Multicultural Comics: From Zap to Blue Beetle*. Edited by Frederick Luis Aldama. Austin: University of Texas Press, 2010.

See also: *Love and Rockets*; *Cancer Vixen*; *Persepolis*; *Fun Home*; *Ghost World*; *Life Sucks*

LAST DAY IN VIETNAM: A MEMORY

Author: Eisner, Will
Artist: Will Eisner (illustrator)
Publisher: Dark Horse Comics
First book publication: 2000

Publication History

Last Day in Vietnam: A Memory was published as a graphic novel by Dark Horse Comics. Will Eisner intended it to be a recollection of his travels while working for the U.S. Army as a consultant and editor for its illustrated training manuals. Already well-respected within the comics community, Eisner released a number of graphic novels in the last few years of his life, and Dark Horse was one of the publishers that introduced readers to some of his work. The book also allowed Dark Horse to introduce a war title into its publishing line.

Plot

Last Day in Vietnam: A Memory includes Eisner's recollections of traveling through Asia while gaining information for his work for the U.S. Army maintenance manual *PS Magazine*. The magazine grew out of his original work with the Army during his service in World War II. The Army considered his work significant to its training, and he was given free rein to create, illustrate, and edit Joe Dope posters. After World War II, this form of illustrated training evolved into *PS Magazine*. During fact-finding trips to South Korea in 1954 and Vietnam in 1967 Eisner heard or witnessed the stories that became the plots for *Last Day in Vietnam*. As Eisner said, the stories in the book were arranged "by personal importance, rather than chronology."

"Last Day in Vietnam," the first story, is told from the second-person perspective and has an almost dreamlike quality at times. A major who serves as an escort gives the reader a tour of a firebase in Vietnam. The major motions the reader to a jeep, then comments that the reader is classified as a brigadier (one star) general; thus, travel is easily obtained. The dialogue is the

Last Day in Vietnam: A Memory. (Courtesy of Dark Horse Comics)

usual sort of idle chatter in which people engage while traveling.

As the helicopter flies along, the major notes that this is his last duty and last day in Vietnam. He then describes the moments that led him to this point in time. He also notes that he had been in the National Guard and then was assigned to headquarters for the duration of his time in Vietnam. He comments on the fighting spirit and capabilities of the Vietnamese. He notes that the goal of the war is to stop the expansion of communism. After the helicopter lands at the firebase, the reader is escorted to the ordnance shack, meets the commander, and sees the interrogation of prisoners. The base is attacked, and the major worries that he will not be able to escape. Only after a mad dash to the last helicopter and the ensuing panic does the major realize that he is going home.

The second vignette is entitled "The Periphery." In the story, a Vietnamese waiter tells of a group of reporters talking about the fighting in the country and the wider picture of the war effort. Two reporters come in from the field and join the discussion; one talks about the Battle of Khe Sanh, and the other simply drinks. At the end of the story, the waiter informs the reader that the son of the silent reporter was killed at Khe Sanh; the discussion of war thus becomes personal instead of theoretical.

The third story, "The Casualty," is a wordless story told from the perspective of a wounded U.S. serviceman. He thinks about how he was enjoying the sights of Saigon, hiring a woman for sexual pleasure. She placed a live grenade under his bed, which exploded, injuring him. He seems to swear off women and heads back to base, but he meets another lovely Vietnamese woman and walks off with her in the last panel.

In "A Dull Day in Korea," a young American officer talks about the boredom of garrison duty along the demilitarized zone. The officer describes his boredom, his abusive father, and his love of hunting. This gives him the idea of shooting at a Korean woman who is gathering wood for a fire. His first shot misses. As he sets up his second shot, he is stopped by a sergeant, who scolds the officer for attempting such an act.

"Hard Duty" shows an enlisted man who is mean and physically strong. He longs for action and complains loudly about being in a maintenance area after a tour in combat. Finally, he begs the reader to come with him on his "hard duty": a trip to an orphanage. While he serves as a jungle gym for the children, the woman who runs the orphanage notes that the children are of mixed race and that no one comes to play with them except for the soldier, who is "such a gentle person."

The final story, and the most personal for Eisner, is "A Purple Heart for George." George, the main character, is a clerk in a stateside unit who becomes inebriated every weekend, laments the fact that he is not serving in a combat unit, and types a request for transfer. Only his bunkmates, who try to stop the letter, know of his actions. As they get ready to leave, they instruct a new man to intercept the letter. However, in one set of panels, the officer in charge reads the request,

signs it, and mails it. After the two friends come back and look for George, they find out his request was not intercepted and that he was transferred. In the last two panels, the two are informed that George was killed in combat not long after arriving. They lament his death, while another asks for his personal information to write his obituary for the camp newspaper.

Characters

- *The major* is an escort in the first story. His intent was to join the National Guard to gain extra money for his family, but he ends up in the Army. His observations on the war are not unlike the conventional wisdom of the day: The Americans are better equipped and have righteousness on their side. He discusses the body counts of the day and asserts that U.S. leadership should consider a "nuke Hanoi" campaign in order to stop communism. He talks of strenuous camp life when picking up reconnaissance troops, but he fears he will be killed during an artillery attack at the firebase.

- *The waiter* is an overlooked storyteller of the Vietnam War. The people of Saigon saw the war from both sides. Civilians often became shields or targets. The waiter notes that for some Americans, the war is academic and does not seem to affect them personally.

- *The wounded GI* is betrayed by a prostitute in Saigon; she detonates a grenade beneath his bed. He is later seen walking off with another Vietnamese woman.

- *George* is a clerk at a stateside base. When drinking, his courage builds and he wishes to be transferred to a combat unit. In the end, his inexperience costs him his life.

Artistic Style

Eisner illustrated and colored *Last Day in Vietnam*, using color, layout, and detail to convey his perceptions of war. Eisner's use of sepia tones is a metaphor for the confusion of the war and represents a rejection of the black-and-white political view held by many of his contemporaries. Actions flow together in panels with undefined borders, giving the stories a type of ethereal, dreamlike feel. The story "The Casualty" uses images in place of dialogue to convey the pleasures and pains of military life. Eisner's use of facial expressions to convey the emotions of combat lends a sense of realism to the stories that is absent from most war comics. Eisner's attention to detail—be it the drunken, slovenly appearance of George or the dressed-to-regulation lieutenant in "A Dull Day in Korea"—adds further realism to the stories. In fact, the only cartoonlike depiction in the book comes in "Hard Duty," in which the rough-and-tumble sergeant is able to straighten out

Last Day in Vietnam: A Memory. (Courtesy of Dark Horse Comics)

metal tubing. This juxtaposes his physical strength with his soft spot for the children in the orphanage.

Themes

Conflict is the major theme of *Last Day in Vietnam*, whether it be internal or external. The reader is exposed to conflicting ideals in the stories, as Eisner illustrates that war and the politics underpinning it are not always black and white. In addition, the stories often illustrate the conflict between differing cultures and societies. The conflict between right and wrong in the international sense is also conveyed in the stories, as when the major discusses what strategies should be used in order to win the war. The reporter who writes of the conflict may see the war through different and biased eyes if a family member is involved. Finally, Eisner examines the conflict between the necessity of appearing strong while in combat and the suppression of emotion and compassion. "A Dull Day in Korea" and "Hard Duty" illustrate a type of conflict different from what one might expect when engaging the topic of war. The stories present conflict in myriad ways, including in realms of sex, love, and family. Ultimately, the stories indicate that war has an impact on everyone in society, soldiers and noncombatants alike. In all of the stories, Eisner's *Last Day in Vietnam* seeks to demonstrate how war provokes both physical and emotional conflict.

Impact

Last Day in Vietnam deals with the human aspect of war and violence. Unlike many of the war-themed comics of the 1950's, which commended valor, self-sacrifice, and the glory of war, Eisner's text shows alternative emotions, such as fear and compassion. The work represents a bridge between antiwar comics such as *Frontline*

Combat (1951-1954) and *Two-Fisted Tales* (1950-1955) from EC Comics and *Blazing Combat* (1965-1966) from Warren Publishing. Eisner's recollections were gleaned from actual trips to combat zones, thus offering a glimpse of the combat life of an earlier time. The release of *Last Day in Vietnam* came at a time when war-themed comics were reassessing the wars that took place in the middle of the twentieth century, a time when most Americans assumed that wars in which the United States was involved were just. The book came out just before the wave of war comics created in the aftermath of the terrorist attacks on September 11, 2001.

Cord Scott

Further Reading

Kubert, Joe. *Dong Xoai, Vietnam 1965* (2010).
Lomax, Don. *Vietnam Journal* (2002).

Sacco, Joe. *Safe Area Goražde: The War in Eastern Bosnia 1992-1995* (2000).

Bibliography

Andelman, Bob. *Will Eisner: A Spirited Life*. Milwaukie, Ore.: M Press, 2005.
Couch, N. C. Christopher, and Stephen Weiner. *The Will Eisner Companion: The Pioneering Spirit of the Father of the Graphic Novel*. New York: DC Comics, 2004.
Eisner, Will. *A Pictorial Arsenal of America's Combat Weapons*. New York: Sterling, 1960.

See also: *A Contract with God, and Other Tenement Stories*; *The Spirit*; *Safe Area Goražde*

LEAVE IT TO CHANCE

Author: Robinson, James
Artist: Paul Smith (illustrator); George Freeman (inker); Jeromy Cox (colorist); Amie Grenier (letterer)
Publisher: Image Comics
First serial publication: 1996-2002
First book publication: 1997-2003

Publication History

Inspired by a *Nancy Drew* pinup drawn by Frank Miller, James Robinson wanted to create a series mainly for girls that would bridge the gap between "kiddie" comics and more adult material. He came up with a character that was a cross between teen detective Nancy Drew and Kolchak the Night Stalker, and he teamed up with artist Paul Smith. The two had previously worked together on *The Golden Age* (1993-1994), a miniseries published by DC Comics.

Originally published as full-color comic books under Image's Homage imprint, *Leave It to Chance* was published sporadically for twelve issues between 1996 and 1999. The twelfth issue of the series was published by DC Comics after the acquisition of Jim Lee's WildStorm imprint (which included Homage) from Image. During this time the first eight issues of the series were collected in two softcover collections in 1997 and 1998. After the series went on a three-year hiatus, Image published a thirteenth issue. Jim Valentino, Image's publisher at the time, announced that the entire series would be reprinted as large-format, European-style hardcover graphic novels similar to *Asterix* (1959-2010) and *The Adventures of Tintin* (1929-1976). Once all thirteen issues were published in this way, the plan was to continue in this format with new stories on a quarterly schedule. After the publication of three hardcover issues, *Leave It to Chance* went on an indefinite hiatus. Issues 12 and 13 from the original series were never reprinted, and new material beyond the original comic book series was never published. As of 2011, *Leave It to Chance* was out of print, and Robinson stated there were no plans to return to the series.

James Robinson

James Robinson is a writer of American superhero comic books, well known for his deep commitment to maintaining the continuity of Golden Age characters and bringing the material forward into the present. His breakthrough work was as the writer of *Starman* for DC Comics, in which he revitalized a Golden Age character for a new generation of readers in the 1990's. His Elseworlds story, *The Golden Age* (with Paul Smith), detailed the experiences of early DC superheroes in the age of McCarthyism. Robinson has also written a wide range of Superman and Batman comics for DC. His most notable work outside of DC is undoubtedly *Leave It to Chance* (also with Paul Smith), which follows the adventures of fourteen-year-old Chance Falconer and her pet dragon, St. George. This was a celebrated adventure graphic novel for young readers, which won several industry awards. Robinson is widely praised for his ability to breathe new life into dated concepts and is a highly sought-after writer.

Plot

Devil's Echo, a city where ghosts and monsters are commonplace, is protected by Lucas Falconer, the latest in a long line of occult investigators who have watched over the city for centuries. Lucas's daughter, fourteen-year-old Chance, is at the age when preparations usually begin for the next Falconer to take the mantle of Devil's Echo's protector, and she is eager to start her training. However, since the death of his wife, Lucas feels that the role is too dangerous and would prefer Chance to live a normal life and allow the mantle be passed to her son. Chance refuses to let her father's wishes discourage her. After overhearing a conversation between her father and police lieutenant Saunders about a catatonic shaman named John Raven and his missing daughter, she sets off to investigate.

Arriving at the hotel where Raven was staying, Chance discovers a dead body and is cornered by a group of monsters, called troggs, who have captured Raven's daughter. Chance is saved by a small dragon (whom she later names St. George) that escaped from the Falconer mansion.

At the police station, Chance recounts her evening to Lieutenant Saunders and is put under the protection of Officer Margo Vela, who is interested in what Chance saw. She brings Chance to reporter Will Bendix, and the three compare notes on the case. Remembering that one of the troggs mentioned the name of mayoral candidate Sonny Abbott, Chance sneaks into Abbott's home and discovers a plot to influence the upcoming election. Abbott has a spy with the current mayor; he has kidnapped John Raven's daughter, but he still wants Raven himself.

Chance and Margo check up on Raven, but he has been kidnapped by a group of troggs. The police try to question Abbott about his involvement in the mayoral plot, but he denies everything. Following Abbott, Chance finds Duncan Bell, the mayor's right-hand man, and Abbott discussing plans to use John Raven's magic to flood the city and tarnish the current mayor's name. However, Bell's plans with Abbott are a diversion for his own plans to destroy the city by raising an ancient god in order to exact revenge on Lucas Falconer, the man responsible for killing his brother, Miles Belloc.

With Raven forced to bring rain using his magic, the city begins to flood. Using Raven's shamanic tokens, Bell raises the Toad God to destroy the city. As the city tries to hold off the Toad God, Chance finds Bell and defeats him, only to discover that Bell's brother was the one who killed her mother. Chance meets with the police and the reunited Raven family, and Raven performs a ritual to send the Toad God back to the sea. Lucas returns from his travels and is angered when Chance, excited about her new role as adventurer, risks her own life.

Unhappy with Chance's involvement in the skirmish with the Toad God and a later incident involving a kidnapped monkey and thugs attempting to gain power from a dark dimension, Lucas sends Chance to a private boarding school to prevent her from getting into danger. Feeling like an outsider, Chance manages to befriend a girl named Ruby. That night, Chance awakens to find that all the students and teachers have been drugged except for the assistant headmistress, Miss Longfellow, and the headmaster, Croft.

The next day, Chance tells Ruby and a group of friends about the unconscious students and guesses that their milk was drugged. (Chance refused to drink it because of an allergy.) Ruby recounts an urban legend about a band of pirates that used the caves beneath the school to hoard their treasure and says that the school is haunted by the ghost of the captain, Hitch.

That night, Chance and Ruby, along with other students, descend beneath the school to find Miss Longfellow and headmaster Croft (dressed as the ghostly Captain Hitch) loading treasure onto a boat. The children are all captured. Before Chance can figure out a way to escape, she is chloroformed and wakes up floating in the middle of the ocean, tied to a dead body. She manages to free herself from the ropes but passes out.

She wakes on the beach to find that her pet dragon, St. George, has saved her from drowning. Making her way back to the school, she discovers a drugged headmaster Croft and realizes that Captain Hitch is actually a ghost and not the headmaster in disguise.

A group of thugs ambush Chance, and while she manages to escape at first, she is captured after finding her friends. After Hitch and Longfellow leave with their boat full of pirates' treasure, the children escape and follow the pirates in a dinghy. Hitch plans to head to Devil's Echo and confront Lucas Falconer, whose ancestor killed Hitch. Just after Chance and her friends board the ship, the Coast Guard arrives. Realizing that his plans have been foiled, Hitch disappears, leaving Longfellow and the rest of the crew in the hands of the Coast Guard.

Patrons of a newly reopened film theater are shocked when four monsters—the Count, Man Monster, the Pharaoh, and the Howler—emerge from the screen to attack first the audience and then the citizens of Devil's Echo. Lieutenant Saunders and the police meet up at Lucas's home to prepare a contingency plan. Chance overhears the conversation and leaves with plans of her own. She finds Margo and another police officer, Roger Howard, at the theater, certain that the theater would be the last place the monsters would be. Suddenly, however, they are attacked by the Pharaoh.

The theater manager, Mr. Granger, is taken away by Man-Monster, and the Howler bites Roger, transforming him into a werewolf. Granger is brought before a man obscured in shadow, who explains his plan to use the monsters to keep the police busy so he can commit crimes. The first crime is the theft of a priceless diamond from the museum in Little Cairo by a young thief named Lightfoot.

Listening in once again, Chance is detected. She manages to escape but almost falls to her death off a building. Lightfoot saves her life, unaware that she is the daughter of Lucas Falconer. Lucas and the police try their best to fight off the monsters, but all traditional methods of destroying them fail.

At the Little Cairo Museum, Chance finds Lightfoot attempting to steal the diamond. She reveals to him that she is a Falconer and decides to let him escape, since he previously saved her life.

After being reminded that the monsters are literally from the movies, Lucas returns to the fight with what looks like a water gun. He threatens to spray the monsters with a film solvent that will disintegrate them but offers them the chance to return to their world. Lucas uses magic to return the monsters to the screen and then attempts to cure Roger of his werewolf form, but he fails.

Believed to be missing during the fight with the monsters, Chance is reunited with her worried father and mentions briefly to him about the shadowed man she spied on.

Volumes

- *Leave It to Chance: Shaman's Rain* (1997). Collects issues 1-4. Includes introduction by writer Robinson and afterword by artist Smith. Volume outlines characters and the town and finds Chance preparing to become the next protector of Devil's Echo.
- *Leave It to Chance: Trick or Treat, and Other Stories* (1998). Collects issues 5-8. Includes introduction by Smith and character sketchbook as well as the story of the ghost of Captain Hitch, who had hidden treasure under what became Chance's school.

- *Leave It to Chance: Monster Madness, and Other Stories* (2003). Collects issues 9-11. Includes introduction by James Robinson. Movie monsters escape from the screen. Lucas threatens to spray them with film solvent but also offers them a chance to return to their world.

Characters

- *Chance Falconer* is the tomboyish protagonist of the series. She is a fourteen-year-old girl and the daughter of the famous occult investigator Lucas Falconer. She has a thirst for adventure and is curious and resourceful. Against her father's wishes, she finds herself involved in many mysteries in their city.
- *Lucas Falconer* is a cross between Dr. Strange and Sherlock Holmes and is the occult investigator of Devil's Echo. He has long black hair and a serious and sometimes gruff exterior. During a battle with his arch nemesis, Miles Belloc, he had his face disfigured and saw his wife killed. This incident has made him protective of Chance, his only daughter.
- *St. George* is a small orange dragon that Chance adopts as her pet. After Lucas has difficulty sending him back to his home dimension, Chance accidentally sets the dragon free. He finds Chance and saves her from being killed by troggs with his ability to breathe fire. He is loyal and affectionate with an acute sense of smell.
- *Duncan Bell* is the main antagonist of the first volume. He is the brother of Miles Belloc, the man responsible for the death of Lucas's wife. He is secretive and conniving and has knowledge of the mystical arts. His main goal is to take revenge on Falconer for the death of his brother.
- *Will Bendix* is the star reporter of the *Devil's Echo Oracle*, the city's major newspaper. He is resourceful and provides information and insight to Chance on her adventures. He also has romantic feelings for Officer Margo Vela.
- *Margo Vela* is an officer on Devil's Echo's police force. She has a strong personality and is courageous. Seeing the potential in Chance, Margo acts as a mentor for the young adventurer. She

is highly dedicated to her position on the police force.

- *Lieutenant Saunders* is the head of the Devil's Echo police force. He has a close relationship with Lucas and works with him to protect the city from supernatural threats. He is African American.
- *Hobbs* is Lucas's butler. He wears glasses and has long gray sideburns and often subtly encourages Chance to explore being an adventurer.
- *Quince* is Lucas's housekeeper and a mother figure for Chance. She is protective of Chance and disapproves of her adventures in Devil's Echo.
- *Captain Hitch* is the main antagonist from Book 2. He is the ghost of a legendary pirate who hid his treasure in a series of caves that years later ended up under a girls' boarding school. He is certain that an ancestor of Lucas Falconer was the one who defeated him.
- *Lightfoot* is a young talented thief employed by a mysterious man in shadows in Book 3. He is dashing and has a flirtatious relationship with Chance even after he discovers who her father is.

Artistic Style

Best known for his short run on Marvel's *Uncanny X-Men* during the 1980's, Smith adapted his realistic superhero style for *Leave It to Chance*. Smith's clear design features a heavy line weight, and his panel construction is dynamic, with a wide range of close-ups, long shots, and action shots. Enhancing the fun, light tone of the series, Smith's characters are rendered in bright colors with expressive faces to contrast the detailed backgrounds and heavy use of blacks that create the moody supernatural quality of Devil's Echo.

After the first few issues, Smith stepped outside his typical style and moved toward more cartoony artwork while maintaining a level of realism. Characters became more caricatured, resembling the odd cast from Hergé's *The Adventures of Tintin* (1929-1976) and emphasizing the varied citizens of Devil's Echo. In particular, the drawing of Chance's eyes moves from realistic to iconic round dots, similar to the eyes of *Little*

Orphan Annie, nostalgically referencing the comics of the past.

Smith's page layouts illustrate his strengths in clear storytelling. Large panels make the book extremely readable and add to the series' fast pace. The addition of inks by George Freeman in Volumes 2 and 3 adds a level of crispness to Smith's already clear artwork. The specific character design of Chance Falconer references other strong female characters, including detective Nancy Drew and two characters from the X-Men, Kitty Pryde and Jubilee, directly opposing the "cheesecake" drawing of female characters that was popular at the time in superhero comics.

Themes

Like many works aimed at children and young adults, *Leave It to Chance* has growing up as its main theme. As a protective father, Lucas Falconer refuses to begin training his daughter to become Devil's Echo's next occult investigator. Chance's sense of excitement drives her to rebel against her father's wishes, and her adventures unfold. *Leave It to Chance* uses a story structure similar to sitcoms, in which every adventure features Chance using her intelligence and resources to escape dangerous situations only to be lightly scolded by her father when she is found to be safe after all. Lucas attempts to stop his daughter from adventuring by sending her to a boarding school, but Chance encounters danger even there. He comes to realize that he must trust his instincts and allow her to explore her passion as an investigator, even though he worries about her safety.

Leave It to Chance has been hailed by many as a prime example of a feminist text, celebrating strong female characters. Chance is unlike many of the examples of female heroines in circulation at the time. She is strong-willed, courageous, and tomboyish, but not unfeminine. She subverts traditional female roles when rejecting her father's suggestion that she should get married, lead a normal life, and allow her son to become the city's next protector. Her decision to become an adventurer may be rebellious, but it is not impulsive. She maintains a level of mature intelligence along with a wide-eyed sense of excitement throughout her adventures. This spirit of feminism is also evident in the character of Officer Margo Vela, who acts as a role model for Chance. As the dominant police officer in the series, she holds her place on the force as a resourceful, highly capable woman in a traditionally male role.

Impact

In the mid- to late 1990's, when dark and violent story lines involving superheroes and hypersexualized female characters were at the height of popularity, *Leave It to Chance* was a rare example of a series written specifically for both young readers and girls, whom many audiences did not consider a good audience for comic books. *Leave It to Chance* blends mystery, adventure, humor, and the supernatural; its fast-paced stories, G-rated violence, and brightly colored artwork have more in common with children's literature and European comics than North American superhero comics of the 1990's. In 2003, DC Comics reprinted issue 5, the beginning of the *Trick or Treat* story line, for Free Comic Book Day, further illustrating the book's potential in reaching a younger audience.

During the 1990's, Image Comics was infamous for its line of superhero comics with incredibly stylized artwork and weak stories. When Valentino became head publisher at Image Comics, one of his mandates was to distance the company from the negatively criticized "Image style" and acquire books to create a diverse line of quality authors and titles. Valentino chose to relaunch *Leave It to Chance* as oversized hardcovers at a low price point to gain attention from the bookstore and library market that were starting to take a serious interest in graphic novels.

Librarians praised *Leave It to Chance* in reviews and included the series on recommended booklists, making Chance Falconer's adventures a must-have series for any start-up children's graphic novel collection. However, Valentino's plans to continue the book as a series of graphic novels never came to be. Robinson took an extended leave from comics to focus on screenwriting and, after his return, to writing mainstream superhero stories for DC Comics. With the three hardcover volumes out of print, *Leave It to Chance* has become a distant memory.

Scott Robins

Further Reading

Foglio, Kaja, and Phil Foglio. *Girl Genius* (2002-2010).

Hale, Shannon, and Nathan Hale. *Rapunzel's Revenge* (2008).

Naifeh, Ted. *Courtney Crumrin* (2003-2009).

Torres, J., and J. Bone. *Alison Dare* (2010).

Bibliography

MacDonald, Heidi. "Image Takes a 'Chance'." *Publishers Weekly* 249, no. 37 (2002): 34.

Robinson, James. Introduction to *Leave It to Chance: Monster Madness and Other Stories*. Orange, Calif.: Image Comics, 2003.

_____. Introduction to *Leave It to Chance: Shaman's Rain*. Orange, Calif.: Image Comics, 2002.

Smith, Paul. Introduction to *Leave It to Chance: Trick or Treat and Other Stories*. Orange, Calif.: Image Comics, 2002.

Yarbrough, Beau. "San Diego, Day 2: *Leave It to Chance* Returns in 2002." *Comic Book Resources*, July 20, 2001. http://www.comicbookresources.com/?page=article&id=87

See also: *The Adventures of Tintin*; *Age of Reptiles*; *The Arrival*

LIFE AND TIMES OF SCROOGE MCDUCK, THE

Author: Rosa, Don

Artist: Don Rosa (illustrator); Susan Daigle-Leach (colorist); Gary Leach (colorist); Todd Klein (letterer)

Publishers: Gemstone Publishing; Boom! Studios

First serial publication: 1994-1996

First book publication: 2005

Publication History

The Life and Times of Scrooge McDuck originally appeared as individual stories in *Uncle Scrooge*, issues 285-296, from Gladstone Publishing, Disney's licensed publisher at the time. Comics creator Don Rosa's run earned critical and popular acclaim, winning the Eisner Award for Best Serialized Story in 1995 and the Comic Buyer's Guide Fan Award for Favorite Comic Book that same year.

In 2005, Gemstone Publishing collected the Rosa stories in book form for the first time. The following year, Gemstone published Rosa's supplemental collection, *The Life and Times of Uncle Scrooge Companion*, which contains stories filling in gaps in the primary narrative as well as author commentary. In 2010, Boom! Studios reprinted *The Life and Times of Scrooge McDuck* in two volumes. The story is told in twelve chapters, each including author commentary, and codifies the various Uncle Scrooge stories created by Rosa's predecessor, Carl Barks. Chapters of the story have also appeared in a number of international editions, including the French *Picsou*, the Dutch *Donald Duck Extra*, the Italian *Zio Paperone*, and the Brazilian *40 Anos de Revista Tio Patinhas*.

Plot

In 1880, after learning from his father of his family's lost legacy, young Scrooge vows to return the clan to its former glory. Shining shoes with a kit given to him by his father, he earns his first coin, an American dime. This dime becomes his lifelong possession and a good-luck charm. While continuing to shine shoes, Scrooge builds a small empire out of peat-moss sales. With the help of an ancestral ghost, he drives intruders

> ### Don Rosa
>
> Don Rosa is best known for writing and drawing *The Life and Times of Scrooge McDuck*, an elaborate effort to establish a canonical timeline of stories based on the work of Carl Barks. Rosa broke into comics working at the student newspaper at the University of Kentucky and contributing to fanzines. In 1985 he began drawing Uncle Scrooge adventure comics for Gladstone Publishing. After breaking with that company, he went to work directly for Gutenberghus (now Egmont), the Danish publisher of Disney comics. In 1991 he began *The Life and Times of Scrooge McDuck*, a chronological retelling of the life of Barks's best-loved creation, which sought to fill in many of the blanks in the life story of the character. He retired from comics in the mid-2000's as a result of eye problems. Rosa's stories are notable for their sense of play and adventure. His drawings hew closely to Disney's character designs but are distinguishable by the presence of cross-hatching and shading, which are seldom used by other Disney artists.

from Castle McDuck, the family home. Scrooge sets sail for the United States, where he becomes steward on his uncle's riverboat. There, he outmaneuvers a gang of thieves called the Beagle Boys that tries to steal from him. After the riverboat explodes, Scrooge is left penniless. Heading west, he bests the James brothers in a railroad robbery, becomes a cowboy, and meets a young Theodore Roosevelt.

Scrooge then takes up prospecting. After laying claim to a valuable copper mine, he bests hordes of claim jumpers. He receives a telegram warning of family disaster and returns to Scotland.

Scrooge plans to use his mining wealth to pay the taxes on Castle McDuck. His rival Angus Whiskerville engages him in an armored duel, during which Scrooge falls to the bottom of the castle moat. The unconscious Scrooge has a visionary encounter with his ancestors and learns pieces of his future. Awakening, he uses his dime as a screwdriver to remove the armor and then surfaces and bests the Whiskervilles.

After failing as a South African gold miner, Scrooge tries prospecting in Australia. In dreamtime prophecy, an Aborigine tells Scrooge of his destiny. Scrooge sees prismatic light through the Aborigine's crystal. Taking it as a sign, he ventures to the Yukon to resume prospecting.

Scrooge's time in the Yukon is catalytic. He discovers an egg of solid gold, known as the Golden Goose Nugget, in a prosperous vein of ore. He finally amasses his fortune. During this time, he meets Goldie O'Gilt, the woman he comes closest to loving. With his first million dollars secured, he invests in the claims of others, always to his advantage but always dealing fairly.

Scrooge returns to Scotland. Expecting a hero's welcome, he is frustrated to learn that the townspeople resent his success. After failing abysmally at the Highland Games, Scrooge decides to move to a parcel of land in the United States, leaving his young employee Scottie to run Castle McDuck. As Scrooge and his family depart, Scrooge's father dies quietly.

In 1902, Scrooge returns to the United States with his family. He crashes his jalopy into the cornfield of his new neighbor, his aunt Elvira, later known as Grandma Duck. Elvira's son Quackmore and Scrooge's sister Hortense meet and fall in love. Scrooge discovers his land is dilapidated. He ejects the occupants, the Junior Woodchucks, who in turn cable authorities in Washington, D.C., that a Scot has occupied an American military base. Theodore Roosevelt, now president, takes up the charge.

Ferrying his barrels of money upstream, Scrooge has a chance encounter with the Beagle Boys. Seeking revenge for the years spent in prison at his hand following the riverboat incident, they follow Scrooge to his hilltop fort. Taking him by surprise, they nail him inside one of his money barrels. At this point, the U.S. Navy, the Marines, and the Junior Woodchucks, led by Roosevelt, attack the fort. After a ferocious battle, Scrooge and Roosevelt face each other for the first time in twenty years. Delighted to see his old friend, Roosevelt halts the charge and arrests the Beagle Boys.

Later, Scrooge builds his money vault on the site of the old fort, which was demolished in the battle.

Now a billionaire, Scrooge invests in railroads and returns to South Africa to join in the Boer War (1899-1902). While there with his sisters, Scrooge insults a voodoo chief and hires local thugs to lay waste to the village, his only dishonest deed. He tricks the chief into signing the village over to him. The chief puts a curse on Scrooge.

When he returns to camp he discovers that his sisters have returned to Scotland, unable to forgive his dishonesty. Scrooge has a crisis of conscience. He prepares to leave but encounters Bombie the Zombie, the being manifest by the chief's curse. He evades the zombie by removing the disguise he used to buy the village.

He joins Robert Peary's arctic expedition, hoping to buy the North Pole. Making his way to Russia during the revolution, he buys a horde of Fabergé eggs and the famous candy-striped ruby. Bombie follows him every step of the way, even onto the sinking Titanic (1912).

Later, Scrooge embarks on a series of treasure-hunting expeditions. In the South Pacific, Bombie reappears. Relenting, Scrooge pays a local witch doctor with the candy-striped ruby to put a binding spell on Bombie, removing the threat that has haunted him for decades.

After twenty-seven years of globe-trotting and treasure seeking, Scrooge returns to Duckburg, the town he founded, where his family throws him a surprise party. He ignores their gesture, and angered, they threaten to never see him again. They all leave, and as they do, his young nephew Donald Duck kicks his behind. After realizing that he now has no family at his side, Scrooge discovers that he is the richest man in the world.

The years pass by, and Scrooge becomes a recluse. Finally, he sends for Donald, who arrives accompanied by his nephews Huey, Dewey, and Louie. Scrooge shows them his money vault.

The Beagle Boys, led by Blackheart, break into the vault. They handily defeat Scrooge and the boys and lock them in a warehouse in the vault. Scrooge is angered that his nephew does not believe his adventures; this disbelief spurs Scrooge back to life. Using mementos of his past and skills accumulated over decades of adventures, he defeats the Beagle Boys.

Scrooge resolves to sell his drafty mansion and resume adventuring.

Characters

- *Scrooge McDuck*, the protagonist, is the heir of
  Castle McDuck in Scotland. Like all characters in the story, he is a humanized animal. He
  evolves from an ambitious youth into a rich,
  secluded old man. In most ways, he is an active
  character, taking initiative to achieve his needs.
- *Hortense McDuck* is Scrooge's younger sister
  and Donald's mother. Her primary physical
  characteristic is her fiery red hair. She tolerates
  Scrooge's meanness and miserly ways but rejects
  him when he behaves dishonorably.
- *Donald Duck* is Hortense's son and, following
  the story line contained in *The Life and Times of
  Scrooge McDuck*, Scrooge's companion on numerous adventures. He is as irascible as his uncle
  but lacks Scrooge's common sense. He appears
  twice: first as a youth, then as an adult with his
  nephews Huey, Dewey, and Louie.
- *The Beagle Boys* are Scrooge's primary adver-
  saries. They are physically identical, aside from a
  white beard on the family elder and the different
  six-digit number each wears on his chest. All
  are stocky, have beard stubble, and wear orange
  shirts and diamond-shaped masks. Their appearances coincide with key moments in Scrooge's
  life.
- *Goldie O'Gilt* is Scrooge's lost love. Their
  romance is only alluded to but is pivotal in
  Scrooge's life.
- *Huey*, *Dewey*, and *Louie* are Donald's identical
  nephews and Scrooge's grandnephews. They are
  proud members of the Junior Woodchucks, the
  Boy Scout-like organization begun on the original site of Scrooge's money bin.

Artistic Style

Rosa's art is replete with detail while maintaining the
deceptively simple design of the characters. His meticulous research on every aspect of the narrative, from
chronology to period design elements, enhances the
narrative flow. The level of detail, though impressive,

is not pure ornamentation but serves the story. For
example, when Scrooge is returning to Scotland and
thinking about the United States as the land of opportunity, the Statue of Liberty is being erected behind his
departing boat.

Rosa's primary page layout is the eight-panel grid
used in most funny-animal comics during the 1950's
and 1960's. This grid encourages quick reading and has
proven an effective way of communicating slapstick
humor in the still images of the comic medium. Rosa
also routinely uses larger panels, open panels, and silhouettes for emphasis. For example, while page 133 is
a straightforward eight-panel layout with only minor
variation in panel widths, page 177 has two equal tiers
in the top half, but the third tier in the bottom half is interrupted by a single panel set in an uncommon shape.
The shape echoes that of the castle in the background.
There are two wordless panels on this page. The first
shows Scrooge's happiness from making a profit on a
simple transaction. The second shows him mourning at
his mother's grave. This is consistent with Rosa's occasional but effective use of wordless panels to demonstrate or reinforce emotional states.

Rosa's palette is specific to mood, location, and
era. The colors of the Australian Outback in chapter
7 are primarily earth tones, while chapter 8, set in the
Klondike, starts with earth tones and segues into cooler
tones. Color reinforces mood in that chapter, as the narrative voice is third person for a flashback page rendered in sepia tones. Rosa's use of nuanced coloring
and more muted tones in his work differs from that
used in many funny-animal books; by contrast, Carl
Barks, Rosa's predecessor in duck narratives, tended
to use flat colors. While some of this may be attributed
to advances in printing techniques, it also reflects a stylistic difference.

The backgrounds are consistent with comics creator
and theorist Scott McCloud's axiom that the best backgrounds serve as environments. Riverboats, trains, and
scenes set in Africa and Russia are all rendered with
accuracy and care. The veracity of talking ducks and
dogs ambling about such carefully rendered settings is
never questioned.

Above all, this is a character-driven narrative,
and the art reflects that. Rosa's strength is showing

character's emotional state. Facial expressions are exaggerated but remain believable and are reinforced with specific and dynamic poses. A cursory examination of the text finds less than a dozen panels in which any character simply stands still. As this is an adventure story, largely modeled on the American convention of the tall tale, every page and pose has a kinetic quality. Images depicting static characters are used for emphasis. The silhouette image, more frequently used, is employed for a similar emotional effect.

Themes

Rosa is the heir apparent to Barks, despite Barks's insistence that Rosa's work was contrary to his and that unifying the narrative was unnecessary. Rosa's work succeeds on a variety of levels.

The Life and Times of Scrooge McDuck is one man's story, a classic definition of a novel. That man (here represented as a duck) embarks on a journey that begins with saving family, works through the abandonment of family for wealth, and circles back to family as a reason to live. These themes are an extension of some of Barks's ideas about characterization in funny-animal comics. They are also a repudiation of some of those ideas. While Barks insisted that these stories were "simple fables" and needed no larger context, by providing that context, Rosa has made a larger statement about the human condition. Ultimately, this story is about the costs and rewards of ambition.

Impact

These stories appeared in the Bronze Age of comics, following the "duck boom" of the late 1970's and early 1980's. Readership of duck books specifically, and funny-animal books in general, was rapidly diminishing. By this time, no new Barks's duck stories

were appearing. The last issue of the alternative title *No Ducks* appeared in 1979.

Rosa came out of comics fandom, applying some of Barks's storytelling principles to his series *Captain Kentucky* (1981-1985) and *The Pertwillaby Papers* (1971-1978), both of which ran in the critically successful *Rocket's Blast Comicollector* magazine. By redefining the genre beginning with his first duck story in 1985, Rosa rekindled interest in funny-animal narratives. His redefinition was, however, quite faithful to the tone of the stories that inspired him. His work is seen as on par with, if not eclipsing, the masters of the form from the 1950's and 1960's. Much of his work has been reprinted over subsequent decades, despite licensing issues with Disney.

Diana Green

Further Reading

Díaz Canales, Juan, and Juanjo Guarnido. *Blacksad* (2010).

Smith, Jeff. *Bone* (1991-2004).

Waller, Reed, Kate Worley, and James Vance. *Omaha the Cat Dancer* (1978-).

Bibliography

Andrae, Thomas. *Carl Barks and the Disney Comic Book: Unmasking the Myth of Modernity*. Jackson: University Press of Mississippi, 2006.

Barrier, J. Michael. *Carl Barks and the Art of the Comic Book*. New York: M. Lilien, 1981.

Rosa, Don. "Don Rosa Part 1." Interview by Dana Gabbard. *The Comics Journal* 183 (January, 1996): 82.

_____. *The Life and Times of Scrooge McDuck Companion*. Timonium, Md.: Gemstone, 2006.

See also: *Age of Reptiles*; *Tales of the Beanworld*; *Omaha the Cat Dancer*

LIFE SUCKS

Author: Abel, Jessica; Soria, Gabe

Artist: Warren Pleece (illustrator); Hilary Sycamore (colorist)

Publisher: First Second

First book publication: 2008

Publication History

Life Sucks was published as a 192-page volume by First Second Books, an imprint of Roaring Brook Press, a division of Holtzbrinck Publishers. Abel has also published *Drawing Words and Writing Pictures* (2008), a textbook for comics creation, with First Second. *Life Sucks* is co-author Gabe Soria's first graphic novel. Illustrator Warren Pleece is a well-established illustrator from Great Britain who works regularly for DC Comics.

Plot

Life Sucks tells the story of Dave Miller, a young convenience-store attendant in the heart of Los Angeles. Unbeknownst to his many patrons is the fact that the owner of the twenty-four-hour convenience store, Radu Arisztidescu, a vampire of Romanian descent, has transformed Dave into a vampire.

The story begins with Dave waking up at night, drinking what appears to be V8 juice and leaving home to cover his shift at the store. That night, the shop is frequented by Goths who patronize nearby establishments. While Dave is talking to Jerome, a fellow vampire, a young Latina walks in, catching Dave's attention. At this point, Dave and Jerome joke between themselves about being young vampires. Radu then walks into the store, checking on Dave.

The following day, Radu calls Dave to cover someone else's shift. As Dave heads to work, Wes, a surfer vampire, cuts him off and damages his bicycle. After finishing his shift, Dave realizes he needs to get home before sunrise. Along the way, he meets Rosa Velasquez, the Latina he saw at the shop, and she gives him a ride. By the time he gets home, Dave cannot get her out of his head.

Next, the convenience store is robbed. Radu arrives and finds Dave wounded. Jerome arrives, having killed the convenience store robber by chance, a fact for which Radu is glad. When Rosa's friend comes in, Jerome hypnotizes her and finds out where Rosa works.

On another night, while Wes is at the store, Rosa walks in and sparks the surfer's interest. When Dave and his friends go to see Rosa at a fashion show, Wes shows up as well, and a rivalry begins. Trying to contain Wes, Dave forces him to take a vampire's oath. Dave's concerns about Wes's treatment of women seem well founded after Wes ruthlessly disposes of one of his vampire brides, Simone, tearing her head off while they surf at the beach.

Rosa and Dave go to the movies to watch a vampire trilogy; it turns out Wes's father owns the films. Eventually, Wes seduces Rosa, intensifying the conflict between him and Dave. One night, while Dave and Rosa are at a diner, Wes walks in with his two remaining vampire brides, making her realize she has been fooled. Dave then takes her to a beach, where, ignorant of his condition, a disenchanted Rosa speaks about her longing to become a vampire, imagining them to be beautiful, artistic people.

Rosa's and Dave's relationship grows, and, in due course, she learns the truth about his identity. (Wes has visited her at her work and insinuated Dave might hold a secret.) However, Dave refuses to turn her into a vampire.

The story's resolution leads to a showdown at a party at Wes's beach house in Malibu. By the time Dave arrives, he finds Rosa in Wes's arms, turned into a vampire at her request. A fight ensues, and Merle, a biker vampire, comes to Dave's assistance. In the end, Dave strikes a bargain with Radu, who forces Wes to renounce Rosa. Dave returns to his night shift at Last Stop, where he repeats the cycle by targeting an aimless child from Ohio, who has just arrived in Los Angeles to try his luck with a band.

Characters

- *Dave Miller*, the protagonist, is a young vampire who works at a convenience store in central Los Angeles. He shares an apartment with his best friend, Carl, and refuses to kill to feed himself, embracing alternate sources of food, such as the blood bank.
- *Rosa Velasquez* is a young Latina Goth with a predilection for vampires. She lives in Boyle Heights, where her mother chastises her for dating Caucasian Americans. She is Dave's love interest, but Wes, the surfer vampire, seduces her. At her request, he makes her into a vampire. In the end, she finds a job at the Sunshine Diner with Sue-Yun, another young vampire.
- *Wes* is a stereotypical Southern California surfer dude, who has turned into vampire. Given his attitude, he failed as a worker at Last Stop, Radu's convenience store. He is given to bouts of aggressiveness and has a dark past. In the course of the story, he savagely beheads three of his vampire brides. According to Dave, he even murdered his own brother. After he makes Rosa into a vampire, he is forced to renounce her as his vampire bride.
- *Radu Arisztidescu* is a Romanian vampire, owner of the Last Stop convenience store, and master of Jerome, Dave, and Wes. He enjoys playing cards with his fellow immigrant vampires, while his slaves assure him a steady income through sales at the convenience store.
- *Jerome* is a young vampire and friend of Dave. Unlike Dave, he has decided to feed himself through victims. In addition, he has developed his vampire skills somewhat better than Dave

has: He practices hypnotism, is able to go through walls, and can transform at will.
- *Carl* is African American and is Dave's best friend and roommate. He knows Dave is a vampire.
- *Merle* is a middle-aged biker who befriends Dave. He encourages Dave to get rid of his master and embrace vampire freedom. At the end of the story, Merle defends Dave and beats Wes at the latter's beach party.
- *Sue-Yun* is a young, independent Asian American vampire who works at the Sunshine Diner. After Wes sets Rosa free, Sue-Yun offers Rosa advice and guidance, getting her a job at the Sunshine.

Artistic Style

Life Sucks is a single, full-color volume, a format embraced by First Second for many of its releases. The notebook-sized format allows for several panels per page, usually, between five and nine, arranged in a straightforward style, emphasizing the humdrum lifestyle of the main characters. Given the nature of the story, most of the action takes place at night or in closed quarters; thus, black is a prevailing color. However, Pleece's art relies on neatly drawn figures and the dexterous use of color to add vivacity to the story. Despite the novel's emphasis on the monotonous existence of these particular vampires, Pleece's illustrations come across as lively and engaging.

Pleece's style of illustration tends to emphasize cleanly shaped forms, with finely drawn shading and minimal scratchiness. Though the story line does not emphasize a sense of place—Wes's house by the beach is one of the few concrete symbols—Pleece's art conveys a clear notion of setting. In it, Southern California appears as a location with solid colors, lacking gradation or tones.

Occasionally, Pleece gives in to cartoonishness, and his characters attain an almost *Archie*-like quality. Faces, in particular, range from careful delineation (Wes, Radu) to iconographic simplicity (a surprised Jerome). Nevertheless, generally speaking, images tend to be realistic and portray characters in a fairly factual manner.

Dialogue appears in balloons with clear lettering, adding to the story's overall sense of realism and consistency, though it mixes in sporadically with the framing of vignettes. In short, vampires become regular, everyday beings without any degree of idealization.

Themes

Life Sucks bears the influence of two main texts: the film *Clerks* (1994), directed by Kevin Smith, and the *Twilight* (2005-2008) fiction series, by Stephenie Meyer. Like *Clerks*, the main action in *Life Sucks* revolves around routine life in a convenience store. In a sense, the novel is a snapshot of the life of slackers, noting how days go by without remarkable differences. However, in this particular case, the duration of routine is informed by the fact that Dave is a vampire, meaning his life is an endless cycle. Thus, the novel not only alludes to but also updates the film.

When juxtaposed with *Twilight*, *Life Sucks* is a critique of vampires. Unlike the well-known book series, *Life Sucks* does not attempt to glamorize vampires. Rather, it portrays vampires as common individuals who must pay the rent, for example, and conform to the forces of capitalism. Centuries of existence do not imply amazing wealth or a sense of refinement but, rather, decades of exploitation at hands of a corresponding master.

Even instances of dramatic action in the novel, such as Simone's decapitation at the beach, are set against the backdrop of laid-back activities—such as surfing—setting the tone for a narrative bent on a more "realistic" view of vampires (as opposed to the idealization of vampires in *Twilight*). It is evident in the power relations between owners and employees, poor and rich slackers, that capitalism is ever-present. Hence, in this case, vampires fit within an economic order based on social inequality, rather than being glorified representations of aristocratic privilege.

Impact

Life Sucks builds on Abel's reputation as an author, even if it results from a collective effort. Thanks mostly to *La Perdida* (2001-2005), which firmly established her as a new talent in the field of graphic novels, new opportunities surfaced for Abel, encouraging creative growth. Accordingly, *Life Sucks* differs greatly in subject matter and style from *La Perdida* and suggests the potential for variety in Abel's work. *Life Sucks* is Soria's first work in the field of graphic novels. Building on the fashionable topic of vampires, the book seems to have generated a solid audience and has consistently enjoyed good reviews. In particular, it has been marketed at a young-adult readership. In September, 2010, Square Fish Books, an imprint of Macmillan, published a new edition of the book, confirming that the book sold well in its first run.

The book is celebrated for its down-to-earth approach to vampires, shying away from romanticization (à la *Twilight*), or violence and action, as in the *Buffy the Vampire Slayer* (1997-2003) television series. Its ability to combine slacker sensibility with postadolescent angst, embodied in the Goth penchant for vampire topics, is an unlikely formula for success.

Héctor Fernández L'Hoeste

Further Reading

Hamilton, Laurell K. *Anita Blake, Vampire Hunter* (1993-2010).

Jensen, Van. *Pinocchio: Vampire Slayer and the Great Puppet Theater* (2010).

Niles, Steve, and Ben Templesmith. *Criminal Macabre: A Cal McDonald Mystery* (2004-).

_____. *30 Days of Night* (2002).

Roberson, Chris. *iZombie* (2010-).

Snyder, Scott, and Stephen King. *American Vampire* (2010-).

Bibliography

Brophy-Warren, Jamin. "Generation Vampire." *Wall Street Journal* 251, no. 97 (April 25, 2008): W2.

Fletcher-Spear, Kristin. Review of *Life Sucks* by Jessica Abel and Gabe Soria. *Library Media Connection* 27, no. 2 (October, 2008): 76-77.

Review of *Life Sucks* by Jessica Abel and Gabe Soria. *Publishers Weekly* 255, no. 8 (February 25, 2008): 59.

See also: *La Perdida*; *30 Days of Night*

LIKE A VELVET GLOVE CAST IN IRON

Author: Clowes, Daniel
Artist: Daniel Clowes (illustrator)
Publisher: Fantagraphics Books
First serial publication: 1989-1993
First book publication: 1993

Publication History

Like a Velvet Glove Cast in Iron was featured in the first ten issues of Daniel Clowes's long-running comic book series *Eightball*, from 1989 until 1993, when it was collected in a trade paperback and published by Fantagraphics Books at the behest of Fantagraphics editor and founder Gary Groth. Written, drawn, and lettered exclusively by Clowes, *Like a Velvet Glove Cast in Iron* was the first extended story to be serialized in *Eightball*. Though the opening panels of the story were originally printed in color, the trade paperback is exclusively black and white. Each of the ten sections of the story has a chapter title in the trade paperback, while an added table of contents provides narrative continuity and cohesion. Before publishing this work, Clowes had been primarily known for his *Lloyd Llewellyn* (1986-1987) comics series, also published by Fantagraphics. *Eightball* remains one of the best-selling independent comics series.

Plot

Like a Velvet Glove Cast in Iron intentionally lacks a cohesive or tight-knit narrative structure. In a general sense, the comic tells the story of Clay Loudermilk's nightmarish expedition as he attempts to track down his estranged wife, chronicling his interactions with a bizarre cast of characters who actively work to either assist or discourage his efforts to find her.

The story begins when Clay, during a visit to an adult theater, witnesses his wife in a sadomasochistic bondage film entitled *Like a Velvet Glove Cast in Iron*. After consulting with a swami who holds court in the theater's bathroom, Clay learns that the film's director, Dr. Wilde, and his production company, Interesting Productions, are both located in the nearby town of Gooseneck Hollow. Immediately after setting out to contact the film's makers, he is stopped and arrested by two policemen, who viciously beat him. Afterward, one of the officers carves into Clay's foot the image of a man wearing a top hat, a novelty icon named Mister Jones.

After regaining consciousness some days later, Clay discovers that he has been rescued by a compulsively naked cult leader named Godfrey who hopes to obliterate the American government and bring about "Harum Scarum," a worldwide war between men and women in which women will be the victors. When Clay is told he must assassinate the columnist Ann Landers, he escapes in Godfrey's car and travels to Gooseneck Hollow.

Once there, he meets the hideously deformed Tina Muskegon and her nymphomaniacal mother. Though he intends to rent their spare room, he flees upon discovering that Tina, in an effort to seduce him, has laid eggs on his bed. The next day, Clay is invited to the home of a man named Billings, a conspiracist who is convinced that the world's superpowers revolve around appearances of Mister Jones. Clay is struck by Billings's orifice-less male dog, Laura, who survives on a single syringe of fresh water per day.

Later than evening, Clay believes he spots his wife in the window of a home, so he rents a room in a motel across the street to spy on her. A few days later, however, he is no closer to finding his wife, and Laura the dog dies of malnutrition. Clay shaves Laura, after finding a note instructing him to do so, and finds a map to the residence of Mr. One Thousand, not only the supposed creator of Mister Jones but also Laura's breeder. Though Mr. One Thousand denies any knowledge of Billings's conspiracy theory, it is apparent that he is, indeed, complicit.

Meanwhile, after discovering Laura's corpse, Billings hires a crazed, violent maniac named Geat to track down and kill Clay in retribution for the dog's death. Completely unaware that he is being followed, Clay locates Interesting Productions, where he watches a new film entitled *Barbara Allen*. In it, he witnesses his wife having sex with another man, only to be shot in the head and buried.

Devastated, Clay wanders into the street to discover that "Harum Scarum" is well on its way; women are openly accosting men in the streets, and Godfrey has successfully managed to infiltrate the White House. Clay travels to the gravestone marking the body of his estranged wife, where Geat attacks him, cuts off his arms and legs, and buries them, leaving Clay alive but immobile. Unbeknownst to Clay, Interesting Productions filmed his dismemberment, which, with Dr. Wilde at the helm, will become the company's new movie. In order to generate new ideas for his pornographic snuff films, Wilde employs the services of a pipe-smoking girl referred to only as Precious, whose obscene fantasies Wilde realizes on film. In a final ironic twist, Clay survives, only to be returned to the care of Tina for the remainder of his days.

Characters

- *Clay Loudermilk*, the protagonist, is searching for his estranged wife after unexpectedly seeing her in a pornographic film. After concluding his search at her gravestone, he is dismembered, though he does survive.
- *Madame Van Damme* is the screen name of Clay's wife. Clay first sees her in the pornographic bondage film *Like a Velvet Glove Cast in Iron* and later in the film *Barbara Allen*, in which she is shot in the back of the head and buried in the wilderness.
- *Godfrey* is a cult leader who hopes to bring about "Harum Scarum," a global battle between men and women in which women will be victorious. He is naked throughout the entire comic. Ultimately, his mission is a success.
- *Tina Muskegon* is a horribly disfigured young woman who falls in love with Clay. Though he initially spurns her advances, she serves as his caretaker after his mutilation.
- *Billings* is a conspiracist who believes that the world's superpowers are intricately bound up with Mister Jones, a novelty icon whose presence he has researched throughout time. He

orchestrates the dismemberment of Clay after his pet, Laura, dies in the latter's care.
- *Laura* is Billings's pet dog. Bred by Mr. One Thousand, he is orifice-less and survives on one syringe of fresh water per day. He dies while living with Clay and is subsequently shaved, revealing a map on his back that leads Clay to Mr. One Thousand's domicile.
- *Geat* is a violent, woman-abusing maniac who dismembers Clay at the behest of Billings.
- *Mr. One Thousand* is Laura's breeder, the inventor of Mister Jones, and, according to Billings, the person who controls all of the world's major superpowers.
- *Dr. Wilde* is the director of *Like a Velvet Glove Cast in Iron* and *Barbara Allen* and the head of Interesting Productions. He gets his ideas for his snuff films from a young woman named Precious, whom he keeps under his surveillance.
- *Precious* is a young pipe-smoking woman whose violent and disturbing fantasies are turned into films by Dr. Wilde and his company, Interesting Productions.

Artistic Style

Like a Velvet Glove Cast in Iron was serialized in ten issues of *Eightball*, which required Clowes to break up the story into distinct sections that would nevertheless feel connected. He accomplished this by formatting each new section of the comic in an identical fashion, featuring on the first page a large, detailed close-up of a character who plays a central function in that particular section, with the first two panels of the chapter underneath it. Each of the close-ups is finely, though grotesquely, rendered, presenting each character in far greater detail than they appear in the actual narrative. This attention to order and sameness is indicative of Clowes's general style, which is exacting and technically exemplary.

Clowes is known for a realistic style defined by clean lines, faithful renderings of both everyday objects and human beings (particularly faces), careful attention to background detail, and contrasting uses of black and white. Heavily influenced by 1950's kitsch, Clowes's work is at times reminiscent of mid-twentieth-century advertising design and typography, particularly his rendering of the novelty icon Mister Jones. In keeping with the comic's surrealistic and disorienting narrative, Clowes allows the detail to clutter individual panels, often overwhelming the reader in much the same way that Clay is overwhelmed by the particularities of his environment.

In an interesting stylistic gesture, Clowes destabilizes the lines of some of the panels, rendering them uneven and sketchy, to indicate when one of Clay's fantasies, remembrances, or dream sequences is taking place. Because of the sameness of the comic, this detail enables the reader to make distinctions between so-called reality and unreality. Even so, the narrative is tangential, uneven, and chaotic. There is no clear plot, and in that regard, the text functions not unlike a dream or a nightmare, introducing characters quickly before dropping them without a moment's notice and changing scenes without clarifying space or place. Clowes employs this technique purposefully, and it represents a significant departure from his other work, which is not only realistically rendered but also more or less straightforwardly narrated.

Themes

Like a Velvet Glove Cast in Iron is notable for its surrealism, absurdity, and egregious use of extreme sex and violence as a means of exploring themes of loss and abandonment. From the very beginning of the comic, Clay routinely encounters flagrant expressions of grotesque sexualities from all angles: He witnesses his wife perform unusual sex acts with men; he is arrested by two policemen who are clearly having a sexual affair; he has sex with Tina Muskegon's mother and is subsequently seduced by Tina in a profoundly disturbing and graphic way; and, after he has been confronted by the reality of his wife's death, he fondly recalls a quiet postcoital moment between them.

Violence is often attached to sex: Geat has rough sex with a woman whom he also physically abuses; immediately after seeing his wife appear in a second pornographic film, Clay witnesses her execution; and after his dismemberment, he is powerless and cared for by Tina, who has powerful sexual feelings for him. In

a similar way, sex is often mingled with loss and abandonment. After Clay witnesses his wife's violent death, he is prompted to remember a tender moment between them. Tina's mother mourns the loss of Tina's father, a beautiful man she had sexual intercourse with only one night and never saw again. After Tina attempts to seduce Clay, prompting him to leave, she falls into a deep depression.

Impact

Though *Like a Velvet Glove Cast in Iron* has been translated into multiple languages, it has been overshadowed by *Ghost World*, Clowes's subsequent and perhaps most popular extended comics narrative series, although its popularity is partly the result of Clowes's and Terry Zwigoff's film adaptation. Because the comic is not entirely in keeping with Clowes's typical narrative style, being completely absurdist, aggressively violent, more sexually charged, and lacking in any organized narrative structure, the trade paperback is not particularly well known or well read. However, its status as the first extended narrative to appear in *Eightball* is significant, particularly given that the series remains one of the most read and most popular independent comics series in print.

Joanna Davis-McElligatt

Further Reading

Burns, Charles. *Black Hole* (1995-2004).
Clowes, Daniel. *Ghost World* (1993-1997).
_____. *Ice Haven* (2005).

Bibliography

Clowes, Daniel. "Conversation Four: Daniel Clowes." Interview by Mike Sacks. *McSweeney's*, 2009. http://www.mcsweeneys.net/links/sacks/clowes.html.

Clowes, Daniel, Ken Parille, and Isaac Cates. *Daniel Clowes: Conversations*. Jackson: University of Mississippi, 2010.

Hignite, Todd. "Daniel Clowes." In *In the Studio: Visits with Contemporary Cartoonists*. New Haven, Conn.: Yale University Press, 2006.

See also: *Ice Haven*; *Ghost World*; *Black Hole*; *Jimmy Corrigan*

LONG TIME RELATIONSHIP

Author: Doucet, Julie
Artist: Julie Doucet (illustrator)
Publisher: Drawn and Quarterly
First book publication: 2001

Publication History

First published by Drawn and Quarterly with a cloth cover in October, 2001, *Long Time Relationship* was later released in a hardcover edition in January, 2002. The book was created by Julie Doucet, a feminist graphic artist from Montreal known for publishing in underground "zines" as well as in *Weirdo*, a quarterly production of little-known comics that ran from 1981 to 1993. She is also known for her Harvey Award-winning series *Dirty Plotte* (1988-1989) and Firecracker Award-winning graphic novel *My New York Diary* (2004). *Long Time Relationship* is Doucet's fifth book of graphic art. Like many of Doucet's works, the book is intended for a mature audience, as it contains graphic depictions of sexuality.

Plot

Doucet conceived the idea for *Long Time Relationship* while working in Germany and New York. The book does not have a specific story line; rather, each page of the project illustrates a different, unnamed character. As such, the work is reminiscent of an artist's sketchbook.

The book is divided into six sections: "Men of Our Times," "Das Herz," "Long Time Relationship," "Sophie Punt No. 1," "Sophie Punt No. 2," "Sophie Punt No. 34," and "Lost and Found Photos." The first section features images of twenty different men and six different women, including a self-portrait of the author. "Das Herz" features fourteen nude images labeled in German. These illustrations represent Doucet's effort to learn the German language.

"Long Time Relationship" is a series of illustrations inspired by personal advertisements placed in the *Village Voice*, a newspaper in which Doucet has published extensively. The title itself refers to Doucet's longstanding history with the paper. "Sophie Punt No. 1,"

Long Time Relationship. (Courtesy of Drawn and Quarterly)

"Sophie Punt No. 2," and "Sophie Punt No. 34" present drawings of various animals and zodiac symbols as well as illustrated fortunes from fortune cookies.

"Lost and Found Photos" is divided into two sections; one includes photographs found in the garbage in Germany, and the other includes photographs found outside of photo booths. Each drawing in this section has its corresponding photograph beside it.

Characters

Due to the book's sketchbooklike format, *Long Time Relationship* has no protagonists or antagonists, and characters are unnamed.

• The characters in "Men of Our Times" are identified by titles such as "One Director of a Comic

Art Museum." This man has bulging eyes, a sweating brow, a receding hairline, and jagged teeth formed into a wide grin. His fellow characters are equally exaggerated and grotesque and include "Eight Comic Artists, Three Fan Boys, Two Publishers, Two Editors of Magazines Specializing in Comic Art, One Journalist, One Concierge, One Grandfather, One Stranger, and Six Discouraged Girls."

- "Long Time Relationship" features different personal advertisements from the *Village Voice*. "I am Waiting 4 U" is written next to a bony woman in a yellow polka-dot bikini with a daisy in her hair, who smiles broadly with exaggerated red lips. "Let's Fall in Love" is paired with an African American man wearing aviator-style sunglasses as well as a sleeveless shirt and leather

Long Time Relationship. (Courtesy of Drawn and Quarterly)

vest that are too short and reveal chest and pubic hairs.

- In "Sophie Punt No. 1," Doucet creates an artist's book ambience, drawing cartoonlike images of small animals such as rabbits, turtles, birds, snakes, and insects. Many of the animals are smiling, and some are given anthropomorphic treatment. For example, birds are shown smoking and butterflies are depicted wearing hats.

- In "Sophie Punt No. 2," Doucet draws the signs of the zodiac. Some of the images are sexual, such as the image of Scorpio that features a character proudly holding his massive phallus with one hand while posing with his other hand behind his head. Others are violent or feature disfiguration or mutilation, such as an image of Gemini, the twins, in which one twin is shown lazily biting the other on its shoulder; the second twin is inexplicably missing a hand.

- "Lost and Found Photos" utilizes a "found art" motif, as the photographs of most of the people drawn were found by Doucet in an abandoned photograph album in Berlin. These are accompanied by linocut illustrations, which were later assembled into Doucet's book *Melek* (2002). These illustrations are professional representations not imbued with the exaggerated features typical of Doucet's other work.

Artistic Style

Doucet's illustrations in this sketchbook-style publication are sharp, edgy, and transgressive. The characters' faces are exaggerated and at times grotesque, as she magnifies each mole, wrinkle, and hair. Noses are often bulbous, hair is frizzy, eyes are bloodshot, and lips are overblown. The first image on the inside cover features a woman and a man on either side of a stack of sharp-toothed gears, levers, and metal objects such as a large keyhole and a double-bell alarm clock. There is no title, caption, or other written message on the page. In this image, the woman is knock-kneed, has drooping breasts, and wears a low-cut dress; her face is wrinkled, and her eyes are completely black. The man on the opposite side stands in a cramped position, his hands hairy beneath diamond-shaped cuff links. His face also features deep wrinkles, protruding ears, and a frown. Most characters, particularly those in "Men of Our Times," are depicted in the same exaggerated style regardless of gender or context.

The book is a departure for Doucet, who worked previously in pen and ink. In *Long Time Relationship*, she uses woodcut, silk screen, and linocut techniques; some images are brush with ecoline ink on Arches paper, and some are placed directly onto the paper without penciling. Most images feature a title near the top or bottom of the page and the date stamped in red below the image.

In "Sophie Punt No. 2," Doucet uses a pink Italian sports newspaper as a background and works mostly in red ink. The symbol for each zodiac sign is rendered in blue and depicted in the corner of the image. "Sophie Punt No. 34" illustrates fortunes that Doucet found within fortune cookies. A fortune appears on the left page of each spread, while various characters act out the fortune on the right page. These images are colored in pink, yellow, blue, and white and are sometimes placed on top of words such as the recurring phrase "skin love," the meanings of which are not explained. One image places "skin love" alongside the phrase "free trial," and the character pictured is a woman with a pink head who literally cries her eyes out.

Themes

Doucet explores the ironic, comic, and grotesque sides of humanity in general and human relationships in particular. She is concerned with the relations between men and women and the personal sides of humanity that most people attempt to hide. Her drawings in the "Long Time Relationship" section in particular demonstrate an interest in the misrepresentation of the self and in the idea of promoting oneself through the uncomfortable form of newspaper personal advertisements. Her work in the "Lost and Found Photos" section shows true artistry, as she depicts loving human relationships and the beauty of the human face in powerful linocuts; this section provides an interesting juxtaposition to the sexual, surreal, and grotesque aspects of the rest of the artwork.

Julie Doucet

One of the most influential female cartoonists of the 1990's, Julie Doucet broke down many barriers in the comics industry, becoming a success with her plain-spoken and confessional autobiographical comics. Doucet developed her style in Montreal's fanzine community at the end of the 1980's, eventually launching her own title, *Dirty Plotte*, with Drawn and Quarterly in 1991. It was in *Dirty Plotte* that she published much of her best-known work (collected as *Lift Your Leg, My Fish is Dead!* [1993], *My Most Secret Desire* [1995], and *My New York Diary* [1999]). Her graphic novel *The Madame Paul Affair* was originally serialized in a Montreal newspaper. Since the early 2000's, Doucet has largely abandoned the production of comics, turning toward gallery art, although her comics diary (*Journal*) was published by L'Association in 2004 and in English as *365 Days* in 2007. Doucet's work has a rough-edged style. Her drawings are confrontational and cartoony, with dark overtones and crowded panels.

Impact

Although Doucet has been nominated for numerous awards for her other works, *Long Time Relationship* is one of her lesser-known comics. Much of the work in this collection was not originally intended for publication, such as the drawings that Doucet used to teach herself German. Since it is not a "graphic novel" in the traditional sense, it may be difficult for readers to pick up and understand unless they are already fans of Doucet.

Shannon Oxley

Further Reading

Coover, Colleen. *Small Favors* (2002).
DiMassa, Diane. *Hothead Paisan: Homicidal Lesbian Terrorist* (1993).
Gloeckner, Phoebe. *Diary of a Teenage Girl: An Account in Words and Pictures* (2001).

Bibliography

Chute, Hillary L. *Graphic Women: Life Narrative and Contemporary Comics*. New York: Columbia University Press, 2010.

Doucet, Julie. "Julie Doucet." Interview by Andrea Juno. *Dangerous Drawings: Interviews with Comix and Graphix Artists*. New York: Juno Books, 1997.

_____. "Julie Doucet's Secretions: A Tête-à-Tête." Interview by the staff of *The Comics Journal*. *The Comics Journal* 141 (April, 1991): 98-99.

Englemann, Jonas. "'Picture This': Disease and Autobiographic Narration in the Graphic Novels of David B and Julie Doucet." In *Comics as a Nexus of Cultures: Essays on the Interplay of Media, Disciplines, and International Perspectives*, edited by Mark Berninger, Jochen Ecke, and Gideon Haberkorn. Jefferson, N.C.: McFarland, 2010.

Miller, Ann, and Murray Pratt. "Transgressive Bodies in the Work of Julie Doucet, Fabrice Neaud, and Jean-Christophe Menu: Towards a Theory of the AutobioBD." *Belphegor: Popular Literature and Media Culture* 4, no. 1 (November, 2004).

See also: *Dykes to Watch Out For*; *Epileptic*; *The Complete Fritz the Cat*

LOST CAUSE:
JOHN WESLEY HARDIN, THE TAYLOR-SUTTON FEUD, AND RECONSTRUCTION TEXAS

Author: Jackson, Jack
Artist: Jack Jackson (illustrator); Samuel Yeates (cover artist)
Publisher: Kitchen Sink Press
First book publication: 1998

Publication History

Kitchen Sink Press published *Lost Cause* as a single volume in 1998, after Jack Jackson worked on the novel for over a decade. Jackson, who began his comics career under the pen name Jaxon, was part of a cadre of cartoonists collectively known as "The Texas Mafia." His early work *God Nose* (1964) is often credited as the first underground comic book. As a founder of underground publisher Rip Off Press, Jackson was a pivotal figure in both the business and artistic aspects of the underground "comix" movement.

Jackson's early work was social satire, as exemplified by *God Nose*. The satire quickly evolved into stronger social commentary on environmental issues, seen especially in his stories in the anthology *Slow Death* (1970), published by Last Gasp. His story "Nits Make Lice," from *Slow Death*, issue 7, was his first significant foray into merging his interest in Texas history with the art of the graphic narrative. Detailing the 1864 Sand Creek Massacre in brutal detail, this story laid the groundwork for his career as a historian working in both comics and prose. *Lost Cause* was Jackson's final historical work in the comics medium.

Plot

Lost Cause is a complex story comprising seven chapters. As a historical western, it provides an elaborate and detailed account of the Taylor-Sutton feud and also chronicles Texas's struggle toward statehood and its place in the United States before, during, and after the Civil War. The narrative can be divided into three primary story lines, which are intertwined. All are told in chronological order.

John Wesley Hardin. (Getty Images)

The first story line details Texas's involvement in the Civil War and its subsequent ostracism within the Union. African American soldiers applying their own standards of justice exacerbate this postwar situation, as do carpetbaggers and other mercenaries, both official and otherwise. Postwar Texas has a tentative legal status. Its senators are denied seating in the U.S. Senate gallery, and the actions of Texans are restricted unless they sign a "loyalty oath" repudiating their involvement with the South during the war.

The second narrative involves ranchers trying to survive after having their herds taken from them, first by rustlers and then by soldiers. Before the Civil War, the practice of taking herds was the result of "mavericking," named for the actions of a rancher named

Samuel A. Maverick, who refused to brand his cattle, possibly in order to stake claim to free-roaming cattle in addition to his own. After the Civil War, range wars erupted over this practice.

Mavericking ties into the third, most complex narrative, which chronicles the Taylor-Sutton feud. Beginning with a dispute between John Wesley Hardin and Buck Taylor over the outcome of a shooting match at a family gathering, the feud escalates between 1866 and 1874. This escalation both parallels and intersects with larger tensions in Texas. Hardin survives the range wars, gunfights, and lynchings of his kindred. He outlasts most of his kin, living long enough to produce heirs before being shot in the back while playing cards.

This final narrative is wrought with twists and turns and two elaborate family trees. The chronicles of both clans are filled with treachery and survival amid the rebirth of Texas as a state following the Civil War. Ultimately, the only measure of success is the peaceful life of Hardin's son in a peaceful Texas.

Characters

- *Creed Taylor*, arguably the protagonist, is the patriarch of the Taylor clan. He is approximately six feet tall, with thick black hair and a full beard. At first intent on keeping the peace, as evidenced by his arbitration of the shooting-match dispute that begins the feud, he later resolves to take any action necessary to defend his family. His efforts are exacerbated by the attempts of mercenaries and corrupt authorities to kill members of the Taylor family.

- *John Wesley Hardin* is the titular hero and antihero. Initially a stern-faced teenager, he grows into a dapper, cautious man who smiles once in the entire story. His role in the feud is minor until most of his family is killed. He becomes an outlaw and flees to Mexico at age eighteen, five years after the shooting match. Following his return, he serves sixteen years of a twenty-four-year prison sentence, writing a florid autobiography in an effort to "set the record straight." He is shot in the back on August 19, 1895.

- *Joe Tumlinson* is the archenemy of the Taylors. Though balding, he wears his hair long. He is

mustached, has a bit of a paunch, and has the overall air of being hardened by life. His efforts continue and escalate the Taylor-Sutton feud

---

Jack Jackson

Jaxon is the pen name of American cartoonist Jack Jackson, co-founder of Rip Off Press and one of the earliest underground cartoonists. Jackson's self-published comic *God Nose* (1964) is frequently credited as the first underground comic published in the United States. He is best known for an extensive body of work that details the history of Native Americans and Texans, including *Comanche Moon*, *El Alamo*, *Los Tejanos*, *The Secret of San Saba*, *Indian Lovers*, and *Lost Cause*. Though his work began with a degree of fictionalization, Jackson's historical comics became increasingly steeped in detailed research as his career progressed. He did not shy away from the depiction of human cruelty in the expansion of the American state and he eschewed what he regarded as political correctness, making his works quite controversial. His images are richly detailed, with extensive crosshatching and shading, and his figures have been strongly influenced by the EC artists of the 1950's.

---

after the early death of Billy Sutton. As Jackson notes in his afterword, the feud might more properly be called the Taylor-Tumlinson feud, as it is not until after Tumlinson's death that the feud ends. Tumlinson loses the horse race following the shooting contest, escalating tensions that had abated as the result of Creed's arbitration of the initial dispute.

Artistic Style

Jackson's art is realistically proportioned, and his subjects are posed. The layouts often resemble vintage photographs, even in action sequences. This is partially the result of his meticulous research and desire for historical accuracy.

The lines in Jackson's illustrations are evenly

weighted, only occasionally varying from their default weight. These lines are inked in heavy blacks, leading to the conclusion that Jackson's primary, almost exclusive, inking tool is the crow quill pen. Despite the scratchy quality this tool can sometimes give, Jackson's work is remarkably textured. Fabrics, furnishings, animals, metals, and even human blood all have definable visual characteristics. Almost all of the tone in *Lost Cause* is created using line work and hatching. There is little use of solid blacks, though the gray values used do tend be darker than 50 percent.

A rare exception to the use of the crow quill pen appears on page 107. This page consists of three banner panels. The first panel shows a trail drive in progress. The middle tier depicts the drivers camping for the night. This particular panel uses the uncommon device of Zip-A-Tone, a dot-pattern shading sheet now largely obsolete, to create the tonal value of the night sky. As the next day's action begins in the third panel, the use of lines and hatching for tone resumes.

Jackson's panel layouts are primarily straightforward six-panel grids with sufficient variation to hold the reader's eye. For example, page 86 begins with a horse and buggy running wild after its occupants have been shot. This wordless banner panel occupies less than one-quarter of the vertical space on the page. The remainder of the page is a standard six-panel grid that equally divides the remaining space.

Jackson depicts characters and scenes from a variety of distances and angles. Nonetheless, almost all his compositions fall on the horizontal plane, and they rarely include views from above or below.

Jackson's use of narrative caption blocks over panels is a recurring device with singular properties. The content echoes or reinforces the images, often seeming to function as stage directions. These captions have two basic visual styles. The first, slightly more dominant, is a bordered caption that intrudes slightly on the panel, either bannered or in the upper-left corner. These caption borders have decorative edges, often featuring scrolling in a manner similar to peeled bark, and wood-grain textures, regularly resembling vintage parchments or signs. The second visual style of caption, only slightly less prevalent, is a "floating" caption

set in the gutter, the space between panels. This device reinforces the narrative omniscience of these captions.

Aesthetically, the cumulative effect of Jackson's illustration and visual narrative is twofold. First, the sense of honesty and visual and historical accuracy resonates. Second, the work conveys a sense of melancholy and inevitability, despite the relatively minimal use of solid blacks.

Themes

Lost Cause deals as much with Texas history as it does with the story of Hardin. Jackson begins the narrative when Hardin is a child and does not introduce Hardin until page 44, when the future outlaw is thirteen years old. Hardin actually appears on fewer than fifty pages, and his story is a small but significant portion of the central narrative. The Taylor-Sutton feud is the crux of the graphic novel. That story, along with its interwoven subplots, reflects the central theme of power struggles in Texas's fight for autonomy and identity before, during, and after the Civil War.

Much of Jackson's oeuvre is concerned with a representation of Texas history from the standpoint of the underdog, and *Lost Cause* is no exception. Even in this context, however, no apology is made for the characters' actions. While the narrative attempts to empathize with Hardin and understand his motivations, Hardin's deeds and misdeeds are presented as matters of fact, rather than heroic or dastardly acts. No moral value is attached, beyond the author's decision about which events to report. Despite his profound efforts, however, Jackson does not claim objectivity in these matters, noting in his foreword, "My ancestors are buried in the feuding ground, and I am a product of what they were."

Impact

Given the page counts of its chapters, it is tempting to presume that *Lost Cause* might have been planned as a set of single-issue comics. The publishers of Jackson's previous underground work, Kitchen Sink Press and Last Gasp, indicated that they were receptive to that possibility. However, given the disappointment over the state of comics that Jackson expressed in interviews at the time of the release of *Lost Cause* and his desire to be accepted as a serious Texas historian, an initial plan for serialization seems unlikely.

Lost Cause was Jackson's fifth graphic novel on Texas history and the second to be initially published as a stand-alone volume. Last Gasp originally printed two of the novel's predecessors, *Comanche Moon* and *Recuerden el Alamo*, as separate series of three comics each. Reed Press collected *Comanche Moon* in a single volume in 2003, while *Recuerden el Alamo* was collected as *The Alamo: An Epic Told from Both Sides* and published by Paisano Graphics in 2002. The third work in Jackson's series on Texas history, *Secret of San Saba*, was originally published as a single volume, also from Kitchen Sink Press, in 1989. Mojo Press published Jackson's stand-alone volume on Sam Houston and the Cherokees, *Indian Lover*, in 1999.

While *Lost Cause* did not receive specific awards, Jackson was made a lifetime fellow of the Texas State Historical Association and inducted into the Texas Institute of Letters. Whether these honors were in recognition of Jackson's graphic narrative work, his prose research of Texas history, or both was not specified, although Jackson stated in interviews that he was primarily recognized for his prose work. Jackson was posthumously inducted into the Will Eisner Comic Awards Hall of Fame in 2011.

Diana Green

Further Reading

Jackson, Jack. *Comanche Moon* (2003).

McCulloch, Derek, and Shepherd Hendrix. *Stagger Lee* (2006).

Truman, Timothy. *Wilderness: The True Story of Simon Girty, the Renegade* (1989).

Bibliography

Estren, Mark James. *A History of Underground Comics.* 3d ed. Berkeley, Calif.: Ronin, 1993.

Rosenkranz, Patrick. *Rebel Visions: The Underground Comix Revolution, 1963-1975.* Seattle, Wash.: Fantagraphics Books, 2002.

Skinn, Dez. *Comix: The Underground Revolution.* New York: Thunder's Mouth Press, 2004.

Witek, Joseph. *Comic Books as History: The Narrative Art of Jack Jackson, Art Spiegelman, and Harvey Pekar.* Jackson: University Press of Mississippi, 1989.

See also: *Blueberry*; *Louis Riel*; *Nat Turner*

LOST GIRL

Author: Kanan, Nabiel
Artist: Nabiel Kanan (illustrator)
Publisher: NBM
First book publication: 1999

Publication History

Nabiel Kanan's *Lost Girl* was first released as a graphic novel in 1999 by NBM Publishing. The same publishing house reissued the novel in 2001. Kanan had previously published *Exit* (1996) and followed up *Lost Girl* with the critically acclaimed *The Birthday Riots* (2001) and *The Drowners* (2006).

Plot

As *Lost Girl* opens, a girl stumbles aimlessly through the woods. The scene shifts to a family, traveling by car to a caravan site for a vacation. Lost, they stop; the parents leave the car to ask directions, while their older daughter, Beth, walks to the local supermarket for some batteries. Beth sees a strange girl sitting on the trunk of a car outside the store. Finding what she needs, Beth proceeds to the register but pauses to witness an encounter between the strange girl and a random man. The girl passes the man a note and leaves. The man, distracted, pays and leaves, throwing the note on the ground. Beth pays for her batteries and, outside, reads the note, signed by P.T.O., which says a naked girl is waiting in the alley for the man. Beth peeks around a corner into the alley and witnesses the strange girl and the random man having sex. The strange girl then steals the man's car and speeds away. Beth returns to her family, and, after some time, they arrive at the caravan site. During the night, Beth awakens and sees the strange girl peering through a window in her room.

Beth's family meets up with her friend Caitlin's family the next morning. Caitlin brings some marijuana and hides it in Beth's room. The two girls avoid spending the day with their families, saying they will relax at the beach. Caitlin does so, but Beth becomes distracted after seeing the strange girl, P.T.O. Beth follows her deep into the woods and sees her enter a house. After the girl leaves, Beth tries to enter the house but

Lost Girl. (Courtesy of Nantier Beall Minoustchine Publishing)

cannot. At the beach together the next day, Caitlin and Beth both find themselves attracted to a local named Paul, who invites them to a party that evening. Paul, interested in Beth, asks Caitlin to help the caterers set up the party while he and Beth leave together.

The next morning, Beth goes to the beach alone. The strange girl appears and tells Beth to follow her to see a patch of flowers in bloom. The strange girl has stolen Caitlin's marijuana from the trailer. The girls agree to meet the next morning, and both smoke the marijuana. The strange girl returns on a horse, extends her hand, and pulls Beth onto the horse. They ride wildly along the beach and through the forest. The strange girl reveals she lives in a caravan at the site and that she has been looking after the house in the woods while the family to whom it belongs is away. Beth and the strange girl part ways, but not before the strange girl suggests they meet again before Beth returns home with her family. After the strange girl leaves, Beth notices a pair of glasses on the ground. She takes them with her and sees, to her dismay, the same glasses worn by the young girl featured on lost-child posters around their caravan site.

Beth fears that the lost child has been taken by the strange girl and hidden in the house in the woods. She dreams of people searching for the girl and the lost child banging on a door. The next day, though, Beth learns that the child has been found and is safe. Beth visits the house in the woods and learns that the family occupying it has not been away and that no one has been watching their home. Beth and her family leave the caravan site and return home. Beth's mother asks her to sort through a trunk of old possessions. Beth looks to her open window, through which a series of butterflies enter her room. Meanwhile, Caitlin arrives and asks to see Beth. When Caitlin arrives in Beth's room, Beth is nowhere to be found. The final cells of the story show Beth walking through the field of flowers she visited with the strange girl. The last scene shows the door that Beth has seen in her dreams; however, the door is now open.

Characters

- *Beth*, the main character, is well behaved and struggling with the process of maturation, both emotionally and physically.
- *P.T.O.*, a.k.a. *the strange girl*, is a character who causes Beth to have a self-awakening. Whether P.T.O. is a real character or a figment of Beth's imagination remains unclear.
- *Caitlin*, Beth's friend, is a rebellious teen who smokes marijuana and becomes jealous when a young man pays more attention to Beth than to her.
- *Paul*, a local young man, receives attention from both Beth and Caitlin. He favors Beth.
- *Anne* is Beth's mother.
- *Jack* is Beth's father.
- *Sally* is Beth's younger sister.

Artistic Style

Kanan's artistic style is clean and concise. The careful employment of vertical and horizontal hashing in most panels culminates in an effect that draws careful attention to the plot and the issues Kanan's work explores. The absence of color requires readers to carefully analyze each panel to fully appreciate the nuances of Kanan's illustrations, such as the arch of a character's eyebrow or his or her stance in a given situation.

Most panels contain a grid that includes between six and ten cells; though, in some cases, the panel is one cell. Kanan employs this technique rarely in *Lost Girl* and does so to emphasize key moments in the story. Only seven pages serve as one-cell panels and capture the strange girl and random man have sex in the alley; Beth and the strange girl alone together on the beach; the strange girl arriving on a horse; Beth and the strange girl riding the horse together; Beth's father asking her to pose on a donkey with her sister for a picture; the strange girl's face; and finally, Beth standing alone on the beach before returning home with her family. Each of these moments is symbolic and crucial in demonstrating Beth's coming-of-age while on a summer vacation with her family.

Themes

Written for a mature audience, Kanan's *Lost Girl* explores themes typical of the bildungsroman genre: sexual awakening, testing boundaries, and developing a personal identity. One of the first topics Kanan explores openly in *Lost Girl* is sexual awakening. When Beth visits the supermarket, her attention is arrested by the strange girl sitting on the trunk of a car outside the store. Beth pays careful attention to the strange girl's appearance, evidenced by the way in which Kanan structures the panel. In Beth's first encounter with the strange girl Kanan explores the girl's body in detail: one cell of the panel provides a view of the girl from behind, and the other two cells emphasize her shapely figure from the front, clothed in only a bikini and wearing a large, dangling cross necklace. The strange girl also smokes a cigarette, which, by the look on her face, intrigues Beth. Beth soon watches the strange girl engage in wild sex with the random man from the supermarket. When Beth and her family arrive at the caravan site, she watches longingly as a man and woman slightly older than her embrace and kiss. She later becomes interested in Paul, an older local boy who, Kanan implies, tries to seduce her. All of these instances combine to poignantly capture the longing for physical contact and pleasure felt by teens navigating the turbulence of puberty.

Another important theme clearly present in *Lost Girl* is testing boundaries. Beth challenges restrictions that have been established for her and takes opportunities to rebel. The most obvious occurrence of this boundary testing concerns Beth and the use of marijuana. Kanan establishes Beth as an innocent girl who follows the rules. When Caitlin arrives at Beth's caravan and hides her marijuana in Beth's room, Caitlin teases her for not knowing a slang term for marijuana. Caitlin then jokingly tells Beth's parents that she came to buy drugs from Beth, a comment that makes Beth's parents laugh since they assume their daughter would never experiment with drugs. Beth is irritated by her parents' response. When she is alone with the strange

---

Nabiel Kanan

One of the most enigmatic cartoonists to emerge in the 1990's—he does not grant interviews—Nabiel Kanan made his early reputation on the strength of his self-published *Exit*, a highly stylized series of comics detailing the lives of British teenagers waiting to take their A-levels. *Lost Girl*, serialized in the early 2000's, follows a young girl on vacation, while *The Birthday Riots* traced the expediency of politics against the idealism of the past. Kanan was nominated for the Eisner Award for both of these works. In 2006, he published *The Drowners*, which tells the story of a powerful man with a shameful past. Kanan's stories are wrought with intrigue and mystery, and he frequently uses flashbacks to develop suspense across the length of his narrative. His earliest comics are notable for their extensive use of blacks and for images that seemed more impressionistic than strictly representational. More recently he has migrated toward a sparse, cartoony style.

---

girl on the beach, she seizes the opportunity to try the drug, likely to disprove the conceptions her friends and family have of her. Kanan reminds readers that simply assuming one will never test a boundary may be all that is necessary to persuade that person to do so.

The crux of *Lost Girl* is Beth's struggle to develop her personal identity. The novel opens with a story line about a lost girl; this girl is a double for Beth, who is also lost figuratively. All protagonists in coming-of-age stories feel lost at some point and seek to establish their identities. The strange girl is also a doppelgänger for Beth; though she may be housed only in Beth's imagination, she embodies Beth's desires to separate herself from her family and to indulge in more adult behaviors, including sexual encounters and experimentation with illegal substances. Whether or not the strange girl exists, Beth is plagued by dreams about searching for the lost girl, which symbolize Beth's own feelings about her identity. Kanan also shows Beth dreaming of a door, behind which is the lost girl, who pounds and shakes the door in the hope of being found. Significantly, the final illustration of the novel is the door, only it is open, but leading to darkness. Kanan suggests Beth has finally opened the door and found herself; however, she is plunged into darkness because the person she is becoming is one unfamiliar to both herself and to those who know her.

Impact

Kanan's risky stories and willingness to confront sensitive issues in his works has made an impact in the comics field by encouraging other writers to explore similar issues unabashedly. His clean black-and-white illustrations remind readers and artists that the strength of a graphic novel emanates from the complexity and beauty of its story, not necessarily from splashes of color.

Karley Adney

Further Reading

Clowes, Daniel. *Ghost World* (1997).
Kanan, Nabiel. *Exit* (1996).
Thompson, Craig. *Blankets* (2003).

Bibliography

Gravett, Paul. "Creator Profile: Nabiel Kanan." *Paul Gravett.* http://www.paulgravett.com/index.php/profiles/creator/nabiel_kanan.

"*Lost Girl*." Review of *Lost Girl*, by Nabiel Kanan. *Publishers Weekly*, January 1, 2003. http://www.publishersweekly.com/978-1-56163-229-9.

Phipps, Keith. "*Lost Girl*." Review of *Lost Girl*, by Nabiel Kanan. *A.V. Club*, March 29, 2002. http://www.avclub.com/articles/nabiel-kanan-lost-girl,6301.

See also: *Blankets*; *Ghost World*; *Hey, Wait...*

LOST GIRLS

Author: Moore, Alan
Artist: Melinda Gebbie (illustrator); Todd Klein (letterer)
Publishers: Kitchen Sink Press; Top Shelf Comics
First serial publication: 1991-1992
First book publication: 1995

Publication History

The *Lost Girls* series first appeared in *Taboo* magazine, starting in 1991. After a six-issue run, writer Alan Moore and illustrator Melinda Gebbie continued to work on *Lost Girls* without immediate serialized publishing, choosing instead to release the completed product all at once. However, the six stories from *Taboo* were reprinted in two graphic novel volumes by Kitchen Sink Press in the mid-1990's. Sixteen years after Moore and Gebbie first began *Lost Girls*, the complete text was published by Top Shelf Comics, debuting at the 2006 Comic-Con International: San Diego. This version was sold in a slipcase format that separated the story into three books. In 2009, Top Shelf released *Lost Girls* in a single hardcover format.

Plot

Clearly aimed at an adult audience, *Lost Girls* began as an attempt to create an alternative form of pornography from that which is typically found in the mainstream media, one that is nonexploitative, emotionally resonant, and deeply contemplative about the roles that sex and sexual fantasy play in the average life. *Lost Girls* tells the story of the physical and emotional relationships that develop among three well-known literary characters—Alice from Lewis Carroll's *Alice's Adventures in Wonderland* (1865), Dorothy from L. Frank Baum's *The Wonderful Wizard of Oz* (1900), and Wendy from the Peter Pan stories—who meet through a chance encounter at an Austrian hotel during the buildup to World War I (1914-1918).

Shortly after arriving at the hotel, Alice is immediately drawn to the free-spirited Dorothy, quickly taking her under her wing. Driven by curiosity and a desire for self-understanding, Wendy soon joins them. The

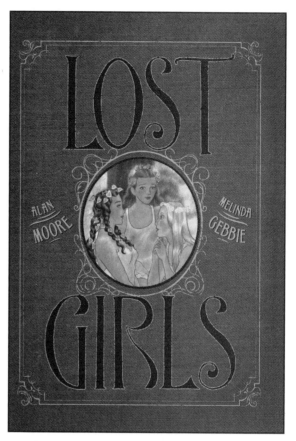

Lost Girls. (Courtesy of Top Shelf Productions)

three women take turns telling their personal sexual histories. Each story, told in flashback, represents a sexualized reinterpretation of the works in which these characters originally appear. The stories kindle further passion among the three women and quickly become a driving force behind the physical and emotional intimacy that develops among them.

Dorothy's story chronicles her sexual awakening, beginning with her discovery of masturbation, which leads to her first orgasm, during a tornado. Driven by a newfound sexual curiosity, Dorothy pursues relationships with three farmhands. Here, the mindless scarecrow, heartless tin man, and cowardly lion of *The Wizard of Oz* are reflected in Dorothy's first three lovers: one who is not intelligent enough for her, one who is not kind enough for her, and one who is not brave enough for her. Dorothy's sexual activities—which later include an orgy with all three men—come to the attention of her parents. This eventually leads Dorothy into an affair with her father.

Wendy's sexual awakening story begins with a glimpse into a forest in a nearby park when she is just sixteen years old. She sees a young man having sex. The young man, Peter, follows her home and climbs into her bedroom at night. He teaches Wendy and her brothers how to stimulate themselves sexually. Enthralled, Wendy and her brothers search for Peter the next day in the park and find him. This leads to a series of sexual encounters between Wendy, Peter, Peter's sister Annabel, and the "Lost Boys" of Peter's gang. However, this also brings Wendy to the attention of a neighborhood pedophile, who happens to have a hooked hand (like Captain Hook). Annabel is soon found dead, presumably killed by the pedophile, and Wendy begins experiencing sexual fantasies that she finds increasingly depraved and disgusting. After narrowly escaping the pedophile, Wendy changes her ways and settles into domestic life as a wife and mother.

Alice's story begins with sexual abuse. A family friend abuses her at a young age, which results in a sense of alienation and the loss of her childhood. Alice is sent to a girls' school and becomes embroiled in a series of lesbian sexual experiences. While at school, Alice falls in love with a teacher and eventually goes to work as her live-in assistant. The teacher exposes Alice to a world of sexual games. During this time, Alice becomes a drug addict and prostitute who helps facilitate the further exploitation of other minors, much to her regret. She is sent to a mental institution before accepting a sort of social banishment to South Africa for the purposes of preserving the good name of her family.

As seen here, the stories reveal progressively the dark nature of each character's sexual past. Alice is deeply traumatized by her sexual abuse; Wendy's sexual curiosity leads her into a dangerous situation and lifestyle; and Dorothy's incestuous affair with her father destroys her family. However, through their continued affairs with one another and with other patrons and staff of the Hotel Himmelgarten, the adult Dorothy,

Alice, and Wendy now achieve sexual expression and emotional healing through the sharing of their stories. During this time, it is revealed that the staff members of the hotel are actually prostitutes assembled by the manager, Monsieur Rougeur, to bring sexual fantasy to life.

This period of discovery is cut short by the outbreak of World War I, and the women are forced to part ways. The novel ends with soldiers arriving at the abandoned hotel and burning it to the ground. Shortly thereafter, the same location is seen as the site of an undisclosed battle, a place of love having now become a place of war.

Volumes

- *Lost Girls:* Book One (1995). Collects issues 1-3. Features the introductions of Alice, Dorothy, and Wendy, flashing back to their previous sexual experiences, which outline the central motifs of the novel.
- *Lost Girls:* Book Two (1996). Collects issues 4-6. Alice, Dorothy, and Wendy begin their affair. By doing so, they are able to deal with the negative or dubious sexual experiences of their past and attain a level of sexual fulfillment before World War I cuts short their escapades.

Characters

- *Lady Alice Fairchild,* a.k.a. *Alice* from *Alice's Adventures in Wonderland,* the first protagonist, is an upper-class, gray-haired woman in her fifties with sharp features and blue eyes. She was sexually assaulted at a young age, an experience that led her to opium addiction and prostitution and, eventually, to be institutionalized. Recently released, she lives off her family's vast fortune and travels at her leisure. The most sexually experienced of the three main characters, she initiates the physical and emotional relationship among the three women.
- *Miss Dorothy Gale,* a.k.a. *Dorothy* from *The Wonderful Wizard of Oz,* the second protagonist, is a nineteen-year-old woman with freckles, brown eyes, and curly red hair. The only notable American character in the series, she is free-spirited, adventurous, and very

much in keeping with the archetypal "farm girl" in terms of her mannerisms, speech, and behavior. Her working-class upbringing and eagerness to experience the world immediately earn her the attention of Lady Alice Fairchild, who takes her on as both a lover and a sort of protégée.

- *Mrs. Wendy Potter*, a.k.a. *Wendy* from *Peter Pan*, the final protagonist, is a middle-aged woman with black hair, green eyes, and a rounded face. Feeling stifled within her loveless, middle-class marriage, she is the most reserved of the three women, yet her sense of curiosity and her desire for self-understanding eventually draw her into a relationship with Dorothy and Alice.

- *Mr. Harold Potter* is Wendy's husband. A fifty-something man with gray hair and a beard, he harbors deep sexual desire for his wife, but because of his repressed nature, he is unable to express this desire and instead treats Wendy like a friend or sister. His sexual desire is then channeled toward pornography, masturbation, and, eventually, an affair with Rolf Bauer.

- *Captain Rolf Bauer* is a handsome young Austrian soldier with a slender gait and slick black hair. Though he is a minor character in the text, he inspires the sexual desire of his two main partners in the novel, Dorothy and Harold. He also harbors an intense sexual fetish for women's shoes. With World War I looming, his presence adds tension to the narrative.

- *Monsieur Rougeur* is a relatively short, round man with carefully coiffed black and gray hair and a mustache. The manager of the Hotel Himmelgarten, he is an ambiguous character. He withholds the truth from other characters and has a natural tendency to embrace fantasy. He is a perhaps unreliable narrator, yet much of his narration concerns essential details that the reader needs in order to piece together Moore's commentary on sexuality, fantasy, and pornography. Because he is fallible, Moore is able to maintain a more ambiguous stance on many of these subjects.

Melinda Gebbie

Melinda Gebbie trained as a fine artist and began creating comics in the early 1970's, contributing stories to underground anthologies including *Wimmen's Comix*, *Wet Satin*, and *Anarchy Comics*. Her 1977 solo book, *Fresca Zizis*, was prosecuted by UK customs in the 1980's alongside other books published by Knockabout and was made illegal to possess in that country. In the early 1990's she began collaborating with writer Alan Moore on *Lost Girls*, a pornographic epic in which the female heroes from beloved children's books share sexual experiences. That work was initially serialized in *Taboo* and eventually collected as a three-volume graphic novel in 2006. With Moore, whom she married in 2007, she created the Cobweb stories in *Tomorrow Stories* from 1999 to 2002. Gebbie's visual style is remarkably ornate, detailed, and florid. She draws strongly on painterly influences, particularly from the first half of the twentieth century.

Artistic Style

Lost Girls is divided into three books, each with ten chapters, with each chapter comprising eight pages. The eight-page format is an homage to the "eight pager" (or Tijuana bible), a form of bootleg comics pornography that emerged during the 1920's. Unlike the vast majority of his comics work, Moore did not draft scripts for *Lost Girls* but instead formed a closer collaboration with Gebbie that involved Moore creating thumbnail sketches of each panel, then consulting directly with Gebbie in the production of the visual imagery.

Lost Girls features some of the most ambitious visual artistry in comics history. Gebbie adopts a distinct visual style for each protagonist's story. Dorothy's stories feature a wide, three-panel-per-page layout, emphasizing the pastoral nature of her Kansas farm upbringing. The colors are warm and earthy, accompanied by smooth and round thin lines and lots of shading. Wendy's stories are rendered in sharp contrast to Dorothy's: These pages depict a four-panel sequence with a wide panel on top featuring full black-and-white contrast, followed by three long vertical panels with full color underneath; here, a thick black line is used for all characters and shading is minimal. This densely structured panel arrangement conveys the sense of structure and order that exists in Wendy's world. Alice's stories are all rendered using three panels per page, with each panel shaped like an ellipsis. This creates a large amount of negative space (the white areas in the margins), which, in turn, suggests distance and confinement. Thus, the paneling mirrors Alice's own emotional turmoil and sense of self-removal following her sexual assault. Gebbie incorporates a wide array of color in these sections, with greater emphasis on secondary colors and dissonant color schemes.

In scenes set in the present, the paneling grid varies wildly according to the needs of the story but also is frequently affected by proximity to a flashback. A scene preceding a Wendy flashback, for example, will frequently take on some, if not all, characteristics of the visual style used for Wendy's stories.

Themes

In the same way that Moore's *Watchmen* is a superhero comic about superheroes, *Lost Girls* is a pornographic comic about pornography. Through processes of self-awareness and self-reflexivity, Moore and Gebbie actively interrogate the role that pornography plays in people's lives. The text features a book within a book. Rougeur places a pornographic book in every hotel room and, as such, the reader watches the effect that this pornography has on the various guests. Furthermore, the three protagonists take turns telling their respective stories of sexual discovery. While one tells the tale, the other two use the story to arouse their passions in order to create and sustain their sexual affairs with one another. Thus, they create their own pornography in order to enhance their sexual encounters. Additionally, the characters are often seen simply discussing the various effects that pornography (in a wide variety of forms) has on them. Finally, by sexualizing iconic characters from children's literature, Moore and Gebbie hint at the subversive sexuality at play within stories that are traditionally perceived as pure and wholesome. The implication is that a closer analysis of *Peter Pan*, *Alice's Adventures in Wonderland*, and *The Wonderful*

Wizard of Oz can reveal the erotic undertones that these stories contain.

As an obvious secondary theme, *Lost Girls* explores the power of sex and sexuality. Moore and Gebbie portray sex at its best as a transcendent force, a great source of joy and emotional healing. At its worst, sex is portrayed as powerfully destructive: a source of trauma, emotional scarring, unfulfilled desire, and shame. The difference between the two potential results seems to be a combination of consent and maturity, which are closely related. When sex is fully understood and embraced by the characters, it dramatically enhances the quality of their lives. When it is not, the results can be downright tragic. Either way, sex is seen to have a tremendous capacity to define the lives of the characters. Furthermore, the juxtaposition of the sexual escapades at the Hotel Himmelgarten with the forthcoming world war hint at the idea that war is simply the result of poorly channeled sexual energies. This juxtaposition is made most clear on the last page of the novel, which depicts a disemboweled soldier with a grotesque and gaping wound that resembles a vagina.

Impact

Lost Girls picks up where the "comix" movement of the 1960's and 1970's left off. Like the works of Robert Crumb in particular, *Lost Girls* defies social and cultural taboos for the sake of creating an open dialogue about sex and sexual fantasy. The length and breadth of *Lost Girls*, however, far surpasses that of Crumb's stories. In this sense, *Lost Girls* offers a more mature perspective on the same sexual issues that underground comics artists were exploring during the 1960's and 1970's. Furthermore, by incorporating fictional and historical figures, *Lost Girls* continues the exploration of intertextuality that has defined much of Moore's work throughout the 1990's and 2000's, as seen most prominently in *The League of Extraordinary Gentlemen* (1999-   ). The impact of *Lost Girls* on the next generation of comics artists has yet to be seen, but the novel has the potential to serve as an important benchmark for discussions of sex and sexuality within the comics form.

J. Andrew Deman

Further Reading

Brown, Chester. *The Playboy* (1992).

Crumb, Robert, et al. *Zap Comix* (1968-2005).

Hernandez, Gilbert, Jaime Hernandez, and Mario Hernandez. *Love and Rockets* (1982-1996).

Bibliography

Alaniz, Jose. "Speaking the 'Truth' of Sex: Moore and Gebbie's *Lost Girls*." *International Journal of Comic Art* 8, no. 2 (Fall, 2006): 307-318.

Hatfield, Charles. "ImageSexT: A Roundtable on *Lost Girls*, A Review and a Response." *ImageTexT: Interdisciplinary Comics Studies* 3, no. 3 (2007).

Wolk, Douglas. "Alan Moore's 'Literary' Porn." *Publishers Weekly* 253, no. 18 (May 1, 2006): 22-23.

See also: *The Playboy*; *Love and Rockets*; *From Hell*

LOUIS

Author: Chalmers, John
Artist: Sandra Marrs (illustrator)
Publisher: Metaphrog
First book publication: 2000-2010

Publication History

Beginning in the mid-1990's, Sandra Marrs and John Chalmers, working under the pseudonym "Metaphrog," self-published the serial *Strange Weather Lately*. It took an enormous amount of effort for the two to self-publish and promote the bimonthly series, so when *Strange Weather* was completed, the duo decided against serializing their next work and focused instead on producing a book-length comic. Marrs had an early concept of creating a story about a character trapped inside a cell. This idea eventually morphed into Louis and his strange, closely monitored world.

Metaphrog soon leveraged their early experience in the comics industry and published *Louis: Red Letter Day* in 2000. Glasgow-based printer Clydeside Press handled the early volumes of the series, and the book was distributed with the support of local businesses and Diamond Comic Distributors. The first volume was highly acclaimed and received Eisner Award nominations for Best Graphic Album—New and Best Title for a Younger Audience. Their early success encouraged them to continue the series and, in 2001 and 2002, they released *Lying to Clive* and *The Clown's Last Words*. The third volume of *Louis* became the first graphic novel to ever receive funding from the Scottish Arts Council.

In 2004, as Metaphrog prepared to release the fourth volume of the series, *Dreams Never Die*, the husband-and-wife team collaborated with musicians Hey and múm to create a soundtrack to accompany and complement their work. Marrs also created a short animated preview of the book, hand drawing the frames individually with a tablet computer in a process that took months to create just two minutes of animation. While Metaphrog continue to self-publish all their work, *Dreams Never Die* was published in association with the label Fat Cat Records. By this time,

Louis: Night Salad. (Courtesy of Metaphrog)

Louis's popularity had outgrown Clydeside Press, and Metaphrog began using other printers; nevertheless, a small portion of *Louis* books continues to be printed in Glasgow. In 2010, Metaphrog released the series' fifth installment, *Night Salad*, which was nominated for an Eisner Award for Best Coloring. In 2011, the duo released a completely redrawn version of *Red Letter Day*, which had been out of print for some time.

Plot

Following the end of *Strange Weather Lately*, Marrs and Chalmers decided to produce a story that was lighter and more accessible than the photorealistic, black-and-white serial. Their intention was to create a story with the apparent simplicity of a children's book but without a clear, simple structure or a resolute, happy ending. The series opens in Louis's strange neighborhood of identical houses, separated by tall fences. Louis is completely isolated within his home, with his mechanical bird Formulaic Companion, or FC, as his only real contact. Louis spends his days manufacturing fruit for a living. His neighbors, the

Quidnuncs, have been screening Louis's mail, intercepting Louis's letters to his aunt, and posing as Louis's aunt in that correspondence. It is never clear who is in charge of Louis's town, Hamlet, but its citizens are all closely monitored; one day, Louis is inexplicably removed from his home and sent to a penal colony. At the prison, known as the Bee Farm, he befriends a bee named Clive. Everyone is subjected to the strange hierarchy at the farm, and the "bees with disease" suffer the most, separated at some distance from everyone else. Eventually, Louis is released and allowed to return home.

After Louis returns from the farm, everyone in Hamlet receives an invitation to a mandatory Fun Day Out, which requires everyone to enter a competition to design a game. Louis is forced to attend weekly sessions at the Cheeseman Information Agency, where he is tortured with various cheeses and questioned about his relationship with the mysterious "underground."

Back at Louis's home, the Quidnuncs continue to intercept Louis's letters to his aunt and appear to steal several of his design ideas. The Quidnuncs then prevent Louis from attending the Fun Day Out festivities by instead directing him toward a dangerous mine, where Louis falls into a deep hole. At the bottom of the hole, Louis finds the bodies of several dead clowns. He discovers a note from one of the clowns describing her feelings of being disconnected with her audience since the advent of the "image boxes." Louis is then rescued by a girl with colored hair, and she tells him that someone is planning to blow up the rollercoaster at the fair with the first-prize winners on it. At the "unfair," the Quidnuncs are accepting first prize after submitting Louis's game when Louis and the girl ride in on a giant rubber spider to disperse the crowd before the bomb explodes.

Louis continues to worry about his Aunt Alison. The Quidnuncs have been sending Louis letters posing as

Louis: Night Salad. (Courtesy of Metaphrog)

his aunt, pretending she is ill. Louis has not received a letter in a long time and is beginning to worry. When the mechanical surveillance system, "The Monitor," breaks down in front of Louis's home, he takes the opportunity to run out into the streets in a desperate attempt to find his aunt. Guards with pointed white hoods respond quickly to the scene, and they begin looking for Louis with robotic dogs and flies. Just when Louis begins to feel desperately lost and confused, the girl appears and leads him through an underground system of tunnels to his aunt's neighborhood. When Louis finds Aunt Alison's house, it appears to have been abandoned for some time. The camouflaged, hooded guards sneak up on Louis and spray him with chemicals to disorient him. Before Louis is captured by a band of guards led by an Adolf Hitler look-alike, he is rescued by the people of the underground.

Louis returns home to his work, but trips while handling toxic chemicals, accidentally poisoning FC. The bird becomes mute and dangerously ill, and Louis is consumed by guilt and anxiety. Louis tries to find relief in books or in his imagination, but he becomes increasingly sick. He reaches out to Aunt Alison, and the Quidnuncs respond that the only cure is from the mythological fruit of the raining tree. The letter warns Louis that he has only a few days to save his friend, sending Louis into a frenzy. He runs from the house, desperate to do something to help FC, but he has become so ill that he collapses in the front yard.

Louis drifts into a dream in which he teams with a guide to find the raining tree. Even in the dream, the Quidnuncs are never far behind, constantly tracking Louis. Louis and his guide become great friends, but, then, a pair of pink clouds begins circling them. The clouds surround Louis's friend and dissolve him, rendering him a pile of dust. As Louis grieves, he notices a new star forming, and the star leads him to the raining tree.

The dream begins to dissolve as Louis hears FC singing; Louis slowly comes to consciousness. The girl with purple hair and a woman find Louis facedown in his front yard, and they restore him and FC to health. As Louis is recovering, the girl teaches him about seed germination; he is skeptical, however, and when he

gets well, he returns to the "normal" way of manufacturing fruit. However, he does have the chemical vats removed from his yard, and begins to prefer fruit grown from seeds to the heavily advertised and ubiquitous Mort™ cereal. Through quiet rebellions like these and in his imagination, Louis is able to temporarily escape the oppressive environment of Hamlet.

Volumes

- *Louis: Red Letter Day* (2000). Features Louis's early adventures in Hamlet and the schemes of the Quidnuncs against him. Explains some of the strange elements of Louis's world.
- *Louis: Lying to Clive* (2001). Tells the story of Louis's imprisonment in Bee Hall and the oppressive conformity there. Introduces the character Clive and Louis's developing friendship with him.
- *Louis: The Clown's Last Words* (2002). Features the story of the Fun Day Out scheme and Louis's creative process in designing his game. The Quidnuncs attempt to ruin Louis's fun day but do not succeed.
- *Louis: Dreams Never Die* (2004). Tells the story of Louis's attempt to sneak past the Monitor in order to find Aunt Alison. Includes a CD with an accompanying soundtrack created by musicians múm and Hey.
- *Louis: Night Salad* (2010). Features the story of a terrible accident, FC's deadly sickness, and Louis's terrifying vision quest to save his friend.

Characters

- *Louis*, the protagonist is a small rounded character with babyish features and a red jumpsuit printed with the number 3120. He is extremely imaginative and longs for a deeper connection with the few people in his life. Through his dreams, imagination, and friendship with FC, he is able to create some happiness in his isolated world.
- *Formulaic Companion* is Louis's mechanical pet bird, who lives in a ringed yellow cage. FC appears to be made of blue metal, with wings and

long legs. FC loves Louis and singing but has difficulty understanding Louis.

- *Jerk Quidnunc*, the antagonist, is Louis's neighbor and has orange hair and a moustache. He wears glasses and a white shirt with a blue bow tie. He has a sick and strange sense of humor and enjoys spying on Louis and causing him pain.
- *Clean Quidnunc*, the antagonist, is Louis's neighbor and a relative of Jerk. Clean is bald and wears a white shirt. He seems to be obsessed with money and status, and shares Jerk's lowbrow, slapstick sense of humor.
- *Aunt Alison* is ostensibly Louis's aunt, though it is unclear whether she is an actual person or if she has been invented entirely by the Quidnuncs to tease Louis. Louis receives regular letters from her, which have actually been written by the Quidnuncs.
- *The Postman*, the antagonist, has a brown moustache and wears a blue postal uniform. It is unclear what the motives of the postman are and how closely involved he is with the power structure of Louis's world. He collaborates with the Quidnuncs in screening Louis's mail.
- *Clive*, the protagonist, is dressed in a hooded bee costume. He is Louis's best friend at the bee farm, and he hopes to learn how to fly, practicing often.
- *The Girl*, the protagonist, is a young girl with long hair that is shaded a different color in each volume. This girl functions as the deus ex machina in the story, often saving Louis and FC at the last moment.

Artistic Style

All five volumes of the *Louis* series have been illustrated by Marrs. While the panels depicting Louis's everyday life are often clear and straightforward, they are interspersed with and overtaken by Louis's rich daydreams. Even with the series' apparent artistic simplicity, Marrs complicates the story by slowly revealing new elements piece-by-piece, showing unfamiliar objects at strange angles, making it difficult for the reader to immediately grasp what is happening. In Louis's dreams, simple objects in his world take on a rich symbolism as they move and morph in his imagination. The first three volumes feature hand-painted illustrations

---

Metaphrog

Sandra Marrs and John Chalmers are a married couple who create comics under the pen name Metaphrog. In the mid-1990's, the duo produced *Strange Weather Lately*, which followed the story of Martin Nitram as he tried to mount a production of a cursed play. The work was drawn in a naturalist style and featured existential overtones. However, the work that they are best known for was a radical departure from *Strange Weather Lately*. *Louis* is a series of graphic novels featuring a round-faced naïf who lives with a mechanical bird. The first volume, *Red Letter Day*, was published in 2000 and the duo has produced a new volume every few years. The stories themselves are quite simple and feature a great deal of fantasy and whimsy. The series has a slightly enigmatic quality that makes it appealing to adults as well as children, and the books have become cult favorites.

---

done in gouache. For the last two volumes, Marrs creates bolder, more vivid illustrations by switching to acrylic inks. The rich colors of the acrylics are better able to render the lush world of Louis's imagination. In fact, the re-released edition of *Red Letter Day* has been completely redrawn in this style.

The series largely follows a nine-panel grid pattern, which matches the regulated and routine lifestyle of the people of Hamlet. Louis's freewheeling imagination, however, is able to break from this structure and tumbles freely across the page, surrounding and incorporating his bleak reality into beautiful and unrestricted images. As the series progresses, Marrs and Chalmers increasingly deviate from the grid pattern, creating a more complex rhythm to the storytelling and accentuating the emotional impact of the story. When Louis begins feeling ill, the panels sway back and forth to underscore his nausea. After Louis's friend and guide is vaporized by the clouds, Louis stands alone in a center panel surrounded by negative space, visually underscoring his loss, isolation, and lack of direction. Despite the clarity and simplicity of this style, the subtle changes to the color scheme, page layouts, and content of the images impart a larger meaning to the series and deepen its emotional impact.

Themes

One of the major themes of the *Louis* series is the difficulty of self-expression and communication in the modern world. As much as Louis loves FC, the two have a fundamental inability to communicate with each other, which often causes Louis to feel lonely. Even Louis's intentions with his friend sometimes get lost in translation. Louis is often caught trying to find the right word or some way to truly express himself.

The Quidnuncs's constant tampering with Louis's mail also touches upon this theme of a modern disconnection in communication. Louis naïvely accepts their bogus correspondence as real, because he has had no real relationship with his aunt against which to gauge it. Conversely, the series also emphasizes the power and importance of words. Louis relies on his small collection of books to inspire him and distract him from his mundane routine. The characters in Louis's dreams often speak in riddles, rhyme, or alliteration, and his guide in *Night Salad* asks him directly, "Do you like words?" before adding in understatement, "Very handy for putting things across." Even Jerk Quidnunc cares deeply about words, poring over Louis's letters to Aunt Alison and commenting, "A careful rereading. . . it's amazing what words will reveal."

The Quidnuncs's long-running interest in spying on Louis speaks to the theme of voyeurism in the series. The basis of the Quidnuncs's sense of humor is schadenfreude, and the two go to great lengths to witness the pain and suffering they cause Louis. More broadly, the residents of Hamlet are constantly monitored and each home is equipped with a *Nineteen Eighty-Four*-esque "entertainment center" (EC). The EC continuously plays "news" and advertisements and all of the town's residents, excepting Louis, seem to watch it constantly.

The series also focuses on the impact of technology on modern life. *The Clown's Last Words*, in particular, touches upon the gap created between performers and their audience by television. The images of the residents of Hamlet dozing in front of their blaring ECs comment on the passivity of many modern viewers. In this vein, the series also examines brand and advertising culture, and the pervasiveness of distracting and hollow ads. The main advertisements in Louis's world seem to be for junk food, with names like "Mort™," "Snak," and "Shok." Even Louis's fruit manufacturing job, in which he adds chemicals to fruits to "discourage prolonged sniffing," speaks to the modern phenomenon of highly processed foods. The volume *Night Salad*, in particular, cautions against the dangerous presence of so many chemical toxins in people's food and homes.

Most important, the *Louis* series is about the power of the imagination to transcend daily life. *The Clown's Last Words* features the profound influence of Louis's dream world on his game design. In *Night Salad*, Louis's visionary imagination allows him to process and cope with his grief. Louis is constantly enriching his daily routines with his daydreams, which is his most important defense mechanism against the strange and shallow world of Hamlet.

Impact

The *Louis* series represents the rare "all ages" genre by conveying a simple narrative but simultaneously imparting a deeper message. As the first graphic novel to be sponsored by the Scottish Arts Council, *Louis* represents the modern trend of wider acceptance of comics among a general audience. The initial success of the *Louis* series led Metaphrog to redraw and rerelease the first *Louis* volume, *Red Letter Day*, in 2011. *Louis*, reminiscent of Hergé's *The Adventures of Tintin* but dealing with Kafkian themes, is a successful example of self-publication, a staple of the Modern Age of comics.

Mary Woodbury

Further Reading

Hergé. *The Adventures of Tintin* (1929–1976).

Chalmers, John, and Sandra Marrs. *Strange Weather Lately* (1999).

Bibliography

Chalmers, John, and Sandra Marrs. "Lies, Letters, and the Strange Weather." Interview by Jennifer M. Contino. *Sequential Tart.* http://www.sequentialtart.com/archive/nov01/metaphrog.shtml.

_____. "The Metaphrog Interview." Interview by Gavin Lees. *The Comics Journal*, September 28, 2011. http://www.tcj.com/the-metaphrog-interview.

Lees, Gavin. "Graphic Youth: *Louis: Night Salad* by Metaphrog." Review of *Louis: Night Salad*, by John Chalmers and Sandra Marrs. *The Comics Journal*, February 21, 2011. http://classic.tcj.com/alternative/louis-night-salad-by-Metaphrog.

Wild, Abigail. "Punks of Publishing." *The Herald Scotland*, September 18, 2004.

See also: *The Adventures of Tintin*; *Give It Up! And Other Stories*; *Good-Bye Chunky Rice*

LOUIS RIEL: A COMIC-STRIP BIOGRAPHY

Author: Brown, Chester
Artist: Chester Brown (illustrator)
Publisher: Drawn and Quarterly
First serial publication: 1999-2003
First book publication: 2003

Publication History

Chester Brown's *Louis Riel: A Comic-Strip Biography* was originally published in ten issues by the Canadian press Drawn and Quarterly between 1999 and 2003; it was collected into a single volume in 2003. Born and raised in Montreal, Canada, Brown was already an established figure in the world of alternative comics at the time, known for autobiographical works such as *The Playboy* (1992) and grimly comedic fiction such as *Ed the Happy Clown* (1989).

Louis Riel, a tightly illustrated and thoroughly researched work of nonfiction, represented a major departure for the author in terms of both content and artistic approach. Brown controlled every aspect of *Louis Riel*, researching, writing, illustrating, and even hand lettering the entire work. Despite the warnings of his publishers, Brown printed the original issues of *Louis Riel* on newsprint with matte, sepia-toned card stock covers in order to lower the price and give a "warmer" tone to the work. The format of the original issues was also slightly smaller than the average comic book, giving them a uniquely austere appearance.

Louis Riel: A Comic-Strip Biography. (Courtesy of Drawn and Quarterly)

Plot

Louis Riel: A Comic-Strip Biography is about the life of the Canadian folk hero Louis Riel, who led rebellions against the Canadian government in 1869 and 1885. Instead of creating an exhaustive biography, Brown focuses only on the events surrounding the two uprisings and Riel's subsequent capture and trial.

The story begins in 1869, as the Canadian prime minister John Macdonald takes control of the Red River settlement and begins to enforce new laws on the area's population of Metis, the mixed-race descendants of French and aboriginal (mostly Cree or Ojibwe) parents. Unhappy that his people are no longer allowed to govern themselves as they had for centuries, the young Metis Riel organizes his people and forms a provisional government to resist Canadian annexation. Tensions mount between the French-speaking Metis and local English-speaking Canadians led by Doc Schultz, leading to a series of violent clashes that leave several dead. The political crisis is brought to a head when Riel sentences a fanatical pro-Canadian named Thomas Scott to death for the brutal murder of a Metis. Scott's execution gives Prime Minister Macdonald the excuse he needs to send in the Canadian military, putting a bloody end to the uprising.

Knowing he will be lynched if captured by the Canadians, Riel goes into exile in the United States.

Spending most of the next decade on the run, he is relentlessly pursued by Doc Schultz, who has offered a reward of five thousand dollars for Riel's capture—dead or alive. The constant flight takes a mental toll on Riel, who begins to suffer delusions and eventually has a total breakdown, during which he receives a vision from God and is anointed as the prophet of the New World. Due to this breakdown, Riel is committed to an asylum.

The story resumes in 1881, as the Canadian government is again encroaching on the land of the Metis refugees of the Red River uprising, this time the western territory of Saskatchewan. Married and living in Montana, Riel is recruited by the Metis military leader Gabriel Dumont to lead the political resistance against the Canadian government. Meanwhile, Prime Minister Macdonald concocts a scheme to drum up political support for his unpopular trans-Canadian railroad by enflaming the conflict between the Canadians and the Metis, allowing him to send in troops using the newly built railway.

The plan works, and a full-scale war breaks out between Canada and the Metis. Although outnumbered and using primitive weapons, the Metis are able to repel the Canadian soldiers thanks to the effective guerrilla tactics of Dumont. Riel continues to show signs of mental instability during the conflict. Believing that he and the Metis are ordained by God, Riel prevents Dumont from engaging in the "Indian tactics" of ambush and sabotage, allowing the Canadians to wear down the Metis's defenses. Left with only a few hundred men, Riel, Dumont, and the Metis make their last stand in the village of Batoche. Out of ammunition, betrayed by the village priest, and facing the advancing army, Dumont and the remaining Metis flee as Riel allows himself to be captured.

The last section of the book details Riel's trial for treason, during which the court assesses his sanity. A series of experts and characters from previous episodes of the novel testify as to Riel's state of mind, with some claiming he is insane and others claiming he is not. The trial ends with an impassioned speech by Riel, who declares that his cause is just regardless of his mental state. The jury returns a guilty verdict, and Riel is hanged.

Characters

- *Louis Riel*, the protagonist, is a French-speaking Metis who has recently returned to the Red River settlement after attending seminary school in Montreal for several years. He is intelligent, educated, and charismatic, making him a natural leader for his people, but he suffers from occasional bouts of madness and at times believes he is a divinely inspired prophet.
- *John A. Macdonald* is the prime minister of Canada during both of Riel's uprisings and is the Metis's greatest political antagonist. He does everything in his power to prevent the nonwhite, French-speaking Metis from gaining the right to govern themselves.
- *Doc Schultz* is an Anglo-Canadian settler who supports Macdonald's annexation of the Red River settlement and leads an armed resistance against the Metis. He becomes Riel's antagonist after being imprisoned during the uprising of 1869, and he spends the next decade pursuing Riel across the United States and Canada.
- *Thomas Scott* is a gaunt, intense Anglo-Canadian and a fanatical supporter of Doc Schultz. He is prone to intense rage, leading him to brutally murder a Metis man with an ax. After being captured by Riel's forces, Scott continuously screams racist and profane threats against his Metis guards. His execution causes the intervention of the Canadian military in the uprising.
- *Gabriel Dumont* is a large, bearded Metis marksman and trapper from the western plains of Saskatchewan. A brilliant tactician and capable warrior, he acts as Riel's general during the rebellion of 1885. He eventually loses confidence in Riel, who claims that God ordered him not to allow Dumont to use guerrilla tactics against the superior forces of the Canadian army.

Artistic Style

The overall aesthetic of *Louis Riel* is one of emptiness, silence, and distance. Brown's black-and-white illustrations are clean and minimal, reducing everything on the page to its simplest visual form. Interior backgrounds are often reduced to solid expanses of black or white, while exteriors capture the cold spareness of the Canadian plains by rendering them as empty horizon lines sparsely punctuated by leafless trees.

Brown makes no attempt to capture his historical subjects realistically. Instead, his characters are rendered in simple line drawings and display cartoonish features such as outsized hands and large noses. Brown almost never depicts his characters in motion, choosing to present them instead in stiff, almost unnatural poses reminiscent of mannequins. The entire effect establishes an emotional distance between the reader and the characters, reminding the readers that they are reading an account of historical events pieced together from

Louis Riel: A Comic-Strip Biography. (Courtesy of Drawn and Quarterly)

various historical sources and not a definitive representation of what actually happened.

Brown has noted that he based the visual aesthetic of *Louis Riel* on Harold Gray's popular *Little Orphan Annie* comic strip (first published in 1924), citing the dramatic restraint of Gray's compositional style and the emotional distance created by his representation of his characters, who have empty eyes that lack pupils or additional details. Although *Annie* did not appear until nearly forty years after Riel's death, Brown's use of Gray's style gives *Louis Riel* the look of a period piece from the early days of comic-strip art.

The sense of authorial distance is reinforced by the composition of the panels. Brown presents his characters as very small relative to the size of the panels, as if readers are observing the action from a distance. This perspective is especially evident in Brown's depictions of battles, during which the point of view shifts to high above the action, reducing the characters to the appearance of toy soldiers or symbols on a tactician's map.

Brown uses the same grid layout, consisting of two columns and three rows of equally sized square panels, for each page of the novel. By forcing the story to conform to an unchanging layout on the page, Brown creates a sense of impartiality, making the reader view the events of the story from a fixed position. Only on the last page of the book, at the moment of Riel's death, does Brown deviate from the regularity of the grid, leaving blank the lower right corner of the page.

Themes

Mental illness and parameters of reality are the overriding themes of *Louis Riel*. Brown explains in a footnote to the novel that he was interested in exploring the question of Riel's sanity. Therefore, Brown chooses to present Riel not as the larger-than-life hero he has become, but as a man of great intellect and charisma plagued by questionable mental stability. Brown believes that Riel's madness was not caused by mental illness and considers that interpretation to be culturally biased; rather, he argues that Riel's mental state was shaped by a strict religious upbringing and the added pressures of political persecution. He suggests that Riel's religious visions of liberation provided the religiously conservative and socially persecuted Metis

with the morale needed to fight against Canadian oppression. The book's exploration of madness as a social, rather than biological, outcome is a continuation of Brown's previous autobiographical work "My Mom Was a Schizophrenic," published in *The Little Man* (1998).

Because the other major theme of *Louis Riel* is the historical mistreatment of Canada's indigenous peoples by the Canadian government, Brown suggests that the question of Riel's mental stability should have no bearing on how one views the justice of his cause. Brown presents Macdonald and other Canadian politicians as greedy, dishonest, and utterly corrupted by corporate interests, drawing them with deformed features such as grotesquely large noses and sunken, skull-like faces. On the other hand, the Metis, to whom Brown gives strong, proportional features, are represented as simple men who want only to protect their lands and way of life. Even though he sympathizes with the Metis, Brown avoids presenting the group as "noble savages." Instead, he shows them bickering, dealing with internal corruption and dissent, and even betraying one another. The representation of the Metis as regular people facing enormous obstacles is intended to make their struggle more comprehensible to nonindigenous readers.

Impact

Louis Riel is part of a larger wave of interest in the expansion of the graphic novel medium that followed the critical and commercial success of Art Spiegelman's *Maus* (1986). While previous nonfiction comics were largely artless affairs produced for schoolchildren, throughout the 1990's and 2000's, comics such as Joe Sacco's *Palestine* (2001) and *Safe Area Goražde* (2000), Scott McCloud's *Understanding Comics* (1993), and Brown's adaptations of the Christian Gospels experimented with the medium as a method of delivering academic-level treatments of complex subject matter.

Brown claimed that he wanted *Louis Riel* to avoid what he saw as the aesthetic failure of many historical comics. Most of these comics, Brown observed, relied on text-heavy narration to present the story. *Louis Riel* features almost no narration, relying on sparse dialogue and the visual elements of the page to convey the story. For those readers interested in the details of the Riel story, Brown includes a twenty-seven-page appendix with relevant quotes from the historical texts on which Brown based his work, as well as an index. In his introduction to *Louis Riel*, Brown notes the anomaly of such academic features appearing in a graphic novel.

Adam Spry

Further Reading

Aaron, Jason, and R. M. Guéra. *Scalped* (2007-   )

Bogaert, Harmen Meyndertsz van den, and George O'Connor. *Journey into Mohawk Country* (2006).

Jacobson, Sid, and Ernie Colón. *Che: A Graphic Biography* (2009).

Bibliography

Brown, Chester. "Chester Brown." Interview by Nicolas Verstappen. *Du9*, August, 2008. http://www.du9.org/Chester-Brown,1030.

_____. "Getting Riel with Chester Brown." Interview by Guy Leshinski. *The Cultural Gutter*, January 5, 2006. http://www.theculturalgutter.com/comics/getting_riel_with_chester_brown.html.

Lesk, Andrew. "Redrawing Nationalism: Chester Brown's *Louis Riel: A Comic-Strip Biography*." *Journal of Graphic Novels and Comics* 1, no. 1 (June, 2010): 63-81.

Siggins, Maggie. *Louis Riel: A Life of Revolution*. Toronto: HarperCollins, 1994.

See also: *Safe Area Goražde*; *Journey into Mohawk Country*; *The Playboy*; *I Never Liked You*

LOVE AND ROCKETS

Author: Hernandez, Gilbert; Hernandez, Jaime; Hernandez, Mario

Artist: Gilbert Hernandez (illustrator); Jaime Hernandez (illustrator); Mario Hernandez (illustrator); Jeff Johnson (colorist); Rhea Patton (colorist); Chris Brownrigg (colorist); Steven Weissman (colorist)

Publisher: Fantagraphics Books

First serial publication: 1982-1996; 2001-2007; 2008-

First book publication: 1985-

Publication History

Soon after brothers Mario, Gilbert, and Jaime Hernandez self-published their first issue of *Love and Rockets* in 1981, it caught the eye of Fantagraphics publisher Gary Groth. In 1982, Groth republished the inaugural issue; the first series of *Love and Rockets* ran for fifty issues, ending in 1996. All issues in the original volume were magazine-size, and the comics were black and white. The art duties for the color covers alternated between Gilbert and Jaime; one would draw the front cover and the other the back cover, then switching responsibilities for the following issue.

After the end of the first series, Jaime and Gilbert began working on separate titles that continued many of the stories in the original *Love and Rockets*. In 2001, the brothers began their second series of *Love and Rockets*, which ran for twenty issues, until 2007. Although these issues were smaller than the originals, they nonetheless retained a similar format: color covers illustrated by Jaime and Gilbert and black-and-white content written and illustrated by all three brothers.

In 2008, the Hernandez brothers returned with a third manifestation of their comic series. The new series, *Love and Rockets: New Stories*, was still in black and white, but the publication size changed again; the comic was published as an annual and in a graphic novel format of about a hundred pages.

Since the mid-1980's, *Love and Rockets* issues have been collected and repackaged in three primary formats: the early *Complete Love and Rockets* series,

Love and Rockets. (Courtesy of Fantagraphics Books)

large omnibus collections, and *Love and Rockets* Library editions.

Plot

Love and Rockets contains a variety of narrative arcs, many of which have convoluted plots. The two primary stories, however, concern the associations of the "Locas," Maggie and Hopey (Jaime's comics), and those of Luba, her extended family, and the fictional Central American town of Palomar (Gilbert's comics).

In "Mechanics," Maggie, a mechanic, goes with her group of prosolar mechanics to a South American town to repair a rocket. While there, they get caught up in a political revolution.

"The Death of Speedy Oritz" is a story of romantic entanglements, focusing primarily on the Maggie's personal relationships. Ray Dominguez likes Maggie but assumes incorrectly that Speedy is involved with her. Speedy professes his love for Maggie, which she cannot handle; he apparently commits suicide.

"Flies on the Ceiling" is a short but significant story, in which Izzy has a nervous breakdown while in Mexico. She becomes involved with a man and his young son, but because she is haunted by her past, she decides to return to Huerta (or Hoppers, as the barrio is called).

"Wigwam Bam" is a complex, sustained narrative and one of Jaime's most ambitious. It begins when Maggie and Hopey are on the East Coast at a party. Angry for being mocked as a "Mexican" and for

Hopey's indifference to this slight, Maggie leaves the party and temporarily runs away from her past. The rest of the story focuses on the relationships of Hopey and the Hoppers crowd. During this time, Izzy searches for the two friends.

In "Ghost of Hoppers," Maggie is back on the West Coast, divorced and managing an apartment complex. Although still in an off-and-on relationship with Hopey, she meets the seductive Vivian Solis and travels with Vivian to her native barrio, Hoppers. There, she undergoes a surreal experience and witnesses the burning of Izzy's house.

Love and Rockets. (Courtesy of Fantagraphics Books)

With "Tri-Girls Adventures Number 34," Jaime revisits the mock superhero genre that he explored in some of his earlier comics. In it, Maggie's friend, Angel Rivera, teams up with several superpowered women to battle another female team and help subdue the renegade Penny Century.

"Heartbreak Soup" is Gilbert's first sustained story of Palomar and its citizens. It involves the entrepreneurial Pipo's ill-fated relationship with the philandering Manuel and establishes the rivalry between Luba and Chelo.

In "An American in Palomar," Howard, an American photojournalist, visits the small town for his new book. Although many citizens believe that he is there to appreciate them, he stereotypes the townspeople and exploits them merely to further his own career.

"Human Diastrophism" is a long serialized narrative involving the arrival of a serial killer in Palomar. As the townspeople and Sheriff Chelo try to solve the mystery, Luba takes up with her former lover, Khamo, and the young artist Humberto inadvertently discovers the murderer's identity.

"Poison River" is perhaps Gilbert's most ambitious narrative arc. It relates Luba's long, convoluted backstory from the early days of Luba's broken family into her marriage at a young age to Pedro and through the many twists of her husband's criminal connections and her own drug habits. Along the way, Luba has a miscarriage, escapes from her doomed marriage, reunites with her cousin Ofelia, gives birth to her first daughter, flees military conflicts, and ends up on the outskirts of Palomar.

"Love and Rockets X" is a highly condensed story with a large cast of characters. Set in Los Angeles and following the exploits of a garage band named Love and Rockets, the narrative is propelled through a series of conflicts surrounding race, class, sexual orientation, and generational differences.

"High Soft Lisp" is an episodic character portrait of Fritz, Luba's younger half sister, covering her high school days, adulthood, careers, and relationships and sexual misadventures. This narrative sets up Fritz as the future B-movie star featured in Gilbert's later non-*Love and Rockets* graphic novels.

Volumes

Complete Love and Rockets

- *Music for Mechanics* (1985). Collects *Love and Rockets* Volume 1, issues 1-2.
- *Chelo's Burden* (1986). Collects *Love and Rockets* Volume 1, issues 3-4, and *Mechanics*, issue 1.
- *Las Mujeres Perdidas* (1987). Collects stories from *Love and Rockets* Volume 1, issues 5-11.
- *Tears from Heaven* (1988). Collects stories from *Love and Rockets* Volume 1, issues 5-7 and 10-12, and *Mechanics*, issues 1-2.
- *House of Raging Women* (1988). Collects stories from *Love and Rockets* Volume 1, issues 13-16.
- *Duck Feet* (1989). Collects stories from *Love and Rockets* Volume 1, issues 6, 9, and 17-20, and Jaime's contribution to *Anything Goes!* issue 2.
- *The Death of Speedy* (1989). Collects Jaime's stories from *Love and Rockets* Volume 1, issues 20-27.
- *Blood of Palomar* (1989). Collects "Human Diastrophism" story from *Love and Rockets* Volume 1, issues 21-26, and *Love and Rockets Bonanza!* (1989).
- *Flies on the Ceiling* (1991). Collects stories from *Love and Rockets* Volume 1, issues 21 and 27-32.
- *Love and Rockets X* (1993). Collects "Love and Rockets X" story from *Love and Rockets* Volume 1, issues 31-39.
- *Wigwam Bam* (1994). Collects the "Wigwam Bam" story from *Love and Rockets* Volume 1, issues 33-39 and 42.
- *Poison River* (1994). Collects the "Poison River" story from *Love and Rockets* Volume 1, issues 29-40.
- *Chester Square* (1996). Collects Jaime's stories from *Love and Rockets* Volume 1, issues 40-50.
- *Luba Conquers the World* (1996). Collects Gilbert's stories from *Love and Rockets* Volume 1, issues 41-50.
- *Hernandez Satyricon* (1997). Collects the remaining stories from *Love and Rockets* Volume 1 not collected in the earlier *Complete Love and Rockets* volumes.

- *Fear of Comics* (2000). Collects Gilbert's stories from *New Stories*, issues 1-6, and his contributions to *Goody Good Comics* (2000), *Hate* (1990-1998), *Zero Zero* (1995-2000), *Mister X* (1984-1992), and *UG!3K* (1999).
- *Dicks and Deedees* (2003). Collects *Love and Rockets* Volume 2, issues 4-5, along with Jaime's solo *Penny Century*, issues 5-7.
- *Ghost of Hoppers* (2005). Collects Jaime's stories from *Love and Rockets* Volume 2, issues 1-4 and 6-10.
- *Luba: Three Daughters* (2006). Collects Gilbert's stories from *Love and Rockets* Volume 2, issues 6, 11-16; along with *Luba's Comics and Stories*, issues 3, 4, 6, and 8; *Measles*, issue 1; and eleven new stories.
- *The Education of Hopey Glass* (2008). Collects Jaime's stories from *Love and Rockets* Volume 2, issues 11-19.
- *High Soft Lisp* (2010). Collects *Love and Rockets* Volume 1, issues 3-5, 7-9, 11, 13-15, and 17-18, along with Gilbert's solo *Luba's Comics and Stories*, issue 7.

Omnibus Editions
- *Palomar: The Heartbreak Soup Stories* (2003). Collects all of Gilbert's Palomar/Luba stories from *Love and Rockets* Volume 1.
- *Locas: The Maggie and Hopey Stories* (2004). Collects all of Jaime's Maggie and Hopey stories from *Love and Rockets* Volume 1.
- *Locas II: Maggie, Hopey, and Ray* (2009). Collects the *Complete Love and Rockets* volumes *Locas in Love*, *Dicks and Deedees*, *Ghost of Hoppers*, and *The Education of Hopey Glass*.

The Love and Rockets Library
- *Maggie the Mechanic* (2007). Reprints parts of the omnibus *Locas: The Maggie and Hopey Stories*. Contains the major story lines "Mechanics" and "Las Mujeres Perdidas."
- *The Girl from H.O.P.P.E.R.S.* (2007). Reprints parts of the omnibus *Locas: The Maggie and Hopey Stories*. Contains the major story lines "House of Raging Women," and "Vida Loca: The Death of Speedy Ortiz," "In the Valley of the Polar Bears," "Ninety-Three Million Miles from the Sun," and "Flies on the Ceiling."
- *Perla La Loca* (2007). Reprints parts of the omnibus *Locas: The Maggie and Hopey Stories*. Contains the major story lines "Wigwam Bam," "Chester Square," "Hester Square," and "Bob Richardson."
- *Heartbreak Soup* (2007). Reprints parts of the omnibus *Palomar: The Heartbreak Soup Stories*. Contains the major story lines "Heartbreak Soup," "Act of Contrition," "The Laughing Sun," "Ecce Homo," "An American in Palomar," "For the Love of Carmen," and "Duck Feet."
- *Human Diastrophism* (2007). Reprints parts of the omnibus *Palomar: The Heartbreak Soup Stories*. Contains the major story lines "Human Diastrophism," "Farewell, My Palomar . . . ," "A Trick of the Unconscious," "The Gorgo Wheel," "Luba Conquers the World," and "Chelo's Burden."
- *Beyond Palomar* (2007). Collects the *Complete Love and Rockets* volumes *Poison River* and *Love and Rockets X*.
- *Amor y Cohetes* (2008). Collects the non-Maggie and Hopey and non-Palomar/Luba stories from the *Complete Love and Rockets* volumes *Music for Mechanics*, *Chelo's Burden*, *Las Mujeres Perdidas*, *Tears from Heaven*, *House of Raging Women*, *Duck Feet*, *Flies on the Ceiling*, and *Hernandez Satyricon*.
- *Esperanza* (2011). Collects the *Complete Love and Rockets* volumes *Ghost of Hoppers* and *The Education of Hopey Glass*.

Characters
- *Margarita Luisa Chascarrillo*, a.k.a. *Maggie*, has remained a central character during the comic's entire run. She is Hopey's best friend and occasional lover. Early in the series she was a mechanic but later works as the manager of an apartment complex. Much of Jaime's stories revolve around her evolving relationships and battles with her weight and self-esteem.
- *Esperanza Leticia Glass*, a.k.a. *Hopey*, is Maggie's best friend. She is unambiguously lesbian

and becomes involved in a variety of relationships. Once a punk rock bassist with a penchant for trouble, she has matured over the years and now lives a more subdued existence as a teacher's assistant.

- *Ray Dominguez* is one of Maggie's former boyfriends. Although he has been involved with others, his heart always returns to Maggie. Growing up in Hoppers, he travels east to study art, returns to the barrio, and eventually moves to Los Angeles. As the series has developed, he has evolved into the central male figure in Jaime's female-dominated comics world.

- *Beatríz García*, a.k.a. *Penny Century*, is *Love and Rockets*' most vivacious and unpredictable character and one of its sexual powerhouses. In contrast to many of Jaime's other female figures, she is decidedly heterosexual. A close friend to Maggie and Hopey and former wife of billionaire H. R. Costigan, she regularly pops in and out of people's lives and often masquerades as a female superhero.

- *Isabel Ortiz Reubens*, a.k.a. *Izzy*, introduced Maggie and Hopey to each other and is deeply devoted to Maggie. Highly perceptive but subdued and dour, she is haunted by the demons of her past, which include a failed marriage, three abortions, a nervous breakdown, and institutionalization.

- *Eulalio Ortiz*, a.k.a. *Speedy*, is Izzy's younger brother and a gang member in Hopper. He had a crush on Maggie, although he did not reveal his feelings to her until near the end of his life. Maggie harbored similar feelings for him, but by the time she acknowledges them, it is too late because he kills himself.

- *Vivian Solis*, a.k.a. *the Frogmouth*, is one of the central sexual icons in Jaime's story world. Her nickname comes from the sound of her croaky voice. A former stripper and would-be actor, she is trashy and unashamed.

- *Angel Rivera* befriends Maggie when the latter becomes manager of an apartment complex. She retains a bit of weight but is athletic and not very self-conscious about the way she looks. In the third series of *Love and Rockets*, she becomes fascinated with some of Maggie's older *Tri-Girl Adventures* comic books. In a dreamlike manner, she even becomes a masked crusader and joins a female superhero team.

- *Luba* is the most central figure in Gilbert's story world and one of the most sexualized characters in *Love and Rockets*. Her unusually large breasts are her distinguishing physical feature. As a young woman, she was promiscuous, becoming involved with a variety of men. She is Gilbert's strongest character and highly entrepreneurial: She ran one of Palomar's bathhouses, owned its sole movie theater, and became the mayor. Twice married and twice widowed, she is the mother of Maricela, Guadalupe, Doralis, Casimira, Socorro, Joselito, and Concepcion; the half sister of Fritz and Petra; and the young cousin of Ofelia.

- *Pipo Jiminez* is a sexually provocative woman popular with the men, but she is also a bit of a tomboy. She has best defined herself outside of the Central American community. A confident entrepreneur, she created a line of clothing and moved to Los Angeles, where she eventually created her own media empire.

- *Chelo* is a onetime competitor of Luba, having once operated a bathhouse in Palomar and been an object of men's desire. She eventually becomes the town's sheriff and, after making peace with Luba, convinces her former rival to run for town mayor. She exudes a muscular sensuality and keeps order without wearing a gun.

- *Heraclio Calderon* is one of the few distinguished male characters in Gilbert's comics world. Palomar's most educated citizen, he works as a schoolteacher. In a brief fling with Luba, he inadvertently fathers Guadalupe. He is married to Carmen.

- *Tonantzín Villaseñor* is one of Palomar's most desirable women. She is known for her fried *babosa*, or slugs. In "Human Diastrophism" she self-immolates while protesting American foreign policy. Her future husband, Khamo, rescues her, suffering lifelong burn scars in the process.

- *Ofelia* is Luba's older cousin. Her world-weariness counterbalances Luba's reckless insouciance. She suffers from a back problem as the result of a politically motivated beating. She has held Luba's family together throughout their adventures.
- *Rosalba Martinez*, a.k.a. *Fritz*, and *Petra Martinez* are Luba's younger American half sisters and play a significant role in her life after her family moves to Los Angeles. Petra is athletic and elects to have major breast reduction surgery. In contrast, her bisexual sister Fritz defines herself largely through her body and her sexuality. Distinguished at first by her prominent lisp, she attains a career as a psychologist, has an on-and-off affair with Pipo, and eventually becomes a B-movie star.

Artistic Style

The styles of the Hernandez brothers are strikingly different. Mario's is the roughest of the three, although his illustrations are a rarity in *Love and Rockets*. Gilbert's art is less realistic and more expressive than Jaime's, and as a result, his illustrations appear less sophisticated to some fans. His work is heavily influenced by the kind of comics he grew up reading, such as those by Jack Kirby and Charles M. Schulz. The artistic debt he owes to Robert Crumb is especially apparent in his explicit, often outrageous depictions of sex. Jaime's illustrations reflect more of a clean-line style. His work has been particularly influenced not only by Dan DeCarlo, but also by Hank Ketcham and Schulz.

Both Gilbert and Jaime employ many of the stylistic gestures common in classic comic strips. These include a variety of emanata (lines indicating shock), grawlixes (symbols replacing expletives), comical facial features, and exaggerations of physical actions, all of which contribute to an occasional cartoony tone. Such moments punctuate their comics in ways that further their storytelling, revealing not only the brothers' grasp of the comics tradition but also their mastery over the entire lexicon of cartoon art.

In terms of subject matter, the Hernandez brothers' work betrays some stylistic differences. Jaime's comics tend to represent more realistic scenarios, whether set

Gilbert Hernandez

One of the famed Los Bros Hernandez, Gilbert Hernandez began publishing *Love and Rockets* with his brothers Jaime and Mario in the early 1980's and it became the defining comic book series of the American alternative movement. Gilbert's contributions to the series revolve primarily around the fictional Mexican town of Palomar, where a vast cast of characters come together to create an epic depiction of an entire way of life. His graphic novels *Human Diastrophism* and *Heartbreak Soup* are among the most important works ever published in comics. In the late 1990's, Gilbert's work came to focus increasingly on just one of the Palomar characters, Luba. He has also published stand-alone graphic novels outside of *Love and Rockets*, including *The Troublemakers*, *Chance in Hell*, and *Speak of the Devil*, each of which is an adaptation of a fictional B-movie. Gilbert Hernandez's work has strong magical realist overtones, and he is renowned for his ability to craft truly believable characters in his fiction.

Jaime Hernandez

The creator, alongside his brothers Gilbert and Mario, of the legendary comic book series *Love and Rockets*, Jaime Hernandez rose to fame as a chronicler of the Los Angeles punk rock scene in the 1980's and is now celebrated as one of the greatest practitioners of the comics form. Jaime Hernandez's contribution to the title he shared with his brothers is generally known as *Locas*. The stories focus on Maggie and Hopey, their on-again off-again relationship, and their circle of friends in the Hoppers neighborhood of Los Angeles. In addition to crafting a truly believable cast of characters and locale, Hernandez is responsible for having created two of the most memorable characters in American comics, and he has chronicled their lives for more than three decades. Hernandez's art is influenced by a wide range of American cartoonists from Hank Ketcham and Harry Lucey to Alex Toth and Jack Kirby. He is one of the most influential cartoonists of his generation and is largely responsible for the turn toward literary-style fiction in alternative comics.

in the West Coast punk scene or in the more mundane environs into which his characters have grown. Occasionally a fantastic side of Jaime's work takes center stage, as in his earlier "Mechanics" stories, where dinosaurs and rocket ships coexist in a contemporary reality. Gilbert's storytelling tends to be more surrealistic and nonrepresentational in form, often expressed in short pieces. However, one of his best-known early works, "BEM," is a long comic that stands as his most fully realized exercise in narrative experimentation. Even Gilbert's more realistic stories contain bits of the fantastic, and many readers have placed his Palomar work within the tradition of South American magical realism. Thus, surreal events are seamlessly interwoven into his realistic story lines.

References to rock and popular tunes saturate *Love and Rockets*, providing a kind of soundtrack to the images. Many characters play instruments and are members of bands, and often music is blaring from a radio or being sung. It is no wonder that the 1980's rock band Love and Rockets took its name from the comic book series.

Themes

One of the most common themes found in *Love and Rockets* is interpersonal relationships, both romantic and sexual. Love affairs, marriages, sexual couplings, and unrequited loves compose a majority of the story lines. What is more, the sexuality represented is largely fluid and nonconventional, leaving the reader to question the role of heteronormativity in the narrative. Homosexuality, bisexual encounters, fetishism, and other sexual practices are represented in such a way that all become normative within the worlds of *Love and Rockets*.

In a similar manner, gender roles and expectations are given broad treatment. Jaime's comics, in particular, have been widely praised for their depictions of women that resist the kind of male-fantasy figures so common in comic books. His female characters struggle with body image, openly discuss their physiques, and come in a variety of shapes and sizes. Gilbert, too, has been praised for his representation of women, especially as powerful individuals controlling their own destinies. However, at the same time, he has

been accused of fetishizing the female figure, falling prey to the same kind of exaggerated "fanboy" fantasies found in mainstream comics.

Another common theme found throughout *Love and Rockets* is the ubiquity of racial and ethnic tensions. Many of the series' characters, some of whom are immigrants, become victims of prejudice and stereotyping. Ethnic discord and immigration are linked to another theme found in *Love and Rockets:* conflicts between the individual and the community. Whether the setting is 1980's punk rock scene in Jaime's comics or the more tranquil and isolated Central American milieu of Gilbert's Palomar, the main characters in *Love and Rockets* are all a part of some community with which they can identify and against which they struggle. In many of Gilbert's stories, conflicts arise between traditional communities and modernity. In narratives such as "Duck Feet" and "Human Diastrophism," the author demonstrates how outside forces can impinge upon, and potentially eradicate, older and more traditional ways of understanding the world. Music undergirds both brothers' comics.

Impact

Along with Daniel Clowes's *Eightball* (1989-2004), Peter Bagge's *Hate*, and Rick Altergott's *Doofus* (1994-1997), *Love and Rockets* helped to define the alternative comics scene of the 1980's and early 1990's. These comics were directly influenced by the underground comics movement of the late 1960's. However, unlike most of the earlier underground comics, the work of the Hernandez brothers moved beyond isolated and episodic story lines to create epic narrative worlds.

Just as *Love and Rockets* is indebted to the comics that preceded it, a younger generation of comics artists has been influenced by the Hernandez brothers. This is perhaps most apparent in the field of minority writing. The brothers began creating their material in a time when ethnic minorities did not or could not foreground their own cultural experiences. In *Love and Rockets*, the Hernandez brothers wrote from the context of their West Coast Latino background, but they did so in a way that normalized those experiences. In other words, their ethnicity was more of a means through which they told their tales, rather than the narrative focus or subject matter. The Hernandez brothers have shown that a comics creator's work can have an ethnic perspective without making that the grand sum of the comics.

Derek Parker Royal

Further Reading

Bagge, Peter. *Hate* (1990-1998)

Clowes, Daniel. *Eightball* (1989-2004).

Sim, Dave. *Cerebus* (1977-2004).

Bibliography

Hernandez, Gilbert. "Palomar and Beyond: An Interview with Gilbert Hernandez." Interview by Derek Parker Royal. *MELUS* 32, no. 3 (Fall, 2007): 221-246.

Hernandez, Gilbert, and Jaime Hernandez. "The Hernandez Brothers." Interview by Neil Gaiman. *The Comics Journal* 178 (July, 1995): 91-123.

Hernandez, Gilbert, Jaime Hernandez, and Mario Hernandez. "Pleased to Meet Them: The Hernandez Bros. Interview." Interview by Gary Groth, Robert Fiore, and Thom Powers. *The Comics Journal* 126 (January, 1989): 60-113.

Hignite, Todd. *The Art of Jaime Hernandez: The Secrets of Life and Death*. New York: Abrams ComicArts, 2010.

Royal, Derek Parker. "To Be Continued … : Serialization and Its Discontent in the Recent Comics of Gilbert Hernandez." *International Journal of Comic Art* 11, no. 1 (Spring, 2009): 262-280.

See also: *Hate*; *Twentieth Century Eightball*; *The Complete Fritz the Cat*

LUCKY

Author: Bell, Gabrielle
Artist: Gabrielle Bell (illustrator)
Publisher: Drawn and Quarterly
First serial publication: 2003-2004
First book publication: 2006

Publication History

Gabrielle Bell began self-publishing comics in small installments known as minicomics. These issues were later collected in larger editions. Her first series, published as *When I'm Old and Other Stories* (2002) by Alternative Comics, features autobiographical vignettes. *Lucky* was the next project in Bell's career; it began as a chronicle of her daily life in the Williamsburg neighborhood of Brooklyn, following her move to New York City. She published three *Lucky* minicomics detailing the events of May, 2003, in *Lucky*, issue 1; September, 2003, in *Lucky*, issue 2; and May, 2004, in *Lucky*, issue 3. These three comics were assembled together into *Lucky*, published in 2006 by Drawn and Quarterly. The collected volume contains a one-page illustrated introduction and four additional stories at the end of the text.

Lucky has been translated into Spanish, published as *Afortunada* in 2008. Bell has since revived *Lucky* in small sections as a new Drawn and Quarterly series entitled *Lucky* Volume 2. *Lucky* Volume 2, issue 1, shares the events of May, 2007, and *Lucky* Volume 2, issue 2, narrates the events of May, 2008. In August, 2009, she began periodically publishing new stories on her Web site entitled *Lucky*. Other of Bell's minicomics such as *L.A. Diary* (2009) and *Diary* (2010) follow the daily autobiographical vignette form of *Lucky* while exploring different cities. Other works, such as *Cecil and Jordan in New York* (2009), fictionalize Bell's experiences in Brooklyn.

Plot

Lucky began as an experiment in which Bell would transform the events of her day into a short story. She understood the work as more than a diary; nonetheless, at first, its production was wedged between more

Lucky. (Courtesy of Drawn and Quarterly)

serious projects. After *Lucky*, issue 1, she began to take the project more seriously, and the work became increasingly introspective.

Lucky, issue 1, is the longest of the comics in the series. Bell pieces together the many fragments of her life, which does not revolve around a nine-to-five career but many freelance jobs. Bell and her work occupy the center of the action, and her time spent drawing is often depicted in the work. The primary narrative arc of the first comic revolves around Tom, Bell's boyfriend, as he searches for an apartment in New York City and his refusal to settle in any one place. Bell gets caught up in his whirlwind when he gives her one of the apartments he finds; she helps him in his search, one that he seems content not to complete, sleeping at Bell's apartment most nights. This anxiety-filled process consumes many panels and resonates through many of the other quotidian moments in Bell's life. Bell and Tom must deal with potential and actual roommates, a variety of living spaces, and the sacrifices of apartment living. By the installment's end, the apartment issue has been resolved as Tom has found a luxurious space with which

he is content. However, Bell's anxieties continue as before; she shows her travails with art modeling at the end of the text, where she feels as disaffected with the task as she did at the beginning of the work.

Lucky, issue 2, does not follow the daily chronological format of *Lucky*, issue 1. Instead, it employs

Lucky. (Courtesy of Drawn and Quarterly)

an extended flashback that ends, roughly, where the issue begins chronologically. Issue 2 starts at the airport, where a hurried Bell loses the original pages for the comic. She is disconsolate at the discovery, and her sense of loss grows as she realizes that she will be unable to recover the work. Her friends convince her to go on a trip upstate to a friend's farmhouse, where she relaxes and starts to redo the lost pages. What follows is the recounting of her life at the end of summer. She tries to sell her cartoon work, and she has a sense of anticipation as she looks forward to her trip to San Francisco. Despite this, a sense of awkward normality reigns, communicated by her extended difficulty in yoga class and a sleeping homeless man in the subway system, whose persistent presence ends the installment.

In *Lucky*, issue 3, Bell organizes each portion of her life into a separate story, each of which has its own arc. She shows the many hats she wears and dedicates time to exploring each experience. As in issue 2, not much time is spent in her apartment other than in the first story, which shows that she has moved and details the particularities of her new dwelling. Her other stories concern her anxiety about working for an established artist, her difficulties in teaching cartooning to two adolescent French boys, and her flights of fancy that emerge while she does repetitive work in a jewelry factory. These stories show Bell negotiating different positions of authority and emphasize the creative ways an artist makes a living.

In the "Extra Stories" in the collected edition, Bell adds self-contained tales that flesh out narrative arcs from earlier *Lucky* stories, such as her work in the jewelry factory, her experience as an art teacher, and her sometimes tense relationship with Tom. Other snippets, such as a son interacting with his mother or the fantasy of a friend getting naked at a bank do not link up with existing story lines but show characters navigating the realm of everyday reality.

Volumes

- *Lucky*, issue 1 (2003). Looks at the unsettled aspects of living in New York City, focusing on Bell's boyfriend, who cannot seem to settle on any one apartment.

- *Lucky*, issue 2 (2003). Bell loses the original second issue; her friends encourage her to redraw the comic. This issue focuses intently on Gabrielle's life at the end of the summer.

- *Lucky*, issue 3 (2004). Bell has moved into a new apartment, and she works in various settings as she refines her art and makes money for rent.

Characters

- *Gabrielle Bell*, the short-haired protagonist, is a cartoonist who chronicles her life and the lives of those around her. She lives in a variety of apartments in Williamsburg, Brooklyn, and holds various freelance jobs to pay her rent. Throughout, she is concerned about her art and whether others appreciate it.

- *Tom*, who has dark, closely cropped hair, is Bell's boyfriend throughout the series. Despite owning a restaurant in Boston, he has moved to New York City to become a filmmaker. He is continually unhappy about his living situation and keeps trading apartments in order to find something more suitable. His unsettled nature becomes a focus of issue 1 and eventually begins to irritate Bell. Even so, in the introduction to the collected series, Bell credits Tom with the success of her series, calling him "the reluctant hero of my 'story.'"

- *Miranda*, one of Bell's friends whose short bob is similar to Bell's, gives Bell advice about her work. In issue 1, she takes Bell and Tom to a lesbian performance-art event, which gives the two a reprieve from the stress of apartment hunting. Although she is a lesbian, she is unable to identify with the women she sees at the event.

- *Alice*, one of Bell's friends, has short, dark hair. She is also a cartoonist; her higher renown slightly bothers Bell throughout the series. In issue 1, she involves Bell and other friends in a documentary being made about her work and life; the documentarians encourage this group of friends to make trouble in Brooklyn for the film. In issue 2, she and Bell sell their comics together at a table along Bedford Avenue, one of the main commercial streets in Williamsburg.

- *Marie*, one of Bell's friends, has a short bob with bangs. She works with Bell as an art teacher in the Bronx. Their interactions with the students appear throughout the narrative, often interspersed in or bookended by other events in Bell's life. She provides Bell the breathing space she needs to deal with the loss of her original version of issue 2, as Bell, Marie, Tom, and Miranda travel to upstate New York to spend a few days at Marie's farmhouse.
- *Jasper*, who wears his long hair in a ponytail, is Bell's brother. He does not live in New York City but is an undergraduate student at the University of Rhode Island. He holds a variety of side jobs in order to fund his studies. When Bell goes to visit him toward the end of issue 1, the two reminisce briefly about their unconventional upbringing.
- *Julien* and *Angus* are two of Bell's roommates throughout much of the series. Both are longtime friends who immigrated to the United States together to pursue their art, but they started to drift apart after they arrived and converted an old warehouse into an apartment. Although they both still reside in the building, they do not talk to each other and often indirectly disagree with each other. Both are fairly accomplished artists but still struggle for respect.

Artistic Style

The pictorial style of *Lucky* fits into the realm of the cartoon. The form of the characters does not vary greatly; they have largely nondescript clothing and similar, simple facial structures. Slight differences in hair style and shade or context often serve to differentiate the characters from each other. This figural simplicity is fairly constant throughout the series, aside from a change in Bell's hairstyle from issue 1 to issue 2. The consistency in representation extends to how objects and backgrounds are delineated with simple lines throughout the series.

Much does change on the formal, structural level however. In issue 1, Bell constructs a vignette for each day she draws; therefore, she relies on six or eight panels on a page to adequately represent and explore the day's events. This large number of panels per page

aligns with the fact that the majority of the stories are represented within one page. In issues 2 and 3, as Bell shifts her narrative style away from that of a daily journal, she switches to a four-panel-per-page format that carries through these two installments. Another formal change introduced here and carried throughout the rest of the series is an introduction of black to color the background. This technique gives more depth to each panel and emphasizes the main character in the foreground. The slightly skewed placement of panels in issues 2 and 3 further draws attention to the movement of the story from panel to panel.

Themes

In the setting of Williamsburg, a neighborhood known for its youthful artistic bent, Bell unfolds a story about the pressures of early adult life that particularly assail those who work in the arts. This autobiographical work highlights the details of daily life, exploring various jobs, friendships, and relationships. Most characters flit seamlessly in and out of the narrative, which largely

---

Gabrielle Bell

Gabrielle Bell is one of the most distinctive voices to have emerged in the American alternative comics scene during the 2000's. Her self-published minicomics, all with titles beginning with "Book of..." were collected in 2003 as *When I'm Old and Other Stories*. That same year she began serializing *Lucky*, a collection of autobiographical reminiscences about life in the Williamsburg section of Brooklyn (collected in 2006). *Cecil and Jordan in New York* is a collection of short stories produced for various comics anthologies, including *Mome* and *Kramer's Ergot*. The title story from that collection was adapted by Bell and filmmaker Michel Gondry as "Interior Design," a short film included in the anthology film *Tokyo!* Bell's visual style is defined by its minimalism and abundant use of text. She draws in a spare fashion, though her panels are often filled to bursting with information. Her stories evince an understated confessional style.

---

revolves around the protagonist's constant battles with creativity and desire for success. Both her interactions with other artists and reactions to her own work figure prominently in the text and underline the central importance of creation, a struggle whose difficulty resonates outward and informs other narrative strains, such as the impossibility of settling on any single apartment.

Relationships are also central to the story line, as almost each tale follows Bell's interactions with friends or other characters. The number of friends who move through the narrative evidence Bell's large support system and premise the importance of friendship. Her brother Jasper shows up only once in the narrative and is treated with the same depth as many of the more minor friendships that Bell introduces. The two discuss their childhood, but issues of familial connection or upbringing do not figure into the rest of the narrative.

The narrative remains superficial in many respects, gesturing toward but not peering into psychological depths. Such psychological concerns certainly inform the commonplace narrative landscape, and through such an intense focus on the details of the outer world, Bell considers the emotional and psychological impact of such elements.

Impact
Lucky's publication as a collected volume came at a time when interest in and production of autobiographical graphic narrative was high. The volume's publication coincided with the release of comics creator Alison Bechdel's coming-out memoir *Fun Home: A Family Tragicomic* (2006) and followed in the footsteps of the translation of cartoonist Marjane Satrapi's coming-of-age memoir *Persepolis* (2003). *Lucky* has not achieved the level of renown of those texts, however, and is still largely ignored by scholars. Even so, interest in *Lucky* and Bell's subsequent works continues to grow. Part of Bell's growing fame derives from her presence in the Brooklyn comics scene, which has become codified with the Brooklyn Comics and Graphics Festival held in the Williamsburg neighborhood in 2009 and 2010. In addition to being one of the event's featured artists, Bell participates frequently in comics events around the New York City area. Moreover, like Canadian comics artist Julie Doucet, Bell has collaborated with famed French filmmaker Michel Gondry. The two worked together on the "Interior Design" segment of the film *Tokyo!* (2008); the scene drew from Bell's *Cecil and Jordan in New York* and was adapted to a Japanese setting.

Margaret Galvan

Further Reading
Abel, Jessica. *La Perdida* (2006).
Bell, Gabrielle. *Cecil and Jordan in New York* (2009).
Doucet, Julie. *My New York Diary* (1999).

Bibliography
Chute, Hillary L. *Graphic Women: Life Narrative and Contemporary Comics*. New York: Columbia University Press, 2010.
Gardner, Jared. "Autobiography's Biography, 1972-2007." *Biography* 31, no. 1 (Winter, 2008): 1-26.
Robbins, Trina. *From Girls to Grrrlz: A History of Women's Comics from Teens to Zines*. San Francisco: Chronicle Books, 1999.

See also: *La Perdida*; *Long Time Relationship*; *Fun Home*

M

MAIL ORDER BRIDE

Author: Kalesniko, Mark
Artist: Mark Kalesniko (illustrator); Paul Baresh (letterer); Dan Dean (letterer); Carrie Whitney (letterer)
Publisher: Fantagraphics Books; Paquet Editions (French); Ponet Mon (Spanish); Poptoon (Korean)
First book publication: 2001

Publication History

Before *Mail Order Bride* Mark Kalesniko had published several comic books and graphic novels, including "Adolf Hears a Who" (1991), published in *Pictopia*; *S.O.S.* (1992); six volumes of *Alex* (1994-1995); and *Why Did Pete Duel Kill Himself* (1997). Kalesniko began writing adult-themed comics after working for years as a character animator on the Walt Disney films *Little Mermaid* (1989), *The Lion King* (1994), *Mulan* (1998), and *Atlantis* (2001). *Mail Order Bride* was published in 2001 by Seattle-based Fantagraphics Books. It and his other books have been published in French. *Mail Order Bride* has also been published in Spanish.

Plot

A social misfit whose world includes toys, comic books, and fantasies, Monty Wheeler feels he is missing out on life because, at age thirty-nine, he has never experienced any kind of relationship with a woman. To substitute for a real person, he has engaged in sexual fantasies using his porn collection. These fantasies have been prompted by pictures and descriptions of Asian women. He becomes convinced that an Asian woman will fulfill him. In his dreams, she will be petite, beautiful, hardworking, submissive, and traditional.

Asian women, he discovers in his magazines, agree to come to Canada as mail-order brides and marry Canadian men who provide them with Canadian

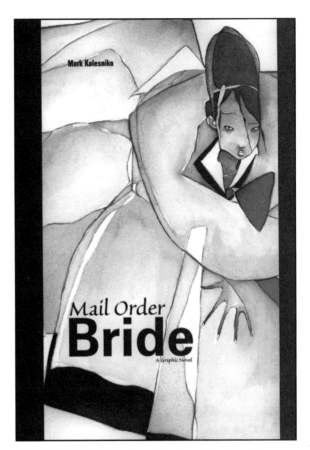

Mail Order Bride. (Courtesy of Fantagraphics Books)

citizenship and a way to escape the limited prospects of their home countries. Thus, Monty orders a bride.

When he meets Kyung Seo at the airport, he is initially disappointed. She is taller than he had imagined; also, she does not embrace him joyously, as he had imagined she would. Kyung Seo is shy and frightened. Her fears are multiplied when she enters Monty's home, which, like his store, is full of crazy toys and games. Those with outlandishly painted features are particularly designed to startle and intimidate. Every surface harbors a malevolent toy that often spontaneously runs amok and attacks. Monty enjoys the practical jokes of these toys.

Delighted with his new wife, he introduces her to his customers, young kids who quickly take advantage of her lack of selling experience, and his friends, who are all older than he. Monty also introduces Kyung to his family, a meeting that clearly reveals a source of Monty's lack of confidence and inability to function with his own peer group.

After some frustrating months inhabiting Monty's world, Kyung ventures out. She meets an Asian-Canadian woman, a photography student, who, with difficulty, persuades her to be her nude model in a series of photos employing the nude figure among huge pieces of industrial equipment. The show is a great success but greatly distresses Monty. Nevertheless,

Mail Order Bride. (Courtesy of Fantagraphics Books)

Kyung pursues the new friendships she is developing, especially with R. Frank, an artist and teacher who persuades her to pursue her intellectual interests and affirm her identity.

All these events push the couple apart as they struggle to maintain their own identities and salvage a relationship, for they do need each other. The story ends indecisively. Neither seems willing or able to sacrifice for the marriage, and both have many reasons to feel lost and alone.

Characters

- *Monty Wheeler* is a self-described geek who is a distributor of comic books, games, and toys and a collector of old toys, games, lunch boxes, and Asian-women themed porn magazines. He orders a Korean bride, whom he expects will fulfill his sexual fantasies and provide friendship and comfort.
- *Kyung Seo* is a mail-order bride from Korea who, though expected to fulfill her new husband's dreams and fantasies, has her own ideas about what life in Canada will be like and hopes to affirm her identity.
- *Mr. Wheeler* is Monty's father. His dominating and berating attitude and words to Monty, even after the latter has developed his own business, furnished his own home, and acquired a wife, do much to explain Monty's difficulties with personal relationships.
- *Eve Wong* is an Asian-Canadian student photographer who befriends Kyung. She encourages her to develop and assert her identity, even though her own goal of marriage is exactly the opposite of what she proposes for Kyung.
- *R. Frank* is an art-history teacher and painter who befriends Kyung, encourages her to explore her intellectual curiosity, and motivates her to discover her artistic talent.

Artistic Style

Color is used for the cover only. The cover features a symbolic, abstract design, which summarizes the themes of the novel. Big pink shapes, suggestive of the thighs of Henri Matisse's voluptuous pink bathers, ensnare the small head of an Asian woman, almost smothering it. Her small head—with intense, desperate eyes and pursed lips—and stiff, tense, outstretched hand, colored in pea green, convey the conflict of the story.

The rest of the novel uses black, sketchy, thin lines to depict the fragility of the characters, with frequent panels of black or panels of speckled black-and-white color, looking like the screen of an inoperative television channel. Black conveys strong emotions—anger, frustration, and passion. Simple as the lines describing characters are, they clearly depict the conflict, exasperation, and melancholy the characters experience and express in the text balloons.

The first several pages present a visual summary of the conflict. Next are the explicit pictures of naked Asian women, women of the pornographic magazines, that prompt Monty to order a bride. These pictures depict an Asian bride as erotic and exotic but also traditional and hardworking.

The next panels are black, reflecting Monty's angry mood from interacting with his bride. The next series present Kyung in nude pictures, but ones very different from those Monty admired. These are of her female form set against large industrial machines. They represent her artistic inclinations and her need for self-realization.

Kalesniko juxtaposes symbolic and realistic shapes and pictures. Some real shapes veer into abstraction, such as the menacing toys and the artistic sets Kyung imagines. This dissonance expresses the novel's theme.

Themes

Mail Order Bride explores the issues that arise when someone orders a life partner from another culture through the mail. Monty envisions the product he is ordering will be similar to the description and the picture presented, but mostly to his own specific needs. Ordering a bride seems to indicate a lack of self-confidence. Seemingly, Monty has been unsuccessful in interacting with his peer group. The bride is subject to exploitation. She is understood to be someone risking personal safety and self-determination for another chance at life. The story presents

Mark Kalesniko

Having graduated from the California Institute of the Arts with a degree in character animation, Mark Kalesniko began a career as a layout artist for Disney. He began publishing comics in 1991 and serialized his first graphic novel, *Alex*, in the early 1990's. *Alex* depicts the life of an alcoholic animator with an anthropomorphic dog's head and is a tale of bitter disappointment. His 1997 graphic novel *Why Did Pete Duel Kill Himself?* features a younger version of Alex, depicting him in a series of poetically rendered scenes as being humiliated and beaten by his schoolmates. *Mail Order Bride* (2001) shifts its attention to a comic shop owner's disappointment in his arranged marriage. Most recently, *Freeway* returns to the life of Alex, who fantasizes endlessly while caught in a traffic jam. Kalesniko's books are often depressing in tone, but are drawn in a lively style that recalls animation traditions, and this disjuncture creates an extremely resonant body of work.

two needy people who place their lives in each other's hands.

The text also explores the theme of the ways people are limited in their abilities to interact normally and positively in society. Monty's family thwarts his social and emotional development. Kyung's circumstances, which she refuses to reveal, demonstrate another variation of societal rejection. Her social position in Korea precludes any opportunity to improve her life and limits her choices so completely that offering herself for sexual exploitation seems to her a positive move.

The story also demonstrates cultural stereotyping. Based on his reading of porn magazines, Monty makes assumptions about Asian women. He imagines every Asian woman will have the qualities of the Asian women in his magazines. Similarly, Kyung expects all Canadians to be like the pictures presented in the media. Neither accepts the other's expectations, yet both must make concessions with each other in the relationship and within themselves in return for an added sense of security that is in essence nothing more than a different form of the loneliness each had experienced before they met.

Kalesniko's interest lies in presenting the complexity of life, one that does not result in the traditional resolution of plot. His works end in a sense of melancholy that does not suggest character epiphany. Monty orders a bride he expects to please him. Instead, his bride is not a commodity but a real person.

The graphics of this novel do more than simply support the story line. The images add meaning allegorically, symbolically, and self-referentially. For example, Kalesniko juxtaposes different images of the nude form. He contrasts the titillating pictures of Asian women in pornographic magazines that inform Monty's fantasies with the nude photos for which Kyung poses, in which she is surrounded by industrial equipment. The former represent Monty's obsessions, fantasies, and his consideration of Kyung as a commodity. The industrial nudes represent, on one level, Kyung's efforts to attain self-realization through art. Nonetheless, both forms objectify women in a general sense and Kyung in particular. Kyung's longing to be a free spirit is represented allegorically by her fantasy of the nude woman dancing in front of the oddly dark, conservative cheerleaders. In these images, she simultaneously sees herself as dancer and cheerleader as well as the photographer who captures this mysteriously complex image.

Mail Order Bride also explores the issues of trauma and poor socialization. Situation, word, and evocative picture depict Monty's and Kyung's struggles and their inability to cope or adapt. The book's themes include isolation, disappointment, separation, and the quest for self-discovery.

Impact

Mail Order Bride, a nominee for the 2001 Ignatz Award for Outstanding Graphic Novel or Collection, extends a subgenre of graphic novels and comics dating to the Tijuana bibles and, later, to Robert Crumb's hero of *My Troubles with Women* (1992). Crumb's series simultaneously describes and satirizes the lustful, repressed male. Kalesniko's male is not satirized, but he is suffering in many ways. *Male Order Bride* is also akin to Posy Simmond's novel *Gemma Bovery* (2000), which presents the female sexual fantasy. Even while Kalesniko utilizes the passionate-lover tradition of comics and graphic novels, he continues to express his own intent. In *Mail Order Bride*, symbolism, allegory, and dramatic situations rendered by graphic art and dramatic structure do not affirm growth and renewal; rather, they serve to define the human condition as one of confusion and frustration.

Bernadette Flynn Low

Further Reading

Katchor, Ben. *The Jew of New York* (2001).
Simmonds, Posy. *Gemma Bovery* (2005).
Tomine, Adrian. *Summer Blonde* (2009).

Bibliography

Eisner, Will. *Graphic Storytelling*. Paramus, N.J.: Poorhouse Press, 2006.
Gravett, Paul. *Graphic Novels: Everything You Need to Know*. New York: Collins Design, 2006.
Paparone, Lesley. "Art and Identity in Mark Kalesniko's Mail Order Bride." *MELUS* 32, no. 3 (Fall, 2007): 201-220.
Zaleski, Jeff. "Mail Order Bride." *Publishers Weekly* 242, no. 22 (May 28, 2001): 51.

See also: *The Jew of New York*; *Gemma Bovery, The Color Trilogy*

MARKET DAY

Author: Sturm, James
Artist: James Sturm (illustrator)
Publisher: Drawn and Quarterly
First book publication: 2010

Publication History

Market Day was published by Drawn and Quarterly in 2010. Drawn and Quarterly had previously published *America: God, Gold, and Golems* (2007), also by James Sturm, which is a compilation of three previously published stories, including *The Golem's Mighty Swing* (2001), one of Sturm's first successes. In his earlier works, Sturm tended to focus on three main topics: Jews, America, and baseball. *Market Day* continues to focus on Jewish experiences, but in eastern Europe. It represents a departure point for Sturm, as it is his first work to be published in color. Throughout, Sturm makes use of the relationship between the main character, his profession as an artist, and color selection.

Plot

Market Day is the story of one day in the life of Orthodox Jewish rug weaver Mendelman and is told from his perspective. Early in the text, the reader learns that Mendelman is content with his profession; he believes that rug making is his true calling as an artisan and that it will provide him with sufficient money to support himself and his pregnant wife, Rachel, in their shtetl (eastern European Jewish village). On the day that the story takes place, Mendelman goes alone to the market while Rachel stays home; he is nervous but also excited about this, as he enjoys the bustling pace and the friends that he will see in town. Upon arrival in the market, Mendelman is unable to sell any of his rugs because his usual buyer has relocated and the new owner is uninterested in additional stock. The rejection weighs heavily on Mendelman because he does not know how he will support himself. This leads Mendelman into a tailspin, as he worries about what he will do to subsist. He begins wandering through the market, eventually arriving at an emporium, where he sells his rugs for

Market Day. (Courtesy of Drawn and Quarterly)

below-market value. This further demoralizes him, and he is ashamed to return home to his wife.

While wandering through the night, he oscillates between depression and the desire to learn a new trade. He encounters a group of homeless men who confuse him for someone else. Later, he even begins to fantasize about another woman. Eventually, Mendelman arrives back in his town, and his friends take him home. The final scenes of the text show Mendelman standing on his porch; the final shot is a picture of just his home, leaving the reader unsure whether Mendelman entered his home, returned to his wife, and will seek new employment or whether he left her to pursue his artistic craft elsewhere.

Characters

- *Mendelman* is an Orthodox Jewish rug weaver who dresses in the style of nineteenth-century eastern European Jews. He wears a dark suit, a white shirt, and a black hat and has a beard. Through reflections on his past, he demonstrates a need for approval. He succeeds in his craft under the tutelage of Mr. Finkler. His talents are recognized by the rabbis of the community; they ask him to weave particular color patterns when they make decisions about Jewish legal matters. On the day the story takes place, he is anxious about his ability to provide for his family after Mr. Finkler moves to a new town and his replacement is uninterested in buying the rugs. This leaves Mendelman with fine rugs but no clients and a pregnant wife at home. Mendelman struggles to adjust to his new situation and acknowledges that he does not have other marketable skills with which to earn a livelihood. Mendelman's life begins to unravel. Whether or not Mendelman has decided to return to his wife is unclear.

- *Rachel* is Mendelman's wife and is absent for much of the text. She has no speaking parts and is seen only at the beginning of the text while sleeping. Despite her physical absence, she is referenced many times throughout and is a central figure in Mendelman's life. She is referred to as Mendelman's better half by the fellow men in the marketplace, and they respect her as Mendelman's wife. However, following his inability to sell his goods, her pregnancy causes Mendelman anxiety because he is unsure how he will provide for her. She expresses concern for her husband

Market Day. (Courtesy of Drawn and Quarterly)

when he does not return home and arranges for his friends to search for him.

- *Mr. Finkler* is an elderly man who sold high-end custom merchandise. He was the first to recognize Mendelman's artistic talent and encouraged Mendelman to practice his skills in order to improve. He purchased many of Mendelman's rugs, not notifying him that sales were tapering off, in order to continue encouraging Mendelman to weave despite putting the shop in financial difficulty. Finkler leaves the town abruptly, abandoning his store and putting it in the hands of his son-in-law. This departure precipitates Mendelman's bad day. The realization that Mr. Finkler continued to buy merchandise from Mendelman though no one was actually buying the rugs causes Mendelman great distress, as he feels that Mr. Finkler misled him about his talents.

- *Mr. Finkler's son-in-law* assumes control of the business, following his father-in-law's decision to retire, and is uninterested in maintaining the rapport that his father-in-law had with his artisans. He approaches the store purely from a business standpoint and refuses to purchase unnecessary stock the way that his father-in-law once did in order to support the development of local artists. It is perhaps not coincidental that he is unnamed, especially given his demeanor and his refusal to develop any type of personal relationship with his customers that would encourage him to share his name or for them to ask him for it.

Artistic Style

Market Day is Sturm's first published work in color and is a departure from his earlier work in black, white, or brown outlines of individuals as is seen in *The Golem's Mighty Swing*. For the most part, colors are muted, but in certain scenes such as those featuring sunrise, sunset, and the fruit stands in the market, the colors are richer but never actually bright. The colors reflect the overall mood of the text as a dark experience.

Throughout, text color is used to reflect the ways in which Mendelman sees the world as an artist. Entire panels are dedicated to depicting the world through Mendelman's perspective, which views everything as a pattern for a future rug. Life is literally an artistic piece for Mendelman, as he sees art everywhere he looks. By presenting scenery in this way, Sturm is reinforcing Mendelman's gift as an artist, yet the scenes also reinforce Mendelman's dilemma that is shared by artists and craftspeople throughout time: Mendelman was born to craft rugs, to create art, yet he is living a world that is increasingly unsupportive of his art.

Sturm also uses scenery for pacing. As Mendelman walks throughout the panels of *Market Day*, the world around him operates at a frenetic pace and Mendelman's day continues to spiral out of control as he is rejected in the market and left forlorn. Through the use of two-page visuals of scenery without any text, Sturm forces his reader to slow down the reading pace and fully internalize and consider what is happening to Mendelman.

Images are also used to convey information that would be difficult to communicate in words yet is essential to the story. For example, Sturm identifies Mendelman as a Jew. One of the panels on the opening page is of a mezuzah, a Jewish ritual object affixed to doorposts. By showing an image of a religious object that many readers would identify as Jewish, instead of entering into an explanation of Mendelman's religious identity, Sturm welcomes the reader into the text and into Mendelman's life in a subtle way. By doing this, Sturm narrows the distance between Mendelman and the reader while still providing important information. Sturm's strategy is particularly effective given the sensitive subject of the text. Without a connection to Mendelman, it would be more difficult to empathize with him and his plight.

Themes

The major theme of *Market Day* is the role of the artist in society. Through his presentation of Mendelman's struggles, Sturm focuses on the relationship between an artist and the society in which he or she lives. Sturm presents a series of examples of this relationship through the reactions of different characters. That Mr. Finkler supports Mendelman's craft despite the fact that he is losing money represents a belief that the artist contributes something beyond financial remuneration to society. On the other hand, Mr. Finkler's son-in-law refuses to support the artist because he stands to make no money from such an endeavor. Between these two poles is Mendelman, who does not know what his role will be after losing his patron. Mendelman wants to create, but he knows that he cannot support himself on his own. Sturm's concluding image, showing Mendelman's home without an indication as to whether Mendelman returned to it, places the burden on the reader to decide what Mendelman should have done. Should he pursue his craft elsewhere and abandon his family, or should he abandon his craft and support his family through some other means? This conundrum forces the reader to consider what society's responsibility is toward artists.

Impact

Market Day is a work of the Modern Age of comics, having been published in 2010. It has received positive reviews from *Time* magazine, National Public Radio, and *The New York Times* and has met with particular acclaim throughout the comics industry. It represents an evolution in Sturm's craft, as he experiments with color, a departure from his earlier work. *Market Day* shows a commitment to the medium and demonstrates the importance of assessing each work independently and what each text needs in order to properly convey

meaning. This accurately reflects Strum's role as a teacher of comics, cartooning, and education through comics.

Matt Reingold

Further Reading

Sfar, Joann. *Klezmer: Tales from the Wild East* (2006).
Sturm, James. *The Golem's Mighty Swing* (2003).

Bibliography

Harde, Roxanne. "'Give 'em Another Circumcision': Jewish Masculinities in *The Golem's Mighty Swing*." In *The Jewish Graphic Novel: Critical Approaches*, edited by Samantha Baskind and Ranen Omer-Sherman. Piscataway, N.J.: Rutgers University Press, 2010.

Kacyzne, Alter, and Marek Web. *Poyln: Jewish Life in the Old Country*. New York: Henry Holt, 2001.

Shandler, Jeffrey. *Adventures in Yiddishland: Postvernacular Language and Culture*. Berkeley: University of California Press, 2008.

Vishniac, Roman. *A Vanished World*. New York: Farrar, Straus, and Giroux, 1999.

See also: *The Golem's Mighty Swing*; *The Jew of New York*; *Maus*; *The Rabbi's Cat*

MAUS: A SURVIVOR'S TALE

Author: Spiegelman, Art
Artist: Art Spiegelman (illustrator)
Publisher: Pantheon Books
First serial publication: 1980-1991
First book publication: 1986; 1991

Publication History

Maus was first introduced as a three-page comic in *Funny Animals* in 1972 and was then serialized in the underground comics magazine *RAW* between the years 1980 and 1991. With the exception of the last chapter in Volume 2, all of the chapters of *Maus* first appeared in altered versions in the magazine. It was then published by Pantheon Press as two separate hardcover books, then as softcover books, and finally as a boxed set. Additionally, in 1994, *Maus* was released on CD-ROM with annotations, maps, and extended video commentary by creator Art Spiegelman on the text as well as examples of his later work. Spiegelman's *MetaMaus*, a commentary on the making of *Maus*, was released in 2011.

Plot

Maus presents two simultaneous stories, Vladek Spiegelman's Holocaust story and Art Spiegelman's experiences as the child of a Holocaust survivor. The two stories are interwoven together, as the framework for the narrative is a series of interviews conducted between Art and his father, Vladek. Through these interviews, the reader learns about Vladek's life before the Holocaust, his Holocaust story, and Art's struggles to live in the shadow of a father who seeks to control all aspects of his life.

The first volume, *My Father Bleeds History*, presents the foundation for *Maus*, relating the story of Vladek's upbringing in Poland and his courtship and early marriage to Art's mother, Anja. Vladek narrates about the family business and the ways that the Jews' lives became restricted after the Nazis took power. At first, Vladek is able to protect his family by paying non-Jews to hide them; however, as the situation deteriorates, he finds it increasingly difficult to do this

Maus: A Survivor's Tale. (Courtesy of Pantheon Books)

and is ultimately deceived in an attempt to flee the country. Vladek's narrative in Volume 1 ends with his and Anja's deportment to the concentration camp at Auschwitz.

In this volume, the reader also learns of the challenges that Art has in his relationship with Vladek as well as his guilt over his mother's suicide some years earlier. These issues are revealed through strained conversations regarding Mala, Vladek's second wife whom he treats poorly, and Vladek's decision to destroy Anja's Holocaust diaries, which Art was interested in using as research for presenting Anja's story in *Maus*. The volume ends with Vladek confessing that he burned the diaries in a fit of depression, which prompts Art to call him a murderer.

The second volume, *And Here My Troubles Began*, commences with Vladek and Anja in Auschwitz and details the ways in which Vladek was able to survive selections, work details, and marches. In Auschwitz, Vladek was adept at making deals with *kapos*, prisoners working as supervisors inside the concentration camp, in order to get better work details for himself and Anja and used his English-language skills to advantage. Both survive Auschwitz, reunite in their hometown after the war, and rebuild their lives, first in Sweden and then in the United States.

In the present, Mala leaves Vladek because she can no longer tolerate his verbal and financial abuse, and Vladek pretends to have a heart attack so that Art will call him. Art and his wife, Françoise, temporarily move in with Vladek at his summer home to help him, but they are quickly burdened by Vladek's demands. Eventually Mala returns and takes care of Vladek until his death at the age of seventy-five. Vladek's death is briefly mentioned but neither shown nor described in the text; the final page depicts Vladek and Anja's reunion followed by an illustration of their shared tombstone.

Volumes

- *Maus I, A Survivor's Tale: My Father Bleeds History* (1986). Relates Vladek's early life prior to the Nazi invasion and his experiences during the Holocaust, culminating with his and Anja's deportation to Auschwitz.
- *Maus II, A Survivor's Tale: And Here My Troubles Began* (1991). Describes Vladek's experiences in the concentration camp, reunion with Anja, and life after the Holocaust.

Characters

- *Art Spiegelman* is not only the writer and artist of *Maus*, but also one of the two main characters. He is interested in Vladek's Holocaust story and how it shaped Vladek's life, but he struggles to comprehend why his father is stingy and intent on micromanaging his and Mala's lives. He is troubled by his mother's suicide and does not understand why she took her life. A breaking point in his relationship with his father comes when Vladek admits to having burned Anja's diaries. He wants to present a realistic portrait of his father but is negatively affected by his father's actions.

- *Vladek Spiegelman* is a Holocaust survivor and the second main character in *Maus*. In his interviews with Art, he explains the different ways that he saved himself and his first wife, Anja, negotiating with people to hide them or give them food and bribing officials to allow him to take jobs for which he was not qualified. His ability to save and store for the future was essential to their survival; however, he is unable to abandon these skills following the Holocaust, ultimately becoming obsessive and controlling. He loved Anja and remains fully devoted to her, even after her suicide and his subsequent marriage to Mala, which seems to be a marriage of convenience in which Mala takes care of him. He is supportive of Art's need to express his feelings through art but is concerned with the way that he will be presented in the text.

- *Anja Spiegelman*, Vladek's first wife and Art's mother, was also a Holocaust survivor. An innately anxious and depressive person, she was devastated when she learned that her first son, Richieu, had died during the Holocaust. To combat her feelings of helplessness, she becomes involved in Art's life to the extent that he feels burdened by her presence. She committed suicide prior to the writing of *Maus*.

- *Mala Spiegelman*, Vladek's second wife, struggles to live up to Vladek's comparison of her and Anja. Vladek micromanages her life, refuses to give her money for her own needs, and accuses her of stealing his life's savings. Eventually, she leaves Vladek but feels guilty for abandoning him and returns to take care of him.

- *Françoise Mouly*, Art's wife, is the person to whom Art confides his difficulties with his father and his struggles in representing their relationship. She supports Art emotionally and helps him care for his father after Mala leaves.

Artistic Style

Maus was drawn by Spiegelman as a black-and-white text that relies heavily on dark shading throughout. Pages are typically arranged in a series of two panels per line with three or four lines per page. This format, however, is not used consistently throughout, and Spiegelman introduces larger panels and pages with more panels at various points.

The most significant aspect of *Maus*'s artwork is the metaphorical way that Spiegelman has chosen to represent his characters. Each nationality is represented as a different member of the animal kingdom: Jews are mice, Nazis are cats, the French are frogs, Poles are pigs, Americans are dogs, and Swedes are reindeer. These choices are intentional, motivated either by the hierarchy that exists in the animal kingdom or by sociocultural associations. Jews are represented as mice to illustrate how they were perceived by Nazis, as lowly, dirty prey. These representations are used both for Vladek's memories and in the present-day stories.

During the Holocaust, Jews often tried to present themselves as Germans or Poles in order to save themselves. In *Maus*, Jews who try to present themselves as another ethnicity are drawn as mice wearing masks with noticeable ties. Spiegelman thereby suggests that ethnicity and religion are aspects of identity that cannot be easily changed and that no amount of subterfuge can truly change.

Importantly, individual characters do not have distinct bodies. Among non-Jews, it is difficult to distinguish between individuals. For Jews, it is not always possible to determine an individual, but main characters are identified by clothing, glasses, or facial features or marks. This ambiguity of identity inverts the Nazi belief that Jews did not have identities and distinct personalities.

The animal imagery is abandoned twice during the series, once in each volume. In Volume 1, Spiegelman includes a previously published short comic entitled "Prisoner on the Hell Planet: A Case History," as part of a dialogue between Art and Mala in which she tells him that his father has already seen the comic. The comic is an autobiographical vignette about Art's experiences, sense of guilt, and suffering following

Anja's suicide; although the comic upsets Vladek, he comforts Art by suggesting its importance as a cathartic creative outlet. The comic's art style is a departure from *Maus*'s animal imagery and instead uses exaggerated poses and facial expressions. The erratic line work reflects the scattered emotions presented in the text.

In Volume 2, Art briefly abandons drawing himself as a mouse and instead draws himself as a human wearing a mouse mask. In this narrative sequence, Art shows the challenges he had resuming his father's narrative about Auschwitz, the unexpected publicity Volume 1 received, his annoyance at the commercialization of his work, and his therapy sessions. In presenting himself as a human pretending to be a mouse, Spiegelman suggests that he felt distanced from his Jewish identity and from the original purpose of the work. Only following a therapy session is he able to return to his father's narrative and to presenting himself as a mouse.

Maus: A Survivor's Tale. (Courtesy of Pantheon Books)

Themes

Through the juxtaposition of the interwoven narratives, *Maus* revolves primarily around the impact that traumatic experiences can have on individuals and their families over a protracted period. By presenting specific examples of how Vladek still lives his life as if he were in Auschwitz, especially in relation to his obsessive need to save, Spiegelman demonstrates that trauma is not easily overcome. Additionally, by presenting his own voice, Spiegelman further illustrates how traumas can be debilitating for the children of survivors, who cannot truly understand their parents' experiences.

Another important thematic concern of *Maus* is the concept of self-sacrifice for loved ones. At Auschwitz, Vladek partially starves himself to be able to make deals that will benefit Anja, only to have his "savings" stolen and have to begin again. He does whatever he can to ease conditions for her and, when caught talking to her, he suffers a severe beating. This suggests that Anja was the lifeline that sustained Vladek throughout the entire ordeal. It is noteworthy that Art and Françoise's relationship also exhibits some of the traits of Vladek and Anja's relationship in relation to sacrifice. Throughout the text, Françoise encourages Art to meet with Vladek and agrees to help take care of him even though she too finds it difficult to work with Vladek for extended periods.

Lastly, Spiegelman makes strong statements about the concept of racial identity. The novel's funny-animal format and use of masks helps to undermine the arbitrary divisions between races, nationalities, and religions. The argument between Art and Françoise about how she should be represented is illustrative of this aim. The second volume opens with Art's various doodles of Françoise as a moose, a frog, a rabbit, a poodle, and so forth. As a Jewish convert of French descent and his wife, Françoise expresses irritation over Art's proposed depictions of her along ethnic lines. This scene's inclusion in the narrative, along with the clear use of masks to indicate Jews trying to pass as a different ethnicity, suggests that identities are partially social constructions, albeit powerful and enduring ones.

Art Spiegelman

Arguably the most influential and important American cartoonist of the second half of the twentieth century, Art Spiegelman created *Maus*, the defining work of alternative and independent comics. Having produced work in the underground comics movement of the late-1960's, Spiegelman turned his hand to editing with *Arcade* (co-edited with Bill Griffith) and *RAW* (co-edited with François Mouly). It was in *RAW* that he began serializing *Maus*, the biographical tale of his parents' experiences of the Holocaust that is presented through the use of anthropomorphic animals. Collected as a two-volume graphic novel, *Maus* proved to a generation of skeptics that comics could produce work on a par with achievements in the arts, and won an entirely new respectability for the form. Spiegelman's reflection on the events of September 11, 2001, *In the Shadow of No Towers*, was also widely praised. Few cartoonists have had the cultural impact that Art Spiegelman has had, and fewer have done so much to advance the common understanding of the art form.

Impact

Maus is considered one of the most significant graphic novels ever produced. Its publication was instrumental in legitimizing comics and graphic novels in the eyes of both scholars and the general population. It was the first graphic novel to win a major literary prize, being awarded a Pulitzer Prize in 1992. It is also included on many college and university syllabi that focus on the Holocaust or graphic novels because of its themes, mode of expression, and critical reception.

Spiegelman's text was the first to represent the Holocaust in graphic novel form. Some deemed the work inappropriate given the sensitive nature of the subject and a perception that the medium of expression delegitimizes and trivializes the Holocaust. For many others, including Vladek Spiegelman as represented in Volume 1, the graphic novel is a genre of communication equal in weight to film, memoir, visual arts, poetry, and other media.

Maus also raised many important questions of historicity, including whether facts can accurately be represented in graphic novel format given the unorthodox mode of presentation. During the book's run on *The New York Times* best-sellers list in 1991, Spiegelman petitioned the newspaper to move it from the fiction list to the nonfiction list. The book's eventual reclassification affirmed that comics and graphic novels can address serious historical events.

Maus is considered the prototypical Holocaust graphic novel, a genre that includes Dave Sim's *Judenhass* (2008), Greg Pak and Carmine Di Giandomenico's *X-Men: Magneto Testament* (2008), Pascal Croci's *Auschwitz* (2003), Joe Kubert's *Yossel* (2003), and Bernice Eisenstein's *I Was a Child of Holocaust Survivors* (2006).

Matt Reingold

Further Reading

Díaz Canales, Juan, and Juanjo Guarnido. *Blacksad* (2010).

Pak, Greg, and Carmine Di Giandomenico. *X-Men: Magneto Testament* (2009).

Spiegelman, Art. *In the Shadow of No Towers* (2004).

Bibliography

Geis, Deborah R., ed. *Considering Maus: Approaches to Art Spiegelman's "Survivors Tale" of the Holocaust.* Tuscaloosa: University of Alabama Press, 2007.

Mulman, Lisa Naomi. "A Tale of Two Mice: Graphic Representations of the Jew in Holocaust Narrative." In *The Jewish Graphic Novel: Critical Approaches*, edited by Samantha Baskind and Ranen Omer-Sherman. Piscataway, N.J.: Rutgers University Press, 2010.

Spiegelman, Art. "A Problem of Taxonomy." *The New York Times Book Review*, December 29, 1991. http://www.nytimes.com/1991/12/29/books/l-a-problem-of-taxonomy-37092.html.

See also: *In the Shadow of No Towers*; *Yossel*

METROPOL: THE COMPLETE SERIES + METROPOL A.D.

Author: McKeever, Ted
Artist: Ted McKeever (illustrator)
Publisher: Image Comics
First serial publication: 1991-1992 (*Metropol*); 1993 (*Metropol A.D.*)
First book publication: 2009

Publication History

In 2009, Shadowline, a privately owned imprint of Image Comics, published the entire *Metropol* series under the title *Metropol: The Complete Series + Metropol A.D.* The two titles were originally published as a series of comic book issues by Epic Comics, an imprint of Marvel Comics. Founded in 1982, Epic provided Marvel an imprint that permitted the creators of the comics to maintain ownership of their work.

Metropol was published in a series of twelve issues from 1991 to 1992; *Metropol A.D.* was published in three issues in 1993. *Metropol* was first published as a single volume by London-based company Blue Eyed Dog in 1995. In 2000 and 2001, Sorhenn Grafiks published *Metropol* in French in two volumes, translated by Serge and Stéphane Philippo. They also published it in English as a single volume and an e-book in 2000.

Plot

Metropol, *Transit* (2008), and *Eddy Current* (2008) form a trilogy of graphic novels by Ted McKeever that address the corruption and decay of an industrialized society. The novel recounts an apocalyptic battle between angels and demons. A plague is devastating the population of a large industrial city. Once people die, they come back to life either as angels or as demons; however, the demons far outnumber the angels. Only a few individuals have the purity of heart to come back as angels, whose mission it is to defeat the demons.

Sarakiel, the leader of the angels, has arrived in the city and is looking for the other angels. Jasper Notochord, who will die of the plague and become the angel Enoch, is embroiled with two unpleasant police detectives, Martin and Verdi, who put him in jail and insist he admit to seeing something that he did not see.

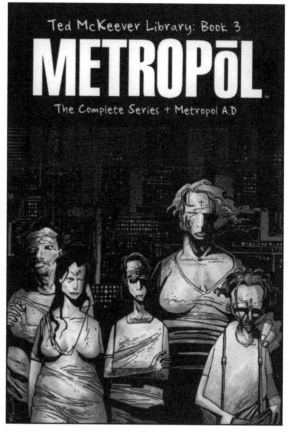

Metropol: The Complete Series + Metropol A.D. (Courtesy of Image Comics)

Trinity, a waitress at the Redd Mecca restaurant, commits suicide by overdosing on pills. Sarakiel comes to her apartment believing she will be one of the angels, but because she has committed the unforgivable sin of suicide, she comes back as a demon with a strong hatred for Sarakiel. They engage in a vicious battle. Humphrey, a clerk in a video store, becomes involved with a street prostitute named Candy. Jack Wack, a Jack the Ripper-type character, kills Candy and her partner. Humphrey kills Jack Wack out of love for Candy and is then killed by a policeman.

Meanwhile, Jasper is resurrected with the knowledge that he is Enoch. Before his death, he had already communicated with this other self. He and Sarakiel soon meet and battle demons. Sarakiel explains the marks that the angels have on their foreheads and helps Enoch with his metamorphosis. Sarakiel and Enoch meet the newly resurrected Candy/Uriel, Humphrey/ Gabriel, and Jack Wack. Once again, Sarakiel makes a mistake in believing that the other three are all angels. Enoch recognizes that Jack Wack is not an angel but a creature from hell. When the angels battle the demons, they undergo a metamorphosis that replaces their skin with metal, and each discovers his or her special knowledge.

The city has been walled in to confine the plague. As the population dies and returns to life, the number of demons increases. The angels go to a gun shop, arming themselves with high-tech weapons and an arsenal of nuclear devices. Meanwhile, Martin and Verdi are killed in a car wreck and resurrected as demons. They kill a policeman, who comes back to life as the angel Noah. Eddy Current has returned and joins Noah, while Jack Wack attempts to organize the city's demons and the angels return to Enoch's apartment. At the end of *Metropol*, Uriel tells Sarakiel that she is pregnant.

In the three-chapter sequel, *Metropol A.D.*, McKeever continues his tale. Jack Wack has become the master of the demons. The angels have been hiding for a year in Enoch's apartment building and are gathering reinforcements. Uriel has given birth to a son, Joshua. Noah and Eddy battle demons as they make their way to the safe house.

The angels make their final stand against Jack Wack and the demons, but much goes wrong, and Gabriel and Noah begin to fight. Noah's anger causes him to break his bond with the other angels. He realizes that he has been defeated by his inability to control his rage and dies fighting the demons. Having decided that self-sacrifice is the answer, Gabriel abandons the others to blow up the city without saving the remaining humans.

Enoch, Sarakiel, Uriel, Joshua, Eddy, and the few humans that are left escape in a truck just before Gabriel sets off a nuclear explosion that destroys the city. *Metropol A.D.* concludes with the three remaining angels discussing their responsibility to watch for the return of the evil and safeguard humankind. They realize that while the future may be safe because of their vigilance, it will still be bleak.

Characters

- *Jasper Notochord*, a.k.a. *Enoch*, the protagonist, is an ordinary, average-looking man who becomes involved in an apocalyptic war between angels and demons. He lives alone in a small apartment and is bothered by dreams that he does not understand. He contracts the plague, dies, and becomes the angel Enoch.
- *Sarakiel* is the leader of the angels. In *Eddy Current*, she was Nun, a large woman who helped Eddy save the world. Both died in the quest. In *Metropol*, she has returned as a large, mannish-looking woman with large breasts.
- *Trinity* is a waitress at the Redd Mecca restaurant. She has the potential to become an angel, but she chooses to commit suicide. Upon her death, she transforms from an average-looking woman with dark hair into a monster with a human female body, a ram's head, and a set of wings.
- *Candy*, a.k.a. *Uriel*, is a prostitute who is shot and killed by Jack Wack. After her death, she becomes Uriel, one of the strongest angels. She gives birth to Joshua.
- *Humphrey*, a.k.a. *Gabriel*, is a mild-mannered, well-intentioned man who is in love with a good-hearted prostitute named Candy. After his death, he transforms into the angel Gabriel.
- *Jack Wack* is from the demons' side. He attempts to pose as an angel and infiltrate their group, but he does not carry an angel's mark on his forehead. Enoch knows he is not an angel and sends him away.
- *Noah*, a former policeman, is the fifth angel. He first appears in the last chapter of *Metropol*.
- *Eddy Current*, the protagonist of McKeever's second work, also called *Eddy Current*, joins the angels in the fight against the demons. He adds humor to the story with both his appearance and his comments.
- *Joshua* is Uriel's son. He represents the continuation of life.

Artistic Style

Metropol and *Metropol A.D.* are drawn in black and white. The action is set in a grim industrialized city filled with corruption and danger, where there is no beauty, no joy, and little compassion. McKeever's renditions of the city, its buildings, and its traffic are heavily inked, giving the impression of overcrowding, pollution, darkness, and decay. The panels are congested with inked-in areas and roughly sketched shapes that express the chaos and discord of the city.

McKeever's characters are hastily drawn and sketchy, with a minimum of detail. They reflect the lack of beauty and joy in the city, as none of them are

Metropol: The Complete Series + Metropol A.D. (Courtesy of Image Comics)

particularly attractive. The angels contrast sharply with traditional portrayals of angels. They do not earn halos and robes; instead, their skin drops from their bodies and is replaced with metal. However, the angels do retain human features, unlike the demons, which are portrayed as monstrous creatures with large eyes, big teeth, horns, and severely misshapen bodies. Jack Wack is always drawn with his hair over one side of his face.

McKeever uses both bubbles and rectangles for dialogue. There is also a considerable amount of commentary. In the first part of the work, the commentary recounts television news broadcasts about the plague and the appearance of demons in the city; in later chapters, it takes the form of biblical prophecy. This technique gives readers the sense of actually watching the story unfold and provides a close investigation of the visual narrative.

McKeever links *Metropol* to his other works with both written and visual references. Sneakers play an important role in the graphic novel and foretell the return of Eddy Current. Sarakiel insists that Enoch wear sneakers. In the sewers, Sarakiel holds up Eddy's sneakers, the only item in her bag not washed away; she has kept them as a reminder of Eddy and as a way to draw him back. The chapter ends with a sequence in which Eddy breaks out of his grave and wants to know where his sneakers are. In another example, while in the gun shop, Enoch says the disposable bazookas remind him of plastic forks. Sarakiel is drawn from behind, with her hair hanging down her back in the form of a dog's hind legs and tail; this portrayal cleverly references McKeever's book about animal experimentation, *Plastic Forks*.

Themes

In *Metropol* and *Metropol A.D.*, McKeever portrays the battle between good and evil on an apocalyptic scale. Overwhelmingly outnumbered angels engage in a violent battle against the demons. McKeever draws upon Christian tradition in his portrayal of the battle, and the names of the angels are either those of biblical angels (Sarakiel, Gabriel, and Uriel) or well-known biblical names (Enoch, Noah). Suicide is viewed as the unforgivable sin. Heaven and Hell exist. However, *Metropol*

is not a modernized retelling of the Christian Apocalypse. Trinity states that Christ has nothing to do with the current situation. The fight is not a question of salvation; it is a war between good and evil, between angels and demons.

In the afterword, added in 2008, McKeever discusses the intent of *Metropol*: to find realistic answers to who people are and whether they possess free will. He states that a human body is twenty-one grams lighter in weight after death, and therefore he recognizes the existence of a soul.

Social criticism is another theme of *Metropol*. McKeever portrays the corruption, vice, and dishonesty of contemporary society. The city is filled with people who have little or no compassion for each other. They are rude, cruel, and uncaring. The police are obsessed with their power and use it to abuse others. Thieves, murderers, and prostitutes abound.

Metropol also addresses the concept of the hero. In contrast to the standard American comics hero, generally an indestructible superhero, McKeever's heroes are vulnerable, and several of them die. Both Noah and Gabriel die, even though they are angels. Eddy Current died in the previous story, his self-titled volume, in which he saved the world, and he returns now to once again be a hero after his death.

Impact

Metropol is one of McKeever's most important works. It is the third in a series of graphic novels that explore the existence of good and evil and critique modern industrialized society. *Metropol* has played a significant role in the expansion of the graphic novel genre and has contributed to the genre's consideration as one of serious literary merit. In contrast to the superhero and crime comics that target a younger audience, *Metropol* illustrates that the medium of comics is suited to more abstract and philosophical considerations.

Metropol is an important addition to the corpus of creator-owned comics, which are becoming readily available to the reading public. In 2010, McKeever began publishing *Meta 4,* another experimental and innovative graphic novel. In addition to his success in producing graphic novels entirely on his own, McKeever has also collaborated with other writers and on major superhero comics, including issues of *Superman*, *Batman*, and *Wonder Woman*.

Shawncey Jay Webb

Further Reading

McKeever, Ted. *Eddy Current* (2008).

_____. *Meta 4: The Complete Series* (2011).

_____. *Transit* (2008).

Bibliography

Eisner, Will. *Graphic Storytelling and Visual Narrative*. New York: W. W. Norton, 2008.

McCloud, Scott. *Making Comics: Storytelling Secrets of Comics, Manga, and Graphic Novels*. New York: Harper, 2006.

_____. *Understanding Comics: The Invisible Art*. New York: HarperPerennial, 1994.

Schwartz, Ben, ed. *The Best American Comics Criticism*. Seattle: Fantagraphics Books, 2010.

See also: *Sin City*; *Walking Dead*; *Dead Memory*

MINOR MIRACLES:
LONG AGO AND ONCE UPON A TIME BACK WHEN UNCLES WERE HEROIC, COUSINS WERE CLEVER, AND MIRACLES HAPPENED ON EVERY BLOCK

Author: Eisner, Will
Artist: Will Eisner (illustrator)
Publisher: DC Comics; W. W. Norton
First book publication: 2000

Publication History

Will Eisner's *Minor Miracles*, subtitled *Long Ago and Once Upon a Time Back When Uncles Were Heroic, Cousins Were Clever, and Miracles Happened on Every Block*, was first published in 2000 by DC Comics. In 2001, it was translated into French as *Petits miracles*, published by Delcourt, and Spanish as *Pequeños milagros*, published by Barcelona Norma. It was republished in English by W. W. Norton in 2009.

Plot

Eisner's *Minor Miracles* contains four, thematically related stories. "The Miracle of Dignity," "Street Magic," "A New Kid on the Block," and "A Special Wedding Ring" all share the theme of modern-day miracles in an urban setting. "The Miracle of Dignity" concerns the Depression-era rags-to-riches-to-rags story of unscrupulous Uncle Amos. Uncle Amos takes advantage of his honest and well-meaning cousin Irving, a well-to-do furniture dealer who takes pity on the impoverished Amos. Amos is given a new lease on life when Irving lends him ten thousand dollars; Amos refuses to sign a promissory note because he has no intention of paying back the money. Amos blackmails Irving emotionally to secure a furniture store on the Concourse and watches nonchalantly as Irving goes bankrupt. Suddenly, Amos and Irving have switched places; Amos has become a financial success, and Irving has become penniless, but no longer naïve. The plot comes full circle as Irving blackmails Amos emotionally, coercing him to pay for the education of Irving's son, who becomes a successful lawyer as Amos reverts to his impoverished, homeless life.

Will Eisner works at his drawing board in 1998. *Minor Miracles* offers a depiction of Jewish life in early twentieth-century New York City. (AP Photo)

The second vignette tells the story of Mersh, an immigrant boy walking through a tough neighborhood with his young cousin. The street-savvy Mersh employs his craftiness to avoid being beaten up. Three hoodlums intercept him the day after they have beaten him up, telling him that immigrants of his kind (the text never indicates what kind) have no right to walk in their territory. One hoodlum writes "GUILTY" on two pieces of paper and places them in a hat, telling Mersh that one paper is blank and the other says "GUILTY." If Mersh selects the one that says "GUILTY," he will be beaten up, but if he picks the one that is blank, he will not be harmed. Mersh selects one paper and, without reading it or showing it to the predators, swallows it. Because the remaining paper says "GUILTY," Mersh announces that the one he swallowed must have been blank; thus, he outsmarts the gang members and is free to walk away with his cousin.

The third story in *Minor Miracles* is a poignant one about a homeless boy who does not know his past or how to speak. Miracles occur around him and are, perhaps, attributable to him; Eisner leaves this point ambiguous. Regardless, characters throughout the story are "saved" or helped with or without the boy's interference. For example, the nameless boy recovers money from a stolen cash register; a man tries to leave his wife for his secretary, but miraculously he ends up staying with his wife because his valise is stolen; neighbors reconcile after a missing garbage can miraculously reappears. The story ends with the boy being taken in by the character Melba, but the boy eventually leaves, never to return.

"A Special Wedding Ring" is a touching tale of Marvin, who is disabled, and Reba who is deaf and unable to speak. The two are thrown together and coerced into marriage by their widowed mothers who fear that their children will be forever alone unless they marry. Marvin and Reba overcome their reluctance and do marry; the marriage of convenience succeeds at first—a blessing attributed to the special ring donated by Shloyma Emmis. Then a miracle occurs: Reba regains her hearing and speech, causing her to be happy and feel that she no longer needs her disabled husband, whom she leaves. Marvin becomes miserable until another miracle occurs—Reba loses her sight and becomes helpless again. When Marvin finds out, he reclaims his former wife, and they live happily ever after.

Characters

- *Cousin Irving* is a furniture-store owner who tries to help Uncle Amos become a successful and dignified man.
- *Uncle Amos* is a *schnorrer*, a deceitful con artist, who takes advantage of Irving, but who, after a brief stint as a successful businessman (which

he achieves at Irving's expense), resumes his rightful place as a beggar.
- *Mersh* is a streetwise immigrant who needs to outsmart bullies in his rough neighborhood in order to survive.
- *Melba* is a bookstore owner who becomes emotionally attached to the unnamed boy and delves into his past to find out who he is. She is a caring person who enjoys helping others, which is a trait that the boy apparently shares.
- *The unnamed boy* may have been kidnapped at a young age and thus never acquired language. He is emotionally fragile and easily scared, which is logical because he was allegedly locked up by kidnappers.
- *Marie Rizzo* is a woman who owns a boarding house and who mistakenly believes that her dead son, Silvio, whom she misses terribly, has returned to her in the form of the unnamed boy.
- *Shloyma Emmis* is a deeply religious Jew who sells jewelry.
- *Marvin* is a disabled man who lives with his mother until she insists that he marry Reba, believing no other woman would want to marry him. He is a caring and forgiving man who is deeply devoted to Reba, even when she is not loyal to him.
- *Reba* is deaf and unable to speak. She marries Marvin unwillingly after being pressured by her mother. Once she recovers her hearing and speech, she leaves her husband, believing herself superior and feeling ashamed to be married to a disabled man.

Artistic Style

Eisner uses black, white, and gray with shadows. He begins the stories with splash pages, which consume the entire page, drawing the reader into the action. He creates panels of different sizes for variety and to emphasize certain scenes within the stories. Eisner employs shadows effectively to portray both the poverty of the tenement community and the unscrupulous nature of some of the characters, such as when Mr. Golin leaves his wife by sneaking out the window to the fire escape, when Marvin and Reba fight after she regains her hearing and speech and wants a divorce, and also when Shloyma Emmis is murdered. Eisner does a wonderful job of creating the visages of the hoodlums who threaten Mersh—delinquents who seem simultaneously realistic and caricatured with bulbous noses, weird hats, and goofy grins. Eisner's shadows also locate the text in time and place—aging, run-down brick tenement buildings in the early part of the twentieth century. Eisner also employs exaggerated facial expressions and hand gestures, such as when Marie Rizzo convinces herself that the nameless boy is the reincarnation of her dead son and when Shloyma Emmis gets excited when he hears about Reba and Marvin's engagement.

Themes

The primary theme is divine miracles and divine intervention versus coincidence and human action. A second theme involves survival in the urban environment. Eisner suggests that the unnamed boy in "A New Kid on the Block" creates miracles because of his innate, unspoiled goodness. During the mysterious boy's presence on Dropsie Avenue, chaos transforms into order, and feuds and unhappy marriages are healed. The narrator leads the reader to question whether the cause is coincidence or the result of the boy's possible divine ability to create miracles.

In "A Special Wedding Ring," when Shloyma Emmis learns that Reba and Marvin will marry, he calls it a miracle from God; God provides for the disabled by allowing them to find, marry, and comfort each other. Emmis gives them a special wedding diamond that seems small or luckless but is miraculous in its symbolic ability to keep the couple together. It seems, perhaps, that Emmis watches over Marvin and Reba through the ring. When Reba leaves Marvin after regaining her hearing and power of speech, thus apparently ending the marriage, Emmis is murdered (perhaps martyred); his death causes Reba to go blind and return to Marvin.

"The Miracle of Dignity" and "Street Magic" involve "fake" miracles, which manifest Eisner's theme of the prevalence of street smarts in poor, immigrant tenement communities. Uncle Amos rises to financial success not because of a miracle or his dignity, but rather because of emotional exploitation. The homeless Amos refuses to accept small acts of charity because he claims he has dignity; he therefore demands large charitable donations such as a ten-thousand-dollar loan that he never repays and a large furniture store on the Concourse. By garnering these large gifts during the Great Depression, he looks like a sagacious businessman, and he attributes his "success" to his dignity (demanding only large acts of charity). However, he has simply received these gifts without earning or working for them. As with most of the characters in *Minor Miracles*, Amos gets what he deserves by losing everything in the end. Irving, who has true dignity, is restored to financial health through his son's success.

The miracle in "Street Magic" consists of Mersh outsmarting the three bullies who terrorize him. In an example of Eisner's false miracles, Mersh's cleverness, not divine intervention, saves him from the bullies. Eisner thus points out to us all that some events can be attributed to miracles while others are simply coincidence, fate, or the result of human intelligence (or the lack of it).

Impact

Eisner was hugely influential on the comic and graphic novel industries. He proved innovative as the genre transformed from comic strip to comic book. He broke new ground in the medium by creating avenues for comic book structure and form. He mastered the "jump cut"; worked with unique perspectives and camera angles, dark shadows, and oddly-shaped panels; and he introduced other innovations as he worked on *The Spirit* (1940-1952). The unusually shaped and frameless panels that he used helped him to redesign the comics format. Eisner influenced comics creators such as Jack Kirby, Lou Fine, Bob Kane, Chuck Mazoujian, Bob Powell, Klaus Nordling, Harvey Kurtzman, Scott McCloud, and Neil Gaiman. Thus, in 1987, the Will Eisner Comic Industry Award for excellence and innovation in the business was created to honor him. The award was also created in part to honor Eisner for his positive impact on future comic book and graphic novel creators.

Eric Sterling

Further Reading

Eisner, Will. *The Contract with God Trilogy: Life on Dropsie Avenue* (2006).

_____. *Will Eisner's New York: Life in the Big City* (2006).

Katchor, Ben. *The Jew of New York* (2001).

Bibliography

Eisner, Will. *Comics and Sequential Art: Principles and Practices from the Legendary Cartoonist.* New York: W. W. Norton, 2008.

_____. *Graphic Storytelling and Visual Narrative.* New York: W. W. Norton, 2008.

Wolk, Douglas. *Reading Comics: How Graphic Novels Work and What They Mean.* Cambridge, Mass.: Da Capo Press, 2008.

See also: *A Contract with God, and Other Tenement Stories*; *The Jew of New York*; *Dropsie Avenue*

MONOLOGUES FOR THE COMING PLAGUE

Author: Nilsen, Anders
Artist: Anders Nilsen (illustrator)
Publisher: Fantagraphics Books
First book publication: 2006

Publication History

Monologues for the Coming Plague represents the contents of two of Anders Nilsen's sketchbooks and depicts a series of sketches that he began in an airport while waiting for a plane. The sketches were collected in the volume entitled *Monologues for the Coming Plague*, which was first published by Fantagraphics Books in 2006. Prior to their publication in this volume, some of these sketches had appeared in other works and collections. As Nilsen notes in his postscript, "The Wilderness, Part 2" originally appeared in *Kramers Ergot*, issue 5, while "The Mediocrity Principle" first appeared in *Blood Orange*, issue 3, and was excerpted in *Best American Nonrequired Reading, 2005.* "Job Hunt" first appeared in *The Chicago Reader*'s year-end issue, 2003. Additional sketches were first published on Nilsen's blog, *The Monologuist.*

Plot

While the book does not present an overarching plot in the usual sense, the various sketched vignettes each follow a story line of sorts. In "Introduction," a woman is spoken to by the bird she is casually feeding. The bird's utterances are hackneyed phrases that seem to be quite random, though the recurrence of these trite phrases highlights their inanity and casts a harsh light on social niceties and the uselessness of many social conventions and icons. The next section, entitled "Semiotics," diverges from this repetitive pattern and introduces two new characters who, through an apparently banal discussion of semiotics, provide insight into contemporary language and the human search for meaning.

One of the book's most compelling mini-narratives is the story that evolves through the sketches in "Pittsburgh." In this section, Scribble-Face and the Other Guy are depicted standing side-by-side, motionless and

Monologues for the Coming Plague. (Courtesy of Fantagraphics Books)

largely expressionless. Through the speech bubbles around them, and through Scribble-Face's constantly morphing head, a story evolves in which the two characters are traveling together to Pittsburgh, though neither is in a condition to drive. Scribble-Head is so tired that he begins hallucinating and then falls asleep at the wheel, crashing the car. Unseen help eventually arrives, but it may be too late for those in the (invisible) car, as they no longer respond.

The story lines of most other sections follow a similar trajectory: Through a series of sketches and related commentary, Nilsen presents a set of ideas and imagery that are variations on a theme and that provide fodder for the reader's separate contemplation. The book does not contain a single unified story in the traditional sense: There is no beginning, middle, or discernible end, and the vignettes, though frequently interrelated, do not together form a story arc. Nevertheless, the sketches in this collection, taken together, encapsulate a set of images and social commentaries that clarify a cohesive conceptual body.

Characters

- *The Bird Lady* is featured in the "Introduction" and appears elsewhere throughout the text as well. In each sketch, she is spoken to by a small bird that she is feeding. The phrases uttered by the birds are most often examples of the clichéd social niceties that permeate everyday conversation, though frequently with a slightly absurdist twist.

- *Scribble-Face* is one of a pair of characters first introduced in the section entitled "Semiotics." With just a scribble for a head and a body that is otherwise largely featureless, Scribble-Face is a minimalistic character who utters profundities without fully understanding their meaning or practical application. He has a dinosaur in his pocket and is eventually dismembered by it.

- *The Other Guy*, Scribble-Face's partner, is also largely featureless. Though he has a face, his expression rarely changes, and his features are only roughly sketched. A typical Everyman, he serves as a supporting character who listens and responds to Scribble-Face's monologues.

- *The Cubic Man* is a roughly sketched figure vaguely resembling Gumby. He first appears toward the book's end in the section entitled "The Mediocrity Principle," in which he announces and is ultimately overcome by his aspirations for mediocrity.

- *The Blank-Faced Man* picks up the "Mediocrity Principle" where the Cubic Man left off and tries to sell the principle to those he meets, including Scribble-Face. He cannot impart the principle and ends up alone, featureless, and seemingly contemplative.

Monologues for the Coming Plague. (Courtesy of Fantagraphics Books)

Artistic Style

Nilsen is widely renowned for his masterful pen-and-ink art. His return in this book to rough-hewn sketches seems to belie his artistic ability. This book is, for Nilsen and readers alike, largely an exercise in stylistic experimentation. Though many readers struggle at first encounter to appreciate the starkness of the illustrations, Nilsen's stylistic choices are the essence of the book and ultimately provide the richness of the reading experience. In a postscript, the author notes that he took the creative liberty of moving some sketches around for purposes of continuity. In certain sketches, mistakes and edits are roughly scratched out and are therefore hidden but are not discounted altogether. These stylistic choices, both in text and imagery, comprise the entirety of the book—there is nothing else. From this nihilism grows a profound examination of contemporary sociocultural experience and modern-day communication. Without color, without background, without the minute-by-minute bombardment of images experienced in modern Western society, communication is stripped of its meaninglessness and is pared down to its essence.

Nilsen's textual design supports his message on all levels; his journal-like format reassures readers with the comfort of the familiar. The reader has the impression of being let in on the artist's innermost thoughts, and of being privy to a stream of consciousness that most are not brazen enough to share. Here the reader has the opportunity to peer into the sketchbook of a renowned artist, to see his designs and ideas at their genesis. The structure of the book itself supports this perception, presenting Nilsen's sketches on two different types of paper within the same volume. The paper used in the two parts of the volume represents the rough brown paper of the first of two consecutive sketchbooks, and the white paper represents the pages of the second. The texture of these pages yields a tactile experience for the reader, making up for some of the perceived sensory deprivation of the unadorned ink sketches.

Themes

Nilsen's stream-of-consciousness sketches address a broad range of themes including pop culture, social stigma, politics, religion, philosophy, language, and relationships. Through absurdist and minimalist sketches, Nilsen renders a striking likeness of modern American society and many of its identifying elements. For example, in a challenging exposé of the apparent ills of Western capitalism, Nilsen sketches a scenario in which Buddha is shot. Though Nilsen does not provide any overt commentary, the juxtaposed images of Buddha and the gun create a statement in themselves. In another example, Nilsen's rendering of a figure practicing highly exaggerated yoga poses, and ultimately attaining freedom simply by envisioning it, conveys the author's commentary on such ideology through imagery alone. In this manner, the minimalist style serves to eliminate distractions and allow readers to focus on the specific details that convey thematic meaning.

In other segments of the book, thematic elements are conveyed through dialogue rather than imagery. Again, the minimalist style and the careful use of page space help to impart specific ideas. By juxtaposing

phrases that seem at odds with each other—phrases that tend to blend into the background behind the daily onslaught of language and imagery—the author is able to highlight significant social absurdities that may otherwise be overlooked. As characters recite lines from advertisements or other inane phrases, Nilsen gently mocks the lack of utility of much daily communication. Though many of his sketches feature dialogue and imagery in support of each other, in all cases the minimalist style serves to underscore his message and accentuate the themes upon which he touches.

Impact

Artistically and philosophically, Nilsen draws heavily on ideals from earlier eras, including the absurdist movement of the nineteenth century and the minimalism movement of the late 1960's and early 1970's. However, his stylistic choices seem inspired more directly by the elegant simplicity of some of the texts on which he grew up. As a child, Nilsen was an avid reader of the comic book series *The Adventures of*

Anders Nilsen

One of the most influential cartoonists to have debuted in the 2000's, Anders Nilsen's mini-comics have been widely collected and anthologized as graphic novels. Nilsen's 2004 book *Dogs and Water* depicts a dreamlike post-apocalyptic world in which a young man wanders the wasteland with a stuffed bear. His follow-up, *Don't Go Where I Can't Follow*, is a heartbreaking collection of drawings, comics, and photographs about Nilsen's fiancée, Cheryl Weaver, who died of cancer in 2005. Both *Monologues for the Coming Plague* and *Monologues for Calculating the Density of Black Holes* are experimental non-linear comics in which the faces of characters are often eradicated. In 2011 he published a graphic novel compiling all of his work on *Big Questions*, which depicts the philosophical life of birds. Nilsen's visual style is highly distinctive and strikingly minimalist. His stories tend to lack strong narratives but are conceptually rich and dense with ideas.

Tintin (1929–1976), and *Monologues for the Coming Plague* reflects a similar lighthearted humor but with a more mature perspective on various sociocultural nuances.

Nilsen's work has also been largely influenced by other members of the Holy Consumption, a Chicago-based group of comics artists—including Jeffrey Brown, John Hankiewicz, and Paul Hornschemeier—who blog about and share their current projects. Nilsen's work has influenced the work of these artists as well. Furthermore, the minimalism and absurdism that characterize the sketches in this volume, and in Nilsen's 2009 volume entitled *Monologues for Calculating the Density of Black Holes*, are becoming increasingly evident among the works of other artists, both online and in print.

Also of note is the role this volume (and of Nilsen's work in general) plays in overcoming the stereotype of illustrated texts being for children only. As Art Spiegelman did in *Maus: A Survivor's Tale—My Father Bleeds History* (1986) and *Maus II: A Survivor's Tale—And Here My Troubles Began* (1991), Nilsen has combined the comic book and graphic novel formats with themes of a far more mature nature than many tend to expect of such works. Additionally, by drawing together themes of philosophy and literature and the graphic novel format, Nilsen's illustrated exploration of these profound themes has helped to bridge any remaining gap between graphic novels and other literary genres. Though his work may be for a niche audience, in targeting an audience beyond the general readership of comics and graphic novels, he has opened the door for further exploration of the genre by both readers and artists.

Rachel E. Frier

Further Reading

Burns, Charles. *Black Hole* (2008).

Nilsen, Anders. *Dogs and Water* (2004).

_____. *Monologues for Calculating the Density of Black Holes* (2009).

Bibliography

Celayo, Armando. "Monologues for the Coming Plague." Review of *Monologues for the Coming Plague*, by Anders Nilsen. *World Literature Today* 81, no. 2 (March, 2007): 70.

Nilsen, Anders. "An Interview with Anders Nilsen." Interview by Matthew Baker. *Nashville Review* (April 1, 2011). http://www.vanderbilt.edu/english/nashvillereview/archives/1902.

See also: *Black Hole*; *Ghost World*; *Maus*

MOUSE GUARD

Author: Petersen, David
Artist: David Petersen (illustrator)
Publisher: Archaia Studios Press
First serial publication: 2006-
First book publication: 2007-2010

Publication History

Mouse Guard is a collection of miniseries published by Archaia Studios Press. David Petersen is the creator, writer, and artist of the series. Each miniseries is six issues. Following the publication of single issues, each miniseries is collected in a hardcover volume by Archaia Studios Press.

Petersen self-published the first issue of *Mouse Guard* in black and white through ComiXpress, a print-on-demand company. He sold this issue at the Motor City ComicCon in May of 2005. Archaia Studios Press became aware of the series and published the first miniseries, *Mouse Guard: Fall 1152*, beginning in February, 2006. The series was published bimonthly, and the sixth issue was released in December, 2006. The hardcover collection was published in May, 2007, with a paperback version released in March, 2008, by Villard Press.

The first issue of the second series, *Mouse Guard: Winter 1152*, was released in August, 2007. There were significant delays in the publication of this miniseries. Though planned as a bimonthly miniseries, the final issue was not published until May, 2009. The hardcover collection was published in July, 2009. The reasons for the delay were related to both the creative and the business sides of publishing. While drawing *Mouse Guard: Winter 1152*, Petersen also worked on a *Mouse Guard* role-playing game, which slowed his production. Additionally, Archaia Press Studios was bought by Kunoichi in 2008, and there were several publication delays during the transition of ownership.

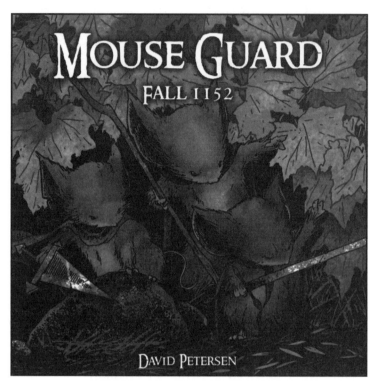

Mouse Guard. (Courtesy of Archaia Studios Press)

In a departure from previous formats, Archaia Studios Press published a four-issue monthly miniseries called *Legends of the Guard* beginning in June, 2010. Each issue featured three short stories by comic book creators who were invited by Petersen to join the project. Each issue also had a framing sequence drawn and scripted by Petersen that introduced the three stories. The hardcover collection *Legends of the Guard* was released by Archaia in November, 2010. *Mouse Guard: The Black Axe*, a six-issue bimonthly miniseries written and drawn by Petersen, had the first issue published in December, 2010, and was scheduled to be completed in 2011.

Plot

Three guard mice, Lieam, Kenzie, and Saxon, search for a merchant mouse who has gone missing. The three mice find the merchant's cart of rice but no sign of the merchant. A snake attacks, and the guard mice retreat and wait for the snake to depart. Believing the snake to be gone, they exit their shelter and discover a hole with snake eggs. While Saxon and Kenzie destroy the eggs, Lieam is attacked by the snake. Lieam kills the snake, and the mice confirm that the snake ate the merchant. Kenzie discovered a map of Lockhaven, the home of the Mouse Guard, in the merchant's grain, which means the merchant mouse was a traitor.

Sadie, a guard mouse, is ordered to discover what has happened to Conrad, a guard mouse stationed near the shoreline of Mouse Territories who has sent no communication for some time. Sadie finds Conrad, who reveals that he has been in hiding and spied a mouse give a map of Lockhaven to a merchant mouse. They plan to take this information to Lockhaven, but crabs attack Conrad's home; so that Sadie can make an escape, Conrad sacrifices himself in battle with the crabs.

Lieam, Kenzie, and Saxon enter the mouse city of Barkstone to search for leads concerning the traitor's plans. While Kenzie and Saxon create a diversion by staging a duel, Lieam disguises himself as a common mouse and asks a map maker if he has a map of Lockhaven. The map maker, believing Lieam to be a part of a rebel group called the Axe, tells him the map has not arrived but that they march at dawn. Lieam is treated as a new recruit of the Axe. At the conclusion of their duel, Saxon and Kenzie are captured by the Axe, bound, and left defenseless outside the city walls. An old mouse, Celanawe, drags Kenzie and Saxon to his house but keeps them tied up.

Celanawe, whose ax was recently stolen, believes Kenzie and Saxon were left outside Barkstone because they were thieves. Celanawe claims to be the Black Axe, a legendary champion of the Mouse Guard, and interrogates Kenzie and Saxon about where they have taken his weapon. Kenzie and Saxon free themselves, explain their situation, and invite Celanawe to join them in defending Lockhaven. Lieam travels with the Axe but is discovered to be a guard mouse and taken prisoner.

Midnight, a member of the Mouse Guard, is revealed to be the leader of the Axe. He has stolen Celanawe's black ax and leads an army to Lockhaven. Celanawe takes Kenzie and Saxon to an old stockpile of weapons and arms them with swords. Sadie reaches Lockhaven before the others and warns the residents of the city that there is a traitor. They prepare their defenses, as Midnight and his army reach the city.

Mouse Guard. (Courtesy of Archaia Studios Press)

Midnight's army is able to breach the doorway of the city, but the portcullis falls, leaving a large number of his army outside the city. Celanawe leads Kenzie and Saxon through a secret passage into the city. Lieam escapes and arms himself. The battle reaches its climax in the chamber of Gwendolyn, the matriarch of the Mouse Guard. She insists the Mouse Guard must protect all mice while allowing each city to remain sovereign, while Midnight argues that uniting the cities under his rule will strengthen all. Lieam, Saxon, Kenzie, and Celanawe arrive in time to save Gwendolyn and capture Midnight. Midnight is banished outside Mouse Territories, but Gwendolyn fears a hard winter is coming.

After winter has fallen, Kenzie leads Saxon, Sadie, Lieam, and Celanawe on a journey to outlying mouse cities. They act as ambassadors, asking the leaders of the cities to come to a council at Lockhaven. They also request supplies for Lockhaven. Using her sling, Sadie blinds in one eye an owl that attacks the group. At Lockhaven, under the care of a healer named Abigail, Rand is slow to recover from an injury he suffered during Midnight's attack. Meanwhile, Gwendolyn worries about their dwindling supplies. While returning to Lockhaven, Kenzie, Saxon, and Sadie fall into an old weasel tunnel. Lieam and Celanawe remain aboveground and plan to complete the journey to Lockhaven with the supplies, while those in the tunnel seek an exit.

Lieam and Celanawe struggle through a freezing rain as Celanawe teaches Lieam to be a complete mouse who does not need others to guide him. Saxon, Sadie, and Kenzie travel in the tunnel, hoping it is abandoned. At Lockhaven, Gwendolyn discovers that Abigail has poisoned Rand with Hemlock.

Gwendolyn orders Lockhaven sealed to search for Abigail. On the way to Lockhaven, Celanawe and Lieam are forced to burrow under the snow to await the end of the freezing rain. Saxon, Kenzie, and Sadie discover that the old weasel tunnel is infested with bats, which leads to a brief battle, during which Saxon is separated from Kenzie and Sadie. Celanawe and Lieam hear a sound outside their burrow, which is the wounded owl waiting for them to emerge.

The owl attempts to eat Celanawe, but his armor protects him. Lieam and Celanawe attack the owl. In the tunnels, Kenzie and Sadie search for Saxon but are unable to find him and fall asleep in each other's arms. Saxon discovers the skeleton Master Loukas, the guard mouse who trained him. An emotional Saxon takes Loukas's sword and buckle. At Lockhaven, Abigail is discovered pouring poison into the city's well. She is shot with arrows and falls into the well.

Saxon reunites with Kenzie and Sadie, and they discover flowing water underground. They plan to paddle upstream. Aboveground, the owl injures Celanawe but Lieam is able to injure the owl as well. Saxon, Kenzie, and Sadie discover a cistern in the river that is cracked at the base. This cistern is the well into which Abigail poured poison. They are pulled up the well into Lockhaven. The owl kills Celanawe, as an enraged Lieam prepares to attack.

Lieam wounds the owl and retrieves Celanawe's black ax to finish the creature. Sadie and Saxon ride on the back of hares to search for Lieam and Celanawe. They find Lieam carrying Celanawe's body to Lockhaven and return to the city. Saxon and Gwendolyn acknowledge their mutual attraction. Celanawe's body is burned as Lieam recalls his friend's final words, in which Celanawe instructed Lieam to carry on the title of the Black Axe.

Volumes

- *Mouse Guard: Fall 1152* (2007). Collects issues 1-6, featuring the rise and fall of the traitorous Midnight.
- *Mouse Guard: Winter 1152* (2009). Collects issues 1-6. Features the journeys of Guard Mice to outlying mouse settlements for supplies, as well as the death of Celanawe, the Black Axe.
- *Mouse Guard: Legends of the Guard* (2010). Collects issues 1-4. Features guard mice telling stories of past exploits of the Mouse Guard.

Characters

- *Lieam* is one of the youngest guard mice. He has red fur, wears a green cloak, and carries a bow and arrow. He will briefly become Celanawe's apprentice before taking on the legendary role of the Black Axe.
- *Kenzie* is a respected leader among the guard mice. He is level-headed and strategic in battle.

He has gray fur, wears a blue cloak, and carries a staff. He develops a romantic relationship with Sadie.

- *Saxon* is a headstrong guard mouse who is always ready for a fight. He has brown fur, wears a red cloak, and carries a sword. He begins a romantic relationship with Gwendolyn.
- *Sadie* is a guard mouse assigned to watch the shoreline of Mouse Territories. She has brown fur, wears a maroon cloak, and carries two daggers. She develops a romantic relationship with Kenzie.
- *Conrad* is a guard mouse who is also assigned to watch the shoreline of Mouse Territories. He has gray fur, a brown cloak, and a peg leg. He carries a fish hook with a segment of fish line as a weapon. He is killed in a battle with crabs.
- *Midnight* is the mouse guard's weaponsmith. He has black fur and a black cloak. He believes the Mouse Guard has been too passive and plans a rebellion to place himself as ruler of a united Mouse Territories. He is banished when his rebellion is thwarted.
- *Rand* is the guard mouse in charge of Lockhaven's security. He has brown fur and wears a yellow cloak. He is a defensive specialist and carries a shield.
- *Gwendolyn* is the matriarch and leader of the Mouse Guard. She is one of the youngest matriarchs the Mouse Guard has had. She wears a blue tunic and light-blue cloak. She believes the Mouse Guard's duty is to protect mice when called upon but to allow each city its own sovereign rule.
- *Roibin* is Gwendolyn's scribe and a poet. He has gray fur and wears a hooded brown cloak.
- *Landra* is a quartermaster of Lockhaven. She has black fur and wears a green cloak. When Rand is injured she is placed in charge of tracking Mouse Guard movements.
- *Abigail* is a healer at Lockhaven. She has dark gray fur and wears a brown cloak. She is discovered to have been a believer of Midnight's ideology and a traitor to the Mouse Guard. She poisons Rand with hemlock to slow his healing and is shot and killed while attempting to poison Lockhaven's water supply.

David Petersen

David Petersen, the creator of the Eisner Award-winning comics series *Mouse Guard* from Archaia Studios Press, entered into the comics industry after graduating from Eastern Michigan University. One of the most notable talents to have emerged in the mid-2000's, Petersen produced work for a number of anthology comics series before launching the title for which he is known. *Mouse Guard* tells the story of mice living in the medieval period, although there are no humans in the story. The titular guards ensure safe passage for their fellow mice, serving as a border patrol against threats. Petersen's work is characterized by its detailed settings and rich characterizations, even while the plots revolve around traditional fantasy elements. The books have become extremely popular with school-aged children due to their mixture of action and comedy.

Artistic Style

Petersen's art style is much closer to realism than cartoon drawing. While the narrative does feature anthropomorphized mice, they are not in the cartoon style popularized by Walt Disney. The mice walk on their hind legs, wear cloaks, and carry weapons, but they are drawn in a natural style. The mice are modeled on the body types of actual mice and rendered in realistic proportion to the natural world around them. Other animals that make appearances, such as snakes, owls, or rabbits, are also drawn in a natural style that avoids a distorted cartoon reality.

Petersen's art style is influenced by his own experience in printmaking, specifically etching and woodcutting. Petersen's backgrounds are detailed, relying heavily on crosshatch and stipple shading. Occasionally there will be large panels in which the mice are drawn small in the foreground, in front of an expansive background with highly rendered details.

Petersen's choice to depict mice as naturally as possible presents a challenge, in that mouse faces do not emote in a way that readers may find familiar. To overcome this problem, characters will occasionally have a word balloon with no text but only a symbol, such as a question mark or exclamation point, to express emotion. This circumvents the difficulty of displaying emotion on the faces of mice while at the same time adhering to the established realistic art style.

The artistic style does not change significantly as the series progresses; the coloring between *Mouse Guard: Fall 1152* and *Mouse Guard: Winter 1152* varies to reflect the seasons. *Fall 1152* is colored with warm, earthen tones, with orange and brown being dominant colors. *Winter 1152* is much starker, with white and gray representing the most dominant colors.

One aspect of *Mouse Guard* that stands out from other comic books is the size and shape of the pages. While a standard comic is roughly 6 x 10 inches, *Mouse Guard* is 8 x 8 inches.

While the number and shape of panels varies greatly throughout the series, the panels are all rectangular. The page layouts may vary, but the grid always conforms to the square page with minimal dead space in the gutter between panes and in the edge.

One sequence that departs from the standard artistic style of the series occurs when Midnight discovers a scroll containing the legend of the Black Axe. The art changes for several pages to a style similar to illuminated manuscripts. The pages have a yellowed background, reminiscent of parchment, and lettering that includes decorative initials and marginalia.

Themes

Many of the themes of *Mouse Guard* are interrelated and become apparent in the duties willingly accepted by the Mouse Guard. Because the mice are drawn in natural proportion to the world around them, the foes they battle are often significantly larger than the mice themselves. The Mouse Guard references an earlier war with weasels and is shown battling a snake, crabs, bats, and an owl in this series. An element of David versus Goliath emerges as these battles unfold, with the mice often being triumphant. The size of the mice is shown to be less important than their skill, bravery, and devotion to their cause. Another aspect of this is stated explicitly in the series, "It matters not what you fight but what you fight for." The mice have inferior size and strength to the animals that naturally prey on

them, but they fight for more than simple food. Additionally, the mice have a culture that provides them with tools and weapons, while the snake, crabs, owl, and bats do not have any additional implements. Part of the Mouse Guard's success can be attributed to the way the mice have pursued learning, giving them more than the simple natural instincts with which they were born.

However, because of their natural disadvantages, they often must be willing to sacrifice themselves for the greater good. The needs of the mouse civilization are shown as outweighing the needs of a single guard mouse. This theme is evidenced not only when a mouse such as Conrad sacrifices himself so that important intelligence can reach the Mouse Guard, but also when guard mice must leave other members in danger for the greater good. For example, Saxon, Kenzie, and Celanawe see that Lieam has been captured by the Axe and are in a position to attempt a rescue, but they know that Lieam would want them to work to protect Lockhaven rather than try to free him.

Learning from the past, or from those with greater experience, is also an important theme. This is explored particularly in the relationship between Lieam and Celanawe, and its antithesis is shown when Midnight misinterprets the past and the legend of the Black Axe and twists it to his own ends.

Impact

Mouse Guard is significant in that represents an independent, self-produced product that has become a success in the industry. Its format size departs significantly from the mainstream, as does its artistic style and narrative topic. Also, in an industry that is most often defined by collaboration among writers, artists, colorists, and letterers, Petersen provides all of the creative input for the series. This auteur-style production is rare.

Because the comic book industry remains dominated by comic books that are in the superhero genre and published by either Marvel Comics or DC Comics, any comic book that is financially viable and falls outside those parameters helps to diversify the marketplace. Petersen's success may have opened doors for other creators with a singular vision that similarly departs from the standard content found in comic book stores. Because of the quality of the story and the targeted age group of the series, *Mouse Guard* has been adopted as a recommended text for many elementary and middle schools.

Joseph J. Darowski

Further Reading

Gaiman, Neil. *The Books of Magic* (1993).

Glass, Bryan J. L., and Michael Avon Oeming. *Mice Templar* (2007-).

Smith, Jeff. *Bone* (1991-2004).

Bibliography

Griffith, Paula E. "Graphic Novels in the Secondary Classroom and School Libraries." *Journal of Adolescent and Adult Literacy* 54 (November, 2010): 181-189.

Stafford, Tim. *Teaching Visual Literacy in the Primary Classroom: Comic Books, Film, Television, and Picture Narratives*. New York: Routledge, 2010.

Withrow, Steven, and Alexander Danner. *Character Design for Graphic Novels*. Burlington, Mass.: Focal Press, 2007.

See also: *Maus*; *Good-Bye, Chunky Rice*

My Mommy Is in America and She Met Buffalo Bill

Author: Regnaud, Jean

Artist: Émile Bravo (illustrator)

Publisher: Gallimard (French); Fanfare/Ponent Mon (English)

First book publication: *Ma maman est en Amérique, elle a rencontré Buffalo-Bill*, 2007 (English translation, 2010)

Publication History

Jean Regnaud and Émile Bravo have been friends since they were adolescents, despite an age difference of four years. They produced their first professional collaboration, *Ivoire*, in 1990. After Bravo joined l'Atelier Nawak (a collective studio for comics artists), they began work on *Aleksis Strogonov*, an adventure series that ran throughout much of the 1990's.

Ma maman est en Amérique, elle a rencontré Buffalo-Bill was originally published in Regnaud and Bravo's native France in 2007 in the *Hors-série BD* ("Special-edition Comic Strip") collection from Gallimard. It was well-received by critics and won the 2008 Essentials Award at the Festival International de la Bande Dessinée d'Angoulême and the Tam Tam Literary Award from the Salon du Livres et de la Presse Jeunesse.

Founded in 2003, the union of British publisher Fanfare and Spanish firm Ponent Mon was known as an international publisher of manga but began expanding its scope in 2008. *My Mommy Is in America and She Met Buffalo Bill* was one of the first works published under this expansion and marked the first English translation of a Regnaud/Bravo's collaboration.

Plot

On the first day of school, Jean is a bit apprehensive. He attended kindergarten in another neighborhood, so he does not know any of his classmates. Once the teacher gets the the students settled into their seats, she begins asking who they are and what their parents do. Jean becomes nervous instantly, trying to figure out what to say his mother does. When he is finally called on, he blurts out that his father is a boss and his mother

My Mommy is in America and She Met Buffalo Bill.
(Courtesy of Ponent Mon S.L.)

a secretary. His tension does not abate immediately, though, and Jean misses what everyone else says.

After school, Jean is picked up by his nanny, Yvette, who has already picked up his brother Paul from kindergarten. At home she makes them iced chocolate milk and, a few hours later, supper. When Jean's father comes home, they all eat around the table. His father asks some superficial questions about the kids' day, correcting their grammar in the process. Though always tempted, Jean never summons the courage to ask where his mother actually is.

The couple next door own kennels. Between their yelling and the dogs barking, the area is often uncomfortably loud. None of the parents in the neighborhood wants his or her children to play with one another, but

Jean and the sligthly older Michele sit on opposite sides of the hedge and play games beneath it. One day, Michele pulls out from under her sweater a postcard from Jean's mother. She promises to read it if Jean swears not to tell anyone about it. Michele reads that Jean's mother is in Spain, eating paella and swimming in the sea.

Jean spends time with his classmates, both in and out of school, and continues to have Michele read him postcards from his mother until the Halloween-All Saint's Day holiday, when he and Paul visit their maternal grandparents. Neither enjoys himself much because Granny Simone is not a very good cook and there is not much for children to do. When Granny Simone takes them into town, they are stopped constantly by her friends, who all sob and dote on the children. As a teacher, Granny Simone works hard to teach Jean how to read and write, which makes Jean look forward to the end of the vacation.

Back in school, the students are introduced to a psychologist. Rumors fly around the classroom about what the psychologist does and where he sends "wacko" children. Eventually, Jean is called and given some basic tests. When asked about his last vacation, Jean does not mention his grandparents and instead relays the contents of the last postcard from his mother, who was in the United States and saw a rodeo featuring Buffalo Bill. That night, Jean begins to seriously wonder about his mother and what happened to her.

As Michele reads Jean another postcard, her father finds her and begins yelling at her as he drags her away. Jean picks up the dropped postcard and tucks it under his mattress. As winter begins, Jean's paternal grandmother, Granny Edith, comes to live with them. Jean and Paul think she is much more fun than Granny Simone because she lets them do just about anything they want. Though she does not partake in the activities herself, she gives the children money to enjoy the St. Martin's festival with Yvette. They come home with cotton candy and toy prizes.

With the holidays approaching, the children get a vacation from school. Yvette goes to spend some time with her family, and Granny Edith is left to babysit them. She helps them write wish lists for Father Christmas and is bemused by their plot to take a picture of him with a Polaroid camera. On Christmas Eve, Jean and Paul try to stay awake and keep an eye on the Christmas tree through the keyhole of their bedroom door. Though Jean falls asleep, Paul wakes him upon hearing a noise. They sneak down to the end of the hall and snap a picture, making a loud racket. Their father steps up to look at the photo, chuckles, and hands it back. Later, Jean examines the photo closely and is excited to see one of Father Christmas's shoes in the otherwise mundane picture. He hides the picture under his mattress, and decides to pull out the postcard, attempting to read the note now evidently made out to Michele.

The next day, after opening the presents, Jean meets Michele under the hedge. He shows her the picture, to which she responds with laughter, telling him that it was his own father's shoe and that Father Christmas does not exist. Jean gets upset and pulls her hair. Michele gets angry and reveals that the postcards were all fake and that, in fact, Jean's mother is dead. Jean races back indoors, sobbing as he tries to tell his father what Michele said about Father Christmas. Jean's father explains that Father Christmas does exist, but only for children, so he should not say anything to Paul about it. That night, in bed, Jean decides that his mother is like Father Christmas and that he is too old to believe in her any more.

Characters

- *Jean* is a five-year-old boy just starting school as the story opens. His extreme youth and inexperience with nearly everything provide the unique lens through which the story is told. Jean is often nervous about new experiences, but he generally does what he is told and takes everything people tell him at face value.
- *Paul* is Jean's younger brother. He acts as a companion but largely just follows Jean's lead.
- *Yvette* is the boys' nanny. She is caring and nurturing toward them and is visibly touched when they present cards and gifts to her on Mother's Day. She appears to be in her early twenties.
- *Jean's Daddy* is not named in the story, but he is the main source of stability for the family. He spends his days working as the manager at a local

bottling factory and frequently has a great deal on his mind, which shows in his graying temples. He is certainly interested in the children's well-being and education but is uncomfortable dealing with them and instead relies heavily on Yvette's guidance. He often masks his emotions and sometimes interferes with Jean and Paul's attempts at having fun.

- *Michele Neunier* is Jean's long-haired neighbor. The two often play under the hedges between their houses. Being two years older than Jean, she is privy to his mother's death and tries to play along with the adults' wishes to keep Jean ignorant by reading him fictional postcards allegedly sent by his mother.
- *Granny Simone* and *Grandpa Pierrot* are Jean's maternal grandparents. They love both of the grandchildren, but the loss of their daughter has grieved them deeply; there is a sense of perpetual sorrow around them.
- *Granny Edith* is Jean's paternal grandmother. Though she smokes incessantly, she is materially generous with the children. Evidently, she convinces her son to get Jean the Native American costume he wants for Christmas.

Artistic Style

Regnaud's story was the result of years of work, and he seemed to have Bravo in mind to illustrate it from the outset. The script, as Regnaud wrote it, was perfectly suited to Bravo's sensibilities; he has claimed that absolutely everything he needed was there, including detailed passages describing what turned out to be entirely silent scenes.

Bravo felt that the story in *My Mommy Is in America and She Met Buffalo Bill* was predicated largely on the pathos of the situation and that his art should in no way detract from that. He consciously and deliberately tried to keep the art as simple as possible in order to force readers to focus on the story. Bravo was actively trying to serve the best needs of the story through simplicity.

The simple style also helped to make the illustrations easier to work on, since Bravo knew many of the people depicted in the story from his long friendship with Regnaud. Bravo was able to work quickly on the

project with the relatively simple style and was able to abstract the characters somewhat from their real-life counterparts; both processes allowed him to avoid dwelling on the personal relationships he had with many of the individuals. Regnaud put his complete trust into Bravo and did not see any of the art for the book until Bravo had effectively completed it.

Themes

My Mommy Is in America and She Met Buffalo Bill is written from five-year-old Jean's perspective. As such, it includes many simple misunderstandings that inevitably arise from not having an adult's vocabulary or view of life. It also presents many situations with little or no context because the adults around Jean conspire to keep his mother's death a secret.

The father's assumption, readers are led to infer, is that Jean is too young to understand death or too immature to deal emotionally with the loss of his mother. This message has been given, directly or implicitly, to the other adults with whom Jean comes into contact, so they all act uncomfortably around Jean, not knowing how to reconcile their grief with his ignorance.

Left to his own devices, though, Jean does in fact come to grips with his mother's absence well before he learns of her death. While he does not, within the story, come to an understanding of mortality, he does show that he has the emotional fortitude to handle the loss. And while his methods of dealing with grief are different than most adults, they are no less valid and serve equally well and perhaps more effectively. Regnaud is, in effect, showing that children are not nearly as inept as adults often think and understand and process more than they are often given credit for.

Impact

Bravo was a founding member of multiple art studios in France, most notably l'Atelier Nawak in 1992 and l'Atelier des Vosges in 1995. The basic concept of these studios was that several artists would share studio space together while working on their independent projects. The studio cost was split among the artists who could also talk freely with one another to work through problems or to share ideas. The support was financial, technical, and intellectual.

Among the artists in l'Atelier Nawak were Lewis Trondheim, Christophe Blain, and Joann Sfar. Sfar has noted that most had fine-art backgrounds and were learning the art of comics together, sometimes having two artists tackle the same story sequence in order to examine different approaches to solving story problems. Many of the artists also came over to l'Atelier des Vosges, where they were joined by Marjane Satrapi. Satrapi was initially skeptical of the comic book format, but she was soon won over. She has cited Bravo and Blain for providing specific pieces of advice, and much of *Persepolis* (2000) was created at that studio.

Sean Kleefeld

Further Reading

Regnaud, Jean, and Émile Bravo. *Ivoire* (2006).
Satrapi, Marjane. *Persepolis* (2008).
Trondheim, Lewis. *Little Nothings* (2007).

Bibliography

Brienza, Casey. "My Mommy Is in America and She Met Buffalo Bill." Review of *My Mommy Is in America and She Met Buffalo Bill*, by Jean Regnaud. *Graphic Novel Reporter*. http://www.graphicnovel reporter.com/content/my-mommy-america-and-she-met-buffalo-bill-review.

Hajdu, David. *Heroes and Villains: Essays on Music, Movies, Comics, and Culture*. Cambridge, Mass.: Da Capo Press, 2009.

McElhatton, Greg. "My Mommy Is in America and She Met Buffalo Bill." Review of *My Mommy Is in America and She Met Buffalo Bill*, by Jean Regnaud. *Read About Comics*, February 18, 2009. http://www.read-aboutcomics.com/2009/02/18/my-mommy-is-in america.

See also: *Persepolis*; *Harum Scarum*; *The Rabbi's Cat*

N

NAT TURNER

Author: Baker, Kyle
Artist: Kyle Baker (illustrator)
Publisher: Harry N. Abrams
First serial publication: 2005-2006
First book publication: 2008

Publication History

Kyle Baker first encountered Nat Turner in elementary school while reading a single paragraph about Turner's rebellion in an American history textbook. Over time, Baker would again find brief mentions of Turner in various books, but not until he read Malcolm X's description of Turner's revolt in *The Autobiography of Malcolm X* (1965) did Baker see the potential of retelling Turner's story in graphic form.

Baker originally intended *Nat Turner* to be a self-published, four-issue miniseries. The first issue was published in June, 2005, the second in December, 2005. Both issues were published by Kyle Baker Publishing and printed in black and white. The remaining issues were never published in the same single-comic format.

In June, 2006, *Nat Turner: Encore Edition*, again published by Kyle Baker Publishing, collected the first two issues of the miniseries. In February, 2007, *Nat Turner: Revolution* was published by Images Comics, collecting the two previously unpublished comics. These editions were both ninety-six pages and were published in black and white.

In June, 2008, the entire series was collected by the publishing house Harry N. Abrams into a single edition. This edition, unlike the previous, was printed in a muted sepia duo tone and includes a two-page preface by Baker.

Plot

Noting the rarity of works about Turner, Baker creates a dramatic retelling of Turner's life, insurrection, and

execution. Baker bases his work on history and legend to fashion a Turner who repudiates the dehumanization of slavery through violence. Baker spares no unpleasantness in depicting the harshness of slavery, racial inequality, and the brutality of Turner's insurrection.

Baker divides *Nat Turner* into four chapters. In the first, an idyllic village market is disrupted when African slave raiders attack marketgoers, attempting to kidnap villagers to sell on the slave market. Turner's mother (though Turner has not been born yet) resists the raiders but is eventually cornered on the edge of a cliff, where she attempts to leap to her death, only to be lassoed by one of the raiders. Later, aboard ship,

---

Kyle Baker

Kyle Baker's first two graphic novels, *The Cowboy Wally Show* and *Why I Hate Saturn*, were unusual for the fact that they contained no in-panel dialogue or word balloons, but placed captions and text below the images. Both books were widely praised for their cutting satire and witty one-liners. Baker also contributed more traditional comics to the superhero genre, notably taking over *The Shadow* from Bill Sienkiewicz in 1988. After moving into animation, Baker returned to comics in the 2000's with *Truth*, a Captain America story about medical experiments on African Americans during World War II, and *Plastic Man*, an update of 1940's character. Baker's drawing style is extremely cartoony and well-suited to his humor as it is dynamic and exaggerated. His writing tends to be politically engaged and socially relevant and explores the edges of what is permissible in the comics industry.

---

she is crammed alongside hundreds of other slaves. Sharks follow the ship, devouring dead slaves who are thrown overboard. One woman gives birth during the voyage and once top-side, throws her baby overboard, at which point a shark devours it. Chapter 1 ends with images of Turner's mother being sold and a young Turner somehow recounting the story of the baby being thrown to the sharks, an event that happened before he was born.

Chapter 2 presents a young Turner growing into a religious revolutionary. As a child, he is excluded from school, but his curiosity and intelligence propel him to learn. He listens at the door of the schoolhouse, teaches himself to read, and reads the Bible ceaselessly, particularly the narratives about Moses freeing the Israelites. Turner experiences visions and realizes he has a divine calling for some great purpose, cryptically prophesying an upcoming cataclysm. Baker also depicts an apocryphal tale of Turner marrying, having two children, and then being separated from them as they are sold to three different owners. Later, Turner, standing in the rain with fists raised to heaven, sees a vision of a battle between white and black spirits. The chapter closes with images of Turner raising a Bible, prophesying to other slaves.

Chapter 3 depicts the insurrection. Turner views an eclipse as a sign to start the slaughter, in which no white person is to be spared. Turner's men kill the Travis family in their beds. Leaving the house, Turner realizes they have forgotten the Travis's infant and orders Henry and Will back to the house to kill the baby. The band continues house to house. Upon returning to his owner's home, Henry, one of Turner's lieutenants, is cheerfully greeted by his owner's young son, whom Henry immediately decapitates with a single ax blow. Turner's group grows to about sixty men, but the group's organization and discipline begin to deteriorate. As Turner's forces become more disorganized, the white community coordinates an attack. Turner and his forces are confronted by a large militia; some flee, but others attack. As Turner's men falter, Turner retreats. Unable to organize a counterattack, Turner hides for six weeks before being captured.

Chapter 4 quickly recounts Turner's imprisonment, confession, and execution. As Turner faces execution,

his lawyer, Thomas Ruffin Gray, asks Turner if he believes the rebellion to have been a mistake. Turner replies by comparing his own fate to that of Christ's. When Turner is taken to be hanged, a small throng mocks him as he looks heavenward. Turner is hanged from a tree; the faces in the crowd turn from excitement to wide-eyed emptiness. The book ends with a young house servant sneaking away to read her master's copy of Gray's *Confessions of Nat Turner* (1831).

Characters

- *Nat Turner*, the protagonist, possesses a superior intellect but must endure the barbarity of slavery throughout his life in Southampton, Virginia. Turner is separated from his father, refused an education, and then forcibly separated from his wife and children. Turner seems to possess special gifts, as he recounts events that happened in the past, sees visions, and communes with the spirit of God. Turner interprets various signs and divine messages as God's endorsement of his leading a revolt against white slave owners.

- *Turner's mother*, born in Africa, has a fearless and indomitable spirit. When slave raiders enter her village, she resists their onslaught, protecting a boy by killing two of the raiders and leading other raiders away from him before being captured. Nat Turner reflects his mother's strength and courage.

- *Turner's father* is an imposing figure with a serious demeanor. He is deeply loved and respected by his son. He listens carefully to secret messages passed through the community through drumbeats and passes information to other slaves through coded whistling. He escapes from his owners in the night, leaving his wife and young Turner behind, never to be seen again.

- *Turner's wife* resembles Turner's mother. She is tall and slender and appears happy to be married to Turner. She has two children but is separated from both her husband and her children when she and her children are sold to different slaveowners.

- *Henry* is a slave who possesses a friendly demeanor, demonstrated by his gentle smile and friendly wave to his owner's young son. He is a muscular man and a foot taller than most everyone around him. His demeanor changes, though, under Turner's tutelage, and he becomes one of Turner's most loyal devotees. He is so devoted, in fact, that during the insurrection, he kills his owner's son without hesitation.

- *Will* is another of Turner's most trusted adherents. Turner refers to him as Will the Executioner for his unflinching ability to kill.
- *Joseph Travers* is Turner's owner and the first to be killed during the insurrection.
- *Thomas Ruffin Gray*, a small, balding, bespectacled lawyer, records Turner's confession after three days of questioning.

Artistic Style

Baker uses heavily shaded sepia duo tone drawings in *Nat Turner*. Each chapter begins with a full-page borderless drawing, while the main work uses various panel constructions, mostly clearly defined rectangular and square panels. Occasionally, Baker employs circles, ovals, and inlaid panels. Word balloons are used only in a single scene when young Turner shouts for his father to run. Sound effects are generally used within panels, while narrative text is generally used outside panels. Baker avoids the exaggerated caricatures found in many of his lighter works, favoring sketches of fairly naturally proportioned characters. Baker's model for Nat Turner appears to be an 1863 steel engraving based on a work by Felix O. C. Darley, which Baker incorporates in the bottom panel on page 111 without disrupting the visual narrative.

The graphic novel relies heavily upon the artwork to present the narrative and includes text only occasionally, primarily from Gray's *Confessions of Nat Turner*. The images often inform and at times conflict with Gray's text. While the text suggests Turner's motivation for the rebellion is of supernatural origin, the images suggest a more earthly motive: revenge. Baker juxtaposes contrasting images to illustrate the inequity and oppression of nineteenth-century slavery in Southampton, Virginia: Images of one slave's rhythmic drumbeats are juxtaposed with the monotone clanging of the town's bell; images of slaves waking from the floor are juxtaposed with images of whites waking in their beds; images of Turner's family being sold are juxtaposed with images of his master, Joseph Travers, tucking his children into bed; images of Turner's wife and children being dragged away by their new owners are juxtaposed with Turner's orders for Henry and Will to kill the Travers's infant. These images create a secondary narrative that makes the text more satisfyingly rich and complex.

Themes

The theme most clearly demonstrated in *Nat Turner* is that violence begets violence. Baker presents a culture in which brutality toward slaves is an accepted, natural occurrence. Chapter 2 begins with an older slave sending messages to other slaves through drumbeats in the middle of the night. The old man is captured, whipped, and literally has salt rubbed into his wounds. His tormentors then cut off his hands and destroy his drum. Later, a female slave is on her knees scrubbing her master's floor when she spots a book with a lion on the cover. Curious, she opens the book only to be caught by her master, who has her strung up by her ankles and whipped by another slave until a pool of blood forms on the ground beneath her head. Unbearable psychological violence is also visited upon Turner when he is separated from his wife and two children when they are sold to different owners. The barbarity of these acts is reciprocated as Turner leads his bloody uprising. Other themes that may be readily found in *Nat Turner* are endurance under oppression, the inextinguishable desire for freedom and justice, the rationalization of violence, the self-destructive nature of violence, the dehumanization of both master and slave in a slave system, religious fanaticism as an instrument for violence, the consequences of racism, and the relationship between education and freedom, among others.

Impact

Since his execution in 1831, Turner has been mythologized as he has been constructed and reconstructed many times over. For some, Baker included, Turner is a hero who resisted slavery's tyranny, becoming a symbol of hope for those suffering under the intolerable weight of oppression. For others, he is a hellish villain, a prototypical terrorist who slaughtered innocent children in his quest to defy subjugation. A third view is that Turner is neither a hero nor a villain but rather the natural consequence of the institution of slavery.

In his introduction to *Nat Turner*, Baker wonders why so few books and films have been made about Turner. The answer, most likely, lies in the brutality of Turner's rebellion, particularly the slaughtering of children and infants. Baker does not shy away from this violence, which allows readers to develop their own opinions as to how Turner should be understood. Filmmakers may also hesitate, remembering the outrage directed toward William Styron's Pulitzer Prize-winning novel *The Confessions of Nat Turner* in the late 1960's.

Baker has claimed that *Nat Turner* is a true story, but as with others who have attempted to re-create Turner's narrative (Harriet Beecher Stowe, George P. R. James, Mary Spear Tiernan, Pauline Carrington Rust, Daniel Panger, and Styron) he has excluded some facts while including a number of historical speculations: Gray's *Confessions of Nat Turner* mentions Turner being influenced by his grandmother; Turner's having a wife is still a source of dispute among historians; women and children taking up arms in support of the insurrection also lacks historical support.

Nat Turner has been well received by critics and reviewers alike. Baker has been praised for his unflinching look into the evils of slavery and has again thrust Turner into the spotlight for this generation.

Films

Goodbye Uncle Tom. Directed by Gualtiero Jacopetti and Franco Prosperi. Euro International Film, 1971. In this Italian film, a documentary team is sent to the nineteenth century, where it films the harrowing inhumanity faced by slaves brought to America: squalid conditions on ships, dehumanizing living quarters, sexual exploitation, and white justifications for slavery. This film is at once a searing indictment of slavery and a highly exploitative film. Turner appears in the last sequence of the film, as an African American man reads Styron's *The Confessions of Nat Turner* on a beach in contemporary times. As he reads passages from the book, he imagines the white

people on the beach taking on the roles of the white victims in the book.

Nat Turner: A Troublesome Property. Directed by Charles Burnett. Subpix, 2003. This PBS documentary presents multiple actors in the role of Turner, each depicting different interpretations of Turner-Gray's, Stowe's, William Wells Brown's, Randolph Edmond's, and Styron's. Turner is presented as a religious fanatic, a sacrificial victim, a heroic revolutionary, and a sexually repressed rebel. Along with the recreated accounts are interviews with Ossie Davis, Henry Louis Gates, Eugene Genovese, Styron, and others.

Possession. Directed by Kevin R. Hershberger. Richmond 48 Hour Film Project, 2010. This short film stars Tyhm Kennedy as Nat Turner and Shawn T. Singletary as Will. The film presents Turner in a way that is similar to Gray's depiction, claiming divine authority and calling his men to prepare themselves to kill everyone but insisting that the primary goal of Turner is to gain freedom for his fellow slaves. As the men attack the first house, Will hesitates to kill those he claims never caused harm. Turner sternly reminds Will that slavery has made him property, that it is their divine obligation to free their fellow slaves; he commands Will to pick up his weapon. The short film ends with Will asking what he should do.

Daniel D. Clark

Further Reading

Burgan, Michael, et al. *Nat Turner's Slave Rebellion* (2006).

McGruder, Aaron, Reginald Hudlin, and Kyle Baker. *Birth of a Nation: A Comic Novel* (2004).

Morales, Robert, and Kyle Baker. *Captain America: Truth–Red, White, and Black* (2004).

Bibliography

Clarke, John Henrik, ed. *William Styron's Nat Turner: Ten Black Writers Respond*. Boston: Beacon Press, 1968.

Davis, Mary Kemp. *Nat Turner Before the Bar of Judgment: Fictional Treatments of the Southampton Slave Insurrection*. Baton Rouge: Louisiana State University Press, 1999.

French, Scot. *The Rebellious Slave: Nat Turner in American Memory*. Boston: Houghton Mifflin, 2004.

Greenberg, Kenneth S., ed. *The Confessions of Nat Turner and Related Documents*. Boston: Bedford/ St. Martins, 1996.

_____. *Nat Turner: A Slave Rebellion in History and Memory*. New York: Oxford University Press, 2003.

Gross, Seymour L., and Eileen Bender. "History, Politics, and Literature: The Myth of Nat Turner." *American Quarterly* 23, no. 4 (October, 1971): 487-518.

Oates, Stephen B. *The Fires of Jubilee: Nat Turner's Fierce Rebellion*. New York: Harper, 1975.

Styron, William. *The Confessions of Nat Turner*. New York: Random House, 1968.

See also: *Birth of a Nation*; *Why I Hate Saturn*

NIGHT FISHER

Author: Johnson, R. Kikuo
Artist: R. Kikuo Johnson (illustrator)
Publisher: Fantagraphics Books
First book publication: 2005

Publication History

R. Kikuo Johnson created his first graphic novel, *Night Fisher*, over the course of three years while he was studying at the Rhode Island School of Design where he was a student of cartoonist David Mazzucchelli. Fantagraphics Books bought the completed *Night Fisher* a year after Johnson finished his program, and the book was received exceptionally well by critics. Johnson was hailed as the "next big thing" in graphic novels. Since then, Johnson has worked as an illustrator, has produced several shorter pieces of comics in various styles, and has published in a variety of venues. Johnson's second graphic novel, *The Shark King*, was published in 2012.

Plot

At the heart of *Night Fisher* is a simple story line with a few short flashbacks that fill in earlier events to help readers understand Loren Foster, the main character. *Night Fisher* has an open ending: Loren is in the middle of a field with little indication of what he will do next. In the context of the realistic story, this ending makes sense from the viewpoint that as in life there are many moments when one's next step is unclear.

The narrative follows Loren for a period of several weeks during his senior year at Winthorpe, an expensive private school on Maui. He has heard rumors that his longtime friend Shane is doing drugs. Indeed, when Shane calls him one night, they go to score methamphetamine, or *batu*, as it is known in Hawaiian slang, and hang out with Jon, a local drug dealer, and a boy called Eustace. Later, the group gets Loren to drive as they steal tires from garages.

Loren had already been losing interest in schoolwork, and it becomes even less of a priority as he spends more time with Shane and buys *batu* with him several times a week. Jem, another classmate at school

Night Fisher. (Courtesy of Fantagraphics Books)

and the school's marijuana dealer, gets expelled for stealing two electronic scales from the chemistry lab. That evening Eustace tells Loren it was actually Shane who stole the scales; he used the money he earned from selling them to buy methamphetamine.

Loren borrows his father's truck, and Jon and Shane take him to steal supplies and a generator from a building site. On their way back, they get pulled over by the police. The police discover the generator in the back of Loren's father's truck, and the group gets taken to the police station.

After Loren has been processed at the station, he is picked up by his father, who is disappointed in his son, and expresses his belief that the years of tuition have been a waste. Loren insists that is not the case. Back at school, Loren reads in a school announcement that Shane has been accepted to the Massachusetts Institute of Technology. When Loren tries to congratulate Shane during a cross-country run, Shane avoids him and says that it is better if they do not talk, at least until their court date is set. Loren trips and falls in the grass. As everyone in the race passes him, he stays behind, staring into the sky as the grass covers him.

Characters

- *Loren Foster* is a straight-A high school senior at an elite private school on Maui, where he has been living for six years. He is 6 feet tall and 140 pounds. He wears glasses, which Johnson often draws without any eyes behind them, giving Loren an inscrutable look. It seems Loren has grown tired of his squeaky-clean reputation, or perhaps he is having trouble dealing with the

Night Fisher. (Courtesy of Fantagraphics Books)

pressure of keeping his perfect grade-point average and deciding what he wants to do after graduation; it seems he deliberately looks for trouble when he connects with Shane again.

- *Shane Hokama* is Loren's longtime friend, but over the previous year, he and Loren have grown apart. Shane and Loren used to go night fishing regularly, but lately, Shane has spent his nights doing drugs and stealing from building sites and his school. He phones Loren unexpectedly, likely because Loren owns a vehicle. He always wears a ball cap and sets it backward on his.
- *Loren's Father* is a dentist with a beard and glasses. He moved to Maui to open a dentistry clinic, "Miles of Smiles." Since its opening, the clinic has lost business and though Loren's father works six days week, he struggles to pay his mortgage and other bills. He has not shared his problems with Loren, but money worries may explain why he puts so much pressure on Loren to excel at school.

Artistic Style

Night Fisher is illustrated in fairly rough brush strokes, with large swatches of black, but the lines can be remarkably fine and subtle when necessary. The lettering of the book is done in the same brush stroke, creating a unity to the look of the entire page. Though Johnson uses a realistic style throughout, he often inserts expressionistic elements, such as bees by Loren's ears to show the effects of the drugs he has just taken or the image of a dead rat to indicate Loren's mental association when a man at a crack house suddenly falls off his seat. Johnson applies many traditional comics devices, such as overlapping text balloons to indicate interruptions or illegible text balloons to show speech that cannot quite be understood. Many of these tropes tend to be used predominately in "cartoony" comics, so they make for an interesting contrast with Johnson's realistic imagery.

Night Fisher creates a new visual vocabulary through the juxtaposition of images from different sources and registers. For example, Johnson inserts textbook illustrations, maps, and graphs often in contrast to the narrative panels. Such images work to show

Loren's state of mind: He is a high school student who uses what he has learned at school to understand the real world, but his preoccupation with learning, as a student under pressure, also makes him emotionally distant. This is exemplified by the ironic contrast between smiling faces on a dentist's office poster and the tense atmosphere between Loren and his father after Loren's arrest.

Even though *Night Fisher* is realistic, its cover is slightly surreal, showing, in stark black relief, a man standing on a cliff high above the ocean, holding a line that leads into the water. The scale is off in the image; the man and the line are too large in comparison to the detailed foliage, which in turn contrasts with the cartoon waves of the blue water. The cover seems to emphasize Loren's dream life, which appears only minimally in the narrative and which Loren seems to want to suppress.

Themes

One of the main themes that Johnson explores is nature versus culture. Before the main character is introduced, the book opens with maps showing the geological formation of the island of Maui. This creates a contrast between the millennia-long history of the island and Loren's brief time there. Loren sits through classes about the native plant and animal species of the islands, and then he recognizes many of the plants covered in class at a local market. Maui's vegetation is constantly changing, as endemic species of plants and animals are threatened by species more recently introduced from elsewhere. As a recent arrival to the island himself, Loren takes these lessons personally. He still feels like an outsider, perhaps even an unwelcome one, and his struggle to make a place for himself on the island is represented in the fight he and his father wage against their lawn, which is under threat to be taken over by the "weeds" that grew there originally.

A second theme that runs through *Night Fisher* is teen angst, as Loren is shown trying to cope in various ways with the pressures of being a high-achieving high school senior and an outsider. In order to gain popularity, he has spread rumors about engaging in sexual activities with Lacey, a friend and romantic interest, which ultimately ruins their friendship. He allows himself be dragged into a nocturnal life of drugs and petty theft to reconnect with his best friend, Shane. The result is additional stress as his grades slide and his father's obvious disappointment pains him. By the end of the graphic novel, it is unclear whether Loren will pull himself together or whether his fall during the cross-country run foreshadows complete disengagement from school and home life.

Impact

Johnson was born and raised on the island of Maui, and his familiarity with the setting is obvious through his drawings and imagery. The emotional turbulence experienced as one crosses the bridge between high school and adulthood is familiar material to many, and in that sense Loren's story is not his own. As a result, *Night Fisher* stands out as a realistic yet fictional graphic novel at a time when autobiographical comics dominate the field of realism in comics.

In *Night Fisher*, Johnson develops the visual language of comics with devices such as the inclusion of various noncomics sources that are juxtaposed with narrative panels to indicate Loren's state of mind, associations that he makes, or visual cues that trigger memories. Johnson also makes small tweaks to the use of text balloons such as using arrows on the text balloon to indicate whom the speaker is addressing, rather than the tail pointing to the speaker in the traditional manner. Johnson is also able to intermix the abstract, convention-based visual language of comics, such as panel use, text balloons, and sound effects, with realistic brush-and-ink representational style, which makes *Night Fisher* an interesting and instructive experiment.

Barbara Postema

R. Kikuo Johnson

R. Kikuo Johnson's *Night Fisher* made him one of the most exciting debut cartoonists of the mid-2000's. Set in the hills of Hawaii, the story revolves around two young men, nearing the end of their high school experience, whose relationship begins to drift apart. Johnson published the work having produced almost no other comics that were widely read, and he was largely praised and compared to other precocious cartoonists, like Adrian Tomine. His follow-up, *The Shark King* (with artist Trade Loeffler), was a children's comic published by Toon Books. Also set in Hawaii, it tells the story of Nanaue, the insatiable son of the shape-shifting shark god Kamohaoali'i. Johnson's visual style is strongly naturalistic with thick, dark lines. He works with heavy blacks and stark contrasts in a very traditional grid framework. His stories draw heavily on his native Hawaii and its myths and traditions.

Further Reading

Abel, Jessica. *La Perdida* (2006).
Clowes, Daniel. *Ghost World* (2010).
Rabagliati, Michel. *Paul Has a Summer Job* (2003).

Bibliography

Attenberg, Jami. "Prime Cuts, Rare and Well Done." *Print* 61, no. 2 (March/April, 2007): 67.
Johnson, R. Kikuo. "R. Kikuo Johnson Interview." Interview by Gary Groth. *The Comics Journal* 277 (July, 2006): 176.

See also: *Ghost World*; *La Perdida*; *It's a Good Life, If You Don't Weaken*

9/11 REPORT, THE: A GRAPHIC ADAPTATION

Author: Jacobson, Sid
Artist: Ernie Colón (illustrator)
Publisher: Hill and Wang
First book publication: 2006

Publication History

Mandated by the White House and Congress, the National Commission on Terrorist Attacks upon the United States, more commonly referred to as the "9/11 Commission," was formed in November of 2002. Chaired by former New Jersey governor Thomas Kean, its job was to conduct a full investigation into the events leading up to the terrorist attacks of September 11, 2001 (9/11). On July 24, 2004, the 9/11 Commission released *The 9/11 Commission Report*, a narrative of the government's official report of these events. This dense and thorough account became the basis and inspiration for *The 9/11 Report: A Graphic Adaptation*, which aims to make this important document accessible and relatable to the general public.

After hearing about the possibility of a film adaptation of *The 9/11 Commission Report*, artist Ernie Colón began to see the advantages of using a visual medium to depict the time line of the events of 9/11, making it easier to process the day's simultaneous proceedings. He contacted longtime friend Sid Jacobson, and the two began corresponding and working on the project over the following year. Although *The 9/11 Report: A Graphic Adaptation* was conceived of and completed without input or assistance from the 9/11 Commission, publisher Hill and Wang sent advance copies to Kean and 9/11 Commission vice chair Lee Hamilton, who, upon reading *The 9/11 Report: A Graphic Adaptation*, enthusiastically supported the project and provided its foreword.

World Trade Center disaster site, New York. *The 9/11 Report: A Graphic Adaptation* offers compelling visuals to aid in the comprehension of the terrorist attacks of September 11, 2001. (Catherine Ursillo)

Plot

Like *The 9/11 Commission Report*, the majority of *The 9/11 Report: A Graphic Adaptation* details the political and global events leading up to the terrorist attacks of 9/11. The first chapter, "We Have Some Planes...," begins on the morning of September 11, 2001, and offers a graphic and textual time line of the hijackings of American Airlines Flight 11, United Airlines Flight 175, American Airlines Flight 7, and United Airlines Flight 93. While the majority of the chapter details the events taking place on the four planes, there is also information interspersed regarding the response of the U.S. government and homeland defense teams.

The text then moves back in time, with chapter 2 chronicling Osama bin Laden's rise to power and the formation of the terrorist network al-Qaeda. This chapter addresses not only the Soviet presence in Afghanistan from the late 1970's through the 1980's but also the events surrounding Bin Laden's 1998 declaration of a fatwa against the United States. Chapters 3 and 4 discuss the 1993 car bombing of the World Trade Center and the U.S. government's response, along with other growing counterterrorism measures in the United States. By the time al-Qaeda bombs U.S. embassies in Kenya and Tanzania in 1998, the U.S. government identifies Bin Laden's role in the original World Trade Center attacks and subsequently acknowledges his role in the African attacks, along with his growing resources and terrorist training camps. Despite this knowledge, no concrete plan of action against Bin Laden is made by the United States.

Chapters 5, 6, and 7 shift back and forth between the plans of the terrorists, chronicling the inception of the "planes operation" that would be executed on 9/11, and the counterterrorism intelligence work being carried out under the presidential administrations of Bill Clinton and George W. Bush. Chapter 8 specifically deals with U.S. intelligence efforts during the summer of 2001. Despite growing knowledge of impending action by al-Qaeda, the lack of a clear plan and communication between government agencies prevents the U.S. government from taking any serious or solid measures against the imminent threat, and, as a result, the public is not warned of any possible terrorist activity.

Chapter 9 returns the narrative to the morning of September 11, 2001, and chronicles the emergency response efforts at the World Trade Center and the Pentagon. Chapter 10 begins with President Bush returning to Washington, D.C., and goes on to detail the U.S. government's response and plans for military action in Afghanistan and Iraq. Chapters 11, 12, and 13 deal with the commission's findings, outlining the government's failures in imagination, policy, capability, and management as they relate to U.S. preparedness for terrorist attacks. The text goes on to outline global strategies for improvement as well as recommendations for the reorganization of U.S. government agencies to allow for greater communication. The graphic adaptation concludes with a "postscript" reminiscent of a report card, which offers a final, dismal evaluation of the president and the congressional response to the commission's findings.

Characters

- *George W. Bush* is the forty-third president of the United States. Serving as president from 2001 to 2009, he is the commander in chief on September 11, 2001, and initiates the "War on Terror" in response to the terrorist attacks, sending thousands of U.S. military troops to Afghanistan and Iraq.

- *Osama bin Laden* is a terrorist leader and son of a Saudi Arabian construction mogul. He becomes involved in the resistance movement against the Soviet invasion of Afghanistan in 1980's. Using his family's considerable wealth, Bin Laden establishes financial support networks and terrorist training camps, eventually becoming the leader of the Islamic terrorist group al-Qaeda. In 1998, Bin Laden issues a fatwa that calls for the death of Americans in the name of Islam. Through al-Qaeda, Bin Laden organizes and funds a number of terrorist activities, including those of September 11, 2001.

- *Khalid Sheikh Mohammed* is considered the mastermind behind the 9/11 plot and known as the "Architect of 9/11." Mohammed is of Kuwaiti descent and holds a degree in engineering from North Carolina Agricultural and Technical State University. In addition to plotting the 9/11 attacks, Mohammed confesses to having a role in a number of other terrorist activities, including the 1993 car bombing of the World Trade Center.

- *Ramzi Yousef* is the nephew of Khalid Sheikh Mohammed and the principal architect of the 1993 bombing of the World Trade Center.
- *Mohammed Atta* is a member of the Hamburg cell of terrorists, which plays a key role in the planning of the 9/11 terrorist attacks. Born in Egypt, Atta studied architecture in Cairo, Egypt, and Hamburg, Germany. After hijacking American Airlines Flight 11 along with Satam al-Suqami, Wail al-Shehri, Waleed al-Shehri, and Abdulaziz al-Omari, Atta pilots the plane into the North Tower of the World Trade Center at 8:46 A.M. on September 11, 2001.
- *Marwan al-Shehhi* is a student from the United Arab Emirates and part of the Hamburg Cell. Al-Shehhi, along with Fayze Banihammad, Ahmed al-Ghamdi, Hamza al-Ghamdi, and Mohand al-Shehri, hijacks United Airlines Flight 175. He pilots Flight 175 into the South Tower of the World Trade Center at 9:03 A.M.
- *Ziad Jarrah* is a student of Lebanese descent who is associated with the Hamburg Cell. Along with Ahmed al-Nami, Saeed al-Ghamdi, and Ahmed al-Haznawi, Jarrah hijacks United Airlines Flight 93 on September 11, 2001. The plane crashes in Shanksville, Pennsylvania, at 10:03 A.M. before reaching its target destination of the U.S. Capitol.
- *Bill Clinton* is the forty-second president of the United States, serving from 1993 to 2001. Clinton is president during the 1993 World Trade Center bombing, al-Qaeda's 1998 bombings of U.S. embassies in Kenya and Tanzania, and al-Qaeda's 2000 attack on the U.S.S. *Cole*. Clinton's administration is aware of Bin Laden's connection to al-Qaeda and al-Qaeda's terrorist activities but is unable to obtain definitive proof of Bin Laden's involvement in these attacks.
- *Donald Rumsfeld* is the U.S. secretary of defense under Bush from 2001 to 2006. In this capacity, Rumsfeld directs the planning of the U.S. response to 9/11 that culminates in the military invasions of Afghanistan and Iraq by U.S. forces.
- *Dick Cheney* is vice president during both terms of Bush's presidency.

Artistic Style

Colón began his career at Harvey Comics, where he worked on series such as *Richie Rich* and *Casper the Friendly Ghost*. It was at Harvey Comics that Colón first met and worked with Jacobson, before the latter left to work on titles for DC Comics and Marvel. Colón's art is reminiscent of the classic adventure style. As *The 9/11 Report: A Graphic Adaptation* depicts contemporary historical figures, he keeps faithful to a realistic style that stays away from caricature or cartoonish representation. Colón matches his art to the various objectives of Jacobson's and the *9/11 Commission Report*'s narratives, employing a number of visual layouts and techniques to aid in the dissemination of information. Maps and diagrams are frequently used, and the first twenty-five pages of the novel offer a visual time line of the hijackings of the four planes.

Sid Jacobson

Writer Sid Jacobson has one of the least conventional career paths in graphic novels, having started as an editor for Harvey Comics (publisher of *Richie Rich* and *Casper the Friendly Ghost*). After working as the executive editor of Star Comics, the children's comics line at Marvel, and Hanna-Barbera Comics, Jacobson became known for his work on two graphic novels: *The 9/11 Report: A Graphic Adaptation* and *After 9/11: America's War on Terror* (both with artist Ernie Colón). Those works were praised for presenting complex history and geopolitics in a format that was easily understood by a wide range of readers, and the books are highly fact driven. Subsequently, the duo collaborated on a pair of *Graphic Biographies*, one of the revolutionary leader Che Guevara and another of diarist Anne Frank. Jacobson's graphic novels are notable for their textual density and for their wide-ranging historical topics.

The time line is the most innovative artistic aspect of the text, as it allows readers to visually situate the various activities of the four planes at any given time. In doing so, Colón re-creates the chaos of the morning's events and demonstrates the confusion and failure of communication among various government and aviation offices. While the majority of nameless individuals and low-level government officials are generically rendered, Colón takes great care in depicting known figures such as Bush and Rumsfeld, often portraying them in serious black-and-white sketches. However, Colón capitulates to ethnic and religious stereotypes in his depictions of the terrorists and other Arabs, which has the effect of weakening any pretense of objectivity. Furthermore, the use of onomatopoeia interspersed with scenes of actual war and terrorism can be construed as insensitive and misplaced alongside the gravity of the text.

Themes

The 9/11 Report: A Graphic Adaptation aims to make the findings of *The 9/11 Commission Report* accessible, relatable, and readable for a general audience. It distills the basic and most important information from the *Commission Report* and places it in a format that offers compelling visuals to aid in the comprehension of the terrorist attacks of September 11, 2001. More than just a chronicle of the day's events, it provides a much-needed history lesson on al-Qaeda and modern terrorist activity aimed at the United States.

In addition to informing the public, the main aim of *The 9/11 Report: A Graphic Adaptation* is to engage audiences and encourage them to understand and support the reforms and suggestions put forth by the 9/11 Commission in an effort to increase awareness and preparedness for future terrorist activity. This is achieved in the graphic adaptation through the textual and visual interplay of narrative and the recommendations and "report card" detailed at the end of the text.

Impact

The political and cultural significance of 9/11, coupled with the praise and critical success of *The 9/11 Commission Report*, generated an interest in *The 9/11 Report: A Graphic Adaptation* even before its publication. Jacobson and Colón were interviewed and featured in a number of mainstream news and media outlets, including National Public Radio (NPR) and *USA Today*, promoting the novel's release. Given its subject matter, the *Graphic Adaptation* appeals to a wide range of audiences, many of whom have no previous knowledge or experience with graphic fiction. It has been used in a number of contexts, including high school and college classrooms, becoming an important text in teaching about 9/11. Its success encouraged Jacobson and Colón to collaborate on other historical subjects, such as Che Guevara and Anne Frank, through the graphic medium. In 2008, Jacobson and Colón published the follow-up graphic novel *After 9/11: America's War on Terror (2001-)*.

Jenn Brandt

Further Reading

Jacobson, Sid, and Ernie Colón. *After 9/11: America's War on Terror (2001-)* (2008).

Spiegelman, Art. *In the Shadow of No Towers* (2004).

Torres, Alissa, and Sungyoon Choi. *American Widow* (2008).

Bibliography

Hassell, Bravetta. "The Bold Outlines of a Plot." *The Washington Post*, July 16, 2006, p. D01.

National Commission on Terrorist Attacks upon the United States. *The 9/11 Commission Report: Final Report of the National Commission on Terrorist Attacks upon the United States*. New York: W. W. Norton, 2004.

Turner, Julia. "The Trouble with Drawing Dick Cheney: Ernie Colón and Sid Jacobson, the Comic Book Vets Behind *The 9/11 Report: A Graphic Adaptation*." *Slate* 10 (September 11, 2006). http://www.slate.com/id/2149231.

See also: *Maus*

NOTES FOR A WAR STORY

Author: Gipi (pseudonym of Gianni Pacinotti)
Artist: Gipi (illustrator)
Publisher: Coconino Press; First Second
First book publication: *Appunti per una storia di guerra*, 2004 (English translation, 2007)

Publication History

Gipi's *Notes for a War Story* was initially published as *Appunti per una storia di guerra* in 2004 by Coconino Press, an Italian publishing house. Since its creation in 2000, Coconino Press has translated and published the work of various popular comics artists from around the world, such as American authors Daniel Clowes, Jason Lutes, and Adrian Tomine; French artists David B., Baru, and Emmanuel Guibert; and Japanese story-tellers Jirô Taniguchi and Suehiro Maruo. In addition to these internationally successful authors, Coconino Press has published both established and new Italian talents such as Davide Reviati, Francesca Ghermandi, and Gipi.

Gipi has been renowned in Italy since 1994 for his subtle use of watercolors and psychologically complex characters. However, he became internationally famous as a result of his *Notes for a War Story*. This work was translated and published into French as *Notes pour une histoire de guerre* by Actes Sud in 2005 and then adapted into English by First Second Books in 2007.

Plot

Notes for a War Story recounts the tale of three young men—Giuliano, Christian, and Little Killer—as they travel in an unknown country ravished by the calamities of war. The story unfolds as a flashback from the perspective of Giuliano, the narrator, who (one discovers in the epilogue) is in fact being interviewed by a news correspondent collecting "notes for a war story" that will be "edited and packaged" for a documentary.

The physical journey of the three young men coincides with their experiences of early adulthood. From the beginning of the story, the trio attempts to take advantage of the chaos engendered by the war to get into what they think will be a lucrative business: selling

Notes for a War Story. (Courtesy of First Second Books)

stolen-car parts. They soon realize, however, that their petty-crime enterprise is bound to fail by conventional means. The war has destroyed not only entire villages but also resources. Nevertheless, they quickly find their way into the militia that is occupying the area and are introduced to its leader, Felix.

Felix is a robust thug who takes a particular interest in the three friends, especially Little Killer because of his experience with manual labor. Felix quickly proposes a "real job" to the boys, giving them a list of items to collect in the city. Thus, the trio ventures into the main town where they soon transform from petty-crime novices into professional thugs, gathering money with both attitude and violence. Their typical and unique strategy involves Christian and Little Killer frightening people with guns while Giuliano stands guard outside. Inevitably, however, one of their jobs ends badly when they are robbed by other bandits. Afraid that Felix will belittle and castigate them for getting duped by another group of criminals, Little Killer vows to find their assailants and eventually kills them.

After regaining their loot, the young men proudly reconnect with Felix and his men. However, during the trio's absence, Felix is injured and the militia is weakened. Felix has other tasks to do to keep the war going. Little Killer, Christian, and Giuliano's assistance is therefore required elsewhere. They are separated and

Notes for a War Story. (Courtesy of First Second Books)

sent away to the war's front lines in militia trucks full of armed men. Alone and afraid, Giuliano jumps off the truck and escapes a dangerous and uncertain fate.

The narrative concludes with Giuliano's interview. The war is over, but Guiliano looks considerably changed and roughened. The journalists are about to leave him to go to the train station and interview the first war prisoners to be released, but Giuliano tags along. The last page of the book shows him on the platform scrutinizing the crowd, hoping to see his friends one more time.

Characters

- *Giuliano*, the narrator, is a young male adult from a well-off family. In contrast to his friends, he is educated and has a house and a family, and therefore has the choice to turn back whenever he wants. He is often not directly involved in much of the crime and generally just observes the situations.
- *Little Killer*, a.k.a. *Stefano*, is a small but violent and sharp young male adult. He grew up in what the local kids called "the war zone" and was baptized Little Killer because during a childhood fight, he drew blood. He witnessed his father's suicide. He is the leader of the trio and is Felix's favorite, who trusts him with the job instructions and a gun.
- *Christian* is a young man who lived in an orphanage. He never had a proper house and is naïve and uneducated. He primarily cares about money and material possessions, and he does not care about how he and his friends acquire them. Similar to Little Killer and in contrast to Giuliano, he cannot choose a different life. His friends are his only family. He helps Little Killer undertake much of the thug action but recurrently asks irrelevant questions.
- *Felix* is a relatively young man who is probably in his thirties. He looks robust, rude, and macho and is the leader of the militia. He cunningly influences the boys and acts as their mentor. He takes Little Killer under his wing because he feels he may be useful to him.

Artistic Style

Notes for a War Story was published as a one-shot graphic novel in a rather small format, typical of European and North American alternative and independent publishing houses such as L'Association and Fantagraphics Books. The small-size format of the book illustrates Gipi's willingness to draw the reader's attention to the proximity of the war that the boys experience as well as to complement his anecdotic take on the topic.

Gipi is famous for a simple, minimalist, and straightforward line style and his use of watercolors. *Notes for a War Story* is no exception. The drawings of the book are not especially sophisticated in that they lack embellishment or superfluous details. In addition to allowing reader identification, this minimalist strategy conforms to the serious tone and subject matter of *Notes for a War Story*, which unabashedly presents the collateral damage of warfare. Gipi's use of black-and-white watercolors, supplemented by a large palette of halftones, also works toward a similar understanding of the trauma that the boys experience. Furthermore, the use of sepia tone coincides with the narrator's flashback.

The artistic style does not change considerably over the course of the book. However, one specific artistic peculiarity is worth mentioning. The narrative is interspersed with several of Giuliano's dreams in which his friends Christian and Little Killer appear headless. This visual metaphor, suggests Alexis Siegel in his afterword to the 2007 English translation of *Notes of a War Story*, is significant in two distinct ways. First, it suggests that the narrator "never stops thinking for himself" and even challenges Felix's authority. Second, the metaphor conveys that Giuliano is different from his friends because he has an "inner life" and "tries to work out his feelings." Interestingly, the war prisoners that Giuliano scrutinizes at the end of the book also appear headless and mark the final episode of the book as inconclusive.

Themes

Notes for a War Story stands out for its treatment of masculinity in the context of war. Although the actual war zone is never directly depicted, the nameless country in which the trio evolves is devastated and can neither provide the boys with future prospects nor inspire them with a clear structure. In this context, Felix rapidly becomes a role model for the three young men. He offers them something to do and, thus, a sense of purpose. In addition, the boys enjoy free enrollment in Felix's "continuous school of life." He teaches them lessons from his perspective about what it means to be a man, and in that sense he influences their behavior.

Notes for a War Story shows similarities to the innocence-experience-consideration model that critics generally employ to discuss the psychological development of soldiers in war literature. The three boys lose their innocence and gradually become more experienced and less naïve as they learn how to operate within organized crime. However, Gipi's book does show how the soldier, after the war, reflects on his mischievous acts. Guiliano's interview at the end of the book hints at the possibility of consideration. However, his interview lacks closure and therefore gives a rather pessimistic twist to both the book and the treatment of masculinity in a war or a postwar context.

Impact

Notes for a War Story was one of the first of Gipi's books to be translated into various languages, including English. In 2006, the French version of the book won the Best Album Award at Angoulême, Europe's most famous international comics festival. The Italian storyteller was at that point only the second non-Francophone artist to receive this prestigious prize since first awarded in 1974. In 2003, American Chris Ware won the prize for *Jimmy Corrigan: The Smartest Kid on Earth*. Before Ware's award, the festival only awarded prizes to non-Francophone artists within the Best Foreign Book category. Since 2003, however, the Best Album Award has considered artists from all over the world. It is in this context that *Notes for a War Story* has participated in the increasing recognition of international comics in Europe. This change in strategy of the Angoulême Festival has allowed artists such as the British Neil Gaiman, the Australian Shaun Tan, or the Japanese Taniguchi to win important prizes.

The Angoulême award that Gipi obtained for *Notes for a War Story* also improved the artist's popularity on an international level. Since then, for example, First Second Books and Fantagraphics Books, two major

---

Gipi

Gipi is the pen name of Gianni Pacinotti, one of the most influential Italian cartoonists of recent years. Having broken into the Italian comics scene with short works in a variety of newspapers, magazines, and anthologies in the 1990's, his breakthrough work appeared in 2005 when he published *Notes for a War Story*, which went on to the win the Grand Prize at the Angoulême Comics Festival. The book tells the story of three young men in an unidentified war-torn European nation. His follow-up, *The Innocents*, deals with a reformed drug addict and a friend who was recently released from prison for a crime that he did not commit. *Garage Band* depicts the trouble that follows a rock band after their only amp blows a fuse. More recently, Gipi has taken an autobiographical turn with *S.* and *Ma vie mal dessinée*. Gipi's art is notable for its fine, thin lines, stylized naturalism and use of delicate watercolors.

American alternative publishing houses, have translated and released various works by Gipi, including *Garage Band* (2007) and *They Found the Car* (2006).

Christophe Dony

Further Reading

Gipi. *Garage Band* (2007).

_____. *They Found the Car* (2006).

Bibliography

Fussell, Paul. *The Great War and Modern Memory*. Reprint. New York: Sterling, 2009.

Gipi. "Taken from Life: An Interview with Gipi." Interview by Nicole Rudick. *Words without Borders* (February, 2008). http://wordswithoutborders.org/article/taken-from-life-an-interview-with-gipi.

Siegel, Alexis. Afterword to *Notes for a War Story*. New York: First Second, 2007.

See also: *The Arrival*; *Jimmy Corrigan*; *Photographer*

O

OMAHA THE CAT DANCER

Author: Worley, Kate; Vance, James; Waller, Reed
Artist: Reed Waller
Publisher: NBM
First serial publication: 1984-1995; 2005-
First book publication: 1987-1998

Publication History

Omaha the Cat Dancer's history begins in 1978, as comics creator Reed Waller's contribution to *Vootie*, a self-published one-shot magazine created by a co-operative of "funny animal" cartoonists. The only erotic piece in the magazine, *Omaha* was picked up by Kitchen Sink Press, which published the continuing adventures of Omaha in *Bizarre Sex*, issues 9 and 10, before the character moved to its own series in 1984 with *Omaha the Cat Dancer*, issue 3. Steel-Dragon Press had published issues 1 and 2. Between 1987 and 1993, Kitchen Sink Press released *The Collected Omaha the Cat Dancer* in six volumes. Not only was Kitchen Sink Press largely responsible for *Omaha the Cat Dancer*'s success, but it also showed its support for the comic by creating the Comic Book Legal Defense Fund (CBLDF), which came into existence in part because *Omaha the Cat Dancer* was often cited in discussions of censorship and obscenity.

Comics writer Kate Worley began writing *Omaha the Cat Dancer* with issue 2. The publication of the series was slowed in 1988, when Worley was in a car accident and Waller had colon cancer. Stress affected the creators' marriage, causing them to divorce in 1995, and the series ceased publication. Worley and Waller, both fighting cancer, reconciled their differences in 2004 and began working on a new sequence of Omaha stories. However, Worley died later that year. Worley's second husband, fellow comics writer

James Vance, stepped in and continued the story-telling based on his wife's notes.

After a short sojourn with Fantagraphics Books in the mid-1990's, Waller and Worley had returned to Kitchen Sink Press, where publisher Denis Kitchen arranged for new comics. He also arranged for collected volumes of *The Complete Omaha the Cat Dancer* to be published by Amerotica, a subsidiary of NBM, starting in 2005. As of 2012, seven volumes have been published; a final, eighth volume is planned. The final stories are written by Vance with drawings by Waller. They appear intermittently in NBM's quarterly erotic graphic magazine, *Sizzle*.

Plot

Omaha the Cat Dancer is an erotic anthropomorphic graphic novel for mature adults in which animals interact as humans and display distinctly human genitalia. The title is a pun on many levels. Omaha is physically a female cat, and "cat dancer" refers to a woman who earns her living as a stripper. Omaha follows this path after leaving her office job and changes her name from Susan "Susie" Jenson. She makes friends with a bisexual female cat, a fellow cat dancer named Shelley, gains fame as a centerfold in a *Playboy*-type magazine known as *Pet*, begins working regularly at the Kitty Korner Club, and falls in love with Chuck Katt (Charles Tabey, Jr.), a male cat and independent artist who frequents the nightclub where she works.

When blue laws are passed, the Kitty Korner Club is closed, and Chuck is forced to go back to work as an artist for media mogul Andre DeRoc. Omaha and Shelley find work at the Underground, a club for the rich and powerful owned by Charles Tabey, Sr., Chuck's father. DeRoc sabotages the opening of the new club, spiking the drinks with drugs. This results in a violent orgy, during which Shelley is shot and disabled. Omaha and Chuck temporarily flee to San Francisco.

Tabey, Sr.'s relationship with Omaha takes a new turn when he offers to let her take care of Shelley. Omaha and Chuck miss each other because of the separation. Corrupt politician Senator Calvin Bonner attempts to possess Omaha, gain power in Mipple City, and have Chuck do his bidding, thereby pitting Chuck against his father.

Tabey, Sr., dies and is buried at sea by Jerry Davidson, his right-hand man. Jerry informs Chuck that there are no other known heirs to the Tabey estate; however, a separation agreement between Tabey and Chuck's mother, Maria, who is believed long dead, is found. JoAnne finds pictures taken during the orgy at the Underground that show Senator Bonner in attendance and decides to feign allegiance with Bonner to discover more about his possible involvement in Tabey's death. Maria arrives at Tabey's house a few days after his funeral and introduces herself to Tabey's assistant Pamela, who does not tell Chuck that his mother is in town.

Omaha and Chuck return to Mipple City, where he buys a house, giving Shelley the first floor and hiring Kurt Huddle as her nurse. Kurt slowly falls in love with Shelley, and their relationship develops throughout the series.

Back in San Francisco, Rob Shaw, who photographed the orgy, is assaulted and his photography shop is burned, but he had already given his negatives to JoAnne. Chuck tries to discover more about Senator Bonner, who is on a campaign to "clean up" Mipple City. Convinced that this is simply an attempt to bring in money for the senator and his rich cronies, Chuck decides to use some of his father's money to block the senator's plans, aligning himself with some streetwise friends in a band called The Herd. Senator Bonner stays ahead of Chuck, though, and has information about Omaha's marriage to David Joplin, whom she has never divorced. All the players converge at the reopened Kitty Korner, where Chuck and the senator nearly get into a fistfight with each other.

Chuck discovers his mother is still alive and has spoken with Omaha. He decides that Maria had abandoned him as a baby (though Omaha knows otherwise). Bitter and increasingly irritable, Chuck dedicates his time to the business he inherited from his father.

Meanwhile, JoAnne convinces Rob to take a hidden video of her and Senator Bonner having sex, which can be released to the press to defame the senator. However, Senator Bonner is killed, shot in the head by a bullet that comes in through his hotel window. JoAnne is immediately arrested for his murder. With Senator Bonner's death, a new mystery story line is introduced, affecting most of the major characters.

Chuck proposes to Omaha, who admits to her marriage. Chuck does not take the news well. Omaha decides to leave him and Mipple City. She goes to Lawrenceville, Wisconsin, where she initially takes a job in an office before rebelling against the company's sexist atmosphere. She then changes her name to "Susan Johnson" and takes a job dancing at Pip's, the town's only erotic club.

Chuck reconciles with his mother. The Herd comes to the attention of a video producer, particularly because of Omaha's dancing in the video. A man named Lopez arrives in town and hires Kurt Hubble as a chauffeur.

Lopez reveals he is Maria's father and Chuck's grandfather and becomes a suspect in the murder of Senator Bonner. Maria reveals to Chuck that she married his father out of love when they both were young. Bonner, then her father's lawyer, had blackmailed her into leaving Charles and Chuck by revealing secrets he knew about the Elandos family dealings. This revelation, coupled with stress from political activity, work, and the loss of Omaha, causes Chuck to have a nervous breakdown.

Omaha returns to Mipple City and Chuck. Senator Bonner's killer remains undiscovered. The final published volume ends on tentative notes: Shelley has broken up with Kurt, now her lover as well as her nurse, and Omaha and Chuck, while together, decide to try to find her husband to ask him to agree to a divorce.

Volumes

- *The Complete Omaha the Cat Dancer*, Volume 1 (2005). Collects independent stories and issues 0-1. Introduces the main characters and reveals their attitudes and motivations. Includes an introduction by Vance, who edits the novels, and another by Waller.
- *The Complete Omaha the Cat Dancer*, Volume 2 (2006). Collects issues 2-5. With Shelley shot, this collection introduces Chuck's father, who dies under suspicious circumstances, as well as many of the secondary characters that remain throughout the series. Includes an introduction by Worley, the series' primary writer, discussing the roles of the female characters.
- *The Complete Omaha the Cat Dancer*, Volume 3 (2006). Collects issues 6-9. Following the death of Chuck's father, major characters return to Mipple City, only to realize how much it has changed under the morality campaign conducted by Senator Bonner. Features an introduction by feminist cartoonist Trina Robbins.
- *The Complete Omaha the Cat Dancer*, Volume 4 (2006). Collects issues 10-13. Chuck confronts his mother, begins an aggressive stance against Senator Bonner, and joins with the musical group The Herd, which produces a video featuring Omaha's dancing. Omaha's marriage

is revealed. Senator Bonner is murdered. Features an introduction by Vance.
- *The Complete Omaha the Cat Dancer*, Volume 5 (2006). Collects issues 14-17. Omaha arrives in Wisconsin, where she tries to establish a new life. Chuck begins to reconcile with his mother. The Mipple City police add JoAnne, Maria, Chuck, and the mysterious Lopez to the murder suspect list. Features an introduction by comics creator Neil Gaiman.
- *The Complete Omaha the Cat Dancer*, Volume 6 (2007). Collects issues 18-20 and independent, self-contained stories. Omaha takes a new lover. Maria explains why she abandoned Chuck and his father, which causes Chuck to have a nervous breakdown. Omaha returns to nurse him. Features an introduction by comics creator Terry Moore.
- *The Complete Omaha the Cat Dancer*, Volume 7 (2008). Collects issues 21-24. Main characters come back together, and newer members of the cast are integrated in the social group. Omaha's husband heads toward Mipple City. Omaha and Chuck get back together, but Shelley and Kurt break up. Features an introduction by publisher Denis Kitchen.

Characters

- *Omaha*, a.k.a. *Susan "Susie" Jenson* or *Susie Johnson*, the major protagonist in the series. She is an anthropomorphic female cat with distinctively human physical qualities. Beautiful and athletic, with flaming auburn hair, she is highly sexual and uses her sexuality to rebel against traditional stereotypes of women. She is in love with Chuck.
- *Charles Tabey, Jr.*, a.k.a. *Chuck Katt*, a tomcat, is an artist and heir to the Tabey fortune. He becomes Omaha's lover. He is a minor protagonist, continuing to side with Omaha and fighting the powers-that-be in Mipple City.
- *Charles Tabey, Sr.*, is a millionaire and Chuck's father. He had relationships with Shelley and JoAnne. He dies mysteriously. He is a minor

antagonist in that he tries to keep Omaha and Chuck apart.

- *Shelley Hine* is a bisexual exotic dancer who becomes Omaha's best friend. She is disabled after being shot at the Underground. She is taken care of by Omaha, Chuck, and Kurt Huddle, who becomes her lover.
- *Andre DeRoc*, a media mogul, is another antagonist. He is represented as a rooster. His competition with Charles Tabey, Sr., negatively affects Chuck. His desire to bring down the Underground affects all of the characters in the series.
- *JoAnne Follett* was the secretary for DeRoc and seems to align herself with Senator Bonner. She had a relationship with Chuck, a one-night stand with Omaha, and a relationship with Charles Tabey, Sr.
- *Senator Calvin Bonner* is a dog, both literally and figuratively. A senator and business tycoon in Mipple City, he is the last of the major antagonists. While he runs his campaign based on appeals to morality, he is sadistic. JoAnne becomes his lover, wanting to expose his hypocrisy. He is murdered by an unknown assassin.
- *Maria Elandos Tabey* is Chuck's mother and Charles Tabey, Sr.'s wife. She was blackmailed into leaving her family.
- *Elandos*, a.k.a. *Lopez*, is Chuck's grandfather and Maria's father. He entered the United States illegally and is a suspect in Bonner's murder.
- *Rob Shaw*, a gay photographer, is a link between Omaha, Chuck, and JoAnne, having taken photos at the Underground on the night of the orgy as well as a film of JoAnne having sex with Bonner.

Artistic Style

Reed Waller's artistry on *Omaha the Cat Dancer* has improved dramatically over his years. For his early art, he used thick lines; this art was almost discarded by the printer because it used too much black ink. In the later stories, Waller's style is lean, alternately focusing on the bodies of the characters to depict sexuality and on their heads for narration. While the comics are rendered in black and white, the covers of the collected editions are color. Designed, drawn, and inked by Waller, they focus mainly on Omaha.

There are usually six panels to a page, unless Waller chooses to emphasize an event. He may use a one-page panel to emphasize an emotion or a variety of "tight" panels to emphasize tension. This works particularly well with Worley's "soap-opera" narrative approach. The art is somewhat reminiscent of the romance comics popular in the late 1950's and early 1960's that were inspired by the rising popularity of the television soap opera.

Other artists, particularly Trina Robbins, a feminist cartoonist, have argued that Waller's sensitivity in depicting sexual relationships moves this graphic novel outside of the realm of pornography and into the erotic, noting that his characters are designed not to surprise or shock, but rather to display human physical relationships familiar to readers.

Themes

The primary theme of *Omaha the Cat Dancer* is the repression of women. Informed by the rise of the women's movement in the late 1960's and early 1970's, Waller and Worley recognize the paradox of the sexually attractive woman's ability to use her sexuality to gain control over her own life. *Omaha the Cat Dancer* focuses on relationships and how the power in relationships shifts based on sex, money, and the designation of gender roles.

Another major theme is hypocrisy. The characters that seem to represent high moral values discard them when it is to their benefit to do so. The moralistic Senator Bonner best exemplifies this. By overcoming their hypocrisy, some of the characters are able to advance their relationships with others.

While sex is important, the love relationships that develop through honesty, trust, and allegiance are ultimately more important in *Omaha the Cat Dancer*. Familial relationships and reconciliations are also addressed in the series. Chuck reconciles with his mother, Maria. Maria's father shows up in support of Maria. Omaha and Chuck determine to marry, creating a new family, and friends such as Shelley and Kurt are brought into this family.

Impact

Omaha the Cat Dancer grew out of the underground comics of the 1960's and early 1970's, and was particularly influenced by Robert Crumb's *Fritz the Cat* (1978). Though Omaha is Fritz's descendant, she (and the story line in general) is more rounded and better developed than Fritz ever was. By virtue of Waller's artistry and Worley's writing talents, Omaha has become a feminist symbol of independence despite her profession.

The series had its share of censorship issues. Banned in Toronto for depictions of bestiality (a charge later dropped, since there are no humans in the novel), *Omaha the Cat Dancer* was later praised by New Zealand's Indecent Publications Tribunal for frank and honest depictions of sexuality in the context of ongoing relationships.

The comic is probably best known among comics fans, artists, writers, and editors for its historic, though unplanned, aid in the creation of the CBLDF, an organization that makes use of donations obtained through sales to disseminate information about censorship in the comics world and help pay legal fees in court battles. Rising sales of erotic comics in U.S. comic book specialty stores caused stores to be closed down and owners to be arrested. In one such case, *Omaha the Cat Dancer* was cited. Denis Kitchen, then publishing *Omaha* through his Kitchen Sink Press, felt obligated to support the specialty-store owners and the reputations of Waller and Worley and therefore formed the CBLDF.

Terry Joseph Cole

Further Reading

Cho, Frank. *Liberty Meadows: Eden*, Book 1 (2008).
Kalesniko, Mark. *Alex* (2006).
Sakai, Stan. *Usagi Yojimbo: The Ronin*, Book 1 (2002).

Bibliography

Pilcher, Tim. *Erotic Comics 2: A Graphic History from the Liberated '70's to the Internet*. New York: Abrams, 2008.

Waller, Reed, and Kate Worley. "An Interview with Reed Waller and Kate Worley." Interview by Rich Kreiner. *Comics Journal* 143 (July, 1991): 93-100.

Wiacek, Win. "Omaha the Cat Dancer Complete Set." Review of *Omaha the Cat Dancer*, by Reed Waller and Kate Worley. *ComicsReview*, April 30, 2011. http://www.comicsreview.co.uk/nowreadthis/2011/04/30/omaha-the-cat-dancer-complete-set-part-i-2.

See also: *Maus*; *The Complete Fritz the Cat*; *Love and Rockets*; *Lost Girls*

One! Hundred! Demons!

Author: Barry, Lynda
Artist: Lynda Barry (illustrator)
Publisher: Sasquatch Books
First serial publication: 2000-2001
First book publication: 2002

One! Hundred! Demons! (Courtesy of Sasquatch Books)

Publication History

While working on the illustrated novel *Cruddy* in the late 1990's, Lynda Barry began to experiment with *sumi* brush painting. As she began playing with the technique, often inspired by a single word or phrase, she began exploring the demons that had haunted her throughout her life, turning them into comic sketches such as "Girlness," "Hate," and "Head Lice and My Worst Boyfriend." The demons eventually took a more formal shape as seventeen comic strips (each with twenty panels) that appeared from April 7, 2000, to January 15, 2001, on the popular online magazine Salon.com.

Following the success of the online publication of *One! Hundred! Demons!*, the anthologized print version of the comic strips was published by Seattle-based Sasquatch Books in 2002. The anthology featured strips that were pared down to eighteen panels, presented with two large panels per page. Barry further polished each of the strips and developed additional features for the printed collection. Working with Tom Greensfelder and Amie Z. Gleed, Barry designed an "Intro," a do-it-yourself tutorial for the "Outro," and elaborate collages for the front and ending pages, as well as detailed, multimedia collages featured between each of the strips. The book was published in paperback by Sasquatch Books in 2004.

Plot

When Barry turned her focus to exploring her own girlhood, she created a new comic form and structure offering the neologism "autobifictionalography" as the term to describe her approach to rendering the self in comic form. In *One! Hundred! Demons!* Barry creates intimate snapshots of her multiple selves, with the girl "Lynda" at the center. Barry frames and constructs her own life story, and in particular her own girlhood, revealing her idea of a dark, disturbing childhood that the narrator ultimately survives by utilizing her own creative impulses to emerge victorious over the demons.

Each strip addresses one of the demons from her life. For example, in "Common Scents" a young Lynda realizes that her Filipino household is different from her neighbors', and though once ashamed of this difference, an older Lynda longs for the smell of home. The book addresses many of these sorts of personal demons, from sexual abuse to the difficulties of fitting in to depression following the 2000 presidential election.

In *One! Hundred! Demons!* Barry shows multiple selves conversing with one another across boundaries of time, space, place, text, and image. Her representations of self–child, teen, and adult–challenge notions of femininity and beauty, of race and passing, and of class and social dictates, exploring how the figure of "Lynda Barry" was both constructed by and in opposition to these discourse communities.

Characters

- *Lynda Barry* appears at various ages throughout the book. Barry as creator is depicted within the strips as a middle-aged woman with red hair, glasses, and a bandanna, drawing her demons and creating the book in the "Intro." Another version of her as the creator of the book is also seen in photographs in the concluding "Outro," in which she demonstrates the process of painting and writing and encourages others to follow her technique for drawing demons. Over the course of the compilation, she is pictured as a young girl, a teenager, a young woman, and an adult. While she is part Filipina, she is generally depicted as pale, with unruly red hair, glasses, and freckles. Her appearance allows her to pass as white in strips such as "Common Scents" and "The Visitor." She is ungainly and full of self-doubt.

- *Kevin Kawula*, Barry's husband, is drawn with glasses, dark hair, and a beard. He functions as a supportive and kindly presence. He appears lying happily in bed with Lynda in "Dogs," and in "The Election." He tries to pull Lynda out of a deep depression after the 2000 presidential election.

- *Lynda's Mother* is a particularly unsympathetic character and something of a villain, berating Lynda and continually putting her down. She was born in the Philippines and suffered hardship during World War II (1939-1945). She scolds her daughter for being ugly in the strip "Girlness." She is depicted with dark skin and dark hair tied back into a severe bun. Her mother is feminine in appearance with long nails and dresses, a striking contrast to her daughter. She frequently smokes and shouts.

- *Lynda's Grandmother* is one of the few sympathetic adults in the book, and she serves as the voice of reason as well as a kindly presence in strips such as "Common Scents" and "The Aswang." She looks after Lynda yet challenges her own daughter, Lynda's mother. She is shown with dark skin and grey hair, rather like an older version of Lynda's mother. She, too, frequently smokes cigarettes.

- *Norabelle* is depicted as a hybrid tomboy/girly girl in the strip "Girlness." She wears her longish hair in a high ponytail and favors sporty striped

One! Hundred! Demons! (Courtesy of Sasquatch Books)

t-shirts along with her feminine bracelets and earrings. The adult Lynda takes her shopping, showering her with the girly items she once desired. When she tries to persuade Lynda to buy herself some especially feminine "Super Monkeyhead" stationery, Lynda balks; however, she assures Lynda that she can still enjoy "girly things."

Artistic Style

Barry is well known for her rough, unstudied drawing style reminiscent of childhood from her cult weekly comic *Ernie Pook's Comeek*. Although a study of her earliest comics indicates her skill in a more representational style, over time Barry's work has come to take on a rough, unstudied style. This childlike approach underscores her attention to youthful concerns. The project *One! Hundred! Demons!* arose when Barry began experimenting with *sumi* brush painting, and the soft lines of the brush are in evidence in the artistic rendering.

At Salon.com each strip comprised twenty panels, but these were edited down to eighteen for the book form. This expanded length allowed Barry to indulge her penchant for extended written narration and afforded additional room for illustration, but it still managed to constrain the artist/author's tendency to indulge in unstructured digressions.

Barry's drawing style in *One! Hundred! Demons!* bears a strong resemblance to her work in *Ernie Pook's Comeek*, but the use of the *sumi* brush results in a looser approach that appears more painterly and less constrained. While still far from representational, Barry's conceptual method appears more polished and composed in *One! Hundred! Demons!* than in the weekly strip. The soft lines and washes of color suggest a calling up and rendering of self from memory, the ambiguity of recollection reinforced in the sinuous lines. This format also made it possible for Barry to work in color, and each panel is awash with bright, brilliant tones and soft strokes in vivid hues.

Barry is well known for being a particularly wordy comics artist, with text taking up a good half or more of each panel, and this project is no exception. The narrative text generally occupies a large portion of each panel, similar to Barry's work in *Ernie Pook's Comeek*, and the writing is most often inked in straightforward capital lettering. Occasionally the font shifts with one word or phrase lettered in a flowery cursive, adding emphasis to particular phrases; this technique slows readers' comprehension, as they must account for the differing fonts while reading. Based on the content, the narrative text further suggests the narrator is an older, wiser Lynda (as pictured in the opening "Introduction") reflecting back on her childhood. The collages interspersed throughout the book add another dimension, bringing in scraps and fragments of a life story–buttons, ribbons, cloth, and paperwork–that reflect the comics within. These collages add yet another element of interpretation and depth.

Themes

One! Hundred! Demons! returns to Barry's childhood, allowing the author to revisit the pain of girlhood and adolescence. Barry touches on struggles with incest and abuse, race and death, gender and femininity, poverty and social class, and becoming an adult. The children shown in the strips, particularly Lynda, grow up quickly and are exposed to sex and violence from an early age.

In the strip "Resilience," Barry explores the resilience of children who try to forget or ignore the pain of sexual abuse but are unable to move past the horror. Strips such as "Common Scents" and "The Visitor" discuss the difficulties of race and ethnicity, particularly for a girl who passes as white. The Lynda figure negotiates shame over her home and background with the desire to fit in with classmates. Barry also has a strong interest in remembering and celebrating the smallest details of youth, a theme she explores in pieces such as "Lost Worlds" and "Magic Lanterns."

Barry further argues for reader participation, particularly in the "Intro" and "Outro," in which she outlines her creative process and encourages the audience to draw and paint their own demons. The strips themselves, such as "Lost and Found," suggest that the way to happiness is through creative pursuits, and once Lynda embraces creativity as a character, she is able to find a measure of happiness.

Impact

One! Hundred! Demons! is notable for several reasons. The book exposed Barry to new audiences through Salon.com and proved to be a turning point in her career. She gained more mainstream acceptance and critical claim, as evidenced by an Eisner Award and an Alex Award. *One! Hundred! Demons!* also marked a turn to the autobiographical for Barry; although the comics were labeled as "autobifictionalographic," the strips were about the life of the author, rather than the characters she created, as in her strip *Ernie Pook's Comeek.*

One! Hundred! Demons! is also significant in that it marks a point where Barry began to experiment with and explore her comics art style, utilizing the *sumi* brush and incorporating more color. Furthermore, the collage pieces foreshadow Barry's later artistic projects, *What It Is* and *Picture This* (published by Drawn and Quarterly in 2008 and 2010, respectively), which showcase Barry's interest in collage and expand on her excitement over her creative process, inviting others to pursue their own creative projects.

Susan Kirtley

Further Reading

Bechdel, Alison. *The Essential Dykes to Watch Out For* (2008).

Gloeckner, Phoebe. *The Diary of a Teenage Girl: An Account in Words and Pictures* (2002).

Lasko-Gross, Miss. *Escape from "Special"* (2008).

Satrapi, Marjane. *Persepolis* (2003).

Schrag, Ariel. *Awkward and Definition: The High School Comic Chronicles of Ariel Schrag* (2008).

Bibliography

Chute, Hillary. *Graphic Women*. New York: Columbia, 2010.

De Jesús, Melinda. "Liminality and Mestiza Consciousness in Lynda Barry's *One Hundred Demons*." *MELUS* 29, no. 1 (Spring, 2004): 219-252.

_____. "Of Monsters and Mothers: Filipina American Identity and Maternal Legacies in Lynda Barry's *One Hundred Demons*." *Meridians: Feminism, Race, Transnationalism* 5, no. 1 (2004): 1-26.

Harris, Miriam. "Cartoonists as Matchmakers: The Vibrant Relationship of Text and Image in the Work of Lynda Barry." In *Elective Affinities: Testing Word and Image Relationships*, edited by C. MacLeod and V. Plesch, eds. New York: Rodopi Press, 2009.

Tensuan, Theresa. "Comic Visions and Revisions in the Work of Lynda Barry and Marjane Satrapi." *Modern Fiction Studies* 52, no. 4 (Winter, 2006): 947-964.

See also: *Dykes to Watch Out For*; *Fun Home*; *Persepolis*; *Blankets*

OUR CANCER YEAR

Author: Pekar, Harvey; Brabner, Joyce
Artist: Frank Stack (illustrator)
Publisher: Four Walls Eight Windows
First serial publication: 1994
First book publication: 1994

Publication History

Our Cancer Year can be regarded as another install-ment of *American Splendor* (1976-2008), Harvey Pe-kar's autobiographical comic book series, but can also be read on its own. Its genesis stemmed from tragic cir-cumstances. When Pekar was diagnosed with cancer in 1990, his wife and fellow comics writer, Joyce Brabner (who edited *Brought to Light*, 1988), proposed that he write a comic book about the experience as a way of helping him deal with the disease. With Pekar having already arranged a book deal with a small literary pub-lisher, the novel was originally conceived as a Pekar solo piece (he was planning on writing about what-ever happened to him during that time). Brabner was brought in as the co-author partially because of Pekar's memory loss from the cancer treatments but also to include her point of view, since the battle against the disease soon engulfed them both.

    Veteran underground comics artist Frank Stack (perhaps best known as the creator of *The New Adven-tures of Jesus*, 1969) joined the pair after writing Pekar a letter of admiration and being invited to collaborate. He used a yearlong sabbatical from his art professor-ship at the University of Missouri to complete the novel, even staying with Brabner and Pekar for a time. Originally published in 1994 by Four Walls Eight Win-dows, *Our Cancer Year* has been kept in print continu-ally, even though the original publisher was absorbed over the years by other companies such as Avalon/Thunder's Mouth Press and Perseus/Running Press.

Plot

Divided into eleven chapters, *Our Cancer Year* docu-ments an approximately twenty-month time span in the lives of Brabner and Pekar. Readers accustomed to either writer's previous work found the novel familiar

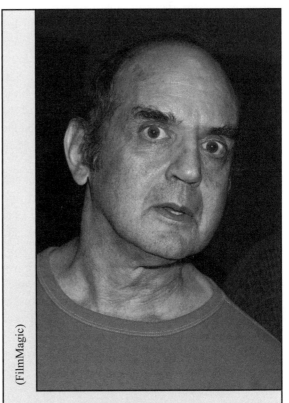

(FilmMagic)

Harvey Pekar

Harvey Pekar is an icon of the American under-ground comics scene. He is best known for the autobiographical *American Splendor* series, illus-trated by a variety of high-profile artists over the decades, though he has ventured into other works of graphic nonfiction. Back when most people thought of comics as the playground of superhe-roes, Pekar was writing his thoughtful, insightful, absorbing nonfiction that covered such diverse topics as the Vietnam War, jazz, and cancer. He takes a literary and savvy approach to exploring the beautiful and the ugly aspects of contempo-rary American life.

territory, but the relationship between the authors also resulted in a marriage of artistic sensibilities (autobiog-raphy mixed with political journalism) that is distinct from their previous individual work. The novel opens in January, 1990, with Brabner and Pekar learning that they may have to move from their apartment, where they have lived for a long time. They decide to buy a house, though Pekar has many misgivings about the move. Brabner attends a student peace conference and meets youth from around the world, many of whom grew up during wartime.

After the couple buys a house, Brabner, working on a comics series about peace activists, travels to visit her young friends from the conference. Her travels are haunted by the unfolding of the Gulf War (1991). Soon after Brabner's return, the work on the new house is challenged when Pekar learns that he has lymphoma.

After receiving surgery, Pekar undergoes chemotherapy and radiation treatment. Pekar's initial refusal to take off work causes many arguments with Brabner. Despite the cancellation of Brabner's comics series by the publisher, she stays in touch with her friends from the conference and worries about her friends in the Middle East while she takes care of and worries about Pekar.

As Pekar's health worsens, the couple battles medical bureaucracy and Pekar considers suicide. Pekar's brother assists them by paying for a home health-care aide. The arrival of the aide, Delores, eases the couple's burdens, and Pekar completes his cancer treatment. However, he suffers from depression after returning to work too early.

Taking some more time off, Pekar recuperates while Brabner's young friends (Dana, Jessie, Ju, Saroeum, and Suy Khim) arrive to visit. The novel ends in the summer of 1991 with Pekar bonding with the peace activists and learning that his cancer has been eradicated.

Characters

- *Harvey Pekar*, the co-protagonist, is a middle-aged, balding file clerk at the Veterans Administration Hospital in Cleveland, Ohio. He writes the comic book series *American Splendor* and is married to fellow comics writer Joyce Brabner. He is somewhat neurotic; his worrying increases when he buys a house and is diagnosed with cancer.
- *Joyce Brabner*, the co-protagonist, is slightly younger than her husband, wears glasses, and

has long hair. She is a social activist who lives in Cleveland. She serves as Pekar's primary caretaker when he is diagnosed with cancer. Working on a comic book series about children during wartime, she meets a number of student peace activists from around the world.

- *Dr. Rhodes* is a female oncologist with long hair who treats Pekar. Having a degree in literature in addition to her one in medicine, she discusses books with Pekar and reads some of his comics. Her description of a chemotherapy course as twelve weeks rather than twelve treatments causes Brabner and Pekar much difficulty, but in general she is highly regarded by the couple since she goes out of her way to work around Pekar's neuroses.
- *Lennie Pekar*, Pekar's brother, has a scar on the right side of his forehead and works for a pharmaceutical company in Indiana. Though they have fallen out of touch somewhat, the brothers reconnect, and Lennie helps his brother through the cancer crisis by paying for a home health-care aide.
- *Delores* is an African American home health-care aide. She helps Pekar develop a routine of errands when he is off work, which helps him deal with depression. Though she has family problems, she grows close to Brabner and Pekar. However, after Pekar's treatment is complete, the characters drift away from one another.

Artistic Style

Stack's expressionistic illustrations adjust themselves to the emotional resonance of the events being depicted by shifting style and layout as appropriate, ranging from impressionism to near photorealism. The one use of color on the pastel cover designed by Brabner strikingly encapsulates the entire novel, depicting a scene of two small figures unloading groceries in front of a house with snow on the ground. The groceries have fallen in the yard, and Pekar is kneeling on the ground, with Brabner bending over him, trying to coax him inside. A yellow ribbon, a symbol of support for American involvement in the Gulf War, is tied on a neighbor's tree. The richness of the cover makes the starkness of the art inside the novel even more striking.

Stack seizes on the emotional intensity of a moment with some panels rendered free of background and shading, which helps readers focus on the interactions among characters. Word balloons and caption boxes tell the part of the story not communicated through the art itself. Even in the many scenes involving characters merely talking, Stack somehow manages to maintain visual interest, often by shifting perspective. However, the dynamism of the illustrations is subtle and always in support of the narrative.

Readers accustomed to the more "meat-and-potatoes" realism of many of Pekar's other collaborators might find Stack's occasional artistic distortion a bit off-putting, but, as Pekar's most famous collaborator, Robert Crumb, noted, no one could have suited the subject matter of the novel, a slice of life punctuated occasionally with the drama of death, better than Stack. Pekar and Brabner were similarly pleased: Even years afterward, Pekar named Stack as one of his best collaborators.

Themes

Though many would regard cancer as the principal topic of the novel, Brabner stated that the book is more about marriage, which is why "cancer year" is prefaced with "our." Accordingly, the novel begins with a home (Brabner and Pekar's apartment) "under siege"– their landlord is rumored to be selling the apartment building, with the tenants likely to be evicted. This happenstance is soon magnified by Pekar's body being under threat from cancer and the whole world being under threat from war.

In fact, invasion of territory, whether by disease or war, seems to be a major preoccupation in the work. Just as Iraq invades Kuwait and refugees search for new homes, the characters in the book weather invasions and search for homes. How people respond to such trying circumstances becomes the major theme of the work, a theme deepened by including the experiences of the student peace activists, many of whom have had to battle similar existential threats. At one point, Pekar is so weakened by the cancer treatment

that his identity completely breaks down, and he wonders if he is a human being or just a character in a comic book.

Through collaboration, determination, and humor, the characters manage to overcome their challenges, and the novel ends with Pekar, free of cancer, and Brabner hosting the activists in their home. This last invasion of territory turns out to be a pleasant one. The wordless final page of Pekar visiting a nearby waterfall with Ju suggests that despite the suffering, life is worth fighting for. However, the inclusion of someone stepping in dog feces on the final page also shows that even in its most pleasant moments, life is far from perfect.

Impact

Our Cancer Year came after the landmark graphic novels of the 1980's such as *Batman: The Dark Knight Returns* (1986), *Maus* (1986), and *Watchmen* (1986-1987), and some critics began to wonder whether the graphic novel had really come of age. In intervening years, some celebrated works, such as Neil Gaiman's *The Sandman* (1989-1996), had appeared, but most of the comics industry was experiencing an overkill of grim and gritty superheroes. An original graphic novel published by a non-comics book publisher, *Our Cancer Year* reminded many that comics could deal with topics far removed from the fantastic and the supernatural.

Unlike many comics (even *Maus*, which, despite the seriousness of Holocaust subject matter, still used the fantasy trope of animals to tell the story), *Our Cancer Year* was thoroughly realistic. As such, it was a milestone critically acclaimed work and helped to solidify the presence of graphic novels in bookstores. It also raised awareness about the presence of alternative and independent comics, an aspect of the comics industry not always widely represented in conventional comic book stores. It showed that serialization was not an artistic necessity and that an audience existed for long-form graphic stories published as a whole.

Pekar's work in general has been influential on subsequent comics creators, particularly those dealing in autobiography and documentary, but *Our Cancer Year* has a particular resonance, being his longest story and perhaps his best work, due to the involvement of Brabner and Stack. It also predated many subsequent cancer stories told in the graphic novel form such as *Lisa's Story: The Other Shoe* (2007) by Tom Batiuk, *Mom's Cancer* (2006) by Brian Fies, *Janet and Me: An Illustrated Story of Love and Loss* (2004) by Stan Mack, and *Cancer Vixen* (2006) by Marisa Acocella Marchetto.

The novel remains in print and continues to inspire beyond the world of comics. For example, in the fall of 2010, Purdue University used the work in a cancer conference in West Lafayette, Indiana, complete with a gallery show and visits from Brabner and Stack. Though the novel has been criticized for being uneven and overly downtrodden, it has encouraged many people dealing with cancer and helped those around them understand the effects of the disease.

Pekar's work in general has been noted for its difference from much of the rest of comics; it was landmark work during the 1970's, serving as a bridge between the underground "comix" of the 1960's and the alternative comics of the 1980's. Though Pekar's work never changed much in tone, modern comics have increasingly come to resemble his work, in the tradition of autobiographical comics, which includes work by authors such as Chester Brown, Joe Sacco, and Seth, and even in the dialogue-heavy superhero work of Brian Michael Bendis.

Films

American Splendor. Directed by Shari Springer Berman and Robert Pulcini. HBO Films, 2003. This adaptation of *American Splendor* and *Our Cancer Year* stars Paul Giamatti as Pekar and Hope Davis as Brabner, though Brabner and Pekar also appear as themselves. Several scenes from the novel are dramatized, and some of Stack's art is used. To form a composite character named Fred, Stack himself becomes merged with another cartoonist, who is the biological father of Danielle, Brabner and Pekar's adopted daughter. The film was well received, winning the Grand Jury Prize at the Sundance Film Festival, and it brought Brabner's and Pekar's work greater renown.

Frederick A. Wright

Further Reading

Brabner, Joyce, et al. *Brought to Light: Thirty Years of Drug Smuggling, Arms Deals, and Covert Operations That Robbed America and Betrayed the Constitution* (1989).

Pekar, Harvey, et al. *American Splendor* (1976-2009).

Stack, Frank. *The New Adventures of Jesus: The Second Coming* (2006).

Bibliography

Harvey, Robert C. *The Art of the Comic Book: An Aesthetic History*. Jackson: University Press of Mississippi, 1996.

Hatfield, Charles. *Alternative Comics: An Emerging Literature*. Jackson: University Press of Mississippi, 2005.

Levin, Bob. *Outlaws, Rebels, Freethinkers, and Pirates: Essays on Cartoons and Cartoonists*. Seattle: Fantagraphics Books, 2005.

Rhode, Michael G., ed. *Harvey Pekar: Conversations*. Jackson: University Press of Mississippi, 2008.

Witek, Joseph. *Comic Books as History: The Narrative Art of Jack Jackson, Art Spiegelman, and Harvey Pekar*. Jackson: University Press of Mississippi, 1989.

See also: *American Splendor*; *The Complete Fritz the Cat*; *Cancer Vixen*

OWLY

Author: Runton, Andy
Artist: Andy Runton (illustrator)
Publisher: Top Shelf Productions
First serial publication: 2003-
First book publication: 2003-

Publication History

The inspiration for *Owly* came from a series of doodles that Andy Runton drew for his mother while he studied industrial design in college. After a stint as a graphic designer, Runton was laid off in 2001 and considered pursuing a career in comics after being reintroduced to the medium through the works created by Scott Morse and Jim Mahfood and published by Top Shelf Productions. After many failed attempts at creating comics, Runton returned to the owl character he created for his mother.

Runton sold minicomics featuring Owly at local conventions and maintained a close relationship with Chris Staros, publisher of Top Shelf Productions. Staros provided editorial advice and, later, table space at conventions for Runton to sell his comics. Following advice from Staros, Runton applied for a Xeric grant to self-publish his Owly stories, but he was rejected. After watching the development of Runton's stories over a year, Staros decided to publish the book himself. The first *Owly* book was published in 2003 and within five years, Runton and Top Shelf had published four more. A picture book featuring Owly and Wormy was also published by Simon & Schuster in 2011, with a follow-up scheduled for 2012. The sixth *Owly* book, *A Fishy Situation*, was scheduled for 2011 release. Runton and Top Shelf have also released several free Owly minicomics that are available to download online.

Plot

Owly is a series of largely self-contained stories with simple plots. Volume 1 includes two short stories, while Volumes 2 through 4 are book-length tales. Volume 5 is a collection of previously unpublished material.

The Way Home (one of the two stories in Volume 1) opens with Owly trying to make friends with three

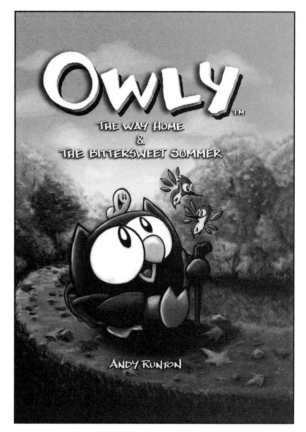

Owly: The Way Home & The Bittersweet Summer. (Courtesy of Top Shelf Productions)

small birds and a pair of fireflies—they are all terrified of him. A discouraged Owly heads home through a rainstorm and comes across a worm drowning in a puddle of water. He brings the worm home and nurses him back to health. When Wormy awakes, he tells Owly how he was separated from his parents during the storm. Owly vows to help Wormy find his family. Lost in the forest, wormy and Owly are guided by two fireflies. Unable to find his home, Wormy spots a broken sign that once indicated where his parents lived, and he assumes the worst. After a tumble down a hill, the two new friends suddenly smell food cooking, and they follow the smell to Wormy's parents' new home. Wormy's parents are happy to see their son but panic when they see Owly. Wormy explains to his parents that Owly helped him. The next day, Owly begins his journey home, and Wormy decides to go with him.

In Volume 1's second story, *The Bittersweet Summer*, Owly and Wormy are tending their garden when something suddenly flies past them. Using his binoculars, Owly spots a mysterious bird, and the two put out birdseed in the hope of catching a closer glimpse of this strange bird. A hummingbird appears for a moment but then flies away. Back at the tree house, Wormy and Owly read about hummingbirds and then visit Mrs. Raccoon's nursery to purchase a flower that will attract them. With a nectar plant in place, two hummingbirds (Tiny and Angel) appear and make friends with Owly and Wormy.

The four spend the summer together. After summer is over, Tiny and Angel explain that they need to seek

Owly: The Way Home & The Bittersweet Summer. (Courtesy of Top Shelf Productions)

a warmer climate for the winter. Months pass; when spring comes, the hummingbirds return.

In *Just a Little Blue,* Volume 2 in the series, Owly and Wormy follow a bluebird back to its nest. Feeling threatened by Owly, the bluebird attacks and tells the pair to go away. While purchasing more birdseed at Mrs. Raccoon's nursery, Wormy spots a poster for a bluebird house. Owly does not have enough money for the house, but Mrs. Raccoon gives him plans to build his own. Discouraged when they realize they have no wood, Owly and Wormy decide to dismantle their gardening cart and use the wood to build the birdhouse. With the help of Flutter, their butterfly friend, Owly and Wormy hang the completed birdhouse on the branch of a tree and wait. The next morning, Owly and Wormy hope to find that the bluebirds have moved into their new home, when suddenly they are attacked by the birds. Utterly discouraged, Owly, Wormy, and Flutter take down the birdhouse. During a storm, the bluebird tries to protect his mate and their fledglings. Owly and Wormy head outside in the rain to tidy their lawn when Flutter arrives and guides them to the bluebird's nest that is nearly toppling over. One of the tiny birds is missing. They find it trapped in a thorny bush. Wormy wiggles between the sharp thorns and convinces the baby bird to come out. With the bluebirds' home destroyed, Owly offers them the birdhouse he and Wormy built.

Volume 3, *Flying Lessons*, again features Owly and Wormy who see a strange creature flying through the forest at dusk. They draw the creature and bring their sketches to Mrs. Raccoon, who identifies the creature as a flying squirrel. Determined to befriend the squirrel, Owly and Wormy fill a bowl with dried fruit and nuts and wait. After dozing off, the pair wakes and sees the squirrel eating. As soon as the squirrel realizes the two are no longer asleep, he hides. Wormy explains to the squirrel that Owly is friendly but the squirrel runs off again.

Alone in the middle of the night, Wormy finds the squirrel, and the two become friends. After a long night of gliding through the sky, Wormy dozes high in a tree with the squirrel. The next morning Owly is upset when Wormy is missing and enlists the help of Flutter, who spots Wormy at the top of a tree with the flying squirrel. At the base of the tree Owly calls to his friend, waking the squirrel, who flies away, leaving Wormy stranded. Since Owly cannot fly to his friend, Wormy jumps down the tree, leaping from branch to branch. One of the branches snaps and Wormy falls, landing on a branch close to the ground. Owly takes his bruised friend home, while the flying squirrel watches. Upset by his inability to help Wormy, Owly is determined to learn how to fly. After many attempts, Owly gives up. Still struggling with the idea of a friendly owl, the flying squirrel shows Owly how to glide through the air. Owly returns home with Flutter and their new friend Rocky, the flying squirrel, to tell Wormy about his new talent.

In *A Time to Be Brave* (Volume 4), Wormy is scared of a dragon that appears in a book Owly reads aloud. To distract Wormy, Owly suggests that the group go outside and play ball. Wormy's worries reappear when he sees a peculiar animal behind a tree. Wormy is convinced it is a dragon. Frozen with fear, Wormy neglects to see the ball that bounces off his head and crashes into a newly transplanted tree. Assessing the damage, Owly supports the tree with some rope and fastens a wire fence around it, protecting it from further harm.

That evening while preparing for bed, Owly and Wormy hear a strange noise. Outside, they find the animal from earlier that day with its paw caught in the fence around the tree. Upset that his actions hurt this creature, Owly tries to help, but the creature snarls at him. Wormy is terrified, still convinced that the creature is a dragon, but remembers how happy he was when Owly helped him when they first met. Wormy crawls through the fence and frees the small animal, which quickly runs off. With the help of Mrs. Raccoon, Owly and Wormy search the forest until they find the small creature. While Owly nurses the creature's sore paw, Mrs. Raccoon consults one of Owly's books and discovers that the animal is an opossum. Owly and Wormy leave the opossum a get-well card by his bed, but when they awake, the little animal is gone. They return to the damaged tree to find the opossum and hand him the card. The opossum reads the card and realizes that Owly is truly a friend. With all their other friends, the three read more fairytales

together, including one with a dragon. Wormy reassures his new friend Possey that dragons exist only in stories.

Volumes

- *Owly: The Way Home & The Bittersweet Summer* (2004). Owly meets Wormy for the first time, and the two meet Tiny and Angel, a pair of hummingbirds.
- *Owly:* Volume 2, *Just a Little Blue* (2005). Owly and Wormy help a bluebird family find a new home.
- *Owly:* Volume 3, *Flying Lessons* (2005). Owly learns how to fly with the help of their new friend, Rocky the flying squirrel.
- *Owly:* Volume 4, *A Time to Be Brave* (2007). Wormy mistakes an opossum for a dragon, but Owly gives his friend a lesson in bravery.
- *Owly:* Volume 5, *Tiny Tales* (2008). A collection of previously unpublished stories, including Top Shelf's Free Comic Book Day stories, the first Owly minicomics, and other short comics.

Characters

- *Owly*, the protagonist, is a caring but often misunderstood owl. He loves making new friends with all creatures of the forest and is extremely protective of them.
- *Wormy* is an enthusiastic worm and Owly's best friend. He also loves making friends and has a strong sense of adventure but often requires Owly's support when facing his fears.
- *Mrs. Raccoon* runs the nursery that Owly and Wormy visit for their gardening needs. She is generous and helpful. She is also resourceful with a vast knowledge of animals and plants.
- *Flutter* is a supportive and helpful butterfly. She often acts as a messenger because of her ability to fly.
- *Tiny* and *Angel*, appearing in Volume 1 only, are a pair of playful and caring hummingbirds who befriend Owly and Wormy.
- *Little Blue* is a baby bluebird who is tentative and afraid to take risks. He is rescued by Wormy in Volume 2.

- *Rocky* is a skittish yet friendly flying squirrel that Owly and Wormy befriend in Volume 3. He also has a strong sense of adventure.
- *Possey* is a misunderstood opossum that Owly and Wormy befriend in Volume 4. He can be quick to anger in order to protect himself from predators.

Artistic Style

Runton's personal connection with nature and love of childhood animal characters saturate the pages of *Owly*. Runton cites characters such as Babar, Paddington Bear, Curious George, and Lyle Lyle Crocodile as major influences for his own characters, ones that display a great deal of charm and personality. All the characters in *Owly* were modeled after silent animal characters like Snoopy, Woodstock, and Dumbo. Without dialogue, Runton relies solely on his artwork to convey the emotion and personality of his characters. Inspired by Disney films and Saturday morning cartoons, Runton gives his own characters the same simplified visual design.

Owly's black-and-white art features Runton's precise brush strokes that look simple but convey subtle emotions and thoughtfulness. Runton's artwork is clean; he strikes a good balance between white space and detail, conveying a strong sense of place while keeping the story readable.

Three to six panels per page make the series a fast-paced read and ideal for younger readers. Throughout the series, Runton highlights select sequences using a single panel in the middle of the page. This is often to illustrate the importance of the passing of time or to bring attention to a particular action sequence. Because *Owly* is a wordless graphic novel series, Runton employs a mix of symbols, icons, and pictograms to convey the dialogue between characters and to move the narrative along at a quick pace.

Themes

After reading any volume of *Owly*, it is clear that the major theme of the series is friendship. The friendship between Owly and Wormy becomes the model to which all other friendships are held: friends should support, help, and protect each other. These qualities

---

Andy Runton

An Eisner Award-winning cartoonist, Andy Runton is best known for his work on *Owly*, the Top Shelf-published graphic novel series for young readers. Largely produced without text or dialogue, *Owly* follows the adventures of a kind-hearted owl who is determined to do good things in the world. With the help of his friends Wormy and Scampy, Owly pursues his adventures. There have been five volumes published in the series as of 2011 and the work has met with a great deal of success, particularly with young children. Runton's art is extremely cartoony, with thick, bold lines and rounded characters in the Disney animation tradition. His pages are un-cluttered and clearly laid out, giving them an ease of reading that is appropriate for the audience that he has targeted.

---

are reflected in each book, as Owly and Wormy attempt to make friends with other creatures of the forest. Owly and Wormy exemplify Runton's values of friendship by saving the baby bluebird in Volume 2, staying persistent in befriending the flying squirrel in Volume 3, and taking care of the opossum's wounded paw in Volume 4. On the surface this may seem sentimental, but for younger readers, it provides a strong sense of security.

One of Owly's more complex themes uses metaphor and allegory to convey the importance of challenging stereotypes and prejudice. Owly's difficulty in making new friends is reminiscent of the stories of Casper the Friendly Ghost, who was so often judged solely on his outward appearance. Many forest animals are afraid of Owly because of his innate predatory nature. Throughout the series, however, Owly subverts this instinct through his kindness, helpfulness, and generosity. Wormy also is able to step outside his perceived capabilities. A worm can be viewed as a weak, passive species, yet Wormy demonstrates a high level of bravery and action throughout the series.

Nature is also an important theme as the forest acts as a venue for learning: Owly and Wormy learn more about the forest and its inhabitants, as do young readers. The series is packed with information about plants and animals. Mrs. Raccoon acts as the conduit for these learning experiences.

Impact

Of the increasing number of comics being produced for children, *Owly* is one of the first graphic novels aimed specifically at very young readers. Recognizing its place in this category, Top Shelf Productions selected *Owly* for six consecutive years as the feature character in its annual Free Comic Book Day offering. Runton's series has been embraced by the general public for its nonviolent subject matter, strong values, and endearing characters. *Owly* has been embraced by educators. As a wordless graphic novel that uses icons, symbols, and pictograms, the series is viewed as accessible for all literacy levels. More important, the series has been used to teach inference to young readers, a key skill in reading comprehension. The series has also been praised for connecting with visual learners, English-language learners, and text-shy readers and for motivating children to attempt more advanced reading. With educators using *Owly* in their classroom, Runton has made available a lesson-plan packet on his Web site.

Librarians have also been extremely supportive of *Owly*, a fact that is reflected in the creation of an Owly and Friends "READ" poster for the American Library Association. *Owly* has received consistently positive reviews in both library journals and book trade magazines. These reviews refer to the series as charming, genuine, delightful, and representative of an innocence found in early children's literature and, by extension, early comics for children, such as classic Harvey and Gold Key comic books.

Owly's wide appeal is also reflective in its fandom. While aimed at young readers, the series has strong reader loyalty of all ages. Runton has expanded this demand for Owly with available merchandise, including T-shirts and plush toys. In addition, Runton's mother handcrafts a limited number of hats, purses, and buttons in keeping with the series family-friendly spirit. With such a devout fan following with both children and adults, Runton is committed long-term to producing *Owly* stories.

Scott Robins

Further Reading

Spires, Ashley. *Binky the Space Cat* (2009).
Tanaka, Masashi. *Gon* (2002).
Varon, Sara. *Robot Dreams* (2007).

Bibliography

Runton, Andy. "Into the Woods: Andy Runton Talks 'Owly.'" Interview by Shaun Manning. *Comic Book Resources* (December 11, 2007). http://www.comicbookresources.com/?page=article&id=12132.
_____. "Declaration of Independents: Andy Runton." Interview by Karen Maeda. *Sequential Tart* (September, 2004). http://www.sequentialtart.com/archive/sept04/doi_0904.shtml.
_____. "What a Hoot: Runton Talks Owly." Interview by Justin Jordan. *Comic Book Resources* (February 23, 2007). http://www.comicbookresources.com/?page=article&id=9435.

See also: *Mouse Guard*; *Good-Bye, Chunky Rice*; *Age of Reptiles*; *The Adventures of Tintin*

P

PALESTINE

Author: Sacco, Joe
Artist: Joe Sacco (illustrator)
Publisher: Fantagraphics Books
First serial publication: 1993-1995
First book publication: 1994, 1996

Publication History

Joe Sacco is a graphic novelist who began his career as a traditional journalist. His comics belong to a genre of graphic novels called "comics journalism" that produces reportage-style story lines in graphic novel formats. After graduating from college, Sacco decided to combine his talent for drawing comics with journalism. Eventually, he established a working relationship with Fantagraphics Books, which published his autobiographical *Yahoo* (1988-1992).

Sacco then traveled to the Middle East, where he spent the majority of his time in the West Bank and the Gaza Strip, after which he wrote and published *Palestine*. *Palestine* was first published serially from 1993 to 1995 in nine issues that range in length from twenty-four to thirty-two pages. In 1994, *Palestine*, issues 1-5, were collected as *Palestine: A Nation Occupied*. The remaining four issues were collected as *Palestine: In the Gaza Strip* (1996). In 2001, the entire series was collected into a single volume that includes an introduction by literary critic and Palestinian advocate Edward W. Said. A special hardcover edition was issued in 2007, which retains Said's contribution and has an additional section by Sacco that includes original photographs and sketches.

Plot

During the late 1980's and early 1990's, the first Palestinian Intifada, or uprising, dominated the headlines from the Middle East. Sacco traveled to the area to witness events firsthand and interview Palestinians

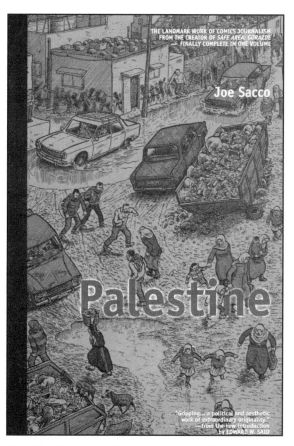

Palestine. (Courtesy of Fantagraphics Books)

affected by Israeli occupation. The collection of his impressions and the stories of the Palestinians he interviewed compose the graphic novel.

Palestine chronicles Sacco's travels from Cairo into the West Bank, followed by an excursion to the Gaza Strip, back to the West Bank, and then into Israel. The first chapter develops the character of "Joe Sacco" and establishes him as an outsider with limited perspective on the conflict. While situating his character in the region, he fills in the background of the conflict. In chapter 2, he continues to develop this history, using the layout of a history textbook, told from the Palestinian perspective.

Next, Sacco recounts the stories of his interviewees. While the structure is episodic, Sacco manages to arrange the chapters around common themes. The theme that emerges from chapter 3 is Israeli confiscation of Palestinian territory, specifically the seizure of olive trees in the name of security.

Chapter 4 focuses on the conditions of imprisonment via the corroborated testimony of men imprisoned in the infamous Ansar III prison. Instead of reporting only the torture they withstood, he transcribes a functioning social system whereby inmates take care of one another and educate each other about Palestinian issues. Different perspectives of imprisonment are related in the sections entitled "Moderate Pressure" and "The Tough and the Dead," which is about an imprisoned woman. Thoughtfully, Sacco inserts a Palestinian joke for comic relief.

The next chapter focuses on the daily humiliation and fears felt by Palestinians instilled by the use of percussion bombs, tear gas, and inflexible curfews. In a poignant section, Palestinians in Hebron recount an attack by Israeli settlers, which is juxtaposed with newspaper clippings that frame the Palestinians as aggressors.

Sacco's trip to Gaza is represented in chapters 6-8. He demonstrates how the law, occupation, and Palestinian resistance movements have robbed a generation of their childhood, fueling the first Intifada. Through the help of a translator, Sacco attempts to reconstruct the early days of the uprising and learns about more daily atrocities that occur in Gaza, mirroring those in the West Bank.

The final chapter is set in Jerusalem again, where Sacco is in the company of two female Israeli tourists who question him about his one-sided journey into history. They encourage him to visit Tel Aviv, which he does. However, this trip only cements his desire to provide a counternarrative centered on the Palestinians' experiences, accounts, and oral history.

Characters

- *Joe Sacco*, the protagonist, is a short Maltese American with glasses. He is a reporter traveling throughout Palestine, collecting stories of the Israeli occupation. He is a complicated character, appearing sympathetic to the Palestinian people but still wanting to hear the next violent story.
- *Ghassan*, a Palestinian man in his thirties and a father, is accused of belonging to an illegal organization, detained without evidence, and tortured over the course of more than two weeks. Sacco conveys basic Israeli torture tactics through the Ghassan episode.
- *Ammar* is a slightly overweight Palestinian man with a weak chin and a scruffy beard. He lives in the Nuseirat refugee camp and does not have a job. He acts as one of Sacco's translators.
- *Sameh* is a slightly balding Palestinian man in his late thirties. He is from the Jabalia refugee camp and works in Gaza with disabled children. He acts as one of Sacco's translators. Unlike other translators, he seems to understand the visual component that Sacco wants to capture and goes out of his way to provide Sacco with every opportunity to experience and record it.
- *Naomi* is an Israeli tourist with blond, medium-length hair who is always shown wearing sunglasses. She meets Sacco, refuses to venture into the Arab market of the old city with him, and eventually invites him to Tel Aviv to experience the Israeli side of things.
- *Paula*, another Israeli, is Naomi's friend. She has shoulder-length brown hair. She agrees to walk through the streets of the old city in the Arab market but appears to be paranoid the whole time.

Artistic Style

Sacco's *Palestine* uses a graphic reportage style that exaggerates emotions through its caricatures, allowing readers to sympathize with the masses, who are meticulously drawn as distinct individuals. There are no thought bubbles; instead, Sacco's thoughts are included in the captions. They move freely through the panels and are not tethered to the Sacco character. When action is more chaotic, the caption boxes move in a correspondingly chaotic arabesque. Dialogue takes place in speech balloons. Palestinian narrators are afforded the same representation; their thoughts and stories become the captions, and only their dialogue is depicted with balloons.

Putting oral accounts and histories into captions gives them more authority. Similarly, in chapter 2, Sacco uses the traditional layout of a textbook, placing the narration in columns and embedding pictures into the format. His choice of layout is used to place this counternarrative on equal footing with the more prevalent Israeli historiography.

In a memorable section in chapter 4, Sacco recounts the story of Ghassan being held without evidence and being tortured during his detention. The number of panels per page gives the reader a sense of expanding and unending time associated with torture. The story begins with three panels, the next page to six panels, then to nine, and finally to twenty. As the panels increase, the prisoner is more confined and the divisions

Palestine. (Courtesy of Fantagraphics Books)

between the panels begin to take on the look and feel like prison bars.

Themes

Palestine is about Israeli occupation and its impact on Palestinians. It is a history of the Palestinian refugees from their own point of view. In a journalistic style, Sacco compiles numerous accounts of displacement, imprisonment, enforced curfew, confiscation, demolition, wounding, and killing with little character development. This accumulation of evidence has two effects: First, it validates the stories; second, it numbs the reader to the violence being presented until the stories begin to sound the same, mirroring the Palestinians' own sense of their surrounding violence. Marketplace percussion bombs exploding are part of day-to-day existence. A family member being imprisoned is common.

The reliability of sources and the framing of stories are constantly brought to the fore. Sacco's *Palestine* is a counternarrative of Palestinian history. When Sacco hears about the attack in Hebron that Palestinians contend was instigated by Israeli settlers, he sees a different narrative in the newspapers. Historical accounts are subjective but are often treated as objective truth. Hence, Sacco includes his own motivations in the text, allowing readers to understand the framing of the novel.

Violent resistance to occupation is another theme better understood through Sacco's attempts to convey the daily humiliation experienced by generations of Palestinians. In the sections set in Gaza, Sacco illustrates the confinement of Gaza and how all activities there are framed through the lens of political resistance. In the final pages, a young Palestinian is forced to stand in the rain while he is interrogated by Israeli soldiers. In this one story, Sacco encapsulates the day-to-day humiliation of Palestinians.

Impact

Joe Sacco is one of the best-known comics journalists. As in New Journalism, the reporter becomes part of the story. Sacco expands the intrusion of the reporter's thoughts and observations and provides metacommentary on his predilection for being a newshound.

Possible influences on his work are Art Spiegelman's biographical *Maus* (1980-1991) series and the work of Robert Crumb and Harvey Pekar, whose autobiographical styles depict real quotidian life, boredom included. Like *Maus*, Sacco's *Palestine* uses comics to illustrate the unseen and the unimaginable. He renders images out of memories and accounts that have eluded camera lenses.

Sacco's graphic novel demonstrates how comics add a dimension of experience that is difficult to articulate. Exaggerated features capture and force emotions on readers in ways that real photos sometimes fail to do. Because of this added dimension, Sacco's work has been included in mainstream media, in publications such as *The Guardian* and *Harper's*.

Because the Palestinian-Israeli conflict is a controversial political topic, *Palestine*'s reception was mixed. Within the pro-Israel camp, the novel was dismissed as unbalanced and slanderous. In many Near Eastern and Middle Eastern studies departments, Edward Said's enthusiasm for *Palestine* opened up a space for it in the curriculum, which in turn opened the door for other forms of popular culture that touch on the stories of marginalized peoples.

While single-panel comics and strips have long been popular in the Arabic-speaking world, the graphic novel has not found a foothold in the region. The publication of *Palestine* inspired many young artists. In 2008, Magdy El-Shafee published *Metro* in Egypt, which has been considered the first adult graphic novel in Arabic. It was confiscated and banned by the administration of then-president Hosni Mubarak. In more liberal Lebanon, the creation of *Samandal*, a journal dedicated to the publication of multilingual comics, has provided many up-and-coming artists space to present their comics, many of whom echo Sacco's autobiographical reportage style.

Kari Neely

Further Reading

Pekar, Harvey, Heather Roberson, and Ed Piskor. *Macedonia* (2007).
Sacco, Joe. *The Fixer: A Story from Sarajevo* (2003).
_____. *Footnotes in Gaza* (2009).

Bibliography

Marshall, Monica. *Joe Sacco*. New York: Rosen, 2005.

Rosenblatt, Adam, and Andrea A. Lunsford. "Critique, Caricature, and Compulsion in Joe Sacco's Comics Journalism." In *The Rise of the American Comics Artist: Creators and Contexts*, edited by Paul Williams and James Lyons. Jackson: University Press of Mississippi, 2010.

Versaci, Rocco. "The 'New Journalism' Revisited: Comics Versus Reportage." In *This Book Contains Graphic Language: Comics as Literature*. New York: Continuum, 2007.

Woo, Benjamin. "Reconsidering Comics Journalism: Information and Experience in Joe Sacco's *Palestine*." In *The Rise and Reason of Comics and Graphic Literature: Critical Essays on the Form*, edited by Joyce Goggin and Dan Hassler-Forest. Jefferson, N.C.: McFarland, 2010.

See also: *Footnotes in Gaza*; *The Fixer*; *Fax from Sarajevo*; *Maus*; *The Wall*

PALOMAR: THE HEARTBREAK SOUP STORIES

Author: Hernandez, Gilbert
Artist: Gilbert Hernandez (illustrator)
Publisher: Fantagraphics Books
First serial publication: 1982-2003
First book publication: 2003

Publication History

Palomar is a compilation of work previously published in the successful *Love and Rockets* series between 1982 and 2003 and traces the lives of the residents of Palomar, a fictional Latin American village. A primary example of the alternative comics revolution of the 1980's, *Love and Rockets* started as a self-published work by Gilbert, Jaime, and Mario Hernandez in 1981. By 1982, after a short stint as an independent, alternative publication, *Love and Rockets* was picked up by Seattle-based Fantagraphics Books, which has continued the successful publication and distribution of Hernandez's work.

In 2003, seeking a wider audience, Fantagraphics released ambitious collections of work by the Hernandez brothers: *LOCAS* for Jaime and *Palomar* for Gilbert. At the time, a six-hundred-page hardcover comics title was an industry novelty. Nonetheless, both volumes brought national recognition to the brothers. Thanks to its commercial success, *Palomar* was reissued in 2004 and 2005. In 2007, in celebration of the twenty-fifth anniversary of *Love and Rockets*, abbreviated volumes were published presenting the Palomar Stories in chronological order.

Plot

While the stories created by Jaime center on the characters of Maggie and Hopey and are strongly evocative of Southern California's punk scene throughout the 1980's, Gilbert's stories exhibit a bond with Latin America and constantly seek a redefinition of the migratory experience. As a compilation, *Palomar* adds to the coherence of Gilbert Hernandez's work, since it collects stories that jump back and forth within the story of the village. Luba, a matriarch and guiding force behind the town, serves as the axis for the narrative,

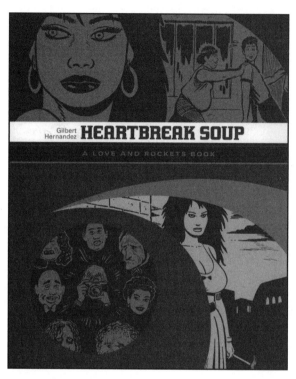

Palomar: The Heartbreak Soup Stories. (Courtesy of Fantagraphics Books)

which begins with her arrival in Palomar and ends with her departure.

The story follows the tension between Luba, who lands in Palomar seeking to remake her fortune, and Chelo, the local *bañadora*, a woman who makes a living by bathing men. When Luba arrives and sets up a competing bañadora business, Chelo trades jobs and becomes the village sheriff. Eventually, Luba's business prospers. She buys an upscale home and the village theater and upgrades her bathing business. In the meantime, she has a series of affairs with locals and with visitors and gives birth to multiple children whose upbringings add to the charm of the story. Eventually, she becomes Palomar's mayor and settles her differences with Chelo.

The volume is divided into chapters, each comprising a different episode of Palomar's history. However, these installments are compilations of narratives that appeared in a more disjointed fashion in *Love and Rockets*.

"Chelo's Burden" introduces Chelo and many of the main characters who were born during the early years when Chelo worked as a midwife. It also traces the village's origins and recounts Chelo's family history and her place in the history as a descendant of Palomar's founders.

"Sopa de Gran Pena" includes the love affair between Pipo and Manuel, Gato's unrequited love for Pipo, and Tipín Tipín's passion for Zomba. Also, it introduces the local gang of teenagers: Heraclio, Jesús, Vicente, Israel, and Sakahaftewa (also known as Satch). It covers the deaths of Toco, Jesus's younger brother, and Manuel, the local Casanova.

Palomar: The Heartbreak Soup Stories. (Courtesy of Fantagraphics Books)

"Act of Contrition" chronicles Luba's economic ascent and her relationship with Archie, a mortician. It also depicts the travails of Heraclio and Carmen as a young married couple and the adventures of some of Luba's children, Guadalupe and Doralis.

"Ecce Homo" narrates the story of Jesús Ángel, who is sent to prison after suffering a nervous breakdown. It also introduces Tonantzin and Diana, the Villaseñor sisters, and covers Pipo's return to Palomar from the city of San Fideo after marrying Gato and giving birth to Manuel's son, Sergio.

"An American in Palomar" tells the story of Howard Miller, an American photographer who visits Palomar. It focuses on Tonantzin, who makes a living selling fried slugs; the affair between Luba and Heraclio, who fathers Guadalupe; and Diana's obsession with running.

"Love Bites" covers Jesús's time in jail and develops further Heraclio's life with Carmen. Along the way, it advances the general story of the village.

"Duck Feet" narrates the events surrounding a visiting witch and further develops the story lines for many characters, such as Israel, who embraces his bisexuality while in San Fideo.

"Human Diastrophism" is a lengthy chapter that starts with a story from Vicente's point of view. It describes the time when Palomar was plagued by monkeys and recounts Luba's affair with the handsome Khamo who fathers Casimira and Doralis. It also includes the episode of Tomaso Marín, a serial killer who becomes the subject matter of Humberto's art, Luba's dalliance with Borro, and Khamo's affair with Pipo. In the end, it hints at Luba's rise to mayor.

"Farewell, My Palomar" opens with Jesús's return to Palomar. It develops the story of Casimira, who loses her arm in an accident, and chronicles Pipo's financial success in the garment industry in San Fideo. It also traces the story of Pito, a town elder, and introduces the mystery of statues at a nearby lake.

"Luba Conquers the World" introduces characters like Petra and Fritz, Luba's sisters, who come to Palomar. Several stories are resolved such as Guadalupe's marriage to Gato and Luba's eventual settling down with a disfigured Khamo.

"Epilog: Chelo's Burden" tells of Palomar's destruction. Ultimately, Luba moves to California when it becomes evident that gangsters have come to Palomar to settle old accounts.

Characters

Palomar has an almost dizzying array of characters. Some of the main ones are listed below.

- *Luba*, the protagonist, is an extremely well-endowed woman of Indian descent. Her arrival to and departure from Palomar signal the story's beginning and end. Her progeny is bountiful and exclusively feminine, marking a lengthy lineage of strong female characters. In sum, she is the axis of a matrilineal order. She is usually the active partner in relationships, and her lovers are, quite frequently, younger men.

- *Chelo*, the town sheriff, is a natural antagonist to Luba. Her ancestors founded Palomar, and her mother taught her to be a midwife. Her sense of authority emanates from her sheriff's badge and the fact that she has known most of the population since they were born.

- *Pipo* grows into a gorgeous woman and is initially seduced by Manuel. She eventually marries Gato, moves to San Fideo, and then gives birth to Manuel's son, Sergio. When she and Gato separate, she returns to Palomar. She eventually sets up a business in San Fideo and becomes a successful businesswoman.

- *Tonantzin Villaseñor* is another beautiful woman in the town. In the beginning she makes a living by selling fried snails. Next, she starts dressing in native clothing and is viewed as mentally unstable. She then becomes obsessed with Howard Miller, the photographer who visits Palomar and whom she thinks will take her to Hollywood. Ultimately, once she has eloped with Khamo, she sets herself on fire during a political demonstration.

- *Heraclio* is perhaps the most emotionally balanced of Palomar's male characters. Luba seduces him when he is a teenager, and he fathers Guadalupe. His marriage to short, strong-tempered Carmen is, in comparison with other relationships in the story, a model of stability. He is the resident teacher in Palomar.

Artistic Style

Hernandez is well known for a style of drawing that evokes the aesthetics of teenage comics of the 1950's and 1960's. The panels are orderly and the images are in black and white with little shading or scratching. In terms of imagery, Hernandez's style of illustration mixes the appearance of post-World War II romance comics such as *Rex Morgan, M.D.* and *Mary Worth* with the playfulness of Bob Montana's *Archie*. His basic scheme resides in narrating unconventional stories by traditional means. While the art emulates the wonders of suburbia, plots are set in cities or far-away villages and contain convoluted story lines, atypical social dynamics, and transgressive sexual politics.

Hernandez offers much more than an Americanized view of Latin America. Hernandez's art is eclectic and mixes aspects from his upbringing and youth with elements from his formal education, which serves to highlight a more complex way of imagining Latin identity in and outside the United States.

As Hernandez has matured as a cartoonist, he has turned more playful. His stories in *Palomar* go back and forth in time, demanding the reader's constant attention, and embrace different points of view in episodic fashion, adding tidbits of information that gradually complete the picture. *Palomar* comes across as almost a direct challenge to chronological order. Many of Hernandez's techniques are evocative of late modernism, and if his drawing style evokes in us a time when the United States was naïve and candid, Hernandez's story lines expose the reader to the fissures and cracks in contemporary society and culture.

Themes

Palomar revolves around a set of recurrent themes, the most prevalent of which is one of strong women who dominate and govern society. Luba and Chelo anchor most of the stories, while Pipo and Tonantzin provide diversions. In contrast, the lives of Heraclio, Jesús, or Israel seem less mandated by their own independent decisions but rather are guided and orchestrated by the women around them.

Gilbert Hernandez

Along with his brothers Jaime and Mario, Gilbert Hernandez formed the trio of Los Bros. Hernandez and created the beloved comic book series *Love and Rockets*. Hernandez's stories are mostly set in the fictional Central American village of Palomar, with tales reflecting the lives, loves, and losses of residents past and present. An element of magical realism reminiscent of such writers as Gabriel García Márquez is found in Hernandez's work, which is noted for its sensuality and strong female characters, such as the iconic Luba.

Despite the loose personal bonds and the muddled way in which many characters combine with each other, another ruling premise of *Palomar* is the importance of family and friendship. Whether they are the product of a long-lasting, stable relationship or the consequence of an improvised spontaneous fling, Hernandez's characters share an inordinate appreciation for loved ones, which perhaps hints at their longing for more conventional interactions.

Another key theme of *Palomar* is the transition between the countryside and the city. The city of San Fideo plays the role of alter ego to the entrenched lifestyle of Palomar, where there is a slower pace and life seems to last longer. Moving to the city means negotiating between the preservation of one's heritage and practical survival. Modernity mixes with customs and rituals to form an elaborate mix, giving the overall impression of an attempt to find a balance between the intricacies and challenges of living in the modern world with new possibilities for maintaining cultural tradition. In this sense, one must not read *Palomar* simply as a picturesque imagining of Latin (or Latin American) identity; rather, the book's main concern is to suggest a pragmatic, less superficial explanation for cultural history while rationalizing a new way of being American.

Impact

As part of the *Love and Rockets* saga, *Palomar* shares a great deal of responsibility for the modern graphic novel boom. In the course of a decade, Hernandez went from being a lesser-known Mexican American cartoonist, who published work independently with the help of family, to being hailed as a master by the likes of *Time* magazine and *The New York Times*. A persistent presence at renowned comics conventions is solid proof of a growing and endearing popularity.

A thorough assessment of Herdandez's work has emphasized the multifaceted nature of his production and has given way to several of the author's post-*Love and Rockets* titles, released by Dark Horse Comics, Eros Comix, and DC Comics. Hernandez has launched a *Love and Rockets* collection titled *High Soft Lisp* (2010) and the third installment of his "Fritz B-Movie" series, *Love from the Shadows* (2011).

Héctor Fernández L'Hoeste

Further Reading

Hernandez, Gilbert. *Beyond Palomar: A Love and Rockets Book* (2007).

Hernandez, Gilbert, and Jared K. Fletcher. *Sloth* (2009).

Hernandez, Gilbert, Jaime Hernandez, and Mario Hernandez. *Love and Rockets* (1981-   ).

Bibliography

Caturani, Khadijah. "*Palomar: The Heartbreak Soup Stories*: A Love and Rockets Book." Review of *Palomar: The Heartbreak Soup Stories*, by Gilbert Hernandez. *Library Journal* 129, no. 1 (January, 2004): 80.

Flagg, Gordon. "Story Behind the Story: Hernandez's *Palomar*." *The Booklist* 100, no. 11 (February 1, 2004): 963.

Hernandez, Gilbert. "Gilbert Hernandez's *Palomar*." Interview by Heidi MacDonald. *Publishers Weekly* 250, no. 42 (October 20, 2003): S12.

See also: *Love and Rockets*; *Dykes to Watch Out For*; *The Complete Fritz the Cat*

PASSIONATE JOURNEY

Author: Masereel, Frans
Artist: Frans Masereel (illustrator)
Publisher: Dover
First book publication: *Mon livre d'heures*, 1919 (English translation, 1922)

Publication History

Frans Masereel was born in 1889 to an upper-middle-class family from Ghent, Belgium. He showed interest in drawing at an early age and studied at the Academy of Arts in Ghent in 1907 before traveling to Paris and Brittany. He started his career as a political cartoonist during World War I and developed a love of the woodcut, which he used in numerous book illustrations and more than fifty wordless books during his life. He coined the term *roman in beelden* (novels in pictures) to describe these imaginative and realistic stories told entirely without text. These stories also are referred to as "woodcut novels," as they are told through black-and-white pictures printed from woodcuts.

Masereel self-published *Passionate Journey* in 1919 on credit from the printer, Albert Kundig, in Geneva. *Passionate Journey* was originally titled *Mon livre d'heures: 167 images dessinées et gravées sur bois*. It caught the attention of the German publisher Kurt Wolff and was published in 1920 as *Mein Stundenbuch: 167 Holzschnitte*. The German edition, which included an introduction by Thomas Mann, was a financial success. As a result of this attention, Kurt Wolff published four more books by Masereel that generated an interest in the wordless book throughout Europe. A limited English edition was first printed in 1922 under the title *My Book of Hours*.

This title was changed to *Passionate Journey* with the American edition, published by Lear in 1948. Two woodcuts were omitted from the Lear edition. One woodcut depicted the story's protagonist having sexual intercourse, and the second displayed him urinating on pedestrians from the top of a tall building. *Passionate Journey* remained the title in subsequent American editions by Penguin, City Lights, and Dover. These American editions included the two woodcuts omitted from

Passionate Journey. (Courtesy of Dover Publications)

the Lear edition. Masereel's most popular book, *Passionate Journey* has been reprinted in many languages and editions throughout the world.

Plot

Passionate Journey portrays the experiences of a man who arrives in a city. The man's youthful innocence is displayed by his amazement and wonder at the industrial innovations in the city and his naïveté with women. With his youthful vigor and caring nature, he revels in the life around him, especially while playing with children or enjoying outdoor activities and sports. He never loses his childlike playfulness and gusto for life, despite his disillusionment with love. He develops an interest in the rights of workers and champions their need for a better life. He rescues a girl from her abusive father and raises her as his own daughter. She lives with him and brings happiness into his solitary life. A few years pass, and he is surprised when he sees her naked and discovers she has grown up to be a beautiful young woman. She unexpectedly falls ill and dies, leaving him stricken with grief.

After spending some time alone, the man decides to travel around the world and take his focus off his loss. On his return to his own country, he goes on a hedonistic spree, drinking, gambling, racing cars, and visiting prostitutes. He then turns his attention toward the hypocrisy around him and acts rebelliously, farting on a group of political dignitaries, offering a hungry family a table at a fancy restaurant, refusing to join the army, and ridiculing the military. A disgruntled crowd eventually chases him out of the city.

He travels through the countryside and eventually wanders off alone into the woods, where he raises his arms in celebration and marvels at the stars. With a peaceful expression, he lies down and dies. His skeleton then comes to life and stomps on his heart in a chaotic dance before skipping nonchalantly off into the universe, one hand in his pocket and the other raised in a friendly wave at the reader.

Characters

- *A Man*, the protagonist, is tall, clean-shaven, handsome, and white. He wears a white shirt and black suit coat throughout the story. The book opens and closes with a wave from the protagonist, first as a young man and then, after his death, as a skeleton skipping through the stars. The protagonist was based on a combination of Masereel, who was reserved and contemplative, and his friend Henri Guilbeaux, who was a biographer of Vladimir Ilich Lenin and possessed eccentricities that served as the model for the protagonist's outrageous behavior.
- *The Girl/Young Woman* represents the one consistent relationship in the man's life. The protagonist stops her father from beating her with a whip and takes her to his home to raise her in safety. She represents the one person he loves and who

loves him unconditionally. After she dies of an illness, he is devastated and never recovers from his grief.

Artistic Style

During World War I, Masereel volunteered as a translator for the International Red Cross in Geneva. He also worked as a political cartoonist for the newspaper *La Feuille* from 1917 to 1920. This job demanded that Masereel create drawings related to the daily news. He used brush and ink to create bold black-and-white images that easily caught the eye of the reader. Such images were well suited for reproduction on the low-grade paper stock, as details and fine lines created using pen and ink did not reproduce well. Masereel later integrated this technique of unembellished black-and-white shapes into his woodcuts and established a distinct style that is immediately recognized as his trademark. This is evident in the figure of the protagonist and the white highlights inside his black figure, making him easily identifiable in the narrative.

Passionate Journey. (Courtesy of Dover Publications)

Masereel was unaware of the expressionist artists' interest in the revival of the woodcut form. He discovered this craft on his own and immediately found his medium of choice. Masereel's skill is particularly evident in his ability to display movement and human emotion within small, flat black-and-white images that have clear, solid lines and do not incorporate cross-hatching. The small woodcuts in *Passionate Journey*, which measure 3.5 inches by 2.75 inches, provide an intimacy between Masereel and the reader.

The woodcut is the oldest printing process and requires simple materials: a block of wood and a knife. In the front of *Passionate Journey*, a woodcut displays Masereel sitting at a table with simple carving tools and blocks of wood. For Masereel, who was suspicious of a growing industrial culture, the woodcut offered a direct link to nature and a simpler way of life. In the skilled hands of Masereel, the woodcut was transformed into a means of storytelling that anyone could read, regardless of language or level of literacy. Writer Stefan Zweig, a friend of Masereel, wrote, "Should everything perish, all the books, the photographs, and the documents, and we were left only with the woodcuts Masereel has created, through them alone we could reconstruct our contemporary world."

Unlike traditional comics, which typically progress from panel to panel, the woodcut novel offers one woodcut per page in scene-to-scene transitions. Many readers find the closure between these transitions difficult to read, in contrast to less demanding progressions of action such as moment-to-moment or action-to-action.

Themes

The major theme is a young man's quest for love that ends in disillusionment and grief. The protagonist has various love affairs, but they all end with him being ridiculed or rejected. The only loving relationship that he experiences is with a girl he raises. After her death and a period of travel, his hopes and desires change to cynicism. He no longer seeks love and chooses a reckless manner of living.

A secondary theme involves the man's search for his place in society. Despite his initial curiosity about modern life, he finds little substance to sustain his

---

Frans Masereel

Born in Belgium in 1889, Frans Masereel is one of the most famous of all Flemish woodcut artists. Trained by Belgian artist Jean Delvin, Masereel settled in Paris in 1910, where he produced his earliest woodcuts before fleeing to Geneva during the First World War. Strongly anti-militarist, Masereel produced thousands of woodcut images and illustrated the work of several writers. In 1918 he produced his first proto-graphic novel, *The Passion of a Man*. His 1925 book *The City* depicts the life of a city in one hundred engravings. His best-known work is undoubtedly *Passionate Journey*, produced in 1926, which similarly traces the urban milieu through the experience of one young man. In 2009, Dover collected three of his works—*The Sun*, *The Idea*, and *Story Without Words*—into a single volume. As the progenitor of the wordless graphic novel, Masereel's art has been tremendously influential on artists like Lynd Ward and Peter Kuper, and his bold black-and-white graphics and powerful compositions make him one of the most important visual artists to work in the comics form.

---

interest. The protagonist is not a person who can fit, like a mechanical part, into a machine. He questions authority, fights against injustice and abuse, and suffers heartache and loss. During his travels, he finds a simpler relationship with others, regardless of religion, culture, or race. He also connects with animals such as monkeys, a camel, and an elephant. He is more comfortable in preindustrial cultures than in a cold metropolis. With the knowledge from his travels, he lampoons and criticizes hypocritical individuals and organizations upon returning to the city.

After being chased from the city for his impetuous and scandalous behavior, he finally finds his place in nature. In these final scenes, Masereel depicts the lush flora with white space, curves, and diagonal lines, in contrast to the ominous black vertical lines of the tall buildings in the city. The man moves more easily in the woods, though his isolation is apparent. As he ponders the stars at night, the moon sheds tears over his solitary figure. However, in the next scene, the man humbles himself in a kneeling position, raises his arms to the heavens, and, with a smile on his face, accepts his place in the world and the experiences that have brought him to this one affirming moment.

One final theme is the integral relationship between humans and nature. Masereel suggests that humanity's place is in a preindustrial culture and in nature, rather than in a commercialized environment.

Impact

Many comics artists, including Will Eisner, have acknowledged the importance of Masereel in the development of the graphic novel. Modern graphic novels owe a great debt to Masereel's woodcut novels, especially *Passionate Journey*, with its wordless narrative and focus on day-to-day events and adult themes. In addition to shaping the genre, Masereel's works have influenced the artistic styles and thematic concerns of comics creators such as Eric Drooker, whose wordless book *Flood! A Novel in Pictures* (1994) examines the inequities of capitalism in contemporary culture. Drooker uses scratchboard, which imitates wood engraving with its fine black-and-white lines, to create his images. Another artist, Neil Bousfield, uses his skill as a wood engraver in *Walking Shadows: A Novel Without Words* (2010), which examines the bitter realities experienced by families caught in a cycle of menial work without hope for escape.

David A. Beronä

Further Reading

Bousfield, Neil. *Walking Shadows: A Novel Without Words* (2010).

Drooker, Eric. *Flood! A Novel in Pictures* (1994).

Masereel, Frans. *"The Sun," "The Idea," and "Story Without Words": Three Graphic Novels by Frans Masereel* (2009).

Bibliography

Avermate, Roger. *Frans Masereel*. New York: Ritzzoli International, 1977.

Beronä, David A. *Wordless Books: The Original Graphic Novels*. New York: Abrams, 2008.

Willett, Perry. "The Cutting Edge of German Expressionism: The Woodcut Novel of Frans Masereel and Its Influences." In *A Companion to the Literature of German Expressionism*, edited by Neil H. Donahue. Rochester, N.Y.: Camden House, 2005.

See also: *Flood! A Novel in Pictures*; *He Done Her Wrong*; *Give It Up! And Other Stories*

PAUL

Author: Rabagliati, Michel

Artist: Michel Rabagliati

Publisher: Les Editions de la Pastèque (French); Conundrum Press (English); Drawn and Quarterly (English)

First book publication: 1999-　　(English translation, 2000-　)

Publication History

Michel Rabagliati was born in Montreal in 1961 and grew up enjoying not only American comic books but also Franco-Belgian works such as *The Adventures of Tintin* (1929-1976), *Gaston* (first appearing in 1957), and *Asterix* (1961-1979). After studying art and typography, he became a graphic illustrator, and his work appeared in such diverse publications as *The Wall Street Journal, Utne Reader, The Advocate,* and *Canadian Business.* After designing a new logo for Canadian publisher Drawn and Quarterly in 1990, Rabagliati regained an interest in comics and began to write and draw comics of his own, just as he had done as a child.

In 1999, the first of his semiautobiographical comics, *Paul à la campagne,* was published by Les Editions de la Pastèque. The following year, Drawn and Quarterly published his story "Paul: Apprentice Typographer" in *Drawn and Quarterly,* issue 3, and later that year published a translation of *Paul à la campagne* entitled *Paul in the Country.* These and the subsequent English editions were translated by Helge Dascher. Both publications were well received, with "Paul: Apprentice Typographer" being reviewed as "a minor-chord masterpiece."

Rabagliati's first full-length graphic novel, *Paul a un travail d'été,* was published in 2002, and the following year, it was released in English as *Paul Has a Summer Job.* This was followed by *Paul en appartement* in 2004, with the translated *Paul Moves Out* published the following year. *Paul dans le metro,* comprising twelve short stories, was published in 2005. The title story was reprinted as "Paul in the Subway" in the pages of *Drawn and Quarterly,* issue 5, and was nominated for an Ignatz Award. Along with "Paul:

Paul Has a Summer Job. (Courtesy of Drawn and Quarterly)

Apprentice Typographer" and an excerpt from *Paul Moves Out,* "Paul in the Subway" was included in *The Adventures of Paul,* Drawn and Quarterly's contribution to the 2005 Free Comic Book Day.

In 2006, *Paul à la pêche* was published; Drawn and Quarterly published the translation in 2008 as *Paul Goes Fishing. Paul à Québec* was published in 2009, and its English translation, *The Song of Roland,* was scheduled for release in May, 2012, with Conundrum Press taking over for Drawn and Quarterly as publisher. *Paul au parc* was published in 2011.

Plot

The stories in the *Paul* series are semiautobiographical and include a small amount of fiction. The main part of *Paul in the Country* deals with a trip that Paul, along with his partner, Lucie, and their daughter, Alice, takes to his parents' home in the countryside. While at his parents' house, which formerly belonged to his great-aunt Janette, Paul remembers his past experiences there, including accidentally killing a bird with a pellet gun and spending time with his friend Alain.

Paul Has a Summer Job primarily takes place in the summer of 1979, when Paul is eighteen. He has dropped out of school and taken a job at a print shop, but he does not like it. His friend Guy invites him to work as a counselor at a camp for underprivileged children located near Lake Morin. He agrees and meets the others at the lake, but he is nervous about sleeping in the woods and encountering bugs and animals. He learns how to climb a nearby mountain, an activity that he will later repeat with the children for whom he is responsible. Shortly before camp starts, he meets his partner at the camp, an attractive young woman named Annie.

Paul and Annie's first group of children is made up of six boys aged eleven and twelve; Paul has some trouble dealing with both them and Annie, but he soon gets along better with both. The next group consists of five older boys, aged thirteen to fifteen. In the time between the boys leaving and the next group arriving, Paul, who is attracted to Annie, learns that she might be attracted to him as well.

The final group is made up of nine- and ten-year-old girls, and Paul becomes close to Marie, who is blind. She is a friendly, funny child who wears a small doll on her necklace, which she later loses. Annie and Paul begin a romantic relationship, and shortly before camp ends, they have sex. It is Paul's first time, and as they lie under the stars, Annie points out a small one, saying that when each of them looks at it they will think of the other. Camp soon ends, and they go their separate ways. While Paul keeps in touch with some of the other counselors, he never sees Annie again.

Years later, Paul, Lucie, and Alice attend a party at a chalet owned by Lucie's friends Dominique and Dave. While there, Paul discovers that the chalet is on the shores of what was once Lake Morin, which was renamed. He searches and finds the old campsite; lifting the platform that was once the floor of his campers' tent, he finds Marie's doll. He gives the doll to his

daughter and points out the star that Annie showed him long before.

Paul Moves Out begins in July, 1983, shortly after Paul and Lucie move into their first apartment. The story then flashes back to October, 1979, depicting their first meeting at the Studio Seguin art school. A new teacher, Jean-Louis Desrosiers, tells his class that they will be concentrating on design, since graphic design has become important. Paul and Lucie begin to spend more and more time together as friends, and they also often spend time with Jean-Louis as well.

Over Easter break, Paul, Lucie, and another student, Danielle, accompany Jean-Louis on a cultural trip to New York City. There, they visit many small art galleries, and Paul and Lucie kiss for the first time. The trip takes an awkward turn when Jean-Louis makes a pass at Paul, which he rejects. However, their friendship recovers by the time the group returns to Montreal. Paul and Lucie continue their relationship and meet each other's parents.

The story then returns to Paul and Lucie in their new apartment, which they have been refurbishing. They make friends with their neighbors, have their bathroom destroyed by a handyman chasing a rat, and go to work and school. Sadness comes into their lives when Paul's great-aunt Janette dies, but they are cheered up a few days later when they babysit Lucie's nieces.

Paul Goes Fishing begins in 1991, with Lucie three months pregnant. The couple visits their friends Francie and Peter, who are also expecting a child. Paul and Lucie take a vacation and share a lakeside cabin with Lucie's sister and brother-in-law, Monique and Clement, and their daughters. Most people, including Clement, visit the lake to go fishing, and Paul recalls the day that he and his father went fishing and their boat almost sank. Other flashbacks shown at this point convey further information about Monique and Clement and explore events from Lucie's and Paul's early lives, including a time when a teenage Paul almost ran away from home.

The trip ends in tragedy when Lucie has a miscarriage. Lucie eventually becomes pregnant again, and her parents bring her gifts for the baby. Two months later, she has another miscarriage. Afterward, when she comes home and finds the baby items, she becomes extremely upset. The following year, with the help of a doctor, the couple tries again; Lucie becomes pregnant and later gives birth to Alice.

Volumes

- *Paul in the Country* (2000). While visiting his parents' home in the country, Paul reminisces about his earlier visits.
- *Paul Has a Summer Job* (2003). At eighteen, Paul works as a counselor at a summer camp and falls in love.
- *Paul Moves Out* (2005). Paul meets Lucie while at art school, and they move in together several years later.
- *Paul Goes Fishing* (2008). Paul and Lucie try to have a child and take a fishing vacation.

Characters

As *Paul* comprises several volumes, there are numerous characters. The primary ones are listed here.

- *Paul*, the protagonist, is a stand-in for the author.

Paul Has a Summer Job. (Courtesy of Drawn and Quarterly)

He is French Canadian and is depicted at various ages. As an adult, he works as a graphic designer.

- *Lucie* is Paul's longtime partner. They meet at art school and eventually have a daughter named Alice. She is a stand-in for the author's companion, Carole.
- *Paul's Family Members* include his parents, Robert and Aline; his sister, Kathy; and his great-aunt Janette.
- *Annie* is a young woman from Quebec City and is Paul's partner at the camp. They become romantically involved, and she is the first person with whom Paul has sex.
- *Marie* is a young blind girl who is part of the third group of campers.
- *Dave and Dominique* are friends of Paul and Lucie who own a house near where the camp once was.
- *Francie and Peter Dube* are friends of Paul and Lucie. Francie is pregnant at the same time as Lucie's first pregnancy and has a daughter, Jeanne.
- *Roland* is Lucie's father.
- *Jean-Louis Desrosiers* is Paul and Lucie's teacher at art school. He is attracted to Paul and rejected by him, but they remain friends for years afterward.

Artistic Style

Rabagliati credits such Franco-Belgian comics creators as Hergé (*The Adventures of Tintin*) and Albert Uderzo (*Asterix*) as his artistic influences, and reviews of his work have noted his style's similarities to the clear-line style made famous by Hergé. Rendered in black and white, Rabagliati's art is generally realistic with some "simplistic" touches, such as eyes drawn as black dots or white circles and noses sometimes drawn with a triangular shape. Male and female nudity is occasionally depicted, but it is not drawn in any exaggerated way. As the stories take place at different points in Paul's life, the characters are shown at various ages, but they remain easily identifiable at all times.

Most, if not all, of the characters shown in the books are based on real people, but since the reader is not shown what these people really look like, it is unknown how accurately Rabagliati has portrayed

---

Michel Rabagliati

Michel Rabagliati was thirty-eight years old when he published his first comics with the Quebec-based publisher La Pastèque. This work, *Paul à la campagne*, introduced the autobiographical stand-in for Rabagliati, a young man growing up in Montreal in the 1970's. *Paul Has a Summer Job* was his first long-form graphic novel and his first book to be translated into English. This was followed by *Paul Moves Out, Paul in the Metro*, and *Paul Goes Fishing*, each of which tells the story of Paul as a rapidly maturing young man. *The Song of Roland* is a dramatic change of pace, detailing the life and death of Paul's father-in-law. This book won the FNAC Audience Prize at the Angoulême Comics Festival and is being adapted for the screen. Rabagliati's art is strongly influenced by European clear-line traditions and is notable for its strong, clean lines and careful compositions.

---

them. The pages are drawn in a standard multipanel format with the number of panels varying from page to page.

Themes

The basic theme of the *Paul* books is life and its issues: love, work, family, and everything else that goes along with those aspects of existence. Some autobiographical works deal with hardships in the author's life, such as illness or abuse, while others deal with successful and unsuccessful romantic relationships and life in general (Harvey Pekar's *American Splendor*, 1987, is a good example of the latter). *Paul* tackles the everyday, commonplace aspects of life but also deals with occasional problems and disappointments, such as Lucie's miscarriages. The comic even discusses the everyday lives of secondary characters, sharing details about downsizing taking place in Clement's company and Monique's work in family services.

Impact

Paul has been well received by critics and readers, some of whom have dubbed the protagonist "The Tintin of Quebec." The stories have gained Rabagliati worldwide fame and accolades, ranging from international awards to inclusion on library association reading lists. *Paul Goes Fishing*, for example, was nominated for the Ignatz Awards for Outstanding Artist and Outstanding Graphic Novel. It was also nominated for an Eisner Award for Best Graphic Album. In addition to French and English, the *Paul* books have been published in Spanish, Italian, and other languages.

David S. Serchay

Further Reading

Brown. Jeffrey. *Clumsy* (2002).

_____. *Funny Misshapen Body* (2009).

Thompson, Craig. *Blankets* (2003).

Bibliography

Boyd, Kevin. "2010 Outstanding Cartoonist: Michel Rabagliati." *The Joe Shuster Awards*, June 23, 2010. http://joeshusterawards.com/2010/06/23/2010-outstanding-cartoonist-michel-rabagliati.

Flagg, Gordon. "*Paul Goes Fishing*." Review of *Paul Goes Fishing*, by Michel Rabagliati. *Booklist*, March 15, 2008.

Serchay, David S. *The Librarian's Guide to Graphic Novels for Adults*. New York: Neal-Schuman, 2009.

See also: *Clumsy*; *The Adventures of Tintin*; *Blankets*; *Asterix*

PEDRO AND ME: FRIENDSHIP, LOSS, AND WHAT I LEARNED

Author: Winick, Judd
Artist: Judd Winick (illustrator)
Publisher: Henry Holt
First book publication: 2000

Publication History

Pedro and Me: Friendship, Loss, and What I Learned, by Judd Winick, is based on events surrounding the 1994 season of the MTV reality show *The Real World*. The program featured a group of six strangers living together for six months in San Francisco. The participants included Winick, then an aspiring cartoonist, and his roommate Pedro Zamora, a young man living with AIDS and committed to educating others about the disease. Soon after the show ended, Zamora died from the effects of AIDS.

A few years later, compelled to chronicle their lives, Winick wrote "The Road from the Real World," based on illustrated journal entries made while he participated in the show. On advice from a friend, he revised it to include more story detail. He gave the result to agent Jill Kneerim. The work was rejected by thirty publishers before Marc Aronson, editor for Henry Holt, recognized its potential and suggested revisions to improve pacing and to create a more coherent structure. The new version of the novel included background of Winick and Zamora, Zamora's AIDS work and his death, and the AIDS mission that Winick undertook.

Plot

This autobiographical graphic novel innovatively describes a relationship between a group of young people involved in a social-living experiment that aired on television as the reality show *The Real World. Pedro and Me* begins a few months after the show was taped. It describes an experience that transformed Winick's life by showing the evolution of the close friendship he developed with Pedro Zamora.

At the beginning, the novel depicts the celebrity that Winick and his housemates experienced after appearing on *The Real World*. The story is framed by the

(WireImage)

Judd Winick

Initially famous as a cast member of MTV's *The Real World*, Judd Winick is now better known as a comic book writer and artist. His teen-oriented work often features racy dialogue and an exploration of social issues, including his acclaimed autobiographical look at his relationship with AIDS activist (and *Real World* roommate) Pedro Zamora. He has worked on many superhero books for a teen audience and older, which often feature a fair amount of sex and violence.

"shuttle guy" incident. A taxi driver takes Winick to the airport on his way to see an ill Zamora, and then, coincidentally, the same driver takes him to the airport again after Zamora's death. On both occasions, the driver helps the distraught Winick by offering words of wisdom and comfort.

Winick carefully unfolds the details of his budding friendship with Zamora. First, he traces his life leading up to the show: college graduation, job hunting in the comics industry, and applying to be a participant on *The Real World*. Then Zamora's pre-*Real World* life is chronicled: living in Cuba, moving to Miami, losing his mother to cancer, looking for love and comfort in the arms of others, and then discovering, as a seventeen-year-old high school honors student, that he has AIDS.

Though Winick and the other cast members knew from the start that one of their housemates had AIDS, Winick was shocked to discover that his handsome, charming, funny, and vital roommate was the victim of the disease that was still mysterious and scary to the average person in 1994 who was uneducated about the disease and how it was contracted.

Winick charts the many good times he, Zamora, Pam Ling, and Cory Murphy have as they get to know one another. As they become friends, Winick sees Zamora's determination to educate young people about AIDS: he travels San Francisco's Bay Area and beyond to talk to young people and impart the facts of the disease—how it is contracted and how it can be avoided—and to help dispel the myths that fuel the prejudice and fear that was so prevalent in the 1990's. Winick shares in Zamora's zest for life and his enthusiasm for his mission. He then watches as Zamora succumbs to illness. As Zamora's condition worsens, Winick takes over Zamora's presentations. In so doing, he discovers the impact of Zamora's life and message.

Characters

- *Judd Winick* is a young cartoonist who tells the story of becoming friends with Zamora while being filmed on the reality television show *The Real World*.
- *Pedro Zamora* is a young gay man who becomes infected with AIDS and then sets out on a mission to help other young people avoid the disease.
- *Pam Ling* is an Asian American woman in her third year of medical school at Harvard University. She becomes good friends with Winick and Zamora.
- *Cory Murphy*, a traditional Christian American,

is a young woman from Fresno, California, who becomes close with Winick, Zamora, and Ling.
- *Sean Sasser* is Zamora's boyfriend who anticipates their marriage in San Francisco after the filming of the television show.
- *Mr. Zamora* is Pedro's father. He is a hardworking man who loves and supports his son throughout his son's short life.
- *Alex Ecarano* is Zamora's best friend who, though living in Miami, talks to Zamora often and encourages him in his struggle with his illness and supports him in his marriage plans.
- *Milly* is Zamora's older sister who becomes a mother figure to Zamora after their mother dies.
- *Bobbi Winick* is Winick's supportive mother.
- *Michael Winick* is Winick's father, who also supports him in his life choices and goals.

Artistic Style

Winick renders his graphic novel in black and white, realistically drawing characters and backgrounds. The highly individualized characters faithfully reflect the people who figure in this story. Adept at depicting facial expressions, he shows the joy, fear, and grief that Zamora's friends and family experience. First, the housemates delight in their newfound friendships and their explorations of San Francisco. Then, they suffer grief and distress as they observe the effects of Zamora's illness.

With vivid characters in the forefront of small panels, backgrounds are simple—a bedroom with a few furnishings, a stage in an auditorium, an outdoor scene focused on the antics of the young people, and a sparse hospital room. While the characters are presented realistically, the anonymous people who recognize Winick and the other participants of *The Real World* tend toward caricature.

With the limited palette of black and white, Winick expresses not only facial detail and emotional state but also generalized mood. Black represents darkness, frustration, anger, fear, and gloom. White represents joy, frailty, and simplicity and even suggests spirituality. Artistic distance similarly depicts emotion and mood. Two faces fill a 2 x 4-inch panel to show roommates having fun. The dying Zamora is shown in an entire page of white space featuring a tiny bed surrounded by little figures.

Winick, who also narrates the story, distinguishes between the narrated story and the dialogue with text boxes and balloons. Text boxes move the story forward, and balloons capture dialogue.

Themes

The title of this novel, *Pedro and Me: Friendship, Loss, and What I Learned*, suggests the primary theme: the story of a young man who experiences the joys of friendship and the sadness of loss. The novel shows the ways in which Zamora tries to cope with his fate by helping others avoid AIDS. Zamora realizes that he was infected with AIDS partly because he knew nothing about it; he did not know how it was transmitted or how to protect himself. To make the time he had left purposeful, Zamora embraces the mission of helping others avoid his fate.

The novel also demonstrates the strength of love. After Winick and the other close friends of Zamora realize the seriousness of his condition and the inevitability of his fate, they rally around him, trying to find ways to help him. Each tries to deal with the loss. Winick carries on Zamora's mission. As he does so, he discovers the many people who were helped by Zamora's story and his message of both empathy and self-protection.

Impact

Pedro and Me continues a tradition of nonfiction graphic novels that describe the lives of individuals during crises or difficult times, focusing on the author's life or the lives of people close to the author. Raymond Briggs's *Ethel and Ernest* (1998), for example, depicts his parent's life in London during World War II and the Cold War; the autobiographical *Our Cancer Year* (1994), by Harvey Pekar and Joyce Brabner, describes the year Pekar battled cancer; Marjane Satrapi's *Persepolis* (2003) describes her youth in Iran; and the two-part *Maus* (1986, 1991) by Art Spiegelman describes his father's experiences during the Holocaust and Spiegelman's ability to relate to his father and his father's past.

Pedro and Me is meaningful to all ages with its message of the inherent inaccuracy of stereotypes. The young adult target audience can especially relate to the impact a friendship can have on an individual as it grows. The fact that relationships can ultimately touch and positively affect so many lives gives this novel added educational import.

The graphic novel is an effective medium for presenting Winick's (and also Zamora's) journey: the joy and fun of young life, Zamora's decline in health and eventual death, Winick's intense feelings of loss and grief, and the ultimate rebirth of Zamora and his work through Winick continuing to spread Zamora's message of protection against AIDS and his commitment to educating young people about the disease. *Pedro and Me* also serves to attach a face to the disease and its effects by showing Zamora full of life and positive energy then as a frail, confused, and sick victim ravaged by AIDS.

Bernadette Flynn Low

Further Reading

Spiegelman, Art. *Maus: A Survivor's Tale: My Father Bleeds History* (1986).

_____. *Maus II: A Survivor's Tale—And Here My Troubles Begin* (1991).

Pekar, Harvey, and Joyce Brabner. *Our Cancer Year* (1994).

Bibliography

Maughan, Shannon. "*Pedro and Me*." Review of *Pedro and Me*, by Judd Winick. *Publishers Weekly* 247, no. 38 (September 1, 2000): 37.

Neace, Melissa. "*Pedro and Me: Friendship, Loss, and What I Learned*." Review of *Pedro and Me*, by Judd Winick. *Library Media Connection* 23, no. 7 (April/May, 2005): 54.

Sieruta, Peter D. "Pedro and Me." Review of *Pedro and Me*, by Judd Winick. *Horn Book Magazine* 76, no. 6 (November/December, 2000): 775-776.

Winick, Judd. "Judd Remembers." *Advocate*, no. 820 (September 12, 2000).

See also: *Maus; Fun Home; Dykes to Watch Out For; Ethel and Ernest; Persepolis*

PERCY GLOOM

Author: Malkasian, Cathy
Artist: Cathy Malkasian (illustrator)
Publisher: Fantagraphics Books
First book publication: 2007

Publication History

Percy Gloom was first published in 2007 by Fanta-graphics Books. The book was the first graphic novel by animation director Cathy Malkasian and marks her transition from one method of storytelling to another. Prior to publishing the novel, Malkasian worked on children's television shows such as *The Wild Thorn-berrys, Rugrats,* and *As Told by Ginger.*

Plot

Percy Gloom tells the story of Percy, a charming old man with a lazy eye who has left home for the first time. He arrives in a small town for an interview with the Safety Now Cautionary Writing Institute. The opportu-nity is a dream-come-true for Percy, who has written to Safety Now for the past twenty years, inquiring about job openings.

Hungry after his long journey, Percy stops at a bakery for three buckwheat muffins and the juice of thirty lemons. According to Percy, these are the only foods he can ingest without suffering terrible night-mares. While there, he meets Tammy, the first of sev-eral characters whose fates Percy affects. Tammy is berating a woman behind the counter. Percy notices her left foot has a terrible infection. Tammy, noticing his stares, turns her aggressions upon him. Percy tries to be helpful by suggesting she treat her infection with medicines. Tammy responds that medicine is poison; when Percy becomes insistent, she violently shoves her foot in his mouth. She states since he does not know of the ancient wisdom of Yagapantha, he need not give her advice.

Percy flees in a panic and searches for a fountain to wash out his mouth. He manages to find one, but before he can gargle, a shepherd with a herd of goats stops him. Distraught, Percy reluctantly heads to Safety Now for his interview.

Percy Gloom. (Courtesy of Fantagraphics Books)

Arriving late, he fumbles through his interview with Margaret, the supervisor for Safety Now. She grows in-creasingly agitated with Percy when his only responses stem from his good-natured desire that no one get hurt. Margaret rejects him, and he leaves the office in de-spair. Fueled by hunger and disappointment, he begins hallucinating the end of his lifelong dreams, and then he faints.

When Percy regains consciousness, he meets Ber-nard, a kindly employee of Safety Now. Bernard first mistakes Percy for an employee, but he apologizes when he learns of his error. Bernard tries to make amends by buying Percy a meal and rescues Percy when he faints a second time. The pair head to Found-er's Park to enjoy a rejuvenating fountain. Bernard also tells Percy more about Tammy and asks about Percy's background.

Feeling invigorated, Percy returns to the Visitor House where he is staying. There, he discovers a basket of buckwheat muffins and a note from Tammy. To his dismay, her feelings of contempt have transformed into obsession for him. He retreats to the solace of his room, where he tells his mother his woes over a radio. She calmly reminds him to turn his head and go to sleep, "for tomorrow is another day."

The next day, Percy discovers Margaret has reconsidered her decision and has hired him. Bursting with excitement, he races toward Safety Now. Before he can continue, he is knocked unconscious by a muffin that is lobbed at his head. When Percy regains consciousness, he discovers he has been taken by Tammy to a vast cavern filled with muffins. Tammy expresses displeasure over his sensitivity and lazy eye, but then

she offers him a muffin to eat. She seems delighted and coy, but a random question causes her to lose her temper once more.

After being literally booted from Tammy's presence, Percy arrives at Safety Now. There, he meets his coworker Leo, a seasoned veteran of the company, and reunites with Bernard. After earning a day off from Margaret, Bernard asks Percy for help in dealing with Tammy. Percy agrees, and Bernard sends him to the Lower Market. There, Percy learns the truth about the cult of Yagapantha: To avoid death, they eat the dying.

Percy also meets Tammy's parents, who reveal Tammy's motivations and inspirations for her cult. They also implore Percy to visit their daughter and to help her come to her senses. Percy leaves the catacombs

Percy Gloom. (Courtesy of Fantagraphics Books)

and confronts Tammy, chastising her for being so un-kind to her parents and other people's relatives. He then departs for home to visit his mother. Over tea and birthday presents, he comes to terms with the regret of never having met his father and the grief stemming from his wife's death.

Filled with renewed confidence, he returns to town to find it destroyed. He also discovers that, in his ab-sence, Tammy has allowed the dying to return to their families. Upon reuniting with Bernard, he learns that Tammy has also found her parents. Percy then visits Margaret, whom he finds weeping over the destruction of Safety Now and her own shortsightedness. Using a telescope his mother invented for his father, he encour-ages her to let go of her failures and try again. The story ends with the line "in the business of caution . . . we are unprepared for happiness."

Characters

- *Percy Gloom,* the protagonist, is an old man with a lazy eye and gap teeth. Polite, kind, and a touch eccentric, he is empathetic and never hesitates to help people. He first comes to the town with the dream of working for Safety Now, but he quickly becomes involved in several of the town's prob-lems.
- *Tammy,* the primary antagonist, is a middle-aged woman with long hair. Angry and stubborn, she bullies everyone in town. Her feelings toward Percy shift from disdain to romantic infatuation. She is also the leader of the cult of Yagapantha, a religion she created as a child to defeat death by devouring the dying.
- *Bernard* is a doctor at the Safety Now Cautionary Writing Institute. Calm and sweet, he quickly be-friends Percy. Despite his calm demeanor, he is the leader of an underground group that combats Tammy's cult, hiding the elderly beneath the city to save them from being devoured by her fol-lowers.
- *Margaret* is the manager at the Safety Now Cau-tionary Writing Institute. She is tall and broad, wears glasses, and has braces. While she has good intentions, she tends to be overemotional

and quick to judge. After the town is destroyed, she feels like she failed to help keep people safe.
- *Lila* is Percy's wife, who died many years before the story begins. Described as a startling beauty, she was a member of the Funnelhead sect, led by a man named Finger. While initially lively and happy, she slowly drifts away from Percy and be-comes more zealous and obsessed with the Fun-nelheads's teachings. In the end, the group is her undoing, as she rolls down a hill to her death, tied to a boulder.
- *Leo* is a dedicated Safety Now employee who is scarred and missing an eye and a hand. The walls in his office are covered with mementos of his safety achievements. Like Percy, he is an older man. He also appears to be in love with his super-visor, Margaret.
- *Tammy's Parents* are a tiny couple with oversized ears who resemble mice. They were once cheese makers, but when Tammy's cult arose, they had to go into hiding or face death at their daughter's hand.

Cathy Malkasian

Cathy Malkasian began her career in the anima-tion industry in the 1990's, working as a designer and storyboard artist before moving into the role of director. Her works include the *Wild Thorn-berrys Movie* and many episodes of the *Curious George* television show. Her first graphic novel, *Percy Gloom*, was published in 2007. Featuring the story of a balloon-headed man who dreams of working for the Safety Now Cautionary Writing Institute, Malkasian propels her lead character through a sinister and dreamlike world with carefully crafted pencil drawings. She won the Eisner Award for Best New Talent for this book. Her follow-up, *Temperance*, tells the story of Lester, a war hero who is unable to recall his past and whose wooden leg is about to abandon him to take off on its own quest. Malkasian's work shows a strong animation influence, and its dream-world logic is carefully situated to create a powerful sense of mood and place in her deeply allegorical stories.

Artistic Style

Malkasian's art strongly reflects her years of working in the animation industry. The architecture and character designs use certain basic shapes to help define and enhance the personalities of both panels and characters.

Percy's body shape is constructed almost entirely of circles and ovals, reflecting his meek and tender demeanor. Bernard has an overly large head to reflect his intelligence and an expressive face to convey his kindness. Safety Now's building resembles a giant egg, and Tammy is drawn in sharp angles and harsh lines. The Gloom household is a large estate, full of bizarre contraptions and stately rooms. In contrast, the homes in which the elderly hide are small and cozy, while Tammy lives in a vast cavern, which is reflective of her lonely life.

The panels are another strength in Malkasian's storytelling; each one manages to further the story without overusing dialogue and to allow the characters to develop and interact naturally. The extra beats and pauses in actions and dialogue give the story an unhurried, natural pace that mirrors human life. Wide shots are used to give a sense of scale and enhance the whimsy by showing off the architecture, and they give depth to the world around Percy and the others. Finally, the choice of sepia tones for the whole comic creates a much warmer feeling than if only stark blacks and whites had been used.

Themes

Percy Gloom's themes revolve around life, happiness, dying, and dealing with the loss of loved ones. Characters like Tammy and Margaret try to fight against aspects of life they feel "threaten" their existence, namely death and danger. However, in their efforts to combat these immutable facets of human life, they both overlook the most important aspect: to enjoy the time one has with those one cares about. On the other hand, Lila, Percy's wife, races to end her time in one life in favor of the next, saying her existence was a sham. Percy's father despaired over the potential for catastrophe and killed himself.

In contrast, Bernard and Tammy's parents have learned to treasure the moments they have. Percy seems to have never thought much about death. Having accepted it as a part of life, he devotes his time to pursuing his dreams and enjoying simple pleasures. His adventures also teach that a person benefits by being open to new experiences. *Percy Gloom* never preaches a right or wrong way to live. Rather, it simply asks that people appreciate the time they are given and try to separate the important worries from the trivial.

Impact

Percy Gloom is Malkasian's first foray into comics after spending many years working in the animation industry for the cable television station Nickelodeon. It was nominated for two Eisner Awards and won the Russ Manning Promising Newcomer Award at the 2008 Comic-Con International: San Diego. *Percy Gloom* is told in a delightful voice; readers find it to be a mature story, full of tender moments and reflections on some of the biggest societal and life questions.

Lyndsey Nicole Raney

Further Reading

Malkasian, Cathy. *Temperance* (2010).

Small, David. *Stitches* (2009).

Thompson, Craig. *Blankets* (2003).

Bibliography

Barsanti, Chris. "PW Comics Week." *Publishers Weekly* 254, no. 23 (June 4, 2007): 36.

Femia, Christine. "Percy Gloom." Review of *Percy Gloom*, by Cathy Malkasian. *Bust* 46 (August/September, 2007): 100.

Goldsmith, Francisca. "*Percy Gloom.*" Review of *Percy Gloom*, by Cathy Malkasian. *Booklist* 103, no. 17 (May 1, 2007): 80.

"*Percy Gloom.*" Review of *Percy Gloom*, by Cathy Malkasian. *Kirkus Reviews* 75, no. 12 (June 15, 2007): 8.

"*Percy Gloom.*" Review of *Percy Gloom*, by Cathy Malkasian. *Publishers Weekly* 254, no. 23 (June 4, 2007): 36.

See also: *Stitches*; *Blankets*; *Jimmy Corrigan*

PERFECT EXAMPLE

Author: Porcellino, John
Artist: John Porcellino (illustrator)
Publisher: Highwater Books; Drawn and Quarterly
First serial publication: 1994-1998 (in *King-Cat Comics and Stories*)
First book publication: 2000

Publication History

John Porcellino made his first handmade, photocopied "zine" in 1982, at the age of fourteen, and began self-publishing his ongoing autobiographical comic series, *King-Cat Comics and Stories*, in 1989. Porcellino photocopied *King-Cat Comics and Stories* and distributed it to his friends and co-workers. As he continued working on the series, his popularity grew, spread by word of mouth. By the early 1990's, Porcellino was one of most recognizable figures in the underground comics scene.

Perfect Example comprises stories that were all originally drawn between 1994 and 1998; the major chapters were completed between 1996 and 1998. The one-off "Live-Evil" appeared in *King-Cat Comics and Stories*, issue 50; the prologue, "Belmont Harbor," was published in *King-Cat Comics and Stories*, issue 47; the epilogue, "Escape to Wisconsin," is from *King-Cat Comics and Stories*, issue 50; and the four central stories in *Perfect Example* ("Haircutting Time," "In-Between Days," "The Fourth of July" and "Celebrated Summer") formed the entirety of issues 52 and 53.

Perfect Example was initially published in 2000 by the small but influential comic book publisher Highwater Books. In 2005, Drawn and Quarterly reissued *Perfect Example* with a new cover design and an updated "Resume and Relevant Information" back page.

Plot

Perfect Example is an autobiographical bildungsroman that takes place during the summer before Porcellino (referred to as "John P." in the book) leaves for college. At the beginning of the summer, John P. starts hanging out with a girl in his class named Tina. The two discover they have similar taste in music and decide to

Perfect Example. (Courtesy of Drawn and Quarterly)

go to a concert together. Their relationship becomes strained, however, when John P. discovers that she drinks and does drugs. After wandering away at a party, John P. imagines his soul leaving his body and floating high above the city.

John P. then falls into a malaise, coming to the conclusion that everything around him feels meaningless. After talking about his problems with his best friend, Fred, John P. calls Kristi, a girl on whom he has a crush, and asks her out on a date. At the end of the night, John P. asks her to be his girlfriend, but Kristi turns him down. Following this rejection, John P. feels even more depressed. A few days later, he goes to a party at John J.'s house, but, feeling awkward about the drinking going on around him, he hides in John J.'s bedroom.

His friend Lita finds him there, and the two begin to talk. They eventually start making out, and John P. leaves the party even more confused about girls than he was before.

A few days later, John P. meets Lita again, but he leaves after being overcome by a wave of depression. John P. then attends a party at Mark Pruitt's house, but feels withdrawn and disconnected. He sees both Kristi and Lita at the party, but he is unable to have a meaningful conversation with either. Later, Fred invites him to see the Fourth of July fireworks with him. However, when John P. sees that Fred has invited Kristi as well, he realizes that the two are dating and gets extremely upset and leaves. Once he gets home, he finds he is locked out and begins crying on his front steps. Mark Pruitt shows up and takes John P. for a ride to help him clear his mind, but John P. cannot help feeling like everything is a dream.

As the summer goes on, John P. begins spending more time by himself. While mowing the lawn one day, he comes to the realization that he creates his own unhappiness and that only he has the power to make himself happy. The next day, he and John Lyons make plans to go to the lake. When John P. discovers Lita

Perfect Example. (Courtesy of Drawn and Quarterly)

has been invited as well, he takes it as an opportunity to overcome his fears. As John P. holds Lita's hand, he feels like he wants to live and be happy for the first time in a long time.

In the epilogue, John P., John J., and John Lyons decide to take a trip to Wisconsin together. The three spend the day skateboarding, and at night, they camp out in the nearby woods. The next morning, as the three take a walk in the woods, John P. feels his depression finally beginning to lift. In the final panel, he assures the reader that he is "very happy."

Characters

- *John P.*, the protagonist, is a teenager preparing to leave for Northern Illinois University in the fall. During the summer, he deals with bouts of depression and anxiety about girls.
- *Lita* is a former classmate of John P. who, after several false starts, eventually becomes his girlfriend. Their relationship is critical to relieving John P.'s depression.
- *Fred* is John's best friend. The two become somewhat distant after Fred starts drinking and begins dating Kristi.
- *Kristi* is a girl on whom John has a crush at the beginning of the graphic novel. She eventually starts dating Fred.
- *John J.* is a friend of John P. who accompanies him on trips to Bluesfest and Wisconsin. He also throws the party where John P. and Lita first get together.
- *John Lyons* is a friend of John P. who accompanies him on trips to Bluesfest, the lake, and Wisconsin. The two often go skateboarding together.
- *Mark Pruitt* is a former classmate of John P. who is described as similar to John P. but smarter. The two become close after Fred starts dating Kristi and Mark invites John P. to his family reunion in Milwaukee.
- *Howard Pruitt* is Mark Pruitt's grandfather. John P. meets him at the Pruitt family reunion, where he encourages John P. to follow his dreams and pursue his interest in music.
- *Harold J.* is a classmate of John P. The two spend their gym class arguing about whether Venom or Hüsker Dü is the better band.

- *Tina* is John P.'s classmate and badminton partner in gym class. The two strike up a friendship, but John P. starts to distance himself from her after he finds out that she drinks and does poppers.

Artistic Style

Porcellino's illustrations are known for their simple, straightforward style. Drawn in black ink (with the exceptions of the prologue, "Belmont Harbor," and the epilogue, "Escape to Wisconsin," which are both drawn in red ink to differentiate them from the main body of the story), there is little detail, shading, or realistic perspective featured in Porcellino's illustrations. His crude figures most closely resemble Charles M. Schulz's *Peanuts* characters. The title page of each chapter, however, features a single panel that, while still simple, features brushwork and shading that suggests the depth of Porcellino's artistic talent. Porcellino has admitted that he purposefully chooses to illustrate his comics in a simple, rough style partially in reaction to his frustrations with the education he received in art school and partially in the belief that it helps make his work more accessible.

Early in his career, Porcellino frequently made the argument, most forcibly in his comic "Well Drawn Funnies #0," that his artwork belongs to a "bad is good" school of punk art that is direct, bold, and embraces ugliness. Since many of the incidents in *Perfect Example* and his other comics are rather bleak (he writes frequently of heartbreak, depression, malaise, and dissatisfaction), he believed it was more honest to create artwork that reflects his dreary outlook on the world. In his later work, however, as he matured as both an artist and as a person, his simple style has become indicative of his interest in Zen. At critical points in *Perfect Example*, Porcellino abandons narrative and lets his simple images of nature and personal serenity speak for themselves.

Themes

Perfect Example is primarily a story about moving out of adolescence and toward some semblance of adulthood. Throughout *Perfect Example,* Porcellino consistently depicts himself as lost and confused, emotionally stunted and ill prepared for the world. Nonetheless, the feelings and circumstances that he describes should be intimately familiar to anyone of a certain age: the difficulty in talking to the opposite sex, the petty squabbles with parents, the days spent doing nothing but "hanging out" at friends' houses, the wide-eyed wonder of watching the world open up. Though at the time Porcellino may have felt misunderstood and out of place, his story turns out to be utterly universal and relatable. There is something reassuring about this fact; though Porcellino has created a testament to the loneliness and difficulty inherent in growing up, he also suggests that no one is truly alone in this pivotal moment.

Looming over this entire story is the theme of depression. As the "Resume and Relevant Information" printed at the back of the book suggests, Porcellino has been struggling with depression for most of his life, starting in high school. The primary struggle in *Perfect Example* concerns Porcellino learning how to deal with his depression, searching (and eventually finding) an outlook on life that will allow him to find meaning and happiness in his world and his personal relationships. The ultimate epiphany of *Perfect Example* is that each person creates his or her happiness or unhappiness.

Impact

Considering that Porcellino's comics have been self-published using only a photocopier, the fact that *Perfect Example* was eventually republished by Drawn and Quarterly, one of the most well-respected publishers of independent comics, is demonstrative of the legitimacy that "zine" culture has obtained in the graphic novel community. When Porcellino began self-publishing *King-Cat Comics and Stories* in 1989, there were few markets available for his unique minimalist style of narrative and illustration. However, looking at the vast number of Web comics being written in the early twenty-first century (many of which feature crude drawing styles and episodic autobiographical narratives that are highly reminiscent of *King-Cat Comic and Stories*) it is hard to overstate Porcellino's contribution to the DIY comics community.

Perfect Example is also remarkable as an example of Porcellino's growth and maturity as an artist. Porcellino's earliest comics were principally known for their anger, dark humor, and punk-rock sensibility. However, while writing and illustrating the minicomics that would become *Perfect Example*, Porcellino shifted his tone as he grew older and eventually married. *Perfect Example* is a much quieter and more sensitive work than many of Porcellino's earlier efforts, which were brazen, where *Perfect Example* is rather sober and melancholy. The honesty and sensitivity about his own depression and suicidal thoughts in *Perfect Example* (and in his other *King-Cat Comics*) has led to a collaboration with the National Film Board of Canada, whereby Porcellino has illustrated *The Next Day* (2011), a graphic novel featuring the true stories of four suicide survivors, written by Paul Peterson and Jason Gilmore.

Stephen Aubrey

Further Reading

Porcellino, John. *Diary of a Mosquito Abatement Man* (2005).

Thompson, Craig. *Blankets* (2003).

Ware, Chris. *Jimmy Corrigan: The Smartest Kid on Earth* (2003).

Bibliography

Arnold, Andrew. "The Complex Simplicity of John Porcellino." *Time*, July 13, 2001. http://www.time.com/time/columnist/arnold/article/0,9565,167115,00.html.

Dodge, Chris. "The Revolution Will Not Be Photocopied." *Utne Reader* 107 (September/October, 2001): 23-25.

Porcellino, John. "Interview: John Porcellino." Interview by Jason Heller. *A.V. Club*, July, 2011. http://www.avclub.com/articles/john-porcellino,14096.

See also: *Diary of a Mosquito Abatement Man*; *Blankets*; *Jimmy Corrigan: The Smartest Kid on Earth*

PERSEPOLIS

Author: Satrapi, Marjane

Artist: Marjane Satrapi (illustrator); Eve Deluze (letterer); Céline Merrien (letterer)

Publisher: L'Association (French); Pantheon Books (English)

First book publication: *Persepolis*, 2000-2003 (English translation 2003, 2004)

Publication History

The first chapter of Marjane Satrapi's autobiographical graphic novel appeared in France in 2000 after Satrapi caught the attention of French comic book artist David B., one of the founders of L'Association, the highly regarded cartoonist collective. Ultimately, *Persepolis* was divided into four books. L'Association published volumes 2-4 in 2001, 2002, and 2003. The series was published to great acclaim, drawing instant comparisons to Art Spiegelman's classic graphic novel *Maus* (1986) and winning the Angoulême International Comics Festival Coup de Coeur Award in 2001. The series was soon translated into several languages and received international acclaim, winning the first Fernando Buesa Blanco Peace Prize in 2003 for its stance against totalitarianism.

The first two French volumes were translated into English by Mattias Ripa and were published in the United States by Pantheon Books as a single volume entitled *Persepolis: The Story of a Childhood* in 2003. Pantheon Books combined the third and fourth volumes, translated by Blake Ferris, into *Persepolis 2: The Story of a Return* (2004). A single-volume edition, *The Complete Persepolis*, combining *Persepolis* and *Persepolis 2*, was made available in the United States in 2007.

Persepolis 2.0, an updated version of *Persepolis* about Iran's 2009 presidential elections, using Satrapi's illustrations and text by two Iranians known as Payman and Sina, has been published online with Satrapi's permission. Although nearly all of the drawings are appropriated from *Persepolis*, Satrapi included one new drawing in which the character Marjane urges her parents to look at Twitter (a Web site that displays

Persepolis. (Courtesy of Pantheon Books)

published text messages) in order to get news about the Iranian elections.

Plot

Persepolis begins at the start of the Iranian Revolution (1978-1980), when Marjane Satrapi is ten years old. Although she dreamed of being a prophet when she was younger, she is resistant to the veil she is suddenly made to wear in school. As she witnesses the rise of the Islamic regime and learns more about the violent history of Iran, her faith in God and her country begins to fade. Marjane eventually becomes enraptured by leftist politics (possibly in imitation of her parents); however, when she meets Siamak and

Mohsen, friends of her parents who had been jailed for their communist convictions, her romantic ideas about political dissidence are put into stark contrast with the horrific tortures Siamak and Mohsen have endured. Her romanticism is further shattered when her beloved Uncle Anoosh is released from prison only to be accused of being a Russian spy and executed.

The Islamic fundamentalists soon gain power in Iran, closing the universities and enforcing sharia (Islamic law) throughout the country. Soon, Iran finds itself at war with neighboring Iraq, and the Satrapi family must endure a life of bomb raids and food shortages.

Marjane, ever the free spirit, starts getting in trouble for mocking the exercises she is taught at her highly religious school. In 1982, Marjane's uncle Taher has a heart attack, brought on by the stress of the war, and dies after being denied a passport to travel to England for open-heart surgery. When the borders are finally reopened a year later, Marjane's parents travel to Turkey and manage to smuggle several gifts for Marjane back from the West. As the war intensifies, many flee Iran, and Marjane has a frightening moment when one of the buildings on her block is destroyed in a bomb. Tensions come to a head when Marjane is finally expelled from a school and her parents decide that it would be safer for her if she left Iran and stayed with one of her mother's friends in Vienna.

In Vienna, Marjane stays with her mother's friend Zozo for ten days, but Zozo eventually decides that there is not enough room and arranges for Marjane to live in a nearby boarding house run by a group of nuns. Marjane eventually falls in with an eccentric group of friends from her new school but is eventually kicked out of her boarding house after getting into a fight with one of the nuns. Marjane then moves in with her friend Julie and begins to experiment with drugs and sex. Later, Marjane's mother comes to visit and helps Marjane find a new apartment leased by Frau Doctor Heller.

Marjane begins dating a man named Enrique, but the relationship fizzles after Enrique realizes he is gay. Marjane then begins dating Markus, a man she calls the first great love of her life. However, that relationship ends when Marjane discovers Markus having sex with another woman. Upset and heartbroken, Marjane fights with Frau Doctor Heller and is thrown out of her room. She spends the next few months homeless, until she eventually catches pneumonia and must be admitted to a hospital. When she finally recovers, Marjane tells her parents she wants to go back to Iran.

Upon her return, Marjane finds it difficult to readjust to living in such an oppressive society. Her family quickly catches her up on the atrocities that have occurred while she was living in Europe. Marjane also visits one of her childhood friends, Kia, who was seriously disabled while fighting in the war. Marjane falls into a deep depression and attempts to commit suicide but soon sets out to become a "sophisticated woman."

At a friend's party, Marjane meets a man named Reza, and the two begin dating even though they are polar opposites. Marjane applies to art school, but after enrolling, she is nearly expelled in her first weeks for expressing her Westernized attitudes about gender. Finding it difficult to be an unmarried couple in Iran, Marjane and Reza decide to marry. As soon as the ceremony is complete, Marjane feels trapped; after only one month of marriage, the two are living in separate bedrooms. Right before Marjane gets her diploma, she and Reza are assigned a project to create a mythological theme park. Despite their best efforts, their proposal is rejected, and Marjane realizes her marriage has fallen apart. After graduating and getting her diploma, Marjane asks Reza for a divorce and decides to immigrate to France, where she can finally be free.

Volumes

- *Persepolis: The Story of a Childhood* (2003). Collects the French editions of *Persepolis 1* and *Persepolis 2*. Recounts Marjane's childhood in Iran until her departure for Vienna.
- *Persepolis 2: The Story of a Return* (2004). Collects the French editions of *Persepolis 3* and *Persepolis 4*. Recounts Marjane's years in Vienna and her eventual return to Iran, ending with her immigration to France.

Characters

- *Marjane Satrapi*, the author and protagonist, begins the novel as a ten-year-old girl living in Iran during the Islamic Revolution in 1980. She grows up during the novel, eventually leaving Iran for Austria in 1984, returning to Iran four years later and, at the story's end, leaving Iran for France in 1994.

- *Ebi Satrapi*, Marjane's father, is a leftist who participated in many protests before the revolution but who becomes less politically active once the

Islamic regime seizes power. An engineer, he attempts to live a Western-style middle-class life despite the restrictions of the Islamic state.

- *Taji Satrapi*, Marjane's mother, is a vocal leftist prior to the Islamic Revolution. She urges Marjane to get an education and further herself despite the restrictions the Islamic regime has placed on women. Although Marjane finds her

Persepolis. (Courtesy of Pantheon Books)

difficult at times, the two still have a close relationship.

- *Marjane's grandmother* lives with Marjane and her parents. Her husband was an Iranian prince who was imprisoned and tortured under the reign of the last shah. She is Marjane's closest confidante and often acts as the voice of reason in the story.
- *Uncle Anoosh*, Marjane's uncle, is a communist who was imprisoned under the shah. He is freed after the revolution and lives with Marjane, but he is later arrested by the Islamic regime and executed under suspicion of being a Russian spy.
- *Markus*, Marjane's first love, is a literature student living in Vienna. They break up when Marjane discovers him having sex with another woman.
- *Reza*, Marjane's husband, is a fellow artist who Marjane meets at a party. They later go to art school together and eventually marry. After several years together, Marjane realizes that she no longer loves Reza and divorces him shortly before leaving for France.

Artistic Style

Persepolis is written in a simple storyboard format. Panels are placed in rows that may vary in size and detail, but the overall page layout is uniform and neat. Panels always move left to right, top to bottom. The layout is more akin to text than to the nonlinear layouts of many contemporary graphic novels. Satrapi makes few experimental forays beyond her basic storyboard format: Full-page spreads are rare, and the illustrations are always contained within neat black frames.

The illustrations are black and white, with elegant black lines rendered into simple stark figures. Using this palette, Satrapi does manage to create detailed, beautiful illustrations on occasion, but in general, she tends toward a minimalist style. Her simple monochromatic illustrations lend the story a sobriety and gloom befitting a depiction of a highly restrictive society. The black-and-white color scheme becomes indicative of Satrapi's own sense of repression living in religiously fundamentalist Iran. However, through the conservativeness of the illustrations, Satrapi is able to create an uncomplicated graphic language. Because her illustrations are so simple and unadorned, there is little fear that readers will miss or misunderstand the graphic novel's plot and nuances; the message behind Satrapi's anecdotes is always clear and explicit. Satrapi's story has no shades of gray, a crucial quality for a graphic novel that intends to impart an important political message. Rather than distract the reader with impressive or artful visuals, Satrapi has chosen an artistic style that places an emphasis on the story's content rather than on its visual context.

Themes

The principle theme of *Persepolis*—and the one that has garnered it the most attention in the United States—is its depiction of the cultural conflicts between Islamic states and the Western world. As a memoir, *Persepolis* offers a truer picture of life inside an Islamic regime than many traditional sources. While some of what *Persepolis* depicts may confirm Western assumptions about Islamic fundamentalist states (such as the oppression of women, an opposition to Western influences, censorship and limits on the freedom of speech), *Persepolis* also depicts a surprising side of life inside Iran. While acknowledging many of the limitations of life inside the Iranian regime, *Persepolis* suggests that life there is, in some ways, not dissimilar from the lives Westerners lead. Marjane, her family, and her friends still manage to find pockets of freedom amid the repressive society; people throw dance parties and listen to the pop music of American singer Michael Jackson, and women wear makeup and attend university. While depicting some of the harsh realities of life inside a repressive Islamic state, Satrapi still manages to convey the basic humanity, the simple commonality, of life in the late twentieth century.

The underlying theme of *Persepolis* is the importance of family. Satrapi repeatedly emphasizes the support her family offers her, how they give her the will to survive and persevere despite the bleak conditions of the Iranian Revolution. At the beginning of *Persepolis 2*, Marjane even returns to Iran from Europe in order to be closer to her family. In this way, *Persepolis* can be best understood as a bildungsroman, a story of a young woman learning to be an artist, supported by a loving and compassionate family until she is ready to finally leave Iran and discover her true purpose. In this way, Marjane's relationship with her family mirrors her relationship to Iran itself. Although both living in Iran and her family are necessary to her development, at the conclusion of *Persepolis 2*, Marjane realizes that she must leave both in order to find herself.

Impact

Although it is a notable entry in the graphic memoir tradition, *Persepolis*'s main impact has been political. Satrapi's books have been internationally celebrated for their depiction of a child living through the Iranian Revolution. They have offered the Western world a unique perspective of life inside contemporary Iran, showing the Islamic state to be both much more terrifying and much more mundane than commonly thought. *Persepolis* has become one of the most popular of a growing number of memoirs being written by first- or second-generation Iranian women living abroad. (Other notable titles include Azar Nafisi's 2003 memoir *Reading Lolita in Tehran* and Ru'yā Ḥakkākiyān's 2004 *Journey from the Land of No: A Girlhood Caught in Revolutionary Iran*.) Since its publication, *Persepolis* has regularly appeared on the syllabi of gender and political science classes in universities across the United States. The popularity of *Persepolis* has brought Satrapi to the forefront of political discussions, particularly during the 2009 Iranian elections. She has used her celebrity both to bring awareness to the plight of Iranians and to stress the common bonds that unite all humanity.

Films

Persepolis. Directed by Marjane Satrapi and Vincent Paronnaud. 2.4.7 Films, 2007. This feature-length French film is animated in a style similar to Satrapi's illustrations. Chiara Mastroianni voices the character of Marjane, and Catherine Deneuve and Simon Abkarian portray her mother and father. (Sean Penn's voice replaces Abkarian's in the English version.) Though a condensed version of the events of *Persepolis* and *Persepolis 2*, the film is nonetheless faithful to the source material because of Satrapi's involvement as a co-writer and co-director. It was awarded the Jury Prize at the 2007 Cannes Film Festival and nominated for a 2008 Academy Award for Best Animated Feature.

Stephen Aubrey

Further Reading

Bechdel, Alison. *Fun Home: A Family Tragicomic* (2006).

Satrapi, Marjane. *Embroideries* (2005).

Spiegelman, Art. *Maus* (1986, 1991).

Bibliography

Chute, Hillary. "The Texture of Retracing in Marjane Satrapi's *Persepolis*." *Women's Studies Quarterly* 36, no. 1/2 (Spring/Summer, 2008): 92-110.

Malek, Amy. "Memoir as Iranian Exile Cultural Production: A Case Study of Marjane Satrapi's *Persepolis* Series." *Iranian Studies* 39, no. 3 (2006): 353-380.

Satrapi, Marjane. "*Persepolis*: A State of Mind." *Literal, Latin American Voices* 13 (Summer, 2008): 44-47.

See also: *Maus*; *Chicken with Plums*; *Embroideries*; *Fun Home*

PHOTOGRAPHER, THE:
INTO WAR-TORN AFGHANISTAN WITH DOCTORS WITHOUT BORDERS

Author: Lefèvre, Didier

Artist: Emmanuel Guibert (illustrator); Frédéric Lemercier (colorist); Didier Lefèvre (cover artist); Danica Novgorodoff (cover artist)

Publisher: Dupuis (French); First Second (English)

First book publication: *Le Photographe*, 2003, 2004, 2006 (English translation, 2009)

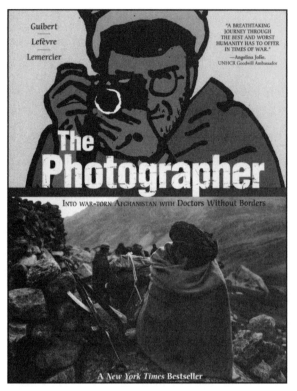

The Photographer. (Courtesy of First Second Books)

Publication History

The Photographer: Into War-Torn Afghanistan with Doctors Without Borders was initially printed to much acclaim by the French publisher Dupuis as part of a three-volume set of graphic novels in 2003, 2004, and 2006. Based on its positive reception, it was then published in the United States in 2009. The photographs, which form the core of the story, were taken in 1986 during Didier Lefèvre's journey with a French branch of the international organization Doctors Without Borders, as they traveled the war-torn mountain regions of Afghanistan providing aid to the regional natives, many of whom found themselves caught in the crossfire between insurgents and their Soviet aggressors. It was not until nearly twenty years later that Lefèvre collaborated with his neighbor, friend, and comics artist Emmanuel Guibert to publish this story.

The Photographer is a unique graphic novel that combines both Lefèvre's powerful black-and-white photos and Guibert's earthy comics art, which continued to win academic, comics, and publisher awards well after its initial release in the United States. Unfortunately, Lefèvre died in 2007 and did not live to see the publication of his novel in the United States or the great acclaimed it received.

Plot

The book opens with an introduction by translator Alexis Siegel, who provides context for the journey, which includes background information about the mission of Médecins Sans Frontières (MSF), the French branch of Doctors Without Borders, that further contextualizes the humanitarian mission in Afghanistan.

Siegel astutely points out that most American readers did not even think about Afghanistan prior to September 11, 2001, let alone maintain any substantial knowledge of the country or its people.

The first part of *The Photographer* depicts the beginning of Lefèvre's journey in July of 1986, in Paris, France, and then Peshawar, Pakistan. Lefèvre recounts his first days in Pakistan as he acclimates himself to the region, its people, and its customs as well as to the members of the MSF team that will travel to neighboring Afghanistan to assist Afghans in need. Part of this preparation includes the need to find armed escorts to accompany (and protect) the MSF team as it crosses the mountain passes from Pakistan into Afghanistan. As Lefèvre points out, Afghanistan's borders were under Soviet surveillance, and convoys faced detainment or even helicopter and artillery fire. Furthermore, the threat of bandits, kidnappers, corrupt regional authorities, and other threats necessitated armed support in the convoy. By the end of August and within one month of arriving in Pakistan, the MSF team sets out on its journey over the mountainous passes into Afghanistan.

Early in the journey, Lefèvre relates the difficulties encountered, such as traveling for long periods at a time, hiking over rough and rocky terrain, making

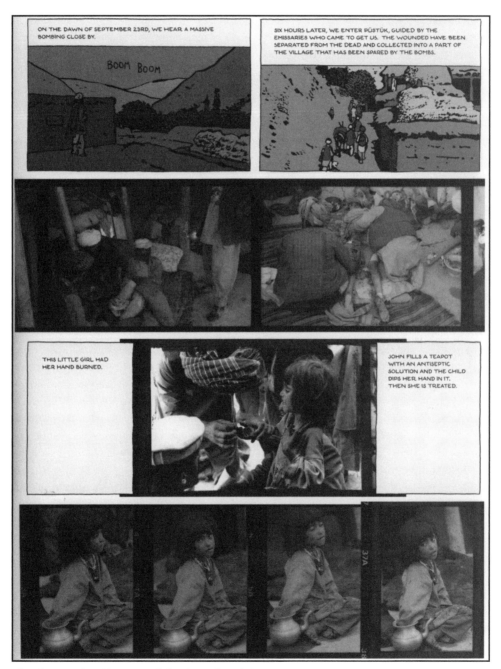

The Photographer. (Courtesy of First Second Books)

do with the lack of substantial food, and other hardships as simple as navigating the social taboos related to relieving oneself. He also documents the culture of Afghanistan prior to the fundamentalist Taliban's rise to power, discussing gender roles and relations. In particular, he highlights the role of Dr. Juliette Fournot, the female chief of the caravan, in a patriarchal society.

The second part of *The Photographer* continues with the journey across the mountainous regions between Pakistan and Afghanistan and the MSF team's arrival at its first destination, the valley of Teshkan. This part of the book covers the team's humanitarian mission and constitutes the bulk of Lefèvre's formal responsibilities as the MSF photographer. However, after spending one month in the country and running low on supplies and patience, he decides that his mission is complete and makes the decision against all guidance from Fournot and others on the team to return to Pakistan and then France on his own.

The final part of *The Photographer* documents Lefèvre's journey back to Pakistan across the mountains. As Lefèvre soon discovers, this is even more lonely and difficult than the trip in the better-supplied and faster-moving caravan on his initial trip. He struggles to navigate the landscape and cultural barrier with uncooperative guides, who eventually abandon him along the way. Lefèvre nearly perishes in a snowstorm alone on a mountain prior to falling into company with his second set of profiteering guides, who lead him to safety, though at the expense of nearly all of his funds. Just as Lefèvre completes his journey out of Afghanistan and crosses the border into Pakistan, a local official temporarily holds him prisoner in his hostel for illegally crossing the border. Shortly thereafter, Lefèvre finally makes his way back to Peshawar, only one day before the MSF team arrives. Days later, Lefèvre flies back to France, reunites with his family, and begins the process of developing his film and his story.

Characters
- *Didier Lefèvre*, the protagonist, is a French twenty-something photographer for an MSF team traveling into Afghanistan to treat the numerous civilian casualties of the Afghan-Soviet conflict. *The Photographer* documents his personal journey from naïve Westerner to a more experienced and worldly messenger and voice for the victims of this conflict.
- *Dr. Juliette Fournot* is the leader of the MSF team in Afghanistan. She worked there for a total of eight years, overseeing and participating in the rotation of MSF teams in the region during five of them. She established and maintained relations with the Afghans until she left for the United States in 1988 with John (the team's surgeon, whom she later married) and established the U.S. arm of MSF.
- *Regis* is a nurse anesthesiologist who accompanies the MSF team on multiple missions out of a desire to help those who have no assistance from their government or other domestic groups.
- *Robert* is a doctor on the MSF team who also participates in multiple missions. He stays behind when the team returned from its rotation. Like Regis, he amicably helps acclimate Lefèvre to the Afghan culture and environment.
- *Mahmed*, the translator for the MSF team, helps Lefèvre adjust to the Afghan culture and environment and teaches him the rudimentary basics of Dari, the Persian dialect spoken there.
- *Najmudin*, a lieutenant of Bassir Khan, leads the security detail for the MSF team and the rest of the caravan as it travels across the mountains. Lefèvre grows to admire and respect him.
- *Aider Shah*, the leader of the Nuristan region, protects and supports the members of the MSF team. Lefèvre initially distrusts him but grows to respect him, especially after Shah rescues him from the profiteering guide "Wolf" and his men.
- *Bassir Khan*, the leader of the Yaftal Valley, helps support the MSF team in its mission to provide aid to the wounded Afghans.

Artistic Style
The Photographer is presented in an oversized format that stands out from most traditional graphic novels because of its unique artistic style: It combines the black-and-white photographs of Lefèvre, the color comics art of Guibert, and the design layouts of colorist Frédéric Lemercier. Guibert eschews a mainstream

comic book approach to his art; instead, he embraces a more minimalist, comic-oriented style in his work. This generalized representation of the Afghans allows for a more universal application of the art to real life and enables the reader to make the reasonable assumption that many Afghans endure similar experiences. The black-and-white photographs are particularly poignant, as these experiences demonstrate many of the "gray areas" in this world seemingly bereft of color. Despite Lefèvre's use of black and white, Guibert incorporates color in his drawings, depending heavily on an earth-toned palette, which reflects the environment where the story takes place. Guibert and Lefèvre also used the photographs as their outline and the art to fill in the gaps; this is clearly seen in such instances as the trip across the mountains. The art is blackened out to reflect the pitch of night. Furthermore, the photographs are displayed as if one were looking directly at the developed film itself; some are viewed as close-ups and others as the actual strips of film. This style gives a less polished and more visceral feel to the overall layout of the book, underscoring the realism of this narrative.

Finally, one cannot overlook the effect of the size of *The Photographer*. The size allows for large, sweeping landscapes and provides the creators with the space necessary to convey a small portion of the epic characteristics of this journey.

Themes

The primary themes present in *The Photographer* involve the two interrelated ideas of the journey from ignorance to knowledge and the need of witnesses to tell the stories of the marginalized groups they come to know. At its most basic level, *The Photographer* recounts the three-month journey that Lefèvre undertakes with the MSF team. This journey results in his departure from the comfort and safety of France to the grueling hardships and dangers of Pakistan and Afghanistan. The reader follows Lefèvre as he grows out of a state of naïveté and a sometimes narrow viewpoint. His personal journey out of ignorance is perhaps best represented in his harrowing snowstorm survival—an isolated and near-fatal experience but one that is not uncommon for the indigenous people. He realizes that

this experience is simply part of the way of life for the Afghans.

Lefèvre's desire to return to Afghanistan indicates he recognizes the significance of his broadening understanding of the world. It also underscores the second theme of *The Photographer*: his acceptance of the role of witness to the burden the Afghans bore under the conflict among themselves and with the Soviets. Even the publication of *The Photographer* highlights Lefèvre's desire to be that witness. This message is one that Siegel points out in the introduction and is one that most Western readers would not have otherwise noted.

Impact

When it was published in the United States in 2009, *The Photographer* garnered significant critical acclaim from both comics and mainstream audiences alike. This book is one representative of an emerging hybrid of comics and journalism. Unlike many journalistic comics publications, however, *The Photographer* relies upon the power of both comics and photography in conjunction with traditional prose and comics text boxes and word bubbles. This mixed-media approach conveys the plight of the Afghans and the hardships endured by Lefèvre and the MSF team through multiple lenses. Furthermore, *The Photographer* informs Western audiences of Doctors Without Borders' mission to provide medical aid to those who do not have access to this basic necessity.

Additionally, the many awards the work received from academic institutions within the first couple of years following its publication serve as an indication that *The Photographer* had an immediate impact in secondary and postsecondary institutions. It further demonstrates the literary credibility of comics and graphic novels and the power of the comics medium to communicate relevant, current, and powerful messages.

Forrest C. Helvie

Further Reading

Folman, Ari, and David Polonsky. *Waltz with Bashir: A Lebanon War Story* (2009).
Sacco, Joe. *Footnotes in Gaza* (2009).
Stassen, Jean-Philippe. *Deogratias: A Tale of Rwanda* (2006).

Bibliography

Goldsmith, Francisca. *The Readers' Advisory Guide to Graphic Novels*. Chicago: American Library Association, 2010.

Hedges, Chris. "What War Looks Like." Review of *The Photographer: Into War-Torn Afghanistan with Doctors Without Borders*, by Didier Lefèvre and Emmanuel Guibert. *The New York Times*, May 24, 2009, BR5.

McKinney, Mark. *History and Politics in French-Language Comics and Graphic Novels*. Jackson: University Press of Mississippi, 2008.

See also: *Waltz with Bashir*; *Footnotes in Gaza*; *Deogratias*; *Burma Chronicles*; *Alan's War*

PLAIN JANES, THE

Author: Castellucci, Cecil
Artist: Jim Rugg (illustrator); Jared K. Fletcher (letterer)
Publisher: DC Comics
First book publication: 2007

Publication History

The Plain Janes (also known as *The P.L.A.I.N. Janes*) was published by Minx, a short-lived American publisher of original graphic novels for teen girls, and was the imprint's first publication in 2007. Minx was an experimental imprint of DC Comics that lasted from 2007 to 2008. Minx's goal was to reach teenage girls who were already reading manga and graphic novels; however, reaching the target audience was difficult because of the unwillingness of comic shops to carry the line.

The Plain Janes is Cecil Castellucci's first graphic novel. Castellucci, a young-adult and short-story author, is a dual citizen of the United States and Canada. *The Plain Janes* takes some inspiration from Castellucci's life: during high school in New York she would see Keith Haring's drawings in the subways.

Illustrator Jim Rugg is best known for *Street Angel* (2005, written by Brian Maruca). He chose to work with Castellucci because he enjoyed her previous books, *Boy Proof* (2005) and *Queen of Cool* (2006).

Plot

Jane moves with her family from Metro City to suburbia after a bomb explodes in a nearby café and nearly kills her. She starts at a new high school with a new personality and a new look. She shuns the popular table to sit with a group of misfits, each named Jane (though spelled differently), whom she feels drawn toward, though they, at first, are aloof.

Jane's mother is overprotective and constantly checks in on Jane, causing her embarrassment. Jane escapes by trying out for different clubs and writing to a John Doe back in Metro City. John Doe was in the explosion too; Jane visited him before she moved. She found his sketchbook in his hospital room and took it to

---

Cecil Castellucci

Writer Cecil Castellucci is a creator who has worn a number of hats, recording music and performing in the band Nerdy Girl under her stage name Cecil Seaskull and writing acclaimed young adult novels, including *Boy Proof*, *The Queen of Cool*, and *Beige*. In 2007 she authored the first graphic novel released by DC Comics' Minx line of young adult works, *The P.L.A.I.N. Janes* (art by Jim Rugg). The story focuses on a teenager named Jane who moves to the suburbs following a terrorist attack on her hometown. There she bonds with three other girls named Jane at the high school reject table and the foursome use art to transform their lives. A sequel, *Janes in Love*, was published the next year, before the Minx line was discontinued. Castellucci's stories bring political overtones into traditional young adult material and attempt to grapple with serious issues within the confines of the young adult format.

---

fill it with her own sketches, one day hoping to return it. Initially Jane does not share her past with anyone, but eventually she opens up.

One day, walking through her new neighborhood, Jane discovers that a strip mall is being planned. She convinces the other Janes by appealing to their special talents to help her create street art in the demolished area in order to get people to think about beauty instead of consumerism. People Loving Art in Neighborhoods or P.L.A.I.N. is formed.

The police are not amused by P.L.A.I.N., and eventually the town sets a curfew, but Jane keeps her group together.

Meanwhile, Jane's letters are returned from the hospital in Metro City. Her friend Damon drives her there to find out what has happened to John Doe. She discovers that John Doe woke up, that his name is Miroslaw, and that he has returned to Poland. His attending nurse gives Jane some information on him, and she decides to try to find him.

Soon, students stand up for P.L.A.I.N. On New Year's Eve, the police chief forbids the annual ball drop out of fear of large groups of people congregating in public, because doing so might lead to an act of art. The Janes fill the New Year's ball with paint and plan to push it off the clock tower, but the plan is abandoned when no one shows up. However, Damon pushes the ball off, splattering paint and glitter into the main town square. He is arrested for vandalism, though Jane confesses her guilt.

The Janes and James, the only boy member, urge Jane to keep the group together. In the end, Jane writes to Miroslaw and plans to send him a blank sketchbook to replace the one she took, hoping he will send it back to her one day filled with his art.

Characters

- *Jane*, a.k.a. *Main Jane*, the protagonist, is a high school girl living in Kent Waters. She organizes P.L.A.I.N. with a group of misfits. She was in an explosion in Metro City and is dealing with trauma stemming from the event.
- *Jane* is a chubby teenage girl involved with the drama club; she thinks she is a comedian. She is a misfit and never gets any roles in the school plays. She becomes one of Jane's friends and joins P.L.A.I.N.
- *Jayne* is the scientific brains of the group. She is also the most shy of the misfits and the only one who wears glasses. She is the first to join P.L.A.I.N. She plans the successful execution of the art project.
- *Polly Jane* is the tallest member of P.L.A.I.N. and is a jock, though she is often the benchwarmer. She joins P.L.A.I.N. because Jane promises to help her get playing time on the soccer field.
- *Cindy* is a popular high school student and tries to make friends with Jane. Initially, she appears as an antagonist, but eventually, she supports P.L.A.I.N. She is a snob and gives preferential treatment to Jane over the others in P.L.A.I.N.
- *Officer Sanchez* is the police chief of Kent Waters and Cindy's father. He is an outspoken opponent

of P.L.A.I.N., calling the group vandals. With the city's support, he imposes a curfew and cancels the New Year's Eve ball-dropping ceremony. He catches Damon, who he thinks is behind all the acts of subterfuge, and refuses to listen to Jane when she confesses to being the group leader.
- *James* is a gay high school student and is daring and outspoken. Though warned by the principal not to do so, he sings in front of the school at noon. Jane asks him to join P.L.A.I.N., and he helps plan its final caper.
- *Damon* is a high school student and Jane's crush. He drives Jane to Metro City to find out about John Doe. He helps Jane pull off the final stunt on New Year's. He is caught by Officer Sanchez and is arrested.
- *John Doe*, a.k.a. *Miroslaw Raminski*, is a young man who was in the explosion with Jane. He is in a coma in Metro City hospital until the end, when he returns to his home in Poland. He is the catalyst for Jane's interest and participation in art. Jane visited him daily and writes to him after she moved.

Artistic Style

Most famous for *Street Angel*, Rugg invested more than one year of work in *The Plain Janes*. Rugg uses clean line work reminiscent of indie cartoonists such as Daniel Clowes and Craig Thompson. He uses gray tones with a high attention to character design. He focuses on natural body language and clothing and fashion, which allow the characters to be quickly identifiable. His use of gray scale for emphasis and eye movement aids contrast within and across panels, and his shading and style do not change with mood or tone. Instead, Rugg relies on the character's body language to convey mood. The characters generate a great deal of movement, and even for a close-up on a character's face, Rugg pays close attention to emotional detail.

The layout of the panels is intuitive and allows for easy reading. Most panels are entirely filled, lending a feeling of closeness. The text is also intuitive, with narrative text in a box, personal thought bubbles, speech bubbles, and portions of Jane's letters and postcards overlaying an image, which helps with the flow of the story and directs the eye across the panel onto the drawing and then into the next panel.

Jared Fletcher is the letterer for *The Plain Janes*. He uses different lettering for sections of Jane's letters and postcards to John Doe and for conversations; however, all characters have the same lettering for their speech. Sound effects, signs, and extra visual items have their own distinct lettering, making the world appear more realistic.

Themes

The Plain Janes is a coming-of-age and a survival story with underlying themes of love and friendship. Castellucci immediately introduces the reader to danger with a retelling of Jane's near-death experience by a bomb explosion, linking the story to modern-day fears of terrorism. Throughout the course of the book, Jane's life slowly improves as she comes to rely on a close-knit group of friends and finds an outlet through creativity. The coming-of-age story is also about surviving overbearing parents and teenage dramas, making new friends, and finding safety in the tumultuous course of teenage years. This book suggests that art is an outlet for frustrations. Further, it compels readers to look at their own neighborhoods and to question how they are living.

The layout enhances the themes of *The Plain Janes*. Rugg portrays emotions in close-up panels, which allows readers to feel empathy. For Castellucci, being an outsider does not mean being alone. The characters also convey that uniqueness can help a person survive rough patches by being independent and confident despite the small insecurities everyone has at one time or another.

Impact

The Plain Janes breaks the mold of Modern Age comics with its female-centric cast and plot. The story line is different from that of the typical hero or superhero comic and takes an introspective look at the healing powers of art and of friendship; Jane does not remain "heroic" throughout, running away from the final art display when no one shows up. The supposed antagonist is portrayed ambiguously, as Cindy remains

in contact with Jane throughout the book and supports P.L.A.I.N. at the end.

The art style represents a departure for Rugg. He uses a more cleanly drawn style and focuses primarily on depicting character emotion, fashion, and movement, helping him to capture the attention of a young female audience. Castellucci's focus on psychological turmoil and healing, and her inclusion of stereotypical misfits allows her to connect with a broad spectrum of young women.

Michelle Martinez

Further Reading

Alexovich, Aaron. *Kimmie66* (2007).
Castellucci, Cecil, and Jim Rugg. *Janes in Love* (2008).
Donner, Rebecca, and Inaki Miranda. *Burnout* (2008).

Bibliography

Alsup, Janet. "One Female Reader Reading YAL: Understanding Norman Holland's Identity Themes Thirty Years Later." In *Young Adult Literature and Adolescent Identity Across Cultures and Classrooms: Contexts for the Literary Lives of Teens*. New York: Routledge, 2010.

Castellucci, Cecil. "Creating Memorable Characters." In *2009 Children's Writer's and Illustrators Market*, edited by Alice Pope. Cincinnati: Writer's Digest Books, 2008.

Rugg, Jim. "Cecil Interviews *Plain Janes* Co-Creator Jim Rugg." Interview by Cecil Castellucci. *Newsarama*, May 18, 2007. http://blog.newsarama.com/2007/05/18/cecil-interviews-plain-janes-co-creator-jim-rugg.

_____. "Jim Rugg Aims to Catch Your Eye with *Plain Janes*." Interview by Arune Singh. *Comic Book Resources*, December 28, 2006. http://www.comicbookresources.com/?page=article&id=8952.

Sherman, Bill. "Graphic Novel Review: *The Plain Janes* by Cecil Castellucci and Jim Rugg." Review of *The Plain Janes*, by Cecil Castellucci and Jim Rugg. *Graphic Novel Review*, May 23, 2007. http://blogcritics.org/books/article/graphic-novel-review-the-plain-janes.

See also: *Blankets*; *Ghost World*; *Scott Pilgrim*

PLAYBOY, THE

Author: Brown, Chester
Artist: Chester Brown (illustrator)
Publisher: Drawn and Quarterly
First serial publication: 1990 (*Yummy Fur*, issues 21-23)
First book publication: 1992

Publication History

The Playboy, first titled "Disgust," is an autobiographical graphic novel that originally appeared in issues 21-23 of Canadian comics creator Chester Brown's serial (and controversial) comic *Yummy Fur*. Brown self-published seven issues of *Yummy Fur* as a minicomic from 1983 to 1986, at which point he began working with publishers; *Yummy Fur* was published as a full-size comic in 1995. During the nine-year span between 1986 and 1995, Brown published thirty-two issues. For issues 21-23, Brown worked with an independent Canadian publisher, Vortex Comics (founded in 1982, but defunct as of 1994). In 1991, he left Vortex Comics and began publishing with the newly established Drawn and Quarterly. *The Playboy* was published as a collection in 1992 and, as of 2011, is out of print. Other works from *Yummy Fur* were also collected as their own publications, including *Ed the Happy Clown* (1989) and the Eisner Award-nominated *I Never Liked You* (1994).

Plot

The Playboy is Brown's autobiographical account of his addiction to pornography, his struggle with the guilt and shame that followed masturbation, his paranoia at the possibility of being caught, and his difficulty relating to other people in his life. It is told in two main parts, and it ends with an epilogue.

Part 1 begins in the summer of 1975. An impish (and older), winged Chester Brown acts as both a time-traveling narrator and as a symbol of young Brown's conscience. Young Brown is unable to see or hear his older conscience. Older Brown escorts the reader to the suburb in which he lived and into a church, where fifteen-year-old Brown sits, unable to concentrate on the sermon because he has been thinking about the *Playboy* magazine he saw at the Bonimart. After this day at church, Brown begins purchasing *Playboy* magazines, masturbating to images of pinups and then hiding, throwing away, or destroying the magazines, only to purchase more (sometimes the same issues) again.

Part 2 begins with young Brown trying to find a safe place to destroy a recently purchased *Playboy*, and he chooses the fireplace in his family's living room. The next day, he wakes, paranoid and worried someone might find evidence, such as the magazine's charred spine, in the fireplace or the ash can. Only after meticulously examining the magazine's burnt spine does he feel assured no one could recognize it. It is not the last *Playboy* magazine he purchases, though.

The Brown family goes on vacation that summer, and his anxiety about being caught masturbating or the chance of someone seeing his recently purchased *Playboy* overwhelms him. At one point, his nervousness makes him ill. This is also the summer his mother dies, though her death is told in passing only. After narrowly avoiding detection by his younger brother Gordon, Brown again attempts to stop purchasing *Playboy*.

In 1982, Brown is with first real girlfriend, Kris, and he throws out all his magazines, not only because he is worried about being caught with them but also because he hopes that having sex regularly will make him want to look at the magazines less. The section ends with narrator/conscience Brown admitting that he likes masturbation better than intercourse and that he still sometimes purchases the magazines. He explains that he only keeps the pictures of the Playmates he likes.

The epilogue brings the story to 1990, around the time of original publication. Brown asks his current girlfriend, Gerbs, if she had gone through his trash basket a year prior and taken from it an issue of *Playboy* he had discarded. Though she says she had not, Brown does not seem to believe her. *The Playboy* ends with her telling Brown that he is confused.

Characters

- *Chester Brown*, the protagonist, is a shy, fifteen-year-old boy who struggles with loneliness, guilt, and an addiction to pornography.
- *Gordon Brown*, Brown's younger brother, appears only three times, but each time, he potentially discovers or actually interrupts what Chester is doing or about to do.
- *Kris* is Brown's first real girlfriend. Brown is in his twenties at the time of their relationship and hopes that having sex regularly will help him stop purchasing and masturbating to *Playboy* magazines.
- *John* is a friend Brown helps to move. He has a dresser full of pornography and tries to hide it at first. Later, Brown tells the story to Kris while they are in bed, and Kris is disgusted.
- *An unnamed friend* is featured in the epilogue. Brown walks and talks with him, keeping from him the secret that he purchased all the *Playboy* magazines he had thrown away.
- *Gerbs* is Brown's girlfriend in the epilogue and is shown stretched out on his bed. He accuses her of taking a copy of *Playboy* out of his trash.

Artistic Style

The most immediate and notable artistic feature of *The Playboy* is its unusual white-on-black format: The pages are black while the images and text are white. Brown uses minimal shading in *The Playboy*, favoring clean lines and more white space.

The page layout and panel organization are equally important. As in other of Brown's books, the panels were created separately and arranged on the page later. Panels are stacked no more than three a page, with the majority of pages having two panels and some only one. They are hand drawn and asymmetrically aligned, rather than ruled and straight. The panels look relatively small on the expansive black background, and this contrast makes the images appear both isolated and vulnerable to exposure, both metaphors for how Brown feels about himself.

Themes

The Playboy is strictly Brown's story. The other characters who make brief appearances—his brother, his neighbors, peers from school, and two of his girlfriends—are mostly foils for his paranoia as people who could potentially catch him masturbating, purchasing a *Playboy* magazine, or hoarding pictures of Playmates.

Furthermore, Brown portrays himself as isolated and incapable of intimacy, either physical or emotional. He rarely talks in the memories, partly because there is never really anybody around. Even when others are present, however, readers are left with the older Brown as narrator. Apart from guilt and shame, other emotions are hardly expressed at all. The young Brown briefly experiences shock and disgust when he encounters a centerfold of a black Playmate, revealing some racial prejudice on his part. Even the death of Brown's mother is mentioned only in passing, as a side note of what else happened the summer he began buying *Playboy* magazines.

The narrator on which Brown relies (a small, older version of himself, with batlike wings, who flies in and out of the scenes) brings to mind the angel and demon that are sometimes seen on opposite shoulders of a protagonist. In fact, the text has deeply religious undertones: The narrative begins with Brown daydreaming in a church; after Brown's mother dies, readers see her on a cloud, with angel wings, potentially watching him bury a copy of *Playboy*; and when Brown masturbates, he uses a nontraditional grip that resembles a pair of praying hands.

Impact

Another collection from Chester Brown, *I Never Liked You: A Comic-Strip Narrative*, also first appeared in original runs of *Yummy Fur*. Like *The Playboy*, *I Never Liked You* is autobiographical and Brown portrays himself as an awkward, introverted youth. It was published as a collection in 1994. Although the time frame is similar to that of *The Playboy*, *I Never Liked You* focuses less on the topics that make *The Playboy* controversial, instead illustrating the young Brown's attempt to connect to others.

The undertone of religious themes in *The Playboy* is given fuller exploration in Brown's gospel adaptations, *The Gospel of Mark* (1987-1989) and *The Gospel of Matthew* (1989-1997). These also appeared in *Yummy Fur* and Brown's later work, *Underwater* (1994-1997). In these gospel adaptations, Brown again exhibits his propensity for controversy. *The Gospel of Mark* is considered finished, while *The Gospel of Matthew* is not, but there is no certainty that Brown will resume work or reprint and publish them as a collection.

Brown's 2011 publication with Drawn and Quarterly, *Paying for It: A Comic Strip Memoir About Being a John*, takes the themes and the struggles portrayed in *The Playboy* to a more current time (Brown as an adult) and a more controversial topic. Again, Brown works in the genre of autobiography and discloses what might be interpreted as sexual deviancy.

Marcy R. Isabella

Further Reading

Brown, Chester. *I Never Liked You* (1994).

Burns, Charles. *Black Hole* (1995-2005).

Seth. *It's a Good Life, If You Don't Weaken* (1993-2003).

Bibliography

Brown, Chester. "Chester Brown." Interview by Nicolas Verstappen. *du9: L'Autre Bande dessinée*, August, 2008. http://www.du9.org/Chester-Brown,1030.

Gallo, Don, and Stephen Weiner. "Bold Books for Innovative Teaching: Show, Don't Tell—Graphic Novels in the Classroom." *English Journal* 94, no. 2 (November, 2004): 114-117.

Hatfield, Charles. "The Autobiographical Stories in *Yummy Fur*." *Comics Journal* 210 (February, 1999): 67.

_____. "Graphic Interventions: Form and Argument in Contemporary Comics." Ph.D. diss., University of Connecticut, 2000.

See also: *I Never Liked You*; *Black Hole*; *It's a Good Life, If You Don't Weaken*; *Ed the Happy Clown*

Poor Bastard, The

Author: Matt, Joe
Artist: Joe Matt (illustrator)
Publisher: Drawn and Quarterly
First serial publication: 1992-1994 (*Peepshow*, issues 1-6)
First book publication: 1997

Publication History

In 1987, Joe Matt began publishing single-page comic strips under the title *Peepshow*. Targeted to an adult readership, these autobiographical strips chronicled Matt's obsessions with women, pornography, and reading and writing comics. The single-page iteration of *Peepshow* ceased publication in 1991. Kitchen Sink Press published a collection of these early one-page strips in 1992 as *Peepshow: The Cartoon Diary of Joe Matt*. Matt published the first *Peepshow* comic book in February, 1992.

Matt's *The Poor Bastard* collects the first six issues of *Peepshow*, which ran until November, 2006 (issue 14). The *Peepshow* issues reprinted in *The Poor Bastard* were originally released between February, 1992, and April, 1994. Subsequently, *Peepshow* issues 7 through 10 were published in 2002 under the title *Fair Weather*, and issues 11 through 14 appeared in the 2007 collection *Spent*.

Montreal-based comics publisher Drawn and Quarterly has produced both *Peepshow* and Matt's subsequent collections. It released the first edition of *The Poor Bastard* in 1997, with second and third editions appearing in 2002 and 2007, respectively. All editions of this title have been published in paperback formats, though a signed and numbered hardbound edition with a print run of four hundred copies was released in 2002. Both *Fair Weather* and *Spent* are available in hardcover editions.

The British publishing house Jonathan Cape published an edition of *The Poor Bastard* in 2007. *The Poor Bastard* has been translated into Spanish, French, and German. Two editions of the Spanish version have been published (2006 and 2008) by noted Barcelona-based comics publisher Ediciones La Cúpula. Parisian

The Poor Bastard. (Courtesy of Drawn and Quarterly)

publisher Delcourt released the French version of *The Poor Bastard* in 2008.

Plot

Organized into six sections, *The Poor Bastard* chronicles the decline of Joe Matt's relationship with Trish, an art student and his live-in girlfriend of four years, and his subsequent attempts at romance. The tensions in their relationship, alluded to in Matt's earliest *Peepshow* strips—namely Matt's selfishness and obsessions as well as Trish's professional aspirations and dissatisfaction with his behavior—finally drive them apart. In this book, these tensions manifest in Matt's attraction to Frankie, a young woman who works with Trish at a local day care center. Though he knows nothing about her as a person, Matt finds both Frankie's appearance and youth tantalizing. While his interest in Frankie ultimately fades after a few embarrassing encounters with her, Matt's impulsive fantasizing about other women and Trish's move to the Toronto suburbs for school ultimately facilitate their breakup.

Matt befriends local hipsters Andy and Kim, who try to set him up with one of Andy's former girlfriends,

a woman named Mary. Attracted to Kim, Matt is reluctant to meet Mary, though he encourages Andy to find him another suitable match. Matt also begins corresponding with Laura, his first significant girlfriend. He regularly meets with his best friends and fellow cartoonists Chester Brown and Seth to discuss his relationships and social interactions as well as to get

The Poor Bastard. (Courtesy of Drawn and Quarterly)

updates on Trish's burgeoning romance with a university student named Graham.

The Poor Bastard concludes with Seth telling him that Trish has left Canada for a job in California. Before learning of this turn of events, however, Matt gives Trish a black eye, alienates his new friends, has an awkward encounter with a possible romantic interest named Jill, and engages in a humiliating sexual episode with Laura during a family visit to Pennsylvania.

Each of the six episodes of *The Poor Bastard* follows a loose narrative trajectory that typically ends on an ironic note that foreshadows events in the next section. Part 5, for example, concludes with Matt's new neighbor, Jill, knocking on his boardinghouse door and asking if a carton of eggs in the refrigerator belongs to him; an important subplot in part 6 concerns Matt's attempt to save a pigeon mangled by cats. Also, in part 1, Matt's concluding words to Trish ("Trust me!") ironically allude to their final breakup in part 2.

Characters

- *Joe Matt*, bespectacled and scrawny with long hair and a receding hairline, is the main character of *The Poor Bastard*. He is an independent comic book artist who occasionally freelances as a comic book colorist. Notoriously opinionated and thrifty, he spends most of his days masturbating and obsessively thinking about his relationships, both real and imagined. Matt is quick to anger around his girlfriend Trish but passively accepts the criticisms and ribs from his friends Chester and Seth.

- *Trish*, an aspiring cartoonist, is Matt's girlfriend of four years. She is enrolled in college and hopes to use her degree to work as a cartoonist or animator. She is slender with long hair. In contrast to Matt, she is outgoing and enjoys making friends and having new experiences. She barely tolerates Matt's masturbatory habits and pornography obsessions, which remain a source of tension for her in their relationship. While she supports her boyfriend's cartooning work, she would prefer that he did not write and draw about their relationship.

- *Seth*, a cartoonist and close friend of Matt, sports round glasses, often wears a coat and tie, and chain-smokes. He exhibits patience and is always trying to temper Matt's delusions about women and romance. He also provides comic relief throughout *The Poor Bastard*. He shares Matt's enthusiasm for vintage comics and rare Fisher-Price View-Master reels.

- *Chester Brown*, a.k.a. *Chet*, is a cartoonist and Matt's other best friend. Casually dressed and lanky with long hair, he speaks far less often than Seth or Matt. When he does voice his opinions, he usually supports Seth's take on Matt's ideas and perceptions.

- *Andy* meets Matt at a local comics shop and professes his enthusiasm for the cartoonist's work. Tall with a goatee and shaved head, he plays bass guitar for a local band. Though he lives with Kim, his girlfriend of five years, he has a wandering eye. He is affectionate and loyal to Matt.

- *Kim* is an attractive young woman in a long-term relationship with Andy. She sports a pixie cut and has a taste for funky clothes. A beauty spot accentuates her smile. Though she is initially cool toward him, Matt is initially attracted to her because of her classic looks and petite frame. She performs tarot readings and claims to be receptive to people's auras.

- *Mary*, Andy's former girlfriend, is slight, fair-haired, and freckled. She works as a server at a local dive. While she is receptive to a friendship with Matt, his aggressive bids for physical contact and a more traditional, exclusive romantic commitment ultimately discourage her. Matt initially insists that she is not his "type" because of her pale complexion.

- *Frankie* is a twenty-year-old woman of West Indian descent who first attracts Matt's attention at a local copy center on account of her exotic looks and dreadlocks. He thereafter associates her with the song "The Girl from Ipanema," which plays on the shop sound system when he first sees her. She works with Trish at a local day care center.

- *Jill* moves into the boardinghouse where Matt lives after he breaks up with Trish. An ethnically Chinese nineteen-year-old, she is studying cuneiform script in the hopes of becoming an expert on ancient Assyria. She seems to find Matt pushy and eccentric.

- *Laura*, Matt's first sex partner, contacts him by letter and phone after getting a divorce. During their correspondence, Matt discovers that she has become sexually adventurous, a fact he finds both distressing and compelling. *The Poor Bastard* concludes with Matt's pathetic tryst with her; she has retained her slender appearance and has grown out the long, dark hair that Matt loved in his youth.

Artistic Style

Matt's bold visual style conveys a remarkable consistency throughout his work over the years. His appreciation for classic comic strips such as *Peanuts* and *Gasoline Alley* is evident throughout *The Poor Bastard*, especially in the way he organizes panels on a page and in his sense of composition in each panel. His use of ink, pen, and brush produces a strong line that maximizes the stark and dramatic effects possible in an adult-themed, black-and-white comic. As a result, Matt suggests to readers that even though the story he tells is autobiographical, his account possesses a certain stability and is therefore credible; an idea he underscores with his use of contrast and composition in each panel on the page.

Generally, Matt renders objects and people in space according to simple perspective and foregrounding to convey depth, and he mostly eschews the use of crosshatching. Because conversation and monologues drive most of the plot, Matt often limits the number of figures and background details in a panel. Also, because *The Poor Bastard* is a textual comic, conversation bubbles and captions typically share the space with one or two figures set against a dark background.

Surroundings, whether domestic interiors or outdoor scenes, usually display some sort of unifying horizontal black space, such as a city skyline or a simple black interior. Matt's panels all exhibit a thick, black frame, and he rarely deviates from a format that situates six frames in three rows of two frames each on a page. This consistent organization draws the reader's focus to the action occurring in the panels themselves and further suggests that the events Matt depicts

Joe Matt

Joe Matt initially made his name with a series of short, autobiographical comics in the late 1980's and early 1990's, collected under the title *Peepshow: The Cartoon Diary of Joe Matt*. He launched his own comic book title with Drawn and Quarterly in 1992, publishing roughly one comic book per year through 2006. *Peepshow* serialized three autobiographical graphic novels: *The Poor Bastard* depicted Matt's relationship with his long-suffering girlfriend, Trish; *Fair Weather* told stories about Matt's childhood in Philadelphia; *Spent* portrayed Matt's addiction to pornography and his friendship with cartoonists Seth and Chester Brown. Matt's work was renowned for its brutal self-depictions, in which the artist frequently portrayed himself in a stunningly unflattering light. Visually, his work is highly detailed, though quite cartoony. His later works are structured with an unvarying grid pattern that gives the story a feeling akin to watching images flash by on a television screen.

throughout follow a logical, cohesive progression toward an inevitable conclusion.

Themes

The Poor Bastard, along with most of Matt's work, centers on the theme of authenticity. Throughout *The Poor Bastard*, Matt's cartoon version of himself constantly questions how he can best maintain his own sense of personal integrity. In turn, he questions how he can maintain this sense of self in his relationships with others, especially in his romantic relationships.

Matt ironically undermines such lines of questioning with his choice of format. The comic book is, after all, a work of art, and Matt's rendering of people, places, and objects is exaggerated and simplified. He contains his drawings in boldly framed panels arranged logically on a page.

Despite the artifice that necessarily characterizes his depiction of life, Matt's view of his struggle for authenticity remains credible. In the end, it is unclear if Matt's seemingly rigid standards of conduct, appearance, and behavior have been at all changed by his experiences. What remains evident, however, is that readers can identify with Matt's double standards, defensiveness, and reluctance to admit fault or defeat as human responses to adversity and confusion.

Impact

Matt's work belongs to the tradition of autobiographical comics pioneered by Justin Green (*Binky Brown Meets the Holy Virgin Mary*) and Harvey Pekar (*American Splendor*) in the 1970's. What distinguishes Matt's work from these seminal titles is his unsentimental and unapologetic portrayal of his life, his personal values, and his proclivities.

The earliest autobiographical comics creators sought to convey everyday experiences and real-life situations in the interest of understanding their values and interrogating their motivations and reactions to people and events. Matt, unlike his predecessors, flips this dynamic to show how the world around him does not necessarily comport with his view of life and how to live it. In other words, Matt suggests that he is happy being who he is and doing what he does. If the people around him have problems with that, then those problems remain their own and do not affect him.

Matt's particular worldview is one he shares with his contemporaries in the Toronto comics scene of the 1990's, Chester Brown (*Yummy Fur*) and Seth (*Palookaville*), both of whom appear in Matt's comics and intermittently include him in their work as well. This referential component to Matt's work is another factor that distinguishes it from earlier autobiographical comic books. Matt's references to and depictions of interactions with his cartooning friends reinforce the documentary quality of his stories. Matt's realism also emphasizes that his personal story is an outgrowth of being part of a creative community and is shaped by peer influence and mutual creative exchange as much as by personal motivations.

Greg Matthews

Further Reading

Brown, Chester. *Paying for It* (2011).
Brown, Jeffrey. *Clumsy* (2002).
Miss Lasko-Gross. *Escape from "Special"* (2006).

Bibliography

Beaty, Bart. "Selective Mutual Reinforcement in the Comics of Chester Brown, Joe Matt, and Seth." In *Graphic Subjects: Critical Essays on Autobiography and Graphic Novels*, edited by Michael A. Chaney. Madison: University of Wisconsin Press, 2011.

Chaney, Michael A. "Terrors of the Mirror and the *Mise en Abyme* of Graphic Novel Autobiography." *College Literature* 38, no. 3 (Summer, 2011): 21-44.

Matt, Joe. "Interview with Joe Matt." Interview by Christopher Brayshaw. *Comics Journal* 183 (January, 1996): 47-75.

See also: *Clumsy*; *The Playboy*; *It's a Good Life, If You Don't Weaken*

Predator

Author: Anderson, Kevin J.; Arcudi, John; Barr, Mike W.; Barrett, Neil, Jr.; Barry, Dan; Collins, Nancy; Dixon, Chuck; Dorkin, Evan; Edginton, Ian; Gilroy, Henry; LaBan, Terry; Lamb, Jason R.; McDonald, Brian; Marz, Ron; Moore, Charles; Prosser, Jerry; Rennie, Gordon; Richardson, Mike; Schultz, Mark; Seagle, Steve; Stradley, Randy; Tolson, Scott; Vachss, Andrew; Vance, James; Verheiden, Mark; Worley, Kate

Artist: Enrique Alcatena (illustrator); Dan Barry (illustrator); Claudio Castellini (illustrator); Howard Cobb (illustrator); Gene Colan (illustrator); Evan Dorkin (illustrator); Leo Durañona (illustrator); Igor Kordey (illustrator); Colin MacNeil (illustrator); Dean Ormston (illustrator); Chris Warner (illustrator); Mitch Byrd (penciller); Scott Fisher (penciller); Alexandra Gregory (penciller); Scott Kolins (penciller); Rick Leonardi (penciller); Brian O'Connell (penciller); Lauchland Pelle (penciller); Roger Peterson (penciller); Ron Randall (penciller); Jordan Raskin (penciller); Duncan Rouleau (penciller); Mel Rubi (penciller); Jim Somerville (penciller); Toby Cypress (penciller and inker); Rob Walton (penciller and letterer); Derek Thompson (penciller and cover artist); Rick Bryant (inker); Sam De la Rosa (inker); Randy Emberlin (inker); Brian Garvey (inker); Armando Gil (inker); Mark Lipka (inker); John Lowe (inker); Rick Magyar (inker); Steve Mitchell (inker); Dan Panosian (inker); Ande Parks (inker); Bruce Patterson (inker); Andrew Pepoy (inker); Jasen Rodriguez (inker); Jim Royal (inker); Dan Schaefer (inker); Robbie Busch (colorist); Chris Chalenor (colorist); Lea Hernandez (colorist); Matt Hollingsworth (colorist); Jimmy Johns (colorist); Julia Lacquement (colorist); Rachel Menashe (colorist); Ray Murtaugh (colorist); David Nestelle (colorist); Cary Potter (colorist); James Sinclair (colorist); Dave Stewart (colorist); Sean Tierney (colorist); Gregory Wright (colorist); Pat Brosseau (letterer); Ellie DeVille (letterer); Steve Dutro (letterer); Gary Fields (letterer); Kurt Hathaway (letterer); Gary Kato (letterer); Sean Konot (letterer); Bill Pearson (letterer); Clem Robins (letterer); Fiona Stephenson (letterer); Michael Taylor (letterer); Vickie Williams (letterer); Den Beauvais (cover artist); Dave Gibbons (cover artist); Igor Kordey (cover artist); Derek Thompson (cover artist)

Publisher: Dark Horse Comics
First serial publication: 1989-1999
First book publication: 1996-1999

On the set of *Predator*. Inspired by the film, the *Predator* comics series centers on the exploits of a powerful alien race that hunts humans for sport. (© Sunset Boulevard/Corbis)

Publication History

On the heels of Twentieth Century Fox's film *Predator*, released in 1987, the first *Predator* comic was released in 1989 by Dark Horse Comics, then only a three-year-old company. The first story line, "Concrete Jungle," is considered a comics sequel to the *Predator* film, serving as inspiration for *Predator 2*, released in 1990 by Fox.

Reportedly, Dark Horse Comics, the sole publisher of *Predator* from 1989 to 1999, acquired licenses to adapt the Predator character, as well as *Aliens* and *Star Wars* characters, as a way of staying afloat in a time when the sales of its independent comics were unpredictable. Over the course of those ten years, the company released *Predator* stories through one-shots and two- and four-part stories in single-issue format and through Dark Horse Comics anthologies. All *Predator* comics have been collected and released as trade paperbacks and omnibuses.

The *Predator* series featured a variety of writers and artists, beginning with writer Mark Verheiden and artist Chris Warner in 1989. Other notable contributors include writer Chuck Dixon and illustrators Gene Colan and Evan Dorkin. No creative team has produced more than three consecutive story lines, thus underscoring that the *Predator* mythos was ripe for interpretation.

Plot

Inspired by the *Predator* film, the *Predator* comics series centers on the exploits of a powerful alien race that hunts humans for sport. It is a series suited for adults, mixing science fiction elements with constant action and graphic violence.

The first story, "Concrete Jungle," takes place during a sweltering summer in New York City. Detective Schaefer of the New York City Police Department is working a drug bust when he first encounters a Predator. Their brief tussle eventually leads to Schaefer's relentless investigation into his brother's disappearance after a mission in Guatemala (as recounted in the first *Predator* film); when reexamining his brother's mission, he encounters another Predator. He kills this one, which sets off a one-day war among Predators, law enforcement, and thugs. In a surprise move, the Predator army leaves when a storm washes the summer heat away.

"Concrete Jungle" is the gateway to subsequent *Predator* stories, which mostly concern how one

individual or team thwarts Predators disrupting a select city or region. Detective Schaefer appears in the second story, "Cold War," which chronicles Predators destroying a Soviet army base in Siberia. Schaefer teams up with Soviet officer Ligacheva to stop the carnage, and both heroes disobey orders from their commanders, causing (and later easing) tensions between the United States and the Soviet Union. Schaefer appears again in the third *Predator* story, "Dark River."

Beyond the Schaefer stories, another compelling pair is "Big Game" and "Blood on Two-Witch Mesa," featuring U.S. Army corporal Enoch Nakai, of Navajo descent, who has an interesting history with Predators. In "Big Game," he has a random encounter with a Predator that destroys an Army base and terrorizes a small town in New Mexico. In the wake of that battle, Enoch is working at a convenience store after an honorable discharge from the Army, questioning his encounter with the Predator. His grandfather reveals that Nakai's great-grandfather witnessed a Predator attack seventy-five years prior. His story underscores tensions between the Navajo tribe and white men who drill oil at Two-Witch Mesa, and how both parties thwart the alien beings. In the end, Enoch is inspired, but his next move is not fully detailed.

With the exception of the aforementioned story lines and a few others, the Predator comics series lacks a chronological plot, although some stories relate to one another. Most *Predator* stories are episodic in that they focus on a particular instance when a Predator or a group of Predators invades.

Volumes

- *Predator Omnibus*, Volume 1 (2007). Collects "Concrete Jungle," issues 1-4; "Cold War," issues 1-4; "Dark River," issues 1-4; "Rite of Passage," issue 1; "The Pride at Nghasa," issues 1-2; "The Bloody Sands of Time," issues 1-2; and "Blood Feud," from *Dark Horse Comics*, issues 4-7. Includes three stories featuring Detective Schaefer and his fight against Predators and the search for his brother, "Dutch" Schaefer (the character played by Arnold Schwarzenegger in the original film).

- *Predator Omnibus*, Volume 2 (2008). Collects "Big Game," issues 1-4; "God's Truth," from *Dark Horse Presents*, issue 46; "Race War," issues 0-4; "The Hunted City" from *Dark Horse Comics*, issues 16-19; "Blood on Two-Witch Mesa," from *Dark Horse Comics*, issues 20-21; the "Invaders from the Fourth Dimension" one-shot; and "1718," from *A Decade of Dark Horse*, issue 1. Includes stories featuring Predator encounters with Navajos, pirates, prisoners, moviegoers, and more; reveals how Predators obtained a flintlock pistol from 1715, the same pistol used in the film *Predator 2*.
- *Predator Omnibus*, Volume 3 (2008). Collects "Bad Blood," from *Dark Horse Comics*, issues 12-14; "Kindred," issues 1-4; "Hell and Hot Water," issues 1-3; the "Strange Roux" one-shot; "No Beast So Fierce," from *Dark Horse Presents*, issue 119; and "Bump in the Night," from *Dark Horse Presents*, issue 124. Chronicles Predators in the sea, suburbia, a bayou, and more.
- *Predator Omnibus*, Volume 4 (2008). Collects "Primal," issues 1-2; "Nemesis," issues 1-2; "Homeworld," issues 1-4; "Xenogenesis," issues 1-4; "Hell Come a Walkin'," issues 1-2; the "Captive" one-shot; and "Demon's Gold," from *Dark Horse Presents*, issue 137. Includes two stories that seek answers to the mysteries of the alien race.

Characters

Predator refers to the hulking alien species equipped with hi-tech weaponry, including a three-point laser, spear, and cloaking device. The species is known for hunting humans for sport, especially in high temperatures. Many humans die from their attacks.

Detective Schaefer, a reoccurring protagonist, is a stubborn, muscular, 6-foot-plus "bad boy" who runs into trouble head on, disobeying laws and battling Predators in Central America, Siberia, and New York City. His tenacity and combat skills are twice employed by the U.S. Army to dispatch the alien species.

General Homer Philips, another reoccurring protagonist and antagonist, is a war veteran with experience in special operations, such as the one involving "Dutch" Schaefer's mission in Guatemala. With earlier experience with a Predator, Philips works for and against Detective Schaefer's actions against the alien species, withholding information about Dutch.

Enoch Nakai, another reoccurring protagonist, is a weak U.S. Army corporal who faces racism from his peers, personal battles with alcoholism, and nightmares about Predators. He survives a Predator attack in New Mexico and later questions the government's cover-up of the event, learning about his family's history with the alien. Unlike Schaefer, he is far from a "tough-as-nails" hero.

Artistic Style

Though the *Predator* series contains a wide variety of creators, the art has common elements. The Predator characters are the most vivid and detailed, with much attention paid to the suit, weapons, and face, likened to a spider and other creatures with mandibles. Coupled with the series' design, many splash pages depict a Predator surrounded by mauled bodies and blood, emphasizing the violence that is also found in the *Predator* films. Clearly, however, artists were not limited to a certain style, though most took a realistic approach (the exceptions being such cartoony stories as "Strange Roux" and "Invaders from the Fourth Dimension").

Among the standout artistry, Dan Barry's art for "Bloody Sands of Time" can be viewed as an evolution of his work on *Flash Gordon* comic strips from 1951 to 1952, linking the series to the Golden Age of comics. Colan's *Predator: Hell and Hot Water* illustrations can be likened to his early 1980's *Batman* and 1970's *Daredevil* work.

Themes

Predator's most prominent theme is survival, as evidenced by the numerous stories chronicling humans combating an alien race with advanced technology. Nearly every story depicts chase scenes and fights, concluding with someone falling prey or escaping.

Mystery is the second most prominent theme. Predators are never deemed "Predators" but assume a variety of other monikers as the protagonists encounter them and seek answers for why they have descended on Earth. Some notable monikers include "Demon of the Forest" (from "Pride of Nghasa") and "The Angry Ghosts of the Old Ones" (from "Blood on Two-Witch Mesa"). The one-shot story "Captive" addresses the mysteries of the Predator species, featuring Dr. Tyler Stern's studies on a Predator in a biosphere, which, of course, takes a turn for the worse.

The theme of war also has a strong presence in *Predator*. Predators disrupt and engage the U.S. Army, Central Intelligence Agency, Soviet army, Confederates, and Central American guerrillas. Some of the best examples are found in such stories as "Cold War" and "Concrete Jungle."

Impact

Predator began in the early years of the Modern Age of comics, when gritty and graphic comics were emerging in the mainstream, departing from the Comics Code Authority, a censor of violence and other adult themes. Before *Predator*'s release, DC Comics released the seminal graphic novel *Watchmen* (1986-1987), about embattled superheroes in an age in which few trust them, and such Batman stories as *The Dark Knight Returns* (1986) and *The Killing Joke* (1988), both of which cast darker iterations of Batman and the Joker than before.

Like DC and others, Dark Horse Comics championed adult-oriented comics, releasing in 1988 a comic series based on the film *Aliens* (1986). Its success, coupled with the company's desire to acquire licenses of popular films, led to the comics adaptation of *Predator*. Later, Dark Horse acquired rights to such films as *Star Wars* (1977) and *The Terminator* (1984), becoming a notable publisher of comics based on popular films. Thanks to the success of the *Aliens* and *Predator* series, Dark Horse also created a crossover series titled *Aliens*

vs. Predator (1991) as well as a number of novels featuring both alien species.

Films

Predator 2. Directed by Stephen Hopkins. Twentieth Century Fox, 1990. This film adaptation stars Danny Glover as Lieutenant Michael Harrigan and Kevin Peter Hall as the Predator. The film is loosely based on the *Predator* comics story "Concrete Jungle," opening with a drug bust that leads the protagonist to the title antagonist. Among the differences, Harrigan replaces Detective Schaefer as the protagonist and dodges the backstory of "Dutch" Schaefer's encounter with a Predator. Also, this Predator exhibits some humanity, sparing a child and a pregnant woman.

Richard L. Shivener

Further Reading

Mark, et al. *Aliens* (1988-1999).

Stradley, Randy, Chris Warner, and Phill Norwood. *Aliens vs. Predators* (1991).

Gibbons, Dave, Adam Kubert, Andy Kubert. *Batman vs. Predator* (1991-1992).

Bibliography

Gustines, George. "A Quirky Superhero of the Comics Trade." *The New York Times*, November, 2006, 1-2.

Warner, Chris. *Aliens/Predator: Panel to Panel*. Milwaukie, Ore.: Dark Horse Comics, 2006.

Voger, Mark, et al. *The Dark Age: Grim, Great, and Gimmicky Post-Modern Comics*. Raleigh, N.C.: TwoMorrows, 2006.

See also: *Aliens*; *Metropol*; *Robots Versus Zombies*

PRIDE OF BAGHDAD: INSPIRED BY A TRUE STORY

Author: Vaughan, Brian K.
Artist: Niko Henrichon (illustrator); Todd Klein (letterer)
Publisher: DC Comics
First book publication: 2006

Publication History

Pride of Baghdad was first published as a hardcover edition by DC Comics' Vertigo line in 2006. It is Brian K. Vaughan's first work in a stand-alone graphic novel. His work often straddles the line between high-concept adventure and social commentary as seen in his work on *Runaways* (2003-2009), *Y: The Last Man* (2002-2008), and *Ex Machina* (2004-2010). Vaughan has said that he was looking to test himself as a writer and challenge his reputation as a "cliff-hanger guy." He was also eager to write a story about his conflicted feelings regarding the war in Iraq. After seeing the report about four lions that escaped the Baghdad Zoo during Operation Iraqi Freedom, Vaughan said, "Everything just kind of fell into place."

Niko Henrichon's previous work on *Barnum! In Secret Service to the USA* (2005) included illustrations of realistic but highly expressive animals. Editor Will Dennis thought Henrichon would be a good fit for the project and facilitated a meeting between him and Vaughan. Previously, Henrichon worked for Marvel and DC, providing interior and cover art for major titles. Since he handled penciling, inking, and painting duties, the project took Henrichon more than a year to complete. When Vaughan first pitched the idea, it was during a time when questioning the war was considered treasonous, so he praised his editors for supporting the project. Despite winning multiple awards for his other series, Vaughan has said, "*Pride of Baghdad* will probably always be the work I'm most proud of."

Plot

The story of four African lions loose in war-torn Baghdad begins with a bird screaming that the sky is falling. Immediately afterward, the leader of the

(Getty Images)

Brian K. Vaughan

The Eisner Award-winning graphic novels of Brian K. Vaughan work on several levels. Readers just looking for a fun read will find fast-moving stories, snappy dialogue, and sex and violence in glorious full color. Readers who want something deeper will appreciate the elaborate social commentary in the books, whether the subject is futuristic gender struggles or the costs of war. Memorable characters and truly inventive plotlines are hallmarks of Vaughan's prodigious output.

pride, Zill, looks up and sees a squadron of incoming American bombers. As the lions try to make sense of the humans' actions, bombs begin to fall, destroying the zoo perimeter and freeing several species from their cages. As the smoke clears, the lions wonder if they are dead, only to discover that they are free.

The lions venture outside the zoo for the first time and are greeted by the panic and horror of war. A stampede of all types of animals rushes out of the zoo, and a giraffe that pauses to praise the gods for his newfound freedom is killed in a direct hit from a falling bomb. The lions continue on past fleeing Iraqi tanks and encounter a turtle that has lost his family to the war. The turtle informs the lions that the humans are fighting over a "poison" called oil and tells them of a large stone statue in Babylon of a lion trying to eat a man. According to legend, "as long as that statue's still standing, this land will never fall to outsiders."

The lions continue downtown, encountering a pack of white stallions roaming the deserted streets. Safa and Noor, the female hunters, pursue the horses and are led into a ruined palace. Inside, they witness the space and luxury of their human keepers. They meet an injured lion, declawed as part of its domestication, and a bloodthirsty bear. The bear attacks, tossing Noor aside and blinding Safa in her other eye. Zill arrives to face the bear and the fight spills into the street, where Noor's cub Ali saves the day by causing the horses to stampede, killing the bear.

Momentarily safe, but still hungry, the lions climb a hill of rubble that used to be a zookeeper's home. At the top of the mound, the lions witness a glorious sunset. As they stare at nature's beauty, they hear a gunshot and Zill falls over dead. As the other lions try to flee, a hail of gunfire cuts them down. A group of American soldiers approach the fallen pride. A blackbird soars over the smoking, backlit Baghdad skyline, and a simple caption reads: "In April of 2003, four lions escaped the Baghdad Zoo during the bombing of Iraq. The starving animals were eventually shot and killed by U.S. soldiers. There were other casualties as well." The final image is the blackbird landing on the statue of a lion. Both the pride and Baghdad have fallen.

Characters

- *Zill* is the leader and the eldest male in the pride. While he is accustomed to life in captivity, he fondly remembers the sunsets he saw while living in the wild. Zill is a "benevolent opportunist," caring more about providing for his pride than seeking freedom. He is the first to venture out of the zoo after American bombs knock the walls down.

- *Safa*, the eldest female lion and Zill's former mate, clearly remembers her days in the wild, but she does not remember them fondly. She bears a scar across her face and one blind eye as reminders of the pride that attacked and raped her. To Safa, captivity is a blessing, and she is reluctant to leave the confines of the zoo and the protection it provides. In fact, when the lion's enclosure is destroyed, she initially chooses to stay behind, hoping that the zookeepers will return and take care of her.

- *Ali*, a young lion cub, has never lived outside the zoo and is eager to venture into the new jungle of Baghdad, where he anticipates being a king. His youthful optimism and curiosity about the world supply the group's energy and levity.

- *Noor*, an adult female lion, is Ali's mother and Zill's current mate. She tries to persuade some of the other animals in captivity to aid her in an escape attempt but cannot persuade them to trust that they would not simply be prey for the lions. Noor is a fierce hunter and a protective mother.

- *Antelope*, the female leader of the antelopes, plots with Noor to escape the zoo.

- *Bukk* is a savage lion who attacked and raped Safa in the wild.

- *Turtle* is an old creature that lost its family in previous wars.

- *Rashid* is a wounded lion that lived as a pet in the Baghdad palace.

- *Fajer* is a crazed and formerly domesticated bear that rules the abandoned palace.

Artistic Style

While the appearance of the animals may remind some readers of Disney's *The Lion King* (1994), the strong line work and detailed shading create a strong sense of realism that separates the illustrations from traditional animation. The lions' movement and physiology are amazingly accurate while still featuring recognizable human emotions. For example, the cover image shows Zill's piercing eyes staring out from behind concrete and metal rebar. At first glance, the lion's face may appear human with the rebar dangling over the eyes like strands of dark hair. Seeing a human face supports the animals' narrative role as dramatic characters. When humans are featured in the story, from fleeing zookeepers to American soldiers, they are always faceless. The lack of recognizable people reinforces the humanizing role of the lions.

Henrichon's color palette favors the red, yellow, and brown of a dusty and sun-ravaged Iraq. The color selection mirrors the burning ruins of the city and the African landscape that was once the lions' home. At times, lush green and blue are used to highlight the remaining beauty of the abandoned world and the natural splendor that exists beyond the walls of the zoo. The landscape reinforces the realistic setting, including recognizable Baghdad landmarks, such as the statue of Saddam Hussein and the hands of victory.

The narrative flow of the story is highly visual and includes several nearly wordless pages. The dialogue bubbles are traditional, relying on bolded text for emphasis and using a jagged and erratic font for the bear alone. Similarly, there are few sound effects, usually reserved for crucial moments. While traditional straight-line borders are used throughout the story, there are a variety of angles and perspectives used to depict the action, including close-ups and extreme long shots, as well as overhead and floor-level perspectives.

Themes

The primary themes of the story are war and freedom. War is a clear narrative force, constantly endangering the protagonists while also raising fundamental questions about the effects of war as an inter-species event. Read as a parable, this interpretation is best expressed by the loss experienced by the turtle, representing the plight of Iraqis caught in the conflict. In a silent moment of remembrance, the reader sees the turtle's family drowning in the oil that spewed into their river. The parable angle also helps explain why the lions continually choose not to eat the other animals they encounter.

Despite being mighty predators, the lions are free in a world that was never meant for them. They are motivated by a quest for food, yet their attempts to eat are continually thwarted as the result of rational and human decision making. They choose not to eat the turtle out of pity and question eating a man's corpse because of their previous relationship with humans. In the historic events that inspired the story, the lions were starving and desperate, which justify the soldiers' actions, however in the story, the lions' conscious decisions not to eat mark them as sympathetic and humanized characters.

Throughout the story, the lions wrestle with the cost of their freedom. Safa and her desire to remain in captivity can be interpreted as an endorsement of zoos and the protection they provide against the threats of the natural and human world. However, as a counterpoint, the domesticated animals in the palace are either mistreated or emotionally scarred by their experiences. The pride has human perspectives on freedom and whether it can be given or if it must be earned. The temporary freedom the lions have leads them on a fatal journey that asks the reader to confront the costs of war on all forms of life.

Impact

Pride of Baghdad earned praise from several notable comic reviewers and crossed into the world of mainstream entertainment. The literary tradition of talking animals expressing human sentiments echoes the work of George Orwell's *Animal Farm* (1946) and Rudyard Kipling's *The Jungle Book* (1894), as well as the graphic novels of Art Spiegelman (*Maus: A Survivor's Tale,* 1986) and Grant Morrison (*We3,* 2004). While many aspects of the story can be read as a parable, the author has clarified that it is not a simple allegory in which each character represents something specific in twenty-first-century Iraq. The anthropomorphic depiction of the lions, in both language and reasoning, complicates their narrative role because it clashes with lions' natural motivations and instincts.

The limited dialogue, vivid art, and layered interpretations make *Pride of Baghdad* a strong introduction to graphic novels, and the book is a popular choice among high school and college teachers. Those interested in exploring comics as literature and animal narratives in fiction will find this book a stellar example of both. The Young Adult Library Services Association (YALSA) selected *Pride of Baghdad* as one of the top ten graphic novels for teens.

The authors were also honored with an invitation to hold a book signing at the Arab American National Museum in Dearborn, Michigan.

Patrick D. Johnson

Further Reading

Morrison, Grant. *We3* (2004).
Smith, Jeff. *Bone* (1991-2004).
Spiegelman, Art. *Maus: A Survivor's Tale* (1986).

Bibliography

Leong, Tim. Interview with Brian K. Vaughan. *Comic Foundry*, July 6, 2006. Available at http://comic foundry.com/?p=1522.

Mangum, Teresa, and K. Corey Creekmur. "A Graphic Novel Depicting War as an Interspecies Event: *Pride of Baghdad.*" *Society and Animals* 15, no. 4 (2007): 405-408.

Richards, Dave. "Joy of the Pride: Vaughan Talks *Pride of Baghdad.*" *Comic Book Resources*, September 11, 2006. Available at http://www.comicbookresources.com/?page=article&id=8051

See also: *Maus*

PYONGYANG: A JOURNEY IN NORTH KOREA

Author: Delisle, Guy

Artist: Guy Delisle (illustrator); Dirk Rehm (letterer)

Publishers: L'Association (French); Drawn and Quarterly (English)

First book publication: *Pyongyang*, 2003 (English translation, 2005)

Publication History

Pyongyang: A Journey in North Korea is Canadian-born cartoonist Guy Delisle's anecdotal memoir of two months in the summer of 2001 that he spent supervising an animation department in the capital of the world's most insular communist country, North Korea. He did not create the book while in North Korea but kept a sketchbook with notes about events and drawings of the things he saw. After returning home to France, Delisle picked the stories and events he considered most interesting and re-created them in graphic novel form, putting them together as if he were telling the story of his adventures to friends and family. He was sensitive about what information he added to his book, knowing that if he portrayed someone as a dissident, the person could be arrested, sent to a reeducation camp, or even executed.

Pyongyang: A Journey in North Korea was first published in France by L'Association in 2003. Drawn and Quarterly released the first English-language translation in hardback in 2005 and paperback in 2007. The book was almost not published at all, however, as Delisle had to sign a confidentiality agreement with Protecrea, the company that had sent him to North Korea. Fortunately for Delisle, the company went out of business and so was unable to prevent him from publishing.

Plot

Pyongyang: A Journey in North Korea opens with Delisle's arrival at the airport in Pyongyang. He brings with him a CD player, a copy of George Orwell's antitotalitarian novel *1984* (1949), and an illegal pocket radio. His sense of being a "stranger in a strange land" begins at the darkened airport (electricity is scarce in Pyongyang). Mr. Kyu, Delisle's guide who must accompany

Pyongyang: A Journey in North Korea. (Courtesy of Drawn and Quarterly)

him everywhere during his time in North Korea, and his driver give him a bouquet of flowers, which are not meant for him. Instead, they are for his first cultural stop: the seventy-two-foot-tall statue of Kim Il Sung, the revered Father of the Nation.

Delisle's work time is spent at the Scientific and Educational Film Studio of Korea (SEK), which used to be a propaganda studio but mostly handles outsourced animation from French and other foreign studios. Delisle's time at work is frustrating, with both a cultural divide and a language barrier getting in the way of production. Most of his free time is spent at his hotel, the Yangakko, one of only three in the city that are open to foreigners. The hotel is set on a small island near downtown Pyongyang, and even though it is forty-seven-stories tall, only the fifteenth floor has power. The hotel includes entertainment facilities and two restaurants, Restaurant 1 and Restaurant 2, both open to foreign visitors only. Delisle and his friends visit with other foreigners—mostly businesspeople, diplomats, and aid workers—partly for entertainment and partly as a way to relax apart from their omnipresent handlers.

Mr. Kyu and Mr. Sin, Delisle's translator, take him on cultural visits, all of which glorify Kim Il Sung and his son, Kim Jong Il. In general, the cultural sites imply that the two leaders are loved and respected worldwide except in decadent and corrupt foreign countries, especially the United States and Japan. Delisle is never given an opportunity to meet with any North Korean citizens other than Mr. Kyu, Mr. Sin, and a select few employees at the animation studio where he works. During their trips around the city, Delisle tries to question Mr. Kyu and Mr. Sin about their country's policies and their leaders' beliefs, but both men remain steadfastly loyal to their nation. Delisle contrasts what he is told by the North Koreans he meets with what he knows from living in the Western world and with the plot of *1984*, which he reads during his stay. At times, he is saddened or appalled by his hosts' naïveté, but at other times, he is amused by the oddities he encounters.

Characters

- *Guy Delisle*, the protagonist, is an animator working for a French animation studio. He has been sent to Pyongyang for two months to oversee work outsourced to North Korean animators at SEK. He is familiar with traveling to Asia for work, but he has not been to North Korea before.
- *Mr. Kyu* is Delisle's official guide, one of the few North Koreans with whom Delisle is authorized to associate. He is required to accompany Delisle everywhere during his time in Pyongyang and arranges for him to tour official sites. He is loyal to his country and its leaders and is shaken by the copy of *1984* that Delisle loans him.
- *Mr. Sin* is Delisle's first official translator. A former military man, he is dour and shows great emotion only at the International Friendship

Exhibition, when overcome by reverence for Kim Il Sung. He explains many aspects of his culture but always from the official political stance of North Korea.

- *Richard*, a foreign national, works for another French animation studio. He befriends Delisle on his first day at work, and they often spend time together after work.
- *David* is the background supervisor for the animation project Delisle is overseeing. He joins Delisle and Richard in their adventures with the other foreign nationals visiting Pyongyang.
- *Fabrice Fouquet* joins the other animation studio after Richard leaves. He and Delisle share stories about their time in North Korea. Two pages at the end of *Pyongyang* are drawn by him and recount how one of his film canisters was taken away and censored because he slipped away from his official guide and took unauthorized photographs.

Artistic Style

While Delisle reproduces several key buildings, landmarks, and monuments accurately enough to be recognizable, most of *Pyongyang* is drawn in a light, cartoonish style. Delisle's portrayal of himself as sharp-nosed and slightly overweight is a good example of his self-deprecating wit. Further touches of humor are added in moments when Delisle is explaining some aspect of North Korean history or politics and creates funny, over-the-top examples to prove his point ("Which One Is the Spy?"). He uses thin ink lines and pencil shading, and his drawings are kept straightforward, relying on the shading to convey his impressions. For example, North Korea's lack of electricity is illustrated by a scene of people scuttling through the dark streets at night, lit only by the lights of the few passing cars. He maintains a simple palette of grey with plenty of white to show the stark cleanliness of the capital city. Delisle also uses cinematic perspective to offer a counterpoint to the events he recounts, either by zooming in for close-ups or by pulling back for long shots. This technique heightens the impact of his story by giving the reader more of a sense that they are present at those events.

Themes

Culture shock is the most pervasive theme in *Pyongyang*. From the beginning, Delisle feels surrounded by incomprehensible behaviors and beliefs. He seeks to learn more, but his only sources of information are his official guide and official translator, who both adhere strictly to the party line. They are loyal to North Korea and are firm believers in the intelligence, munificence, and benevolence of Kim Il Sung, known as the Eternal President, and Kim Jong Il, known as the Supreme Leader. As he tours official cultural sites with his guides, Delisle contrasts what he knows from living in the Western world with what the North Koreans are told happens both within and outside their borders.

Rebellion is a minor theme because Delisle's acts of rebellion are small. Outside radios are banned by the North Korean government, and local ones are locked onto the official station. Delisle manages to bring an AM/FM pocket radio with him, though he is able to pick up only a single station. He insists on walking

Pyongyang: A Journey in North Korea. (Courtesy of Drawn and Quarterly)

many places, when his guide and translator would rather drive him; he occasionally journeys places without them, which is a violation that could get them in more trouble than him. Delisle makes jokes and asks pointed questions about North Korean political beliefs, though to no avail, and he flies paper airplanes out of his hotel window. During his free time, he reads *1984*, Orwell's classic novel about an oppressive society and contrasts Orwell's fictional world with the real one of North Korea. None of the North Koreans Delisle meets rebel in any way, with the exception of one man who complains that propaganda films are boring. Even when Delisle loans Orwell's novel to his guide, the man soon gives it back, claiming not to have enjoyed it at all.

Impact

Pyongyang: A Journey in North Korea benefited from being released during a time when the tense global political situation—U.S. president George W. Bush's references to an "Axis of Evil" included North Korea—offered a ready-made audience for books that explained complex political issues in simple, engaging, and innovative ways.

Additionally, graphic novels in general were growing in popularity at the start of the twenty-first century. Nonfiction graphic novels, especially journalistic ones that offered glimpses into complex and seemingly alien countries and political situations, were in demand. Cartoonist Marjane Satrapi's memoir *Persepolis*, about growing up in revolutionary Iran, was published in France three years prior to the French publication of *Pyongyang* and released in the United States two years prior to the English translation of *Pyongyang*. The popularity of *Persepolis*, along with works by creators such as Joe Sacco and Art Spiegelman, set the stage for *Pyongyang*'s success.

In general, critics were highly favorable toward *Pyongyang*, citing its humor and its anecdotal nature as bringing a human touch to journalistic writing. They not only recognized the likelihood that readers might choose a graphic nonfiction work before choosing a denser, less-accessible prose nonfiction work, but also mentioned that *Pyongyang* was likely to inspire readers to seek out more information about the reclusive communist nation. Feelings about Delisle's behavior toward North Korea and its people were divided. Some reviewers felt that Delisle's Everyman, first-person look at his experiences treated his subjects with respect and humor; others were concerned that Delisle exhibited a high-handed Western snobbery toward the people's naïveté, instead of accepting that each country will have its eccentricities and that people have difficulty seeing through political rhetoric when their information is limited.

Despite critics' concerns about Delisle's attitude, the overall critical success of *Pyongyang* bridged the gap between nonfiction for adults and that for teenagers, leading to its inclusion on a number of best-of lists aimed at both audiences. Among these were Amazon.com's Best Books of 2005: Comics and Graphic Novels; *Time* Magazine's Best of 2005: Comix; CBC Radio Talking Books' Top 25 Books of the Year: Graphica (2005); and the Young Adult Library Services Association's Best Books for Young Adults (2006), Great Graphic Novels for Teens: Nonfiction (2007), and Outstanding Books for the College Bound: History and Cultures (2009). Additionally, Delisle was nominated in 2006 for two Eisner Awards (Best Reality-Based Work and Best Writer/Artist) for his work on *Pyongyang*.

Snow Wildsmith

Further Reading

Delisle, Guy. *Burma Chronicles* (2008).

Thompson, Craig. *Carnet de Voyage* (2004).

Willems, Mo. *You Can Never Find a Rickshaw When It Monsoons: The World on One Cartoon a Day* (2006).

Bibliography

Arnold, Andrew D. "From Ming to Kim." *Time*, September 23, 2005. http://www.time.com/time/columnist/arnold/article/0,9565,1108801,00.html.

Delisle, Guy. "A Talk with Guy Delisle: Looking for the Details." Interview by Ada Price. *Publishers Weekly*, October 20, 2009. http://www.publishersweekly.com/pw/by-topic/new-titles/adult-announcements/article/1868-a-talk-with-guy-delisle-looking-for-the-details-.html.

Koelling, Holly, and Betty Carter. *Best Books for Young Adults*. 3d ed. Chicago: American Library Association, 2007.

See also: *Persepolis*; *Burma Chronicles*; *The Photographer*; *La Perdida*

Q

QUEEN AND COUNTRY

Author: Rucka, Greg; Johnston, Antony

Artist: Steve Rolston (illustrator); Jason Shawn Alexander (illustrator); Rick Burchett (illustrator); Leandro Fernandez (illustrator); Mike Hawthorne (illustrator); Brian Hurtt (illustrator); Carla Speed McNeil (illustrator); Christopher Mitten (illustrator); Mike Norton (illustrator); Stan Sakai (illustrator); Chris Samnee (illustrator); John K. Snyder III (illustrator); Christine Norrie (inker); Bryan Lee O'Malley (inker); Guy Major (colorist); Dave Stewart (colorist); John Dranski (letterer); Sean Konot (letterer); Doug Sherwood (letterer); Matthew Hollingsworth (cover artist); Scott Morse (cover artist); Tim Sale (cover artist); Durwin Talon (cover artist)

Publisher: Oni Press

First serial publication: 2001-2007

First book publication: 2002-2007

Publication History

Queen and Country began as a bimonthly comic in March, 2001, though the release schedule varied from monthly to sporadic from 2003 onward. Individual story arcs were completed within three to five issues. Each group of stories was subsequently collected into a paperbound graphic novel. The series, which ran for a total of thirty-two issues until August, 2007, was reprinted in eight volumes between 2002 and 2007. A related three-volume series, *Declassified*, was issued between 2003 and 2006 to provide backstories for key characters. The entire series, including *Declassified*, was reprinted, with supplemental material, in four "definitive" volumes between 2007 and 2009. Greg Rucka, the series author, also published three novels—*A Gentleman's Game* (2004), *Private Wars* (2005), and *The Last Run* (2010)—that bridge or expand upon events referred to in the comics.

Queen & Country. (Courtesy of Oni Press)

Queen and Country was the second major collaboration between Oni Press and Rucka, following the author's award-winning series *Whiteout* (1998). *Queen and Country* showcased Rucka's particular strength: writing tough, resourceful, independent, angst-ridden female protagonists.

It is testament to Rucka's reputation as a storyteller that many across the graphics spectrum—series creators, artists, letterers, inkers, and colorists—have contributed to *Queen and Country*. Seasoned professionals such as Stan Sakai (*Usagi Yojimbo*, 1987-) and Tim Sale (*Batman*, *Spider-Man*) and emerging stars such as Leandro Fernandez (*Punisher*) have found Rucka's terse, action-filled prose easily adaptable to sequential illustration. Several artists, including Steve Rolston and Brian Hurtt, achieved their first major success in the pages of *Queen and Country*.

Plot

Queen and Country is a fictional saga based upon a genuine secret organization: the special operations arm of the Secret Intelligence Service (SIS) in the United Kingdom. London-headquartered SIS, also known as MI6, carries out missions abroad for the British government at the behest of the Ministry of Defense; the domestic counterpart of SIS, responsible for national security, is MI5. Special operations is a clandestine unit that plans covert missions to be executed on foreign soil via as many as three highly trained field operatives known as "Minders."

The SIS gathers information through various agencies. If intelligence suggests the potential to affect British interests somewhere in the world, upper-echelon politicians decide whether and how to react, and orders are passed down the chain of command. When action is warranted, the Minders are sent to carry out objectives—such as infiltration, assassination, or extraction of people or objects—intended to defuse volatile situations, eliminate threats, or provide favorable national advantages. Goals may be general or specific, and individual Minders must be highly adaptable in adjusting to actual conditions once they are in place. As in real life, in *Queen and Country*, human nature is unpredictable, information is sometimes unreliable, and the best-laid plans do not always unfold smoothly.

The first story, *Operation—Broken Ground* sets the tone for the series. The initial scene unfolds in London in the map-dominated SIS operations room, where personnel await news from their operative in Kosovo. The scene shifts to that location, where Minder Two, Tara Chace, is hiding in a bombed-out building. When a former Russian general, now an arms dealer and mafioso, arrives, Tara shoots him dead. Chased by the

Russian's angry henchmen, Tara is wounded and must rely on her wits to escape the area. Meanwhile, back in London, Tara's superior, Paul Crocker, justifies the mission to his boss: It was undertaken as a favor for the U.S. Central Intelligence Agency (CIA), which is now beholden to the SIS.

In chapter 2, Russian arms dealers retaliate, firing a rocket into SIS headquarters, killing several workers. Though such an attack would normally be the province of MI5, Crocker wants the SIS to take revenge for the assault and argues with his superiors and with MI5 for the chance to do so. Crocker learns the Russians have placed a million-dollar bounty on Tara.

In chapter 3, Tara is used as bait for bounty hunters stalking her, with other Minders standing by as protection. Since they are operating within England, the Minders are ordered to turn in their firearms. Tara and the other Minders must make do with realistic-looking pellet guns and their superior physical skills to defeat a quartet of thugs. Contrary to Crocker's wishes, MI5 takes surviving Russians into captivity. In the final chapter, Crocker tries to mount an assassination attempt on the captive bounty hunters, but his plans are foiled when the Russians are secretly traded to the U.S. Federal Bureau of Investigation.

Subsequent entries in the series deal with a variety of issues. Missions are mounted in global hot spots such as Afghanistan, Germany, Egypt, Sudan, Japan, and Zimbabwe as the SIS works to counter kidnappings, undermine brutal dictatorships, assist in defections, or dismantle terrorist plots. Operatives are damaged physically or emotionally in the course of their work and must be rehabilitated through medical and psychological care. Operatives and other members of the SIS die, become incapacitated, or leave the service and must be replaced. Conflicts rise and fall among the ranks, between the various rival British governmental bodies, and between the SIS and their foreign equivalents to further complicate matters.

Volumes

- *Queen and Country: Operation—Broken Ground* (2002). Collects issues 1-4. The cast of characters is introduced through dossier-like visual and brief verbal portraits. Individual character qualities are exhibited through the examination of a tension-filled mission and its equally stressful aftereffects.

- *Queen and Country: Operation—Morningstar* (2002). Collects issues 5-7. Drinking heavily and plagued by insomnia, Tara undergoes psychological counseling, as the other Minders risk death

obtaining hidden information during a mission in Afghanistan.

- *Queen and Country: Operation—Crystal Ball* (2003). Collects issues 8-12. Shaken by the September 11, 2001, terrorist attacks, the SIS Minders globetrot to Berlin, Cairo, Sudan, northern Iraq, and Japan on the trail of a clever terrorist scheme.

Queen & Country. (Courtesy of Oni Press)

- *Queen and Country: Declassified*, Volume 1 (2003). Collects issues 1-3 of *Queen and Country: Declassified*. Flashes back to 1986 in West Berlin. Newly married Crocker, then a Minder, aids the defection of Soviet Valery Karpin. Despite Crocker's best efforts, Karpin is killed at the border. Meanwhile, Minder One, Lindsay Mills, is killed in the Ukraine.
- *Queen and Country: Operation—Blackwall* (2003). Collects issues 13-15. French officials blackmail British billionaire Colin Beck (via sexual videos of his daughter Rachel) to obtain business concessions. Tara, Rachel's friend from Cambridge University, ends her own affair with Minder Ed Kittering and goes to Paris to neutralize the threat.
- *Queen and Country: Operation—Stormfront* (2004). Collects issues 16-20. Ed Kittering dies in Venezuela and is replaced by Brian Butler. In Tbilisi, Georgia, Russian businessman Lasha Karpin—son of would-be defector Valery—is kidnapped. Tara and Brian are sent to free Karpin, and Brian is killed in the effort.
- *Queen and Country: Operation—Dandelion* (2004). Collects issues 21-24. Supercilious Frances Barclay takes over as "C," Chief of Service at the SIS. Tara goes undercover in London to tease information out of Daniel Mwamba, who has aspirations of replacing brutal Robert Mugabe as head of government in Zimbabwe.
- *Queen and Country: Operation—Saddlebags* (2005). Collects issues 25-28. Tara visits her jet-set mother in Switzerland. In London, Minder One Tom Wallace resigns; Tara replaces him, and Chris Lankford becomes new Minder Three. Tara fails in her mission to prevent a British national from selling secrets to the Russians.
- *Queen and Country: Declassified*, Volume 2 (2006). Collects issues 1-3 *Queen and Country: Declassified*, Volume 2. Flashes back to 1995 in Bosnia. North Atlantic Treaty Organization (NATO) troops, including Royal Marine sergeant Tom Wallace, battle insurgents. Wallace is recruited as new Minder Three and sent to Hong Kong before the Chinese takeover to determine the significance of the murder of a British official.
- *Queen and Country: Declassified*, Volume 3 (2006). Collects issues 1-3 of *Queen and Country: Declassified*, Volume 3. Flashes back to 1981 in Northern Ireland. Examines the interwoven careers of Irish Republican Army terrorist-attack survivor Lauren Mullen, terrorist Liam Finnegan, and Special Air Services trainee and future SIS Minder Nick Poole over the course of twenty years.
- *Queen and Country: Operation—Red Panda* (2007). Collects issues 29-32. Tara returns from Saudi Arabia, where her lover, Tom Wallace, has been killed. She and Minder Nick Poole are sent to Iraq disguised as journalists. They are kidnapped; in a rage, Tara kills all their captors. Returning to London, she discovers she is pregnant.

Characters

- *Tara Chace* is the main character. Blond, attractive, and in her mid-twenties, she is skilled in languages, firearms, and martial arts; she smokes, drinks to excess, and engages in meaningless sex to relieve stress. She has been Minder Two for several years. By the final issues, she has moved up to Minder One.
- *Paul Crocker*, a chain-smoking former Minder, is director of operations in charge of the Minders. A married forty-something with two children, he acts as a buffer between those at the top who issue commands and those at the bottom who carry out orders. He does not always agree with government strategies or decisions and employs creative methods to accomplish goals.
- *Donald Weldon*, formerly stationed in Prague, is deputy chief of service and Crocker's immediate superior. An ambitious, middle-aged man, he is often torn between supporting those above and below him in the SIS hierarchy.
- *"C,"* the codename for the head of the SIS, is ultimate arbiter for all departmental activities. For most of the series, Sir Wilson Stanton Davies, a soft-spoken, pipe-smoking older man occupies the position. After Davies suffers a stroke,

the balding, bespectacled former Prague station chief Frances Barclay replaces him.

- *Kate* is Crocker's personal assistant. Young, pert, blond, and capable, she is both deferential and sarcastic toward her boss.
- *Alexis* and *Ron* are SIS operations room staff. Alexis, with short dark hair and glasses, is mission-control officer; she is responsible for communications between field operatives and headquarters. Ron, who is chubby, blond, and efficient, gathers and evaluates incoming information and arranges travel schedules and accommodations for operatives leaving on missions.
- *Angela Chang*, later *Cheng*, is the CIA station chief in London. She is a young, attractive Asian American known for her foul mouth. She often meets in secret with Crocker to exchange intelligence or to ask for or grant operational favors.
- *Minder One* for most of the series is former Royal Marines sergeant Tom Wallace. An eight-year veteran of the SIS, he sometimes goes on field missions but most often sends one of the other Minders. He is killed in Saudi Arabia.
- *Minder Three* designates the field operator with the least seniority. It is often an unlucky position. Edward Kittering is Minder Three when the series opens. After Kittering dies, Brian Butler replaces him but is immediately killed. Trooper Nick Poole replaces Butler and later moves up to Minder Two. Inexperienced Chris Lankford becomes new Minder Three.
- *Simon Rayburn* is SIS director of intelligence, at an equivalent level with Crocker, with whom he occasionally meets to discuss proposed missions resulting from the information his department has acquired and evaluated.
- *David Kinney* is the burly, blunt, mustachioed operational chief at MI5. He and Crocker often butt heads over jurisdictional issues. Kinney is contemptuous of Tara, and the feeling is mutual.

Artistic Style

Both the *Queen and Country* comic books and collected volumes feature evocative color covers, ranging in style from near photorealism to impressionism.

Interiors, however, are entirely black and white, which act as a metaphor for aspects of the subject matter: the shadowy world of espionage, the "us-versus-them" mentality that operates within the intelligence community, and the darkness that lurks at the core of the human soul.

Unlike most long-running comics series, which typically feature a single creator as writer and artist or creative teams that remain together for many issues, *Queen and Country* showcases the talents of more than a dozen illustrators. Each story arc offers new artists for covers, chapter breaks, and panel layouts, which serves to shatter preconceived visual notions, provide variety, and keep readers alert.

The styles of the individual volumes are incredibly diverse, and thanks to the crisp, cinematic quality of Rucka's writing, they all work. The light, clean, cartoonlike drawings of Rolston (*Operation—Broken Ground* and *Operation—Saddlebags*) could have been pulled from an adult coloring book. They contrast sharply with the high-contrast, ink-saturated, fine-line renderings of Fernandez (*Operation—Crystal Ball*) that veer from realism to exaggeration. Nonetheless, each artist skillfully draws the reader into the story, which always takes precedence over the art.

The sketchily realistic style of Jason Shawn Alexander (*Operation—Blackwall*) is quite different from the stark chiaroscuro efforts of Chris Samnee (*Operation—Red Panda*), but each is appropriate to the subject at hand. The various artists are all equally capable of creating interesting layouts that propel the narrative forward while fracturing the expected grid pattern and dividing the visuals into readable, aesthetically pleasing segments that can be appreciated singly or as a whole. Individual issues feature a plethora of eye-catching techniques: across-the-page horizontal panels, double-page spreads, overhead and low-angle views, trapezoidal frames, silhouettes, long-distance and close-up shots, and out-of-frame bursts to emphasize action.

One of the most fascinating aspects of the use of various artists is in the interpretation of protagonist Tara Chace. Most of the illustrators draw her as reasonably attractive, with subtle touches that enhance or downplay her physical appeal. Bryan Lee O'Malley, for example (*Operation—Morningstar*), shows her wearing a ponytail, with bags under her eyes and a haunted expression. Carla Speed McNeil (*Operation—Storm Front*) gives Tara a shag haircut and a boyish figure that deglamorizes her. Mike Hawthorne (*Operation—Dandelion*) imparts Tara with a fragile beauty. Fernandez, at the far end of the scale, makes Tara gorgeous and positively voluptuous, with a *Playboy* Playmate body.

Themes

One major thread that runs throughout *Queen and Country* is the contrast between appearance and reality. To the public at large, spying is an adventurous profession. The modern model of the spy is novelist Ian Fleming's James Bond. His is a world of fast cars, exotic locations, fancy gadgets, designer clothing, and romantic encounters with beautiful women. The indestructible hero takes on and single-handedly defeats a diabolical, larger-than-life villain.

The reality as depicted in *Queen and Country* is far different. Much of intelligence collection is drudgery: endless yawn-inducing days of observation, documentation, collation, and interpretation leading nowhere. There is considerable downtime for field operatives between missions, during which they often indulge in self-destructive behavior. Field assignments are not always clear-cut but can rather be mazelike, with complications requiring contingency plans at every turn and hazy objectives at the end. Villains are less often megalomaniacal masterminds and more often simply greedy individuals or groups of ordinary people willing to take extreme measures to support a cause. Missions do not always succeed. Sometimes the villain gets away. Sometimes a hero dies.

Another theme concerns the deleterious effects of espionage work. Minders must be well versed in "tradecraft": the ability to spot and lose followers, to glibly assume cover identities, to improvise, to become confident liars, to act brutally if necessary. Such habits can bleed into personal life. Outwardly, Minders present tough, impenetrable facades, but internally they are in turmoil because they are humans, not machines. Slippery issues such as ethics combined with the uncertainties and the life-or-death peril of missions, all take their

toll. It is no wonder Rucka shows battered operatives suffering from post-traumatic stress disorder after completing missions and drinking to excess or engaging in empty sex to forget what they have experienced.

Impact

The concept of *Queen and Country* was inspired, as Rucka has freely admitted, by the television series *The Sandbaggers* (1978-1980), which realistically depicted British-style espionage. Though Rucka retained the structure of the secret organization and the downbeat tone of the television series, he put his own stamp on the face of modern espionage: the story behind the story ripped from the headlines. In Rucka's version, more sex is shown than was allowed when the television show was airing. More violence is depicted, though not glorified. The language can be coarse at times.

For *Queen and Country*, Rucka created a complete cast of well-realized characters who act in believable fashion within an established hierarchy: They try hard, make mistakes, suffer consequences for their actions,

---

Greg Rucka

Novelist Greg Rucka established himself as the creator of the Atticus Kodiak series, which was widely praised for its attention to detail and realism. He moved into comics with *Whiteout* (art by Steve Lieber), a crime thriller set in Antarctica, which was subsequently adapted for the screen. In 2001 he began writing his signature series, *Queen & Country*, with art by a number of contributors. This spy thriller, set in the world of the British Secret Intelligence Service, is a more realistic adventure series than is typical of American comics. Rucka's writing is distinctive for its seriousness and its attempt to create fully developed characters and political intrigue within the generic confines of the spy thriller. In the 2000's Rucka became one of the most sought-after writers of superhero comics, writing *52*, *Adventures of Superman*, *Wonder Woman*, and *Gotham Central* for DC Comics and *Wolverine*, *Elektra*, and other titles for Marvel Comics.

and if they survive, carry heavy baggage afterward. Rucka's account of the SIS focuses on modern global issues: control of oil reserves, corporate dirty tricks, manipulation of foreign governments, and fanatical splinter groups. *Queen and Country* particularly emphasizes the stultifying effect of bureaucracy on an occupation like espionage. Ultimately, *Queen and Country* is both a tribute and a creative extrapolation of *The Sandbaggers*, which coincidentally ended with a mystery worthy of a spy thriller. The television series creator and writer Ian Mackintosh, a former intelligence officer, disappeared off Alaska during a flight in 1979. No trace of him has since been found.

Jack Ewing

Further Reading

Bartoll, Jean-Claude, and Renaud Garreta. *Insiders* (2009-).

Fleming, Ian, et al. *James Bond Omnibus* (2009-).

O'Donnell, Peter, et al. *Modesty Blaise* (2003-).

Bibliography

Davies, Barry. *The Spycraft Manual: The Insider's Guide to Espionage Techniques*. London: Zenith Press 2005.

Hitz, Frederick Porter. *The Great Game: The Myths and Reality of Espionage*. New York: Vintage Books, 2005.

Jeffery, Keith. *The Secret History of MI6*. New York: Penguin, 2010.

See also: *Hard Boiled*; *Richard Stark's Parker*; *The Fixer*; *Whiteout*

RABBI'S CAT, THE

Author: Sfar, Joann

Artist: Joann Sfar (illustrator); Brigitte Findakly (colorist)

Publishers: Editions Dargaud (French); Pantheon Books (English)

First book publication: *Le Chat du Rabbin*, 2002-2006 (English translation, 2005, 2008)

Publication History

The Rabbi's Cat is a French graphic novel series written and drawn by Joann Sfar, consisting of five volumes as of 2011, originally published by Editions Dargaud. By the time Sfar wrote *The Rabbi's Cat*, he was already a critically acclaimed graphic novelist in France, having created multiple graphic novel series on his own and collaborated on others. *The Rabbi's Cat* was a deeply personal project for Sfar, inspired by his own family's history, as his father was an Algerian Jew who immigrated to France.

The first volume to appear was *La Bar-Mitsva*, in 2002. Next was *Le Malka des Lions* (2002), followed by *L'Exode* (2003), *Le Paradis terrestre* (2005), and *Jérusalem d'Afrique* (2006). The popularity of *Le Chat du Rabbin* led to an English edition, published by Pantheon in 2005 and translated by Alexis Siegel and Anjali Singh. This book contained the first three volumes of the series.

In 2008, Pantheon published a sequel, *The Rabbi's Cat 2*, which contained the fourth and fifth volumes. Although many readers have assumed that the series was finished, in late 2010, Sfar announced tentative plans for a sixth volume. Also in 2010, Dargaud issued a single-volume compilation, *Le Chat du Rabbin l'intégrale*, intended to coincide with the release of the film based on the series.

Plot

A blend of fantasy, history, philosophy, autobiography, travel narrative, and political critique, the series defies easy classification. Set in Algiers during the 1930's, the story is a set of loosely connected episodes revolving around the family of Rabbi Abraham Sfar, which

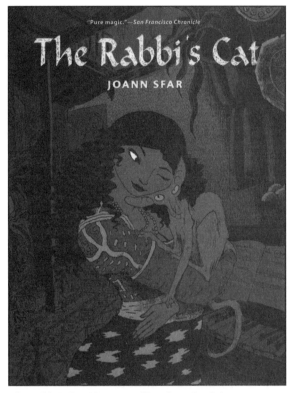

The Rabbi's Cat. (Courtesy of Pantheon Books)

includes his talking cat, his daughter Zlabya (and later her husband Jules Nahum), and his cousin Malka. Although the cat remains the narrator throughout, its role changes from a mischievous figure driving the plot to an observer and commentator on the action.

The cat acquires the power of human speech after eating the family's pet bird. Declaring himself a Jewish cat, it announces its desire to have a Bar Mitzvah. The rabbi begins to teach the Torah to the cat but is defeated by the cat's arguments.

Awaiting his cousin Malka's visit, the rabbi dreads the French exam required by the Central Consistory of French Jews. Hoping to help its master, an Arabic speaker whose knowledge of French is minimal, the cat utters a curse and abruptly loses the power to speak. When a Parisian rabbi, Jules Nahum, appears soon after, the rabbi fears the young man is his replacement.

Unable to face the prospect, he takes a short trip. On the way, he meets an old friend, the Muslim Sheikh Muhammed Sfar, and they pray together. He learns he has passed the exam and returns home to find that Jules and Zlabya are engaged to be married.

The rabbi and his cat accompany the couple on their honeymoon to Paris, to meet Jules's family. Dismayed by Jules's nonobservant parents, the rabbi seeks shelter in a church, then in a restaurant, before calling his nephew, Raymond Rebibo, a musician now living in Paris. While the rabbi is at first appalled to see Raymond in an Arab costume singing in the street for money, he concludes philosophically that sometimes compromises are necessary to survive.

Temporarily leaving the rabbi, the cat travels through the desert with the nomadic Malka and his tame lion. Near the end of the volume Malka meets up with the rabbi in Oran, where they both are shocked to hear a French priest delivering a virulently anti-Semitic speech.

Next, a Russian Jewish painter arrives as a stowaway in a crate of Talmuds, explaining that he is searching for a mythical African Jerusalem to serve as refuge for his oppressed countrymen. Vastenov, a wealthy Russian émigré, offers to sponsor the expedition, which the rabbi and Sheikh Muhammed Sfar join. The route they take follows that of an iconic French colonial car journey, La Croisière noire (1924-1925), across Africa; the rabbi carries a copy of *La Croisière noire: Expédition Citroën Centre-Afrique* (1927; *The Black Journey*, 1927), a memoir of the journey by Georges-Marie Haardt and Louis Audouin-Dubreuil.

There are also a number of similarities between incidents in the memoir and those in Sfar's graphic novel. In the desert the cat is bitten by a scorpion; miraculously revived by a Muslim healer, Professor Soliman, it now can speak all human languages. Later Soliman offers the rabbi the choice of converting to Islam or being killed. Coming to his friend's defense, the Sheikh incurs Soliman's wrath. After Vastenov dies in a duel, they depart.

Along the way, the Russian Jew falls in love with a young African woman and asks the rabbi to marry them. The Russian Jew and his bride, along with the cat, enter "Jerusalem," where the Russian Jew is told that he cannot be Jewish because he is white and must leave or be killed. He reports back to the rabbi that his African Jerusalem does not exist after all.

Volumes

- *Le Chat du Rabbin: 1, La Bar-Mitsva* (2002). Concerns the cat's coming to terms with its ability to speak and his desire to become Bar Mitzvah.
- *Le Chat du Rabbin: 2, Le Malka des Lions* (2002). Introduces the rabbi's cousin, Malka, and Jules Nahum, who falls in love with the rabbi's daughter.
- *Le Chat du Rabbin: 3, L'Exode* (2003). Relates the rabbi's disastrous trip to Paris, tagging along on his daughter's honeymoon.
- *Le Chat du Rabbin: 4, Le Paradis terrestre* (2005). Reveals Malka's secret life and his fear of growing old.
- *Le Chat du Rabbin: 5, Jérusalem d'Afrique* (2006). Involves the trip across Africa in search of a hidden Jewish utopia.

Characters

- *The cat*, who has no name, is a skinny gray house cat with striking green eyes. It is devoted to the rabbi and Zlabya. As the narrator of the series, it acquires the ability to speak when it eats the family's pet bird. Its linguistic skills as translator prove invaluable in volume 5.
- *Rabbi Abraham Sfar*, the protagonist and moral center of the series, is the cat's widowed master. A short, overweight man, bald with a bushy gray beard and round nose, he looks slightly comical and is usually dressed in a sleeveless white undershirt and short brown pants. He loves his daughter Zlabya and his books.
- *Zlabya Sfar*, the rabbi's beautiful but spoiled and hot-tempered daughter, has large dark eyes, long curly black hair, and freckles and always wears red or orange. She relishes her independence, and resents her husband's telling her what to do.
- *Malka* is the rabbi's cousin, a charismatic storyteller who enjoys spreading legends about himself. A tall thin man with piercing blue eyes,

flowing white hair, and a moustache and a beard, he is always accompanied by his tame lion.

- *The rabbi's rabbi* is a tall, thin, serious-looking man with a long nose and long face. He is narrow-minded and superstitious, horrified by the idea of a talking Jewish cat. Later he tries to murder the Russian Jew, believing him to be a golem, an artificial being made by magic.
- *Jules Nahum*, a French-born rabbi, of North African descent, marries Zlabya. A muscular man

with broad shoulders, he sports a fashionably thin moustache and wears European suits.

- *Sheikh Muhammed Sfar* is a Muslim musician and a good friend to the rabbi. He is a kindly looking man with a long white beard; he wears glasses and a flowing robe and travels with a donkey. His intervention saves the lives of both the cat and the rabbi in volume 5.
- *Raymond Rebibo*, the rabbi's nephew, is a musician living in Paris. A tall, thin man with a pointed nose and thin moustache, he dresses up

The Rabbi's Cat. (Courtesy of Pantheon Books)

in a red fez and long robe, singing on the street to earn money because no one values his North African music.

- *The Russian Jew* arrives as an unnamed stowaway in a crate of Talmuds. He stands out because of his pale white skin, orange hair, and blue eyes. A nonobservant Jew, he regards painting as a form of spirituality.
- *Vastenov* is a wealthy, bored Russian émigré who sponsors the Jerusalem trip. Tall and thin, with glasses, a thin moustache, and short gray hair, he lives in a mansion outside Algiers. His arrogance leads to his death.
- *Professor Soliman* is a tall, angry man. A devout Muslim healer, he reluctantly brings the cat back from the dead after a scorpion bite. He despises the rabbi for not renouncing Judaism and the Sheikh for befriending a Jew.
- *The African woman* has no name and no family. A former slave, she is a beautiful woman with short and braided black hair. She agrees to convert to Judaism in order to get married.

Artistic Style

Sfar's highly expressionist pen-and-ink drawings are well suited to the fantastic, magical, and dreamlike qualities of the series. The most striking aspect of *The Rabbi's Cat* may be the unnerving variability with which he draws his characters, so that individuals may appear quite different from panel to panel and from the first volume to the fifth volume. Sfar's loosely drawn, sketchy style suggests characters instead of reproducing them identically each time they appear. In some cases, characters are distorted, their outward appearance providing clues to their moods and emotions. Thus, the cat changes size and shape, growing ominously large at one point, when it is jealous of Zlabya's husband, Jules, and turning into a half-human, half-cat creature at another, when it is in the throes of an identity crisis. The exception to the drawing style is the rabbi's cousin, Malka, whose face is drawn in a consistently more realistic style.

Another element of the artistic style in *The Rabbi's Cat* is Sfar's attention to intricate patterns and geometric shapes in the furniture, the floor, the walls, and

Zlabya's clothes, reflecting Moorish influences. Colorist Brigitte Findakly's muted palette of earth tones—shades of yellow, orange, red, and brown—seems to suggest the sympathetic connection between the characters and the North African landscape, their sense of belonging and of being part of this environment. Color is also used to convey mood or daydream states; at times, an entire panel may be one color, or a character in a panel may be one color or may be shown in silhouette. When Malka gets angry, the panel's background is red with black slashing marks.

The scenes in Paris are markedly different in tone than those in Africa, dominated by shades of gray, reflecting not only the colder, damper climate but also the characters' profound sense of being out of place. Zlabya, still in her distinctive red and orange, frets that she does not fit in and does not look like a Parisian woman, and the rabbi, surrounded by non-Jews and nonobservant Jews, feels that he has entered an alien and ambiguous moral space.

Themes

The central theme of *The Rabbi's Cat* is the destructive nature of prejudice—ethnic, racial, and religious—and the need for tolerance. The cat embodies the irrationality of prejudice, since its ability to speak, read, and argue, as well as its ability to feel compassion, love, and jealousy, are all human qualities. Nonetheless, it looks like an ordinary cat and so it faces discrimination from the rabbi's rabbi, the officials at the school where the rabbi takes his French test, and Professor Soliman, the healer. As an immigrant in Paris, the rabbi's nephew, Raymond Rebibo, discovers that an Algerian Jew is as impossible as a talking cat.

Sfar also demonstrates that racial, ethnic, and religious prejudices exist within Judaism. The appearance of the white-skinned Russian, an Ashkenazi Jew, creates panic in the rabbi's Sephardic Jewish community, where he is denounced as a golem. In a case of reverse racism, the black Jerusalemites claim that the Russian Jew cannot be Jewish because he is white.

Colonialism is another theme, as the colonizing French redefine indigenous Algerians—Arabs and Jews—as trespassers and drive a wedge between them.

In Volume 4, the malignant Abbé Lambert publicly calls for the eradication of Arabs and Jews in Algeria.

Family is another important theme. Although the rabbi does not always agree with his family or approve of what they do, he loves them unconditionally, and they support him. The eclectic community of travelers in Volume 5 forms an extended family that transcends ethnic, racial, religious, and linguistic differences and serves as an idealized version of society.

The series also highlights the theme of faith, through a range of Jewish and Muslim characters. Despite belonging to different religions, the rabbi and Sheikh Muhammed Sfar share a similar approach to spirituality, valuing pragmatism over strict dogmatic interpretation.

Impact

The Rabbi's Cat represented a reaction against the Franco-Belgian comics tradition closely identified with Hergé. In a parodic allusion to *Tintin in the Congo* (1931), Sfar stages a playful brief encounter between his characters and Tintin and Snowy. Volume 5 can also be read as a critique of the colonial attitudes toward Africans exemplified by *Tintin in the Congo*.

Although Jewish-themed graphic novels have a long tradition in the United States, beginning with Will Eisner's *A Contract with God* (1978), in its exposition of Sephardic Jewish culture *The Rabbi's Cat* introduced readers to a significant part of Jewish life that had been left out of American Jewish graphic novels, rooted as they have been in Ashkenazi Jewish experience. Additionally, because writing about explicitly Jewish issues was not part of the French comics tradition, *The Rabbi's Cat* broke new ground in subject matter for the French graphic novel by foregrounding Jewish history, identity, and religion.

Even more significantly, *The Rabbi's Cat* performed an important role in educating readers about Algerian history, drawing attention to the once-thriving Algerian Jewish community that began to decline in the second half of the twentieth century. Sfar's focus on Algerian Jews, and on a time when Jews and Muslims lived side by side, sharing culture and language, was a revelation to many readers. Although novels had been written about North African Jews and graphic novels had been written about Algeria, no graphic novel had previously addressed this particular topic.

Marla Harris

Further Reading

Banerjee, Sarnath. *The Barn Owl's Wondrous Capers* (2007).

Eisner, Will. *A Contract with God, and Other Tenement Stories* (1978).

Sheinkin, Steve. *The Adventures of Rabbi Harvey* (2006-2010).

Bibliography

Beaty, Bart. *Unpopular Culture: Transforming the European Comic Book in the 1990's*. Toronto: University of Toronto Press, 2007.

Eisenstein, Paul. "Imperfect Masters: Rabbinic Authority in Joann Sfar's *The Rabbi's Cat*." In *The Jewish Graphic Novel: Critical Approaches*, edited by Samantha Baskind and Ranen Omer-Sherman. New Brunswick, N.J.: Rutgers University Press, 2008.

Harris, Marla. "Borderlands: Places, Spaces, and Jewish Identity in Joann Sfar's *The Rabbi's Cat* and *Klezmer*." In *The Jewish Graphic Novel: Critical Approaches*, edited by Samantha Baskind and Ranen Omer-Sherman. New Brunswick, N.J.: Rutgers University Press, 2008.

Kaplan, Arie. *From Krakow to Krypton: Jews and Comic Books*. Philadelphia: Jewish Publication Society, 2008.

Joann Sfar

An important part of the new generation of Franco-Belgian comic creators, Joann Sfar is an acclaimed writer, artist, and filmmaker. He has occasionally collaborated with other French comics creators, including David B. and Lewis Trondheim. Sfar blends historical, theological, and personal elements in his work to create humorous and poignant stories. In addition to his adult-oriented work, he has done an acclaimed adaptation of the classic children's novel *The Little Prince*.

Roth, Laurence. "Drawing Contracts: Will Eisner's Legacy." *The Jewish Quarterly Review* 97, no. 3 (Summer, 2007): 463-484.

Shasha, David. "Rediscovering the Arab Jewish Past." *The American Muslim*, October 26, 2005. http://www.theamericanmuslim.org.

See also: *Maus*; *A Contract with God, and Other Tenement Stories*; *The Golem's Mighty Swing*; *Aya of Yopougon*

REX MUNDI

Author: Nelson, Arvid

Artist: Eric J. (pseudonym of Eric Johnson, illustrator); Jim Di Bartolo (illustrator); Juan Ferreyra (illustrator); Brian Churilla (penciller); Guy Davis (penciller, inker, cover artist); Jeromy Cox (colorist); Jason Millet (colorist); Dave Stewart (colorist, cover artist); J. H. Williams III (cover artist); Arvid Nelson (letterer)

Publisher: Image Comics; Dark Horse Comics

First serial publication: 2002-2009

First book publication: 2004-2010

Publication History

In 1999, comics writer Arvid Nelson met comics creator Eric Johnson (who uses the pseudonym Eric J.) and made his first visit to Paris; the latter experience sparked Nelson's interest in European history and architecture and conspiracy theories surrounding the Holy Grail. Nelson and Johnson collaborated to combine these interests, resulting in a self-published black-and-white issue of *Rex Mundi* that they sold at the 2000 Comic-Con International: San Diego.

Deciding their first effort was too raw, Nelson and Johnson reworked it with colorist Jeromy Cox. Image Comics published a trial issue (known as issue 0) in August, 2002, which sold out as the result of the buzz created by a *Rex Mundi* Web comic. The trio worked on fourteen issues of the series, but because of creative differences and scheduling difficulties, Nelson replaced Johnson and Cox with Jim Di Bartolo. Johnson retained a co-creator credit for the remainder of the series. Di Bartolo drew two issues before deciding to pursue other forms of art, and Nelson enlisted Argentinean artist Juan Ferreyra to complete the series. Three issues after Ferreyra joined, *Rex Mundi* switched to Dark Horse Comics' line of horror comics. Nelson remarked that he admired Image Comics' model of having creators produce their entire comic, but editorial and production support from Dark Horse allowed him to concentrate on completing the series.

Rex Mundi: The Guardian of the Temple. (Courtesy of Dark Horse Comics)

Plot

Rex Mundi occurs in an alternate historical time line in which the Inquisition mostly suppressed the Protestant Reformation and the Bourbon Restoration ended the French Revolution in 1799. France has an ostensible constitutional monarchy with a national assembly: an upper Hall of the Sword and a lower Hall of the Robe. Aristocrats who trace their lineage back to the First Crusade serve in the Sword, while the monarchy appoints the members of the Robe. In practice, the monarchy and the Robe always overrule any militaristic initiatives of the Sword.

These changes stunt the development of democratic, feminist, and radical thought, and the American experiment in self-government is seen as a dismal failure. The Confederate States of America (CSA) retained their independence from the Federal Republic of America (FRA) thanks to British support, and the CSA and FRA are two backwater powers engaging in endless border wars over their western territories. Slavery in the CSA and the transatlantic slave trade endure, as do many institutions and features of feudal and medieval Europe: Guilds and Italian merchant princes control economic life, the Catholic Church wields significant political power, the Inquisition serves as an international police force, the Holy Roman Empire and the Ottoman Empire endure, and the Islamic emirate of Cordova controls most of the Iberian Peninsula. In this alternate world, kabbalistic magic is real but tightly controlled by the Sorcerers' Guild and the Inquisition.

Rex Mundi fleshes out these details by including a couple of supplementary newspaper pages in the back of most issues. These newspapers give glimpses of world events in the alternate time line and feature stories that illustrate the workings of the French government, the guild system, and magic, among other details.

The main plot of *Rex Mundi* occurs in 1933-1934 and begins in Paris. Several characters quest to determine the nature of the Holy Grail and locate it. Dr. Julien Saunière is a mash-up of detective Philip Marlowe and archaeologist-adventurer Indiana Jones; he is enlisted by his friend and mentor Father Gérard Marin to locate a scroll stolen from Marin's church after the priest had a postcoital conversation about it with a prostitute. The scroll, written by the Knights Templar, specifies the burial grounds of Merovingian kings; it could potentially lead to the Grail. The prostitute, her pimp, his gangster boss, the latter's Italian merchant prince contact, and Marin are all ritualistically murdered by a mysterious sorcerer clad in all white, and Dr. Saunière spends the rest of the series trying to discover who sponsored the assassin and the reason behind those murders.

Parisian street urchins and Rabbi Albert Maiselles assist Dr. Saunière in his quest, and, at one point, the Inquisition, which also seeks the Grail, deputizes the doctor. Another ally of Dr. Saunière is his colleague and sometime lover, Dr. Genevieve Tournon. Dr. Tournon's loyalties remain divided between Dr. Saunière and her new lover, the duke of Lorraine, who, in a series of political maneuvers, transforms France into a fascist state based on myths of Frankish racial purity and Christian crusading.

Lorraine incites a world war that resembles both the Napoleonic Wars and World War I and World War II, with the Axis powers of France, the United Kingdom, and Russia warring with the invading Allies: the Cordovan, Prussian, Holy Roman, and Ottoman empires. Lorraine's imperial ambitions and his ethnic cleansing of Jews and Muslims spring from his mysterious connection to the Grail. These mysteries mostly resolve in a series of violent, occult confrontations at a secret castle in the Pyrenees, as Saunière, Tournon, Saunière's implacable nemesis Grand Inquisitor Gervase Moricant, oppressed Muslim shepherds, and Lorraine's daughter, the socialite-cum-sorcerer Lady Isabelle, battle Lorraine and his forces.

Volumes

- *Rex Mundi*, Book 1: *The Guardian of the Temple* (2004). Collects issues 0-5 and Web comic "Brother Matthew, Blessed Are the Weak." Dr. Saunière investigates four ritual murders and a Templar scroll theft, and Dr. Tournon enters the duke of Lorraine's political circles.
- *Rex Mundi*, Book 2: *The River Underground* (2005). Collects issues 6-11. Dr. Saunière learns the secret, contradictory histories of the Grail, and he and Dr. Tournon discover Lorraine's connections to the Templars.
- *Rex Mundi*, Book 3: *The Lost Kings* (2006). Collects issues 12-17. The Inquisition deputizes Dr. Saunière, and he believes he has discovered the truth of the Grail and the Crucifixion; Lorraine forces war with Muslim rule in Cordova.
- *Rex Mundi*, Book 4: *Crown and Sword* (2007). Collects issues 18 of the Image series, issues 1-5 of the Dark Horse series, and a short story from *The Dark Horse Book of Monsters*, "To Weave a Monster." Saunière and Tournon flee to the south of France, and war engulfs Europe.
- *Rex Mundi*, Book 5: *The Valley at the End of the World* (2008). Collects issues 6-12 of the Dark Horse series. Inquisitor Moricant and a drunken Dr. Saunière locate the Grail, and Dr. Tournon

rejoins a victorious Lorraine who seeks to reunite Europe.

- *Rex Mundi*, Book 6: *Gate of God* (2010). Collects issues 13-19 of the Dark Horse series and the story "Hill of Martyrs." The Grail seekers are forced to revise their opinions on the nature of the Grail, and Lorraine launches a Tenth Crusade to capture Jerusalem from the Ottomans.

Characters

- *Novate Inquisitor Matthew* is a brilliant detective-monk squeamish about the Inquisition's methods.
- *Father Gérard Marin, S. J.*, was the veteran priest of L'église de la Madeleine in Paris's 8th arrondissement and charged with the secret task of guarding the church's cache of Templar and Merovingian texts.
- *Master Physician Julien Saunière* is an alcoholic doctor of obscure origins whose ministrations to the Parisian poor, French Jews, and the underworld put him at odds with his guild and the Inquisition.
- *Father Eugene Calvet, S. J.*, delivers the final message of his older friend Father Marin to Dr. Saunière.
- *The Man in White* is an unknown sorcerer whose assassinations draw Dr. Saunière into the mystery.
- *Grand Inquisitor Gervase Moricant* serves Archbishop Ireneaux and his faith with fanatical ruthlessness.
- *Rabbi Albert Maiselles*, an expert on the occult and golems, is a friend of Dr. Saunière, but he wishes to keep a low profile because of rampant anti-Semitism.
- *Master Physician Genevieve Tournon* is the personal physician of the duke of Lorraine, an aspiring politician, and an occasional lover of Dr. Saunière.
- *Emile-Jean Ireneaux*, the archbishop of Sens, heads the Inquisition in Paris and secretly seeks the Grail.
- *David-Louis Plantard de St. Clair*, the forty-ninth duke of Lorraine and speaker of the Hall

of the Sword, foments a militaristic French nationalism and has personal colonial experience in Indochina and Algeria.

- *Baron Robert Teniers* is an associate of Lorraine. Lorraine frequently treats him with condescension.
- *Mayor of the Court Charles Martel* is the king's proxy negotiator and opposes Lorraine's expansionism.
- *Baronet Aristide de Mandeville*, the speaker of the Hall of the Robe, is a former supporter of royal policy.
- *Lady Isabelle Plantard de St. Clair* is Lorraine's daughter and a notorious socialite who can be a liability for her father, whose attention she craves.
- *First Lord of the Admiralty Winston Churchill* is Lorraine's counterpart in the British government and a fellow imperialist who supports Lorraine's warmongering and hostility toward Muslims.
- *The Marquises of Aragon, Navarre, and Catalonia* are three autonomous noblemen entrusted with defending France's southern border with Cordova. They ally with Lorraine.
- *King Louis XXII* conducts dealings through intermediaries but publically opposes expansionist policies.
- *Aleron* is an anchorite (Church-sanctioned mystic) and a long-standing ally of Father Marin in his search for the Grail.
- *Madame Flóra Tamássy* was Lady Isabelle's governess who appeared to perish while protecting the young Isabelle from an attack by a Swiss vampire.
- *Shaykh Ibrahim al-Rashid* is the elder of a village of Muslim shepherds whom Lorraine's ancestors have kept enslaved for generations.

Artistic Style

Johnson draws *Rex Mundi* in a clean, detailed style. In the early issues, he renders many scenes of talking heads ruminating over arcane Grail lore or machinating over the still-feudal stage of European and French politics. Johnson is the only main artist on *Rex Mundi* not to do his own colors, and Cox's coloring garnered praise for the moody noir tones they give to Johnson's detailed renderings of the medieval Paris cityscape. Johnson and Cox's replacement, Di Bartolo, did two issues as the regular artist, but his most striking contribution is a later fill-in issue that flashes back to the fairy-tale encounter of young Lady Isabelle and her governess with vampires in a Swiss Alpine château.

Ferreyra's initial style on the book evokes the neoclassical paintings that Dr. Saunière attempts to decode early in the narrative, and Ferreyra uses innovative panel layouts similar to J. H. Williams III's work on *Promethea*. Coinciding with Dark Horse's acquisition of the series, Ferreyra's work begins to use simpler layouts and more typical adventure comic naturalism. As the story shifts toward a climax, talking heads became less important, the urban landscape of Paris is abandoned for the countryside of southern France and the Pyrenees, and Ferreyra draws striking versions of

horror set pieces, such as a crumbling castle and an aerial occult battle between Lorraine and his daughter. Ferreyra's visual sense revitalizes some of the more cliché aspects of these set pieces; particularly striking is his coloring of Lady Isabelle in issue 14 of the Dark Horse run. She battles her father's soldiers with Grailinduced magic, and her nose begins to bleed from the exertion. Such a scene is common in adventure stories when a character exerts mental powers, but Ferreyra's coloring emphasizes a startling contrast between the red blood and the pale, almost white of Lady Isabelle's skin and hair.

Themes

The religious trappings of *Rex Mundi* are manifest and frequent, and Nelson describes himself as a convert from Episcopal Protestantism to Baha'i faith.

Rex Mundi: The Guardian of the Temple. (Courtesy of Dark Horse Comics)

Nelson envisions the series as a Baha'i allegory on the unity of the prophetic and mystic traditions of the Abrahamic faiths: Judaism, Christianity, and Islam. Despite his intentions, however, the series is primarily concerned with the political uses of religion. Most of the series was published during the U.S. presidential administration of George W. Bush, one that became notorious for its pursuance of two wars in the Middle East and its adamant support of Israel's position in the region. Bush's vocal conservative Christian rhetoric and faith in democratic capitalism became a touchstone for many critiques that labeled his Middle Eastern policies as messianic, millennial, or crusading. Lorraine deploys religious imagery to sanctify his imperial incursions into the Holy Land, his domestic persecutions of Muslims, and his lineage, becoming a pulpy, exaggerated caricature of what many critics saw in the Bush policies.

Alternate history's facility for political critique does have limits. Such narratives often celebrate the current political status quo and the progress of actual history by showing deviations leading to undesirable outcomes, thereby foreclosing the possibility of radical and positive changes to history. An extreme example of

this tendency comes in Nelson's other alternate history series, *Zero Killer* (2010), in which the U.S. failure to use nuclear weapons against Japan leads to an apocalypse by the 1970's. *Rex Mundi* mostly bypasses this myopic celebration of how history unfolds by showing the seeds of fascism as not being limited to Germany and Italy. Winston Churchill and the United Kingdom serve as Lorraine's primary allies, and this decontextualization of Churchill and the British Empire provides a telling reminder of their long-held racism and imperial ambitions despite popular idealization of the British roles in the real World War II.

Impact

Rex Mundi's impact and influence on the wider art of comic books seems limited, except as an example of a successful creator-owned comic. It began as a self-published piece hawked at a convention but managed to tell its entire story with successful runs at two of the bigger American independent publishers.

In a broader cultural sense, the most notable thing about *Rex Mundi* is its similarities to Dan Brown's novel *The Da Vinci Code* (2003). Nelson and Johnson are quick in interviews and letter columns to disavow influence and point out that they began publishing issues the year before the best seller debuted. The similarities between the two works are numerous and recall similar questions of whether Jack Kirby's *Fourth World* saga (1970-1974) influenced the original *Star Wars* trilogy (1977, 1980, 1983) and if Grant Morrison's *The Invisibles* (1996) provided a model for *The Matrix* films (1999, 2003). Both *Rex Mundi* and *The Da Vinci Code* feature doctors with female companions racing through Paris trying to decode cryptograms and the secret messages of paintings that lead to the Grail, while being pursued by sinister Catholic forces. Some of the similar subject matter emerges from both works' reliance on the speculative work *Holy Blood, Holy Grail* (1982) by Michael Baigent, Richard Leigh, and Henry Lincoln as a primary source. *Rex Mundi* and *The Da Vinci Code* also both have a key character named for the corrupt French priest Bérenger Saunière. The major difference comes from Brown accepting most of Baignet, Leigh, and Lincoln's thesis, while Nelson criticizes

Arvid Nelson

Best known as the writer on the thirty-eight-issue series *Rex Mundi* from Image Comics and Dark Horse Comics, Arvid Nelson turned to writing comics in Paris while working on a documentary project about the *Paris Review*. Set in an alternate reality in 1933 where the Protestant Reformation was thwarted, *Rex Mundi* tells the story of a quest for the Holy Grail in the context of a murder mystery. The book is deeply influenced by Nelson's Bahá'í faith. Since concluding this work, Nelson has written for both Marvel Comics and DC Comics, produced a Kull limited series for Dark Horse, and created a Thulsa Doom series for Dynamite Entertainment. Nelson's work has a strong fantastic element to it and he is known for adventure stories that have a high degree of historical and spiritual interest.

it as absurd and uses it to examine obsessions with lineage, purity, and religious justifications of political rule.

Bob Hodges

Further Reading

Davis, Guy. *The Marquis* (2009).

Mignola, Mike, et al. *Hellboy* (1994-   ).

Moore, Alan, and Eddie Campbell. *From Hell* (1989-1996).

Bibliography

Grant, Steven. "Permanent Damage: Issue 86." *Comic Book Resources*, May 7, 2003. http://www.comicbookresources.com/?page=article&id=14428.

Nelson, Arvid. "Arvid Nelson talks *Rex Mundi*." Interview by David Press. *Comic Book Resources*, July 18, 2008. http://www.comicbookresources.com/?page=article&id=17297.

_____. "Nelson Talks *Rex Mundi* and Religion." Interview by Edward Carey. *Comic Book Resources*, September 17, 2008. http://www.comicbookresources.com/?page=article&id=18089.

Snodgrass, Mary Ellen. *Encyclopedia of Gothic Literature*. New York: Facts On File, 2005.

Willard, Thomas. "Occultism." *The Handbook of the Gothic*. 2d ed. Edited by Marie Mulvey Roberts. New York: New York University Press, 2009.

See also: *From Hell*; *The Adventure of Luther Arkwright*; *Glacial Period*

RICHARD STARK'S PARKER

Author: Stark, Richard (pseudonym of Donald E. Westlake)
Artist: Darwyn Cooke (illustrator)
Publisher: IDW Publishing
First book publication: 2009-

Publication History

The first *Richard Stark's Parker* illustrated novel, *The Hunter*, was published in June, 2009. The second installment, *The Outfit*, was published in 2010. Two additional volumes were planned for publication. Illustrator and adapter Darwyn Cooke is a multiple-award-winning writer and artist best known for his work on *DC: The New Frontier* (2004).

Crime novelist Donald E. Westlake wrote the *Parker* paperback novels between 1962 and 1974 under the pen name Richard Stark. They were adapted to film several times, and Cooke based his vision of Parker on Lee Marvin's portrayal of the character in one of those adaptations, *Point Blank* (1967). In 2000, Cooke decided that the *Parker* books would be his next major project. He began to negotiate for permission to adapt *The Hunter* via a series of e-mails between Westlake, initially through his agent, and himself, assisted by IDW Publishing editor Scott Dunbier. Cooke had illustrated many characters for DC and Marvel, and he allowed Westlake to see scanned pages from *DC: The New Frontier*, as the series was set in the same approximate time frame as the *Parker* novels. The directors of the various film adaptations had glamorized and glorified Parker, against Westlake's wishes, and thus no previous adaptation had been allowed to use the name "Parker." After about a month of e-mails and presentations, however, Westlake realized that Cooke's vision of the character was much more in line with his own and thus allowed Cooke to use the name.

Prior to the publication of *The Outfit*, IDW released a saddle-stitched edition of the first forty pages of the second *Parker* novel, *The Man with the Getaway Face*. Cooke explains in the introduction that he did not want to illustrate the entire novel but that a certain scene

needed to be shown in order for future adaptations to make sense to readers.

Plot

The Hunter is set in the early 1960's. Parker, the main character, is completely amoral, involved in one criminal enterprise after another. He is a brutal man who can be only temporarily diverted from his goal. The story opens with him walking across the George Washington Bridge, refusing an offer for a ride, and eventually hopping a subway turnstile. He falsifies a driver's license, then goes to several banks, claiming to have lost his checkbook. One bank teller allows him access to "his" account, and Parker buys an entire new wardrobe to replace his threadbare one. Then he sets out to find the people who double-crossed him prior to the beginning of the story: his heist partner, Mal Resnick, and his wife, Lynn.

Darwyn Cooke

After working in the animation industry, Darwyn Cooke began illustrating comics with his work on Catwoman with Ed Brubaker. *The New Frontier*, his 2004 miniseries, which he also wrote, re-imagined DC's superheroes in the Cold War context of the 1950's and drew its visual inspiration from the graphic styles of the immediate postwar period. In 2006, he produced a re-envisioning of Will Eisner's *The Spirit*. Since 2009 he has been adapting *Richard Stark's Parker* novels as graphic novels, with the artwork particularly influenced by the high modernist aesthetics of 1960's furniture design. Cooke's art draws heavily on his background in animation, particularly with its round lines and wide-eyed characters. His style is frequently backward-looking and borrows heavily from the design traditions of the past. This tends to give his work a nostalgic feeling of innocence, a tone that is interestingly problematized by the violence in the *Parker* graphic novels.

Parker goes to see Lynn, who lives rent-free in midtown Manhattan as part of a payoff from Resnick. He finds out when Resnick's messenger will bring the rent money and coldheartedly encourages Lynn to overdose on sleeping pills. When she does, he cuts up her face and leaves her in the woods. The messenger gives Parker the name of Arthur Stegman, who runs an auto dealership in Queens, but even Stegman is afraid to tell Parker of Mal's exact whereabouts. On the subway ride back into Manhattan, Parker reflects on the crime gone wrong. After the job he did with Resnick's gang, Lynn shot him and Resnick took the money. Parker had always been involved with armored-car heists or gun smuggling but had never before dealt with the Outfit, the crime syndicate to which Resnick now belongs.

After checking in with several prostitutes, Parker confronts Mal and learns that the entire haul from the robbery, minus the monthly stipend for Lynn, was given back to the Outfit, which is working out of Frederick Carter Investments. The first volume ends with Parker visiting the office, wanting only his share of the money. Carter is killed, as are Mal and Stegman, and an arrangement is made for Parker to get his money delivered to him at a stop along the Long Island Rail Road. After avoiding several ambushes, he drives one of the getaway cars into the darkness, contemplating whether he should go to Miami or the Florida Keys.

Cooke wanted to adapt the third Parker novel, *The Outfit*, next. First, however, he adapted a small portion of the second Parker novel, *The Man with the Getaway Face*, as certain plot points in it are important to understanding the subsequent *Parker* installments. In this story, following the events of *The Hunter*, Parker gets plastic surgery to change his face, then starts looking for his next job. Some new characters are introduced, and Parker avoids a double cross. Now lantern-jawed and looking older, Parker believes he has hidden himself from the mob.

The Outfit opens in Miami Beach, a year after the events in *The Hunter*, with Parker now using the name Chuck Willis. While in bed with a woman, Bette Harrow, he manages to avoid an attempt on his life. The would-be hit man tells him that he was hired by Jim St. Clair, who runs the mob-owned Three Kings Club in Utica, New York. Parker is amazed to find that Skim

Lasker, a bookie and an old friend from Cincinnati, has revealed his whereabouts. Sixteen months before, after removing the bandages from his plastic surgery, Parker met up with Lasker to undertake an armored-car heist in New Jersey. In Brooklyn, they and Handy McKay, one of Parker's few friends, meet with Alma, a woman who works at a diner where the armored-car drivers often stop to eat. After the robbery goes off as planned, the group leaves in two cars. Alma, who is riding in the lead car, stabs Lasker, and Parker and McKay kill her as she tries to flee. Lasker survives the stabbing, and, after weeks of recuperating, he tells Bronson, a representative from the Outfit, where Parker is. After learning this, Parker finds Lasker and kills him.

Parker then sets up a new crew in Scranton, Pennsylvania, where he is joined by McKay and a part-time actor named Grofeld. They pull off ten robberies, including a high-profile one at the Club Cockatoo in New York, costing the Outfit more than one million dollars. The book ends with Parker and McKay killing Bronson and his crew.

Volumes
- *The Hunter* (2009). Parker is double-crossed by his wife and partner, shot, and left for dead. Sixteen months later, he returns to New York City to settle scores.
- *The Outfit* (2010). Tying up loose ends from *The Hunter*, Parker organizes a string of robberies, each affecting the Outfit, in order to take his revenge.

Characters
- *Parker*, whose first name was supposedly known only by his dead wife, is in his thirties. Enlisted during World War II, he is now a career criminal who assembles crews in various cities to help him rob jewelry stores and armored cars.
- *Lynn Parker* is Parker's wife, who shot him during a robbery after they had sex in an abandoned beach house. She is the only person for whom Parker has ever felt emotion, a compassion that he "feared." He encourages her to commit suicide by overdosing on sleeping pills, which she does.

- *Mal Resnick* is a former business partner of Parker. Owing gambling debts to the Syndicate, he double-crosses Parker and leaves him for dead so he can take Parker's share of the stolen money.
- *Handy McKay* is a criminal who helps Parker in several heists, often rounding up a crew while Parker scouts the designated establishment to rob. Always chewing on a toothpick, he hopes to make enough money to retire from crime and purchase a diner on Presque Isle, Maine.
- *Arthur Stegman* is the owner of an auto dealership in Rockaway, Queens. He is questioned by Parker about Resnick's whereabouts and later tells Resnick about Parker's visit.
- *Frederick Carter* runs an investment company that is a front for the Outfit. Parker confronts him regarding the money from the robbery, which Parker believes to be his.
- *Bette Harrow* is a rich woman who knows Parker by the alias Chuck while he is living in Florida. Once she realizes what kind of work Parker does, she helps him subdue the man sent to kill him.
- *Clint Stern* is a Miami Beach hit man.
- *Jim St. Clair* is the owner of the Three Kings Club in Utica, New York. He is one of Parker's targets during a string of robberies.
- *Skim Lasker* is a bookie and an acquaintance of Parker who tells him about a small-time robbery involving an armored car. After being stabbed and left for dead by the waitress who helped set up the heist, he later resurfaces, and Parker is forced to kill him.
- *Alma* is a waitress at a New Jersey diner. She is shot and killed by Parker after stabbing Lasker and attempting to flee.
- *Grofeld* is another associate of Parker, a part-time actor in Scranton, Pennsylvania.
- *Bronson* is a high-ranking member of the Outfit.

Artistic Style

The *Parker* books are illustrated and colored in a single tone. *The Hunter* is entirely in black and white with blue tones. Cooke works in a grid pattern in which only the pastel washes act as borders, a technique he perfected when working on *DC: The New Frontier*. In *The Hunter*, a full twenty pages elapse before the reader even sees Parker's face, and even then it is only his reflection in a mirror.

The *Parker* novels are set in the early 1960's, so the background characters, such as businessmen on the street and pert young women lounging in apartments, have a glamorous look. Cooke occasionally breaks away from his grid format to allow for a single image that provides several paragraphs of exposition, at times ending with a line of dialogue that leads directly to the full-page illustration. He also implements this method when setting up the details of an intricate heist, providing a map of sorts, with images of vehicles, highball glasses, and road routes. The end result is one in which the art and the prose are mutually complementary.

Themes

The *Parker* novels provide a view of a man without a moral compass. Classic, pop-art pulp, *Parker* reads fast and smooth, portraying a character who is smart and completely amoral. The books touch on numerous themes involving the main character's nihilistic attitude. Crime, corruption, and greed surround all of the characters, and all are driven by selfish desires. Westlake, writing as Stark, created a character engaged in violence and motivated by avarice, which are attributes that Cooke picks up on and accentuates.

Impact

DC's Vertigo crime imprint was certainly influenced by the hardcover novel format of the *Parker* series, in tone at least. Although Westlake wrote the stories, Cooke sets up the scene, and his illustrations perfectly convey the characters' thoughts and emotions. Building on Cooke's prior work, the novels demonstrate an evolution in his use of single-color tones in storytelling.

Wayne Allen Sallee

Further Reading

Brubaker, Ed, and Sean Phillips. *Criminal* (2007-2010).
Cooke, Darwyn. *DC: The New Frontier* (2004).
Cooke, Darwyn, and Matt Hollingsworth. *Selina's Big Score* (2002).

Bibliography

Rubin, Brian P. "*Richard Stark's Parker: The Hunter*." Review of *Richard Stark's Parker: The Hunter*, by Darwyn Cooke. *Graphic Novel Reporter*. http://www.graphicnovelreporter.com/content/richard-starks-parker-hunter-review.

Sante, Luc. "The Gentrification of Crime." *The New York Times Review of Books*, March 28, 1985.

Smart, James. "*Richard Stark's Parker: The Outfit*, Adapted and Illustrated by Darwyn Cooke." Review of *Richard Stark's Parker: The Outfit*, by Darwyn Cooke. *The Guardian*, November 26, 2010.

See also: *Hard Boiled*; *A History of Violence*; *Road to Perdition*; *Stray Bullets*

ROAD TO PERDITION

Author: Collins, Max Allan
Artist: Richard Piers Rayner (illustrator); Bob Lappan (letterer)
Publisher: DC Comics
First book publication: 1998

Publication History

Road to Perdition by Max Allan Collins was published by the DC Comics imprint Paradox Press in 1998. From its inception in 1993, Paradox Press tried to break out of the traditional superhero format. *Road to Perdition* fit well in the Paradox Press line, as the company published adult graphic novels in black and white. While prior books from Paradox Press were nominally successful, *Road to Perdition* was perhaps the most well known and commercially viable, given the boost in sales it received after the release of the film adaptation in 2002. Both the film and the book spurred three smaller "sequels" that told of the interim travels of the characters from Rock Island, Illinois, to Perdition, Kansas. Ironically, the book sequels and the film adaptations of *Road to Perdition* came after the Paradox Press line was phased out in 2001. The books that were originally published by Paradox Press continued to be published by the DC imprint Vertigo or simply went out of publication.

Plot

Collins used the real history of the Quad Cities of eastern Iowa and western Illinois during the Prohibition era as the basis for his fictional work. The story is one of gang vengeance and honor during the early 1930's.

The story is told from the viewpoint of a man recollecting his childhood. In the first chapter, entitled "Archangel of Death," Michael O'Sullivan, Jr., recounts the reality and the myth of his father, Michael O'Sullivan, Sr., "the Archangel of Death." His father was a triggerman for the Looney gang that controlled the Rock Island, Illinois, area.

Young Michael reveres his father, who seems to lead an exciting secret life that involves carrying a

(WireImage)

Max Allan Collins

Max Allan Collins is a prolific author of detective fiction, who has drawn inspiration from a number of sources, including the hardboiled detective mysteries of Dashiell Hammett, Raymond Chandler, and Mickey Spillane. While Collins's characters are frequently more complex and flawed than those of the authors who inspired him, his textured characters, such as Nathan Heller—a fictional protagonist who becomes involved with crimes involving historical figures—ring true.

gun. Following a dare from his brother Peter, Michael stows away in a car and later witnesses his father and Connor Looney (the boss's son) assassinate several rivals. When confronted by Connor about what the boy saw, O'Sullivan swears the child to secrecy. Connor does not like the thought of there being any witnesses to the crime and so eventually plots to kill O'Sullivan and his family. The wife and younger O'Sullivan son are killed when the intended target, Michael, is late coming home from a party. At the same time, O'Sullivan himself is endangered when a club owner who owes money to the Looney family is offered amnesty for killing him. O'Sullivan later discovers a note from Connor exposing the assassination attempt.

The remaining two chapters chronicle the damage O'Sullivan inflicts on those who shelter Connor. The second chapter, "Village of the Dead," also details the hazards of the trip to Perdition, Kansas, where relatives take in Michael. O'Sullivan tries to bargain with the notorious Chicago Outfit, but mobster Frank Nitti states that, while the O'Sullivan murders were horrible, business must continue. In response, O'Sullivan begins to kill those who oppose his quest for retribution. He goes on a spree, taking money that the Chicago Outfit had deposited in banks around the Midwest as a way of forcing the mob to give up Connor. While his vengeance against those criminals is long and violent, O'Sullivan is tormented, taking no pleasure in such acts and often seeking absolution in Catholic churches.

The final chapter, entitled "Road without End," tells how the principal characters deal with their isolation and punishment. Connor pays in the form of his own death, which is the result of violence against those he felt had betrayed him. Looney is arrested on his New Mexico property by federal authorities and later imprisoned; he also deals with the knowledge that he has lost both his son and his close confidant. O'Sullivan gains vengeance but dies. Michael is haunted by the knowledge that his father's profession led directly to the demise of the family, and he is left to ponder what is gained from destruction. In the end, all the characters have to deal with psychological demons and their own personal "perdition."

Characters

- *Michael O'Sullivan, Jr.*, the narrator, recounts his childhood and the violence perpetuated by his father and him during the 1930's. He often notes that his story had to be corroborated with questionable histories and that the facts often change from person to person, making any true tale difficult to decipher.
- *Michael O'Sullivan, Sr.*, a.k.a. *the Archangel of Death* and *the Angel*, is a World War I veteran, hired gun, and loyal henchman to Rock Island crime boss John Looney. He is adept at killing, though not as a perverse joy but as a necessary act of survival.
- *John Looney* is the head of an organized crime gang in the Quad Cities area of eastern Iowa and western Illinois. He is a father figure to O'Sullivan and a shrewd businessman with interests in New Mexico and the Quad Cities. He also has ties to Al Capone's Chicago Outfit.
- *Connor Looney*, a.k.a. *Crazy Connor*, is the son of crime boss John Looney. He has grown up amid privilege and violence. His violent temperament exposes both his sociopathic and psychopathic tendencies. He is hotheaded and willing to kill anyone who impedes his lifestyle. His distrust of both O'Sullivans is the catalyst for the primary action of the book.
- *Frank Nitti* was the real-life assistant to infamous Chicago mobster Al Capone and is a critical player in the story. His willingness to continue business with the Looney family, even while expressing regret for what Connor has done, triggers O'Sullivan's quest to kill Connor.

Artistic Style

The artwork is central in *The Road to Perdition*. Illustrator Richard Piers Rayner often tells the story in small panels—no more than four per page, often with minimal writing—and effectively displays the black-and-white imagery. Since the illustrations are done exclusively in black ink, shading is particularly critical to the artwork.

Realism is integral to the novel's overall artistic style. The inclusion of actual figures and places from the 1930's—such as mobsters Nitti and Capone, federal agent Eliot Ness, and the Lexington Hotel in Chicago—serves to ground the story in reality. The violence, necessary for the story line, is not necessarily gory in representation, but the characters are drawn realistically and historical figures are drawn according to actual photographs. As the story develops, Rayner depicts the characters in a manner that emphasizes the stress of their lives. For example, O'Sullivan often appears unshaven and slightly disheveled to reflect the chaos around him while Connor's features convey instability without being unduly caricatured.

Rayner also took great pains to render buildings in an authentic manner. Minor details such as certain styles of cars, the use of specific weapons, and the depictions of the Wrigley and Lexington Hotel buildings in Chicago all give the story added depth. In fact, Rayner's attention to detail made the progress of *Road to Perdition* quite lengthy, with a total of four years invested in the story artwork.

Themes

As with the series *Lone Wolf and Cub* (1970-1976), a major influence on *Road to Perdition*, the story revolves around a violent or evil person seeking retribution against other violent or evil persons. The story borrows from the film noir style, in which all characters have some sort of repulsive or reprehensible aspect of their nature. As the story progresses, however, readers begin to feel empathy for Michael O'Sullivan, Sr., and understand the motivation behind his acts of aggression. While one cannot condone his violent lifestyle, the reader can empathize with his desire to seek some sort of retribution for the death of loved ones. His experience begs the question of what lengths one would go to for justice. While O'Sullivan is almost heroic in his vengeance and is juxtaposed against others who seem even more vicious and corrupt, the fact remains that O'Sullivan himself is a killer, which makes him, and in turn all the characters, antiheroic. Through O'Sullivan, Collins indicates that no matter how one is portrayed in history, a person's character and actions can always be viewed from several vantage points.

Impact

The relative success of *Road to Perdition*, as well as John Wagner's *A History of Violence* (1997), helped renew interest in the crime comic book, which had died off as a result of the Comics Code in 1954. The story was also successful enough that Collins wrote three smaller "interlude" books that told the details of the six-month odyssey of the O'Sullivans. Drawn by José Luis Garcia-Lopez, Steve Lieber, and Josef Rubinstein, these three books came out in 2003 and 2004, just after the release of the film adaptation. The minicomics also introduced other aspects of gang life that are not as widely known, such as the reign of gangster Thomas Joseph Pendergast in Kansas City during the 1930's. In 2011, Vertigo published a sequel entitled *Return to Perdition*, which follows Michael's son as he too becomes involved in organized crime.

Films

Road to Perdition. Directed by Sam Mendes. Dreamworks/Twentieth Century Fox/The Zanuck Company, 2002. This live-action film adaptation by screenwriter David Self starred Tom Hanks as Michael Sullivan, Sr., Paul Newman as John Rooney, and Daniel Craig as Connor. Graphic novelist Max Allan Collins later stated that while he regretted not writing the adaptation, the film remained true to the story's intent. The film differs from the book in several regards, including the principal characters' surnames. A new character was added: crime-scene photographer Harlen Maguire (Jude Law), who moonlights as a mob assassin and plays a key role in the plot. The film ends with Michael (Tyler Hoechlin) living on a farm, rather than becoming a priest after a life in a Catholic orphanage. The film won an Academy Award for Best Cinematography.

Cord Scott

Further Reading

Koike, Kazuo, and Goseki Kojima. *Lone Wolf and Cub* (2000-2002).

Kubert, Joe. *Jew Gangster* (2005).

Vance, James, and Dan Burr. *Kings in Disguise* (2006).

Wagner, John, Vince Locke, and Bob Lappan. *A History of Violence* (1997).

Bibliography

Arnold, Andrew D. "The Original *Road to Perdition*." Review of *Road to Perdition*, by Max Allan Collins. *Time*, July 16, 2002. http://www.time.com/time/columnist/arnold/article/0,9565,321312,00.html.

Collins, Max Allan. "Just the Facts Ma'am: Max Collins Talks *Road to Perdition*." Interview by Arune Singh. *Comic Book Resources*, June 16, 2002. http://www.comicbookresources.com/?page=article&old=1&id=1240.

Singh, Arune. "Collins' 'Road' to the Future." Review of *Road to Perdition*, by Max Allan Collins. *Comic Book Resources*, August 7, 2002. http://www.comicbookresources.com/?page=article&id=1373.

See also: *A History of Violence*; *Kings in Disguise*

ROBOT DREAMS

Author: Varon, Sara
Artist: Sara Varon (illustrator)
Publisher: First Second
First book publication: 2007

Publication History

Robot Dreams, published in 2007, is Sara Varon's first book with First Second, but it draws from themes and story lines with which she has worked since her first published book of comics, *Sweaterweather* (2003). *Sweaterweather* included friendships between various creatures, including dogs, as well as a story about the temporary nature of a snowman's existence. With *Robot Dreams*, Varon has drawn on her previous work but has been able to create a longer and more focused and nuanced narrative.

Plot

In August, Dog literally makes a friend when she assembles the robot kit she ordered through the mail. Dog and Robot spend quality time together, going to the library and watching movies, but events turn tragic after a trip to the beach. Though initially wary, Robot joins Dog in the water; but after Robot has rested on his towel for a while, instead of drying up, he has rusted solid. Robot is too heavy for Dog to carry, and as night falls, Dog has to abandon Robot on the beach. Robot stays behind on his beach towel.

In September, after a dream about Robot on the beach, Dog reads about robot repairs and returns to the beach. However, the beach is closed for the season, and though she can see Robot in the distance, she has to leave him behind again. Over the following months, she makes various new friends, but none of these relationships quite work out. The ducks with whom she goes camping migrate to Florida for the winter; she has fun in the snow with a pair of anteaters, but their food disagrees with her. In January she makes a snowman (who borrows a coat, hat, and scarf from her), and Dog and Snowman meet a new friend in Penguin. In March, however, the penguin returns Dog's scarf, hat, and coat: Snowman has melted.

Robot Dreams. (Courtesy of First Second Books)

All this time, Robot stays on the beach and dreams of escaping or of being saved. One of his toes is taken by some rabbits that use it to fix their boat, and all winter he is covered in a blanket of snow. In April, after the snow melts, a robin builds a nest in the crook of his arm, and Robot watches as the eggs hatch and the chicks eventually fly off with their mother. In May, a monkey scavenging for metal on the beach finds Robot and sells him to a scrap yard. Consequently, when Dog returns to the beach in June, she finds no sign of Robot except for the leg the rabbits broke off. Lonelier than ever, Dog buys another build-it-yourself robot kit.

In July, Raccoon is building a radio, but when it only produces garbled sounds, he visits the scrap yard to look for more parts. There, Raccoon finds Robot's head, arms, and one leg, and he buys these to fix his radio. At first, it does not work, but when Robot makes some adjustments to his new radio body, the result is music. Raccoon and Robot dance and become good friends. In August, Dog takes her new robot friend, Square Robot, to the beach. This time, she knows better than to let Square Robot in the water, and after a relaxing day, they head home together. Robot happens to look out the window at Raccoon's house and sees Dog and Square Robot walk by. His first reaction is sadness,

but then he reconsiders. He tunes his radio to let the music follow Dog and Square Robot along the street, and as the sounds reach them, Dog walks off wagging her tail and whistling.

Characters

- *Dog* is an outgoing city dweller with a light-blue collar. She is lonely from time to time, and so she sends out for a mail-order robot kit. Though the

Robot Dreams. (Courtesy of First Second Books)

drawings of Dog are relatively gender neutral, it is appropriate in this case to refer to Dog as "she" and "her." Varon has mentioned that this story was partly inspired by the death of her own dog, a close companion, and furthermore, many of Varon's stories are at least partly autobiographical. Therefore, it is possible that Dog functions as an alter ego for Varon.

- *Robot* arrives at Dog's house by mail, as a build-it-yourself tin robot kit. He has a bullet-shaped head and body and very long arms. He and Dog share an interest in movies about robots and music. Once he gets a new lease on life after Raccoon salvages him, Robot discovers new aspects of his personality: Like Raccoon, he loves music and dancing and is a fan of alternative comics.

- *Raccoon* enters the story toward the end. He is a DIY enthusiast and needs parts for a radio he is building. When he goes to the scrap yard, he finds pieces of Robot and decides to use them for his project.

- *Square Robot* is Dog's second robot pal, built from a store-bought tin robot kit. The catalog at Modern Robots: Robots and Robot Supplies claims that this Robot is a "fine companion . . . tells good stories [and] knows a lot of jokes." She is also supposed to be "Improved!" Dog has learned from experience and now knows how to take care of Square Robot.

Artistic Style

Varon creates deceptively simple drawings. Her figures are friendly, the pages are open, and her lines are slightly uneven, but the results are clear, emotionally expressive, and nuanced. The book is done in a soft palette, with occasional bright colors. Publishing with First Second also allowed Varon the use of color, which *Sweaterweather* did not have. Robot's dreams are set apart stylistically from the rest of the narrative through the use of wobbly panel lines (straight ones are used elsewhere) and, initially, by the use of sepia tones in the dream sequences. Once Varon establishes the wobbly panel for dreams, later dreams introduce bright colors.

Like most of Varon's previous work, *Robot Dreams* does not contain dialogue, so that the panels are not

Sara Varon

One of the most distinctive voices to have emerged in the 2000's, Sara Varon is known for her simple, cartoonish figures and deceptively straightforward stories. *Sweaterweather* is a collection of mostly wordless short stories featuring characters including turtles, rabbits, and snowmen drawn in a stripped-down, spare style with stark black-and-white contrasts. *Robot Dreams* is a wordless color book about the relationship between a robot and a dog. This work deals with substantially more complex relationship issues than does her previous work, using the aesthetics of children's comics to explore more difficult themes. Varon has also produced two children's books depicting the relationship of a cat and a chicken: *Chicken & Cat* and *Chicken & Cat Clean Up*. Varon is known for producing work that displays a childlike enthusiasm, drawing upon the traditions of children's comics even when subverting them.

broken up by word balloons. A constant in Varon's work is the minimal use of text: Varon does not use dialogue, and her comics generally do not contain text balloons. Instead, the body language and expressions of her characters convey their emotions and intentions. That is not to say that her comics are completely mute, since words for various sound effects appear next to actions throughout; also, she uses "iconotexts" copiously, where words appear as part of the image. Store signs, book covers, and newspapers are examples of this. Varon has mentioned that she has not felt the need to use dialogue; but because her stories are getting more complicated, writing dialogue may be the next step in her development as an artist.

Varon uses a fairly regular three-tier page structure, with one or two panels per tier. She varies this with bigger panels, switching from lined panels to panels without borders, and occasionally using full-page illustrations that run to the edges of the paper. The book is broken into months rather than chapters, and Varon uses pages with single, small panels to bridge chapters and transition between scenes. Varon's style has remained remarkably consistent since her first book was published in 2003, with the main development being the introduction of color.

Themes

Friendship is a recurring theme in Varon's work and is central to *Robot Dreams*. Dog searches for friends throughout the book and experiences the many obstacles to creating close friendships: incompatibility, drifting apart, carelessness, and even death. Using animals and mechanical beings as her characters enables Varon to explore some of the most painful aspects of friendship and its mutability, without making these observations too direct or painful. Readers may recognize their own experiences in some of the events. For example, Dog's shame and guilt over having to abandon Robot are clear, but they are also softened by the fact that she is not human.

The second, though less explicit, theme of *Robot Dreams* is loss. Dog loses the friend she made, and Robot's dreams enact loss and mourning. When, in his dream, he sees Dog with a new robot friend, Robot returns to his beach and buries himself under sand and snow. Later, after he has been rescued by Raccoon and sees Dog walk by with Square Robot, the loss strikes him again, but he quickly moves beyond his sadness, sending Dog on her way with music. The book shows that loss can be felt acutely, but that it is something that can be lived with and through. This is also evident from Snowman's fate. Snowman melts at the end of the winter, but both Dog and Penguin understand this to be part of snowmen's life cycle. Furthermore, with Snowman's "death," Dog and Penguin also cease to be friends. It seems it was their mutual affection for Snowman that drew Penguin and Dog together.

Impact

Varon writes illustrated children's picture books as well as comics. Much of her work, including the Scholastic publications *Chicken and Cat* (2006) and *Chicken and Cat Clean Up* (2009), is a crossover between the two genres. Stylistically and narratively, they are clearly suitable for young readers; formally, they fall between the larger illustrations of picture books and the sequential panels of comics. *Robot Dreams* is clearly a comic book and is suitable for children age eight and older, but it has strong appeal for more mature readers as well. Varon's work demonstrates that comics that are appealing to children do not have to be simplistic. This work carries an emotional impact that perhaps comes across best for older readers who have experienced loss. It is hard to say whether this book will have a lasting impact, but it is a good example of the renaissance of comics publication for children. First Second is one of the publishers becoming increasingly interested in publishing well-made comics specifically for children.

Barbara Postema

Further Reading

Crane, Jordan. *The Clouds Above* (2008).
Tan, Shaun. *The Arrival* (2006).
Thompson, Craig. *Good-bye, Chunky Rice* (1999).

Bibliography

Bush, Elizabeth. "*Robot Dreams*." Review of *Robot Dreams* by Sara Varon. *Bulletin of the Center for Children's Books* 61, no. 3 (November, 2007): 155.
Postema, Barbara. "Mind the Gap: Absence as Signifying Function in Comics." Ph.D. dis., Michigan State University, 2010.
Roback, Diane. "About Our Cover Artist." *Publishers Weekly* 254, no. 28 (2007): 1.

See also: *Good-Bye, Chunky Rice*; *The Arrival*; *Mouse Guard*; *Owly*; *Tales of the Beanworld*

Rose
Prequel to Bone

Author: Smith, Jeff
Artist: Charles Vess (illustrator)
Publisher: Cartoon Books
First serial publication: 2000-2002
First book publication: 2002

Publication History

The miniseries *Rose*, published by creator Jeff Smith's company, Cartoon Books, was conceived as a single story arc that derived from a parent series, Smith's *Bone* (1991-2004), and portrayed some of its backstory. Smith, who had both written and illustrated *Bone*, collaborated with illustrator Charles Vess to produce *Rose*. This arrangement worked well; Smith needed a respite from what had become an exhausting cycle of writing and drawing, and Vess was fascinated with the idea of depicting an episode from Smith's microcosm and establishing his own version of its setting, the Valley. Smith was comfortable with sharing his creation, as he greatly respected Vess's award-winning work on Neil Gaiman's *The Sandman* (1989-1996) and *Stardust* (1999).

Rose was published initially in three square-bound, forty-eight-page books: Issue 1 was published in November, 2000; issue 2 in April, 2001; and issue 3 in February, 2002. After reprinting *Bone* in a new, full-color series of books, Scholastic, Inc., under its Graphix imprint, reprinted the three volumes of *Rose* as a single volume in 2009. This edition comprised fourteen chapters and 160 pages.

Plot

Rose opens with a history of the Valley that describes the ordering of the world, the life force underlying the universe, and "the dreaming." This sequence is nearly identical to the creation myth described in *Bone*: A dragon, Mim, keeps the spiritual essence of life and death in balance by clenching her tail within her teeth—similar to the mythological figure of the Ouroboros. The Lord of the Locusts, a demonic spirit, enters the world by infecting Mim's mortal body, driving her

Rose: Prequel to Bone. (Courtesy of Cartoon Books)

insane. The other dragons are forced to bring the world back into balance by turning Mim and her parasite into stone, a struggle that creates the mountain range that separates the Valley from the outside world. As the first episode of *Rose* opens, this history is being told to two young princesses as a part of their royal training.

The princesses, Briar and Rose, are sisters, but they are estranged from each other because of the competitive nature of their upbringing. Magical aptitude—the talent of "dreaming" and its related abilities—rather than seniority determines who will become crown princess and eventual queen of the ancient city of Atheia. As understood by the two girls, "dreaming" is not merely conscious awareness during sleep and the ability to manipulate dreams but a connection between the dream world and external reality that allows the dreamer to alter the "real world" by altering his or her dreams. The younger princess, Rose, is known to have a strong "dreaming eye," which expresses itself as prescience about future danger and the ability to understand animals. The elder girl, Briar, is said to be "blind" to the dreaming world. Thus, since childhood, Rose has been favored over her older sister.

As both girls are reaching adolescence, which the book refers to as the time of "the turning," the king and queen of Atheia decide that the time is ripe for a crown princess to be chosen from between them. Both are sent to "Old Man's Cave" to have their final test, riding in the company of the young and handsome Lucius Down, the captain of the queen's guards. Rose almost immediately develops a crush on the handsome soldier, but Briar, as envious as always, moves in to take away Lucius's honest affection for Rose.

This story, as related in *Rose*, is not original; Smith revealed many elements of *Rose* as narrative sequences in *Bone*. The two princesses, Rose and Briar, and the captain of the guards, Lucius Down, although altered greatly by the passage of years, are all characters in Smith's oeuvre. The Great Red Dragon, too, makes a significant appearance in *Bone* as he seeks to protect Rose's granddaughter, Thorn, from danger. The plot of *Rose*, too, sheds light on enigmatic statements made by the older Rose and curious events occurring to the young Thorn and her friends.

While the girls are being tested by the headmaster, Rose has a waking dream of walking up a winding path. She hears someone cry for help and, out of pity, rescues a small river dragon from a swiftly running creek. Then, ignoring her dogs' warnings, Rose follows the river dragon into a cave where her parents are standing in intense communion with a hooded figure and a giant locust—the Lord of the Locusts. Rose startles awake, immediately realizing that she is facing a spirit of great evil. The Lord of the Locusts is another character who provides continuity between *Bone* and *Rose*, serving as the primary villain of both series.

Unfortunately, just as in *Bone*, waking from a nightmare does not provide an escape from a dreamer's troubles. Rose's "rescue" of the little dragon in her dream was, in fact, a sign of Rose's maturing power of dreaming. She has truly freed a very troublesome, vicious river dragon named Balsaad. Rose's decision to slay Balsaad by herself comes on the heels of her discovery that her sister, Briar, has seduced Lucius. Rose does not truly understand what she is facing, and in the process of tracking down Balsaad, she again encounters the Lord of the Locusts and is nearly seduced by him into giving up her quest.

This plotline explains why Briar is so committed to Rose's destruction in *Bone* and rather blatantly reveals one of the parent series' biggest plot twists: the connection of Princess Briar with the evil "Hooded One." Rose stands before the Lord of the Locusts, utterly captivated by delicious images he has placed in her mind—images of Lucius loving her, rather than Briar. Only when Briar, inflamed with jealousy, thrusts her aside is Rose is able to break free of the evil spirit's power and kill Balsaad in the swift waters, which prevent him from regenerating. The end of the novel places Rose's coronation as crown princess in the context of the revelation of Briar's treachery.

Characters

- *Rose Harvestar*, the protagonist, is the younger of the two princesses of Atheia and, by her own admission, not as smart as her older sister, Briar. She is physically strong and resourceful, understands the speech of animals, and has the ability to sense when bad events are about to unfold. She has a crush on Captain Lucius Down.
- *Captain Lucius Down* is the captain of the queen's guard in Atheia and a huge man with broad shoulders and black hair. Although he is fond of Rose because of her sweet nature and friendliness, he is diverted into romancing her sister, Briar. He spends the rest of his life regretting his decision, not realizing that he was being controlled by magic.
- *Briar Harvestar*, an antagonist, is the elder of the two princesses of Atheia. She is highly intelligent and has the ability to magically influence human beings, but she is driven to evil by her jealousy of her younger sister. She swears her allegiance to the Lord of the Locusts in exchange for promises of power and vengeance against Rose.
- *Balsaad*, an antagonist, is a river dragon. By manipulating Rose's dreams, he is able to leave his river, gaining his independence. He can immediately heal and reattach dismembered parts of his body.

- *The Lord of the Locusts*, an antagonist, is an evil spirit who is the primary villain of both *Bone* and *Rose*. Although he lacks a body, he tries to enter the mortal world several times. Initially, he infects Mim, the queen of the dragons. When she is turned into stone, he whispers to powerful dreamers, hoping to entice them into helping him escape. He frequently appears as a giant locust and can easily control swarms of locusts to do his bidding.
- *The Great Red Dragon* is one of the more ambiguous characters in *Rose*, which is a change from his heroic portrayal in *Bone*. He is the son of the great dragon Mim and, along with the others, decides to turn her into stone when she becomes possessed. He sets himself apart from the other dragons by attempting to guide and protect human beings. He tries to guide Rose, although she does not trust him and deceives him in order to protect her sister.

Artistic Style

Vess's vision of the Valley in *Rose* is different from Smith's depiction in *Bone*. Because of his history as a fantasy artist, Vess creates art more along the lines of that found in illustrated novels than that associated with the comic book format. His personal fondness for sculpting can be seen in his backgrounds; many of his scenes have a three-dimensional quality to them that suggests a reality beyond the edge of the panel.

Vess's boundary pushing affects the pacing of his graphic panels. Regular, evenly spaced panels suggest an even passage of time. Thus, varying the size and position of panels within the outline of the page, as well as the amount and position of dialogue, changes the perceived time and movement of characters within the panels. Time seems to pause when Vess transitions between a series of short, interlaced panels and a full-page splash panel. Vess also plays with the selection and presentation of background figures and the careful use of color to vary the mood of each scene. For example, one can almost sense Briar's vicious nature when observing her glowering in the background of a scene while Rose has some pleasant exchange in the foreground. The shift

of light and dark colors also emphasizes the relative moodiness of the "darker" princess.

Themes

Like *Bone*, *Rose* is a study of the maturing of a young woman. Rose is a dynamic, original character placed alongside fairly static fantasy stereotypes. Briar, the villain of the piece, is almost a stereotypical scheming blond. Likewise, *Bone*'s bartender-turned-hero, Lucius, is transmuted into a handsome captain of the guards, noted as looking markedly similar to Marvel Comics' hero Superman. The king and queen of Atheia are somewhat flat also, as they are engaged in the suppression of one daughter for the benefit of the other.

The unique aspect of *Rose* is the presentation of the titular character. She is not especially feminine, not especially attentive to her study of magic, and utterly outmaneuvered by the clever machinations of the humans and creatures around her. The fact that she grows out of amazing naïveté into the deceptive wisdom of her later self, Gran'ma Rose Ben of *Bone*, suggests a keen appreciation of the demand for more prevarication and

---

Charles Vess

One of the most popular and distinguished artists working in the fantasy tradition of American comics, Charles Vess achieved his most lasting fame with a series of award-winning collaborations with writer Neil Gaiman. *The Books of Magic* miniseries inspired a long-running monthly series of the same name, while the Vess-illustrated issues of *Sandman*, focusing on Dream's relationship with playwright William Shakespeare, are among the most celebrated chapters in that saga. Vess has won three Eisner Awards for his work on *Sandman* and *Rose*, a painted miniseries produced with Jeff Smith. His comics are notable for their elegant and intricate lines and delicate compositions. His images are highly detailed and lushly conceived. With his turn toward painted comics, Vess took greater control over the way his images were colored, blending elements to create more harmoniously muted balances between line and color.

---

less idealism in the harsh world of reality as opposed to the absolute idealism of traditional fantasy.

Another theme, again reminiscent of *Bone*, is the keenly felt awareness of the destructive power of myth in shaping human life. The humans of Atheia live and die according to tradition and prophecy. It is painful to watch how these very traditions become barriers between people who should, by all rights, love and trust one another. Because only one princess can become the next ruler of Atheia, Rose and Briar are set at odds with one another from early childhood. The kinship of their names is also at variance with their roles here; in traditional stories, the briar nurtures and protects the rose, whereas here, Rose is the target of Briar's suppressed rage. Rose struggles against the expectations of her spiritual teachers just as Briar struggles against the disappointment of her parents.

Impact

Rose is a work typical of the post-1980's Modern Age comic book in that it challenges some of the conventions of the genre in previous eras. For example, the terms of the collaboration between Smith and Vess allowed Smith to act as writer and storyboard director while handing over the penciling, inking, and painting to Vess. In comparison to some of the fixed roles that Golden Age and Silver Age writers and illustrators accepted, this flexibility of responsibility between collaborators within a single microcosm seems startlingly unusual in what has sometimes seemed a particularly territorial artistic venue. Some modern graphic artists, including Smith and Vess, have resisted the "Marvel versus DC" or "superhero comics versus alternative comics" sort of binary that is the norm in the comics world; both *Bone* and *Rose* seem to challenge that fixity of purpose.

The intertwining plots of the two works, however, also caused problems. Vess and Smith discussed the possibility of creating *Rose* prior to 2000 and determined that the plot of the prequel necessitated revealing several key plot points significant to, but not yet revealed in, *Bone*. As a consequence, the prequel could not be published until after the relevant plot points were no longer "secrets."

Vess took over the artistic reins of *Rose* with an attitude of reverence for Smith's characters. Both works, for example, not only attract and appeal to a larger number of female readers than most other graphic novels but also have broad "acceptable age" ranges. On the other hand, differences have been noted between Smith's and Vess's respective visions of the characters and scenarios. *Rose* is decidedly somber and lacks *Bone*'s lighter, humorous touch. *Rose* also is a "purer" work in the sense that it does not cross genres; *Rose*'s adherence to fantasy conventions strictly regulates the appearance and behavior of most of the characters.

Julia M. Meyers

Further Reading

Lee, Tanith, and Trina Robbins. *The Silver Metal Lover* (1985).
Pini, Richard, and Wendy Pini. *ElfQuest* (1978-1985).
Speigelman, Art. *Maus* (1980-1991).

Bibliography

Arnold, Andrew. "No Bones About It." *Time*, September 17, 2004, 26-27. http://www.time.com/time/columnist/arnold/article/0,9565,698456,00.html.
Nolen-Weathington, Eric. *Charles Vess*. Modern Masters 11. New York: TwoMorrows, 2007.
_____. *Jeff Smith*. Modern Masters 25. New York: TwoMorrows, 2011.
Smith, Jeff. "Interview with Jeff Smith." Interview by Jeff Mason. *Indy Magazine*, January 21, 1994.

See also: *Bone*

S

SAFE AREA GORAŽDE
THE WAR IN EASTERN BOSNIA 1992-95

Author: Sacco, Joe
Artist: Joe Sacco (illustrator)
Publisher: Fantagraphics Books
First book publication: 2000

Publication History

Graphic journalist Joe Sacco traveled to the small town of Goražde four times in late 1995 and early 1996 to conduct interviews and take photographs in the almost entirely Muslim enclave designated a United Nations (U.N.) Safe Area during the Bosnian War (1992-1995). Sacco's access to the region was facilitated by North Atlantic Treaty Organization (NATO) air strikes on Serb positions around Goražde in response to the Serbian takeover of Srebrenica. Before that, Goražde had been effectively cut off from outsiders; the Blue Road (so called because of the color of U.N. peacekeepers' helmets) connecting it to the city of Sarajevo had become contested territory. During that time, Sacco transported goods, currency, and letters between Goražde and Sarajevo.

Sacco worked on his book for the following few years, publishing several stand-alone comics titles. Fantagraphics Books published the first edition of *Safe Area Goražde: The War in Eastern Bosnia, 1992-1995* in a deluxe hardcover format with a foreword by British writer Christopher Hitchens in June, 2000. Fantagraphics published the first softcover edition of this title in January, 2002. The London-based publisher Jonathan Cape released *Safe Area Goražde: The War in Eastern Bosnia, 1992-1995* for the British market in 2007. Various European publishers have produced Bosnian, Italian, Serbian, and Spanish translations of Sacco's account. In May, 2011, Fantagraphics published a special edition presenting a

Safe Area Goražde: The War in Eastern Bosnia 1992-1995. (Courtesy of Fantagraphics Books)

selection of Sacco's sketches, photographs, interview transcripts, and excerpts from his notebooks, along with the original work.

Plot

Safe Area Goražde: The War in Eastern Bosnia, 1992-1995 follows a narrative trajectory similar to the one Sacco presented in his groundbreaking, award-winning 1994 book *Palestine: A Nation Occupied.* Frustrated with the journalistic opportunities available to him as a recognized member of a foreign press, Sacco attempts to integrate into the community to get unofficial, ground-level accounts of what has taken place.

Sacco's account begins with him sitting in a bar with his friend Edin, waiting for news of the peace agreements that will eventually become the historic General Framework Agreement for Peace in Bosnia and Herzegovina (also known as the Dayton Accords). The news does not arrive. Sacco shifts from this episode to relate how and why he got to Goražde—and this historically ambiguous moment in the bar—in the first place.

Sacco entered Goražde in a somewhat official capacity, as a journalist covering the Bosnian War. Because access to the small town had been virtually impossible before the NATO bombing of Serb positions around the enclave, foreign journalists and film crews glut the area, seemingly anxious to provide proof of the NATO progress in the war. Sacco and his colleagues are fêted by local dignitaries and given access to the finest lodgings and food available. Sacco, however, feels increasingly frustrated by the dissonance between the official line about what has occurred in Goražde and the stories he hears from locals. After a dizzying five-day stint, during which he meets several like-minded colleagues and makes some key local contacts, especially Edin, Sacco resolves to return to Goražde to gather more information.

Befriending Edin is a pivotal moment for Sacco. This Bosnian soldier, schoolteacher, and translator becomes Sacco's guide, helping him navigate through the decimated landscapes of Goražde as well as the historical and cultural complexities that underpin the memories and opinions of the people Sacco interviews and comes to know. Sacco nevertheless attempts to portray Edin and others he meets in a neutral light, and he supplements their accounts with his own research into the region's history and geography.

The book closes with Sacco reuniting with many of his Bosnian friends and contacts in Sarajevo after the signing of the Dayton Accords in Paris, France, on December 14, 1995. He observes that many of those he came to know seem restless and frustrated by life

after war. The hopes that sustained them through the horrors of the previous few years now seem inadequate or insufficient in some way. The book closes as it began, on an ambiguous note.

Characters

- *Joe Sacco* is the narrator and a caricatured version of the author. His most prominent feature is his glasses, which are colored white, revealing nothing behind their frames. As the author, Sacco attempts to portray himself as an objective observer.
- *Edin* speaks fluent English and is Sacco's primary contact, translator, and friend in Goražde. He is an engineering student at the University of Sarajevo who returns to his hometown of Goražde at the beginning of the Bosnian War. There, he enlists in the Bosnian forces defending the almost exclusively Muslim enclave, translates for peacekeeping troops, and teaches math to secondary school students. He introduces Sacco to many eyewitnesses of Serbian atrocities. His own anecdotes provide a majority of the material Sacco covers in the book.
- *Riki*, a friend of Edin, befriends Sacco. He serves as a soldier in the Bosnian army. He exhibits a quixotic nature and spontaneously bursts into snatches of English-language pop tunes and Bosnian folk and patriotic songs. A University of Sarajevo student whose studies have been interrupted by the war, he dreams of someday leaving Bosnia to travel in the United States.
- *Emira*, a nineteen-year-old, works as a translator for journalists covering the Bosnian War in Goražde. She epitomizes the tragic experiences and sometimes ironic hopes of Goražde's youth. She longs for escape and material luxuries, especially original Levi's 501 jeans, while she struggles to come of age and eke out an existence in a war zone.
- *Dr. Alija Begovic*, the director of a hospital in Goražde, verifies the extent of atrocities that Sacco hears about; he also offers his own

horrific accounts of what it is like to work in a medical facility during wartime, sharing anecdotes about performing amputations with kitchen knives and anesthetizing patients with brandy.

Artistic Style

Sacco's artistic style in *Safe Area Goražde* is consistent with his previous work in comics and journalism.

Consisting of a distinctive mix of life drawing and caricature, Sacco works in black and white, and his ink illustrations exhibit a variety of techniques, especially his virtuosity with pen and brush. One of the most compelling characteristics of Sacco's style is his almost cartoonish depiction of himself, which emphasizes his short stature, his wide, toothy mouth, and his round spectacles. This last point is particularly important in light of Sacco's tendency to convey emotion in

Safe Area Goražde: The War in Eastern Bosnia 1992-1995. (Courtesy of Fantagraphics Books)

his renderings of people's eyes. Sacco rarely, if ever, draws his own eyes, and his white, owl-like eyeglasses suggest both objectivity and blindness. With this deceptively simple visual detail, consistent throughout his body of work, Sacco underscores the idea that he is, at best, an imperfect but committed witness to events taking place in the world.

Sacco is a master with line, and he utilizes cross-hatching to tremendous effect as both a method of illustrating depth and texture and a means to convey mood. Much of the action in *Safe Area Goražde* takes place in dark interiors (living rooms, cafes, and clubs), where Sacco's cross-hatching suggests an air of intimacy as well as a conspiratorial tone. His use of this technique is most dramatic in his rendering of Edin's account of his journey to Grebak, a distant Bosnian supply outpost in the midst of Serb-controlled territory that can only be reached on foot. Sacco's dark treatment of men and women marching pell-mell through forests at night, passing the forms of others too exhausted to complete the trip, suggests the nightmarish fear that compels desperate people to survive in hellish circumstances.

Sacco adheres to a conventional comics format in his illustrated journalism. Pages are divided into sequential panels set against a variety of frames or borders. Sacco alternates situating regular panels against a flat black background with superimposing panels on illustrations presented on white backgrounds. In general, Sacco uses regular panels on black pages for documentary passages in which he and his sources are explaining or providing anecdotes about historical events and causes that illuminate what is happening in the present. Narrative and dialogue appear in frames and bubbles contained in the sequential panels. By contrast, Sacco's white pages exhibit less order and regularity. Text and dialogue appear in bubbles and boxes of various shapes and sizes that crowd into adjacent panels, overlap borders and frames, or otherwise compete with imagery. Sacco's depiction of Riki's singing, for example, crams musical notation and bold, capitalized, undulating letters into thickly outlined bubbles, all of which transmits the singer's volume and gusto and provides an ironic and poignant counterpoint to the tragic events Sacco describes.

Themes

In his foreword to *Safe Area Goražde*, Hitchens observes that, though Sacco adheres to a fairly objective treatment of events, he does demonstrate a "contempt . . . for the temporizing, buck-passing, butt-covering 'peacekeepers' who strove to find that swamp of low moral and 'middle' ground into which the innocent end up being shoveled by the aggressive." Sacco persistently interrogates this idea of the innocent throughout his work. Reluctant to settle for tidy and ultimately specious arguments that foist blame "on all sides," Sacco attempts to show and practice an unflinching objectivity that honestly portrays the effects of atrocity on real people. His interest in this tragic dimension of human experience transcends the impulse to justify the actions of one group over another, though Sacco also makes it clear that he understands the temptation to blame.

Complicating his treatment of this theme is Sacco's ambivalence about his own role as a comics artist and journalist. He invites readers to consider his own innocence as an observer, for example, but also seems to question his own purpose and role as a reporter. The question remains, however, whether Sacco and his readers would be better off if he did not attempt to document the tragedies that he covers. The very existence of his work emphasizes that traditional reporting and media fail to account for details crucial to a fuller understanding of events taking place in the world, especially on a human level that could, suggests Sacco, provide some common ground.

Impact

Widely considered an innovator in print journalism and comics, Sacco opened the door to utilizing comics to represent historical events in ways that were credible to a general readership. While Sacco was not the first artist to treat historical subjects in a comics format, his vision is a unique combination of the ironic, first-person point of view characteristic of independent comics published in the late 1980's and early 1990's and traditional print reporting. In many ways, his portrayal of the Portland, Oregon, music scene in early comics such as *Yahoo* (1988-1992), for example, highlights the distinctive elements of his comics journalism: The artist depicts himself as both insider and outsider, witnessing a historical moment in the life of a particular community. Sacco's own role in this account is both deliberate and dubious, though his work on *Palestine* and *Safe Area Goražde* abandons some of the self-referential irony present in his earlier comics in favor of an urgency to tell and draw a significant story as accurately as possible. In this respect, Sacco's enduring impact remains his integrity as an artist and journalist. His commitment to represent what he sees and hears, even if offered self-consciously, lends his work a credibility and honesty that undercuts the arbitrary distinctions between media that reward academic pretensions or corporate interests.

Greg Matthews

Further Reading
Modan, Rutu. *Exit Wounds* (2007).
Sacco, Joe. *Palestine* (1996).
_____. *War's End: Profiles from Bosnia, 1995-1996* (2005).

Bibliography
Baker, Bill. Review of *Safe Area Goražde: The Special Edition*, by Joe Sacco. *ForeWord* October 17, 2010). http://www.forewordreviews.com/reviews/safe-area-gorazde.
Bartley, Aryn. "The Hateful Self: Substitution and the Ethics of Representing War." *Modern Fiction Studies* 54, no. 1 (2008): 50-71.
Rieff, David. "Bosnia Beyond Words." *The New York Times Book Review*, December 24, 2000. http://www.nytimes.com/2000/12/24/books/bosnia-beyond-words.html?scp=1&sq=Bosnia+Beyond+Words&st=cse&pagewanted=all.
Walker, Tristram. "Graphic Wounds: The Comics Journalism of Joe Sacco." *Journeys* 11, no. 1 (Summer, 2010): 69-88.
Wolk, Douglas. "Drawing Fire." *Print* 62, no. 1 (February, 2008): 76-83.

See also: *Exit Wounds*; *Fax from Sarajevo*; *Persepolis*; *Burma Chronicles*; *Palestine*

SCARY GODMOTHER: THE BOO FLU

Author: Thompson, Jill
Artist: Jill Thompson (illustrator)
First book publication: 2000
Publisher: Sirius Entertainment

Publication History

Jill Thompson's *Scary Godmother: The Boo Flu* is the fourth graphic novel installment of the *Scary Godmother* story. Thompson released the first of the series, *Scary Godmother*, in 1997. She published *Scary Godmother: Revenge of Jimmy* in 1998 and *Scary Godmother: The Mystery Date* in 1999. Thompson also crafted some single-issue and miniseries comics to complement the four anchoring novels of the series.

Plot

While preparing for Halloween, Scary Godmother falls ill with the Boo Flu. The Scary Godmother's monster cronies begin to worry. Hannah informs them that she can fulfill Scary Godmother's duties and that all Halloween festivities can proceed as planned. Before long, Hannah becomes overwhelmed by the number of tasks she must complete. She must build scarecrows, create cobwebs, sew monsters together, spread dry leaves on the streets, vacuum the fur of Halloween cats, oversee the howling of wolves, and carve pumpkins (this task finally unnerves her, since so many pumpkins need to be carved). Dejected, Hannah cries because she will be unable to complete the Scary Godmother's job. Her tears awaken a vampire family who come to her aid. Using their teeth, the vampires help carve the pumpkins.

Meanwhile, the doctor (Professor Toad) administers medicine to Scary Godmother, who makes a full and quick recovery by morning. The first light sends the vampire family back into hiding. Hannah realizes that she still has many tasks to complete and fears that Halloween will not be celebrated because of her. Scary Godmother finds Hannah and reminds her that celebrating Halloween comes from the spirit within, not just from carved pumpkins or seeing goblins and ghouls. This provides Hannah with some peace, and

Jill Thompson

Best known as an artist, Jill Thompson has created art that ranges from manga-inspired illustrations to a more elaborate watercolor style heavily influenced by classic picture books. Her artistic style evokes a combination of playfulness and darkness. She has worked on a number of characters created by Neil Gaiman for his *Sandman* series and enjoyed success with several of her own creations, which range from Halloween stories for younger readers to darker horror tales intended for an older audience.

she spends her Halloween evening sleeping, recovering from her hard work the night before.

Characters

- *Hannah*, the protagonist, is a young girl befriended by the Scary Godmother. She is helpful and kind and works hard to make Halloween a success.
- *Scary Godmother* is a witch who oversees the success of Halloween. She has a group of friends who help her complete this task.
- *Mr. Pettibone* is a friendly skeleton and a close friend of Scary Godmother.
- *Bug-a-Boo* is a kind monster who is also a close friend of Scary Godmother.
- *Orson*, a vampire, brings his wife and son to help Hannah carve pumpkins for Halloween.

Artistic Style

The four main works in the *Scary Godmother* canon were published as large hardcover books, typically with no more than three panels per page. Most pages, however, are splash pages lush with color. Thompson relays her story primarily through narrative outside the panel frame, though she also incorporates speech bubbles throughout her work. The narrative and speech bubbles combine to provide readers with a work that rhymes, an especially useful technique when writing for a juvenile audience. The cadence of the narrative instills an air of fun and light-heartedness.

Thompson's rich illustrations fully depict the scenes described in the accompanying (and brief) text. These visuals are crucial to her juvenile audience who may be unable to read the text for themselves. Including large, detailed panels allows young readers to comprehend and enjoy the story. Thompson depicts Scary Godmother as a tall, thin woman in typical witch garb, though her bright red hair and purple and green wardrobe convey playfulness instead of fear. Hannah always appears cherubic, with dark brown curls and a round, full face. She typically wears a pink shirt and purple leggings; the healthy use of purple in both Hannah and Scary Godmother's wardrobe creates a visual link between the characters.

Thompson typically infuses a wealth of bright colors in her panels, juxtaposing a rainbow with Halloween, a day typically associated with darkness. While some of Thompson's illustrations rely on gray or black, Hannah still shines brilliantly. For example, when Hannah visits a pack of storm clouds, the clouds and the night sky are illustrated in shades of gray, but Hannah is adorned in bright colors. This technique also instills feelings of hope and fun in readers who may otherwise find reading about Halloween frightening.

Thompson utilizes different techniques that culminate in her unique artistic style. For example, the final page of *Scary Godmother: The Boo Flu* shows Hannah, arms behind her back and eyes closed, extinguishing the candle inside a jack-o'-lantern. Wafts of smoke drift lazily up the page. This final illustration does not appear in a traditional panel as all other illustrations in the text do; instead, white space surrounds the image. The artistic choice not to include borders around this illustration creates a feeling of openness rather than finality. Since *Scary Godmother* is one of Thompson's most popular works (with sequels both in graphic novel and single-issue-comic form), perhaps the avoidance of a defined panel reminds readers that another *Scary Godmother* story is to come.

Themes

Scary Godmother: The Boo Flu incorporates numerous positive and uplifting themes, well suited for Thompson's intended juvenile audience. Some of the most prominent themes include friendship, challenging expectations, perseverance, and spirit.

Without hesitation, Hannah offers to serve as Scary Godmother's substitute so that Halloween celebrations can occur uninterrupted. Though she is young and unaware of the depth of Scary Godmother's responsibilities, Hannah happily takes on the role of bringing Halloween to people everywhere because she is a good friend. The job might be scary and difficult, but as a dedicated friend, Hannah does what she must to offer assistance to Scary Godmother, who has always been a good friend to Hannah. Thompson reminds her young readers that sometimes people must take chances and do extra work to help those they care about, as Hannah does for Scary Godmother. Similarly, when Hannah thinks she will never be able to complete the duty of carving myriad pumpkins for Halloween, Orson the vampire appears with his family to help Hannah complete her task. Though no evidence exists that Hannah and Orson know each other well, his choice to help her emphasizes the theme of friendship and friendliness.

The theme of challenging expectations also resounds in Thompson's work. Transported into a fantastic world focused on celebrating Halloween, readers must examine their preconceptions about the characters, namely Scary Godmother, the monsters, and Hannah. Scary Godmother is actually anything but scary; she is a kind witch who works hard to make sure everyone can enjoy Halloween. Her friends, a bevy of monsters, including a talking skeleton, are also kind and supportive. This depiction provides a stark contrast to what most juvenile readers would associate with monsters. The monsters in *Scary Godmother: The Boo Flu* only wish to do good. Readers must also examine their expectations about Hannah, a child. Perhaps they assume her incapable of helping Scary Godmother because of her age and stature; on the contrary, Hannah accomplishes much in a short amount of time. Thompson implicitly reminds readers that appearances can be deceiving. The importance of learning about a person and their character remains one of Thompson's strongest messages to her young readers.

Another important theme in *Scary Godmother: The Boo Flu* is perseverance. When Hannah offers to serve in Scary Godmother's place, she finds herself with a daunting list of activities to complete. Hannah has no one to assist her. She keeps a positive attitude but, in a few instances, feels downtrodden and doubts her abilities to successfully complete her mission. Thompson reminds her young readers to work hard and persevere, even in difficult times. Hannah continues to work diligently and her mentor, Scary Godmother, both acknowledges and celebrates her commitment to the cause of bringing Halloween to everyone. Though Hannah was unable to complete every job, she was still successful in bringing the spirit of Halloween to all.

The concept of spirit is important in Thompson's work. Hannah fears that Halloween will not be celebrated by everyone since she was unable to finish all of the tasks the Scary Godmother usually completes to guarantee a lively and exciting celebration. Comforting the young girl, Scary Godmother explains to Hannah that enjoying Halloween does not depend solely on the presence of monsters, bats, howling wolves, screeching owls, and jack-o'-lanterns. What matters most, Scary Godmother confides, is people feeling the spirit of Halloween. This knowledge comforts Hanna and allows her to spend Halloween relaxing, rather than worrying. Scary Godmother's message to Hannah also encourages Thompson's readers to remember that attitude and feelings hold greater value than material objects.

Impact

Celebrated as a leading woman creator in the comics industry, Thompson has produced works for many leading publishers in the field, including Sirius Entertainment, DC Comics, and Marvel Comics. Her *Scary Godmother* series remains appreciated by diverse audiences and has spawned several film adaptations. The animation in these films drew critical attention and was compared by some critics to the distinctive style of Tim Burton's films. Thompson also wrote a play based on the *Scary Godmother* series, which was performed in 2001 in Chicago for several months.

Films

Scary Godmother: Halloween Spooktacular. Directed by Ezekiel Norton and Michael Donovan. Mainframe Entertainment, 2003. This film adaptation, released in Canada, follows the story of Hannah Marie. Her cousin Jimmy teases and tries to frighten her, and Scary Godmother rescues Hannah Marie and takes her on an adventure.

Scary Godmother: The Revenge of Jimmy. Directed by Ezekiel Norton and Terry Klassen. Mainframe Entertainment, 2005. This film adaptation builds on the existing *Scary Godmother* canon and includes the same cast from the first *Scary Godmother* film.

Karley Adney

Further Reading

Thompson, Jill. *Scary Godmother* (1997).

_____. *Scary Godmother: Mystery Date* (1999).

_____. *Scary Godmother: Revenge of Jimmy* (1998).

Bibliography

Moltenbray, Karen. "Witches' Brew: Mainframe Entertainment Mixes Up a Wide Range of Graphic Styles to Create a Unique Look for *Scary Godmother*." *Computer Graphics World* 26, no. 10 (October, 2003).

Thompson, Jill. "Interview: Jill Thompson Talks *Scary Godmother*, *Beasts of Burden*, and More." *MTV Geek*, March 7, 2011. http://geek-news.mtv.com/2011/03/07/interview-jill-thompson-talks-scary-godmother-beasts-of-burden-and-more.

_____. "Jill Thompson Interview." *Westfield Comics*, June, 2001. http://westfieldcomics.com/wow/low/low_int_050.html.

See also: *Tales of the Beanworld*; *Age of Reptiles*; *Owly*

SCOTT PILGRIM

Author: O'Malley, Bryan Lee
Artist: Bryan Lee O'Malley (illustrator)
Publisher: Oni Press
First serial publication: 2004-2010

Publication History

Bryan Lee O'Malley is a Canadian-born writer and illustrator. After working with Oni Press and then creating his first original work, *Lost at Sea* (2003), O'Malley began work on *Scott Pilgrim*. O'Malley has admitted that the characters were originally grounded in his own life, but after the first book, the story ceased to be autobiographical. The books were wildly popular and gained acclaim with each release.

When the first book was released, O'Malley was approached about rights to a film adaptation. The film was released in 2010 to critical success and coincided with the release of the final book, signaling the height of the series' popularity. O'Malley decided to end the series at the sixth book for personal reasons, saying that he did not want to continue to do *Scott Pilgrim* for the rest of his life.

The books were popular among young adults, featuring references to music and old Nintendo games. The lighthearted atmosphere generated by cultural allusions overshadowed the slow character life that developed throughout the series. This was all well received; O'Malley garnered international attention for his work and was nominated for many awards. The series itself was also lauded and received awards throughout its publication.

Plot

The story begins with the titular Scott Pilgrim dating seventeen-year-old Knives Chau. Scott is an unemployed slacker who lives with Wallace Wells, who more or less pays for everything. Scott is in a rock band with his friends Steven Stills and Kim, and Knives falls for him after seeing him play. However, one night, Scott has a dream in which a girl skates through his head on Rollerblades, and Scott becomes obsessed with finding out who she is.

Scott Pilgrim's Precious Little Life. (Courtesy of Oni Press)

After asking around, Scott discovers her name is Ramona Flowers; the two begin seeing each other, and she agrees to come watch his band play. She also reveals that Scott has a "subspace highway" in his head, which is part of a vast transportation system, entered by doors with stars on them. At the concert, Ramona's evil "ex" attacks Scott. They fight, and Scott wins. He and Ramona duck out of the club and agree to start dating.

However, Scott has forgotten to break up with Knives. When he does, she believes Ramona has stolen him from her, and she vows revenge. She attacks Ramona in the library, but Ramona manages to make her retreat. During this time, Scott defeats Ramona's second evil ex by tricking him into doing a deadly skateboarding trick.

Afterward, Scott gets a call from his former girlfriend, Natalie, who is now a successful musician going by the name of Envy. They are playing a show in town, and she invites Scott to come see them play and to talk business afterward. Scott, Ramona, and the rest of the band go to see them play, and Ramona points out that their bassist is her third evil ex.

After the show, Scott begins fighting with Ramona's third evil ex, but after he activates his psychic vegan powers, Envy intervenes and postpones the fight. Envy's presence puts a lot of pressure on Scott and, by extension, his relationship with Ramona. While their relationship gets more and more difficult, it is revealed that Todd has been cheating on Envy and is not truly a vegan.

At the show, Envy catches Todd cheating, and he and Scott begin to fight. This time, thanks to outside help, Scott is able to beat him. Scott's band ends up playing the show, and Scott gets his first glimpse of Gideon, Ramona's seventh evil ex and leader of the league of evil exes.

After his lease expires, Scott is left to find a new place to live. Tension emerges when Scott's old friend, Lisa, comes back to town. Lisa brings back a lot of Scott's past, including his relationship with Kim. This tension makes Ramona uneasy about letting Scott move in, so he instead has to stay at friends' houses. To make matters worse, a man has been chasing Scott with a samurai sword, and he is attacked by a "half-ninja" girl in an alley.

Meanwhile, Scott has gotten a job at a restaurant and sees Ramona with the girl who attacked him. She is Ramona's fourth and female evil ex, from when she went through a "bi-curious" phase. She attacks, but Scott runs away with Ramona. With nowhere else to go, Scott is forced to stay with Lisa, where she admits an attraction to him and suggests they get together; however, Scott confesses that he actually loves Ramona. He goes to see her, but on his way he is attacked by the swordsman, who is actually Knives's father. He runs into a subspace door, which takes him into Ramona's head, where she was chained up by a shadowy figure. She sees Scott and throws him out, telling him to forget everything he saw.

Ramona's fourth evil ex then appears, having spent the night at Ramona's. She attacks Scott, but he distracts her with Knives's father while running away. After realizing how cowardly he is being, not only in the fight but also in his relationship, he tells Ramona he loves her and a sword appears in his chest called "The Power of Love." He uses it to defeat Ramona's fourth evil ex and apologizes to Knives's dad, who leaves him alone. Ramona and Scott then move in together.

At a Day of the Dead theme party, Ramona's fifth and sixth evil exes, a set of twins, show up. They have their robots attack Scott at one of his band's shows. While this is happening, Knives finally tells Ramona the truth: Scott cheated on both of them in the beginning. Ramona is unhappy and wonders if Scott is just another evil ex waiting to happen. Scott is worried about their relationship. Before he can do anything about it, however, the twins kidnap Kim, and Scott is forced to rescue her. After a difficult fight he manages to beat them but returns to Ramona's place to find her leaving, saying she had fun while it lasted.

After Ramona leaves, Scott is incredibly depressed. Gideon is still trying to kill Scott, but Scott runs away. Wallace sends him on a wilderness sabbatical with Kim, where Scott confronts "the nega-Scott," who is made up all of the bad things he chooses not to remember. Scott loses and is reminded of the terrible things he has done in all of his relationships. With newfound confidence, he confronts Gideon. Using his new sword, "the Power of Understanding," and with Ramona wielding the Power of Love, the two manage to defeat Gideon and start over together.

Volumes

- *Scott Pilgrim's Precious Little Life* (2004). Scott Pilgrim meets Ramona and the two start dating. He fights Ramona's first evil ex.
- *Scott Pilgrim Versus the World* (2005). Scott defeats Ramona's second evil ex, and Scott's former girlfriend returns with her new band.

- *Scott Pilgrim and the Infinite Sadness* (2006). The return of Scott's former girlfriend causes tension between Scott and Ramona, but he manages to defeat Ramona's third evil ex and gets his first look at Gideon.
- *Scott Pilgrim Gets It Together* (2007). Scott gets a job and actually becomes a functioning member of society. He defeats Ramona's fourth evil ex and tells Ramona he loves her; the two move in together.
- *Scott Pilgrim Versus the Universe* (2009). Scott defeats Ramona's fifth and sixth evil exes, but after finding out about Scott's relationship with Knives, Ramona leaves.
- *Scott Pilgrim's Finest Hour* (2010). Scott accepts his past, beats Gideon, and wins Ramona back, all while finally growing up.

Characters

- *Scott Pilgrim* is twenty-three years old at the start of the series. He is skinny and generally good looking. He is affable but immature. All the events of the story center on him, his relationship with Ramona, and his maturing while defeating her evil exes.
- *Ramona Flowers* is attractive and consistently changes her hair color and style. She is confident and forthright, but at the same time, she is insecure and afraid to get hurt after a string of bad relationships, culminating with Gideon. She motivates Scott to grow up and face life in order to win her over.
- *Gideon Gordon Graves* is the primary antagonist of the story. He sends the evil exes after Scott before finally fighting him himself. He is tall and skinny and wears glasses. In addition to

Scott Pilgrim's Precious Little Life. (Courtesy of Oni Press)

being a brilliant inventor, he is egotistical and self-centered.

- *Steven Stills* is the lead singer and guitarist for the band. He gets Scott a job at the restaurant where he works. He and Scott have been friends since college, and he dates Julie on and off. He is revealed to be gay in Book Six.
- *Kim Pine* is Scott's oldest friend and former girlfriend. She is still fairly bitter after being hurt by Scott in high school and being unsure of what to do with herself. However, she still helps Scott and tries to keep him and Ramona together.
- *Knives Chau*, Scott's high school girlfriend in the first book. Even after they break up, she still is part of his group of friends. She obsesses over him but moves on and goes to college at the end of the sixth book.
- *Wallace Wells* is Scott's gay roommate. He is sarcastic and acts as a guide for Scott, finding information on the evil exes. He moves out in the fourth book to go live with his boyfriend, but he continues to help Scott.
- *Stacey Pilgrim* is Scott's younger sister and is far more mature than Scott. She is friends with Ramona, since Ramona often goes to the coffee shop where she works.
- *Natalie "Envy" Adams* is an incredibly attractive singer whom Scott dated in college. She causes a lot of tension between Scott and Ramona for bringing in his past. She is dating Gideon in the sixth book, and Scott sees parallels between himself and Gideon, earning him the power of understanding.
- *Lisa Miller* was a high-school friend of Scott who appears in the fourth book. She is a perky actor who has been attracted to Scott since they were young. She causes tension between Scott and Ramona, but she gets Scott to confess that he is in fact in love with Ramona.

Artistic Style

The art of *Scott Pilgrim* is styled after Japanese manga and anime. The books themselves are the same size and length of a typical manga, except they are read left to right instead of the traditional right to left customary

in Japan. In keeping with the format, the entire series is done in black and white, save one colored section at the beginning of the fourth book. Again, this is along the lines of traditional manga books.

O'Malley uses bold, thick lines on all of his panels, except on the occasions when the story requires a fade, such as in subspace or when Scott dies. This is his signature style and is part of his earlier work, *Lost at Sea*, as well. These clean lines and sharp black and whites have garnered O'Malley acclaim as an artist.

One of the trademarks of the *Scott Pilgrim* series is the use of black caption boxes with white lettering. These often sarcastic details serve as narration and provide basic information about characters and also may serve as Scott's voice in the series, showing himself as "Awesome." His point of view is one of the themes in the stories, and the caption boxes serve to work along with self-esteem and awareness.

The location of *Scott Pilgrim* is incredibly grounded in reality. O'Malley often includes actual locations from Toronto and sets scenes there. He uses obscure restaurants or bars, which adds to an overall sense of realism despite the fantasy nature of the story, and creates a unique universe of fantastic actions in a realistic setting.

Themes

At its heart, *Scott Pilgrim* is a story about growing up. Scott is a character who has a large ego despite not having a job or really anything else going for him. The major conflict in the story ends up not being Scott versus the league of evil exes but Scott versus his own issues that prevent him from being a "grown-up" and a decent boyfriend to Ramona. A stable relationship with Ramona motivates Scott to be a better person, to act like an adult, and to confront his problems, not only with Gideon and the league but also with himself.

The power of love is another major theme. In the sixth book, after Ramona is stabbed by Gideon, the "Power of Love heals her wounds." The Power of Love is a physical sword that represents the ability of love to provoke change. Love motivates Scott to get a job so he can prove his worth to Ramona and to fight her evil exes despite the danger and his general desire not to fight them. Also, when Ramona is healed by the

Power of Love, it implies that Scott has healed the wounds from her relationship with Gideon and that she can get on with her life.

One of the final and most important themes of the story is the characters' self-image, specifically Scott. Scott begins the story saying forthrightly that he is "awesome." He sees himself as a paragon of virtue, despite conveniently forgotten indiscretions. While Scott has a specific image of himself as a fantastic boyfriend, it is only in the way he remembers himself. Other characters throughout the series introduce the reader to Scott's actual past, which includes his relationships with Envy and Kim. Scott's relationship with Knives shows some of his true character and things he will have to deal with if he wants his relationship with Ramona to last.

Often these themes are buried underneath pop culture, music, and video-game references, but they are the underlying ideas of the story and what make it echo beyond Nintendo jokes. Scott's journey from man-child to man and to becoming an actually likable character is what makes the series resonate beyond its fun attitude and artwork.

Bryan Lee O'Malley

One of the most influential cartoonists of his generation, Bryan Lee O'Malley broke into comics as one of the artists on the *Hopeless Savages* series written by Jen Van Meter. After publishing his first original graphic novel, *Lost at Sea* in 2003, he began to work on the series for which he is best known: *Scott Pilgrim*. This six-volume series, released roughly annually from 2004 through 2010 became a cultural phenomenon unlike any other graphic novel produced during that decade, inspiring the movie *Scott Pilgrim Versus The World* and selling hundreds of thousands of copies worldwide. *Scott Pilgrim* was produced in the format of Japanese manga and the story delved deep into its study of Toronto's nerd-culture-obsessed hipsters. A romance with components of video game culture and magic realist elements, *Scott Pilgrim* is drawn in a hyper-kinetic and style-conscious, cartoony fashion.

Impact

The *Scott Pilgrim* series was both critically and popularly acclaimed; each book was on recommended-reading or best-of-the-year lists. While the series itself contributed little to the development of mainstream comics or innovations in styles or ideals, it is a phenomenal example of success by a smaller publisher and individual work.

Scott Pilgrim resulted in a cult following, leading to merchandise, a film, shorts on Cartoon Network, and even a video game. This devoted following made the graphic novel a successful enterprise, and the series gained incredible mainstream success, which is rare for a book from an independent publisher such as Oni Press. Further, the book's success showed the available audience for comics outside superheroes or other traditional comic books and also opened up a new readership for graphic novels.

The novel also featured a glorification of geek culture and the Nintendo generation. Many things in the books are references to old Nintendo games, some of which are obvious and some of which are obscure. O'Malley actually uses his book to criticize the idea of selling out the geek culture; the character of Gideon markets himself directly to Scott, representing corporate culture attempting to woo the geek culture.

Films

Scott Pilgrim Versus the World. Directed by Edgar Right. Universal, 2010. This film adaptation stars Michael Cera as Scott Pilgrim and manages to retain most of the original style of the books, if not the plot. The film differs from the series in that it removes a lot of Scott's growth, such as him getting a job. It also emphasizes the relationship between him and Knives and removes most of the backstory with Kim. The film was stylized, featured music by many popular musicians, and was well received critically, but it failed to appeal to a mass market and failed at the box office.

Television Series

Scott Pilgrim Versus the Animation. Titmouse, 2010. A short animation that appeared on Cartoon Network's Adult Swim, it explores the backstory between Scott and Kim in high school. It is drawn like the novel and features the voices of the actors from the film.

Sam Otterbourg

Further Reading

Larson, Hope. *Salamander Dream* (2005).

Millar, Mark, and John Romita. *Kick-Ass* (2008-2010).

O'Malley, Bryan Lee. *Lost at Sea* (2003).

Bibliography

Medley, Mark. "Bryan Lee O'Malley's Finest Hour." *National Post*, July 20, 2010. http://arts.national-post.com/2010/07/20/bryan-lee-omalleys-finest-hour.

O'Malley, Bryan Lee. "Bryan Lee O'Malley." Interview by Jason Heller. *The Onion AV Club*, November 9, 2007. http://www.avclub.com/articles/bryan-lee-omalley,14171.

_____. *Scott Pilgrim and the Infinite Sadness*. Portland, Ore.: Oni, 2009.

See also: *American Born Chinese*; *Blankets*

SHENZHEN: A TRAVELOGUE FROM CHINA

Author: Delisle, Guy
Artist: Guy Delisle (illustrator); Dirk Rehm (letterer)
Publisher: L'Association (French); Drawn and Quarterly (English)
First book publication: *Shenzhen*, 2000 (English translation, 2006)

Publication History

First published in French by L'Association in 2000, *Shenzhen: A Travelogue from China* depicts Canadian-born cartoonist Guy Delisle's experiences in Shenzhen, China. In North America, it was published in English by Montreal's Drawn and Quarterly in 2006. Previously, in 2005, Drawn and Quarterly published Delisle's critically acclaimed *Pyongyang: A Journey to North Korea*, an illustrated chronicle of his visit to North Korea, which was selected as one of the Young Adult Library Services Association's Best Books for Young Adults and nominated for two Eisner Awards. *Shenzhen* works as a sequel, following *Pyongyang* in style and content. The book belongs to a trilogy, as Delisle published a third installment in 2008, *Burma Chronicles*. *Shenzhen* was translated and published in Spanish in 2006, German in 2010, and Dutch in 2011.

Plot

Shenzhen chronicles Delisle's second trip to China, a three-month stint in Shenzhen, a rapidly growing city on the southern tip of China's Guangdong Province, immediately north of Hong Kong. One of China's most successful Special Economic Zones, Shenzhen exemplifies the accelerated rate of economic growth experienced by China, with the city increasing from one to ten million in population in the two decades before the book was published; thus, Delisle's account serves as a postcard of a particularly awkward moment of global expansion. (In fact, Delisle's narrative identifies Shenzhen as the fastest growing city in the world at the time of his account.)

Hired to direct a team of animators for a television series by Dupuis, a Belgian publisher, Delisle spends most of his time in China between the workplace, his

Guy Delisle

Guy Delisle is the most famous travel comics creator in the world. Early works published by L'Association, including *Aline et les autres* and *Albert et les autres*, showed an experimental tendency, but it was his travel diaries—initially serialized in *Lapin*—that shot him to fame. Working as an animation supervisor in China, Delisle recorded his experiences in *Shenzhen* and a sequel set in North Korea, *Pyongyang: A Journey in North Korea*. These autobiographical works focused on the artist's sense of alienation in cultures that were so distant from his own. After producing a series of slapstick police comics with the three volumes of the *Inspecteur Moroni* series, and children's comics *Louis au ski* and *Louis à la plage*, Delisle returned to travel comics. *Burma Chronicles* details time spent in Myanmar with his wife, an administrator for Doctors Without Borders, and he has also completed a book about his year in Jerusalem with the same organization. His art style is spare and cartoony but with a great deal of pencil shading.

hotel, and various restaurants, sharing incidental encounters with a wide array of people. Along the way, he experiences increasing isolation and cultural disorientation, eventually embracing his freedom from conventions as a foreigner. The author shares anecdotal information about Chinese dentistry, massive construction sites, public toilets, miniature theme parks, the politics of space in transportation, the neighborhood Gold's Gym, and local cuisine, equating the city with Dante's circles of Hell. His frustration with subordinates becomes evident when the Chinese illustrators prove unable to draw Caucasian eyes correctly and fail to grasp variable dynamics of the human body.

Delisle's increasing alienation in a homogeneous Chinese population climaxes when he depicts himself amid a sea of Asian faces. By the end of the journey, Delisle transforms into an alternate version of Hergé's character Tintin, embracing the ethnographic disposition of his experience in China. Delisle's time in Shenzhen contrasts with his trips to Canton and Hong Kong, both of which seem to offer more amenable, appealing lifestyles that are more in sync with Western sensibilities.

Characters

- *Guy Delisle*, the main character, is a lonely westerner amid myriad Chinese citizens (a fact emphasized by the angularity of his face and his rounded eyes). True to his Canadian upbringing and European background, Delisle tries to engage the locals in a number of ways and observes them with keen attention, patience, and, at times, detachment. His experiences mostly lead him to puzzlement and astonishment. Usually portrayed with a jacket and a turtleneck shirt, he looks for clues to Chinese culture in areas relevant to Canadian and French culture, such as food, space, and social conventions; thus, his experience of the country is limited by his own cultural identity.
- *The translators* embody Delisle's frustration with China, given his general lack of linguistic competence and his muteness. At times, responses bear little relation to Delisle's inquiries. At other times, the translators leave the author to his own devices, when he could have easily used some assistance. In a sense, they are highly representative of the cultural chasm between East and West, since, though they may manage the language, they fail to acknowledge any of the implicit cultural codes. They are among the few female characters in the story.
- *Mr. Lin the illustrator*, in a singular display of friendliness, invites the author to celebrate Christmas at his apartment. However, the celebration includes viewing tai chi videos, discussion of Rembrandt's work, and the serving of coffee, which demonstrates the degree of cultural disconnect. At the end of the night, having returned Delisle to his hotel by taxi, Mr. Lin runs off to catch a bus. Later, in a gesture of reciprocity, Delisle gives him a book on Rembrandt, which he accepts in a rather cursory fashion.

- *The boss* is a tall, quite elegant man who gets along well with his employees. A seasoned conversationalist, he personifies the social dexterity and competent attitude of a new generation of Chinese businesspeople, contrasting markedly with the enigmatic nature of the Chinese masses, which seem to misinterpret the singularities of Western culture and thrive in their alleged conformism.
- *Cheun* is Delisle's most consistent acquaintance during his time in China; they meet during Delisle's trip to Canton. He accompanies Delisle to some distinctly Chinese venues, such as a restaurant that serves dog. Later, he invites Delisle to his condominium in downtown Shenzhen, where they play basketball and Delisle meets his girlfriend.
- *The hotel porter*, perhaps more than anybody else, personifies an irritating, vexing version of China. Every time Delisle arrives, he is greeted with a phrase that bears little logical connection to context. His behavior does not even suggest a concern for pretense, but rather a penchant for self-interest, willing to do or say anything to appeal to the foreigner and gain his or her favor. In short, the porter evinces China's eagerness to embrace the West as an economic resource.
- *Tom the foreigner* is the stereotypical fortune-seeking westerner, living in China to make money through e-commerce and the Internet. Fluent in Chinese, he personifies the other side of the cultural disconnect: the westerner who, though linguistically competent, does not master local cultural codes (a fact that he readily admits). His sense of worldliness is provincial and rooted in deep American ethnocentrism, as he argues about the differences in taste between hamburgers in big cities and small towns.
- *The English Canadian*, with a ponytail and round eyeglasses, is a compatriot to Delisle, who the latter meets toward the end of his time in China. The encounter allows Delisle to posit a puzzling, self-mocking theory about what he singles out as Canada's only national issue: cultural identity. The character reifies stereotypes about

anglophone Canadians since, for a change, he speaks fluent French.

- *The restaurant cook* is linked to Delisle by his gestures, which allude to the egg dish that plays a big role in the author's diet during his stay in Shenzhen. His presence at the end of the story, when Delisle is almost locked in his workplace and may miss his flight home, signifies an instance of refreshing familiarity amid a culture that, for the most part, remains incomprehensively baffling.

Artistic Style

Shenzhen's black-and-white illustrations are rendered in a charcoal-drawing style. This style emphasizes China as a country in a never-ending process of construction, still far from attaining economic maturity. The only exceptions are Delisle's reproductions of a beautiful book of children's drawings and the art books discovered in local bookshops, featuring authors such as Wang Chi Yun and Hu Buo Zhong. The latter leads to a full page of the author's work emulating Chinese use of clean line. Delisle also incorporates a few images of the animated heroine from his work for Dupuis to highlight the locals' inability to grasp the subtleties of the Caucasian physique. Occasional flashbacks to his earlier time as a cartoonist are depicted with a cleaner, less sketchy quality, as are the images from Chinese television channels or a photograph of a French-style table setting. The contrast between styles underlines Delisle's intentional depiction of China with charcoal.

To evoke a more traditionally Asian rhythm of illustration, Delisle intersperses full-page images throughout the narrative. A number of these depict the changing landscape of the city: a skyscraper in the process of construction, concealed in scaffolding; a construction site with towering cranes; an electrical tower with power lines and a transformer; a building with towering billboards; and scaffolding improvised with what appears to be striped blankets. Others pointedly address cultural difference, including his anonymous presence amid a torrent

of Chinese passersby; a facade covered with signs in Chinese characters but topped by a sign with Roman letters, hinting at the prestige of the West; Delisle dressed as Tintin, with Snowy by his side, in a veiled critique of Hergé's representation of China. Rather than suggest the Zen-like pace of Asian narratives, however, the images appear jerky and abrupt, given their contextualization in Shenzhen's speedy growth.

Themes

Above all, *Shenzhen* problematizes cultural difference. True to his French Canadian origins, Delisle appears fascinated by cultural identity. However, as he narrates his travails in Shenzhen and lists the ways in which he experienced the cultural disconnect, Delisle seems to gain awareness of limitations implicit in his Western perceptions. Most likely, the quality of his representation informs the reader equally about China's intricacy and Canadian ethnocentrism. Along the way, it is an adequate snapshot of sweeping changes brought forth by globalization. China's nerve-racking pace of growth is best appreciated in places like Shenzhen, where conventional priorities appear dislocated. Thus, as an exercise of cultural inquiry, *Shenzhen* works better as a personal exploration than as an attempt to grasp faithfully the complexities of Chinese society and its idiosyncrasies. As portrayed by Delisle, China appears as a place so different from the West that the experience of otherness becomes almost visceral.

Impact

Shenzhen tried to reproduce the success of *Pyongyang*, which dealt with Delisle's experiences working and living in communist North Korea. Nonetheless, given the lack of specific critique of a political system (an agenda again embraced in *Burma Chronicles*), *Shenzhen* did not enjoy the same eager praise as its forerunner. For this very reason—the absence of judgmental militancy—the book suggests a more measured approach to cultural difference, coming across as more neutral and sincerely anecdotal than its two counterparts.

Héctor Fernández L'Hoeste

Further Reading

Delisle, Guy. *Burma Chronicles* (2008).

_____. *Pyongyang: A Journey in North Korea* (2005).

Thompson, Craig. *Carnet de Voyage* (2004).

Bibliography

Flagg, Gordon. "*Shenzhen: A Travelogue from China*." Review of *Shenzhen: A Travelogue from China*, by Guy Delisle. *Booklist* 102, no. 22 (August 1, 2006): 60.

Ling, Chuan-Yao, and David Shook. "*Shenzhen: A Travelogue from China*." *World Literature Today* 81, no. 2 (March/April, 2007): 65.

Publishers Weekly. "*Shenzhen: A Travelogue from China*." *Publishers Weekly* 253, no. 37 (September 18, 2006): 42.

Shaer, Matthew. "Graphic Novels, All Grown Up." *Christian Science Monitor*, June 27, 2008. http://www.csmonitor.com/The-Culture/Arts/2008/0627/p13s01-algn.html.

Yang, Andrew. "Globality in Comics." *197* (Summer, 2008): 193-194, 201.

See also: *Pyongyang*; *Burma Chronicles*; *The Photographer*